Estate Planning and Taxation

14th EDITION

D1614159

by **JOHN C. BOST,** J.D., M.S.(Tax)

Professor Emeritus
Department of Finance
San Diego State University

KENDALL/HUNT PUBLISHING COMPANY
4050 Westmark Drive   Dubuque, Iowa 52002

Disclaimer: This textbook is intended solely as an educational tool. The materials contained herein are not legal advice and should not be construed as such. For specific issues, the reader must do his or her own research and/or engage professional advisors with experience in the area in question.

Formerly entitled *Introduction to Estate Planning.*

Copyright © 1987, 1989 by Richard D. Irwin, Inc.

Copyright © 1992, 1993, 1994, 1995, 1996, 1997, 1998, 1999, 2000, 2001, 2003, 2006 by Kendall/Hunt Publishing Company.

ISBN 0-7575-2606-3

Printed in the United States of America
10 9 8 7 6 5 4 3 2 1

CONTENTS in Brief

CONTENTS in Detail

ILLUSTRATIONS TABLE

PREFACE

Estate Planning and Taxation is a textbook designed to be used in an academic program. Its concepts are introduced logically rather than encyclopedically; and as the reader's knowledge grows, more advanced principles are covered.

Estate Planning and Taxation is for the professional or student pursuing a career in financial services, taxation, or law in which estate planning and estate and gift taxation is but one of several principal areas of practice. Applicable careers include law, tax accounting, financial planning, insurance sales, paralegal work, banking, trust management, investment brokerage and management, and real estate. Since much of the subject matter is Internal Revenue Code driven, the textbook draws heavily on primary sources of the law, both Code and cases. The textbook is adaptable to law school courses in estate planning and taxation, giving the law student a strongly quantitative slant that is often overlooked in traditional law books, even those dealing with taxes.

The organization of *Estate Planning and Taxation* seeks to present a concise, integrated overview, highlighting the essence of concepts without confusing the reader with every technical qualification and reference, a problem which has impaired the readability of many books in the field. For example, the text expects the student to learn only those case names and Code section numbers that have attained the status of common industry jargon (chapter endnotes cite many others). Nonetheless, the book's content is comprehensive. For example, with its quantitative orientation, it demonstrates numerically, wherever possible, the consequences of planning, and of the failure to plan, on family wealth.

Many pedagogical devices are used to aid comprehension. Numerous examples are included to clarify concepts. Each chapter contains end-of-chapter questions and problems, many with solutions. Appendixes include a glossary, tax and valuation tables relevant to estate planning. An instructors manual containing a test bank is available to instructors who adopt the book.

The Teaching Aids CD ROM disk contains ETAX 2006, an EXCEL program that can be used to calculate estate and gift taxes. Also on the disk are numerous federal tax forms and Treasury publications in Adobe Reader format (pdf). The National Conference of Commissioners on Uniform State Laws has again kindly granted permission to include over a dozen estate planning related uniform laws. Like the estate planning relevant Internal Revenue Code sections included on the disk, these are in MS Word format.

Estate Planning and Taxation can be used in a two-hour or three-hour quarter or semester introductory college undergraduate course, graduate, or law school course. It can be read in conjunction with a correspondence, certificate-type course offered to the financial services industry; and it can be read independently by anyone seeking a moderately technical overview, including the practitioner in accounting or financial services, the law student, the attorney in general practice, and the very determined lay reader.

DEDICATION AND ACKNOWLEDGMENTS

DEDICATION This edition is dedicated to the teachers and students who have made suggestions that have helped improvement of this textbook. Your continued support and advice is sincerely appreciated.

RECOGNITION FOR WORK ON THIS EDITION Credit for improving this textbook must be given to steadfast friends and colleagues. Special praise and thanks to the following people: attorney Robert E. Barnhill III, Adjunct Professor, Texas Tech University in Lubbock, Texas, for once again collaborating on Chapter 8, with special attention to fiduciary income tax concepts and planning; attorney Zuzana Colepeper, Adjunct Professor, Thomas Jefferson School of Law and California Western School of Law both in San Diego, California, for thoughtful comments on the last edition and review of Chapter 8; and one of my former estate planning students, Ehson Salaami, SDSU, for numerous suggestions.

RECOGNITION FOR PAST CONTRIBUTIONS My thanks to the many individuals whose previous contributions continue to be reflected in this textbook: Michael Ahearn, Martin Anderson, Robert Barnhill, Karen Booth, J. Buckhold, Daniel J. Burnside, Paul M. Cheverton, Neil Cohen, Larry Cox, Jeffrey Dennis-Strathmeyer, D. J. Devin, Mark Dorfman, W. W. Dotterweich, Jon Gallo, Randy Gardner, William S. Gray, Keith Fevurly, Mark Greene, Benjamin Henszey, Carole Hill, Joseph W. Janick, Jerry Kasner, Fred Keydel, James K. Leese, Russell H. May, Shekhar Misra, Karen Molloy, Burton Nissing, Gregg Parish, Mary Reese, Phelder St. Germain, Janice Samuells, John Schooling, Jack Stephens, and Richard Wellman.

SPECIAL THANKS To past, present, and future students of estate planning for whom this text was created and for whom it continues; to the late Professor Chris J. Prestopino (1943 - 1994), who initiated this textbook; and to my wife, Jennifer, and our two daughters, Heather and Laura, my personal reason for learning about estate planning.

Thank you readers of earlier editions for your suggestions. I welcome and encourage comments from students, instructors, and professionals who use this textbook. Through a continuing dialog we can make this book even better in the future. Of course, I take full responsibility for any errors that remain.

John C. Bost
email: john.bost@sdsu.edu

Please visit Sushibrain.com for updates and corrections. If you find an error or a questionable statement, check the "Corrections Table" for the 14th edition at the website to see whether the matter has already been covered, and if not, please contact me by email.

ETAX Program Information

On the Teaching Aids CD ROM that comes with this textbook is a spread sheet program, ETAX 2006, for use with EXCEL (Microsoft). Any revised or update of this program will be available for downloading from my website at <Sushibrain.com>. ETAX 2006 is an estate and gift tax spreadsheet program designed for educational use only. However, it will do basic estate tax, state death tax credit, and cumulative gift tax calculations. It will not add to the gross estate the gift taxes paid on gifts made within three years of death (IRC § 2035(b)); it does not calculate the tax for pre-1977 transfers; and it will not calculate the prior transfer credit (IRC § 2013).

Once you bring the file into EXCEL, save it to your hard drive. Only certain cells will allow data entry:

- Estates: the **year of death**, the **gross estate**, and **deductions** (you will have to do your own total for marital, charitable, debts and expenses).
- Gifts: the **year of the current gifts**, the **year of prior gifts**, the **current year's gifts** (you must subtract the annual exclusions), and **prior year's gifts** (i.e., the taxable amount after subtracting the annual exclusions).
- After entering the data, hit calculate. Your spreadsheet setup should be set for at least five iterations, ten if you want to try to do inter-related calculations such as net gifts. To determine whether you have the iterations set high enough, enter figures high enough to generate a tax at the cells for prior gifts, current gifts, and the gross estate and see whether the resulting tax amounts change after you hit calculate a second time. If they do, notice how many times you must hit calculate before they do not change and set the iterations accordingly.

CHAPTER 1

Introduction to Estate Planning

WHAT IS ESTATE PLANNING?

Two threads intertwine in estate planning, one focused on personal matters and the other on financial matters. Planning for the transfer of personal responsibilities for one's self include such issues as how one handles healthcare, management of property and personal care if the person becomes incapacitated. What arrangements have been made to care for children or other dependents? Planning for the transfer of assets and liabilities includes ensuring assets are efficiently transferred to the chosen recipients and that liabilities are paid.

Figure 1 - 1 The Estate Planning Process

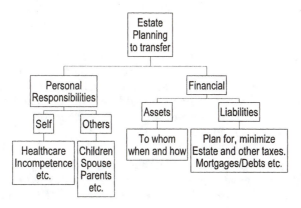

Because all elements of estate planning are so closely intertwined, it is difficult to separate them. As estate size increases, the importance of estate taxes as a financial issue increases. Planning for future wealth transfers may require the preparation of contracts, such as life insurance policies, and other documents including wills, trusts, deeds, and powers of attorney. Successful estate planning requires an understanding of many areas of law, including the law of property, wills, trusts, future interests, estate administration, intestacy, insurance, and taxation.

How can knowledge of such an extensive subject benefit you, the reader? As a knowledgeable planner, you can help clients, and your own family, avoid the adverse consequences of inadequate or faulty estate planning. Must adults are somewhat familiar with wills as documents that guide disposition of a person's property at death. Trusts are less familiar. These are documents that allow a person–the trustee–to manage the property of another, the trustor, also called the settlor. The documents can be used to transfer the trust property when the settlor dies. Some trusts are designed to keep the settlor's property out of probate. Probate is the process of having a court settle a deceased person's estate. It is guided by the decedent's will, if there is one, and, if not, then by the laws of intestate succession. Here are some hypothetical situations, based on real life examples, which highlight problems that arise when estate planning goes awry.

EXAMPLE 1 - 1. Joanne died intestate, i.e., without a will. She is survived by her husband and their two young daughters. The intestate laws of her state require a significant portion of her $600,000 estate *pass to her daughters*. As they turn 18, each daughter's share must be turned over to her. Joanne's husband is shocked that he is not inheriting the entire estate. He is also troubled with having, as guardian of the daughters' estates, to file annual accountings with the court.

EXAMPLE 1 - 2. Marge and Henry, parents of five-year-old twins, died in an accident. They had no estate plan. The probate court appointed Marge's sister Julie as *guardian* for the twins. Marge and Henry had been quite critical of how Julie and her husband were raising their own children, but they had not formally selected guardians for their twins. In selecting Marge's sister for the job, the court simply followed statutory guidelines.

EXAMPLE 1 - 3. Maggie's will left her estate to her son, Charlie. Six weeks prior to her death, she gave him her ABC common stock worth $90,000. Maggie's $14,000 basis in the stock is now Charlie's basis. If he sells the stock he will recognize considerable capital gains. Had Maggie kept the stock until her death, Charlie's basis in the stock would have been its value as of her date of death.

EXAMPLE 1 - 4. Christine was elderly and in poor health when she had her family lawyer draft a *simple will*, leaving her sizeable estate to her husband, Evan. After her death, Evan, who is quite ill, realizes that, as owner of all the family wealth, estate taxes may be due after he dies. Much of the tax could have been avoided if Christine's estate plan had incorporated the estate planning device known as a *bypass trust*. He still might be able to decrease the tax on his estate by using a *disclaimer*, but he will need competent legal advice to make the disclaimer tax effective.

EXAMPLE 1 - 5. Suppose that instead of receiving the property by will (as in the preceding example), Evan received it as surviving *joint tenant*. The estate tax problem would be the same.

EXAMPLE 1- 6. Leslie is the founder of a highly successful real estate company. Unfortunately, she has not done any estate planning and is now very ill. Her children are struggling with several problems, including how to generate sufficient *liquidity* to pay the estate taxes and whether to sell the business. Because only a person with a real estate license (which none of the children have) can operate a real estate office, they fear that the business will sell for much less after Leslie dies compared to its present value. Indeed, it could have sold for even more money several years ago when Leslie could have been active in seeking buyers and working with them on a transition.

EXAMPLE 1 - 7. Elmer, a wealthy man, had a severe stroke three months ago. Unable to communicate, he is hooked up to machines that keep him alive. The doctors say his prognosis is very poor. His family realizes that they should have encouraged Elmer to consult an estate planner years ago while he was still able to express his desires. Documents could have been drafted that would have nominated a person or persons to manage his wealth during his incapacity and would have directed the eventual distribution of his wealth after his death. Other documents would have articulated the appropriate level of medical intervention. Whether the decisions of the doctors and the family concerning his care or the pattern of wealth distribution mandated by the laws of intestate succession really match his desires will never be known. In addition, if the family cannot reach agreement on medical treatment, a costly court battle could ensue.

EXAMPLE 1 - 8. Several years before he died, Marty executed a revocable living trust leaving all his property to several close friends rather than to the few relatives who had been rather cool to him for years. Marty completed the trust by filling in the blanks of a form photocopied from the pages of a popular how-to-avoid-probate book. Thinking that the trust took care of his estate, Marty tore up his will (the one that left everything to the same set of friends as specified in the trust). He failed to transfer his assets into the trust and he did not make a new will. A careful reading of the how-to book would have called to his attention the need to fund the trust by transferring assets to the trustee of the trust and the importance of something called a *pour-over will*. Marty did not realize that his self-made estate plan was ineffective in avoiding probate. Worse yet, it did not control who received his estate. Because he did not transfer his property to the trustee of the trust and because he died without a will, Marty's estate will probably be distributed to his relatives in a manner specified in his state's intestate succession laws.

EXAMPLE 1 - 9. At his death, Carlos owned real estate in six states, including his state of residence. His simple will left his estate to his three children. In addition to the *probate* in his state of domicile, there were five ancillary probates, forcing Carlos's family to pay court filing fees and hire probate attorneys in all six states. Had Carlos's estate plan used a *living trust*, these probates could have been avoided.

EXAMPLE 1 - 10. Many years before her death Lola bought Sammy's $30,000 life insurance policy for $5,000. They jointly notified the insurance company to change the beneficiary designation to Lola and to send all further premium notices to her address, but they did not request a change of ownership. Lola insisted they complete a "Bill of Sale" form she obtained at a stationery store. It set forth the details of the sale, including the identification of policy, and had Sammy's notarized signature. She recorded this document at the county recorder's office. Eventually Lola had paid sufficient premiums to completely pay up the policy. As soon as Lola went into a nursing home, Sammy used a change of beneficiary form supplied by the insurance company to change the beneficiary back to his daughter. When Lola died, her son discovered the Bill of Sale and contacted the insurance company only to learn that Sammy had died two years earlier and the proceeds were paid to Sammy's daughter. Because the company had never been notified of a change in ownership, they correctly followed Sammy's change of beneficiary designation. His daughter might have been liable, but she lived in another state and had spent almost all of the money. Lola's son concluded that the uncertainty of collecting anything made it unrealistic to spend money to pursue his claim. If Lola had just had Sammy make an irrevocable assignment of the policy to her, and sent it to the insurance company, he would have lost the power to change the beneficiary designation.

Problems like these occur because people tend to avoid estate planning or attempt ill-conceived "do-it-yourself" solutions. Misconceptions about estate planning abound because it is a technical subject and the laws vary from state to state. Many people choose to ignore their estate planning needs because estate planning forces them to discuss matters related to their own death. Overcoming inertia requires the thoughtful, caring encouragement of loved ones, and the sensitive approach of the estate planner.

DEVELOPING AN ESTATE PLAN

Developing an estate plan should result in a set of recommendations and related documents that skillfully allow for the best use, conservation, and transfer of the client's wealth. In 1996, the Certified Financial Planner Board of Standards, Inc., (the Board or the CFP Board) identified the following steps in the financial planning process: (1) establishing and defining the client-planner relationship; (2) gathering client data, including goals; (3) analyzing and evaluating the client's financial status (an income statement and net-worth balance sheet); (4) developing and presenting financial planning recommendations and/or alternatives; (5) implementing the financial planning recommendations; and (6) monitoring the financial planning recommendations.

Establishing the Client-Planner Relationship

The planner usually takes the lead by explaining to the client the financial planning process. Some of the issues and concepts will already be familiar to the client, e.g., the purpose of a will, but other matters such as estate taxation or the use of trusts might be quite foreign. The role of the estate planner should be made clear and should be set forth in an engagement letter that spells out the services to be performed. The cooperation of the client is important to building a successful plan. So the planner must make the client aware of his or her responsibilities, including gathering information, working with the planner to implement the plan, and keeping the planner informed of changes that might require its modification.

Acquiring Client Facts and Goals

To make meaningful recommendations, the planner must acquire sufficient information about the client and the client's family. Essential information must be collected to give the planner a fairly complete picture of the client's family, his or her financial situation, and what the client expects to achieve by implementing an estate plan.

The importance of family. The estate planning opportunities for a wealthy married couple seeking to transfer an estate to the next generation are greater than those available for a single wealthy parent. Likewise, the estate planning needs of a young couple with minor children will be quite different from a couple whose children are grown. Family members may also be suitable choices for fiduciary positions such as executor, guardian, and trustee. A *fiduciary* is a person who holds a position of trust and confidence in the management of the affairs of another. A fiduciary has an obligation to the persons being served to carry out the duties of the office with the highest order of loyalty, care, and honesty. The planner needs to be aware of special concerns, e.g., a child with special health needs or a child who has a drug addiction. In these situations, special trust planning that provides for long-term asset management may be appropriate.

The client's financial situation and objectives. To understand the client's financial situation, the planner will require several types of statements. First, he or she will need a current *balance sheet*, showing the fair market value of all assets and liabilities. Information on each asset should include the manner in which title is held, the date of acquisition, and current adjusted tax basis. Many lawyers verify real estate title information through a title company or by checking the records at the recorder's office.

> EXAMPLE 1 - 11. Relying on Marlene's representation that all her property was in her name alone, her lawyer prepared a will that left all her property to her husband. After she died, it was discovered that the most valuable parcel of real estate (acquired by Marlene long before the couple had married) was held in *joint tenancy* with Marlene's niece. Of course, the niece became the sole owner.

For liabilities, the client should list the lender and the loan terms (maturity, a payment schedule, interest rate, collateral, etc.). Depending on the nature of the engagement, the planner might request, or aid in preparing, a *cash flow statement*, describing sources of income and estimates of expenses.

The planner will also need other facts, such as whether the client expects to receive significant gifts or inheritance, and the names of the client's other advisers, including accountants, lawyers, investment brokers, life underwriters, real estate agents, physicians, and religious advisers. Further, the planner will want a description of the client's financial objectives, a self-appraisal of his or her ability to manage finances, and the location of any estate planning documents such as wills, trusts, and advanced directives for health care.

The process of gathering client data, organizing it and putting it in written form is extremely important. Often clients use the planner's summary document as a convenient reference. Gathering information can alert a client to important issues so they can be considered calmly and preemptively rather than in the stress of damage control. For example, when gathering documents, a client may realize an insurance policy is missing and easily contact the company to obtain a replacement copy.

The client's objectives. The planner also needs an understanding of the client's objectives, especially with regard to dispositive preferences (i.e., the plan as to who gets what) for the spouse, children, and charities; and whether significant transfers are likely to be made during the person's life or only after death.

Many planners develop questionnaires to help them acquire information as efficiently as possible and checklists to help them avoid overlooking important issues. A sample questionnaire is included in Appendix 1A at the end of this chapter.

The planner should routinely examine existing documents, such as the will and evidence of title to property to make sure client responses on a questionnaire are correct, especially about matters such as how title is held. Double-checking as much information as possible can help avoid mistakes that would be damaging to the client or embarrassing to the planner.

Analyzing and Evaluating the Client's Financial Status

After acquiring the financial information and the client's goals, the planner will prepare a plan with preliminary recommendations and, where appropriate, alternatives. The most common recommendations fall into two areas: financial planning for property transfers and personal planning to provide help for the client's incapacity and death.

Developing and Presenting Recommendations and/or Alternatives

Depending on the nature of the engagement, i.e., the services contracted for by the client, the plan may focus on both financial matters and personal matters or just financial matters. Indeed, the parties might agree to have the planner focus on just a very narrow set of issues, such as whether the client has investments appropriately diversified or whether there is adequate life insurance.

Financial planning for property transfers. The major purpose of the plan is to efficiently distribute the client's wealth to the proper persons, in the proper amount, and at the proper time. To do this, the planner must keep in mind the following considerations that relate to more specific estate planning goals:

- Deciding whether to use a trust or some other means to *avoid probate* as a means of transferring property at the death of the client
- Examining alternatives to reduce and possibly eliminate *transfer taxes* at the death of the client
- Considering *lifetime transfers*, partly to reduce transfer costs and partly to shift income to family members with income in lower tax brackets
- Arranging to provide the needed *liquidity* at the client's disability or death
- Devising a strategy to unwind the client's *business affairs* in a manner that maintains the greatest income and value for the survivors

Personal planning for incapacity and death. Personal planning for a client's incapacity tends to focus on arranging for someone to care for the client and the client's property if the client becomes incapacitated. It may also include making funeral or cremation arrangements, and assuring that at the time of death certain religious formalities will be faithfully followed. Personal planning also includes the important task of arranging for someone to care for the client's children if both parents become incapacitated before the children reach adulthood. In subsequent chapters, we will consider these objectives, and others, plus various methods to meet them.

Implementing the Plan

After the specifics of a plan are agreed upon, the planner and client should implement it. Transfer documents are drafted by an attorney and executed by the client. An insurance agent may be needed to secure the appropriate insurance contracts. If a trust is included in the plan and the client wants a bank trust department named as either initial trustee or as a successor trustee, one of the bank trust officers should be contacted for authorization and advice before the trust document is completed. The trust officer may want the bank's legal department to review the document to make sure that its terms are ones they are willing to carry out. The client should feel comfortable with the bank trust department's personnel, including their investment philosophy and how they interact with trust beneficiaries.

A person "executes" a document by taking all of the steps necessary to render it valid. For example, execution of a will normally requires, among other things, that the client sign the will in the presence of witnesses who, by their own signatures, attest to the authenticity of the client's signature. Certain documents have other technical requirements, such as a notarized signature, which is required on a real estate deed in order for it to be recorded.

Monitoring the Financial Planning Recommendations

Depending on the scope of the engagement, the estate planning process may include monitoring the estate plan over a long period of time. By keeping current with the client's situation and with the law, the planner can suggest appropriate revisions to the plan when such are appropriate. Events that are likely to require plan revision include marriage, divorce, birth of a child, or changes in the law.

For example, in 2001, the Economic Growth and Tax Relief Reconciliation Act of 2001 (EGTRRA) was enacted. It provides dramatic increases in the amount that can pass estate tax free, from $675,000 in 2001 to $3,500,000 in 2009, with a temporary repeal of the tax for those dying during 2010. The tax-free amount is called the applicable exclusion amount, or AEA for short. EGTRRA has a sunset provision that causes the estate and gift tax law to revert back to the pre-EGTRRA law with the AEA falling to $1,000,000. However, few estate planners believe that Congress will allow that to happen. Predictions are that the AEA for estates is likely to increase to $3,000,000 or $4,000,000; or perhaps the estate tax repeal, rather than lasting just one year, will be made permanent. To assure that both of their AEAs are used, many modestly wealthy couples, e.g., worth a million or two, have estate plans that call for the creation of at least one irrevocable trust when the first spouse dies. With the AEA increasing to $2,000,000 in 2006, many of these couples will find that their existing estate plan is needlessly constricting, given that estate tax is unlikely even if the combined total estate is taxed at the second death. Many planners contacted their clients to encourage them to update their plans in light of the change in the law. Thus, many estate transfer documents, such as wills and trusts, have been revised to take advantage of the more beneficial tax provisions, often with alternate provisions that will kick in if the AEA amount really does fall back to $1,000,000.

THE ESTATE PLANNING TEAM

Generally, estate planning is a team effort by a group of professionals. The job requires the diverse knowledge and skills of a number of practitioners, including attorneys, accountants, life underwriters, trust officers, and financial planners. These professionals are referred to as the *estate planning team*. Next, we describe the unique contribution each team member makes to the overall planning process.

Attorney

In most states, only an attorney may legally accept payment for rendering legal advice and drafting legal documents. This makes the attorney an indispensable team member in the estate planning process. If the documents are to correctly express the client's estate plan, their preparation requires an attorney with the ability to make precise legal distinctions. The working years for these documents may be measured in decades, operating long after the client is deceased, and they are likely to be viewed as the final authority concerning the client's estate planning objectives. Thus, by putting an estate plan in print, the attorney puts his or her professional skill to the test. Eventually, the results (good or bad) will be there for all to see.

Most attorneys accept the responsibility of coordinating the actions of the other members of the estate planning team. This is especially true if the attorney specializes in estate planning and taxation.

The attorney's role might not end at the client's death. He or she may be hired to advise the estate's personal representative. The attorney is likely to aid in the transfer of the client's assets to surviving beneficiaries or in the allocation of assets to various trusts. In addition, the attorney may engage in postmortem tax planning, a job which, as we will see in Chapter 16, entails choosing certain tax options, and perhaps the preparation of various estate tax returns.

Accountant

By preparing the client's financial statements and yearly tax returns, the accountant is likely to be the professional having the earliest and most frequent contact with the client. Typically, these forms are so financially revealing to accountants that financial planners have described them as the client's "annual financial report."

The accountant may spot specific financial problems requiring attention, especially with regard to the client's business interests. Perhaps the accountant's most important service to the client, insofar as estate planning is concerned, is to encourage the client to seek estate planning help. Once the process begins, the accountant may be hired to prepare the client's financial balance sheet and cash flow statement. After the client's death, the accountant will probably be called upon to complete the required income tax returns and, if necessary, an estate tax return. It is not unusual for the attorney to prepare the estate tax return (Form 706) and the accountant the fiduciary income tax return (Form 1041), although often the accountant prepares both.

Life Underwriter

The life underwriter's crucial role is to help the client select appropriate insurance to meet the liquidity needs that arise in the event of the client's disability or death. The efficient use of life insurance requires an understanding of estate planning to minimize transfer costs and assure an adequate level of financial support for the client's surviving beneficiaries.

Given life insurance's natural connection to wealth transfer planning, the life underwriter may be the first professional to recommend estate planning to the client. He or she may therefore be in a position to select the other members of the client's estate planning team.

Trust Officer

A skilled professional executor and trustee, the trust officer performs fiduciary services for clients and estates. A *fiduciary* is a person having a legal duty to act for the benefit of another. The word fiduciary is derived from the Latin word for "trust." A fiduciary is any person in a position of trust, loyalty, and confidence, who has the legal duty to act for the benefit of another person, putting that other person's interests above his or her own. Besides trustees, fiduciaries include executors, administrators of estates, guardians, and agents (see Chapter 2 for a further discussion).

If selected to serve as the *executor* of the client's estate, the trust officer manages assets that are transferred through the probate process. Similarly, if selected to serve as *trustee* of a trust created by the client, the trust officer manages assets placed in the trust. Thus, the trust officer can be particularly helpful in the planning for the long-term management of assets. It is wise in the planning stages to determine what parameters have been set by various trust departments with regard to the trusts or estates each is willing to handle, e. g., a bank trust department might not accept a fiduciary position for estates below a certain value, or it might refuse to serve as trustee if too much supervision of a beneficiary is expected, or if it is required to retain difficult-to-manage assets.

EXAMPLE 1 - 12. Martha's trust named her local bank's trust department to serve as successor trustee of her living trust. After her death, the trust is to provide income during the life of her son, Curtis, and after his death, it is to be distributed to his issue (children, grandchildren, etc.) if any. Otherwise, it will be distributed to Martha's brother William, or William's issue. Because Curtis had a long history of substance abuse, the trust had a clause that required the trustee to withhold distribution of income if Curtis failed to stay free of drugs and alcohol. It also allowed the trustee to distribute *trust corpus* (trust principal) if the trustee thought it would contribute to Curtis's well-being. When Martha died, Curtis was 50, unemployed, and childless. The bank's trust officers had not been consulted when the trust was drafted and the bank refused to serve as trustee. It considered the responsibility of deciding when and whether to distribute income and corpus to Curtis to be too great a burden. Eventually, a court appointed a private fiduciary to take on the task.

Financial Planner

The financial planner is the newest member of the estate planning team. The financial planner is the professional skilled in integrating the various parts of a client's financial plan, e.g., making recommendations concerning insurance, investments, retirement planning, income tax planning, and estate planning. He or she may be best suited to serve as the team captain, coordinating the work of the others. The financial planner does not, however, draft the legal documents. As stated earlier, in most states only an attorney is legally permitted to accept payment for creating the documents. As the profession matures, it is expected that the financial planner's role will increase.

THE GOALS OF ESTATE PLANNING

This part of Chapter One introduces the commonly encountered estate planning goals and the planning techniques used to accomplish them. The goals are categorized as financial and nonfinancial. Some techniques accomplish more than one goal, and, unfortunately, some goals may be in conflict. Some techniques foreclose other techniques. The strategies and tactics of estate planning involve many intricacies and interdependencies, feedback loops and trade-offs. It is easy for the planner to become process driven and lose sight of the main goal. Estate planning is not just about avoiding estate taxes and complicated trust arrangements, but about meeting real needs with real solutions. Estate planning should be needs driven, not process driven. A sense of perspective comes with experience.

A major goal of estate planning is preserving options. Many people think creating an estate plan is like building a home; once the roof is on, it will be hard to make changes. Actually, good planning incorporates the means for long-term flexibility. A good plan sets guidelines for surrogate decision makers to follow.

In creating any plan, the planner should consider the options the plan creates and those it forecloses.

As you read this book, keep in mind that individuals invariably have one fundamental goal in common, which may be far more important than saving taxes or attaining any narrower goal. The primary goal is happiness and peace of mind, and specific estate planning strategies may conflict with this primary goal. For example, large gifts may reduce transfer taxes, but they may also jeopardize happiness by imperiling the donor's sense of financial security or they may provide a disincentive for children to lead productive lives. The planner should be especially attuned to the individual's emotional and psychological preferences and not persist in recommending techniques that are in conflict with them. Planning strategies are not ends in themselves; they are a means to an end, the client's well-being.

NONFINANCIAL GOALS

Some specific objectives in estate planning cannot be measured in dollars and cents. These nonfinancial goals, often called "personal planning," include caring for one's dependents, transferring property promptly and privately, and managing assets prudently.

Caring for Dependents

One main objective is to provide care for family members affected by a person's disability or death. For example, disability may trigger the need for someone to care for the disabled person, for his or her property, and, perhaps most importantly, for his or her minor children. Estate planning makes it more likely that the actual wishes of the person will be carried out. Various methods to accomplish these tasks are examined in Chapter 15.

Accomplishing Fair and Proper Distribution of Property

Good estate planning seeks to dispose of a person's property to the appropriate parties in the proper amounts at the right time. Many factors will influence the choice of the best succession and distribution techniques, and almost every ensuing chapter will discuss them.

Maintaining Privacy in the Transfer Process

Other things being equal, most people prefer that their wealth be transferred as privately as possible. They want their intended beneficiaries to avoid the stress of public scrutiny. Different methods of property transfer have different degrees of privacy. Probate is the court supervised transfer of a decedent's property. The probate process is considerably more public than the process of transferring property by trust. Trusts are private arrangements whereby one person holds the property of another in trust with the understanding that the person, the trustee, who takes title will use the property in keeping with a trust agreement (the trust) for the benefit of the persons designated as beneficiaries in the trust. We will cover trusts in great detail in the next several chapters. If privacy were the only criterion, no one would prefer the probate alternative. Probate does, however, offer some advantages, and each person should weigh the advantages for his or her own estate against the disadvantages and decide accordingly. The probate process, its advantages and drawbacks, is the covered extensively in Chapter 4.

Prompt Property Transfer

After a person dies the persons entitled to the decedent's estate generally want it to be turned over promptly. Prompt distribution is less likely with the probate alternative when compared to transfer from a trust that was funded while the creator of the trust was alive. The person who creates a trust is called the settlor or the trustor. On the other hand, joint tenancy is probably the quickest way to transfer property at the death of a co-owner, but it is also very inflexible. Where title to property is held in joint tenancy it goes automatically upon the death of one joint tenant to the surviving joint tenants. Various ways of holding title to property, and the estate planning significance of each, are discussed in Chapter 2. Living trusts are expensive to establish, but allow flexible, long-range estate planning. As discussed later, "living trust" just means that assets are transferred to the trustee while the creator of the trust is still living, rather than being funded after death by the probate process. Speed, flexibility, economy, and privacy are goals that might involve trade-offs. We will discussed some of the trade-offs in the chapters that follow.

Maintaining Control Over Property

As we shall see in later chapters, many lifetime estate planning strategies require that a person relinquish interests in property by making transfers. Few people relish this; they would rather hold on to their property for as long as possible. But estate planning goals, such as reducing estate taxes, might motivate some to make lifetime transfers.

Further, different lifetime transfer strategies require different degrees of transfer. Usually, the more complete the transfer, the more likely other goals, such as estate tax reduction, can be accomplished. Some of the more complex strategies involve giving up control but retaining an interest, e.g., a retained income interest in an irrevocable trust, or retaining control but giving up an economic interest, e.g., a family limited partnership. As you read about the various estate planning techniques, consider whether the benefits of each seem worth the complexity that is added to the client's life. Of course, the answer will depend on each client's individual goals and tolerances.

FINANCIAL GOALS

We will divide our discussion of financial goals into those that are nontax-related and those that are tax-related.

Nontax Financial Goals

Financial goals that are not tax-related include maintaining a satisfactory standard of living, attaining lifetime and postmortem flexibility, maximizing benefits for the surviving spouse, ensuring proper disposition by careful drafting, assuring adequate liquidity, minimizing nontax transfer costs, and preserving business value.

Maintaining a satisfactory standard of living. Some tax objectives are achieved with lifetime transfers. The planner should ensure, however, that the client will retain sufficient assets and income to maintain a satisfactory standard of living. This may require foregoing certain tax-saving transfers, such as outright gifts, in favor of retaining property. Or it may call for making less complete or less costly transfers, such as an installment sale, that generate cash flow for the client. These alternatives are explored in detail in Chapters 11 and 12, where lifetime transfers are the main topics.

Attaining lifetime and postmortem flexibility. Flexibility in estate planning means that as circumstances change, the client or the individual's surrogates can intelligently alter arrangements to accomplish desired goals. A surrogate is a person who stands in for another person. While the client is still alive and mentally competent, flexibility can be maintained by the client periodically reviewing the estate plan and revising it when necessary. After the client either loses mental capacity or dies, flexibility, although not entirely impossible, is more difficult to sustain. Yet, as we will see next, considerable flexibility can be maintained if a person provides in advance for surrogate decision makers such as nominating an agent to make health care decisions should the need arise.

The critical need for flexibility emerges in the context of providing for children in the event that both parents become severely disabled or die prematurely. For example, without planning, their property might be held by a court-chosen guardian until it is transferred outright to the children at age 18. Most parents would prefer to delay outright distribution until the children are older and, hopefully, wiser. Such can be accomplished by designating responsible parties (whether as trustees, agents, or holders of limited powers) to act on their behalf. Flexibility, through the use of surrogate decision makers, is made possible by granting flexible guidelines to the trustee of a trust, (discussed in Chapter 4), through the use of powers of appointment (usually found in trusts, see Chapters 7, 9, and 10) and durable powers of attorney (a written agency arrangement designed to carry out certain tasks, see Chapter 15).

Maximizing benefits for the surviving spouse. Most wealthy couples want to be assured that the surviving spouse will live comfortably and at the same time minimize transfer taxes. Poor planning may result in an inefficient transfer, accomplishing one goal at the expense of another, when both could have been obtained.

EXAMPLE 1 - 13. Wealthy Cliffton saves money by writing his own will. He is married to Pamela and they have three middle-aged children. Having heard that each person can leave a couple of million dollars without paying estate taxes, he leaves that much outright to their children, even if Pamela survives him. Cliffton's estate plan succeeds in utilizing his the tax-free amount, called the applicable exclusion amount (AEA) and the property bypasses Pamela's estate, but in so doing, he has unnecessarily denied her the use of the property. There are plans that use the first spouse to die's AEA by placing property in a trust without claiming a marital deduction on it, allow the surviving spouse to use the income from the property, and not have the property included in the survivor's estate.

Chapters 9 and 10 discuss tax-reducing plans that provide for the surviving spouse's welfare without sacrificing other important objectives.

EXAMPLE 1 - 14. Continuing the prior example, Cliffton could achieve his goals by leaving the property in trust for the benefit of Pamela and the children. Without causing any increase in transfer tax, the trust could give Pamela the following rights: (1) the right to the income from the property for her life; (2) the power to invade the trust corpus for reasons of health, education, support, or maintenance; and/or (3) the power to determine whether the property should continue to be held in trust for their children after her death or be immediately distributed at that time.

Ensuring proper disposition by careful drafting. In the planning process, most people assume that no matter what happens, their intended beneficiaries will in fact receive their accumulated wealth. People trust their attorney to draft transfer documents properly. However, drafting skill varies greatly, and poor drafting can frustrate an individual's dispositive preferences in many ways. The examples below are illustrative.

EXAMPLE 1 - 15. Martha's simple will does not include a survival clause, creating the risk that her property will be inherited by her in-laws rather than by her parents.

EXAMPLE 1 - 16. Unaware of trust planning, an attorney drafts a simple will for Francis which leaves all of his property outright to his second wife, running the risk that she may neglect to adequately provide for her stepchildren (Francis's children from his prior marriage), who are living with Francis's first wife. There are trust plans that give a beneficiary income from a trust without allowing the beneficiary full access to the trust assets.

EXAMPLE 1 - 17. A trust-will is drafted that provides for estate property to be held in trust until the youngest of the client's grandchildren reaches age 25. The disposition may be ruled invalid for violation of a rule that keeps trust from going on for too many generations. The rule against perpetuities, as it is know, is discussed in Chapter 3.

EXAMPLE 1 - 18. Donald's attorney drafted a tax-saving testamentary trust. However, because most of Donald's property is held in joint tenancy with his wife, that property will not pass to the trust at his death but will go to his wife by right of survivorship. She could transfer the property into a trust but it will be in her estate, assuming the trust is for her benefit. This would have been avoided had the trust property come directly from Donald's estate.

In each of these situations, more careful planning and drafting would have eliminated the risk of these unintended dispositions without significantly altering the person's objectives.

Ensuring adequate liquidity. The death of a person may trigger the need for liquidity to pay taxes, administration expenses, claims, and for the needs of a surviving family. Many, if not most, wealthy people lack sufficient liquidity to immediately take care of all of these things. This is especially true if much of the person's wealth was tied up in real estate or a closely held business. Chapter 13 covers the role of life insurance in estate planning and will describe the major methods of increasing liquidity.

Minimizing estate transfer costs. Nontax estate transfer costs include attorney and trustee fees, executor commissions, court costs, and probate fees and expenses such as the bond premiums. Chapter 4 will examine cover various aspects of probate.

Preserving business value. The death of a business owner can precipitate a serious and rapid decline in the value of that business. In Chapter 14, we see that certain arrangements by an owner will minimize (or even avoid) the decline in value, thereby greatly increasing the likelihood that the pre-death value of the business passes to the owner's heirs. We will also discuss a number of business related estate tax relief provisions found in the Internal Revenue Code.

Tax-related Financial Goals

Income taxes and transfer taxes are a significant cause of estate shrinkage for larger estates. Many of the planning strategies covered in this text are designed to reduce these taxes.

Income tax savings goals. Planning strategies designed to save income taxes generally seek a step-up in basis, shift income to lower bracket taxpayers, and to defer the recognition of income.

Obtaining a stepped-up basis. When property is inherited, its basis for the devisee/legatee is reset to its current value. For assets that have appreciated, this is called a step-up in basis. Thus, other things being equal, planners recommend deferring the transfer of appreciated assets until the owner's death. Achieving a step-up in basis is especially important to a transferee who wants to sell an appreciated asset. However, for other reasons, estate planning often favors lifetime gifts, where the basis is not stepped up but carries over. Determining the basis of transferred property is covered in Chapter 8. Of course, basis is just one of many considerations involved in making lifetime transfers. Lifetime transfers, whether by gift or exchange, are thoroughly explored in Chapters 11 and 12.

Shifting income to a lower bracket taxpayers. Wealthy people are usually in the highest income tax brackets, whereas the income of other family members, such as parents and children, may be in lower tax brackets. Under our progressive income tax rate structure, rates increase with increasing taxable income. Thus, there is an incentive to reduce overall income tax rates by shifting income to family members who are in lower tax rate brackets.

However, tax reform legislation in the 1980s directed a three-pronged attack on popular methods of shifting income to a lower-bracket family member. First, it adopted the "kiddie tax," described in Chapter 11, that virtually eliminates any benefit of shifting income to children who are under the age of 13. Income shifting has become a less pressing goal as the maximum marginal rates have decreased over the years. In the 1950s and 60s, the top rate was 91%, declining over the next several decades, hovering between 35 and 40% in recent years.

Of course, taxpayers in the highest tax bracket are the most likely to be interested in making income shifting transfers. In 2005, taxable income in excess of $326,450 reaches the top federal marginal rate of 35% whether the tax payers are single individual or married couples filing jointly. The greatest tax savings occur when the additional income collected by the transferee is either not taxed or taxed at the 10% marginal rate. Thus, the most likely persons to benefit from income shifting include minor children over age 13, young adults in college, and, perhaps, the donor's parents. This is especially true where the wealthy person is presently making after-tax gifts to the lower tax bracket donee.

Figure 1 - 2 illustrates the progression of maximum marginal federal income tax rates since 1952. The highest during that time period was 91% from 1952 through 1963 and the lowest was 28% from 1988 through 1990.

Figure 1 - 2 Maximum Marginal Federal Income Tax Rates 1952 - Present

---

Can all income potentially receivable by one person be taxed to another? The answer is no, because tax law distinguishes two types of income: personal service income and other income. Under the *assignment of income doctrine*, earnings from services performed will always be taxable to the person performing those services. However, income from investment property can be taxed to another if the property is transferred before the income is realized. Hence, interest accrued, or dividends declared, after the date of a gift are taxed to the recipient; those accrued or declared before the date of the gift are taxed to the donor, even if the interest or dividend is paid to the donee.

Usually income is shifted by a complete transfer (i.e., an outright gift) of the income-generating property. However, with some techniques the transfer is intentionally partially incomplete. The custodial gift and the irrevocable trust discussed in Chapter 11 are partially incomplete gifts. We will also see in Chapter 16 that income shifting to save income taxes can be accomplished by the timing of distributions from an estate to its beneficiaries. And there are some opportunities to use multiple taxpaying entities rather than just one, such as electing to treat a trust held for the children of deceased parents as separate trusts for each child rather than just one trust. This is referred to as taking multiple "trips up the rate ladder." Since the income tax rates are progressive, taxes are saved by having multiple taxpayers.

Tax reform since 1986 has dramatically reduced the benefits of shifting income to trusts and estates. When legislation radically lowered the maximum marginal tax rate for individuals, it greatly reduced the tax bracket amounts for trusts and estates that are subject to the lower rates. Thus, incremental income taxed to estates and trusts hits the top of the rate ladder at a much lower income level than for income taxed to individuals. A trust reaches the top tax bracket by the time its taxable income reaches about $10,000 (see Table 6 in Appendix A).

Deferring recognition of income. Careful planning can defer tax on a gain from its sale to later years. Examples of transfers that defer taxable gain are the installment sale and the private annuity, covered in Chapter 12. In Chapter 16, we will see that an estate can defer income by choosing its fiscal year end. Deferral of the tax enables the taxpayer to use the money to earn income until the taxes finally have to be paid.

Transfer tax savings goals. Techniques designed to reduce transfer taxes generally do so by accomplishing one or more of the following: reducing (maybe to zero) the amount deemed to be taxable; freezing the estate tax base; deferring taxes; and leveraging the use of exclusions, exemptions, or the unified credit. To some extent, all three techniques make use of unified transfer tax system imperfections described at the end of Chapter 5.

Reducing the estate tax base. Certain planning arrangements reduce the estate tax base, subjecting less of the person's wealth to transfer taxation. Each dollar of value that is removed from the transferor's tax base and still makes it to the intended beneficiary represents money saved at the transferor's highest transfer tax marginal rate, i.e., in 2007 anywhere from 41% (gifts) to 45% for estates.

EXAMPLE 1 - 19. A month before she died in 2005, Sharon, a widow whose net estate was worth more than $3 million, gave each of her children, their wives, and their adult children checks in the amount of $11,000. There were 10 donees in all. Due to the annual exclusion, none of the gifts were taxable. Her estate tax base was reduced by $110,000, lowering her estate tax by $51,700, given that the 2005 top marginal rate is 47%. Gift tax and the annual exclusion are covered in Chapters 5 and 7. For gift and estate tax rates see Table 1 in Appendix A.

Other reduction techniques examined in later chapters include:
- Gifts into trust (Chapter 11)
- Judicious use of the unlimited marital deduction (Chapters 9 and 10)
- Bypass planning (Chapters 9 and 10)
- Election of the alternate valuation date (Chapters 6 and 16)
- Special-use valuation for farm or other closely held businesses that rely on real estate property (Chapter 14)
- Valuation discounts for gifts of family limited partnership interests, fractional interest discounts, and conservation easements (Chapter 14)

Freezing the estate tax base. Certain property arrangements are designed mainly to *limit the future increase* in the estate tax base by freezing a portion of the person's wealth at its current value, thereby excluding future appreciation is from transfer taxation.

EXAMPLE 1 - 20. In 2006, Nicky, a single parent, sells one of his vacation homes to his son Donny at its actual market value of $128,000, receiving $15,000 as a down payment and a secured installment note for $113,000 with interest-only payments (at 7.5%) for 10 years followed by interest and principal payments amortized over another 15 years. If Nicky dies in the next 10 years, his estate includes the note valued at approximately $113,000 (actual value depends upon how well it is secured and prevailing interest rates), whatever is left of the $15,000 down payment (or the investments therefrom), and the interest payments. Even if the value of the vacation home at the time of Nicky's death is considerably more than it was when he sold it to Donny, that increase is not included in Nicky's estate.

Transfers are often a blend of reducing and freezing a portion of the tax base, rather than being exclusively one or the other.

EXAMPLE 1 - 21. Assume that Nicky, from the last example, gave the vacation home to Donny. He would file a gift tax return and report a taxable gift of $117,000 ($128,000 market value less $11,000 annual exclusion.) Assuming no prior taxable gifts, no gift tax is due because of the shelter of the unified credit. If Nicky dies 10 years later when the value of the vacation home is $200,000 (or, for that matter, any amount), Nicky's estate tax base will include just the taxable gift value of $117,000. Nicky's estate tax base has been partially reduced (the $11,000 annual exclusion portion) and partially frozen (the taxable gift portion). If Nicky's estate is taxed at a marginal rate of 45%, the saved by making this gift is $37,350, i.e., 45% of $200,000 - $117,000.

Leveraging the use of exclusions, exemptions, and the unified credit. Much of estate planning leveraging seeks to magnify the end results of transactions. Many of these transactions, if successful, greatly reduce the estate tax and, if not successful, leave the transferor no worse off than had he or she simply not made the transfer (other than the modest costs associated with making the transfer).

EXAMPLE 1 - 22. Wendy gave a life insurance policy on her life to her son Matthew. Although it had a face value of $500,000, it was valued at only $30,000 for gift tax purposes. When Wendy died six years later, Matthew collected the $500,000 proceeds and Wendy's estate reported a $20,000 adjusted taxable gift. Had Wendy died within three years of the transfer, then IRC § 2035(a) would have applied and the $500,000 would be included in her estate (the adjusted taxable gift would be reduced to zero). Thus, if successful, the transfer greatly leverages the transfer of wealth at a very small transfer tax cost. If it is not successful, the result is basically what would have occurred had no transfer taken place.

The use of life insurance and life insurance trusts in estate planning is covered extensively in Chapter 13. A discussion of when a transfer of life insurance, or a transfer into trust, is later included in the transferor's estate is discussed extensively in Chapter 6. Examples of techniques that use leveraging are the benefits of the grantor retained income trust (GRIT), the qualified personal residence trust (QPRT), and the private annuity are covered in Chapter 12. Legislation that has reduced corporate recapitalization as a method of freezing the value of business interests is covered in Chapter 17. Many of these transactions are a blend of reduction, freezing, and leveraging with the characterization being based upon what is expected to produce the greatest reduction in transfer taxes.

Delaying payment of the transfer tax. In certain situations, transfer taxes can be deferred, even though a completed transfer has taken place.

EXAMPLE 1 - 23. Danny and Barbara Brown have equally large estates. Each could live well on his or her own assets. Generally, transfers between spouses are not subjected to transfer tax so if Danny gives his wealth to Barbara there will be no immediate estate tax on that property. In effect, though, the estate tax will only be deferred, not eliminated because the property will probably be taxed at Barbara's later death. In fact, the gift to her will probably increase the overall estate tax on that property since the transfer to Barbara (a) foregoes the use of Danny's unified credit at his death; and (b) will increase the size of Barbara's gross estate, possibly pushing it into a higher marginal rate. If he left the property outright or in trust to the children at his death, there might be a small tax at his death but the property would not be taxed at Barbara's death. Thus, Danny faces the alternative of immediately incurring a (smaller) estate tax on his wealth or deferring a potentially larger tax.

Chapters 9 and 10 discuss the interrelationship between the marital deduction and the applicable exclusion amount. Other transfer tax deferral devices include the application of IRC § 6166, covered in Chapter 14, dealing with the payment of the estate tax in installments, lasting almost 15 years, for certain estates that include closely held businesses; IRC § 6163, which allows the deferral of that portion of the tax attributed to a vested remainder interest; and IRC § 6161, pertaining to the deferral of the tax for good cause (the latter two are covered in Chapter 6).

THE NEED TO ENCOURAGE PLANNING

Many individuals need estate planning but fail to seek it. They simply ignore issues involving their own death, refusing to accept the fact that death can occur quite unexpectedly, and that all of us must die someday. Others are so busy pursuing their careers that they do not make time for planning. Still others lead lives that seem too unsettled to undertake long-range planning. Finally, some fear the family conflicts and expenses that are likely to arise at their death—without considering that good planning is likely to minimize the potential problems, even if not all problems can be resolved.

For these reasons, members of the estate planning team should actively encourage individuals to create estate plans. As mentioned earlier, good planning will help dispose of assets fairly, minimize taxes and expenses at death, provide for the care of disabled family members, generate sufficient liquidity, provide for continued income for dependent survivors, and arrange for efficient business succession.

ORGANIZATION OF THIS BOOK

Chapters 1 and 2 introduce the major estate planning concepts used throughout the text. Described are the basic concepts of estate planning and definitions of many estate planning terms.

Chapters 3 and 4 provide an understanding of the documents used in estate planning and the mechanics of transferring property within the family.

Chapters 5 through 7 cover the principles of transfer taxation (gift tax and estate tax). These are subjects of great importance to estate planning for wealthy families. Chapter 8 covers income tax issues related to gifts, trusts, and estates.

The rest of the book demonstrates how the fundamentals covered in the first eight chapters are used in estate planning.

Chapters 9 and 10 considers the various methods used to defer, reduce, or completely eliminate a wealthy couple's estate taxes with the focus on estate plans that utilize bypass trusts and marital deduction elections.

In Chapters 11 and 12, a wealth of other matters are covered, such as: planning for lifetime transfers to members of the family, friends, and charities. Chapter 13 looks at the important role of life insurance as part of an estate plan.

Chapter 14 explores the special planning needed for owners of closely-held businesses and some of the Internal Revenue Code sections that provide some tax relief for their estates.

Chapter 15 considers some of the most important matters addressed by estate planning, such as how one provides for the care of minor children, selects a successor trustee, or plans for his or her own incapacity.

Chapter 16 discusses those issues that must be dealt with immediately after a person dies, covering both personal matters such as funeral arrangements and tax matters, such as returns that must be filed and tax elections that should be considered.

In Chapter 17, we cover advanced topics. Many of these are topics are covered briefly in the earlier chapters, then in great depth here. This depth is probably not needed for someone in general practice, whether as a financial planner, accountant, or lawyer, but is important to anyone specializing in the area of estate planning.

CONCLUSION

This chapter has introduced estate planning, the main goals that planners seek, a brief introduction to some of the techniques used to achieve these goals, and an overview of the topics covered in the text. The next chapter continues our study by covering basic estate planning concepts.

QUESTIONS AND PROBLEMS

1. At a dinner party, one of your clients asks you what estate planning entails. Define estate planning for her, and name the areas of the law embraced by it.

2. Write an essay that addresses the issue of why many people avoid doing even the simplest estate planning, e.g., not even having wills or durable powers for healthcare.

3. Interview in person or by telephone a financial planner to find out the type of services offered, what the planner recommends as preparation for a career in financial planning, how fees are determined, the extent to which there is a "team" involved with the practice, and any other questions you would like answered, e.g., how satisfying or frustrating he or she finds the practice. Summarize the information gathered.

4. What is the definition of "estate planning" found in Merriam-Webster's Dictionary of Law at the website <http://dictionary.lp.findlaw.com>?

5. A man comes into your office to inquire about your services. You find out that he owns a closely-held business and has a wife and two young children. He has not yet done any estate planning. Explain briefly how failure to plan could lead to adverse consequences.

6. Visit Pennsylvania attorney Robert Clofine's webpage (estateattorney.com). Find and describe at least one item that appears there that has relevance to estate planning–hopefully one with information that was new to you.

7. Review the questionnaire in Appendix 1A. Which items are likely to be the most difficult to complete? Why?

8. Interview by telephone or in person a trust officer to find out the type of services that are offered, the fees charged, and whether his or her organization has minimum trust values below which it will not serve as trustee. Summarize the information gathered.

9. Outline the steps required to develop an estate plan.

10. Assuming an estate planner is competent and makes recommendations appropriate for his or her client, what action or lack of action is (are) most likely to eventually cause a conflict between the planner and the client?

11. Explain the unique contribution made by each member of the estate planning team.

12. Should state law be changed to allow competent financial planners to draft estate planning documents such as wills and trusts without a law degree? Before taking a position one way or the other, state the merits and demerits of doing this. If it were to be done (not that you would support it), what safeguards should be put into place?

13. Consider that goals sometimes conflict. (a) What is do you think is likely to be the typical client's principal estate planning goal? (b) Give an example of how some other goal might conflict with it.

14. Should the primary concern of the financial planner be to recommend strategies that will provide optimal financial results for the client?

15. Describe a situation where there might be a conflict between nonfinancial goals and financial goals in estate planning.

16. List and briefly describe a person's nonfinancial estate planning goals.

17. Using your favorite web browser do a search for "estate planning goals." Compare two sites: (a) What is the purpose of the site? (b) What were some of the suggestions for goal setting? (c) Could you tell whether it is being kept current? (d) What does it give as the maximum annual exclusion? In 2005 the maximum is $11,000 per year but it will probably be $12,000 by 2006. (e) What does it say is the maximum estate that can pass estate-tax free? In 2005 the amount is $1,500,000, increasing to $2,000,000 for years 2006, 2007, and 2008.

18. What issues are more likely to be of concern to a couple with a blended family, i.e., one or both spouses have children by prior marriage, as compared to a couple whose children are all from their union?

19. List and briefly describe a person's nontax financial estate planning goals.

20. (a) What does it mean to have flexibility in estate planning? (b) What are some methods of maintaining flexibility given the possibility of losing mental capacity? (c) What are some of the methods for maintaining flexibility insofar as caring for surviving dependents in the event of one's disability or death?

21. Describe the advantage of selecting a surrogate decision maker in the estate planning process.

22. Describe some major reasons for seeking liquidity for a decedent's estate. How is this accomplished?

23. List and briefly describe a person's income tax savings goals.

24. List and briefly describe a person's transfer tax savings goals.

25. What steps have you taken toward having your own estate plan in order? What goals have you not addressed?

26. Tony is 92 years old and in poor health. He has securities valued at $500,000 and a basis in them of only $100,000. He told you that it has always been his goal to give his daughter Angela something special and added, "I am going

to give her these securities tomorrow. I know I won't be living much longer and nothing will make me happier than to see her sell these securities and buy something that she will enjoy." Comment on Tony's plan.

ANSWERS TO QUESTIONS AND PROBLEMS *(odd numbered only)*

1. Estate planning is the study of the principles of planning for the use, conservation, and efficient transfer of an individual's wealth. It embraces the law of property, wills, trusts, future interests, estate administration, intestacy, insurance, income taxation, gift taxation, and death taxation.

3. Answers will vary.

5. Examples of how failure to plan could lead to adverse consequences include the following:

   a. Premature death of husband and wife in a common accident resulting in the court appointing an undesirable parental guardian for the children.

   b. Inability to sell the business after the premature death of the owner.

      Please refer to examples 1-1 through 1-10 for common illustrations of the failure to plan.

7. Clients may have difficulty completing the portions of the questionnaire that inquire about how title to property is held, ask for the fair market value of assets, or request information concerning employee benefit plans. Individuals with minor children may find it difficult to choose guardians for their children.

9. Steps required in developing an estate plan: The following is taken from the CFP Board of Standard's definition of the financial planning process adopted 9/14/96:
   i. Establishing and defining the client-planner relationship
   ii. Gathering client data including goals

   iii. Analyzing and evaluating the client's financial status

   iv. Developing and presenting financial planning recommendations and/or alternatives

   v. Implementing the financial planning recommendations

   vi. Monitoring the financial planning recommendations

11. The unique contribution made by each member of the estate planning team includes:

   a. Attorney: drafting legal documents

   b. Accountant: preparing the client's financial statements and tax returns often gives him or her the greatest and earliest financial contact with the client

   c. Life Underwriter: providing insurance contracts to meet liquidity needs at the client's death

   d. Trust Officer: providing fiduciary services as experienced trustee and/or executor

   e. Financial Planner: potentially capable of creating a complete financial plan, one including recommendations concerning insurance, investments, retirement planning, income tax planning and estate planning

13. (a) The client's principal goal is happiness and peace of mind. Estate planning deals principally with property transfer decisions, many of which are fundamentally unsettling for some individuals. (b) Answers will vary. One example would be that making large gifts may decrease a person's estate tax but make him or her feel less financially secure.

15. To reduce estate taxes one might making large gifts to children, but this might result in the children losing their drive to be productive.

17. There are numerous sites that come up in response to "estate planning goals." Some of them are selling trust services, investment management, retirement planning, or attorney referral services. Some are out of date as indicated by using $10,000 as the maximum for the annual gift exclusion or $600,000 as the maximum for tax free estate transfers. Others appear to be current and have useful articles and links to other estate planning related sites.

19. Nontax financial estate planning goals:(a) Minimizing nontax estate transfer costs. (b) Maintaining a satisfactory standard of living. (c) Ensuring proper disposition. (d) Preserving business value. (e) Attaining pre- and postmortem flexibility. (f) Maximizing benefits for the surviving spouse.

21. The advantage of selecting a surrogate decision maker is the person chooses someone he or she trusts to "get things done right" in the event of incapacity or death, rather than having a court choose the person(s) to make decisions.

23. Income tax savings goals: (a) Obtaining a stepped-up basis. (b) Shifting income to a lower bracket taxpayer. (c) Deferring recognition of income.

25. An important question that everyone should answer, but each in his or her own way.

Sample Client Fact-Finding Questionnaire

Susan R. Goodall
5556 Long Street, Suite 245
Anytown, ST 54321
888/555-3456

DATA SHEET FOR ESTATE PLAN
Married Persons
(With Minor Children)

Please print or type the following information. If you need more space, use the reverse side (include the question number). If you are not certain about an answer, write a question mark next to it. If you have questions, write them down at the end of this data sheet. *It is more important that you return this in a timely fashion than that it be complete.*

1. Husband's (H) full name _____
   Name used on real estate documents _____
   Other or former names _____
   Wife's (W) full name _____
   Name used on real estate documents _____
   Other or former names _____
   Citizenship: Husband _____ Wife _____

2. a.   Residents of _____ County.
   b.   Address _____
   _____
   c.   Home phone # _____   Business # _____

3. Date of Birth: (H) _____   (W) _____
   Place of Birth: (H) _____   (W) _____
   Date of Marriage: _____ Place: _____
   Approximate dates moved to California   (H) _____   (W) _____
   Social Security #: (H) _____   (W) _____
   Occupation: (H) _____
                  (W) _____

4. Family:
   a.   Children of this marriage:

Name	Birth date	Residence (If still living with you, put "Home")
_____	_____	_____
_____	_____	_____
_____	_____	_____

   b.   Are there children by prior marriages?   Yes/no. Whose child? Please give full information below:

Name	Birth date	Residence (If still living with you, put "Home")
_____	_____	_____
_____	_____	_____
_____	_____	_____

   c.   If there are deceased children who left issue, please give information below:
   _____
   _____

    d.   Living parents (names/addresses):

        (H) _____

        _____

        (W) _____

        _____

    e.   Brothers and Sisters (names/addresses):

        (H) _____

        _____

        (W) _____

        _____

    f.   Should you or your children adopt a child (or children), should they inherit on the same basis as natural children and/or grandchildren? __

5. Friends to whom you intend to leave bequests (names/addresses):

    a. _____

    b. _____

6. Estate information (to nearest $10,000)

    a.   The net value of our assets is approximately $_____

    b.   Our three major assets and their approximate net values are:

    (1) _____ (value $_____)

    (2) _____ (value $_____)

    (3) _____ (value $_____)

7. How is title to your property actually held? Bring title documents with you when you come to see me.

8. Give the following information about your life insurance:

Whose Life? H or W	Company/ Policy No.	Owner H/W/Both	Beneficiary & 1st Alternate	Amount
____	_____	_____	_____	_____
____	_____	_____	_____	_____

9. Have you entered into a community property agreement? Yes/no
   Have you entered into a prenuptial or postnuptial agreement? Yes/no

10. Distribution. Put your thoughts in general terms at part (b). We will discuss
    details at the time of interview.

    a.   Specific gifts (show gift, i.e., heirlooms, money, etc. and the
         beneficiaries' names and addresses).
         1. _____
            _____
         2. _____
            _____
         3. _____
            _____
         4. _____
            _____

         For specific gifts, indicate which alternative:
           1st alternative: Property left free and clear _____
           2nd alternative: Property left with encumbrances _____

    b.   Residue (1st) _____
         _____
         (2nd) (if people in 1 predecease me) _____
         _____
         (3rd) (if people in 1 & 2 predecease me) _____
         _____

11. Please circle the answer to the following questions. (If yes, give details and,
    if appropriate, approximate values on the reverse side. If a document is
    involved, attach a photocopy.)

    a.   In any year, have you made gifts to anyone of more than $3,000 prior to
         1982 or $10,000 after 1981? (H)Yes/no (W) Yes/no

b. Does either of you expect to inherit or receive gifts totaling in excess of $100,000 from your parents and/or from others? (H) Yes/no (W) Yes/no

c. Do you have powers of appointment? (H) Yes/no (W) Yes/no

d. Do you have Wills already drawn? (H) Yes/no (W) Yes/no

12. If a trust is contemplated: Proposed Trustee (give the relationship, name, and address if not already listed):
1st choice: _____
2nd choice: _____
3rd choice: _____

13. If there are minor children: Proposed Guardian (relationship/name/address if not already listed):

1st choice: _____
2nd choice: _____
3rd choice: _____

14. Proposed executor (relationship/name/address if not already listed):

(H) 1st choice: _____
    2nd choice: _____
    3rd choice: _____

(W) 1st choice: _____
    2nd choice: _____
    3rd choice: _____

15. Are specific burial instructions available to the executor? If yes, explain:
(H) _____
(W) _____

16. Do you have a safe deposit box? Yes/no
    a.   Where? _____
    b.   Who has access? H _____ W _____ Other _____

17. Where shall the original of the will be kept? (check one)
    a.   Client's (your) safe deposit box _____
    b.   Other place _____ Where? _____

18. How many photocopies of each will do you want, i.e., in addition to the original? H _____ W _____ (Giving a copy to your executor is optional.)

19. Questions to ask your attorney:

    a.   _____

    b.   _____

    c.   _____

    d.   _____

    e.   _____

    f.   _____

    g.   _____

    h.   _____

CHAPTER 2

Basic Estate Planning Concepts

OVERVIEW

This chapter introduces the basic concepts regularly employed in estate planning. They will be referred to throughout the text. Some of these concepts are so straightforward that mere use of them in a sentence will make their meaning clear. More involved concepts and terms are defined and illustrated. The terms, along with others introduced in later chapters, are included in the Glossary at the end of this book.

CONCEPTS DEALING WITH ESTATES

An *estate* is a quantity of wealth or property. *Property* represents something over which the owner may lawfully exercise the right to use, control, or dispose. More simply, property is anything that can be owned.

Ordinarily, for a person or a family, an estate represents the total amount of property owned. However, the word *estate* is used in several other contexts in estate planning to mean some other amount. In certain situations, estate means the *net* value of property owned, calculated by subtracting the amount of the estate owner's liabilities from the value of all property owned. Estate might refer to the *probate estate*, which constitutes all property that passes to others by means of the probate process after the death of the owner. Estate may mean the *gross estate* or the *taxable estate*, two concepts used only in connection with taxation at death. As we will see later, the probate estate and the tax-related estate may be very different in size and composition. The net estate and the probate estate are generally less than all property owned; the net estate is less because liabilities are subtracted, and the probate estate is less because many things owned, e.g., held in joint tenancy and life insurance, pass outside the probate process. The gross estate will equal or exceed the value of all property owned because it includes all things owned and may also include things that are not owned, such as gift taxes paid on gifts made within three years of the donor's death. In Chapter 6 we will cover the concepts of the gross estate and the taxable estate in detail.

CONCEPTS DEALING WITH TRANSFERS OF PROPERTY

One of the primary areas of emphasis in estate planning is the transfer of property. This section will cover the terminology used in this area.

Transfers of Legal and Beneficial Interests

A *transfer* or *assignment* of property refers to any type of passing of property in which the *transferor* gives up an *interest* to the *transferee*. The interest transferred can be purely legal, purely beneficial, or both legal and beneficial. *Legal interest* refers to a situation where title passes. For example, an independent trustee of a trust takes title to all trust assets in order to manage the trust property, but cannot use it in a manner inconsistent with the trust agreement. A mother who takes title as custodian of a bank account established for her child's benefit under the Uniform Transfers to Minors Act[1] has legal title, but the beneficial interest is owned by the child.

On the other hand, a purely *beneficial interest* occurs when a transferee receives something that carries an economic benefit, but not title. Examples of beneficial interest in property include the temporary or permanent right to possess, consume, pledge, or otherwise benefit from property. If a friend lends you her car while your car is in the shop, you have a beneficial interest in the car without having title. As we will see, a trust beneficiary's rights may be purely beneficial.

Finally, an interest given up by the transferor can be both legal and beneficial, such as where the transferee receives both title and the beneficial interest. An *outright transfer* occurs when one receives both legal and beneficial interests, without restrictions or conditions, as typically happens when one person gives another a birthday present.

Complete versus incomplete transfers. A transfer of property is said to be *complete* and *irrevocable* when it is no longer rescindable or amendable, i.e., when the transferor has totally relinquished all dominion and control over that property. For example, after you purchase a magazine at the store, you have made a completed transfer of money and the store has made a complete transfer of title to the magazine. On the other hand, a transfer is said to be *incomplete* and *revocable* while it is still rescindable or amendable. In some states, if you purchase a time-share property, you have three days after signing the purchase agreement to change your mind and receive a total refund of your deposit. The transaction is incomplete until the three days pass without the buyer's rescission of the contract. When a trust is established, the settlor might or might not retain the right to revoke or amend it. If it is a revocable trust, the settlor has the right to take back the trust property. Even if it is irrevocable, the transfer is deemed incomplete if the settlor has retained control over who gets to benefit from the trust even if the benefits cannot possibly favor the settlor.

EXAMPLE 2 - 1. In 2006, using property worth over $500,000, Samantha establishes an irrevocable trust for the benefit of her two nieces, Anna and Virginia, 15 and 18 years old, respectively. A private fiduciary serves as the trustee. The terms of the trust allow Samantha to decide each year how to allocate the income between the two nieces, and requires that when Anna turns 25, the trust must terminate with the trust property divided evenly between Anna and Virginia. Because of the retained right to determine who receives the income, the gift is incomplete. It will not become complete until Anna turns 25. The gift will be based upon the value of the assets at that time. Of course, because the gift is incomplete, the income is taxed to Samantha and each distribution of income is considered a completed gift from Samantha to the niece receiving it.

Property as a bundle of rights. To fully distinguish between complete and incomplete transfers, one must grasp that ownership of property is really a bundle of rights that can sometimes be separated. So if one sells something, such as 100 shares of ABC stock, we would understand that to mean the entire asset, including all rights and interests that go with ownership. However, the bundle of rights inherent in property ownership are sometimes divided, hence when one speaks of an *interest in property* the reference is to one or more of these individual rights. In estate planning, more than one interest in a piece of property may be transferred in a way that highlights the divisibility of the interests associated with property ownership.

> EXAMPLE 2 - 2. Tom transfers 100 shares of stock in trust to Terry. The trust terms give Alan the right to all income for five years, followed by Barbara having the right to receive income for ten years, and finally, after 15 years, the trust is to terminate with the trust assets distributed to Carl. Each person has received an "interest" in the stock. Terry's interest is a legal one (title), Alan and Barbara each have a beneficial one (really in the trust, and only indirectly in the stock), and Carl's interest is both beneficial and legal in the sense that he will benefit from the trust and will take title to assets when the trust terminates. We'll take a more detailed look at trusts in the next couple of chapters.

Giving up control makes a transfer complete. A transfer of each specific interest in property is either complete or incomplete. To be complete, the transferor must part with control over the property.

> EXAMPLE 2 - 3. Continuing with the same facts as above, if Tom retained the right to revoke or amend the entire trust, his transfers of property into trust would be incomplete. On the other hand, if Tom retained the right to revoke or amend only Alan's interest, the transfer of Alan's interest would be incomplete, and the transfer of Barbara and Carl's interests would be complete. Finally, if Tom retained no right whatsoever over the trust, the transfers to Alan, Barbara, and Carl would all be complete.

When we study gift taxes, it will become clear that this issue of whether a transfer is complete or incomplete is important because gift tax law generally treats completed transfers, even of just a partial interest, as gifts subject to gift taxation and any attempt to retain control, even if the right retained has no economic benefit for the transferor, makes the gift incomplete.

Fair Market Value Concept. The value of a transfer is measured by its fair market value at the time of the transfer. Determining fair market value (abbreviated as FMV) is the subject of several sections in the text. A generally accepted definition of *fair market value* is "the price at which the property would change hands between a willing buyer and a willing seller, neither being under any compulsion to buy or sell, and both having reasonable knowledge of the relevant facts." The IRS uses this definition in the regulations for valuing gifts and estates.[2] For gifts the value is determined as of the date of the gift. For estates it is the date of death value that generally matters, although in some instances the executor can elect to use the value as of six months after the date of death but we will save a discussion of the *alternate valuation election*[3] until Chapter 6.

Sale Versus Gift

Most commonly, completed transfers of property interests are undertaken by sale, by gift, and more rarely by a combination of both sale and gift. A *sale* is a transfer of property under which each transferor exchanges *consideration* regarded as equivalent in value. By contrast, a gift is a transfer of property for which the transferor takes back little or nothing of economic value in exchange. The most common methods of making gift transfers are *outright* and *in trust*.

Arm's-length transactions. Where two parties to a transaction are not related and are each negotiating to secure the best advantage for his or her own-self, it is said to be an "arm's-length" transaction. The fact that one of the parties greatly underestimates the FMV of what he is selling does not make it a bargain sale, indeed, it might just be a bad bargain, e.g., there would be no gift involved if a person sells an old painting for $100 at a garage sale and the painting turns out to be a Cezanne worth hundreds of thousands of dollars.

A bargain sale. A bargain sale occurs when a person (the transferor) transfers property in exchange for other property that the transferor knows has an economic value less than the property he or she is giving up. A bargain sale involves a transfer that is a part sale and part gift. The notion of the bargain sale requires us to define a gift somewhat more broadly than in the last paragraph. Usually a gift means the donor takes nothing in return; however, a bargain sale is obviously a gift even though property is received by the donor. A *bargain sale* occurs when there is an exchange of considerations significantly unequal in value, and the parties know and intend them to be unequal. In tax law, the amount of the gift is the difference between the values of the exchanged property.

Transfers Now or Then

A transfer of property can be *inter vivos*, meaning that it is made while the transferor is alive, or it can be made at death. Inter vivos is Latin for "among the living." Transfers at death are guided by legally binding documents prepared by the owner before death (e.g., will, trust, title by joint tenancy, or insurance beneficiary designation), or pursuant to state law (intestate succession) in the event that there is no document to guide or control the transfer. A will or trust document is sometimes referred to as an *instrument*.

Beneficiaries. A *beneficiary* or *donee* is a person who receives a gift of a beneficial interest in property from a transferor. The transferor is called a *donor*. Although, in the most general sense, donee and beneficiary are synonymous, in certain contexts one or the other term is more commonly used. For example, the recipient of an outright *inter vivos* gift from the donor is usually called a donee, whereas, the recipient of a bequest by a will or an interest in a trust is usually called a beneficiary. Occasionally, the term *donee* is used to describe one who has received something without also receiving any beneficial interest, such as where one is given a limited power of appointment, an estate planning tool discussed later in this chapter and again, in the context of the estate tax, in Chapter 6.

WILLS, TRUSTS, AND PROBATE

There is a fair amount of misconception about the relationship between wills and probate, between wills and trusts, and between trusts and probate. Having a will neither causes nor avoids probate. Having a trust does not do away with the need to have a will. Having a trust drafted may or may not avoid probate depending upon the type of will and whether it is funded or not.

Estate Matters

In estate planning, a *decedent* refers to a deceased person. When a person dies, property owned by the decedent must be transferred. Each state takes special interest in ensuring that all property owned by the decedent is transferred to the proper parties. State law recognizes certain documents prepared by the decedent (wills, trusts, joint tenancy arrangements, life insurance policies, etc.) as legally binding guides for the proper disposition of the decedent's property. A *will* is a written document that expresses a person's desired distribution of his or her property at death. The person making a will is called the *testator*. The will is said to make *testamentary* transfers, and the actual process by which transfer is accomplished is the probate process. At the death of a person, his or her will controls the transfer of property only if there is no guide to the transfer that is recognized as superior. Thus, the will controls property in the decedent's name alone or held with another as a tenant in common, but not property held in trust or in joint tenancy. Property held in trust will be transferred according to the terms of the trust, not according to the terms of the settlor's will. An attempt to direct the transfer joint tenancy property by a decedent co-owner's will fails, since by law the right of survivorship inherent in joint tenancy title prevails over provisions in a will.

A trust is a fiduciary relationship in which one person (the *trustee*) is the holder of the title to property (the *trust estate* or the *trust corpus*), subject to an equitable obligation to keep or use the property for the benefit of another (the *beneficiary*). The *trust instrument* is the written agreement between the *settlor* (the person creating and funding the trust) and the *trustee* that sets forth for whose benefit the trust is created, how the trust estate is to be managed, its duration, and to whom the corpus must be given when the trust terminates. Another term for settlor is *trustor*. Trusts are described in greater detail later in the chapter.

Will or no will. If a valid will is found, the decedent is said to have died *testate*. If the will does not dispose of all the decedent's property, the decedent is said to have died *partially intestate*. If no will is found, the decedent is said to have died *intestate*. However, if all property is disposed of by alternative means (e.g., trusts, joint tenancy), a will may not be necessary, and the absence of a will would not cause any problems as there would be no property without some mechanism of transfer.

In some cases, the moment that death occurs has significance because it determines the rights of beneficiaries, and, quite obviously, it is extremely important if the dying person has authorized organ donations. The Uniform Determination of Death Act addresses this issue by defining death as follows:

> § 1. [Determination of Death]. An individual who has sustained either (1) irreversible cessation of circulatory and respiratory functions, or (2) irreversible cessation of all functions of the entire brain, including the brain stem, is dead. A determination of death must be made in accordance with accepted medical standards.[4]

Probate. *Probate* is the legal process of administering the estate of a decedent with some degree of court supervision. The probate estate consists of all property belonging to the decedent for which there is no other mechanism of transfer. Thus, the probate estate is that property whose disposition is guided by either the decedent's will or the state laws of intestate succession. Generally, *probate assets* fall into one of three groups: property owned by the decedent as an individual, interests of the decedent held with others as tenants-in-common, and, in some community property states, the decedent's one-half interest in community property. Some community property states, such as California, no longer require a probate for property going to the surviving spouse whether that property is the decedent's half of the community property or is the decedent's separate property. *Non-probate assets* include property held in trust, property with title in joint tenancy, the proceeds of insurance policies on the life of the decedent (unless payable to the decedent's estate), and most retirement plan assets. More on this later in the chapter.

The estate's personal representative. In probate administration, the judge of the probate court determines the validity of the will, if any, and (after a period of administration) authorizes distribution of the probate estate to creditors and beneficiaries. The court appoints a *personal representative* to act as fiduciary to represent and manage the probate estate. If the court appoints the person nominated in the will to be personal representative that person is called the *executor*. An *administrator* is a person appointed by the court to represent the estate of a person who died intestate. In some states, a female personal representative is called an executrix or administratrix, however the trend is to use the title of executor or administrator regardless of gender. At times courts appoint someone other than the person(s) nominated in the will. The person nominated may have predeceased the testator, may be incapacitated, or perhaps is unfit (e.g., is serving time in prison for bank robbery). If the decedent died with a valid will, but the court appoints someone other than the person nominated in it, the personal representative is called an *administrator with will annexed*.

The word "fiduciary" is derived from the Latin word for "trust." A *fiduciary* is a person in a position of trust, loyalty, and confidence, who has the legal duty to act for the benefit of another, putting that person's interests above his or her own. Besides personal representatives, fiduciaries include trustees, guardians, and agents.

Recipients of probate property. Beneficiaries of a decedent's probate property are called heirs, devisees, or legatees. An *heir* is a person who inherits property from a decedent whether by will, intestate succession, or any other mechanism of transfer such as through a trust or by joint tenancy. *Heir at law* refers to the person (or persons) who would have a right to inherit if the person died intestate. Degrees of blood relationship, which are important in determining heirs at law, is a topic covered in Chapter 4. A *devisee* is a beneficiary, under a will, of a gift of real property. A devisee is said to receive a *devise*. A *legatee* is a beneficiary, under a will, of any property other than real property. Non-real estate is called *personalty* or personal property. Personal property does not mean personal use property, it just means that it is not real estate. For instance, a cash register used in a store is clearly business use property but in a technical sense it is considered personal property. A legatee is said to receive a *legacy* or a *bequest*. The trend in modern usage is to use the term bequest for any testamentary gift, whether of real or personal property. The Uniform Probate Code (UPC), discussed in extensively in the next two chapters, uses the term "devise" both as a noun and a verb, to mean a bequest or the act of making a bequest (whether of real or personal property) in connection with transfers by will.

Issue refers to a person's offspring or progeny, including children, grandchildren, great-grandchildren, and the like. A *descendant* is one who is descended from a specific ancestor. Thus, the terms issue and descendants are used interchangeably. Be careful not to mix up the term decedent (the one who died) with descendant (a child, grandchild, etc.).

Types of bequests. Bequests are categorized as specific, pecuniary, general, residuary, and/or class gifts. A *specific bequest* is a gift of a particular item of property capable of being identified and distinguished from all other property in the testator's estate, e.g., "I leave all my household furnishings to Sally Ann," and "I leave my high school ring to my brother Bill." If the property subject to a specific bequest is sold, given away, or lost before the testator's death, under the common law doctrine of *ademption* (from the Latin *ademptio*, a taking away) the bequest fails, meaning the person does not receive anything to replace the missing property. Although most states follow the common law doctrine, some states' statutes have exceptions that do not result in ademption in certain circumstances, e.g., an asset was acquired by the decedent in a manner that made it clear it was intended to replace specific devised real or tangible property.[5] A *general bequest* is a gift that can be satisfied out of the general assets of the estate, e.g., the bequest "I leave 10 percent of my estate to my brother Henry."

At common law the term *legacy* meant a testamentary gift of money or personal property; however, it has come to mean any bequest. *Pecuniary bequest* is the term used to describe a bequest expressed as a specific dollar amount. The term comes from the Latin *pecunia*, meaning money. It is a pecuniary bequest even though the executor has the option of satisfying it with cash or with assets worth the specified dollar amount. Since the bequest could be paid from any account, or be satisfied by the transfer of any asset not specifically bequeathed, a pecuniary bequest is a type of general bequest.

What remains of the estate after all the foregoing bequests are taken into account is called the *residue* of the estate. A *residuary bequest* is a gift of that part of the testator's estate not otherwise disposed of by the will, e.g., "I leave the rest of my estate to Robert Moon." Generally, debts are paid out of the residue and not charged against the specific bequests.

A *class gift* is a gift to a group of individuals that may not be completely defined at the time the gift is made (e.g., "I leave the residue of my estate to my grandchildren living at the time of my death.")

A person might die leaving insufficient assets to satisfy all bequests and pay all creditors. Under a procedure called *abatement*, bequests are eliminated or reduced so that all debts (and administration expenses) are paid in full, or else the estate is exhausted. In those states that follow the UPC, shares of the beneficiaries abate in the following order: (1) probate property not disposed of in the will, if there are no residuary bequests, (2) residuary bequests, (3) general bequests, and (4) specific bequests. Some state statutes abate gifts to a spouse, or to issue, only after the abatement of gifts to persons not so closely related to the decedent.

> EXAMPLE 2 - 4. Lawrence died in a UPC state. Lawrence's will leaves his car to his son, Sam, $20,000 cash to his sister, Vira, and the residue of his estate to his wife, Mary Ellen. Assume that at his death Lawrence owned only the car and $25,000 in cash, and he owed $6,000 in debts. Most states (perhaps all) would require the $6,000 debt be paid, leaving just $19,000 in cash. The UPC abatement would result in Vira getting the $19,000 balance, the car would go to Sam, and Mary Ellen would receive nothing. As discussed later, many states allow a widow or widower to claim a statutorily determined share of the deceased spouse's estate instead of taking what is left by will. Claiming an elective share would probably give Mary Ellen the entire $19,000, leaving sister Vira with nothing.

Disclaimers

Most people would welcome a large bequest, especially if it came from a distant relative. After all, such gifts may make for financial security. Yet there are times when it makes sense for a beneficiary to refuse a gift or bequest. A *disclaimer* is an unqualified refusal to accept a gift or bequest. Disclaiming may be preferable when it avoids, reduces, or delays transfer taxes. The person refusing the gift is called the disclaimant. If the disclaimer is done "right" it will not be treated as a gift by the disclaimant. This is referred to as being a *tax effective* disclaimer, meaning that the act of disclaiming does not generate a transfer tax. Usually, a person will disclaim property only if it will then pass to a person the disclaimant wants to have it.

To be tax-effective, the disclaimer must meet the requirements of both state property law and federal tax law. Under property law, a disclaimant is treated as having *predeceased* the decedent-donor.[6] Consequently, the disclaimed property will pass under one of two possible sets of legal guidelines. Either it will pass to the "alternate taker" in accordance with the terms of the decedent's transfer document (which is usually a will or trust) or, if no such document exists or if the document does not name an alternate taker, the property will pass under laws of intestacy.

> EXAMPLE 2 - 5. Bachelor Barry died recently, and his will left an estate valued at $500,000 to his brother Mike, if living, otherwise to Mike's issue. Mike, age 87, wealthy and in poor health, has three living children. If he immediately disclaims the inheritance, it will pass under the will to his children. The transfer will not be treated as a gift from Mike, but rather as though it passed to them directly from Barry.

> EXAMPLE 2 - 6. Changing the facts in the previous example a bit, assume Barry's will stated that if Mike predeceased Barry, then the bequest would go to Barry's long time friend Charlie. If Mike disclaims, Barry's estate will pass to Charlie rather than to Mike's children. Of course, Mike could assign his interest in the estate to his children, but that would be a gift from him to them.

When we take up estate and gift taxes, we will cover in detail the requirements for a tax-effective disclaimer, and we will illustrate ways in which disclaimers are used to improve estate plans.

LIFE INSURANCE

A *life insurance* policy is a contract in which the insurance company, in exchange for the payment of premiums, agrees to pay a cash lump-sum amount (called the *face value* or *policy proceeds*) to a person designated in the policy to receive it (the *beneficiary*) on the death of the subject of the insurance (the *insured*). Usually, the policy names alternate beneficiaries who will receive the proceeds if the named beneficiary dies. One other important party in the life insurance contract is the *owner*, who has title to the policy, and who generally possesses both legal and beneficial interests in the policy. As beneficial owner, the policy owner has the right to benefit from the policy. Beneficial rights usually include the right to receive policy dividends, the right to designate and to change the beneficiary, and the right to surrender the policy. These rights can have economic value, even before the death of the insured. Whether a life insurance policy has economic value prior to the insured's death depends on the type of policy. If the owner holds title to the policy as the trustee of an irrevocable life insurance trust, then the owner will have legal title but will most likely not have a beneficial interest. Irrevocable life insurance trusts are used to keep life insurance proceeds out of the estate of the insured. Such trusts are discussed in detail later.

Most *term life insurance* policies have minimal cash value prior to the death of the insured because the premium charged, which increases over time along with the increasing risk of death, simply buys pure protection. If the insured dies during the policy term, the company will pay the face value; otherwise, it will pay nothing. Some multi-year term policies (called *level term*) have a constant premium for a stated period (e.g., five or ten years). This requires a cash build-up during the term's early years that is used to pay the higher mortality risk in the later years.

In contrast to a term policy, a *cash value* policy accumulates economic value because the insurer charges a constant premium that is considerably higher than mortality costs require during the earlier years. Part of this overpayment accumulates as a *cash surrender value*, which, prior to the death of the insured, can be used by the owner in one of two ways: (1) at any time the owner can surrender the policy and receive this value in cash, or (2) the owner can request a policy loan and borrow up to the amount of this value.

Life insurance makes a significant contribution to estate planning because a policy can have value prior to the insured's death, can pay cash to the beneficiaries on the insured's death, and can be structured to avoid estate tax. It is said to be the only asset that can create an *instant* estate of substantial magnitude for a person of otherwise modest wealth. For a family that includes dependent children, this may be an important means of assuring the financial well-being of the surviving family members if a parent dies. For the wealthy family, life insurance may provide needed cash to pay the death taxes. A discussion of the types of life insurance and irrevocable life insurance trusts is found in Chapter 13. To use life insurance properly, the planner must be aware of the impact of taxes, a subject explained in detail in Chapters 5 through 8.

TAXATION

In estate planning, the two principal types of taxing authorities are the individual states and the federal government. The four major types of taxes are gift tax, death tax, generation-skipping transfer tax, and income tax.

A *gift tax* is a tax on a lifetime gift; that is, a lifetime transfer of property for less than full consideration.

A *death tax* is essentially a tax levied on certain property owned or transferred by the decedent at death. There are two basic types of death tax statutes, which, depending on the format, are referred to as either an estate tax or an inheritance tax. An *estate tax* is a tax on the decedent's right to transfer property, while an *inheritance tax* is a tax on the right of a beneficiary to receive property from a decedent. Either way, the tax is usually paid by the executor out of the decedent's estate before the property is transferred to the heirs. If most of the property is held in trust, then the trustee will make sure the tax is paid before distributing the trust property. With an inheritance tax, the amount of death tax paid on any given size inheritance is likely to be greater for remote relatives as compared to close relatives, and greatest for non-relatives. For example, amounts going to a surviving spouse might not be taxed at all, and bequests to a child might have a high exemption amount and/or a lower tax rate than property going to a non-relative. The federal death tax is referred to as the federal estate tax. The characteristic of an estate tax is that, for any given net estate (i.e., after debts and expenses), the tax will be the same regardless of who receives it. For example in the year 2007, the federal tax on a $5 million bequest would be $1,815,000 whether the estate went to the decedent's children or went entirely to non-relatives.

However, the federal estate tax is not a pure estate tax because it has two deductions based on the status of the beneficiary. A complete marital deduction is allowed for all property going to a surviving spouse (for a non-USA citizen spouse a special trust might be required, but we'll save that discussion until later), and a complete charitable deduction is allowed for property going to qualified charities. Since these are complete (100%) deductions, subtracted from the gross estate before arriving at the taxable estate, and they are the only two deductions based on the character of the beneficiary, little is lost in our thinking of the federal death tax as an estate tax.

A *generation-skipping transfer tax* is a tax on certain property transferred to someone who is more than one generation younger than the donor - a "skip person." Thus, the surviving spouse and the children of a decedent are not skip persons, but grandchildren and great-grandchildren are. Without this tax, wealth could skip several generations and escape one or more levels of transfer tax. For example, without the GST tax, a gift or estate transfer of a $10 million parcel of land to a grandchild would be subject once to a gift tax or death tax, but it would not be taxed twice. It would be taxed twice if it went through the natural succession, i.e., once when the property passes from the client to the child, and again when it passes from the child to the grandchild. Chapter 5 introduces this topic and Chapter 17 covers it in more detail. It is enough to say here that the generation-skipping transfer tax has a per transferor exemption that makes careful planning in this area necessary only for clients with fairly substantial estates.

An *income tax* is essentially a tax levied on income earned by a taxpayer during a given year. Income tax laws usually distinguish five different taxpayers or entities that must report income by filing income tax returns: individuals, partnerships, corporations, estates, and trusts. Principles of taxation can differ substantially for each. For instance, partnerships generally do not pay income taxes because the partnership is treated as a *passthrough* entity, income and deductions are passed through to be reported by the individual partners. Trusts and estates are partially passthrough entities and tax-paying entities, depending mainly on whether income is retained or distributed. Each taxpayer, including partnerships, must submit an annual income tax return that reports certain items including income, deductions, credits, and the tax due (calculated by using tax tables applicable to that entity). Married individuals may file a joint income tax return in which they report their combined income, deductions, and other information on one return. This textbook will not try to cover income taxes in detail as it is beyond the scope of this course; however, a good introduction to the income taxation of trusts and estates is found in Chapter 8.

PROPERTY INTERESTS

Estate planning seeks to preserve and efficiently transfer an individual's wealth. Wealth is generally thought of as the property a person owns. This section will describe some of the ways in which property can be owned. Essentially, ownership can be classified in the following six ways:

- The physical characteristics of property (e.g., real versus personal)
- The extent of ownership interest in property (e.g., fee simple or a life estate)
- The type of co-ownership (e.g., joint tenancy versus tenants in common)
- A legal versus a beneficial interest (e.g., property held in the name of the trustee versus a trust beneficial interest)
- A present versus a future interest (e.g., an income interest in a trust versus a remainder interest)
- A vested versus a contingent interest (e.g., outright ownership of land versus a contingent remainder interest, where the remainderman must outlive the income beneficiary or the trust property reverts back to the trustor's estate)

Classification of Property by Physical Characteristics

Property is classified as real or personal. *Real property* includes ownership interests in land and any improvements, such as buildings, fences, trees, and the like, that are attached to the land. Curiously, an interest for years (a leasehold) in real estate is considered personal property. Accordingly, a good functional definition of *personal property* is all property except interests in land and its improvements.

Property is further divided into tangible and intangible property. Something is tangible if it can be perceived by the senses as having a physical existence. *Tangible personal property* is personal property whose utility comes primarily from its physical characteristics rather than the legal rights conferred on the owner or possessor of the property. Conversely, *intangible personal property* derives its value from the legal rights it represents. Thus a newspaper is tangible personal property because its value is based on the news printed therein. Initially, one might pay 35 cents to read it. A few days later, the value may drop to almost nothing, being useful only to wrap dead fish or as recycled newspaper. Yet, a very old paper with an article of historical significance on the front page may be worth a lot to collectors of old newspapers. On the other hand, a stock certificate is valuable to the owner of the certificate if the company is a going business, not because of the physical characteristics of the paper it is printed on, but because of the rights it represents, such as the right to vote for the board of directors, the right to dividends when they are declared, and certain liquidation rights. If the company has gone out of business, then the stock certificate has become tangible personal property. The certificate may be worth only the value of the paper it is printed on, or, if it is old or unusual for some reason, it may be of some value as a collector's item.

Intangible personal property includes a *chose in action*, which is a claim for money or property that could be recovered from another in a lawsuit, if such is necessary. A chose in action, pronounced "shows," represents the right to money or property that is owed to the holder of the chose. That right can be transferred, sold, or assigned to another, who can then act on it in his or her own name. The person holding the chose as a result of a transfer is entitled to keep any recovery.

> EXAMPLE 2 - 7. Betty borrows $9,000 from Lenny, agreeing to pay it back by December 31 of this year. Lenny signs a piece of paper assigning to his daughter, Christine, his right to collect the debt. Since the debt could be collected by a lawsuit if necessary, it is considered to be a chose in action, and the assignment to Christine gives her the right to collect it.

Basic Interests in Property

The three basic interests in property are fee simple, life estate, and estate for years.

Fee simple. A *fee simple* interest, often called a *fee* or a *fee simple absolute*, represents the greatest interest that a person can have over *real* property and corresponds to our usual notion of full ownership. Common rights include the right to possess, use, pledge, or transfer the property. If you own a house, even if it is subject to a mortgage, you probably have it in fee.

Life estate. A *life estate* interest in property, like a fee simple, is a powerful form of ownership, but is different in that the interest ceases on someone's death. Ordinarily, the *measuring life* is that of the owner of the interest. However, it could be any other person.

> EXAMPLE 2 - 8. Doctor Bud assigns his interest in a house to Gladis, his widowed mother, for her to use and enjoy until her death. Gladis has received a life estate in the house. Her own life is the measuring life.

A life estate for the life of someone other than the owner of the interest is called an estate *for the life of another*. These are rarely used.

EXAMPLE 2 - 9. Facts are similar to the previous example, except that Gladis's interest will cease on the death of Bud. Gladis still has a life estate in the house but now Bud's life, rather than her life, is the measuring life. She has an estate for the life of another.

Ordinarily, the owner of a life estate enjoys, for the length of a measuring life, complete ownership, nearly equivalent to a fee, except that it will end on the life tenant's death. However, life estates are sometimes created so that the recipient enjoys only a partial present interest in the property.

EXAMPLE 2 - 10. Aunt Jane, owner of dividend-paying common stock, gives to her niece Barbie the right to receive the dividends for as long as Barbie lives. Barbie has received a life estate in the income of the stock. Under the customary arrangements, Barbie does not have many rights in the stock itself. For example, she does not have the right to possess or sell the stock, or to use it as collateral against a loan. The stock will be held by someone else, either the original owner, or more commonly, a trustee under a trust arrangement.

Trusts are used extensively in estate planning and will be discussed in every chapter of this book. An introduction to trusts follows this discussion of property.

Interest for years. Often, a person transfers possession and/or enjoyment of property to another for a fixed period. This is called an *estate for years*—even if the fixed period is something other than a certain number of years.

EXAMPLE 2 - 11. Professor Jackson rents his cottage to Dr. Johnson, a visiting professor, for the spring semester. Dr. Johnson has an estate "for years" even though the semester is only four months long.

EXAMPLE 2 - 12. Mary is presently enjoying a life estate, for her life, in the income from certain common stock. Today Mary transfers to Mark her interest for the next ten years. If Mary does not survive the full ten years, Mark's interest will be cut off on Mary's death. Mary cannot transfer any greater interest than she actually owns, and Mark's interest is limited to that which Mary can legally give; thus, Mark has an income interest in the stock, ending at the earlier of ten years or Mary's death.

A common example of an interest for years is a *leasehold*, which entitles the lessee to possess and use the property (e.g., a house or computer) for a specified time, usually in exchange for a fixed series of payments. Leasehold interests can amount to a valuable part of a lessee's wealth if the fixed payments are below current market rates, and if the lessee is permitted to "sublet" the property.

EXAMPLE 2 - 13. Five years ago, Freda acquired a 15-year leasehold interest in a commercial building and is obligated to pay $15,000 per year for the entire period. If the rent for comparable buildings is $25,000 per year for the next ten years, and assuming a discount rate of 8%, the value of Freda's leasehold is the present value of $10,000 for ten years, discounted at 8%, or $67,101 [see Table B, annuity factor of 6.7101]. Freda could possibly sell her interest for that amount.

Annuities. Generally, an annuity is a series of payments for a period of time. The source could be a pension or it could be an investment annuity. The person receiving the annuity is called the annuitant and the entity (often and insurance company) or the person making the payments is called the obligor. With an investment annuity, the investor may pay in a lump sum and start receiving payments almost immediately or may delay the payments for a period of time, e.g., timing them to start when the annuitant retires. The payments may be for the annuitant's lifetime or may be for a period of years. On the other hand, the investor-annuitant might pay money into the annuity account for a period of years, called the accumulation phase, and then start drawing out the annuity. Finally, when working with an annuity provider such as an insurance company, the annuitant may have the option of having set payments (the dollar amount will not fluctuate) or might have the payments vary based upon the performance of selected mutual funds or some other indicator.

Concurrent Ownership

Property may be owned individually, in which case one person owns and uses it, or it may be owned concurrently by two or more persons. Where there is *concurrent ownership*, title may be taken as joint tenancy, tenants by the entirety, tenants in common, or as community property.

A common characteristic of all types of concurrent ownership is the *undivided* right to use the entire property, not just a physically identifiable portion. In addition, the co-owners usually each have the right, in the event of a dispute, to have the property physically divided (partitioned), at which time concurrent ownership ends. If the nature of the property is such that it cannot be partitioned, a court may order it sold and the proceeds divided among the owners according to their respective shares.

Joint tenancy interests. The defining characteristic of property held in joint tenancy is that, on the death of one co-owner, the decedent's interest automatically passes to the surviving owner(s). The owners are said to hold title in *joint tenancy*, or it may be said that they are *joint tenants*. Property law, developed as part of our common law, requires that the interests all be equal, and the owners' respective shares should not be stated as part of the title, thus, "Jim, John, and Jose, as joint tenants," not "Jim, John, and Jose, as joint tenants each owning a one-third share." Because tenants in common can own unequal shares, the share of each is usually expressed in the title; therefore the second statement, with the shares defined as "one-third," might result in a claim by the heirs of a deceased co-owner that tenants in common was actually intended and that the one-third interest belongs to them and not to the surviving co-owners.

Under joint tenancy, ownership passes to the surviving cotenant automatically at a cotenant's death by *operation of law,* meaning that the law recognizes the transfer as immediate on the cotenant's death without any action required by the survivors. However some authorities, such as banks, will require document revision in order to transact further business. A title company will want proof of the death of a joint tenant before it will issue title insurance should the survivors try to transfer title to someone else.

EXAMPLE 2 - 14. John and Mary own a house as joint tenants. At John's death, Mary automatically becomes the sole owner of the house. However, as a practical matter, she might have to record an affidavit establishing the death of a joint tenant, with a certified death certificate attached, in order to clear the title.

The automatic right of survivorship inherent in joint tenancy prevails over other means of transfers at death, including the will and the trust instrument.

EXAMPLE 2 - 15. Continuing the prior example, if, John had executed a will that left his one-half interest in the house to his son, Mary would still receive it by right of survivorship. The joint tenancy designation supersedes the will.

However, in certain jurisdictions, agreements can be executed between joint owners to nullify a joint tenancy designation.

EXAMPLE 2 - 16. Continuing prior examples, if John and Mary were to execute a written *agreement* stating their intention that the house, presently held in joint tenancy, is in fact to be held by them as community property or as tenants in common (see description below), many jurisdictions will honor the agreement, and the house would not pass to Mary by automatic right of survivorship.

Joint tenancy interests in real estate are created by a written document called a deed. In most states, one cotenant can unilaterally "sever" the joint tenancy without the knowledge or consent of the other tenant(s).

> EXAMPLE 2 - 17. Oscar, Ray, Sam, and Clark own Green Acre Ranch as joint tenants. Without telling the other three, Sam deeds his interest to his friend Ed. Sam has broken the joint tenancy insofar as his interest is concerned. Ed owns a one-fourth interest as a tenant in common with the other three holding title to three-fourths as joint tenants. If Ray then dies, Oscar and Clark will own the three-fourths as joint tenants, and Ed will continue to own one-fourth. If Ed dies, his share will go to his heirs, not to the other co-owners.

Joint tenancies are commonly created among family members, as they are the most likely to appreciate the simplicity of this means of transfer and are least likely to be concerned that the ultimate owner of the property may be determined by whom among them lives the longest.

Tenants by the entirety. Holding title as *tenants by the entirety* is like a joint tenancy in that it carries that key characteristic of joint tenancy, the right of survivorship; however, an interest by the entirety can be created only between husband and wife. Unlike joint tenancy, neither spouse may transfer or encumber the property without the consent of the other. Tenants by the entirety is a common law concept, generally not recognized in the community property states. In addition, a few of the common law states no longer recognize this form of ownership and will treat an attempt to create it as merely joint tenancy. Since tenants by the entirety is available only to married couples, a divorce causes said title to automatically transmute, from a legal standpoint, into tenants in common.

Tenants in common. Like joint tenancy, *tenants in common* interests are held by two or more persons, each having an undivided right to possess property. Unlike joint tenancy interests, however, interests in common may be owned in unequal percentages, and when one owner dies the remaining owners do not automatically succeed in ownership. Instead, the decedent's interest passes through his or her estate, by will or by the laws of intestate succession. The interest can also be transferred to the trustee of a trust and pass according to the provisions of the trust.

EXAMPLE 2 - 18. Jack owns a 16 percent real estate interest in common with two other individuals who, combined, own the other 84 percent. Jack's will leaves his entire estate to his wife, Deanna. On Jack's death, his will determines who will get his interest. Therefore, the 16 percent interest will pass by the probate process to his wife, Deanna, not to the other cotenants.

Interests in common are the title of choice for non-related parties since this form of title, in contrast to joint tenancy interests, creates a means of enjoying common ownership without any of the co-owners losing the right of disposition at death.

Community property interests. In the eight states recognizing it, *community property* is that property acquired by the efforts of either spouse during their marriage while living in a community property state, and other property which by the agreement of the spouses is converted from separate property into community property. *Separate property* is all other property owned by the spouses (e.g., acquired by only one of the spouses by gift, devise, bequest or inheritance, or by a spouse domiciled in a common law state, or acquired by either spouse prior to their marriage). The traditional community property states are Arizona, California, Idaho, Louisiana, Nevada, New Mexico, Texas, and Washington. In addition, Wisconsin has adopted the Uniform Marital Property Act (UMPA)[7], which creates a presumption that property owned by the spouses is property of the marriage, and, as such, it does not belong to just one spouse. This presumption holds even if title to property is in one spouse's name alone. The "marriage property" presumption can be overcome by evidence that sufficiently establishes otherwise, e.g., evidence that it was owned prior to the marriage or acquired by inheritance.

When it comes to classifying income, most of the community property states follow what is referred to as the California rule, which is that income from community property is community property, as is anything bought with that income, and income from separate property is separate property, as is anything bought with that income. Three community property states, Texas, Idaho, and Louisiana, follow what is called the Texas rule and treat income earned from separate property during the marriage as community property. Likewise, Wisconsin law provides, with some exceptions, that "income earned or accrued by a spouse or attributable to property of a spouse during marriage and after the determination date is marital property."[8] The "determination date" is the later of the couple's marriage, their domicile in Wisconsin, or the enactment of Wisconsin's Marriage Property Act. Even Texas-rule states treat the gain on separate property that is sold as separate property, and, of course, anything bought with the proceeds of the sale is separate property.

Community property is owned equally by both spouses. Generally, both spouses must consent to a gift of community property. Community property states allow couples to convert community property to separate property, and vice versa, although some states require a written agreement wherein the spouse whose interest is reduced acknowledges the fact that something has been lost. Separate property is considered entirely owned by the acquiring spouse. In states without community property provisions, of course, all property is separate property. In those states, it would simply be referred to as "the property owned by" Sam, Wanda, or whomever.

> EXAMPLE 2 - 19. Pat and Mary live in New Mexico, a community property state. When they married two years ago, Pat owned a sports car that Mary now uses. Last year Mary's father gave her 100 shares of XYZ stock, which pays a quarterly dividend. Mary used the last dividend check to buy a bicycle. Pat bought a rowboat from money saved from his July paycheck. The stock and bicycle are Mary's separate property. The car is Pat's separate property. All the other assets, including both salaries and the rowboat, are community property.

Community property laws represent the attempt by certain state governments to impose greater fairness in property ownership by married couples. Under old English common law, the husband owned all property that either husband or wife acquired during their marriage. Even after most states recognized the right of married women to own property, during pre-World War II America, the husband typically earned most of the outside income while the wife performed the non income-producing household chores; therefore, husbands usually acquired title to almost all the family wealth. At early common law, a wife was entitled to own none of this property until her husband's death, at which time she received a life estate in one-third of her husband's real property. Called a "dower" interest, it has been modified by most common law states; however, it seldom gives the non-working spouse the advantages inherent in the law of community property, which automatically gives both spouses an immediate equal share in all the property acquired by their efforts during the course of their marriage.

Arizona, California, Idaho, Washington, and Wisconsin have a concept called *quasi-community property*, which is defined as that property, acquired by a resident while domiciled in a non-community property state, which would have been community property had the resident been domiciled in a community property state at the time of acquisition. For example, if a married couple moves to California owning common stock acquired with salary earned during the marriage while they were residents of New York, the stock is quasi-community property. Essentially, quasi-community property is treated as separate property of the acquiring spouse until divorce or death. If the parties divorce, the property is divided in a manner similar to community property. Treatment at death depends on which spouse dies first. If the acquiring spouse dies first, the surviving spouse is entitled to one-half of the property. On the other hand, if the non-acquiring spouse dies first, his or her interest in the property ceases.

Joint tenancy (JT) and community property (CP) have several major similarities and differences that are summarized in the outline below:

1. Major Similarities:
   a. Both involve ownership by more than one person.
   b. The owners have equal ownership rights and equal rights to use the entire property. Their interests are undivided.
   c. Any owner may demand a division of the property into separate, equal shares.
2. Major Differences:
   a. CP exists only between spouses. JT can exist between any two or more persons.
   b. CP rights arise automatically, by operation of law under state statute, even if title or possession is taken by just one of the spouses. Hence, CP is created immediately on acquisition of the property. JT rights are usually created by an agreement of the parties (e.g., they ask that stock be issued in their names as joint tenants) and are not governmentally imposed.
   c. JT includes automatic right of succession to ownership (right of survivorship) by surviving joint owners. This right takes priority over any will. In contrast, CP includes no automatic succession to ownership of the decedent's share by the surviving spouse. Therefore, at death, a spouse can transfer his or her share of CP, by will, to someone other than the spouse. However, intestacy will ordinarily result in succession by the surviving spouse under most state laws of intestate succession.
   d. Property held in JT will not be subject to the probate process. In contrast, the decedent's share of CP may be subject to probate. However, as mentioned earlier, some CP states no longer require a probate if the property is left to the surviving spouse or if, because of intestacy, the surviving spouse will receive the property by the laws of intestate succession.

It is important to make two observations regarding item 2c: First, some states, such as New York, recognize an agreement between the spouses declaring that specified property is held in joint tenancy "for convenience only;" and second, Arizona, California, Idaho, Nevada, and Washington have enacted statutes that allow the designation "community property with right of survivorship." This results in the property being treated like joint tenancy. This means that the decedent spouse's will does not control disposition, and the property transfers to the surviving spouse by operation of law, meaning there is no need for probate.

Introduction to Trusts

Usually, the owner of property has all the rights to possess and enjoy it; however, these interests can be divided so one party has just the "bare legal title" and is responsible for preserving and managing property for the benefit of another, and the other is entitled to enjoy the property in specified ways. The former holds the *legal interest* while the latter holds a *beneficial interest*, also called an *equitable interest*, in the property. Trusts are the most common legal arrangement to employ this division.

The parties. There are three major parties to the trust: settlor, trustee, and beneficiary. The *settlor*, also called *grantor*, *creator*, or *trustor*, is the person who creates the trust, and whose property is used to *fund* the trust. The property held in a trust is called the *principal*, but also the *corpus,* the *res* (Latin for things)*,* or the *trust estate*. The *trustee* is the person, persons, or entity (e.g., bank trust department) who takes legal title to the trust property and manages the trust estate. Usually the trust instrument names an initial trustee and several alternates. The trust *beneficiary* is the person or persons who are named to enjoy beneficial interest in the trust. Placing property in a trust is called *funding* the trust. Funding is accomplished by transferring title of the property into the name of the trustee. Since trusts often last for a long period of time, there are likely to be income beneficiaries, who, as the name implies, receive distributions of trust income. How much of the income will depending on how the trust was written. For instance, some trusts designed to qualify for the estate marital deduction require the surviving spouse receive all of the income from the trust distributed at least annually. Other trusts might give the trustee discretion as to how much income to retain and how much to distribute. Eventually, trusts end and property remaining is distributed, either back to the settlor or the settlor's estate, or to someone else depending on the terms of the trust. If the trust requires the property return to the settlor, this retained interest is referred to as a *reversion*. The property is said to revert to the settlor. If the trust is silent on who receives the property on the termination of the trust, then it will revert to the settlor. Often, the trust does not return to the settlor, but rather goes to someone else, in which case the person is called the *remainderman*, or if more than one person, the *remaindermen*, and the interest is call a *remainder* interest. Figure 2-1 illustrates the relationship between the parties to the trust.

FIGURE 2 - 1   The Parties to a Trust

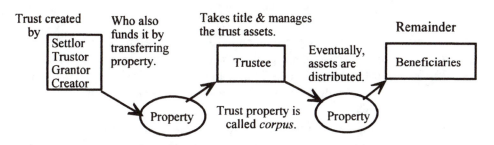

A trust can be *living* or *inter vivos*, meaning it is funded during the life of the trustor, or it can be *testamentary*, to take effect at the trustor's death with the funding mechanism being the probate process. A testamentary trust is one created by the trustor's will. An example of the provisions of a testamentary trust can be found in Chapter 3, Exhibit 3-3.

> EXAMPLE 2 - 20. On November 23, 2006, trustor Harold Stuart transferred 1,000 shares of ABC stock in trust to Uncle Jay as trustee, with the income payable to Harold's son, Chet, for 11 years, after which the corpus of the trust reverts to Harold. Jay receives only legal title which would probably read, "Jay Stuart, as trustee of the Chet Stuart Trust, dated 11/23/2006." Jay is responsible for managing the property during the term of the trust. He can sell the stock and buy other investments in his name, as trustee, but he may not use trust assets for his own benefit, and he is required to distribute all income to Chet, the income beneficiary. Chet has a beneficial interest, that is, an estate for years in the income of the trust.

Reasons for creating trusts. Clients may wish to include trusts in their estate plans for five principal reasons: to provide for multiple beneficiaries, to manage their property if they become incapacitated, to protect beneficiaries from themselves and others, to avoid probate, and to avoid or reduce transfer taxes.

Since these factors are discussed in detail in numerous sections of the text, the following commentary will be brief.

First, clients may wish to *leave their property to more than one person*, either at the same time or successively, over a period of time, and may need an arrangement that will fairly protect each beneficiary's individual property rights.

> EXAMPLE 2 - 21. After his death, Constantine wants to let his second wife enjoy the use of his property for the rest of her life. After her death, Constantine wants the income from his property to be payable to the children of his first marriage until they reach age 30, at which time he wants them to receive the principal outright. By executing a trust, Constantine can appoint a responsible trustee (even his second wife, if both of them are comfortable with the arrangement) to manage the property for what may turn out to be a very long time.

A transfer into a trust is sometimes called a *split interest* transfer, because it divides rights to the corpus into two or more interests, usually an income interest for a specified period of years or for the beneficiary's life, and a "remainder" interest in the principal. Remainder interests will be described shortly and income versus principal interests will be covered a little later.

Second, clients may create trusts to *manage their property if they become incapacitated*. If, due to injury or old age, a person becomes unable to manage his or her property, who will do so? On petition, a court will appoint someone to manage the estate of a disabled person. Depending on the jurisdiction, the court-appointed caretaker is called a *conservator* (i.e., one charged with "conserving" the disabled person's assets) and the arrangement a *conservatorship*, or a *guardian* (i.e., one "guarding" the person's interests) and the arrangement a *guardianship*. Some states use the term guardian only for minors and use the term conservator for adults (the person being cared for is called the *conservatee*). Other states use guardian whether the person cared for is a minor or an adult. In either case, the person caring for the estate must make annual reports to the court and, depending on the circumstances, may have to get court approval for certain expenditures or to sell certain assets.

> EXAMPLE 2 - 22. Several years ago, Linda Smith created a *revocable living trust*, changing the title of all her property to read "Linda Smith, trustee of the Linda Smith Revocable Living Trust, dated March 19, 1998." The terms of the trust provide that if Linda becomes incapacitated during her lifetime, her brother Tom will become successor trustee. Linda has taken steps to avoid expensive court procedures to determine who should be appointed guardian or conservator of her property if she becomes incapacitated before death. The trust has the added benefit of allowing Linda's estate to avoid probate when she dies.

Third, clients may wish to create trusts to *protect beneficiaries from themselves and others.*[9] As we will see in the next chapter, trust documents typically contain provisions restricting use of the property by beneficiaries. For example, trust instruments often provide that the trustee's discretion will determine the amount and timing of distributions to beneficiaries. In addition, they often prohibit any beneficiary from pledging his or her interest in the trust property as collateral for a loan. Many other restrictions can be included.

Fourth, a trust that is funded during the trustor's lifetime allows the property that is placed in the trust to *avoid the probate process*. Trusts funded while the trustor is alive are called *living trusts*. Trusts can also be funded through the probate process, either by means of a *pour-over will* (a will that has a previously established trust as its primary beneficiary) or by means of a *testamentary trust* (a trust is a substantial part a will and is not in existence until after the testator dies). The probate process, and various means of avoiding probate, are discussed in more detail in Chapter 10.

Fifth, clients may wish to use trusts to *avoid or reduce taxes*. On the inside front cover of the textbook is a table that shows the amount that can be passed tax-free (meaning without the payment of gift or estate taxes), e.g., for the year 2006, the applicable exclusion amount for estates is $2,000,000. In general, the applicable exclusion amount has little relevance when property is transferred from one spouse to the other because there is a 100% marital deduction, but it is very important when property passes to other family members, e.g., to the children. A fair amount of estate planning revolves around using the both parents' applicable exclusion amounts while keeping the couple's combined estate intact for as long as either of them is alive. This is usually accomplished by holding in trust, for the benefit of the surviving spouse, the estate of the first spouse to die, with the children named as the remaindermen. By doing this, the trust estate is not merged with the surviving spouse's estate, and both spouses' applicable exclusion amounts are used. After examining the taxation of gifts, estates, trusts, and beneficiaries in Chapters 5 through 8, Chapters 9 and 10 will have a great deal to say about tax planning using trusts.

Power of Appointment

In arranging property transfers into trusts or otherwise, clients can add con-siderable flexibility to their estate plans by granting a power of appointment. A *power of appointment* is a power to name someone to receive a beneficial interest in property. The grantor of the power is called the *donor*. The person receiving the power is called the *holder* or *donee*. The parties to whom the holder may appoint (i.e., give) property by *exercising* the power are called the *permissible appointees*, and the parties whom the holder actually appoints are called the *appointees*. In addition, the persons who receive the property if the holder permits the power to *lapse* (i.e., does not exercise the power within the permitted period) are called the *takers by default* and are also know as the *default beneficiaries*. In some cases, the holder of a power of appointment can *release* the power by formally relinquishing the right to exercise the power.

Depending on how it is written, a power of appointment can be exercisable either during the lifetime of the holder or at his or her death, or both during lifetime and at death. If exercisable during lifetime it is exercisable either sometime during the holder's entire lifetime, or only for a stated period. A *testamentary* power is only exercisable at the holder's death, usually by a provision in the holder's will. The broadest powers allow the holder to exercise both during lifetime and at death.

> EXAMPLE 2 - 23. Assume that Dona grants Harold a power of appointment over her 100 shares of ABC stock, permitting Harold to appoint the stock to Anna, Bobby, or Carol, and designating Terry as the taker in default should Harold fail to appoint the stock within 90 days. Shortly thereafter, Harold appoints Bobby to receive the stock. Dona was the donor, Harold was the holder (of the power), Anna, Bobby, and Carol were the permissible appointees, and Bobby was the actual appointee (of the stock). Terry, the taker in default, didn't get to "take" because the holder did not permit the power to lapse.

Comparing the relationship between the parties to a power of appointment with the parties to a trust, the donor of the power is usually the trustor. The holder is commonly the trustee but may also be one or more beneficiaries or a trusted friend of the trustor. The permissible appointees are usually the trust's beneficiaries. Trustee powers of appointment may be over trust income, principal, or both income and principal. Trustees may also be granted the power to *distribute income* among a group of beneficiaries, which is referred to as "sprinkling the income" of the trust. Where the trustee has this discretion, the trust is referred to as a *"sprinkling trust."* Almost humorously (we estate planners are always looking for a good laugh), the term *"spray"* is sometimes used to describe a trust clause that gives the trustee discretion to *distribute principal* in different amounts among permissible beneficiaries. Trust powers of appointment are extremely important estate planning tools and will be discussed frequently in this book.

Powers of appointment are most often established within the framework of a trust. Figure 2-2 illustrates the relationship amongst the parties involved in a power of appointment.

FIGURE 2 - 2   The Parties to a Power of Appointment

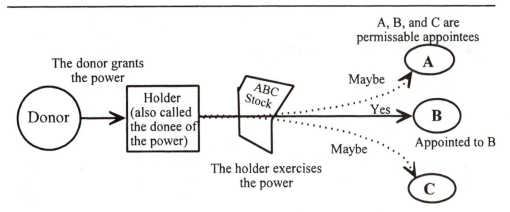

In the chapter on estate taxes, we will see that death taxes play an important role in the use of powers of appointment—so much so that we commonly classify two types of powers using Internal Revenue Code classifications. Under the Code, a power of appointment is either a *general* power of appointment or a *non-general* power of appointment, also called a *limited* or *special* power of appointment. We'll define these terms in greater detail when we start working on estate taxes, noting how the wording of a power can cause property to be included in the holder's estate, subjecting it to tax. The next example shows a common use of a power of appointment.

> EXAMPLE 2 - 3. Charles, a single parent, died recently, and his will placed some of his property in trust for the benefit of his children. A bank is named trustee and is given a non-general power of appointment over the corpus. The bank has, among other things, discretion to distribute corpus to the children in accordance with their needs "for their proper support, health, and education." This year, the trustee has distributed $16,000 to one son and $14,000 to a daughter to pay their college tuition.

Powers of appointment can add great flexibility to a person's estate plan by enabling someone to direct trust dispositions after taking into account changes in circumstances that occur long after the person's death. According to common law, property subject to a power of appointment is not considered legally owned by the holder, rather, the holder is treated as merely a proxy for the donor. However, when it comes to federal estate and gift tax law, some powers cause the holder to be treated as if he or she owned the property, at least to the extent that the holder has control over the property. We will consider powers of appointment as they relate to the estate tax in Chapter 6 and gift tax in Chapter 7.

Present Versus Future Interests

A beneficial interest in property may be classified as a present interest or a future interest, depending on whether the owner has the immediate right to possess or enjoy the property. The owner of a *present interest* has an immediate right to possess or enjoy the property while an owner of a *future interest* does not, because the latter's right to possess or enjoy the property is delayed, either for a specific period of time or until the happening of a future event. The most common types of future interests are reversions and remainders. A *reversion* is a future interest in property that is retained by the transferor after the transferor transfers to another some interest in the property. The reversion is said to be *vested* if it will become a present interest of the transferor, or the transferor's estate, at the termination of all interests that were transferred, i.e., at some point in time the donor will get the property back. It is said to be contingent if the reversion is conditional, e.g., it will only come back if the transferor is still alive, and if not, it will go elsewhere.

> EXAMPLE 2 - 25. Jerry transfers property, in trust, to Eve for her life. The trust document was silent as to what should happen to the property after Eve's death. By not designating a remainderman, Jerry has retained a vested reversion, also called a reversionary interest. The trust property will belong to Jerry, if he is still alive when Eve dies, otherwise, it will belong to his estate (the interest will pass according to his estate plan).

> EXAMPLE 2 - 26. In the prior example, suppose the trust provided that the property would return to Jerry if he was still alive, otherwise it would go to his brother, Ned. Jerry has retained a contingent reversion. The trust property will belong to Jerry, if he is still alive when Eve dies, otherwise, it will belong to his brother.

Technically, a *remainder* is the right to use, possess, and enjoy property after all prior owners' interests end, and all interests must have been created at the same time by a single document. As mentioned earlier, it is a future interest held by someone other than the transferor and it will become a present interest when all other interests have ended. In estate planning, remainders usually arise in the context of trusts, where the remainderman is entitled to the remaining trust assets at the termination of the trust. In many, if not most, trust situations, the remaindermen are the settlors' children or grandchildren, who will receive the remainder at the death of both settlors. In some of these estate plans, the trust changes at the death of one spouse into several trusts, including one or more irrevocable trusts. Where multiple trusts are formed at the death of one spouse, the survivor usually has a life estate in all the trusts, even those that are irrevocable, and the children wait as remaindermen until the surviving spouse dies.

EXAMPLE 2 - 27. George irrevocably transfers property to Sally for her life, then to John or his estate. John's future interest in the property is a remainder. It is not a reversion because it does not return to George.

Vested Versus Contingent Future Interests

A *vested remainder* is a remainder that is non-forfeitable; it is a remainder whose possession and enjoyment are delayed *only by time*, and is not dependent on the happening (or not happening) of any future event. Note that the property might go to the remainderman's estate if he or she is dead when the preceding interests end, in which case it will be the remainderman's heirs and beneficiaries that get to enjoy use of the property, but it is still considered vested.

EXAMPLE 2 - 28. With regard to the transfer by George in the previous example, John's remainder is vested. Nothing prevents him or his estate from receiving possession, except the passage of time. Morbidly but accurately speaking, eventually Sally will die. If John dies before Sally, it is John's estate plan that determines who will own the property.

A *contingent remainder* is a remainder that is not vested; that is, it is a remainder whose possession and enjoyment are dependent on the happening of a future event, not on just the passage of time.

EXAMPLE 2 - 29. Catherine transfers property to Flo for her life, then outright in fee simple to Jason, if alive, otherwise to Chris, if alive, and if not, then it reverts to Catherine. Jason and Chris each have a contingent remainder interest in the property and Catherine has a contingent reversionary interest. If Jason outlives Flo, the property is his; Chris is next in line if Jason doesn't make it. Finally, Catherine, or her estate, will get the property back if neither Jason nor Chris lives.

A few more examples, presented in the context of common transfer devices, should help to clarify the distinctions discussed above.

EXAMPLE 2 - 30. When Gary died, his will created a trust funded with his entire estate. The terms of the trust give income to his wife, Joan, for her life. At Joan's death, the trust terminates and the property passes outright in fee to Gary's son Max, if still alive, otherwise to the Salvation Army. At Gary's death, Joan received a present interest called a life estate in the income, and Max and the Salvation Army each received a future interest, called a contingent remainder. Max and the Salvation Army share something in common; only one of the interests can ever become a present interest since an event will occur which will defeat one or the other interest. Max's interest will cease if he predeceases Joan. The Salvation Army's interest will cease if Max survives Joan. Therefore, both have contingent remainder interests because possession is dependent on the happening of a future event, not on just the mere passage of time.

EXAMPLE 2 - 31. Sam left property in trust, giving his wife, June, income for life with the remainder going to Sam's son, Kurt, or Kurt's estate. Kurt has a vested remainder in the property. Although initially a future interest, it is certain that it will become a present interest someday; it cannot be defeated. Only the passage of time keeps Kurt's interest from being a present interest. Of course, Kurt may not be alive to enjoy the property, but the beneficiaries of his estate will.

We have seen that the transfer of property in trust results in a division into two interests, with the trustee receiving the legal interest and the beneficiaries receiving the beneficial interests. In addition, transfers into trust typically result in a second type of division of interests when the beneficial interests are split among two or more beneficiaries. Ordinarily, one group of beneficiaries, called the *income beneficiaries,* receives a life estate or estate for years in the trust income, while the other group, called the *remaindermen*, receives the remainder at the termination of the income interests. The many reasons for splitting beneficial interests into a life estate, or into an estate for years and a remainder, will be explained in later chapters. At present, the reader should simply be aware of the interest-splitting nature of the trust. You should recognize that, at the time of the transfer into the trust, the life estate and estate for years are usually, but not always, present vested interests; the remainder is a future interest, either vested or contingent.

Quantifying Present and Future Interest

It is important to understand the quantitative nature of remainders, reversions, life estates, and interests for years. The estate tax is based upon the date of death value of property included in a decedent's estate. What value should be assigned if the property is an interest that only last for a period of time or is an interest that comes into possession only in the future interest? What value is assigned to an annuity that will pay the survivor $50,000 for the next 20 years? How much would one include if the decedent owns a vested remainder in a $1,000,000 trust that does not terminate until the death of the 65-year-old income beneficiary? Sometimes we must value a present or future interest to determine a taxable gift. Indeed, in determining the gift tax we subtract an annual exclusion, an $11,000 deduction in 2005, but only if the gift qualifies as a present interest. If $40,000 is placed in an irrevocable trust that gives one beneficiary income for 5 years after which the trust terminates in favor of someone else, is there a present interest? If so, how is it valued? Generally, we use must use a discount rate to take into account that the property is either being received over a period of time or will be received only after a delay for a period of time.

The value of an annuity, life estate, or remainder interest is determined by using a factor based upon the discount rate applicable for the month when the interest was created. The appropriate discount rate, referred to as the §7520 rate, is published by the Treasury in the monthly Internal Revenue Bulletin.[10] For practical reasons, this text cannot include all of the factors for all of the rates since it would require a supplement the size of a typical phone book.[11] Appendix A includes part of IRS Tables "S," "B," "K," and " 90CM," the four most commonly used tables in estate planning. Table S is used when the property being valued either lasts a lifetime or is being postponed for someone's lifetime, e.g., income from a trust for as long as the beneficiary lives. Table B is used where the interest being valued lasts for a specific period of time or is postponed for a specific period of time, e.g., an annuity for 10 years or a remainder interest that won't be received until 10 years have passed. Table S and Table B are abridged to list a sampling of present value factors for discount rates of 3, 4, 6, 8, 10, and 12%. Tables S and B assume for annuities and life estate an annual payment, with the first payment at the end of the first year. Table K gives adjustment factors where annuity payments are made other than annually. We will be using the actuarial factors in examples and problems as they are especially helpful in the *planning* stage, when estimates are useful in calculating the values of life estates, remainders, and the like. Table 90CM is a one-page mortality table, useful for valuing interests that are contingent on survival, e.g., the value of a remainder interest that will come into possession 10 years from now, but only if you are still alive, is much higher if you are 25 years old than if you are 85 years old. With Table 90 CM you can figure out the probability of a 25-year-old living 10 years compared to the probability of an 85-year-old doing so.

The following series of examples will illustrate the use of these four tables for the valuation of four basic property interests: remainders, reversions, annuities for life, and annuities for a *term certain*. The choice of table for a particular problem depends on whether the interest valued is predicated on someone receiving either all income or a fixed annuity (1) for a fixed number of years, or (2) for life. All examples will assume payments start at the end of the first year after the interest is created.

Interest based on a term of years. We use Table B, Appendix A, to determine the value of an income interest that is for a *fixed period of time* (also called an interest for a *term certain*) or the value of a remainder interest that follows another interest that lasts for a fixed period of time.

> EXAMPLE 2 - 32. When the 7520 rate was 10%, Dana created an irrevocable trust by transferring $200,000 in property to the Fish-Net Bank Trust Department. By the terms of the trust, the trustee must distribute all the income to Harry (or his heirs) for a period of ten years, then terminate the trust by distributing the remainder to Stephen (or his heirs). The value of Harry's ten-year annuity is calculated as follows: the income interest (Inc. Int. column) factor for 10 years is 0.614457, thus the current value of Harry's income interest is $122,891 [$200,000 * 0.614457]. What is the value of Stephen's remainder interest? Since the income interest and the remainder represent the entire value of the trust at the outset, the value must be $77,109. In Table B, REM stands for remainder value and we could arrive at $77,109 either by multiplying the factor found there for 10%, 10 years (i.e., .385543) by $200,000 or by subtracting the income interest ($122,891) from the $200,000 initial value of the trust.

In determining the value of a reversionary interest, one takes the same steps as if it were a remainder interest, i.e., use the REM column.

> EXAMPLE 2 - 33. For this example, we revise the terms of the trust in the prior example such that on termination the trust corpus comes back to Dana (or her

heirs). The initial value of Dana's reversion is $77,109 found by multiplying the REM factor by the initial value of the trust. Of course it is the same as the value of a remainder interest since in both instances the value is based upon a delay of ten years with the value of the trust and the 7520 rate being held constant.

With an annuity interest, we must use the annuity column (A) whether we are valuing the income interest or a remainder interest. The values in the annuity column are the present value factors for an annuity of $1 for a set period of time.

EXAMPLE 2 - 34. At a time when the 7520 rate was 4%, Brett established an irrevocable trust by transferring $200,000 in property to the Fish-Net Bank Trust Department. The trust gives him the right to receive an annual distribution of $16,000 for 15 years, after which the trust would terminate and be distributed to Brett's two children. The value of Brett's 15-year retained interest is calculated by finding the factor in Table B that corresponds to a 15-year payment period discounted at 4%, i.e., 11.1184, and multiplying it by the annual payment. Thus the current value of Brett's annuity interest is $177,894 [$16,000 x 11.1184]. For gift purposes, the important value is not what Brett kept, but what he gave away, which of course is the remainder interest. What is its value? The difference between his retained interest and the initial value of the trust, i.e., $200,000 - $177,894 = $22,106. Brett would report this value on a gift tax return.

Interest based on a life estate. We use Table S, Appendix A, to determine the value of an income interest that lasts for a person's lifetime, i.e., a *life estate* (also referred to as *income for life*), or the value of a remainder interest that follows a life estate.

Valuation of a life estate. Table S indicates what portion of a property's total value is reflected in the value of a beneficiary's income or annuity interest for life. We cannot use Table S where the person with the measuring life (e.g., the person with a life estate) is terminally ill at the time the interest is being valued. The regulations define terminal illness as "an incurable illness or other deteriorating physical condition . . . if there is at least a 50 percent probability that the individual will die within one year." However, if the person actually lives 18 months or longer, there is a presumption that the person was not terminally ill, unless the contrary is established by clear and convincing evidence.[12] In the examples that follow we will assume the person was not terminally ill.

EXAMPLE 2 - 35. The 7520 rate was 6% when Martha created an irrevocable trust with assets worth $100,000. The terms give Charles, age 50, with a life estate and Samuel (or his heirs) the remainder interest. The 6% "life estate" factor corresponding to age 50 is 0.76498, hence the value of Charles's interest is $76,498 [$100,000 x 0.76498]. Of course we can determine the value of Samuel's remainder interest by using the remainder column (REM) factor of 0.23502 to arrive at $23,502 or simply subtract the value of the life estate from the initial value of the trust.

Valuation of reversion after life estate. As with reversions after an income interest or an annuity interest for a term certain, reversions after a life estate are calculated in exactly the same manner as remainders.

Valuation of annuity for life and a remainder that follows. If the payments are a fixed amount, rather than all the income, we use the annuity column (A) from Table S.

EXAMPLE 2 - 36. Muhammad is the beneficiary of a testamentary trust that must pay him $2,000 per month for life, with the remainder designated as going to Ali or Ali's estate. Since Ali died before Muhammad, the remainder value must be included in his estate.[13] At the time, the 7520 rate was 6%, the trust was worth $750,000, and Muhammad was 70 years old. To determine the value of the annuity, turn to Table S, 6%, age 70, to find the factor 8.4988 in column A. Since the payments are made monthly, we will have to adjust the value using Table K. Thus, the value of this life annuity is $209,519 [8.4988 * $2,000 * 12 * 1.0272]. The vested remainder is the difference between the annuity value and the value of the trust, i.e., $750,000 - $209,519 = $540,481. Remember, when a monthly payment is given, you must multiply by 12 to get the annual amount, likewise, 52 for a weekly payment. It may be obvious, but it is a step easily overlooked.

Future interest contingent of survival A remainder interest that is contingent on the remainderman's survival for the duration of the trust is calculated by determining the value of the remainder as shown above, then reducing the remainder by the fraction that represents the probability of the person being alive at the end of the trust. IRS Mortality Table, 90CM, Appendix A, shows the number of people expected to be living at each age based on statistics for the 1990 census (since this table was made available in 1999, the next one, based on the 2000 census, is not expected to arrive much before 2010). According to the table, out of 100,000 live births (age 0 = birth), only 95,373 of them are expected to be alive at age 40. Calculating the probability of a person age X surviving to age Y is determined by dividing the number of people alive at age Y by the number alive at age X. Thus, the probability of a newborn reaching age of 40 is 0.95373 [95,373 ÷ 100,000]. Since one of the goals in estate planning is to transfer property with a minimum of transfer tax, the smaller the value of a gift the better, especially if we are able to transfer a significant amount without using up too much of the donor's AEA (the estate or gift tax free amount).

EXAMPLE 2 - 37. At a time when the 7520 rate was 4%, Mavis, age 60, established an irrevocable trust by transferring property worth $1,000,000 to the

Hip-Hop Bank Trust Department. The trust gives her the right to receive an annual distribution of $5,000 per month for 10 years, after which the trust terminates and is distributed to Mavis's three children. However, the trust states that if Mavis dies before the trust ends, the trust corpus reverts to her estate. What is the value of the gift to the children? First, determine Mavis's interest using Table B, 4%, 10 years, $5,000 per month for 10 years, i.e., 8.1109 * $5,000 * 12 * 1.0182 = $495,511. This is the value of what Mavis kept; the remainder interest is $1,000,000 minus $495,511, i.e., $504,489. What is the probability that the children will receive the remainder instead of seeing it revert to Mavis's estate? According to the table, 71,357 of the 85,537 alive at 60 will make it to 70, hence the value of the remainder after taking the contingency into account is: $504,489 * 71,357/85,537 = $420,857. This would be the value of the gift Mavis must report on a gift tax return.

These IRS tables will be used to value property interests in several sections of the text, covering such estate planning techniques as annual exclusion gifts (Chapter 7), minor's income trusts (Chapter 11), private annuities and charitable remainder trusts (Chapter 12).

TRANSFER ON DEATH ARRANGEMENTS

Somewhere between sole ownership and joint tenancy are several title arrangements that avoid probate without giving immediate rights to the designated beneficiary. These arrangements, called pay on death accounts, transfer on death securities, and Totten trust accounts have in common that the initial owner retains full control of the account or security, and not until his or her death does ownership shift to the designated beneficiary.

Pay on death accounts. Probably all states now accept *pay on death* (POD) *accounts* as valid probate avoidance arrangements. Generally, the account has the account owner's name in the title, followed by "in trust for" and then the name of the person who will take the account if the owner dies before closing the account. Most states allow POD accounts to be used with checking and savings accounts, money market accounts, and certificates of deposit. It can be an account at a bank, credit union, or savings and loan. The depositor maintains control of the account so long as he or she is alive. Upon death, assuming the account is still open, transfer to the designated beneficiary is accomplished without probate. POD accounts are often referred to as Totten Trusts, a name derived from an early New York appellate case that recognized the arrangement as a legitimate way to transfer a cash account to a designated beneficiary at the account owner's death.[14] Other states followed New York's lead and recognized these POD arrangements either by court approval or by legislative action. Once assets are transferred into joint tenancy they can generally be withdrawn by any of the joint tenants and are subject to the liabilities of each joint tenant, whereas, the owner of a POD account maintains control and can revoke the beneficiary's interest by revoking or changing the beneficiary designation, or closing the account. Obviously, the creditors of the designated beneficiary have no way of reaching the account as long as the owner is alive.

Transfer on death. By the end of 2005, all states had adopted the Uniform TOD Securities Registration Act, bringing to owners of securities the same benefits already recognized for cash accounts, this Act permits issuers of securities (stocks, bonds, mutual fund shares, security accounts) to offer owners the ability to name death beneficiaries to whom securities transfer when the owner dies. TOD is an acronym for "Transfer on Death." While there is no separate uniform code governing POD accounts, the Uniform TOD Securities Registration Act recognizes it as a type of TOD registration, keeping both terms mainly because the POD is already widely accepted at financial institutions. During his or her life, the owner retains complete control over the securities or the brokerage account, including the power to revoke or change the beneficiary designation without needing to obtain the beneficiary's consent. As with POD accounts, the owner's will has no control over the disposition of the TOD property. Generally, the beneficiary can obtain possession of the property by presenting the death certificate of the deceased owner and identification that establishes that he or she is the person designated in the title as next in line. The Act frees issuers and financial institutions of any liability for making a good faith transfers to a named beneficiary. It also preserves the rights of a deceased owner's creditors where the securities have been used as collateral.[15]

CONCLUSION

We have covered a wide range of topics in this chapter: estates, property interests and transfers, wills, trusts, probate, disclaimers, a little about taxation and about insurance, also POD and TOD arrangements, Totten trusts, and much more. The concepts and terms listed in the table on the next page are ones that we will use often in our study of estate planning. The next chapter explores the major documents used in the property transfer process.

IMPORTANT CONCEPTS AND TERMS COVERED IN THIS CHAPTER

Estate
Property
Probate estate
Gross estate
Taxable estate
Transfer
Assignment
Transferor and Transferee
Legal interest
Beneficial interest
Transfer
Outright gift
Complete (transfer)
Irrevocable (transfer)
Incomplete (transfer)
Revocable (transfer)
Interest in property
Partially complete (transfer)
Sale
Consideration
Gift
Bargain sale
Inter vivos
Instrument
Beneficiary
Donee
Donor
Decedent
Will
Testamentary
Executed
Testator
Trust
Intestate
Testate
Partially intestate
Probate
Personal representative
Fiduciary

Executor
Administrator
Heir
Devisee
Legatee
Legacy
Issue
Descendant
Specific bequest
Ademption
General bequest
Pecuniary bequest
Residuary bequest
Residue
Class gift
Abatement
Disclaimer
Life insurance
Insured
Term life insurance
Level term life insurance
Cash surrender value
Cash value life insurance
Unified transfer tax
Gift tax
Death tax
Inheritance tax
Estate tax
Generation-skipping
    transfer tax
Fee simple
Life estate
Measuring life
Interest for years
Leasehold
Real property
Personal property
Tangible personal property
Intangible personal property

Chose in action
Concurrent ownership
Joint interest
Joint tenancy
Interest by the entirety
Tenants in common
Community property
Separate property
Trust
Trustor, grantor, creator
    or settlor
Trust principal or corpus
Trustee
Trust beneficiary
Living trust
Testamentary trust
    or trust-will
Power of appointment
Donor or creator (of a power)
Holder or donee (of a power)
Permissible appointee
Appointee
Exercise (a power)
Release (a power)
Lapse (of a power)
Taker in default
Present interest
Future interest
Reversion
Remainder
Vested remainder
Contingent remainder
Income beneficiary
Remainderman
Totten trust
Pay on Death Account
Transfer on Death securities

QUESTIONS AND PROBLEMS

1. Much of estate planning is related to ownership of property. How different would our society be if individuals did not own anything but everyone could use whatever was available? Or, if ownership was limited to things that one made and to animals one captured?

2. How would our society be different if at death one's property could not be passed on to others? What effect would drastic limits on wealth transfer have on society, for instance if one could only leave a certain amount (i.e., $1,000,000 worth) with the rest required to go to charity?

3. If society retains a tax on wealth transfers, is there a justification for taxing gifts less heavily than transfers at death? What arguments might be made in favor of doing so? Against doing so?

4. (a) What is probate? (b) What types of assets are subject to probate administration? (c) What types of assets are not subject to probate? (d) Does having a will avoid probate?

5. Tristan's mother left him real estate worth almost half a million dollars. Her will provides that if Tristan is not alive, the property passes to his children. Tristan would rather the property pass immediately to his children. (a) What is the legal term given to Tristan's refusal to accept this bequest? (b) How might making this refusal enhance Tristan's estate plan?

6. At the moment of Lou's death, a life insurance policy was in force in the amount of $250,000, which had a cash surrender value of $60,000. Lou had the power under the policy to change the beneficiary. After Lou's death, his wife, Mary, received a check from the insurance company.

   a. Identify by name the: (1) Insured, (2) Beneficiary, and (3) Owner.
   b. Did Lou's wife receive $60,000, $190,000, $250,000, or $310,000? Why?
   c. What is the likely purpose of a policy such as this one?

7. Use a web browser to find a definition of "estate planning." Give the location of the site and the definition.

8. Use a web browser to find a definition of "fair market value." Give the location of the site and the definition.

9. Characterize each of the following items as either: i) tangible personal property; ii) intangible personal property; iii) real property; or iv) in need of explanation:
   (a) antique gold watch
   (b) RMOP Common Stock
   (c) classroom wall clock
   (d) a park bench
   (e) a $5 gold piece (worth $100)
   (f) a $5 bill

10. Characterize each of the following items as either: i) tangible personal property; ii) intangible personal property; iii) real property; or iv) in need of explanation:
    (a) stock certificate for a 1885 gold mining company no longer in business
    (b) a $5,000 certificate of deposit
    (c) a timeshare unit
    (d) Christmas trees growing on a tree farm
    (e) Christmas trees for sale in a Christmas tree lot

11. Define community property and separate property.

12. Compare community property with joint tenancy.

13. Warren Willis died six weeks ago. In an envelope marked "open after my death was found the following hand written message, "This is my will. I want my car to go to my brother Charlie, my paintings to go to my sister Sally, and my savings accounts to be split 75% to Sally and 25% to Charlie. Signed, Warren Willis." In addition to the car and some paintings, Warren owned an investment account, a checking account, household furnishings and furniture that included valuable antiques. There were no savings accounts although there was an interest bearing checking account with almost $60,000 in it.

Charlie, with his sister's blessing, has applied to be the estate's personal representative. Charlie and Sally are the only known relatives. (a) Did Warren die testate or intestate? Explain (b) If appointed, what is the term for that describes Charlie's position as the estate's representative? (c) Would Sally get 75% of the bank account? Discuss. (d) Are the investment accounts part of the probate estate? What determines who gets them or will they escheat to the state?

14. Woody Lionheart transferred all his property to his living trust. He was the initial "owner-manger" of the trust property. A provision in the trust called on his son, Marcus, to take over if Woody resigned, became disabled, or died. After Woody's death, the trust terminates with distribution going to his three children, namely Marcus Lionheart, Alice Myers, and Gary Lionheart. Use the correct legal terms to describe: (a) the document Woody created; (b) Woody vis-a-vis his relationship to the trust; (c) Marcus, if he takes over; and (d) Marcus, Alice, and Gary.

15. Use the internet [http://www.ca-probate.com/wills.htm]to find copies of the wills of some famous people. (a) Review the copy of David Packard's will. He was a co-founder of Hewlett-Packard. Who or what will receive the residue of his estate? What is the estimated worth of his estate? (b) Review several other wills, what patterns do you notice? (c) Find something of interest in one of the wills to share with the class.

16. If you are the holder of a power of appointment, how might you be assisting in the donor's estate plan?

17. Lori Stienbock transferred all of her considerable property to the trust department of Thirteenth National Bank & Trust company. Lori's husband David was in poor health, suffering from dementia, and needed considerable care. The trust officers at 13th NB&T are to manage the trust funds and to pay bills for Lori and David as long as either of them is alive. After the death of both of them the trust property was to pass to their two children. (a) Give reasons that Lori might put her property in trust. (b) Who has legal interests and who has beneficial interests? (c) Who has present interests and who has future interests?

18. In the preceding problem, the Stienbock trust stated that in the event that Lori died before her husband, his brother, Matthew Stienbock, could hire additional care for David and direct the bank trust officer to pay for it. Matthew was given the authority to have some of the trust assets transferred to Lori and David's children so long as he was comfortable that the remaining assets were sufficient to continue David's care. (a) Describe Matthew's position; (b) What is the purpose of this kind of arrangement? (c) Is the bank trust department likely to view this arrangement as beneficial or as a burden? Explain.

19. (a) What is the term that describes the situation of a person dying without a will? (b) Does that mean that there will be a probate to dispose of the person's estate? Explain. (c) If there is a probate and the decedent left no will, what determines who shares in the decedent's estate?

20. (a) If Cheryl named Paul today to be the remainder beneficiary of her probate avoiding trust, is Paul's interest most likely a present or future interest? (b) If future, is it most likely to be a vested or contingent one? (c) If contingent, when will it vest, if ever? Explain each answer carefully.

21. When he was 65, Edward transferred his home worth $300,000 to an irrevocable trust. By the terms of the trust, Edward has the right to remain in the house for a period of four years. At the end of that period, the trust will terminate and the house will be distributed to his son, Kevin, age 44 (or to Kevin's estate). (a) At a rate of 8%, calculate the current value of Kevin's remainder interest. (Note: this would be a vested gift to Kevin). (b) Recalculate Kevin's remainder interest if it was contingent on Edward surviving the four-year income period (i.e., he kept a contingent reversion).

22. On her 75th birthday, Gertrude transfers her home worth $700,000 to an irrevocable trust. The trust terms provide that Gertrude has the right to remain in the house for a period of 10 years. At the end of that period, the trust will terminate and the house will be distributed to her issue. (a) At a rate of 8%, calculate the current value of the remainder interest. (Note: this would be a vested gift to the issue). (b) Recalculate the remainder interest if it was contingent on Gertrude surviving the income period.

23. Roberta created an irrevocable trust using investment assets worth $700,000. Her friend Mo, age 65, will receive all the income, payable annually for his lifetime. At his death, all principal will pass outright to Roberta's niece Sherrie (or to her estate). (a) At a rate of 6%, calculate the current value of Mo's and Sherrie's property interests. (b) Also, calculate the values at 12%. (c) Comment on the influence of a higher discount rate.

24. Melissa created an irrevocable trust using investment assets worth $300,000. The rate for calculating split gifts was 6%. Melissa's friend Murray, age 50, will receive all the income, payable annually for his lifetime. At his death, all principal will pass outright to another friend, Marci, age 30, or to Marci's estate. (a) calculate the current value of Murray's and Marci's property interests. (b) Calculate the values if Murray was 60 and Marci was 80 when Melissa established the trust. (c) Comment on the influence of the parties' ages on the values.

25. Keri, age 30, is the beneficiary of an annuity that will pay her $300 per week for life. (a) At 6%, calculate the current value of this life income interest. (Remember to adjust for the weekly payment.) (b) At 12%?

26. Dako, age 80, is beneficiary of a trust that will pay him $2,000 per month for life. (Remember to adjust for the monthly payment.) (a) At 8%, calculate the current value of this life income interest. (b) At 10%?

27. What happens if George places property in an irrevocable trust with terms that give his brother James a life estate, but are silent as to what should happen to the trust property when James dies?

28. Discussion Case: Stanley Pigeon was found dead in his luxury New York condominium apartment. All indications are that he died of natural causes. An envelope was found in his desk with a note reading, "open after my death, Stanley Pigeon." A note inside read as follows:

> *If you are reading this, I must be dead. If there is anything left after paying my debts, I want my friend Lee to have all my tangible personal property, including my XYZ stock held at Bixby Brokerage. I give my real estate in New Jersey to my friend Fred. I give $10,000 from my First National Bank account to my card buddies, Marcia, Pam, and Phil. I want my son Mark to have $5,000 as that should be enough for him. There aren't any other kids, so don't look for them. Anything else that I own should be given to my friend Susan. She can handle getting my stuff to the right people.*
>
> *Signed on 6/30/03 by Stanley Pigeon*

As it turns out, Marcia predeceased Stanley. There were hardly any debts. The Bixby Brokerage account was held in joint tenancy with Julie, Stanley's mother. Although not financially well off, Julie does not want the Bixby account or anything else from the estate other than some photo albums. It appears true that there are no children other than Mark, and he has no issue. State law for transferring property where there is no will, or where the will fails to cover all the estate, typically gives all the estate in this order: first to a surviving spouse, next, if no spouse, to issue, and if there are no issue, then to the decedent's parent(s). The only relatives are Stanley's mother and his son.

At this point in your study of estate planning you are not expected to know the answers to all the questions raised here. The goal is to get you to think about the issues and suggest possible, reasonable solutions. (a) What is likely to happen to the XYZ stock? Is there a problem with it being referred to as tangible personal property? How should it have been categorized? (b) What is the term for the part of the estate left to Marcia? Given that she predeceased Stanley, what happens to this part, i.e., who is likely to get it? (c) Given Marcia's death, if the court appoints Fred to represent the estate, what is the correct term for his position? What are the proceedings that will eventually sort out this estate called? (d) What is the term for a bequest stated in a specific monetary amount? Is it clear whether Marcia, Pam, and Phil were left $10,000 each or was the intent for Marcia, Pam, and Phil to split $10,000 three ways? How should a court resolve this? Would statements that Stanley made around the card table be relevant evidence, e.g., "you can all go on a real nice cruise in my memory after I'm gone"? Does it matter whether there is $40,000 in the account or just $12,000? If the court concludes the intent was to give just $10,000 shared by the card players, should Pam and Phil each get $5,000 or $3,333? What should Stanley have written to make it clear one way or another? (e) If the law is as stated above, who would get Marcia's share of the estate? Might the statement about Mark just getting $5,000 be considered a disinheritance clause as to anything above that amount? If that was Stanley's intent, how could he have made it clearer? (f) If Julie does not want the Bixby account and would like Lee to have the XYZ stock what should she do? If the court has ruled that Mark is disinherited insofar as anything other than the $5,000, what will happen to the property that Julie refuses to accept? Would it be better for Julie to take the property and then give it away?

ANSWERS TO QUESTIONS AND PROBLEMS *(odd numbered only)*

1. Think this one through for yourself, then let me share my thoughts (opinions really). One would expect very primitive capital development. In some ways society might be better, it would certainly eliminate keeping up with the Jones. On the other hand, we see how the communist systems failed. The desire to acquire (own) things seems almost to be innate.

3. If one goal is to break up large estates, then encouraging gifts does so earlier as compared to the estate tax that waits until the wealthy person dies. An argument against doing so is that it complicates the tax laws, creating a separate rate structure for what is essentially generational wealth transfer.

5. (a) He would make a tax effective disclaimer. (b) One reason might be that Tristan is already very rich and does not want to add additional wealth on top of what he already owns, especially if he doesn't need it and believes it will

be taxed at the highest estate tax marginal rates. That would result in almost half of it being taken away by estate taxes. If he is dying, then another reason might be that there is no sense in having the property pass through his estate (whether probate or trust), and then on to his children; rather he might as well disclaim it to quicken the outcome.

7. Numerous sites, so answers will vary but all should mention wealth transfers.

9. Property categories:

Item	Character and/or explanation
(a) antique gold watch	*tpp*
(b) RMOP Common Stock	*ipp*
(c) classroom wall clock	*rp (fixture)*
(d) a park bench	*either tpp or rp, depends on how "attached" to the earth.*
(e) a $5 gold piece (worth $100)	*tpp (value is in what its physical characteristics rather than the rights conferred*
(f) a $5 bill	*ipp (value is in the abstract rights rather than in its physical characteristics).*

11. *Community property* is any property acquired by the efforts of either spouse during the marriage while domiciled in a community property state. It also includes any property that by agreement the couple convert from separate into community. Some states require said conversion to be in writing. Excluded is property acquired by gift, devise, bequest or inheritance and the income from separate property. Texas, Idaho, and Louisiana treat income from separate property as community property.

Separate property is defined as any property that is not community property, i.e., all property acquired by a person not during marriage, or during marriage in a common law state, and property acquired during a marriage by gift, devise, bequest or inheritance, or often, income earned on property so acquired.

13. (a) Testate, but partially intestate because not all property is covered. Needed a residuary clause that covers everything not specifically given away. (b) Charlie would be the administrator with will annexed.(c) Good question. It depends upon whether the court would determine the checking account to be a "savings account" given that it earns interest. If not, then no. What evidence? What if it was the only account that WW had at the time the will was signed? (d) Yes, they aren't held in joint tenancy or as pay on death accounts. Intestate succession laws would control, e.g., equally split between the two children.

15. Internet: (a) A charitable foundation named after Mr. Packard and his wife: the David and Lucile Packard Foundation. Header above the will estimates the value of the estate to be $7 billion. (b) Obviously what different people find interesting will vary.

17. (a) To avoid probate, management for her and her husband, perhaps to reduce estate taxes. (b) 13th National Bank & Trust, as trustee, has the legal interest (i.e., title) and Lori, her husband, and the children have beneficial interests. (c) Lori and her husband have present interests, whereas the children have future interests.

19. (a) "intestate" (b) No, if the estate is transferred by other means, e.g., joint tenancy or through a trust, there is no need for there to be a probate. On the other hand, if there is property in the decedent's name alone or co-owned as tenants in common there may be a probate. Most states have small estate set aside statutes that allow the collection and transfer of the decedent's property if the estate is below a certain level, e.g., CA PC§13100 allows up to $100,000 be transferred without a probate proceeding. Basically, the will serves as a guide as to who gets what and who handles the estate. (c) Intestate succession laws.

21. Edward: Note that Kevin's age is not relevant to the calculations. (a) Using Table B, 8%, four years: $300,000 * .735030 = $220,509. (b) contingent: $220,509 * 73186/79519 = $202,947.

23. Roberta: (a) Table S, 6%, life estate for 65-year-old. $700,000 * .58291 = $408,037 as Mo's interest. Sherrie's interest is $700,000 * $.41709 =

$291,963. This is of course the same as $700,000 - $408,037. (b) Same, except using 12%: $700,000 * .77305 = $541,135 for Mo and $158,865 for Sherrie. (c) As the discount rate increases, the value of the remainder interest drops and the value of the life estate rises. Since the rate is the assumed rate of return, the higher it is, the greater the value of the income interest with a corresponding decrease in the value of the remainder interest. For a term certain, the remainder value is determined by the fraction one, as the numerator, and a denominator of the quantity one plus the discount rate, raised to the power of the number of years, e.g., with a six percent rate, the remainder value at the end of ten years is $1/(1.06)^{10}$ which equals 0.558395, whereas with a 12% rate the value of a remainder after ten years, expressed as $1/(1.12)^{10}$, giving us a factor of 0.321973 for the remainder interest.

25. Keri: (a) Table S, 6%, age 30, weekly annuity: $300 * 52 * 15.078 * 1.0291 = $242,062. (b) same @ 12%: $300 * 52 * 8.1274 * 1.0577 = $134,103.

27. A basic rule for gifts is that what is not given away must have been kept; hence George must have kept a reversionary interest.

ENDNOTES

1. Completed by the Uniform Law Commissioners in 1983 and amended in 1986. As of November 2002, the Uniform Transfer to Minors Act had been adopted by all states except South Carolina and Vermont. However, the Vermont legislature is considering adoption. See *http://www.nccusl.org/index.htm*.

2. IRS Reg. 20.2031-1(b).

3. IRC § 2032.

4. The National Conference of Commissioners on Uniform State Laws, Uniform Determination of Death Act, Approved and Recommended for Enactment in All the States (1980). As of 2002, adopted in 40 states and the District of Columbia, Puerto Rico, and the Virgin Islands. See *http://www.nccusl.org/index.htm*.

5. For the Uniform Probate Code's six exceptions. See UPC § 2-606.

6. The rules for a tax effective disclaimer are found in IRC § 2518.

7. UMPA, completed by the Uniform Law Commissioners in 1983, has been adopted, as of 2000, only by Wisconsin. See *http://www.nccusl.org/index.htm*.

8. Wisconsin Statutes, § 766.31 (4). See *http://www.legis.state.wi.us/rsb/Statutes.html*, click on the link to Chapter 766, "*Property rights of married persons; marital property.*"

9. Somewhat humorously, Edward Schlesinger has described the trust as capable of protecting assets from "inability, disability, creditors, and predators."

10. For the latest rate at http://www.irs.gov/index.html put 7520 in the search box, and for rates going back 15 years try http://www.tigertables.com/7520.htm.

11. The Alpha volume, Publication 1457, can be purchased from the U.S. Government Printing Office. These tables are also available in the form of easy-to-use computer software. For example, *Tiger Tables*, available from Lawrence P. Katzenstein at http://www.tigertables.com, computes all Alpha values plus many other factors, including unitrust remainder factors for from one to ten lives, probabilities of survival, annuity adjustment factors for annuities due, the value of an income beneficiary's interest in a trust with a 5 and 5 power, and commutation tables.

12. IRC § 1.7520(b); Reg. §§ 20.7520-3(b)(3)(i); 25.7520-3(b)(3).

13. Students of finance may notice that traditional financial mathematics can *not* derive this number. It is based not only on the time value of money, but also on life expectancy.

14. In re Totten, 179 N. Y. 112, 71 NE 748 (1904).

15. The Uniform TOD Securities Registration Act is included on the Teaching Aids CD Rom. Also see The National Conference of Commissioners on Uniform State Laws' official website (maintained by the University of Pennsylvania Law School) at *<http://www.law.upenn.edu/bll/ulc/>*.

CHAPTER 3

Estate Planning Documents

OVERVIEW

Estate planning seeks to facilitate the transfer of the client's wealth as efficiently as possible. Efficiency in estate transfer usually requires the preparation of one or more formal documents that will be accepted by the authorities who ultimately authorize and make the transfers. For example, the proper preparation and execution of a will are essential to the efficient disposal of any probate property. The will must be drafted clearly to ensure that the testator's desires are correctly expressed, and it must be signed and witnessed according to law so the probate judge will accept it as the guide for the title transfer process.

This chapter, the first of two introducing the principles of property transfer, explores the documents commonly used in the process of transferring wealth. Specifically, it examines the creation of four common property transfer mechanisms: joint tenancy, contract, the will, and the trust. The next chapter examines the actual process of property transfer whether guided by these documents or by the law of intestate succession.

Generally, property transfers are regulated by state, not federal, law. State laws in this area vary, but there are definite patterns we can discuss. For instance, more than half the states have adopted all or a significant part of the Uniform Probate Code (UPC) and, therefore, have many property distribution laws in common. The UPC was introduced in 1966, partly in answer to the criticisms that probate procedures in the United States were too costly, too time-consuming, and too complicated. Idaho was the first state to adopt it in 1972. To read Idaho's version of the UPC and to see which other states have adopted it, visit the web site maintained by University of Pennsylvania Law School, *http://www. law.upenn.edu/bll/ulc/ulc_frame.htm.*[1] In presenting the material in this and the next chapter, we will often refer to the laws of those states that have adopted the UPC, especially in three major areas: will execution, intestate succession, and probate administration.

JOINT TENANCY ARRANGEMENTS

The acquisition of title in joint tenancy is ordinarily a simple matter, requiring the completion of one or two preprinted forms. Transfers can be done with or without the aid of an attorney. Deeds to transfer real property into joint tenancy are usually drafted by an attorney, although in some states the job may be done by a real estate agent, by the title company, or by an escrow agent. Similarly, when two or more people open an account such as a stock brokerage account or bank account, the professionals involved generally will ask whether title will be in joint tenancy or tenancy in common. There really is no limit to what kind of property can be held in joint tenancy. Where there is no title document, it might be more difficult for the survivor to establish that property was held as such, e.g., we bought the couch and television together and intended joint tenancy title. On the other hand, vehicles and boats generally have title documents that are likely to establish whether or not a particular property was held in joint tenancy.

Later in the text the reader will learn several significant disadvantages to taking title in joint tenancy. Deciding whether joint tenancy is appropriate is not always clear; however, our focus at this point is on how title in joint tenancy is taken, not whether it should be taken.

Similar to joint tenancy are assets whose title simply lists the names of the owners separated by "or," e. g., Frank Smith or Alice Smith, husband and wife. Bank accounts, automobile titles, and savings bonds, to name a few, are assets that can be held in this way. Either party can deal with the asset without the knowledge or consent of the other. Generally, these accounts are treated as joint tenancy accounts.

PROPERTY TRANSFER BY CONTRACT

A significant part of a person's estate plan may be transferred pursuant to a contract. Examples of property that is transferred after the death of the owner (or the insured) are life insurance, pension and profit sharing plans, and individual retirement accounts (IRAs).

Life Insurance

Wealth derived from life insurance comes in two forms: the policy itself and the policy death proceeds. Almost all states require that the applicant for insurance have an insurable interest in the property or person being insured. This is to reduce the likelihood of insurance being used as an instrument of gamble or, worse, as an inducement that causes the loss. In the context of life insurance, an insurable interest means that the person obtaining the insurance would suffer a loss as a result of the insured's death. The loss may be economic and/or result from the diminishment of family life. All state laws give a person an insurable interest in his or her own life, and in the life of a spouse. There is no requirement that designated beneficiaries have an insurable interest, e.g., a person can name a friend or lover as beneficiary. Most states require that the insurable interest exist when the policy is issued, without requiring it exist when the insured dies, hence one can take out a policy on one's own life and then transfer it to a friend. The friend, lacking an insurable interest in the insured, could not have obtained the policy but is allowed to own the policy, indeed, keeping it even if the friendship ends. Where the applicant of a life insurance policy is the trustee of a trust, most states look through the trust to the beneficiaries to determine whether the requisite insurable interest exists, hence if the beneficiaries are the surviving spouse or other family members, the requirement is satisfied. If the beneficiaries of the trust do not satisfy the insurable interest requirement, the insured can obtain the policy and transfer it to the trustee, however, if estate tax avoidance is a reason for creating the trust, then there is a risk that the insurance will be included in the insured's estate under a special three year rule. We will discuss this in Chapter 6 and 13.

Arranging the transfer of title to a life insurance policy itself from one owner to another is fairly simple; all that is required is the completion of a short assignment form that can be obtained from the insurance company. Even where an interest exists, many states require the insured's consent before a policy can be obtained, e.g., a husband would have to have his wife's consent to obtain insurance on her life.

During the policy application process, the applicant designates the beneficiary who will receive the proceeds at the insured's death. Once the policy is issued, up until the death of the insured, the policy owner can easily change the beneficiary designation by giving the company written notice using its beneficiary designation form. Very rarely, there is an irrevocable beneficiary designation, i.e., the designation cannot be changed without the consent of the beneficiary or someone besides the owner. Such irrevocable designations may be the result of a divorce settlement or as a condition of a personal loan. Once certain conditions are met, the owner-insured may be free to change beneficiaries, e.g., once the children are grown or the loan is repaid.

Pension and Profit Sharing Plans

Pension and profit sharing plans are contracts between the employee-client and the employer. Ordinarily, the employer requests that the employee fill out a written form designating the beneficiary, the party who will be entitled to any benefits paid after the employee's death. Thus, the actual process of beneficiary designation for most retirement plans is simple and straightforward.

WILLS

Many people die leaving no formal directions as to the disposal of their property, who should manage their estate, or who should care for their minor children. In such cases, the state seeks to make these decisions equitably and sensibly, applying statutory rules to the surviving family situation. However, state law may conflict with the wishes of a decedent, whether unstated or even as recollected by the survivors. Compared to a properly planned estate, intestacy can result in unsuitable property disposition and higher taxes. Individuals can avoid an undesirable outcome by expressing, while still alive, their desires in a legally binding document that serves as a set of directions to be followed by those who survive. The will is the most common formal document for this purpose.

A will is a legally enforceable document that expresses the testator's directions for disposing of his or her probate property at death. In some states, wills can be oral, but laws usually greatly restrict the scope of their ability to dispose of wealth, generally limiting the application of oral wills to personal property worth less than a modest amount, such as $2,000. In addition, the testator, on execution, is often required to be a member of the armed forces or in peril of death. Practically speaking, wills prepared in the estate planning process are written.

Who May Execute a Will

In most states, any individual 18 or older who is of sound mind may dispose of his or her property by will. The implications of this are twofold. First, individuals under age 18 cannot transfer property by will unless they are emancipated minors. A minor is emancipated if a court, after a petition and hearing, determines that the child should be free from parental control and given the status of an adult for contractual and other legal matters. In most states, a person under age 18 is considered an adult if he or she is married. Thus, in most instances, a deceased minor's property will pass according to the laws of intestate succession, which will usually result in the property passing to the child's parents or if the parents are also deceased, then to siblings. Second, a will can be denied probate if it can be established that the testator, at date of execution of the will, lacked testamentary capacity, was subject to undue influence or fraud, or acted mistakenly. These four concepts are discussed next.

Testamentary capacity. *Testamentary capacity* concerns the testator's mental ability to execute a legally enforceable will. A testator has testamentary capacity if he or she possesses each of the following three attributes:

1. Sufficient mental capacity to understand the nature of the act being undertaken (executing a will).
2. Sufficient mental capacity to understand and recollect the general nature of his or her property.
3. Sufficient mental capacity to remember and understand his or her relationship to the persons who have natural claims on his or her bounty and whose interests are affected by the provisions of the will.

Essentially, in addition to being an adult, testators must know that they are executing a will, they must be aware of what they own, and they must be cognizant of family and friends. On its face, this test seems quite severe; strictly construed, it might prevent many older testators from executing a valid will. However, mere age and physical disability do not negate testamentary capacity. Probate courts have admitted to probate wills executed by individuals who were forgetful, absent-minded, alcoholic, or behaving peculiarly—even persons declared mentally incompetent, insane, under conservatorship, or who committed suicide shortly after executing a will. Indeed, the threshold is lower than that for contractual capacity, which may be as it should, given that the formation of a contract requires the ability to negotiate with another person, whereas executing a will does not. Nonetheless, failure to meet one or more of these three requirements will result in a finding of insufficient testamentary capacity. Examples of sufficient evidence of incompetence include senility, ongoing hallucinations, irrational beliefs, irrational behavior, and totally groundless beliefs about the testator's spouse, children, or other family members. Generally, the outcome hinges on whether, at the time the will was executed, the three-prong test was met. Appellate courts are reluctant to "set aside" a will. They have reversed many cases where the jurors found that the testator lacked testamentary capacity, especially those cases where the testator disinherited immediate family members in favor of newly found friends. As a consequence, affirmed findings of testamentary incapacity are very rare.

Anticipating the possibility of a will contest based on lack of testamentary capacity, some attorneys videotape the will execution of a testator who may have questionable capacity, believing that the taping will make capacity more credible. Others believe that videotaping can enhance the success of a contest, reasoning that testators may look terrible on the screen (especially if they are shown lying in a hospital bed), and that the taping constitutes evidence that even the will drafting attorney lacked confidence in the testator's capacity.

Undue influence. A will executed by a testator who was subject to undue influence by someone who stands to benefit, directly or indirectly, may also be denied probate. Undue influence is influence by a confidante that has the effect of overcoming the testator's free will. Examples include improper persuasion and psychological domination, as when "Snake Oil Sam," the smooth-talking newcomer, makes a romantic play for the 92-year-old widow, "encouraging" her to disinherit her children and leave her entire estate to him.

Winning an undue influence case can be difficult. These cases often involve a person with a weak, unsound, or impaired mind. Indeed, the family may not be aware of a new, less favorable will until after the testator is dead. An element of fraud or deceit is a common thread in these cases. Juries tend to side with family members against outsiders whom they see as meddling non-relatives. Thus, a jury is likely to "rewrite" a will in keeping with what the jurors think is fair to the family. But, unless the evidence of undue influence is clearly in the record, this type of verdict is likely to be reversed on appeal.

Fraud. *Fraud* involves deception through false information. Some courts distinguish two types of fraud based on the action of the deceiver. *Fraud in the inducement* is where the testator is persuaded by lies of the wrongdoer to change his or her estate plan. For example, fraud exists if a niece tells her great-uncle she is penniless when, in fact, she is wealthy, or a daughter incorrectly tells her mother that her sister instigated a conservatorship proceeding, when actually they acted together. The other type is called *fraud in the execution*, where the person is deceived into signing a document not knowing that it is a will. An example would be obtaining a person's autograph on a blank sheet of paper, then, with the help of accomplices, placing will language above it and witness signatures below to create what appears to be a genuine will.

Mistake. Very rarely, a will can be successfully contested on the basis of a mistake. Examples include: (a) the testator leaves her estate to only one son, mistakenly believing that the other is wealthy; (b) the testator mistakenly leaves out an intended clause; or (c) the will mistakenly includes an unintended clause.

Ordinarily, a finding of lack of testamentary capacity will invalidate the entire will, while a finding of undue influence, fraud, or mistake might invalidate only those provisions that relate to the specific problem.

Statutory Requirements for Wills

Most states, including those that have adopted the Uniform Probate Code, recognize at least two types of wills, the *witnessed will* and the *holographic will*.

Witnessed will. Although state laws vary, a witnessed or *attested will* must meet the following three requirements:

1. It must be in writing (handwritten, typed, etc.).

2. The testator must sign the will in the presence of two witnesses (three in Virginia). A testator can execute a will by directing another person to sign for him or her in the presence of the witnesses.[2] If the testator is unable to sign and is directing someone else to do so on his or her behalf, it might be a good idea to videotape the signing ceremony.
3. The witnesses must sign their names to the will. Generally, this follows a paragraph that states they witnessed the testator sign the instrument which they understand to be the testator's will.

The main purpose of requiring witnesses is to prevent forgery and coercion of the testator. Beneficiaries should not be witnesses to a will because that could imperil their right to receive some or all their bequest. In some states, a bequest to a witness is void unless the witness is also an heir, and in that case, the witness can take no more than his or her intestate share. In most states, a beneficiary can serve as a witness, but if someone raises an undue influence challenge, the "interested witness" may take more than the intestate share only if he or she is able to rebut a statutory presumption that the bequest was procured by undue influence. Inability to rebut this presumption might not totally invalidate the will, but might invalidate some or all the bequest to the witness.

Holographic will. If a will does not meet all the requirements for a witnessed will, in most states, including those adopting the UPC, it can still be admitted to probate if it meets the requirements for a holographic will. Typical state requirements for a holographic will are:

1. Signature is in the testator's handwriting.
2. All the "material provisions" of the will are in the testator's handwriting.

In the past, courts often refused to admit to probate holographic documents unless it was clear from reading just the handwritten portions that the document was the decedent's will. In determining what parts of the will must be in the testator's handwriting, some still follow the old rule, but many states now allow a preprinted will form to be treated as a holographic will so long as both the material provisions and the signature are in the decedent's own handwriting.[3] The material provisions are the dispositive ones (who gets what), the identity of the executor, the nomination of guardians, and the like.

Document intended to be a will. The Uniform Probate Code allows a court to accept as testamentary documents instruments that do not meet the formal execution requirements of a witnessed will or the handwriting requirements of a holographic will if it can be establish by "clear and convincing evidence" that the writing being offered was intended by the decedent to be his or her will (or a codicil).[4] Section 2-503, *Writings Intended as Wills, etc.* reads as follows:

> Although a document or writing added upon a document was not executed in compliance with Section 2-502, the document or writing is treated as if it had been executed in compliance with that section if the proponent of the document or writing establishes by clear and convincing evidence that the decedent intended the document or writing to constitute (i) the decedent's will, (ii) a partial or complete revocation of the will, (iii) an addition to or an alteration of the will, or (iv) a partial or complete revival of his [or her] formerly revoked will or of a formerly revoked portion of the will.

Clear and convincing evidence is a higher standard of proof than the usual civil case burden known as a preponderance of the evidence.

> EXAMPLE 3 - 1. Marcia and Ted Parkhill had no children and desired to leave their estate to friends. When they went to their attorney's office to sign their wills, a mix-up occurred whereby each signed the other's will. Their property was in joint tenancy when Ted died so the error went unnoticed. When Marcia died one of her friends who was named in both wills as the alternate executor, petitioned to probate the will intended for Marcia even though it was signed by Ted. Attached to the petition was the attorney's explanation of the inadvertent mix up at the execution of the wills. Marcia's next of kin, who stand to take the estate by intestate succession if the wills are invalid, object to the probate of this will. The court is likely to accept the will as Marcia's. Acceptance is almost certain if the two wills are mirror images of each other, i.e., both have the same pattern of bequests.

No-contest Clause

In the last few pages, we have described several technical requirements for a valid will including testamentary capacity, absence of undue influence, fraud, mistake, and certain specific execution requirements such as signatures by witnesses and the testator. Anticipating that dissatisfied persons may claim that one or more violations of these requirements have occurred, as a pretext for obtaining more of the estate, testators may insert in their will a "no-contest" clause such as the one that follows:

I have purposely made no provisions herein for any other person or persons, other than as set forth in this will, and if any person contests this will, I revoke any share or interest given such person, and said share or interest shall be disposed of as though said person predeceased me without leaving issue.

This usually discourages will contests. There are several reasons, however, that it may not be effective: First, it will discourage only beneficiaries named in the will, not disinherited persons who stand to lose nothing by contesting. Second, beneficiaries may still wish to contest if they expect to gain considerably more than they will lose. Finally, in states that have adopted the UPC, such clauses are unenforceable if the contestant has probable cause for instituting the proceedings.[5] Perhaps most testators would desire the latter result anyway.

What situations tend to invite will contests? The most common are where the testator chooses to disinherit family members in favor of a friend, a charity, a spouse married shortly before death, or where a testator treats children unequally. If the testator is very old or is ailing physically or mentally, a contest is even more likely.

Will contests are infrequent, and successful contests are very uncommon. One study showed that fewer than three percent of wills offered for probate were challenged, and more than two-thirds of those challenges were unsuccessful. However, will contests may become more common for several reasons. As the general population continues to age, more elderly people of means will acquire "friends" who offer to assist them in their finances and work their way into the person's estate plan. A high divorce rate has increased the number of children of former marriages, a group that is less likely to get along with the surviving spouse of a later marriage. When any of these situations or factors apply to a particular client, attorneys should take special precautions in drafting and executing the will.

The Simple Will

Wills can be quite lengthy and complex, but this section focuses on a relatively simple will. A *simple will*, as it is generally called, is a will prepared for a family having a small, or even a modest estate, where death taxes are not a significant concern. We will cover estate taxes in Chapter 5 and you will see that we are in a period of transition. The amount that can pass tax-free (assuming the decedent has not made significant lifetime gifts) is increasing, growing from the pre-1998 figure of $600,000 to $3,500,000 in 2009. Complete repeal of the estate tax takes place in 2010. However a "sunset" provision repeals the repeal as of 2011. There is considerable agreement that Congress will not allow this provision to take effect, so the shape of post-2010 tax law is uncertain. The estate tax repeal may be made permanent or the tax-free amount may be set at a high level and indexed for inflation.

The simple will usually includes all the following: nominating an executor and, if there are minor children, a guardian; a waiver of the probate bond; and, in most cases, giving the testator's property to the spouse, if alive, otherwise to the children per stirpes.

Exhibit 3-1 presents a simple will that demonstrates the essential nature of this probate property transfer document. The reader is encouraged to study it carefully so that the analysis that follows is more readily understood.

EXHIBIT 3 - 1 Simple Will

WILL OF
WILLARD THOMAS SMITH

I, Willard Thomas Smith, a resident of Mytown, Anystate, declare this to be my will. I revoke all prior Wills and Codicils.

First: Family and Guardian I am married to Sue L. Smith, referred to in this will as "my wife." I have three children, all from this marriage, whose names and birthdays are:

Kristi M. Smith	June 27, 1987
Heather L. Smith	April 19, 1989
Todd R. Smith	May 11, 1991

Reference to "my children" or to "my child," shall include children born later and children adopted by me. I have no deceased children.

If my wife does not survive me, and it is necessary to appoint a guardian, I appoint Curtis J. Quint guardian of the person and estate of each such minor child. If for any reason Curtis J. Quint does not act as guardian, I appoint Maria S. Cruise as guardian of the person and estate of each such minor child.

EXHIBIT 3 - 1 Simple Will *continued*

Second: Executor The executor shall serve as follows:

A. *Designation* I appoint my wife as my executor. If for any reason she does not so act, I appoint James A. Reliable to be my executor. If for any reason neither my wife nor James A. Reliable acts as executor, I appoint Third National Bank of Mytown to be my executor.

B. *Bond waiver* My executor shall not be required to post bond or other security.

Third: Disposition of Property I make the following gifts of property:

A. *Tangible personal property* If my wife survives me by 30 days, I give her all my interest in our tangible personal property. If my wife does not survive me by 30 days, I give my tangible personal property to my issue, per stirpes, provided they survive me for that period. My executor shall consider their personal preferences in making the division. My executor has my permission to sell any of that property and distribute the proceeds to equalize the shares. My executor shall be discharged for all tangible personal property so given to any minor child if the child, or adult having the child's custody, gives a written receipt to my executor.

B. *Residue* If my wife survives me by 120 days, I give her the residue of my estate. If my wife does not survive me by 120 days, I give the residue to my issue, per stirpes, provided they survive me for that period. If neither my wife nor any of my descendants survives me by 120 days, I give the residue of my estate according to Anystate's laws of descent and distribution, one half as if I had died with no will on the last day of that 120-day period, and one half as if it were my wife's estate and she had died with no will on that last day.

C. *Taxes from residue* All death taxes imposed because of my death, as well as interest and penalties on those taxes, whether on property passing under this will or otherwise, shall be paid by my executor from the residue of my estate.

Fourth: Powers of Executor My executor shall have unrestricted powers, without court order, to settle my estate as this will provides. In addition, my executor shall have the following powers:

1. To make interim distributions of principal and income to those entitled to it.
2. To sell, exchange, mortgage, pledge, lease or assign any property belonging to my estate.
3. To continue operation of any business belonging to my estate.
4. To invest and reinvest any surplus money.

I have signed my name to this instrument on March 19, 2006, at Mytown, Anystate.

Willard Thomas Smith

Willard Thomas Smith

EXHIBIT 3 - 1 Simple Will *continued*

Statement of Witnesses We, the undersigned the witnesses, on March 19, 2006, sign our names to this instrument, being first duly sworn, and do hereby declare to the undersigned authority that the testator signs and executes this instrument as his last will and that he signs it willingly (or willingly directs another to sign for him), and that each of us, in the presence and hearing of the testator, hereby signs this will as witness to the testator's signing, and that to the best of our knowledge the testator is eighteen years of age or older, of sound mind, and under no constraint or undue influence.

_____*John Meeks*_____ _____*Jennifer Jarrett*_____
1341 Park St., Little Town, Anystate   42 Short Rd., Little Town, Anystate

---

Analysis of the simple will. Let's analyze the major provisions of this will, section by section.

Will of Willard Thomas Smith. In this introductory paragraph, the testator "declares" the document to be his will, satisfying the legal requirement that there be evidence of testamentary intent.

A *codicil* is a separate written document that amends or revokes a will. It is executed if the testator wishes to make changes or additions to his or her will. It must meet all the legal requirements of a will, including subscription by witnesses, although in states that recognize holographic wills, a holographic codicil even to a witnessed will is acceptable if the codicil meets that state's requirements for a holographic will.

One of the more common methods of revoking a prior will is by executing a later will that declares such revocation, as is done in the Smith will. Revocation by "cancellation" with a "subsequent instrument," as it is termed, can also be undertaken in any other signed, witnessed statement. A will can also be revoked by a physical act, such as burning, tearing, canceling, or otherwise destroying it, when such is done by the testator with an intent to revoke.[6]

Revoking all prior wills and codicils eliminates the danger that provisions in prior wills that are inconsistent with the present will may cause confusion. Without a revocation clause, needless litigation might arise over whether the provisions in two or more wills are inconsistent. For example, in one state supreme court case, a decedent-testator had written two "last" wills within three weeks. The first simply left "a tract of land" to a friend. The second contained no revocation clause and left "all my effects" to siblings Y and Z. The court permitted a trial to determine whether the first will should be construed along with the second, reasoning that they were not necessarily inconsistent because the testator could have used the word "effects" to mean only personal property.[7] If the testator's intent was to leave everything to Y and Z, inclusion of a revocation clause would have assured this result. If the intent was to preserve the gift of the land to the friend, then that should have been clearly stated in the second will.

First: Family and guardian. Naming all members of the immediate family assists the personal representative in finding relatives and locating assets.

Including *after-born children* in the will prevents a child born after the execution of the will from inheriting under the laws of intestate succession, a consequence which would probably conflict with the testator's intent.

A child who is still a minor when both parents are dead will have a *guardian* of the person and of the estate appointed by the probate court. A guardian of the person is responsible for the minor child's care, custody, control, and education, while a guardian of the child's estate is responsible for managing the minor child's property. A testator's nomination carries great weight and is usually followed; however, the probate judge does have the power to appoint someone else if there is good cause for not following the nomination. Nominating an alternate guardian increases the likelihood that the testator's preferences will be followed.

Second: Executor. Similar to the nomination of a guardian, the nomination of an executor and an alternate executor is helpful to the probate court in its selection process. The court will follow the recommendation of the testator unless there is good cause to do otherwise.

Unless the bond is waived in the will, the executor is required to post a *fiduciary bond.* A bonding company, for a fee, insures the estate assets against losses caused by the personal representative's breach of fiduciary obligations, whether the breach is the result of negligence or willful misconduct. The will can waive the bond requirement. The testator may consider a bond unnecessary because it results in additional expense to the estate, and/or because the executor is a highly trusted member of the testator's family, such as the surviving spouse, and/or is also one of the major beneficiaries of the estate. Ordinarily, the bond amount will be set by the court to be equal to the total value of the personal probate property plus one year's estimated income from all the probate property. The idea here is that the personal representative could run off with everything but the real property.

Third: Disposition of property. This simple will essentially leaves all property to the testator's spouse, if surviving, otherwise to the children. The contingent interest of the children is sometimes referred to as a "gift-over" to the children. The will distinguishes the tangible personal property from the residue, which consists of all other probate assets. Thus, the spouse must survive by 30 days to take tangible personal property and 120 days to take the residue. If the spouse does not survive the requisite time period, the property passes to the children who do so survive.

Inclusion of a survival requirement, such as 30 days or 120 days, reduces the likelihood that the death of both spouses in a common accident will result in subjecting some of the family property to two successive probates. This *survival clause*, as it is called, helps in situations not covered by the Uniform Simultaneous Death Act (USDA).

Enacted by every state, the USDA provides that when transfer of title to property depends on the order of deaths, and when no sufficient evidence exists that two people died other than simultaneously, the property of each is disposed of as if each had survived the other. Thus, in the case of a childless married couple, the husband's estate would pass to his blood relatives and the wife's estate would pass to her blood relatives. This statute is of limited value, however, because it does not avoid double probate when the order of deaths can in fact be established. In some states, if it can be established that one spouse survived the other, even only by seconds, then the USDA will not apply and, absent a survival clause, there will be a double probate of the property owned by the first spouse to die. Perhaps worse, all the property may ultimately pass to that spouse's in-laws, rather than the surviving relatives. Some states, including California, have legislated safeguards against inheritance by in-laws by requiring that the portion of the decedent's estate attributable to the predeceased spouse pass, in some circumstances, to the predeceased spouse's children, parents, or other kin.[8] The Uniform Probate Code requires a beneficiary of an estate to outlive the decedent by 120 hours or be deemed to have predeceased the decedent. This rule is not applied if it would cause the decedent's property to escheat (revert) to the state.

With regard to insurance on the life of a decedent, the USDA states that, in the event of an apparent simultaneous death of the insured and the beneficiary, the policy proceeds are to be distributed as if the insured survived the beneficiary. Thus, the proceeds will be paid to the contingent beneficiary, and if none, then to the owner's probate estate.

Section B of Article Three, covering the "residue," is called the *residuary clause*. Failure to include it in a will can result in partial intestacy. In a recent case, the attorney who had drafted the decedent's will admitted that he mistakenly omitted the residuary clause, but his notes showed that the decedent wanted the residue to go to a specific friend. The court would not allow admission of this evidence, ruling that extrinsic evidence is admissible to explain poorly drafted parts of a will, but cannot be used to put in parts that are missing.[9]

Disposing of estate property by differentiating the tangible personal property from the residue can speed up probate distribution and can often save income taxes. In the chapter on fiduciary income taxes, the concept of distributable net income, or DNI, is discussed. A *specific bequest* of property, such as when the testator specifies a bequest of the tangible personal property, prevents the distribution from being labeled DNI. This generates less taxable income to the distributees (often the spouse and/or children), and correspondingly more taxable income to the estate, which is (hopefully) in a lower rate bracket.

Instead of "tangible personal property," some wills ill-advisedly use the term "personal effects," which really means "tangible personal property, worn or carried about the person or having some intimate relation with the person." Since automobiles and some other property are not considered "personal effects," the broader term *tangible personal property* is preferred. Early distribution of this property also allows the executor to avoid the cost and trouble of storing it.

Distribution by *per stirpes* is a method of allocating a bequest of the decedent's property such that it follows the natural line of descent (e.g., the children of a predeceased child share that child's portion of the estate.)

The laws of intestate succession, also known as "laws of descent and distribution," vary somewhat from state to state. They spell out the priority of succession rights of the decedent's spouse and kin in the event of intestacy. In the event that his wife and all his descendants fail to survive him by 120 days, the testator has generously chosen to divide his property in halves, with one half going by intestate succession to his relatives and the other half going by intestate succession to his wife's relatives.

Fourth: Powers of executor.   Granting explicit powers to the executor can eliminate the need to secure permission of the probate court to undertake certain administrative actions. Ordinarily, testators would like their executors to act without undue delay.

Signature clause and the statement of witnesses. Every state imposes formal requirements regarding the signing of the will by the testator and the role of the witnesses. The paragraph above the witnesses' signatures increases the likelihood of compliance with these formal requirements by explicitly stating them and having the witnesses, by their signatures, acknowledge that such were carried out. The last sentence above the signatures of the witnesses offers some additional evidence of the testator's capacity to execute a will. The Statement of Witnesses is also referred to as the *attestation clause*. When a will is signed and witnessed in the proper manner, such that it is a valid will, it is said to be executed.

Other aspects of the simple will. Simple wills are most commonly drafted by attorneys for clients with modest estates where death taxes are not a concern. For a married couple, a simple will is usually prepared for each spouse. In most cases, the dispositive clauses are almost identical. Thus, the husband's will leaves all to his wife, if she survives, otherwise to their children. And the wife's will leaves all to her husband, if he survives, otherwise to their children. Such simple wills are commonly called *reciprocal wills*, *mirror wills*, or *mutual wills*.

Occasionally, clients will want *contractual wills*, ones that cannot be revised once one of the parties (usually a spouse) dies. Sometimes these are done in the form of a single will for two people, called a *joint will,* although a joint will need not be contractual. Contractual wills are rare because most clients want the flexibility of being able to change an estate plan after one spouse dies. Joint wills should be avoided unless the clients really want a contractual will, because even if the clients did not intend the joint will to be irrevocable once one of the testators dies, a court may rule that this was the intent because there can be little other reason to create one will for two people. Wills that are more complex are less likely to be reciprocal in content. Typically, they are prepared by attorneys specializing in estate planning.

Where should the original copy of the will be kept? The client's safe deposit box makes good sense in those states (e.g., California) that do not seal boxes at the owner's death. In states where safe deposit boxes are sealed at the owner's death, access to the will is delayed until a state official can join the prospective executor in inventorying the contents of the box so as to ensure that the executor accounts for any jewelry, bearer bonds, and the like that might be there. Some attorneys recommend their own safe. Some people might view this as self-serving, since the executor will have to come to the attorney's office to take charge of the will, thus giving the attorney a good chance of serving as the probate attorney. However, since the testator selected that attorney to draft the estate plan, it would seem reasonable to select that attorney to handle the probate. Some attorneys simply recommend a secure, handy place in the client's home.

TRUSTS

The principal parties to a trust are the trustor, the trustee, and the beneficiary. As a legal arrangement, a trust is created by the trustor and divides and transfers interests in property between two or more people. Any interests or control over the trust not given to the beneficiaries are either retained by the trustor, granted to the trustee, or held by both.

A trust can take effect during the lifetime of the trustor, or it can take effect at the trustor's death. The former is called a *living* (or *inter vivos*) *trust*, while the latter is called a *testamentary trust* - a complex will that is also called a "trust-will." The testamentary trust document is covered later in the chapter.

At any given moment, a trust is either revocable and amendable, in which case the trustor is capable of voiding (canceling) or amending it, or it is irrevocable, that is, not voidable or amendable. A living trust usually contains specific language stating whether it is revocable or irrevocable. A revocable living trust usually, but not always, becomes irrevocable at the death of the trustor(s). Like the contents of most wills, the provisions of a testamentary trust can be amended or revoked before the testator's death by codicil, revocation, or destruction of the document. At the testator's death, a testamentary trust takes effect and becomes irrevocable since the only person capable of amending or revoking it, the testator, is, of course, permanently unavailable.

A trust usually contains two different legal types of property, principal and income. The *principal* of a trust is its invested wealth (also called the *corpus* or the *res*). Its size will fluctuate with changes in its market value, by additions (income or additional property), by charges (expenses or losses), and by distributions from it. In contrast with trust principal, the *income* of a trust is the return in money or property derived from use of the trust principal. Examples of income include cash dividends, rent, and interest. Trust income also has charges against it, most of which reflect expenses incurred in managing the trust property (e.g., insurance premiums and some portion of the trustee's fee). Any trust income not distributed to beneficiaries is said to be accumulated in the trust and is generally accounted for as retained income, not principal, unless the trust agreement requires that accumulated income be added to principal.

The accounting distinction between principal and income is particularly important, because most trusts contain provisions that bestow rights to principal and income to different beneficiaries. In the chapter on fiduciary income taxes, we will see that the distinction between principal and income will influence trust income taxation.

The beneficiaries of an irrevocable trust are usually either *income beneficiaries* (i.e., those having an interest in the income) or *principal beneficiaries* (for example, a remainderman who stands to receive principal outright when the trust terminates). These two types of beneficiaries may have conflicting or "adverse" interests, because the increased distributions to one will generally decrease the distributions to the other. For example, high-yield/low-growth stock would tend to benefit the income beneficiaries more than the remaindermen whereas low-yield/high-growth stock would favor the remaindermen more than the income beneficiaries.

The following material describes a living trust and a testamentary trust. Keep in mind that individual trusts vary greatly, so it is a stretch to call any trust used as an example here typical. These examples are merely to illustrate the basic form of each document. There are other ways of classifying trusts, especially in connection with tax planning. The chapters in Part 3 introduce several tax-saving trusts, including the bypass trust, the Crummey trust, and the QTIP trust.

Living Trust Instrument

A living trust is created by a document of agreement between the trustor (or settlor) and the trustee. Before we examine the actual instrument, let's compare and contrast the characteristics of a living trust with a will.

Similarities between trusts and wills. The will and the living trust instrument are similar in three important ways. First, both serve as the guide to the disposition of property at death. Second, both have a fiduciary (the executor or the trustee) who is responsible for managing property for a period of time until the transfers can be completed. Third, both instruments are generally amendable and revocable, at least until the person creating the instrument dies. The will can nearly always be amended by a codicil, or revoked by its destruction or by execution of a later will that explicitly revokes earlier ones. One exception, of course, is the *contractual will*, which becomes irrevocable after the death or incapacity of the first co-testator. The living trust is either revocable or irrevocable. In most states, a trust must state that it is revocable, otherwise it becomes irrevocable upon execution. In the other states, the opposite rule is in effect, such that a trust is revocable unless stated to be irrevocable.

Differences. The will and the living trust instrument are different in three important ways. First, they dispose of a totally different set of property. A living trust instrument disposes of property owned by the trustee in trust for the trustor (decedent), while a will disposes of probate property owned by the decedent at death. Thus, with regard to property transfers, the living trust instrument and the will are mutually exclusive; property owned by the trustee is not probate property, while probate property is owned by the decedent, not the trustee. Of course, the decedent's will can transfer property, by way of the probate process, to the trustee of his or her living trust, or even to the trustee of a trust he or she did not create, such as one created by one's spouse. A will that transfers property to a trustee is called a *pour-over will,* because it scoops up property and "pours" it into an existing trust.

Second, with regard to choosing a fiduciary, a living trust instrument *appoints* a trustee whereas a will *nominates* an executor. A testamentary trust must nominate both an executor and a trustee. Since the trustor of a living trust is alive when the trustee is appointed, the trustor has control over the appointment. The trust instrument is a legal contract between the trustor and the trustee. On the other hand, the probate judge appoints the executor of a will after the testator's death. The judge may appoint someone other than the nominated executor for any number of reasons, including the nominee's inability to serve due to death, disability, or incompetence.

Third, while the formal execution requirements for writing a will are quite strict, the requirements for properly executing a trust instrument are simple to meet. In most cases, the trust document is simply dated and signed by the trustor and the trustee. Witnesses are not required. However some attorneys have the trustor's signature notarized to assure others of its validity, especially those who might have to rely on the document at a time when the trustor is incapacitated or deceased. Although the formalities surrounding the execution of a trust document are simpler than those for a will, the mental capacity necessary is set at a higher standard. The settlor must have contractual capacity. Given the nature of the trust document, this would be, in addition to testamentary capacity, the ability to understand and enter into a bilateral contractual agreement. In most states, one contesting a settlor's (or a testator's) capacity has the burden of proving the lack of capacity by "clear and convincing" evidence. This is a more difficult (i.e., higher) standard than the typical "preponderance" of evidence burden generally placed on the plaintiff in a civil case.

Exhibit 3-2 presents a fairly simple living trust. It is not designed to break into several irrevocable trusts at the trustor's death as some do in order to save estate taxes. We will discuss those later.

EXHIBIT 3 - 2 Living Trust Instrument

JOHN C. JONES
Revocable Living Trust Dated March 19, 2006

TRUST AGREEMENT made March 19, 2006, between John C. Jones, as trustor, resident of Common County, Anystate, and John C. Jones, resident of Common County, Anystate, as trustee.

1. Trust property. The trustor has set aside and holds in trust the property described on Schedule One, attached to this instrument. The trustee agrees to hold such property and any later accepted property, in trust, under the terms and conditions provided herein.

2. Successor trustee. If John C. Jones for any reason ceases to act as trustee, his wife, Sarah E. Jones, shall serve as trustee. If Sarah E. Jones is unable or for any reason ceases to act as trustee, then First National Bank of Anytown shall serve as trustee.

3. Power to amend or revoke. The trustor reserves the right at any time to amend or revoke this trust, in whole or in part, by an instrument in writing signed by him and delivered during his lifetime to the trustee.

4. Operation of trust during trustor's lifetime. During the trustor's lifetime, the trustee shall administer and distribute the trust as follows:

a. Trust income. The trustee shall pay the net income to the trustor at convenient intervals but at least quarter-annually.

b. Trust principal. The trustee shall pay to the trustor from time to time such amounts of the principal of this trust as the trustor shall direct in writing or as the trustee deems advisable for the trustor's support and comfort.

5. Operation of trust after trustor's death. On the death of the trustor, the trust estate shall be held, administered, and distributed as follows:

a. Wife survives by four months. If the trustor's wife survives trustor by four months, the trustee shall distribute the entire trust estate to the trustee of her revocable trust, dated the same date as this trust, to be held and administered according to its terms. If said trust is no longer in existence, then distribution shall be to trustor's wife, free of trust.

b. Wife does not survive by four months. If the trustor's wife does not survive the trustor by four months and if no then-living child of the trustor is under age twenty-one, then the trustee shall divide the trust into as many equal shares as there are children

EXHIBIT 3 - 2 Living Trust Instrument *continued*

of the trustor's then living and children of the trustor's then deceased with descendants then living. Each share set aside for a child then deceased with descendants then living shall be further divided into shares for such descendants, per stirpes. The trust estate shall be held, administered, and distributed in the manner described in subsections 5(b)(2)(a) and (b), below.

If neither the trustor's wife nor any of the trustor's descendants survive the trustor by four months, the trustee shall distribute the entire trust estate according to Anystate's laws of descent and distribution, one half as if the trustor had died with no will on the last day of the four-month period and one half as if it were the trustor's wife's estate and she had died with no will on the last day. If the trustor's wife does not survive the trustor by four months and if any then-living child of the trustor is under age twenty-one, then the trust estate shall be held, administered, and distributed as follows:

(1) *Any child under age twenty-one.* So long as any of the trustor's children are living who are under twenty-one, the trustee shall pay to or apply for the benefit of all the trustor's children as much of the net income and principal as the trustee in the trustee's discretion deems necessary for their proper support, health, and education, after taking into consideration, to the extent that the trustee considers advisable, the value of the trust assets, the relative needs, both present and future, of each of the beneficiaries, and their other income and resources made known to the trustee and reasonably available to meet beneficiary needs. The trustee may make distributions under this provision that benefit one or more beneficiaries to the exclusion of others. Any net income not distributed shall be accumulated and added to principal.

(2) *Youngest child reaches age twenty-one.* When the youngest of the trustor's then-living children reaches age twenty-one, the trustee shall divide the trust into as many equal shares as there are children of the trustor's then living and deceased children who left issue. Each share set aside for the issue of a deceased child shall be further divided into shares, per stirpes, for such descendants. Each such share shall be distributed, or retained in trust, as hereafter provided.

(a) Each share set aside for a descendant shall be distributed to that descendant free of trust when he or she reaches age twenty-one.

(b) Each share set aside for a descendant who has not then reached age twenty-one shall be retained in trust. The trustee shall pay to or for the benefit of that descendant as much of the income and principal of the trust as the trustee, in the trustee's discretion, considers appropriate for that descendant's support, health, and education. When that descendant reaches age twenty-one, the descendant's share shall be distributed to that descendant, free of trust. If that descendant dies before receiving distribution of that descendant's entire share, the undistributed balance of that descendant's share shall be distributed, free of trust, to that descendant's then-living descendants, per stirpes, or if there are none, to the trustor's then-living descendants, per stirpes. The share of a descendant for whom there exists a trust created by this instrument, shall augment that descendant's trust.

EXHIBIT 3 - 2 Living Trust Instrument *continued*

---

6. Restriction against assignment, etc. No interest in the principal or income of this trust shall be anticipated, assigned, encumbered, or subject to any creditor's claim or to legal process before actual receipt by the beneficiary.

7. Perpetuities saving. Any trust created by this will that has not terminated sooner shall terminate twenty-one years after the death of the last survivor of the class composed of my wife and those of my descendants living at my death.

8. Powers of trustee. To carry out the purposes of this trust, the trustee is vested with the following powers with respect to the trust estate and any part of it, in addition to those powers now or hereafter conferred by law:

a. To continue to hold any property, including shares of the trustee's own stock, and to operate at the risk of the trust estate any business that the trustee receives or acquires under the trust as long as the trustee deems advisable.

b. To manage, control, grant options on, sell (for cash or on deferred payments), convey, exchange, partition, divide, improve, and repair trust property.

c. To lease trust property for terms within or beyond the term of the trust and for any purpose, including exploration for and removal of gas, oil, and other minerals and to enter into community oil leases, pooling, and unitization agreements.

d. To borrow money and to encumber or hypothecate trust property by mortgage, deed of trust, pledge, or otherwise.

e. To invest and reinvest the trust estate in every kind of property, real, personal, or mixed, and every kind of investment, specifically including, but not by way of limitation, corporate obligations of every kind, stocks (preferred or common), shares of investment trusts, investment companies and mutual funds, and mortgage participations, which persons of prudence, discretion, and intelligence acquire for their own account, and any common trust fund administered by the trustee.

f. In any case in which the trustee is required, pursuant to the provisions of the trust, to divide any trust property into parts or shares for the purpose of distribution, or otherwise, the trustee is authorized, in the trustee's absolute discretion, to make the division and distribution partly in kind and partly in money, and for this purpose to make such sales of the trust property as the trustee may deem necessary on such terms and conditions as the trustee shall see fit.

IN WITNESS THEREOF this instrument has been executed as of the date set forth on the first page of this instrument.

John C. Jones
_____
John C. Jones, Trustor

John C. Jones
_____
John C. Jones, Trustee

[Notarization of the signatures would appear here]

Analysis of the living trust instrument. Let's examine the major provisions of this living trust instrument section by section.

Trust agreement. A trust is, in effect, a contract or agreement between two parties, the trustor and the trustee. Both sides agree to perform certain tasks: among other things, the trustor agrees to deliver property described in Schedule One (not shown) to the trustee, and the trustee agrees to hold, administer, and distribute the trust property in keeping with the terms of the trust.

In this living trust instrument, the trustor names himself to be initial trustee and names alternate successor trustees to take over when he resigns, becomes incapable of performing because of incapacity, or death. In other words, he might want to travel without worrying about managing the trust property or he might become too ill to manage it.

1. Trust property. The instrument specifies that additional assets may be put in trust in the future, even after the trustor's death. For example, a trustor's will can be directed to "pour over" probate property into a trust.

2. Successor trustee. Since the trust instrument states the trustee's name in the opening paragraph, this section needs only name successor trustees. It is usual to name one or more of the remaindermen, if they are adults, as successors, since the remaindermen have a vested interest in managing and transferring the property efficiently. Sometimes the children are named as successor trustees, with the requirement that they have reached a certain age (e.g., twenty-five), in order to serve. Naming a bank, or other corporate entity, as a successor trustee virtually ensures that an experienced trustee will be available to serve for the duration of the trust. Some corporate fiduciaries will not assume the position of trustee unless the corpus is some minimum value. Where a corporate trustee is being considered, a meeting with the trust officers should be arranged to decrease the likelihood that the position will be refused later.

3. Power to amend or revoke. This trust can be amended or revoked by a written document signed by the trustor and delivered to the trustee. An amendment is similar to a codicil to a will but without the strict formal execution requirements.

4. Operation of trust during trustor's lifetime. During the trustor's lifetime, the trustee is required to pay to the trustor all income at least quarterly and any principal as requested. The reader will notice the wording assumes the trustor and the trustee are different parties. However, as mentioned above, most living trusts name the trustor as the initial trustee. Nevertheless, this paragraph is used in anticipation that, at some point, a successor trustee will take over the management of the trust.

5. Operation of trust after trustor's death. This section is substantially longer than the Disposition of Property section in the simple will. It provides for several alternative outcomes depending on who survives. First, the trust terminates if the trustor's spouse survives the trustor by four months, with the result that all trust property will pass to her revocable trust or, if it is no longer in existence, then outright to her.

Second, if the trustor's spouse does not survive by four months and all the trustor's children are over age twenty-one, the trust will terminate and distribute all assets free of trust to the children. However, if one or more of the trustor's living children are younger than twenty-one, the trust continues as one trust. The trustee is instructed to collectively use trust principal and income to provide for all the children's support, education, and other reasonable needs. Thus, the trustee has a limited power of appointment over the entire trust income and principal, with all living descendants named as permissible appointees. Then, when the youngest child reaches twenty-one, the trust is divided into equal shares, one for each child then living, and one for each deceased child for whom there are living descendants. The trust directs distribution to the younger generations per stirpes, a concept more fully explained in a the next chapter. Each share is then distributed outright to each descendant when he or she reaches age twenty-one. Thus, at the time the corpus is split, each child and any other descendant beneficiary who is at least age twenty-one will receive his or her share.

Third, if the trustor's spouse fails to survive the trustor by four months and no living child is under age twenty-one, the trust may or may not terminate, depending on whether there are underage descendants of deceased children. In any event, however, the trust estate is immediately divided into shares, and each child immediately receives his or her share. The balance of the trust corpus (held for these underage descendants of deceased children) will be administered in a manner (described below) quite similar to the way it is administered for a living child under age twenty-one. As each of these descendants reaches age twenty-one, he or she will receive an outright distribution of his or her share. Accordingly, the trust will terminate when the youngest living descendant of deceased children reaches age twenty-one.

Finally, if the trustor is survived by neither a spouse nor descendants, the trust terminates and the trust property passes by intestate succession, with one half to the trustor's relatives and the other half to the trustor's spouse's relatives. The laws of intestate succession are covered in the next chapter.

The above disposition, using a trustee, has much to recommend it over the will's provisions making outright gifts to the minor children, which requires a court-appointed guardian.

6. *Restriction against assignment.* This is an example of a *spendthrift clause*. Without it, the laws of many states would allow trust beneficiaries to transfer and encumber their interests in the trust property, and would enable the beneficiaries' creditors to seize trust assets to satisfy their claims. For example, beneficiaries may not borrow money secured by their share of trust property, sell a future interest in it, or devise it. A spendthrift clause restricts such transfers. However, it only protects trust property while held by the trustee, not after it has been transferred outright to a beneficiary.

7. *Perpetuities saving.* This clause is included to prevent a contingent gift from being ruled invalid because it violates a law found in almost all states that requires interests to vest within some reasonable time after the transfer. This law is called the rule against perpetuities.

8. *Powers of trustee.* Since a trustee is likely to manage trust property for a considerably longer period than an executor is likely to manage an estate, the powers granted to the trustee are usually stated in more detail than those granted in a will to an executor. In addition to these powers, both the executor and trustee automatically have other implicit powers derived from statutory law and from case law, unless the document specifically prohibits such powers. For example, trustees have the power to defend against claims brought against the trust property, whether that power is specifically granted in the document.

This living trust is uncomplicated primarily because it does not attempt to save estate taxes. If the other spouse survives the trustor spouse by four months, all corpus will pass to the surviving spouse's revocable trust or outright to her. Like the simple will, it is created for families with modest estates, for whom death tax planning is not a significant concern. We will introduce a more complicated tax-saving living trust in the two chapters that deal with estate plans for the wealthy, where estate taxes are a concern.

Testamentary Trusts

The testamentary trust, or trust-will, is the third principal document of property disposition commonly prepared by attorneys in the estate planning process. In essence, a testamentary trust is actually one type of will; it serves as the guiding document for the distribution of the testator-trustor's probate property at death. In addition, it disposes of some, or all, of the probate property to the trustee of a trust that is newly created according to trust terms that are set forth as part of the will. This trust takes effect after the testator's death at the end of the probate process. The actual creation of the trust, and the funding mechanism, is the order for distribution. The order names (appoints) the trustee, sets forth all the terms of the trust (generally quoting verbatim from the testamentary trust document), and orders the executor to distribute the estate to the trustee. The trustee uses the order as the governing document when dealing with third parties, such as banks, brokers, and title companies, rather than the original trust-will. Recording a certified copy of the order in those counties where real property is located serves to transfer the property from the estate to the trustee.

As a will, the testamentary trust must conform to all legal requirements for the execution of a will. It therefore contains all essential provisions found in any will, such as nomination of a guardian of the person and estate of the testator's minor children, nomination of executors, and a section for the attestation by witnesses. It may also have provisions that make outright gifts of certain property (e.g., the tangible personal property may be given to the spouse or children free of trust).

In addition to containing all provisions customarily found in other wills, the testamentary trust, like the living trust, must include other unique clauses that relate to the trust itself. Thus, it will include provisions for distributing probate property into the trust, for naming one or more trustees, for stating who will be the trust beneficiaries, for specifying how much income and principal they will receive and when they will receive it, and for describing the trustee's duties and powers in connection with managing the trust property. Of course, all but the first clause just mentioned are also included in a living trust.

It should be noted that being a will, the testamentary trust is not an "agreement" between testator and future trustee. In fact, the potential trustee may not even be aware that he or she will one day be asked to perform this task, and may not even be born when the testamentary trust was signed. Before the court order of distribution, the nominated trustee will have to file with the court a consent to serve as trustee. Exhibit 3-3 presents a relatively uncomplicated testamentary trust.

EXHIBIT 3 - 3 Testamentary Trust (Trust-Will)

WILL OF
WILLARD THOMAS SMITH

I, Willard Thomas Smith, a resident of Mytown, Anystate, declare this to be my will. I revoke all prior Wills and Codicils.

First: Family and Guardian I am married to Sue L. Smith, referred to in this will as "my wife." I have three children, all from this marriage, whose names and birthdays are:

Kristi M. Smith	June 27, 1987
Heather L. Smith	April 19, 1989
Todd R. Smith	May 11, 1991

Reference to "my children" or to "my child," shall include children born later and children adopted by me. I have no deceased children.

If my wife does not survive me, and it is necessary to appoint a guardian, I nominate Curtis J. Quint guardian of the person and estate of each such minor child. If for any reason Curtis J. Quint does not act as guardian, I nominate Maria S. Cruise as guardian of the person and estate.

Second: Selection of Fiduciaries I nominate the following fiduciaries:

A. *Designation of Executor* I nominate my wife as my executor. If for any reason she does not so act, I nominate James A. Reliable to be my executor. If for any reason neither my wife nor James A. Reliable acts as executor, I nominate Third National Bank of Mytown to be my executor.

B. *Designation of trustee* I nominate such of my children as are over age twenty-five as co-trustees. If my children are unable to serve as trustees, then I nominate James A. Reliable as the trustee of all trusts provided for under this will. If for any reason neither my children nor James A. Reliable are available to serve as trustee, I nominate Third National Bank of Mytown as trustee.

C. *Bond waiver* No bond, surety, or other security shall be required of my executor or of my trustee.

EXHIBIT 3 - 3 Testamentary Trust (Trust-Will) *continued*

Third: Disposition of Property I make the following provisions for my probate property:

A. *Tangible personal property* If my wife survives me by 30 days, I give her all my interest in any tangible personal property. If my wife does not survive me by 30 days, I give my tangible personal property in equal shares to those of my children who survive me by 30 days. My executor shall consider their personal preferences in making that division. If my children are still minors, my executor has my permission to sell any of that property and distribute the proceeds to equalize the shares. My executor shall be discharged for all tangible personal property so given to any minor child if the child or adult having the child's custody gives a written receipt to my executor.

B. *Residue* If my wife survives me by four months, I give her the residue of my estate. If my wife does not survive me by four months and all my living children are then over age twenty-one, I give the residue in equal shares: one to each child who survived me by four months, and one share for each deceased child whose issue is then living. If any issue of a deceased child entitled to a share is under age twenty-one, his or her share shall be administered as set forth at subparagraph two of this Third Article.

If my wife does not survive me and if any child of mine is under age twenty-one, then the residue of my estate shall not vest in the children as provided above; rather, such property shall be distributed in trust to the trustee named above, to be held, administered, and distributed as follows:

1. *Any child under age twenty-one* So long as a child is under age twenty-one, the trustee shall pay to or apply for the benefit of my children, as much of the net income and principal as the trustee in the trustee's discretion deems appropriate for their proper support, health, and education, after taking into consideration, to the extent that the trustee considers it advisable, the value of the trust assets, the relative needs, both present and future, of each of the beneficiaries, and their other income and resources made known to the trustee and reasonably available to meet beneficiary needs. The trustee may make distributions under this provision that benefit one or more beneficiaries to the exclusion of others. Any net income not distributed shall be accumulated and added to principal.

2. *Youngest child reaches age twenty-one* When the youngest child reaches age twenty-one, the trustee shall divide the trust into as many equal shares as there are children of mine then living and children of mine then deceased with descendants then living. Each share set aside for a child of mine then deceased with descendants then living shall be further divided into shares for such descendants, per stirpes. Each such share shall be distributed, or retained in trust, as hereafter provided.

EXHIBIT 3 - 3 Testamentary Trust (Trust-Will) *continued*

---

a. Each share set aside for a child, or for the descendant of a deceased child who has reached age twenty-one, shall be distributed free of trust.

b. Each share set aside for a descendant who has not reached age twenty-one shall be retained in trust. The trustee shall pay to, or for the benefit of, that descendant as much of the income and principal of the trust as the trustee, in the trustee's discretion, considers appropriate for that descendant's support, health, and education. When the descendant reaches age twenty-one, that descendant's entire share shall be distributed to that descendant, free of trust. If that descendant dies before receiving distribution of that descendant's entire share, the undistributed balance of that descendant's entire share shall be distributed to that descendant's then-living descendants, per stirpes, or if there are none, to my then-living issue, per stirpes. In the latter event, the share of a descendant for whom there exists a trust created by this instrument shall augment that descendant's trust.

C. *Taxes from residue* All death taxes imposed because of my death and interest and penalties on those taxes, whether on property passing under this will or otherwise, shall be paid by my executor from the residue of my estate.

D. *Restriction against assignment, etc.* No interest in the principal or income of this trust shall be anticipated, assigned, encumbered, or subject to any creditor's claim or to legal process before its actual receipt by the beneficiary.

E. *If all beneficiaries die before full distribution* If neither my wife nor any of my descendants survives me by four months, I give the residue of my estate according to Anystate's laws of descent and distribution, one half as if I had died with no will on the last day of that four-month period, and one half as if it were my wife's estate and she had died with no will on that last day.

F. *Perpetuities saving* Any trust created by this will that has not terminated sooner, shall terminate twenty-one years after the death of the last survivor of the class composed of my wife and those of my issue living at my death.

Fourth: Powers of Executor My executor shall have unrestricted powers, without court order, to settle my estate as this will provides. In addition, my executor shall have all powers my executor thinks necessary or desirable to administer my estate, including the following:

A. To make distributions of principal and income on an interim basis to those entitled to it.

B. To sell, exchange, mortgage, pledge, lease, or assign any property belonging to my estate.

C. To continue operation of any business belonging to my estate.

EXHIBIT 3 - 3 Testamentary Trust (Trust-Will) *continued*

D. To invest and reinvest any surplus money.

Fifth: Powers of Trustee To carry out the purposes of any trust created under Article Three, and subject to any limitations stated elsewhere in this will, the trustee is vested with the following powers with respect to the trust estate and any part of it, in addition to those powers now or hereafter conferred by law:

A. To continue to hold any property, including shares of the trustee's own stock, and to operate at the risk of the trust estate any business that the trustee receives or acquires under the trust as long as the trustee deems advisable.

B. To manage, control, grant options on, sell (for cash or on deferred payments), convey, exchange, partition, divide, improve, and repair trust property.

C. To lease trust property for terms within or beyond the term of the trust and for any purpose, including exploration for and removal of gas, oil, and other minerals and to enter into community oil leases, pooling, and unitization agreements.

D. To borrow money and to encumber or hypothecate trust property by mortgage, deed of trust, pledge, or otherwise.

E. To invest and reinvest the trust estate in every kind of property, real, personal, or mixed, and every kind of investment, specifically including, but not by way of limitation, corporate obligations of every kind, stocks (preferred or common), shares of investment trusts, investment companies and mutual funds, and mortgage participations, which persons of prudence, discretion, and intelligence acquire for their own account, and any common trust fund administered by the trustee.

F. In any case in which the trustee is required, pursuant to the provisions of the trust, to divide any trust property into parts or shares for the purpose of distribution, or otherwise, the trustee is authorized, in the trustee's absolute discretion, to make the division and distribution in kind, including undivided interests in any property, or partly in kind and partly in money, and for this purpose to make such sales of the trust property as the trustee may deem necessary on such terms and conditions as the trustee shall see fit.

I have signed my name to this instrument on March 19, 2006, at Mytown, Anystate.

Willard Thomas Smith

Statement of Witnesses We, the undersigned witnesses, on March 19, 2006, sign our names to this instrument, being first duly sworn, and do hereby declare to the undersigned authority that the testator signs and executes this instrument as his last will and that he signs it willingly (or willingly directs another to sign for him), and that each of us, in the presence and hearing of the testator, hereby signs this will as witness to the testator's signing, and that to the best of our knowledge the testator is eighteen years of age or older, of sound mind, and under no constraint or undue influence.

John Meeks	*Jennifer Jarrett*
1341 Park St., Little Town, Anystate	42 Short Rd., Little Town, Anystate

Notice that, unlike the living trust shown in Exhibit 3-2, this particular testamentary trust creates only a *contingent trust* (i.e., a trust that comes into existence only if a certain combination of events happens, specifically, if the testator's wife fails to survive him and one or more beneficiaries is under age twenty-one). Not all testamentary trusts are contingent. For example, a testamentary trust could provide that a trust be created that gives the surviving spouse a life estate, followed by a life estate for the children, with the remainder going to the grandchildren.

TRUST DURATION

Because using trusts allows settlors to control use of property long after the settlor is dead, the use of trusts for long-term planning is sometimes referred to as "ruling from the grave." How long can a trust last? Is it good estate planning to tie up property for generations? Is it even good for the settlor's descendants? The common law answer was to limit the duration of private trusts by what is known as the Rule Against Perpetuities. Some states have abolished the rule and the rest have modified it in some way. Long duration, multi-generation trusts established in states that have abolished the rule are called *dynasty trusts*.

The Rule Against Perpetuities

The Rule Against Perpetuities (the rule) originated in English common law. The rule acts to prevent a transferor from controlling the disposition of property for an unreasonably long period after making the transfer. The rule is generally stated as follows:

No interest is good unless it must vest, if at all, not later than twenty-one years after some life in being at the creation of the interest.

Thus, the rule has the effect of invalidating a future contingent interest which might not vest within twenty-one years after the death of certain people alive (the measuring lives) at the time the document creating the interest became irrevocable.[10] The statutes of all states except Alaska, Idaho, Wisconsin, North Dakota, and South Dakota contain some variation of this rule. Charitable trusts are exempt from the rule, making them potentially infinite in duration.

In estate planning, an interest in property can take effect during the transferor's lifetime, or it can take effect at the transferor's death. A transfer into an irrevocable living trust is an example of the creation of a property interest that will take effect during the transferor's lifetime, whereas a transfer into the typical revocable living trust and a transfer by will are examples of transfers that create interests that do not take effect until the transferor's death.

Thus, to satisfy the requirements of the rule, the interest must vest, if at all, within twenty-one years after the death of someone alive at the moment of transfer into an irrevocable trust, or at the moment of the transferor's death, for interests created by will or by revocable living trust.

The rule is satisfied if an interest vests (or fails) immediately on its transfer. Thus, a statement in a will giving a bequest "to John, for his life, then to Mary or her estate," creates vested interests for both John and Mary at the testator's death. Nothing (except, in Mary's case, the passage of time) will prevent them from receiving possession of the property. Of course, if John dies before the testator, his interest (a life estate) will immediately fail. Therefore, the rule need only be used to determine the validity of contingent future interests; that is, interests that are not vested when created.

The requirement that the interest must vest "if at all" means that a contingent future interest will not violate the rule merely because it failed to vest due to the happening of a contingency that did not work in favor of a named party. Thus, the transfer "to Jane if she survives Margo" gives Jane a contingent future interest that must vest or fail to vest within the permitted time. Failure to vest will not violate the rule, so long as that failure (or non-failure) must occur within the required period. Thus, Jane will or will not survive Margo, an outcome that will be determined as soon as one of them dies. If one cannot be sure that one or the other of these outcomes will definitely happen during the period, then the interest violates the rule.

To qualify under the rule, an interest must vest or fail to vest "not later than twenty-one years after some life in being at the creation of the interest." The "life in being" concept is difficult to explain precisely. For our purposes, however, we can say that the persons permitted to be "lives in being" are usually those mentioned or identified in the transfer document itself. Thus, for the transfer "to Carrie for her life, then to Carrie's living children," Carrie would be the sole measuring life. She is alive at the creation of the children's interest, and the length of her life span will determine the devolution of the property. Taking a second example, the provision that a trust will terminate "twenty-one years after the death of the last survivor of the class composed of my wife and those of my issue living at my death" identifies the measuring lives as all the people in the class. This "perpetuities saving clause," included in the testamentary trust in Exhibit 3-3, is a clause that can further protect an interest from vesting too remotely.

The requirement of vesting within "twenty-one years" after the death of a life in being was originally included to enable the transferor to control the disposition of property for his or her life, for the lives of the children, and for the period of the grandchildren's minority, but no longer. For those individuals, all interests created which are contingent solely on parent survival will usually vest within the required period. The children's interest will vest by the time of the death of the transferor, and the grandchildren's interest will vest within twenty-one years of the death of the last surviving child. Thus, their interests will vest within the required period. On the other hand, a great-grandchild's interest will typically (but not always) vest after the twenty-one year period, and thus will usually fail.

A violation of the rule will cause that interest to be void. It is said to be an all-or-nothing rule. If there is the possibility that an interest to one member of a class of possible takers will vest beyond the prescribed time, then all gifts to that class fail. As an example, if a testator's will creates a trust giving income to several generations of descendants, with directions that it will terminate in favor of the decedent's issue still living when the last grandchild dies, the rule is violated since a grandchild could be born after the decedent died, i.e., we would have a measuring life that was not "in being" when the trust was established. Rather than allowing the measuring lives to be limited to those that were alive (and thus avoid violation of the rule), the common law would cause the interest to vest in the farthest generation that does not violate the rule, i.e., the decedent's children in this case would take the property in fee rather than merely receiving a life estate.

Let us consider some examples. In each case, assume that the transferor has died, leaving a will containing the disposition clause shown as the initial quote.

EXAMPLE 3 - 2. Ted's will stated, "To my wife, Mary, for her life, then to Bill or his estate." Both Mary's and Bill's interests vested immediately when the will took effect (at Ted's death) because at that point, nothing except the passage of time could delay their possession or enjoyment. Therefore, neither interest is contingent, that is, dependent on the happening of a future event, other than the passage of time. Applying the rule, their interests "must vest...not later than...." Thus, both interests are valid under the rule.

EXAMPLE 3 - 3. Continuing with the prior example, assume the following is also included in Ted's will: "...then to my great, great, great-grandchildren..." Assuming that Ted is survived only by children and grandchildren, it is possible that the great, great, great-grandchildren's contingent interest will vest more than twenty-one years after the death of all children and grandchildren, who are the only apparent lives in being at Ted's death. Thus, their interests are void.

EXAMPLE 3 - 4. Theresa's will stated, "To my husband, Bert, for his life, then to my son James, if still living, otherwise to Ron or his estate." Bert's vested interest is valid under the rule for the same reason that Mary's was in the preceding example. Both James and Ron have contingent interests in the property. Thus, we must ask whether they must vest within the specified time. Both James's and Ron's interests will vest, if at all (either one or the other will never vest, depending on whether James survives Bert), within "twenty-one years after some life in being." Bert is "a life in being" at the time of Theresa's death, and both interests will vest or will fail to vest at his death well within the time limit of the rule. Therefore, both James's and Ron's interests are valid under the rule.

EXAMPLE 3 - 5. Tom's will stated, "To my wife Sarah, for her life, then to my son Greg, for his life, then equally to Greg's living children when the youngest child reaches age 25." Are Greg's children's interests valid under the rule? Sarah, Greg, and any children alive when the trust became irrevocable at Tom's death are "lives in being" at the creation of the interest. But more children could be born to Greg, and they would not be lives in being at the time the trust became irrevocable, yet they would (by the terms of the trust) each have an interest that could vest, more than twenty-one years after the deaths of Sarah, Greg, and any of the children that were born when the trust became irrevocable. Therefore, the grandchildren's interests are void, and Tom or his successors would receive a reversionary interest that follows the death of Greg. Since Tom's only living issue is Greg, violation of the rule probably means that Greg would have the interests in fee. Note that had the trust called for the interests to vest when Greg's oldest living child reaches age twenty-one, then all the children's interests would vest within a life in being plus twenty-one years, even if none of the children were born when the trust became irrevocable, since all children would be born within Greg's lifetime.

Here are two general rules of thumb when applying the rule to transfers of interests to surviving issue:

1. Transferors usually can create valid contingent interests for their grandchildren, as long as the interests must vest by the time their grandchildren reach age twenty-one. The law tacks on the period of gestation to the twenty-one years; hence a grandchild born after the father's death can have his or interest vest at age twenty-one without violating the rule.
2. Transferors usually can create valid interests for their great-grandchildren only if they outlive their children or specify the measuring lives as persons alive at the transferor's death, e.g., "all interests shall vest no later than twenty-one years after the death of the last survivor of settlor's issue who was alive when this trust became irrevocable."

Today, not all dispositions in violation of the rule are invalid. Two types of safeguards designed to overcome the rule are available to transferors. First, most states have enacted statutes that limit application of the rule, or even invalidate it entirely. For example, many states have enacted a "wait and see" statute which, in effect, finds an interest void only if the interest turns out in fact not to vest within the required period. In addition, some states have a type of wait-and-see statute stating that any interest which actually vests within a certain period of time (e.g., 60 years) after its creation cannot be declared void, even if it violates the rule. In 1986 the National Conference of Commissioners on Uniform State Laws approved the Uniform Statutory Rule Against Perpetuities, recommending that all states enact it. It includes a wait-and-see period of 90 years after creation.

Another statutory safeguard is the application of the "*cy pres*" rule to enable the courts to correct violations of the rule, if at all possible, so that the transferor's intentions can be respected. *Cy pres*, French for "as near as possible," is a principle used primarily in the context of charitable bequests, to permit the substitution of one beneficiary for another when the original charitable purpose is impossible, illegal, or impractical to carry out. For example, over a century ago, one testator left property in trust to fight for the cause of abolition. After the 13th Amendment, a court applied *cy pres* to permit the trust to continue by assisting freed slaves.

The second type of safeguard is to protect against a perpetuities violation and involves the lawyer's insertion in the document of the earlier mentioned perpetuities saving clause, similar to the one in the testamentary trust in Exhibit 3-3. Such a provision, however, may act to prevent the client from making an otherwise valid transfer, perhaps simply because the attorney chose not to test the interest against the rule. In fact, none of the above safeguards is as effective as the thoughtful analysis and planning of an expert.

Yet, one must have some sympathy for the lawyers who use the clause. The rule often requires complex analysis to test a given interest, and it can even puzzle experts. One state supreme court held that, given the complexity of the rule, an attorney who created a will that violated the rule was not liable because he had used the ordinary skill commonly exercised by lawyers.[11] It is doubtful that a similar case would be decided the same way today.

Dynasty Trusts

Running counter to common law wisdom that saw a danger in tying up property in perpetuity, many states have enacted legislation that either abolishes the rule against perpetuities (RAP) or have expanded the duration allowed such that for all practical purposes it is abolished. The arguments for abolishing it seem tend to be along these lines: (1) everyone should be allowed to do with his property whatever he or she wants; (2) it allows financial protection for one's descendants; and (3) it allows asset protection for one's descendants. An empirical study of competition amongst states to attract trust assets by abolishing RAP indicates that doing so meets with success. Through 2003, states that did so increased trust assets by about $6 billion (a 20% increase on average). The abstract of the article points out that, "Interestingly, states that levied an income tax on trust funds attracted from out of state experienced no increase in trust business after abolishing the Rule. This is a striking finding for the theory of jurisdictional competition, because it implies that abolishing the Rule does not directly increase a state's tax revenue." [12]

Googling "Dynasty Trusts" on the Internet will turn up literally thousands of sites, most of which will tout the advantages of establishing a perpetual trust. Common examples demonstrate that by avoiding transfer taxes and with the power of compounding, putting $1 million dollars in a dynasty trust that escapes transfer taxes and compounds at 7% per year will be worth $50 million in 50 years and over $800 million in100 years.

Status of Dynasty trusts (as of 2005)
RAP Abolished: Alaska, Arizona, Colorado, Delaware, Idaho, Illinois, Maine, Maryland, Missouri, Nebraska, New Hampshire, New Jersey, Ohio, Rhode Island, South Dakota, Virginia and Wisconsin.

States with a maximum duration:

Wyoming, Utah	1,000 years
Nevada	365 years
Florida	360 years
Washington	150 years

In a thoughtful article by economics professor Neil E. Harl, the argument is made that allowing trusts to last beyond 150 years creates problems at least in part by to the sheer number of progeny that would trace their ancestry back to the settlors.[13] Even with very modest growth rates, it is estimated that the settlors' living issue would number 100 in 100 years, 2,500 in 250 years, and 45,000 in 350 years. Society will have to decide whether tying up capital for so long is really beneficial.

CONSIDERATIONS COMMON TO WILLS AND TRUSTS

There are a number of considerations that one must take into account whether the controlling estate planning document is a will or a trust. To receive a share of the estate, should a beneficiary have to outlive the testator, or settlor, for some minimum period of time?

Survivorship Clauses and Anti-lapse Statutes

The phrase "If A survives me, I give her. . ." is a survival clause and is commonly included in will and trust instruments, mainly to avoid the consequences of a lapse.

Effect of a lapse. A *lapse* occurs when a beneficiary named in a will fails to survive the testator. Each state's probate code contains sections that determine, in the absence of a provision in the will, to whom a lapsed testamentary bequest will pass. A very common type of *antilapse statute*, as it is called, provides that bequests to one of the testator's predeceased blood relatives will instead pass to that relative's surviving issue. The UPC limits the antilapse to predeceased grandparents and descendants of grandparents.[14]

> EXAMPLE 3 - 6. Rudolph died. His will left his car to his brother, Randall, and the residue of his estate to his friend James. Randall predeceased Rudolph. Due to the state's antilapse statute, the bequest of the car will pass to Randall's only son, Jeremy.

Antilapse statutes expressly apply only to wills, not living trust instruments or property held in joint tenancy. However, some courts have applied their antilapse statutes to living trust instruments by analogy. On the other hand, the interests of predeceased co-joint tenants are always cut off by their death; thus, the surviving co-tenants will share a greater percentage of the property.

If the state has no antilapse statute, or if the particular statute does not apply, perhaps because the lapsed bequest was to a beneficiary not related to the deceased, or in a UPC state to a remote relative, then a lapsed specific bequest will ordinarily pass to the residuary beneficiary.

> EXAMPLE 3 - 7. In the prior example, if the car was left to Rudolph's predeceased friend Josef instead of to Randall, the car will pass to James, the residuary beneficiary, because the state's antilapse statute applies only to relatives.

This result is unfortunate if the testator actually wished, in the event the named beneficiary predeceased the testator, to leave property to someone else, for instance the surviving spouse of the predeceased beneficiary who might have also been close to the testator.

> EXAMPLE 3 - 8. Samuel's will left his estate to his brother Arthur. It was silent as to disposition in the event Arthur died first which is what happened. Arthur left a wife, Mary, and three young children. The estate passes to Arthur's children based on the state's antilapse statute and Mary receives none of it. Guardianships must be established for the children and Mary will need court permission to use any of the assets.

If a residuary gift lapses in the absence of a specific antilapse statute provision, the property will pass by intestate succession.

EXAMPLE 3 - 9. In EXAMPLE 3 - 6, if James also predeceased Rudolph, the residuary bequest will lapse, and the estate will pass according to intestacy laws.

Survival clause. A lapse can usually be avoided with a survival clause designating an alternate taker.

EXAMPLE 3 - 10. Continuing the series of examples above, if Rudolph's will instead left the car to Isaac "in the event that Randall fails to survive me," and Isaac survives Rudolph, then Isaac, the alternate taker, receives the car.

A survival clause may require survival for some period beyond the testator's death. An example would be the phrase, "...if she survives me by 30 days..." Extending the survivorship requirement reduces the likelihood that bequeathed property will be subject to two successive probates in situations when the beneficiary dies shortly after the decedent.

EXAMPLE 3 - 11. In Example 3- 6, if Randall survived Rudolph by a month, the car will still pass to Randall and also be subject to administration in his estate. If instead Rudolph's will bequeathed the car to Randall "if he survives me by six months, otherwise to Isaac," then Isaac will receive the car, which will be subject to administration only in Rudolph's estate.

How long should the survival period be? Making it at least several months in duration will provide for the multiple death event which, relatively speaking, probably occurs most frequently: death of the decedent and the intended beneficiary in a common accident. However, specifying too long a survival period can delay distribution of estate assets since the executor will be required to wait that long to determine whether the named beneficiary in fact survived that period. Further, as mentioned previously in the discussion of the terminal interest rule, a bequest will not qualify for the marital deduction if it is contingent on the spouse surviving the decedent by a period greater than six months.

Many planners use a survival period of about one month for tangible personal property and between four and six months for other property. The shorter period for tangible personal property reflects the usual testator's desire to permit the surviving beneficiary to be able to use such property almost immediately, if even for only a short while, and to avoid storage and other additional costs.

CONCLUSION

This chapter has introduced the documents used in the transfer of an estate, with particular emphasis on the simple will, the living trust, and the testamentary trust. The next chapter focuses on the actual process of transfer of the property disposed of by these documents, with particular emphasis on the probate process and its handling of intestate succession. Later chapters will again discuss trusts in connection with saving estate taxes, with special emphasis on what are called bypass trusts and marital deduction trusts.

QUESTIONS AND PROBLEMS

1. (a) Which of the following can be held in joint tenancy: real estate, stocks, vehicles, bank accounts, and/or tangible personal property? (b) What is the main advantage to this form of title?

2. Why is an attorney more likely to be involved in creating a joint tenancy interest in real estate as compared to creating one in a brokerage or bank account? Explain.

3. Does the right to choose or change the beneficiary designation reside with the insured? Explain.

4. Is the insured the only one allowed to own life insurance on his or her life? If not, how does one go about changing ownership to a life insurance policy?

5. Merril owns a $300,000 life insurance policy on her husband's life. She is named as the beneficiary, however she wants the proceeds to go to their two children. There are cash reserves of $20,000 that could be borrowed. She is considering either naming the children as beneficiaries or transferring the ownership of the policy to them. Discuss the advantages and disadvantages of each alternative. If ownership is changed, what else should be done?

6. (a) What is a codicil? (b) Why is it mentioned in the typical will?

7. (a) Why does the will nominate two types of guardians? (b) Must the probate judge follow the testator's nominations?

8. Why might it be a mistake to waive (as part of one's will) the requirement of an executor's bond? When does waiving the bond make sense?

9. Consider what you would do in creating a will for yourself. On a separate sheet of paper write the answers to the following: (a) Who would you nominate to serve as executor? (b) If (or when) you have children, who would you ask to serve as guardians? Would you have the same or different people serve as guardian of the person and of the estate? (c) To whom would you leave your property? (d) Are there any items that you would want to go to

specific persons? (e) Which of these decisions was hardest to make? Which was the easiest? Explain.

10. What is the purpose of a residuary clause? In a typical family situation, e.g., a spouse, 2.3 children, who is likely to be given the residue of an estate? What else should be stated in case the first choice dies before the testator?

11. What is the purpose of having a minimum survival period before an estate beneficial interest vests?

12. Frida was diagnosed as suffering from bi-polar disease. In her manic phases she tended to give away property that she regretted parting with when she came down from the high. To avoid the further loss of property she allowed a conservatorship to be established by which a court appointed conservator took control of her property. She handwrote a will leaving all her property to her brother, Ted. She signed and dated it. After her death, her other two siblings challenged the validity of the will, arguing that the estate should be distributed three ways in accordance with intestate laws. Discuss the probable arguments that the siblings would use, the counter arguments, and the probable outcome.

13. In the preceding problem, if Ted was serving as Frida's conservator and, at her request, furnished her with the pen and paper with which she wrote the will, what additional issues would that bring up and how would be the likely disposition of those issues? (For medical information on bi-polar illness see http://www.psycheducation.org/depression/Psychotherapy.htm)

14. Visit the website [http://www.elder-law.com/search_fm.html] of Arizona lawyers Fleming & Curti, P. L. C to answer the following questions: (a) Was the will prepared by the old gentleman's bookkeeper valid or was it procured by undue influence? (b) Was the "no-contest" clause enforced? (c) Make a table to compare the division of the estate given these possible outcomes: (i) the will was invalid and hence he died intestate, (ii) the will was valid and there was no will contest, and (iii) as decided by the court.

15. Visit the website [http://www.elder-law.com/search_fm.html] of Arizona lawyers Fleming & Curti, P. L. C., to answer the following questions: (a)

did Mr. Ferber include a "no-contest" clause in his will? (b) What facts support the argument that the Ferber brothers were slow to get things done? (c) How was Sandra Plumleigh able to get around the no-contest provision? (d) Compare California law's treatment of no-contest clauses to that of Arizona.

16. (a) Describe, in general, how the living trust included in Exhibit 3-2 disposes of income and principal. (b) Which parties stand to receive a contingent future interest? (c) When, if ever, will each future interest become vested?

17. Holly's will leaves her property in trust, with income to her living children for their lives, then income to her grandchildren for their lives, and finally, distribution to her then living great-grandchildren. Is there a rule against perpetuity issue? Who will get Holly's property?

18. Generally, how do drafters of trust documents avoid violation of the rule against perpetuities?

19. Wills and trusts differ from contracts insofar as the number of parties involved in making them legal documents. Explain.

20. Ask a friend or relative who has a trust as part of his or her estate plan and who is willing to answer the following questions in order to help you with this assignment: (a) How long has he/she had the trust? (b) What is its main goal? Or are there several goals? (c) Has it been easy or difficult to deal with having a trust? Explain. (d) Was it expensive to have drafted? Has it been costly to keep it going?

21. Consider what you would do in creating a trust for yourself: (a) Who would you name as trustee? As successor trustee? (b) What would you want to accomplish with your trust?

22. (a) What is the main difference between a testamentary trust and a living trust? How is each trust funded? (b) What are the commonly used alternative names for each of these trusts? (c) Are all testamentary trusts established in wills? (d) How do pour-over wills relate to these two trusts?

23. To answer the questions about dynasty trusts that follow, visit Merrill Lynch's Individual Investor website for a description of these trusts and read at Harvard's website the short "developments note" by Professor Joseph William Singer about changes in state law regarding the rule against perpetuities. Questions: (a) What is a dynasty trust? (b) How does one "leverage" the GST tax exemption? (c) Which states are identified in Dr. Singer's note as directly abolishing the rule against perpetuities? (d) How long does Florida allow a trust to continue without the trust property vesting? How long in Washington State?

    The Merrill Lynch article can be found at <http://askmerrill.ml.com/>, under estate planning, look for Dynasty Trusts; Professor Singer's note about state law changes to the rule against perpetuities can be found at <http://www.law.harvard.edu/faculty/jsinger/developments/stateperprules.php>]

24. To answer the questions that follow, visit the article by Professor Harl, "To Repeal Or Not Repeal the Rule Against Perpetuities," Agricultural Law Digest Agricultural Law Digest, at <http://www.econ.iastate.edu/faculty/harl/Vol14No16.pdf>. (a) According to Professor Simes, as quoted in the article, what are the two reasons for the rule? Which is the more important reason? (b) What is the thrust of Professor Harl's economic based argument against repealing the rule?

ANSWERS TO QUESTIONS AND PROBLEMS *(odd numbered only)*

1. (a) All the property listed can be held in joint tenancy, indeed it is hard to think of any that cannot be. It might be harder to establish that form of ownership for tangible personal property unless one has some type of title certificate (e.g., car registration would make it clear how title is held). Nevertheless, three friends could buy a kayak together and agree that they will own it equally, if one dies the survivors will own it, etc., and the owners would joint tenants. (b) Advantage? The good old right of survivorship. The simplicity of transfer of title if one co-owner dies.

3. No, the right belongs to the owner of the policy. It is very common for the owner and the insured to be one and the same, but the children of the insured or the trustee of a life insurance trust could be the owner. Usually, when the owner is not the insured, the owner names him or herself the beneficiary. Naming someone else is likely to be a gift by the owner to the beneficiary when the insured dies.

5. Five major reasons why a will may not be admitted to probate:

   (a) Lack of testamentary capacity; that is, failure to be aware: (1) that they are executing a will; (2) of what they own; (3) of their heirs
   (b) Undue influence, or over-persuasion
   (c) Fraud
   (d) Mistake
   (e) Format (formality) problems, e.g., one witness where the state of domicile requires two

7. In many states, a valid will can theoretically meet the typical requirements for both the witnessed will and the holographic will because the formal requirements are not usually mutually exclusive. Such a will would usually have to be written, with all material provisions written in the testator's hand, and signed in the presence of two witnesses.

9. (a) A codicil is a separate written document that amends or revokes a prior will. (b) It is mentioned in the revocation clause to prevent needless litigation over the construction of two or more wills.

11. A survival clause avoids the risk of (1) double probate, and (2) unintended disposition to in-laws, etc., when one spouse survives the other a short period.

13. This might bring up an issue of undue influence (UI) in the creation of the will. Undue influence means that one wrongly persuaded another to do something against his or her will. UI is more likely to be found where the person accused held a position of trust, i.e., was in a fiduciary position vis-a-vis the testator. Serving as conservator is a fiduciary position. Once this relationship is established, a fiduciary receiving more than his or her intestate share of an estate has the burden of proof to show there was no such wrongful influence if another beneficiary challenges the will Depending on the circumstance, Ted might be able to show that he furnished all of his sister's paper and pens, along with doing the grocery shopping, providing for house cleaning, etc., and that he was not present when the will was drafted and did not know its contents until after Freda died. Assuming these things to be true, he would probably be able to carry the burden of proof. If she was in a hospital at the time, evidence of the medical staff concerning whether Ted was present when Freda drafted the will (assuming they know) would probably be the best evidence to either convince a jury one way or the other.

15. This is a web assignment. Once you arrive at the site, you should be able to enter "Ferber" in the search box to find the article and the answers. Let's just say, both Ferber brothers took time administering the estates under their respective charge.

17. Both Holly, her children, and any grandchild alive when she dies are lives in being insofar as this trust is concerned. The income interests of the children and the grandchildren vest within the rule's outer limits but the remainder to the great-grandchildren violates the rule. The great-grandchildren's interests fail because there is a chance that a child could give birth to a child (Holly's grandchild) after Holly died. That grandchild would not be a life in being, hence any child born to that grandchild (i.e., the child would be Holly's great-grandchild) would have, according to the trust, an interest that was not within the outer limits of the rule. Due to the violation of the rule, the remote interests of the great-grandchildren are cut off and the grandchildren would end up with remainder interests instead of just income interests. Note that the

common law rule does not take a wait and see approach, e.g., it does not allow us to wait and see whether any grandchildren are born after Holly dies.

19. Contracts always have two parties, often with very different interests. For instance, someone buying property wants the lowest price whereas the seller wants the highest price. A "meeting of the minds" might require negotiations. A will has just one party, the testator. The witnesses might be needed to make the will valid but they are not considered "parties" to the instrument. Trusts have two parties to the document, the settlor (trustor) and the trustee. The settlor creates the document and the trustee must agree to serve as trustee. The beneficiaries are not really parties in the sense of initiating or carrying out the trust, but like the beneficiaries in a third party beneficiary contract, e.g., life insurance, they can enforce the trust if the trustee fails to carry out its terms. Contrasting to the contract, the parties to a trust generally are on the same side, that is having the interest of the beneficiaries come first. As a practical matter, the initial settlor, trustee, and beneficiary are likely to be the same person or persons.

21. Answers will vary. (a) Most people serve as the initial trustee of the their trust. The harder part is deciding who to ask to serve as successor trustee. (b) This answer will vary. Influencing the answer will be whether the estate is larger or small, whether there are children, and if so, whether they are young or mature adults, and whether there are special needs that should be addressed.

23. (a) A Dynasty Trust, also known as a Perpetual or Legacy Trust, is an estate planning tool that provides income and support to unlimited generations of your family. Income and appreciation is free from future estate, gift and generation-skipping transfer tax. (b) Answer is implied in the article where it is stated, "If the GST tax exemption (currently $1,060,000 and increasing to $3,500,000 in 2009) is properly allocated to contributions, the trust assets will never be subject to the GST tax." Note that the GST tax exemption increased to $2,000,000 in 2006. (c) The three states mentioned as having directly abolished the rule against perpetuities are Rhode Island, New Jersey and South Dakota. (d) Florida allows trusts to last 360 years and Washington for 150 years.

ENDNOTES

1. According to the National Conference of Commissioners on Uniform State Laws, (see Legislative Status & Information on Uniform Acts at <http://www.nccusl.org>, the following states have adopted all or part of the UPC: Alaska, Arizona, Colorado, Hawaii, Idaho, Maine, Massachusetts, Michigan, Minnesota, Missouri, Montana, Nebraska, New Jersey, New Mexico, North Dakota, Pennsylvania, South Carolina, South Dakota, Utah, Vermont, and Wisconsin. Numerous other states have borrowed heavily from the UPC.

2. UPC § 2-504, see South Dakota's Title 29A-2-504 at <http://legis.state.sd.us/statutes/index.cfm>.

3. See California Probate Code § 6111(c) at <http://www.leginfo.ca.gov/calaw.html>.

4. See UPC § 2-503, see South Dakota's Title 29A-2-503 at <http://legis.state.sd.us/statutes/index.cfm>.

5. UPC § 2-517, see South Dakota's Title 29A-2-517 at <http://legis.state.sd.us/statutes/index.cfm>.

6. UPC § 2-507, see South Dakota's Title 29A-2-507 at <http://legis.state.sd.us/statutes/index.cfm>.

7. *Wolfe's Will,* 185 NC 563 (1923).

8. Cal. Probate Code § 6402.5 @ *<http://www.leginfo.ca.gov/calaw.html>.*

9. *Knupp v. District of Columbia*, 578 A. 2d 702 (D.C. Ct. App., 1990).

10. For an interesting discussion of the rule against perpetuities, see *<http://www.wwlia.org/ruleperp.htm>.*

11. *Lucas v. Hamm*, 56 Cal. 2d 583 (1961).

12. Sitkoff, Robert H. and Schanzenbach, Max Matthew, "Jurisdictional Competition for Trust Funds: An Empirical Analysis of Perpetuities and Taxes" (April 25, 2005). Northwestern Law & Econ Research Paper No. 05-07. <http://ssrn.com/abstract=666481>.

13. Harl, Dr. Neil E.,"To Repeal Or Not Repeal the Rule Against Perpetuities," Agricultural Law Digest Agricultural Law Digest, 121 Volume 14, No 16 August 22, 2003 ISSN 1051-2780, see article at <http://www.econ.iastate.edu/faculty/harl/Vol14No16.pdf>.

14. UPC § 2-603, see South Dakota's Title 29A-2-603 at <http://legis.state.sd.us/statutes/index.cfm>.

CHAPTER 4

Property Transfers

OVERVIEW

This chapter considers the actual processes by which property is transferred, emphasizing transfers taking effect at death. We will consider both probate and nonprobate transfers. We will also review the laws of intestate succession that serve as a guide where no other legally recognized guide exists.

WHY PROBATE?

When a person dies, steps must be taken to transfer ownership of his or her property interests to the proper beneficiaries. Probate means the entire court process supervising the distribution of any part of a decedent's property according to a will or the rules of intestate succession. Each of the 50 states and the District of Columbia has enacted a probate code that establishes the rules for transferring a decedent's property. These codes serve a dual purpose; they attempt to protect both creditors of the decedent's estate and assure that the appropriate beneficiaries eventually end up with the property after debts and expenses are paid. Where a will exists, the codes seek to assure that the nominated executor is appointed unless there is good cause for appointing someone else. The notice provisions seek to assure that the creditors have a chance to file their claims and that potential beneficiaries, including heirs that have been disinherited, are aware of the proceedings so that the interested parties can raise an issue if the will being offered for probate is not the last will or if there is some irregularity concerning the will being offered. The code specifies the contents of the petition that starts the probate process and the steps that the estate's personal representative must take from start to final distribution. The probate procedures are much the same whether there is or is not a will. The main difference is that without a will intestate succession laws serve as the guide to distribution. What does not change are the notices, marshaling of assets, filing of an inventory, reports and accountings prepared for the court, and obtaining an order authorizing distribution of the estate.

DETERMINING THE PROBATE ESTATE

In a sense, the probate process stands last in line. Only that property for which there is no other mechanism of transfer is swept into the probate process. As discussed in the previous chapter, other mechanisms include certain contract, trust, and title arrangements. After nonprobate mechanisms are taken into account one is left with the probate property, mainly property held in the decedent's name alone or with others as tenants in common. In some states property left to the decedent's surviving spouse does not have to be probated. Most states allow the collection and distribution of small estates without court involvement. The threshold as to what constitutes a small estate varies greatly, e.g., the Uniform Probate Code (UPC) suggests $5,000[1] whereas in California it is $100,000.[2]

Like probate, the nonprobate mechanisms for transfer are sanctioned by law. However, they are subject to much less state supervision. With title held as *tenancy by the entirety* or *joint tenancy,* the right of survivorship results in the automatic transfer of ownership to the surviving co-tenants, with the right previously held by the decedent-owner ceasing immediately on death. This automatic transfer is said to be a transfer by *operation of law*. Although title may pass automatically, as a practical matter, additional steps may be necessary to clear title to the property. The decedent's name will need to be removed from the actual documents. Fortunately, this is usually processed quickly by the authorities (officers at banks, personnel at the department of motor vehicles, etc.) when a surviving cotenant appears with a certified copy of the death certificate. For real estate, to satisfy title companies personnel, the survivors will have to record in each county where the jointly held land is located a notarized "affidavit of death of joint tenant" verifying that the person identified in the attached certified death certificate was the co-owner of the parcels identified in the affidavit.

Property that, at the decedent's death, is held in a revocable or irrevocable *living trust* is not held in the decedent's name, but rather the legal title is in the name of the trustee. Since probate administration is concerned with transfer of property held in the decedent's name (individually or concurrently), property held by a trustee is not subject to probate administration. If, in accordance with the underlying trust document, the settlor's death triggers a transfer out of trust to the remainderman, the transfer process is uncomplicated. The trustee simply makes the distribution by deed or assignment, depending on the nature of the assets.

Where the decedent settlor (trustor) was serving as trustee at the time of his or her death, most state laws allow the successor trustee to immediately take over the administration of the estate, hence no probate administration is required. The successor will have to establish for the benefit of those involved with the transfer process (e.g., brokerage houses, title companies, etc.) that the settlor is dead, by producing a certified death certificate, and that he or she is the successor trustee, by some reliable means such as an official photo identification (e.g., the successor trustee's driver's license).

Property owned by the decedent to be transferred at death *into*, rather than out of, a trust will be subject to probate administration. In such instances, the probate process is the funding mechanism for the trust. This will occur for all testamentary trusts because no separate trust exists prior to the death of the testator. Near the conclusion of the probate, the court order for distribution to the trustee has a dual purpose: (1) it serves as the trust funding mechanism, and (2) it serves as the trust document since the terms of the trust, taken from the will, are repeated as part of the order. Where real property is transferred pursuant to a probate order for distribution, whether to the trustee of a testamentary trust or to someone else, no deed is necessary. Rather, the executor records a certified copy of the order in the county where the real property is located. Generally, when a living trust is used, a probate is unnecessary. Nevertheless, the settlor will have created a pour-over will, so called because it scoops up assets left out of the trust and "pours" them into it. This "pouring" is done through the probate process, which concludes with an order for distribution to the trustee of the living trust. Of course, with the living trust, the order does not include the language of the trust because it is already in existence as a separate document.

Property disposed of by contract, including *life insurance proceeds* on the life of the decedent and *retirement benefits*, is not subject to probate administration because title to such assets is not held by the decedent. Instead, the insurance company pays the insurance proceeds directly to the named beneficiary at the death of the insured and the pension payments shift to the alternate beneficiary as per agreement once the employee-beneficiary dies. The insurance company or pension fund pays the named beneficiary in accordance with the payout option selected by the decedent or by the beneficiary.

In contrast with title held in joint tenancy, title held by a decedent either as an *individual*, as a *tenant in common*, or as *community property* does not in itself create a mechanism (or guide) for title transfer. As a result, the states have established the probate process to transfer title, using either the decedent's will or the laws of intestate succession as the guide.

Although it is difficult to gather accurate statistics, it is generally estimated that about half of all adults die without a will. In such circumstances, the state's intestate succession laws serve as the guide for the distribution of all property for which there is no other guide. Generally, the mechanism for intestate distribution is the probate process, although there may be a simplified "claiming process" that avoids probate court involvement for small estates. The claiming process generally requires the person with the successor interest in the decedent's property to present the holder of the property with an affidavit (a written declaration signed under penalty of perjury with the signature notarized) setting forth the basis of the successor's claim, i.e., by virtue of the decedent's will, through intestate succession law, or as a creditor. The document must include a statement that the estate's value meets the state's small estate definition and that no probate is pending.[3]

Figure 4-1 diagrams the probate and nonprobate interests of a decedent at the moment of death. The left side contains probate assets, including the decedent's one-half interest in community property, the decedent's interests in probate held in common with others, and the catchall--all other probate property owned individually by the decedent. This would include the value of life insurance *on the life of another* owned by the decedent. Of course, where there is co-ownership, the portion of the interest held *by others,* whether as tenants in common, joint tenants, or as community property, is not part of the decedent's probate or nonprobate estate. One should also note that some community property states, such as California, no longer require a probate for property going to a surviving spouse, whether going to her (or him) by virtue of the decedent's will or by intestate succession. Those states may require the surviving spouse to file a simple request for confirmation by the court of the survivor's right to take the property, followed by notice to interested parties, then a hearing, and, finally, a court order granting the confirmation. If decedent's half interest in community property is left to someone other than the surviving spouse, then it would be probated.

FIGURE 4 - 1 A Decedent's Property Interests

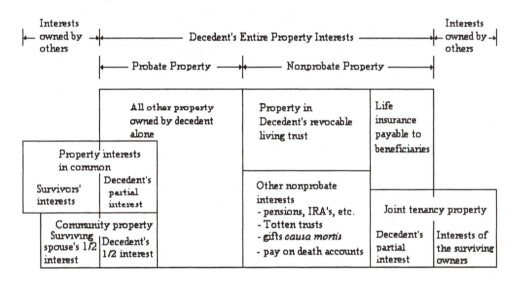

The right side of the diagram contains the nonprobate property, including interests in living trusts, property held in joint tenancy or as tenants by the entirety, life insurance policies on the decedent's life other than those payable to the decedent's estate, and certain other nonprobate interests. Life insurance proceeds payable to the decedent's estate are collected by the estate's representative and become part of the probate estate. Policies issued since World War II are not likely to be paid into the insured's probate estate. In addition to having several layers of alternate beneficiaries, the policy will probably have a provision very similar to intestate succession designating the order of beneficiaries in the event that the named beneficiaries predecease the insured and only as a last resort have the proceeds payable to the decedent's estate.

The logic of Figure 4-1 suggests a relatively straightforward *procedure* to determine which of a decedent's assets will be subject to probate administration. First, list all the decedent's property interests held immediately prior to death, including all insurance policies. Then remove from the list all assets for which there is a nonprobate mechanism of transfer, such as property in living trusts, joint tenancy property, and interests payable to a designated beneficiary, such as life insurance, pensions, and finally miscellaneous nonprobate interests such as Totten trusts, pay-on-death, and transfer-on-death accounts. What is left is the probate estate, mostly property in the decedent's name alone or held with others as tenants-in-common, and for states that still require probate for community property even when it goes to the surviving spouse, the decedent's half of the community property.

So far, we have seen how the decedent's probate property is determined. The next step is to decide who will receive this property. For this, one first looks to the will. If there is no will, the state laws of intestate succession are applied.

INTESTATE SUCCESSION LAWS

We have seen that a person who dies without a will is said to die intestate and that any probate property will then pass according to the state's laws of intestate succession. Further, a person receiving property under these laws is called an heir and is said to inherit the property.

In determining who should inherit, the members of the various state legislatures have used their knowledge of human nature to design estate plans for persons dying intestate. Thus, these state codes usually give priority to the decedent's spouse, next to the decedent's issue, and, if there is neither spouse nor issue, then to the decedent's other blood relatives, with priority given to the closest relatives. We will review the Uniform Probate Code's version of intestate succession after we cover degrees of consanguinity (kinship) and several alternative patterns for allocating property among a decedent's issue. These concepts are relevant to both intestate and testate property distribution. They are important to understand because the alternative allocation methods can make a big difference in how property is distributed.

Degrees of Consanguinity

Degrees of consanguinity refers to the level of closeness in the blood relationship between a decedent and the decedent's various relatives. As we have said, and as Figure 4-2 depicts, descendants (issue) of the decedent (the dead person) include children, grandchildren, great-grandchildren, and so on. Ascendants (ancestors) include parents, grandparents, great-grandparents, and the like. Descendants and ascendants of a person are said to be in the person's *lineal,* or vertical line. Generally, after spouses, intestate succession laws favor lineal descendants over all other relatives. Relationships are said to be *collateral* if they share with the decedent a common ancestor, but they are neither ascendants nor descendants,

FIGURE 4 - 2 Degrees of Consanguinity

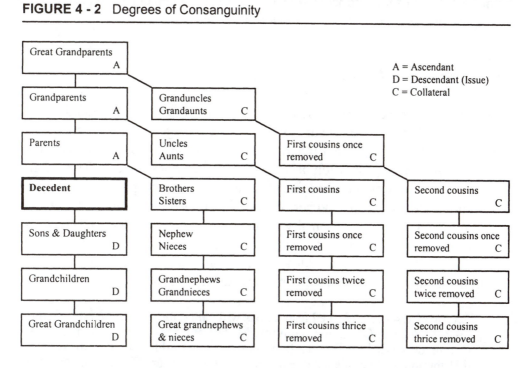

and thus are not in the lineal or vertical line. For example, a nephew of a person is not his or her issue, but shares a common ascendant with the person, namely the person's parent.

The most common method of measuring a collateral relative's degree of consanguinity to the decedent is to count the "steps" along degree lines, the lines shown linking the boxes. Degree lines run only between child and parent and parent and child. To find degree of closeness or consanguinity we first count ascendant lines to the common ancestor, then collateral lines until we reach the person of interest. For example, the decedent's brother is two steps from the decedent. We count one ascendant step to the common ancestor parent and then one collateral step to the brother. The decedent's uncle is three steps from the decedent because we first count two ascendant steps upward to the common ancestor and then one collateral step to the uncle. Figure 4-2 can be helpful in determining relative closeness to the decedent of distant surviving relatives, especially in those states that have not adopted the more restrictive succession rules of the Uniform Probate Code. Generally, only persons of the same degree of closeness share an intestate decedent's estate.

Per Stirpes or Per Capita

If an intestate decedent's only heirs are one living son and two grandchildren who are the daughters of the decedent's predeceased daughter, how much will each one inherit? Will they each inherit one-third of the estate, or will the son be entitled to a larger proportion because he is a closer descendant? The technical terms used to answer questions like these are per capita and per stirpes. Per capita is Latin for "by the head" and per stirpes is Latin for "by the roots." A *per capita* distribution gives each person alive at the top of a line of descent an equal share of the estate, or "share and share alike." On the other hand, a *per stirpes* distribution gives each line of descent an equal share, which means that a share will be subdivided if it drops down below the next generation.

> EXAMPLE 4 - 1. Bob died testate. His will called for a per capita distribution to his descendants. Of his four children, Martha and Max survived him; David and Carl predeceased him. David left two children and Carl left three. With a per capita distribution, the top of each line of descent gets one share. The seven people at the top of descent lines are Martha, Max, and each of David and Carl's children. They will each receive a one-seventh share. It does not matter how many children Martha and Max might have, likewise, whether any of David or Carl's children also have children does not change the distribution since the distribution does not drop below a living descendant.

EXAMPLE 4 - 2. In the prior example, if Bob's will called for a per stirpes distribution the shares would be quite different. First, the estate would be divided into shares based upon lines of descent; here there are four. Martha and Max would each receive a one-fourth share. David's two children would each receive a one-eight share and Carl's three children would each receive a one-twelfth share.

The Uniform Probate Code (UPC) uses a method of allocation called *"per capita at each generation."* This form is important as it is becoming more common in estate plans and is likely to replace per stirpes as the preferred method of allocating an estate amongst one's issue. Indeed, the UPC suggests it as the model for intestate succession. With per capita at each generation, the shares are divided by the number of lines of descent, starting with the top generation (i.e., nearest the decedent) having living descendants, each living descendant at that upper-most level then gets one share. The remaining shares are combined and one moves to the next generation with living descendants. The combined shares are again divided by the lines of descent with those alive at this next highest level each get one share and what remains being combined to move to the next level to be divided again in like manner. This may be difficult to explain but it is fairly easy to demonstrate by example.

EXAMPLE 4 - 3. In the prior example, consider the distribution that would occur if Bob's will called for a per capita at each generation distribution. Since the nearest generation with living descendants is the next generation, i.e., there are two children surviving, we divide by the four lines of descent and Martha and Max would each receive a one-fourth share. At the next level, there are five lines of descent, one for each of the children of David and Carl. They would each receive one-fifth of the remaining half, i.e., a one-tenth share of the estate.

Described next are three patterns of distribution used so often in estate planning documents and in intestate succession laws that they have been given names. Each has a set of rules for determining the shares of descendants. Regardless of which of the three is used, the same set of people receive a share of the estate and only the portions change depending on the pattern chosen. For all three, as one goes down a line of descent, only the surviving members of the *generation nearest the decedent* receive a share. In other words, if an ancestor is alive then those descendants below do not receive anything.

Consider the following family tree illustrated in Figure 4-3. Cross-marks in the diagram indicate descendants who have predeceased the decedent. Keep in mind that the person who died is the decedent and children, grandchildren, great-grandchildren, etc, are descendants.

FIGURE 4 - 3 Distributions Per Capita, Per Stirpes, Per Capita at Each Generation

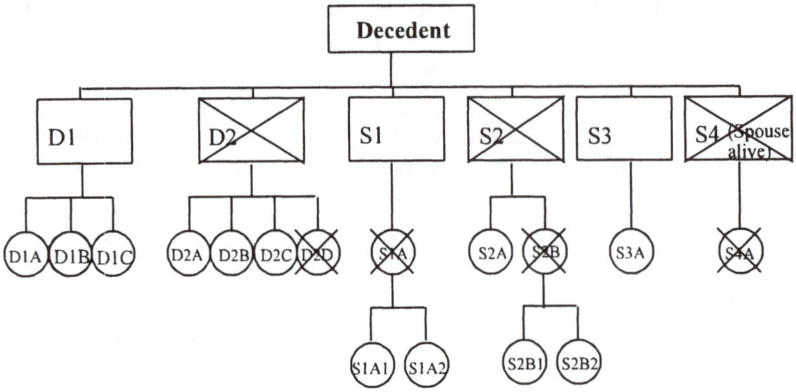

In our example, the decedent had the following descendants: daughters D1 (alive) and D2 (dead); sons, S1 (alive), S2 (dead), S3 (alive), and S4 (dead).
D1 three children (all alive): D1A, D1B and D1C
D2 three children alive, one dead: D2A, D2B, D2C (alive); and D2D (dead).
    D2D no issue.
S1 one child: S1A (dead).
    S1A is survived by two children (both alive): S1A1 and S1A2.
S2 two children: S2A (alive) and S2B (dead).
    S2B is survived by two children: S2B1 and S2B2.
S3 one child: S3A (alive).
S4 one child: S4A (dead) no issue; S4 left a spouse.

Regardless of which pattern of distribution is used, given that only the living descendant at the top of each line of descent receives anything, the following (and only the following) nine descendants receive property: D1, D2A, D2B, D2C, S1, S2A, S2B1, S2B2, and S3. Why do the others receive nothing? Either because they did not survive the decedent (D2, D2D, S2, S2B, S4, and S4A), or because there is a surviving ancestor in a generation between them and the decedent (D1A, D1B, D1C, S1A1, S1A2, and S3A). It also follows that no property will be allocated to a line where all descendants in the line have predeceased the decedent. For example, S4's bloodline (S4A) receives nothing. Spouses of deceased descendants receive nothing.

The discussion below will analyze each pattern separately. Once you "get it" the rules applicable to these patterns are easy to apply.

Per capita. A per capita distribution requires that all eligible descendants receive an *equal amount.* Thus, D1, D2A, D2B, D2C, S1, S2A, S2B1, S2B2, and

S3 would each receive a one-ninth share. Historically, the per capita method has not been very popular. The two methods of allocation described next are much more prevalent.

Per stirpes. *Per stirpes* has been used for hundreds of years. Under it, surviving descendants of predeceased children may take unequally depending on how many in their family survive. First, the property is divided into shares, one share for each surviving child and one share for each of the decedent's predeceased children having living issue. Each surviving child gets his or her share directly. Second, the share for each predeceased child with living issue is divided equally among the issue - one share for each living child and one share for each predeceased child with living issue. Step two is just like step one but at the next generation. The process repeats until all the shares are taken. A share only goes to the next generation if the previous generation is not alive to take it. The next living generation is said to "represent" its parent.

- In our example, each living child, D1, S1 and S3, will receive a 1/5 share and their descendants receive nothing.
- D2 is a predeceased child with three living children and none who died with issue. The three children each take 1/3 share of their mother's 1/5 share or 1/15.
- S2 is a predeceased child with one living child and one predeceased child with living issue. Thus, S2's share is divided in two; one share goes to his living son, S2A who gets 1/2 of his father's 1/5 share or 1/10.
- S2B is a predeceased child with living issue. His share is divided among his issue. Thus, his 1/2 of his father's 1/5 share is divided between his two children, each of whom takes 1/20.

Summarizing, a per stirpes distribution of the decedent's estate will be divided as follows:

D1, S1 and S3	1/5 each;
D2A, D2B, and D2C	1/15 each (i.e., 1/5 x 1/3);
S2A	1/10 (i.e., 1/5 x 1/2); and
S2B1 and S2B2	1/20 each (i.e., 1/5 x 1/2 x 1/2).

Per stirpes has also been called "by right of representation." To avoid confusion, we will only use per stirpes for the above pattern because some states define "by representation" to mean "per capita at each generation."

Per capita at each generation. Per capita at each generation is becoming more common in estate plans. In the Uniform Probate Code it has replaced per stirpes as the preferred intestate succession distribution pattern.[4] Under the UPC, if a statute or an estate plan "calls for property to be distributed 'by representation' or 'by per capita at each generation,' the property is divided into as many equal shares as there are (i) surviving descendants in the generation nearest to the designated ancestor which contains one or more surviving descendants (ii) and deceased descendants in the same generation who left surviving descendants, if any. Each surviving descendant in the nearest generation is allocated one share. The remaining shares, if any, are combined and then divided in the same manner among the surviving descendants of the deceased descendants as if the surviving descendants who were allocated a share and their surviving descendants had predeceased the distribution date."[5] Per capita at each generation distributes the property that goes to the decedent's three living children the same as per stirpes. The difference is in the property that goes to the descendants of the deceased children, i.e., to grandchildren and great-grandchildren. The shares of those entitled to receive a portion of the estate at each generational level are combined and then divided equally.

First, the property is divided into shares, one share for each surviving child and one share for each of the decedent's predeceased children having living issue. Each surviving child gets his or her full share. Second, all the shares for the predeceased children who left issue are combined and divided equally, one share for each living grandchild and one share for each deceased grandchild who left issue. The living descendants at this generation level take their shares. The shares for those grandchildren that predeceased the decedent are combined and go to the next generation. The process repeats until all the shares are taken.

- Thus, in the illustration, similar to per stirpes, each living child, D1, S1, and S3 would receive a 1/5 share and their descendants receive nothing.
- D2 and S2 died leaving issue. Their shares are combined and go to their combined descendants.
- D2 has three living children and none who have died leaving living issue. S2 has one living child, S2A, and one predeceased child with living issue, S2B. The total combined number is 5. Thus, the four living children of D2 and S2 each get 1/5 of the combined 2/5, or 2/25. If they had descendants, their descendants would receive nothing.
- The 2/25 share for S2B, a predeceased child with living issue is divided at the next generation. Since there is only one share to divide, and there are only two living issue to share it, each takes half their predeceased parent's share, or 1/25.

Summarizing, a per capita at each generation distribution of the decedent's estate will be as follows:

D1, S1 and S3:	1/5 each;	
D2A, D2B, D2C and S2A:	2/25 each;	(2/5 x 1/5)
S2B1 and S2B2:	1/25 each.	(1/2 x 2/25).

Notice that each eligible grandchild inherits the *same amount* (2/25), rather than different amounts as in the case of per stirpes. Whew!

Comparison of the three rules. One advantage of per capita at each generation is that it gives equal shares to those who are equally close in relationship to the decedent, e.g., grandchildren who receive a share will all get the same share. One advantage of per stirpes is that it passes the same share that the descendants would receive had their ancestors survived and then died bequeathing the property to the next generation. One advantage of the per capita rule is that it treats everyone equally. This issue is important in planning because clients may strongly prefer one of these types of distribution over the others, and their will or trust document should reflect that preference.

All three distribution rules are similar in that they dispose of an intestate estate to the same descendants. For each, all descendants who are more remotely related to the decedent will not inherit if an ascendant in a generation closer to the decedent is alive. Preventing inheritance by more remote descendants has the advantage of reducing the number of heirs, thereby making inheritable property more marketable and minimizing the likelihood of inheritance by minors and the need for court-appointed guardians.

Finally, answering the question posed at the beginning of this section, under per stirpes or per capita at each generation, the son would inherit one half and the granddaughters would each inherit one quarter of the estate. Under per capita distribution, the son and each granddaughter would inherit one-third of the estate.

Intestacy in UPC States

We are now ready to look at the rules of intestate succession used in states that have adopted the Uniform Probate Code. Note that the UPC uses the term descendant rather than issue, reflecting a modern trend to avoid a biological connotation and extend inheritance rights to adopted children.

The UPC's principal intestate sections are reproduced in Exhibit 4-1. These and more are found on the Teaching Aids CD. In general, § 2-101 makes it clear that the Code's intestate succession rules apply only if the will does not dispose of all of the decedent's estate or if there is no will. The intestate share of the surviving spouse is determined by referring to § 2-102 for common law states, or to § 2-102A for community property states. The intestate share of heirs, other than the surviving spouse, is determined by referring to § 2-103. Section 2-104 requires an heir to survive 120 hour longer than the decedent to qualify for an intestate share. Finally, if there are no "takers" under the above sections, § 2-105 has the estate pass to the decedent's state of domicile. The property is said to "escheat" when there are no heirs, meaning that the decedent's property becomes the property of the state. Examples applying UPC intestate succession rules follow Exhibit 4 - 1.

EXHIBIT 4 - 1 Intestate Succession under the Uniform Probate Code

---

2-101 Intestate Estate

(a) Any part of a decedent's estate not effectively disposed of by will passes by intestate succession to the decedent's heirs as prescribed in this Code, except as modified by the decedent's will.

(b) A decedent, by will, may expressly exclude or limit the right of an individual or class to succeed to property of the decedent passing by intestate succession. If that individual or a member of that class survives the decedent, the share of the decedent's intestate estate to which that individual or class would have succeeded, passes as if that individual or each member of that class had disclaimed his (or her) intestate share.

2-102 Share of Spouse (Common Law States)

The intestate share of a decedent's surviving spouse is:
(1) the entire intestate estate if:
   (i) no descendant or parent of the decedent survives the decedent; or
   (ii) all of the decedent's surviving descendants are also descendants of the surviving spouse and there is no other descendant of the surviving spouse who survives the decedent;

(2) the first ($200,000), plus three fourths of any balance of the intestate estate, if no descendant of the decedent survives the decedent, but a parent of the decedent survives the decedent;

(3) the first ($150,000), plus one-half of any balance of the intestate estate, if all of the decedent's surviving descendants are also descendants of the surviving spouse, and the surviving spouse has one or more surviving descendants who are not descendants of the decedent;

EXHIBIT 4 - 1 Intestate Succession under the UPC *(continued)*

(4) the first ($100,000), plus one-half of any balance of the intestate estate, if one or more of the decedent's surviving descendants are not descendants of the surviving spouse.

2-102A Share of the Spouse (Community Property States)

(a) The intestate share of a surviving spouse in separate property is:
  (1) the entire intestate estate if:
    (i) no descendant or parent of the decedent survives the decedent; or
    (ii) all of the decedent's surviving descendants are also descendants of the surviving spouse and there is no other descendant of the surviving spouse who survives the decedent;
  (2) the first ($200,000), plus three fourths of any balance of the intestate estate, if no descendant of the decedent survives the decedent, but a parent of the decedent survives the decedent;
  (3) the first ($150,000), plus one-half of any balance of the intestate estate, if all of the decedent's surviving descendants are also descendants of the surviving spouse and the surviving spouse has one or more surviving descendants who are not descendants of the decedent;
  (4) the first ($100,000), plus one-half of any balance of the intestate estate, if one or more of the decedent's surviving descendants are not descendants of the surviving spouse.
(b) The one-half of community property belonging to the decedent passes to the surviving spouse as the intestate share.

2-103 Shares of Heirs Other than Surviving Spouse

Any part of the intestate estate not passing to the decedent's surviving spouse under Section 2-102, or the entire intestate estate if there is no surviving spouse, passes in the following order to the individuals designated below who survive the decedent:
  (1) to the decedent's descendants by representation;
  (2) if there is no surviving descendant, to the decedent's parents equally if both survive, or to the surviving parent;
  (3) if there is no surviving descendant or parent, to the descendant of the decedent's parents or either of them by representation;
  (4) if there is no surviving descendant, parent, or descendant of a parent, but the decedent is survived by one or more grandparents or descendants of grandparents, half of the estate passes to the decedent's

---

EXHIBIT 4 - 1 Intestate Succession under the UPC *(continued)*

---

paternal grandparents equally if both survive, or to the surviving paternal grandparent, or to the descendants of the paternal grandparents or either of them if both are deceased, the descendants taking by representation; and the other half passes to the decedent's maternal relatives in the same manner; but if there be no surviving grandparent or descendant of a grandparent on either the paternal or the maternal side, the entire estate passes to the decedent's relatives on the other side in the same manner as the half.

2-104 Requirement that Heir Survive Decedent for 120 Hours

An individual who fails to survive the decedent by 120 hours is deemed to have predeceased the decedent for purposes of homestead allowance, exempt property, and intestate succession, and the decedent's heirs are determined accordingly. If it is not established by clear and convincing evidence that an individual who would otherwise be an heir survived the decedent by 120 hours, it is deemed that the individual failed to survive for the required period. This section is not to be applied if its application would result in a taking of intestate estate by the state under Section 2-105.

2-105 No Taker

If there is no taker under the provisions of this Article, the intestate estate passes to the state.

Intestate share to surviving spouse. In *common law states*, under UPC § 2-102, the surviving spouse is entitled to all the decedent's intestate estate if the decedent leaves no parent or descendant, or if the decedent does leave descendants, but neither the decedent nor the surviving spouse have other descendants (e.g., child of a former marriage). Alternatively, the spouse takes the first $100,000 to $200,000, plus a fraction of the rest ranging from one-half to three-fourths, depending on whether parents or descendants of the decedent and/or spouse survive. An example of § 2-102(3) is where the decedent and surviving spouse leave a child and the surviving spouse has a child from a former marriage. An example of § 2-102(4) is where the decedent leaves a child from a former marriage.

Under § 2-102A, the surviving spouse's intestate share in *community property states* is identical to that for common law states, except for an additional provision for the distribution of the community property. Thus, that spouse takes the same share of the decedent's separate property as he or she would take in a common law state. In addition, the surviving spouse is entitled to the decedent's entire half of the community property.

Intestate share to others. According to § 2-103, other relatives of the decedent are divided into a hierarchical list of classes, corresponding to the degree of blood relationship to the decedent. Thus, to determine which class is entitled to succession of an intestate decedent's property, one would move down the list, stopping at the first class containing at least one living member. Distribution would be made only to members within that class. A summary of this prioritized list follows:

1. Surviving descendants, by right of representation
2. Parents
3. Descendants of parents, by right of representation
4. Paternal and maternal grandparents and their descendants, one-half to each side, by right of representation

The UPC calls for a "per capita at each generation" form of distribution whenever a document has property pass by right of representation.[6]

Under § 2-104, any heir must survive the decedent by 120 hours to take by intestate succession. This state-imposed survival requirement has the effect of avoiding double probate in some common accident situations.

Finally, under § 2-105, if none of the above relatives survive, then the decedent's intestate property passes to the state, under the doctrine of *escheat*. In English feudal law, escheat meant that the feudal lord received a reversion in the property, either because the tenant died without issue or because the tenant committed a felony. In American law, escheat has come to mean a reversion of the decedent's property to the state because no individual is "competent" to inherit. In most states, including California, there will be no escheat unless the decedent is not survived by *any* kin, no matter how remote the relationship. The UPC, on the other hand, limits inheritance to the closer relatives, under the arguable premise that more remote "laughing heirs" would be receiving a windfall not ever intended by the decedent. One wonders whether the typical decedent really would have preferred leaving property to the state or a favorite charity, rather than to some distant relatives. "Heir hunting" firms exist to locate beneficiaries who cannot be found by the estate's personal representative. They routinely pull probate court files to see whether a missing heir is mentioned in the proceedings. If so, the firm will try to locate the missing heir and give the person the information necessary to claim the inheritance, but only if the heir agrees to pay a fee. The fee is usually a percentage (e.g., 25 to 33%) of the value of the inherited property.

The examples listed next illustrate the principles of intestate succession. In each case, assume that D is a decedent who died a resident of a common law UPC state, and owned $300,000 in property. Relevant UPC sections are given in brackets.

> EXAMPLE 4 - 4. D is survived only by spouse and a cousin. His spouse will inherit all. [§ 2-102(1)(i)].

> EXAMPLE 4 - 5. D is survived by spouse and their five children, one of whom has a daughter. The spouse will inherit all. [§ 2-102(1)(ii)].

> EXAMPLE 4 - 6. Facts similar to EXAMPLE 4 - 4, above, except that spouse also has a child of a former marriage. The spouse inherits $150,000 plus one-half of the rest, or a total of $225,000. Each of the five children inherits an equal share of the rest, i.e., $15,000. D's granddaughter inherits nothing. [§ 2-102(3) and § 2-103(1)].

> EXAMPLE 4 - 7. Facts similar to EXAMPLE 4 - 4, above, except that decedent also has a child of a former marriage. The spouse inherits $100,000, plus one-half of the rest, or a total of $200,000. Each of the children inherits an equal share of the rest, i.e., S16,667 (i.e., $100,000/6). D's granddaughter inherits nothing. [§ 2-102(4) and § 2-103(1)].

> EXAMPLE 4 - 8. Facts similar to EXAMPLE 4 - 4, above, except that spouse survived decedent by only five hours. The spouse will not inherit. Each of the five children will inherit one-fifth of the total, i.e., $60,000. D's granddaughter still inherits nothing. [§ 2-104 and § 2-103(1)].

> EXAMPLE 4 - 9. D is survived by parents and two children. The children take all. [§ 2-103(1)].

> EXAMPLE 4 - 10. D is survived by spouse, a parent, and a sister. The spouse inherits $275,000 and the parent inherits $25,000. The sister receives nothing. [§ 2-102(2) and § 2- 103(2)].

> EXAMPLE 4 - 11. D is survived by a sister and two nephews, the sons of D's deceased brother. Based on the required by right of representation distribution, sister inherits $150,000 and each of the nephews takes $75,000. [§ 2-103(3)].

> EXAMPLE 4 - 12. D's closest surviving relative is a second cousin. All property will escheat to the state. [§ 2-105].

If the decedent had been a resident of a community property state, each of the above dispositions of the decedent's individually owned property (i.e., separate property) would still be correct. In addition, the decedent's half of the community property would pass to the surviving spouse, with the result that the surviving spouse would own all of the community property.

Intestacy in Non-UPC States

The intestate succession laws in non-UPC states vary somewhat, but like the UPC states one would expect as common thread a surviving spouse to have priority, followed by descendants (using either a per stirpes or a per capita at each generation pattern), and, if neither spouse nor descendants then more remote heirs' interests are determined by degrees of consanguinity. For example, if an intestate decedent is survived by children but no spouse, the children usually take all. If the decedent leaves a spouse and children, the spouse and the children will usually share the property, with the spouse receiving one-third to one-half of the estate and the children the rest. If the decedent is survived by a spouse but no children, the spouse usually receives all. If, in addition to the spouse, the decedent's parents are still alive, while in some states the spouse gets all, in others the spouse shares a portion with the parents. Since state's intestate succession laws do vary, the reader is urged to make an independent investigation of these laws as adopted by his or her own state. One source for accessing state laws is the Washburn University School of Law's website (*http://www.washlaw.edu/uslaw/statelaw.html*).

Advancements

An *advancement* is a lifetime gift that the donor wants to have treated as an advanced distribution from the donor's estate to be taken into account when the donor dies. Nearly all states have statutes spelling out what is needed to prove that such was the donor's intent. Most states, including those adopting the UPC, require that the donor's intent be in writing or that the donee acknowledge that the gift was understood to be an advancement. If the recipient of the property fails to survive the decedent, the property is not taken into account in computing the intestate share to be received by the recipient's issue, unless the declaration or acknowledgment provides otherwise. Where advancement occurs, the value of the gift when given is added to the net value of the decedent's estate before determining intestate shares. The donee's share is then reduced by the value of the gift. If the donee's intestate share is less than the value of the gift, the donee does not have to return the excess, but will not otherwise share in the estate. The other heirs' shares are redetermined excluding the donee and the gift to the donee.

> EXAMPLE 4 - 13. Sherry died intestate, survived by her three children, Marie, Dean, and Barbara. Her estate was valued at $120,000. Two years before she died, Sherry gave Marie XYZ stock valued at $30,000. With the gift was a typed letter from Sherry saying that she knew Marie needed the income from the stock and she should not have to wait until Sherry died to get it, but Marie should understand that it would be taken into account when her estate was divided up. Even though the letter would not qualify as a will (it was neither holographic nor witnessed), the gift will be treated as an advancement. The children will inherit the following amounts: $20,000 to Marie and $50,000 each to Dean and Barbara, and the date-of-death value of the stock is immaterial. If Sherry's gift had not been an advancement, each of the children would inherit $40,000. In either outcome, Marie will keep the $30,000 gift.

> EXAMPLE 4 - 14. Same as before, except Sherry's estate was valued at $45,000, not including the gift to Marie. When the gift is added back, each child's share is $25,000. This is less than what Marie has already received. Therefore she receives nothing, the gift is ignored, and the $45,000 is split equally by Dean and Barbara.

The advancement rules apply only to intestate succession, on the assumption that a testator wishing to reduce a beneficiary's share would do so in the will itself or by codicil. A handwritten statement evidencing an advancement may be treated as a holographic codicil in those states that recognize holographic wills.

OMITTED RELATIVES

To what extent can one fail to provide for a surviving spouse? What about children? Does it matter whether the failure to provide appears to be deliberate or by inadvertence? Needles to say, state law answers these questions but the answer may vary depending on the jurisdiction.

The Rights of Omitted Children

An omitted child is defined as any living child (or living issue of any deceased child) who was not provided for in his or her deceased parent's will. This may occur because the child was born after the will was executed and the parent's will did not have a clause providing for later born children, or the child may have been alive at the time the will was executed but the parent chose, for whatever reason, not to mention the child. An omitted spouse, an omitted child, and the omitted issue of a deceased child, are referred to as *pretermitted* heirs, meaning overlooked or forgotten heirs. As a general rule, states protect, if at all, only the interests of surviving spouses and issue, and other kin have no legal claim against a decedent's estate plan.

Children born after the will was executed. In most states, including UPC states,[7] an after-born child is entitled to take the share he or she would have received had the decedent died without a will, unless any one of the following is true: (a) the omission was intentional; (b) the will left substantially all of the estate to the other parent; or (c) the testator made some other provision for the after-born child. The child's intestate portion can be the entire estate where the child has no brothers or sisters and the decedent-parent was unmarried, or it might be nothing, as in community property states where the surviving spouse inherits all the community property. In a community property state, the omitted child might have a claim to a share of the decedent's separate property. Generally, if the estate plan leaves a portion of the estate to the surviving spouse and a portion to children who were alive when the will was executed, the after-born child shares only in the portion going to the other children.

EXAMPLE 4 - 15. When Haylie executed her will she had two children, Jon and Joyce. Her will left each child $48,000 and the balance of her estate to her husband, Frank. She had another child, Jeanne, but neglected to update her will. Each child is entitled to $32,000, i.e., $96,000 divided three ways.

EXAMPLE 4 - 16. If Haylie's will left Jon $72,000 and Joyce $24,000, Jeanne would still get $32,000 but the other two would have their shares proportionally abated, hence 1/3 from $72,000 leaves Jon $48,000 and 1/3 from Joyce leaves her $16,000.

The most common planning strategy to avoid a claim, counter to the estate plan, by after-born children is to treat them similar to other children. This is done by using class gift terminology such as the terms "descendants" or "issue" in the will or trust to designate the persons who will inherit, rather than specifically naming children.

Children born before the will was executed. While some states still permit an omitted child who was born at the time the will was executed to take an intestate share, most states, including UPC states, generally bar such claims with the one exception being where there is evidence that the testator mistakenly believed the child was dead.[8]

Disinheriting issue. Generally there is no prohibition against disinheriting one's descendants. However, most states will allow a family allowance during probate administration for children that were dependent upon the decedent. The amount and duration of the allowance is likely to be at the discretion of the probate court.

Adopted children. Most states, probably all, including those that have incorporated the UPC, treat *adopted children* the same as the birth children of their *adoptive parents* for intestate succession purposes.[9] So, an adopted child will inherit from the adoptive parents (and their blood relatives), and the adoptive parents (and their blood relatives) will inherit from the adopted child. Conversely, most states give the *biological parents* of a child adopted by another no rights to inherit by intestate succession from their biological child. Similarly, adopted children usually have no succession right to the interests of their biological parents. Called the "fresh start" policy, this rule, breaking inheritance rights between adopted children and their biological parents, reflects public policy belief that implementing a complete substitution of the adoptive family for the biological family is in the child's best interest. Of course any of the parties can change the results by creating an estate plan that does not follow the intestate pattern, hence the biological parent who has established a relationship with her adopted child can leave that child property if she so chooses. If she does not so choose, and fails to mention the child, the child is not considered a pretermitted heir.

EXAMPLE 4 - 17. Sam and Sue placed their infant child, Gloria, up for adoption. She was adopted by Kevin and Kay. If Sam later dies intestate, in most states Gloria would not inherit any of Sam's property. If Kay then dies intestate, Gloria would inherit equally with Kay's biological children. If Gloria subsequently dies intestate, Kevin and Kay's issue could inherit, but neither Sue, her issue, nor Sam's issue would. Of course, any of these individuals may receive property if they are named in a given decedent's will.

The fresh start rule does not usually apply in the case of a "stepparent adoption," where an adult child is adopted by a stepparent, usually after divorce or after death of a biological parent. An exception is made, allowing inheritance by these adopted children from both their biological parents and their stepparents, reflecting public policy belief that such children will be better off maintaining contact with their biological relatives.

EXAMPLE 4 - 18. Mike was six years old when his biological parents, Edith and Frank, divorced. Edith subsequently married Archie, who adopted Mike. In most states, Mike will inherit from both Edith and Frank and from Archie.

Omitted heir situations have a peculiar consequence. They result in the limited application of the intestacy laws to a decedent who actually died testate (i.e., with a valid will). Another example of the need for intestacy proceedings when a valid will exists is the situation called *partial intestacy*, in which a will does not dispose of all the decedent's probate property, as when it fails to contain a residuary clause. The latter is more likely to occur when a layperson does a holographic will than when an attorney drafts the will.

The Rights of an Omitted Spouse

Can one spouse totally "disinherit" the other? Most states have laws designed to prevent this. States handle the potential problem of a penniless widow (or widower) by enforcing one or more of the following concepts: community property, dower and curtesy, the spousal right of election, family allowance, and homestead property.

A spouse is most likely to be omitted when the testator married *after* executing a will. In most states, the spouse takes an intestate share unless the omission was intentional or unless provision was made elsewhere for the spouse.[10] And, as in the case of omitted children alive at the execution of the will, an omitted spouse whom the testator married *before* executing the will may or may not take an intestate share, depending on the applicable state law. In UPC states the spouse could elect to take against the will.

> EXAMPLE 4 - 19. Prior to Claude and Betty's engagement, Claude prepared his only will. Claude died in a skiing accident on their honeymoon. In most states, since Claude's premarital will *does not provide* for Betty and the omission appears unintentional, the will can be admitted to probate but Betty will receive her intestate share of Claude's property. If, on the other hand, the will *has provided* for Betty, in some states she will receive just the amount devised to her, which could be more or less than her intestate share. In states that allow a surviving spouse to elect to claim an interest in lieu of the amount left by will, Betty could choose to take the "elective share" rather than what the will has provided.

What is generally referred to as a forced widows election is discussed below.

Community property. As we have seen, *community property states* protect spouses by attributing to each spouse ownership of one-half of all property acquired by his/her efforts during the marriage while domiciled in a community property state. One would expect spouses to have nearly equal estates if they have been married most of their working years and they lived those years in community property states. Of course, a significant inheritance by one of the spouses will result in unequal wealth unless that spouse decides to convert the inherited property into community property. Recently married spouses or spouses that marry late in life, especially after retirement, may own little or no community property. The laws of the community property states do not require the decedent to leave the survivor any of the decedent's half of the community property or any of his or her separate property. Nevertheless, some protection is available under the Retirement Equity Act of 1984, which provides that after a person is married for one year to an employee who is a participant in a retirement plan, the only payment option is a joint annuity unless the nonparticipant spouse consents in writing to some other option.

Dower and curtesy. Originating in English common law, a *dower* represented a surviving wife's life estate interest in a portion of the real property owned by her deceased husband. A *curtesy* represented a surviving husband's life estate in a portion of the real property owned by his deceased wife. These interests have all but disappeared from our legal landscape.[11]

Spousal right of election. Most common law states have enacted legislation replacing dower and curtesy with a spousal right of election, which essentially gives a surviving spouse a choice. Either the spouse can "take under the will," that is, accept the provisions of the deceased spouse's will, if any, or the spouse can "take against the will," that is, elect instead to receive a statutorily specified "elective share." In some states the "elective share" is equal to one-third of the decedent spouse's estate.

The problem with having the elective share as a percentage of the decedent's estate is that it might result in the survivor's heirs getting a windfall at the expense of the heirs of the first spouse to die. This is especially true if the survivor already has a substantial estate.

EXAMPLE 4 - 20. Damon and Sylvia had been married seven years when he died. He left his house, worth about $180,000, to Sylvia with the balance of the estate left to his two children by a prior marriage. The estate, including the house, was valued at $900,000. Sylvia was entitled to an elective share of one-third, which she claimed even though her own estate was worth $1,500,000. Damon's children shared the $600,000. She died a year after Damon, leaving an estate worth almost two million dollars to her relatives.

The elective share provisions of the Uniform Probate Code were revised in 1990 in an attempt to be more equitable and less arbitrary than elective share statutes predicated solely on intestacy or some arbitrary fraction of the decedent's estate. See below Exhibit 4-2, Elective Share. The share is equal to a percentage of the "augmented estate," which "consists of the sum of the values of all property, whether real or personal; movable or immovable, tangible or intangible, wherever situated, that constitute the decedent's net probate estate, the decedent's nonprobate transfers to others, the decedent's nonprobate transfers to the surviving spouse, and the surviving spouse's property and nonprobate transfers to others."[12]

EXHIBIT 4 -2 UPC § 2-202. Elective Share

2-202. Elective Share.

(a) [Elective-Share Amount.] The surviving spouse of a decedent who dies domiciled in this State has a right of election, under the limitations and conditions stated in this Part, to take an elective-share amount equal to the value of the elective-share percentage of the augmented estate, determined by the length of time the spouse and the decedent were married to each other, in accordance with the following schedule:

If the decedent and the spouse were married to each other:	The elective-share percentage is:
Less than 1 year	Supplemental Amount Only.
1 year but less than 2 years	3% of the augmented estate.
2 years but less than 3 years	6% of the augmented estate.
3 years but less than 4 years	9% of the augmented estate.
4 years but less than 5 years	12% of the augmented estate.
5 years but less than 6 years	15% of the augmented estate.
6 years but less than 7 years	18% of the augmented estate.
7 years but less than 8 years	21% of the augmented estate.
8 years but less than 9 years	24% of the augmented estate.
9 years but less than 10 years	27% of the augmented estate.
10 years but less than 11 years	30% of the augmented estate.
11 years but less than 12 years	34% of the augmented estate.
12 years but less than 13 years	38% of the augmented estate.
13 years but less than 14 years	42% of the augmented estate.
14 years but less than 15 years	46% of the augmented estate.
15 years or more	50% of the augmented estate.

These provisions allow shares ranging from 3 percent if the spouses were married less than one year, to 50 percent for marriages of 15 years or more, with a minimum share of $50,000.[13] This reduces the significance of the manner in which the decedent and the surviving spouse held title.

EXAMPLE 4 - 21. Suppose Damon from the last example died in a UPC state. Since they had been married 7 years, Sylvia's elective share would be 21% of the augmented estate (i.e., their combined wealth) reduced by what she already owned, i.e., 21% * $2,400,000 equals $504,000 which is reduced to zero by the fact she already owns more.

Note that when the two estates are about equal in size, the elective share is likely to be less than what the surviving spouse already owns, hence there is nothing to take from the deceased spouse's estate. This is especially true for very short marriages. The longer the marriage and the greater the disparity in wealth, the more likely that the elective share will be attractive to the surviving spouse if she or he is the poorer of the two.

EXAMPLE 4 - 22. Jane and Harold had been married 20 years when she died. Her will gave Harold a life estate in her house with the rest of the estate left to her children by a prior marriage. Her estate was worth $3,000,000 and his was worth $400,000. He elected to claim his share of the augmented estate, i.e., 50% * $3,400,000 equals $1,700,000. This is reduced by what he already owns, such that he will take an elective share of $1,3000,000 from her estate and give up the life estate in the home.

In the above example, had Jane and Harold been married less than four years, his property would have been worth more than the elective share, hence he would have taken nothing by way of an election against the estate and would settle for the life estate in the home.

Family allowance. All states give the probate court legal authority to grant a family allowance to support the decedent's spouse and minor children during the period of estate administration. The family allowance takes precedence over claims by taxing authorities and unsecured creditors. Even a disinherited spouse or a disinherited dependent child might be given a family allowance.[14] The amount of the family allowance, usually paid in installments, will vary depending on the survivors' needs and the size of the estate.

Homestead and other exempt property. Finally, most states protect surviving family members from losing certain property to the decedent's unsecured creditors or by the terms of the decedent's will. The *homestead*, as it is called, includes the family home and adjacent property, perhaps subject to maximum acreage limitations. State statutes may also exempt other property, such as household furnishings, a vehicle, wearing apparel, and the like. Depending on the state, such assets may be exempt from forced sale while used by the surviving spouse or for as long as she is taking care of the decedent's minor children. These statutes vary greatly from state to state. The UPC also grants a monetary homestead allowance of $15,000 for the surviving spouse, however, if there is no surviving spouse, then $15,000 is divided among the surviving minor and dependent children.[15]

Most states have laws that prevent the death of one spouse from impoverishing the surviving spouse. Generally, surviving children are not afforded the same protection. In some other countries, such as France and Switzerland, most of a parent's estate must be left to the spouse and children. It may seem unfair that children in the United States are not similarly protected, since spouses have the ability to protect themselves when they marry but children have no choice when they enter the parent-child relationship. In addition, young children cannot support themselves. However, our society's refusal to protect children likely stems from a policy interest in discouraging expensive guardianships on the assumption that the protected spouse will support the minor children. Nonetheless, this is not an ideal solution in a world filled with second and third marriages, where the surviving spouse and the decedent's children may not be related.

Effect of Divorce

Given that almost half of all marriages end in divorce one should be concerned about how it impacts estate planning. Obviously, once a divorce is initiate, both parties, husband and wife, should immediately review their estate plan. They each need their own attorney since their respective goals and interests are likely to be in conflict. Divorce is usually very stressful and changing one's estate plan might take a back seat to other matters.

What happens to the estate plan if it is not immediately changed? UPC §2-804 provides that divorce (or an annulment) not only terminates the former spouse's interest in the decedent's probate estate (i.e., he or she takes nothing under decedent's will and has no intestate succession interest) but also revokes any interest in property passing by any other means if the decedent at the time of his or her death had the power to terminate the interest. This means that the former spouse neither receives life insurance proceeds from the deceased spouse's policy even if named as the beneficiary nor is he or she entitled to distributions from the decedent's trust. The couple's joint tenancy and/or tenancy in the entirety property converts to tenants in common. The section also revokes any provisions for relatives of the divorced individual's former spouse. Not surprisingly, also automatically revoked are designations of the former spouse, and his or her relatives, as personal representative of the estate and as trustee of the decedent's trust.

If the divorce decree requires a spouse to keep life insurance in force for the benefit of the former spouse, then the section does not apply since the decedent would not have the power to terminate the interest. A decree of legal separation that maintains the couple's status as husband and wife will not revoke either spouse's interest in the other spouse's estate. In contrast to a divorce decree, mere legal separation leaves insurance designations and trust interests intact unless the couple take the steps necessary to change the governing documents.

Next, we direct our attention to the administration process associated with probate.

PRINCIPLES OF PROBATE ADMINISTRATION

The principles underlying our system of probate administration originated in England, where public officials and the Church of England took control of a decedent's property, or at least supervised those individuals taking control, and then distributed it to the heirs and devisees. The word *probate* stems from the Latin word *to prove*, meaning to certify the validity of a will. When a will is "approved," it is admitted to probate. Today, the term probate is seldom used in the restrictive sense of proving the validity of a will. In modern usage, probate refers to the entire court-related process of the administration of a decedent's estate, including those estates of people who die intestate, and thus have no will to prove.

Probate has been said to have three main *purposes*. First, it *protects creditors* by mandating that valid debts of the decedent be paid. Second, it implements the dispositive wishes of the testator by *supervising the distribution* of estate assets to beneficiaries. And third, it creates an authoritative record of *title transfer* to those who receive property from the estate.

Presenting a comprehensive overview of the principles of probate administration in the United States requires generalization since each state has its own set of laws. There are, however, many similarities. Nearly all *formal probate* procedures have the following five attributes:

1. Probate is initiated by a petition for the appointment of the personal representative. The court hearing to consider the petition is heard after written notice has been given to all interested parties, e.g., beneficiaries, creditors, and executors. Notice to creditors is usually done through newspaper publication.
2. After the hearing, the court appoints the estate's personal representative.
3. Signed court orders, issued after a noticed hearing, are a precondition to the performance by the personal representative of certain major steps, e.g., the sale of real property, the payment of attorney's fees, or the distribution of property.
4. Review and approval, by the court, of one or more financial accountings and reports on significant matters of concern to the interested parties.
5. The court's order authorizing the final distribution and closing of the estate.

These requirements reflect the strong interest each state has in protecting creditors and beneficiaries. In addition to providing these elaborate procedures, many states offer the option of *less formal* settlement procedures. These states have adopted all or most of the provisions of the Uniform Probate Code. Flexibility under the UPC enables the estate's interested parties to choose whether to be extensively supervised by the court, to be supervised only with regard to certain specific acts, or to be almost totally unsupervised.

This section will examine the traditional approach and the flexible approach to estate administration, partly to show that their underlying philosophies are very different, and partly to give the reader an indication of the current trend in probate reform. Actually, this reform has influenced all states to some degree, including those offering much less flexibility.

Formal Supervision in Non-UPC States

We will use California as a model for non-UPC states that use *formal probate* procedures realizing, of course, that details will vary from state to state. In UPC states, the executor has the option of using the formal or informal method, unless the probate court registrar (clerk of the court) determines that there is a reason the probate should be formal.[16] Sections of the California Probate Code (CPC in the endnotes) are found at *http://www.leginfo.ca.gov/calaw.html*.

Opening the probate. After a person has died, the executor is expected to start the formal probate process as soon as is reasonably possible. The person nominated as executor is required to file a petition for probate within 30 days of gaining knowledge of the testator's will and of his or her nomination.[17] The original will is filed with the clerk of the superior court in the county where the decedent resided. California law recognizes a tort cause of action that can be brought against a person for fraudulently destroying, concealing, or "spoiling" a will.

Any person "interested" in the estate may make a file a petition to initiate the probate.[18] Where there is no will, hence no executor, the interested person is likely to be a close relative. Rarely is more than one petition filed. On filing the petition, the court clerk must schedule a hearing on the petition within 45 days.[19] Ordinarily, the executor nominated in the will files the petition requesting: (1) probate of the will, (2) letters testamentary, and (3) authorization to administer under the Independent Administration of Estates Act. Each request will be described briefly.

1. *Probate of the will:* If, after the hearing, the will is "admitted to probate," that will is thereby considered to be the only valid will and, except in the most unusual circumstances, it will serve as the blueprint for distribution.

2. *Letters testamentary* or *letters of administration:* Also known as "letters," this document, usually just one page long, contains the court's formal identification of the person selected by the court as representative of the decedent's estate. A court-certified copy of the letters empowers the personal representative to deal with third parties on behalf of the estate. They are called "letters testamentary" if the person selected was nominated in the decedent's will, and "letters of administration" where the selected personal representative was not named in the will. Where there is no will, the personal representative is referred to simply as the administrator. The administrator is called an *administrator with will annexed* if there is a will admitted to probate but either no executor was named in the will (probably a homemade will done without attorney involvement) or neither the named executor nor the alternate executors were appointed by the court (perhaps they were unsuitable or unavailable).

What happens when more than one person asks to be named administrator? State statutes and the UPC have a preferential priority list that the court will follow in selecting an administrator. Priority is likely to go first to a spouse, followed by adult children, then other relatives.[20] Of course, the court cannot force anyone to serve. When willing persons of equal standing put their names forward, the judge chooses the person (or persons) he or she thinks will do the best job. Some statutes favor the selection of a beneficiary if he or she will receive more than 50% of the estate or has the backing of beneficiaries with more than 50% of the estate.

3. *Authorization to administer under Independent Administration of Estates Act*: The California Probate Code allows a somewhat simplified formal probate administration. Essentially, it eliminates the requirement of obtaining court approval for many of the common transactions undertaken by the personal representative. However, some actions are not exempt and require either express court approval or written notice to all beneficiaries of a proposed course of action, giving them a period of 15 days in which to lodge an objection before the action is taken.[21]

In addition to making these requests, the petition also makes several representations, including facts about the bond, the heirs, and the beneficiaries. A *probate bond* (also called a *fiduciary bond*) is required unless the will waives it or unless all beneficiaries agree to waive it.[22] The bond protects the estate from a financial loss in the event of wrongful conduct by the personal representative. If the personal representative misappropriates estate property or loses it due to negligence, the bonding company must make the estate whole and then has the right to pursue the personal representative. This right of the bonding company to seek to recover from the personal representative any money it had to pay the estate is called a *right of subrogation*. Ordinarily, the bond amount will be equal to the total value of the personal probate property plus one year's estimated income from all of the probate property. The bond amount does not include the value of real estate because it almost impossible to misappropriate.[23] The bond premium, typically one-half to one percent of the amount of the bond, is charged to the estate. The petition for probate must state either that the will waived the bond, that the beneficiaries all request the waiver of the bond (in which case the waivers should be filed with the petition), or that the requirements for a bond will be met. Where a bond is required, evidence that it has been issued is required before the court will issue letters. As a second representation, the petition for probate is required to identify all beneficiaries named in the will and any heirs at law even though not named as beneficiaries.

Two other forms are ordinarily filed with the court clerk at the time of filing the petition for probate. First, a *Proof of Subscribing Witness* is submitted, in which at least one witness to the will declares that he or she signed the original document, that the decedent appeared to be of sound mind and over age 18 at the time of the signing, and that the witness knows of no evidence that the will was signed under duress, menace, fraud or undue influence. If a witness cannot be found, or if all witnesses have died, proof can be offered by handwriting analysis. To make this task unnecessary, in the spirit of probate simplification, most states now recognize what is called a *self-proved* will, also called a *self-executing* will, that eliminates the need to locate witnesses to attest to a will's validity perhaps years after its execution. To be self-proved under the UPC, the execution takes place before a public officer, generally meaning a notary public, who acknowledges that the required formalities were observed. Other states, such as California, just require a formal affidavit as part of the attestation portion of the will. Therein the witnesses state, under penalty of perjury, that all formalities were followed. This statement stands unless an interested party challenges the validity of the will. Even then, the self-proved will creates a presumption that all formalities were correctly followed thus putting the burden on the challenger to prove that such was not the case. The self-proved wills found in Exhibits 3-1 and 3-3 have the affidavit type attestation clauses.

The second form ordinarily filed along with the probate petition is the *Notice of Petition to Administer Estate* and contains the same information as the announcement notice that must be published (three times prior to the hearing) in a newspaper of general circulation in the city (or county) in which the decedent resided. Exhibit 4-3 shows an example of the information that might be found in a published notice.[24]

The notices, both filed and published, announce to interested parties and to the public the following:

1. That a petition for probate has been filed.
2. That a hearing will be held, identifying the time and place.
3. That interested parties may attend the hearing to object to the granting of letters to the petitioner.
4. That creditors must file claims against the estate within four months after the issuance of letters.

EXHIBIT 4-3 Replica of a Newspaper Notice of Petition to Administer Estate

---

NOTICE OF PETITION TO ADMINISTER ESTATE OF
JOHN PAUL JONES, a.k.a. J. P. JONES
CASE NUMBER: P781431

To all heirs, beneficiaries, creditors, contingent creditors, and persons who may otherwise be interested in the will or estate, or both, of JOHN PAUL JONES, a.k.a. J. P. JONES.
A PETITION has been filed by Mary Jones in the Superior Court of Anystate, County of Anycounty.
THE PETITION requests that Mary Jones be appointed as personal representative to administer the estate of the decedent.
THE PETITION requests the decedent's WILL and codicils, if any, be admitted to probate. The will and any codicils are available for examination in the file kept by the court.
A HEARING on the petition will be held on 03-10-06 at 8:30 a.m. in Department 1 located at Superior Court of Anystate, County of Anycounty, 25 County Center Drive, Anycity, Anystate 99999.
IF YOU OBJECT to the granting of the petition, you should appear at the hearing and state your objections or file written objections with the court before the hearing. Your appearance may be in person or by your attorney.
IF YOU ARE A CREDITOR or a contingent creditor of the deceased, you must file your claim with the court and mail a copy to the personal representative appointed by the court within four months from the date of first issuance of letters as provided in Section 9100 of the Anystate Probate Code. The time for filing claims will not expire before four months from the hearing date noticed above.
YOU MAY EXAMINE the file kept by the court. If you are a person interested in the estate, you may file with the court a formal Request for Special Notice of the filing of an inventory and appraisal of estate assets or of any petition or account as provided in Section 1250 of the Anystate Probate Code. A Request for Special Notice form is available from the court clerk.
Attorney for petitioner: Gordon C. Brown, BROWN & BROWN,
P.O. Box 0000, Anycity, Anystate, 99999-1111.
PUBLISHED: February 13, 21, and 27, 2006.

---

5. That anyone may examine the probate file.
6. That the petitioner is requesting authority to administer the estate under the Independent Administration of Estates Act.

At least 15 days prior to the date of the hearing, copies of the notice must be mailed to all heirs and beneficiaries.[25]

The hearing. If there are no objections to the petition, the initial hearing for any particular probate estate may last less than a minute. The judge gives anyone in the courtroom the opportunity to object. Objections are rarely raised. Grounds for objection include the allegation that a more recently executed will exists or that even though the will in question is the only one or the most recent one, it should not be admitted to probate because it was not properly executed due to the testator's lack of capacity, undue influence, fraud, or mistake. If there are objections, the judge will set the matter for further proceedings to settle the dispute, which, if not immediately resolved, can turn into a *will contest*. If the petition for probate is granted, the judge signs an *Order for Probate* that states the court's findings:

1. All notices have been given as required by law.
2. The decedent died on the specified date.
3. The will filed with the court should be admitted to probate.
4. The petitioner is the appropriate person to serve as the estate's personal representative, either as executor or as administrator with will annexed.

Then, the order generally specifies:

1. The will is admitted to probate.
2. The named personal representative is appointed.
3. Whether a bond is required and, if so, states the amount.
4. Whether the personal representative is given authority to administer the estate under the Independent Administration of Estates Act.
5. Letters are issued (on the posting of the bond, if such is required).

Once the court grants the Order for Probate, the personal representative must satisfy any conditions, such as obtaining a fiduciary bond, before he or she secures certified letters from the probate clerk, thus completing the first stage of formal probate proceedings.

Administering the estate. Next, usually in conjunction with the estate's attorney, the personal representative undertakes the marshaling of estate assets and expected claims. Within three months of appointment, the personal representative must file with the probate court a formal document called *Inventory and Appraisement*.[26] This document lists all probate assets showing their fair market value. The personal representative is permitted to determine the value of cash items (e.g., bank deposits, etc.). Other assets may be valued by an appraiser who, depending on state law, may be selected by the court from a list of court-approved independent appraisers or may be chosen by the personal representative. In UPC states the personal representative just sends a copy of the

Inventory and Appraisement "to all to interested persons who request it." Filing a copy with the court is optional.[27]

The Inventory and Appraisement performs several important functions. First, it lists those assets for which the personal representative is responsible. Second, as a document available for public inspection at the courthouse, it describes the contents of the probate estate to all interested parties, including potential heirs, legatees, devisees, and creditors. Third, it provides information to the court to determine, among other things, the proper fiduciary bond amount, the amount of the family allowance, and, if property is sold, the minimum bid that the court will approve. Finally, the values are generally accepted on the estate tax return and for income tax purposes, e.g., for capital gains and depreciation.

During the *creditors' claim period*, which in most states lasts for four months after the date the letters are issued, each creditor is expected to file with the court, or estate's personal representative, a form called a *creditors' claim*. Failure to file the form within the claim period bars later collection, unless an exception is allowed.[28] Exceptions include creditors who did not have actual knowledge of the proceedings,[29] and taxing authorities since the back taxes are not barred by the creditors' claim period.[30] The availability of a shortened creditors' period is said to be a major advantage of the probate process compared to other mechanisms for the transfer of a decedent's estate, at least for estates that anticipate potential problems with creditors.

During estate administration, the personal representative is responsible for handling the financial affairs of the estate, such as: paying bills (rent, utilities, property insurance premiums), marshaling liquid assets so that debts and expenses can be paid (e.g., credit cards, income taxes, and legal fees), and protecting assets from exposure to loss by insuring and safeguarding them

Closing the probate. Generally, the estate will be distributed to the beneficiaries only after all debts and taxes have been paid. However, a partial distribution to beneficiaries may be made on court approval of a *Petition for Preliminary Distribution*. Ordinarily, this petition is filed after the end of the creditors' period. To grant the request, the court must be satisfied that the distribution can be made "without loss to creditors or injury to the estate or any interested person." No more than 50 percent of the estate can be distributed in a preliminary distribution.[31]

"Final Distribution" is made upon approval of a petition at a hearing, after the court determines that all current debts and taxes have been paid.[32] At the same time, the judge usually approves the estate's final accounting, and the request for authority to pay attorney's and executor's fees.[33] The order will include the legal description of any real estate and identify the person or persons to whom it is distributed. A certified copy of the order is recorded in each jurisdiction where real estate is located. This serves to record the transfer to the beneficiaries. After distribution and the payment of fees, the executor requests and receives a final discharge.[34] Formal probate generally takes 8 to 24 months to complete.

Attorneys' fees for California probate administration work are determined by statute, in the absence of a different agreement by the parties. Statutory probate fees are summarized in Table 4-1.

TABLE 4-1 California Statutory Probate Fees [35]

Probate Estate		Rate	Cumulative: Estate/Fee	
First	$15,000	4.0%	$15,000	$600
Next	$85,000	3.0%	$100,000	$3,150
Next	$900,000	2.0%	$1,000,000	$21,150
Next	$9,000,000	1.0%	$10,000,000	$111,150
Next	$15,000,000	0.5%	$25,000,000	$186,150
Over	$25,000,000	Reasonable amount set by the court		

These fees are based on the *gross* probate estate, not net of liabilities, plus gains from the sale of assets, plus income, and less losses from the sale of assets. Gains and losses are based on the date-of-death appraised values. California executors are entitled to the same amount as shown above for attorneys.[36] California is one of the states that has statutory fees; however, additional fees are allowed for "extraordinary services" such as the sale of real property, handling litigation, and preparing tax returns. In most states, probate administration fees must simply be "reasonable" and specific amounts or percentages are not mandated. In other states, probate fees must be "reasonable," but not in excess of a certain percentage, e.g., Iowa sets an upper limit of 2 percent times the value of the probate estate that exceeds $5,000.[37]

EXAMPLE 4 - 23. California attorney Spector works with executor Gregory to probate a $500,000 estate. Included in the estate is a house worth $200,000 that has a $150,000 mortgage. Both the attorney and the executor receive a fee of $11,150 based on the gross (not the net) value of the estate. [4% * $15,000 + 3% * $85,000

+ 2% * $400,000]. Note that the combined charge is 4.46% of the gross value of the probate estate.

Sometimes attorneys are asked by survivors to act as both estate attorney and executor. Whether they will receive a full double fee will depend on several factors, including state law and the attitude of the specific probate judge. Some states, including California and New York, have made this "double dipping" illegal in the absence of prior court approval. In other states, probate judges may reduce the fee in such situations.

Summarizing the essential components of formal supervision: Formal probate in most non-UPC states requires at least four document filings (petition for probate, a certification establishing that notice of death has been published, an inventory and appraisement, and a petition for authority to distribute the estate and pay fees), requires at least two formal court hearings (one for the admission of the will to probate and to appoint the personal representative, and another to approve the final accounting and the request for authority to distribute the estate), and at least one accounting (unless it is waived by all estate beneficiaries).

We now turn to the second major type of state probate supervision, the flexible approach found in the Uniform Probate Code.

Estate Administration in UPC States: A Study in Flexibility

Personal representatives in non-UPC states usually must use formal probate, although summary probate procedures may be available for smaller estates and for property passing outright to the surviving spouse.

In contrast, probate procedures in a UPC state are much more flexible, allowing interested parties to determine the degree of supervision desired. The basic choices are: court-supervised administration (formal probate); almost totally unsupervised (informal probate) administration; a combination of unsupervised and supervised administration; or, some simplified procedure for small estates.

Court-supervised administration. Some complex or unusual estates in UPC states may be subject to supervised administration. Generally, UPC supervised administration is a bit less regulated than a formal probate in a non-UPC state such as California. Under UPC, the personal representative is given greater freedom to act independently. Usually, there is no court involvement between the time letters are issued and the time the personal representative petitions the court for closing of the estate. Most personal representatives in UPC jurisdictions choose not to be subject to supervised administration. Occasionally, an interested party will lack trust and request formal probate supervision because he or she wants notice of what the personal representative is doing. In contrast, probate administration in non-UPC states, as we have seen, requires court approval of all major transactions.

Informal and formal administration. In UPC jurisdictions one of two types of procedures is followed: informal or formal administration.

Informal administration usually requires few, if any, court appearances and very little notice. The application for informal appointment is the simplest way for a personal representative to be appointed. The prospective personal representative files an application with a court registrar, whose role is administrative rather than judicial. Once appointed, the personal representative has the powers needed to perform the job, including the power to deal with creditors and distributees. The personal representative is required to give notice of the appointment to all heirs and devisees by ordinary mail within 30 days of appointment. Within three months, the personal representative must prepare an inventory of the estate and mail it to all parties requesting it. The entire inventory can be valued by the personal representative unless an interested party objects.

Even with informal administration, the personal representative must publish an initial newspaper notice, similar to the procedure for a formal probate, in order to limit the creditors' claim period to four months from date of first publication. Without published notice, the limitation period is one year measured from the decedent's date of death.[38]

Six months after appointment, the personal representative can apply to the registrar to close the estate. After another six months, assuming no one has lodged an objection, the personal representative is discharged from all liability except due to fraud or other major offenses. Unless the newspaper notice was given, distributees of estate property will continue to be liable for estate debts until the earlier of the regular statute of limitations for each claim or for one year after decedent's death.

Formal administration procedures under the UPC include the petition for *formal testacy* (proving the will), petition for formal appointment of the personal representative, and petition for formal closing. Each is undertaken in a manner similar to that for supervised administration and requires giving proper notice to interested parties, filing a petition with the court, and appearing at a court hearing.

During informal proceedings, a dissatisfied interested party can petition the court for a hearing to resolve the controversy, whereupon the matter will be taken up "in" court. Once the dispute is settled, administration can resume in informal proceedings "out" of court. The UPC's unique method of settling disputes has been described as an "in and out" method.

In addition to the right to petition the court, interested parties have other protective remedies, including the right to request that the personal representative obtain a bond even though it was waived in the will, the right to request a restraining order to keep the personal representative from doing some specific act (such as selling a family heirloom), and the right to demand notice by receiving a copy of any filings or orders in connection with the estate. With the exception of the right to notice, the requests are subject to the court's discretion.

We can now see the relationship between informal and formal proceedings under the UPC. At each significant step in the probate process, the interested parties can elect a different degree of supervision. For example, the probate process may begin with an application for informal supervision of the personal representative. Then a controversy may arise that requires court resolution. Finally, the personal representative may feel compelled to file a formal petition for closing. Only rarely will an interested party petition for completely supervised administration. Generally, it is the desire of all beneficiaries to minimize judicial supervision because supervision tends to prolong the probate process thereby delaying final distribution.

Small estate procedures. Most states have non-probate settlement procedures for small estates. These generally fall into one of two categories, either a *claim-by-affidavit* procedure or a *summary administration* requiring at least one court hearing. The statutes of many states provide for both procedures, generally with a lower estate value limit for the affidavit procedure than for the summary procedure. Summary proceedings generally require a written agreement signed by all beneficiaries and either a statement by the petitioner that there are no unpaid creditors or an assurance that all creditors who file claims within the statutory claims period will be paid, up to the value of the estate, before the estate will be distributed. Some statutes require publication of a notice identifying the time and place of the hearing to consider summary administration, others just require the publication of a notice to creditors that specifies where, when, and to whom claims must be submitted, and, finally, some have no publication requirement. Presumably, the person handling the estate has an obligation to pay known creditors even if publication is not required. While the summary administration statutes vary considerably, they are all considerably less burdensome on the personal representative than even informal probate.

The UPC provides a simple claim-by-affidavit procedure for estates made up of personal property only. The section allows a person to claim by affidavit assets of a decedent, but only if the "value of the entire estate, wherever located, less liens and encumbrances, does not exceed $5,000."[39] Most state claim-by-affidavit statutes require a waiting period, usually 30 days from the decedent's death, during which no probate is initiated before claims can be made by affidavit. The claim is submitted to those in possession of the decedent's property and is generally made by the decedent's heirs, although some states also allow creditors to use the procedure. States have limits that range from net estates as small as $3,000 for Alabama to as high as $150,000 for Wyoming.[40] Generally, following the UPC model, the limit is based on the value of all estate assets less encumbrances and liens. Many states restrict the claim procedure to estates made up entirely of personal property; others, such as Wyoming, cover real estate as well. In Wyoming, if real estate is involved, the affidavit claim procedure is really a summary proceeding in that the claimant must apply to the court for an order establishing who is entitled to title. Information concerning the application must be published for two consecutive weeks before the court hears the matter. If the facts stated in the application are not in dispute, the court enters "a decree establishing the right and title to the property." A certified copy of the decree recorded in the office of the county clerk is "presumptive evidence of title to the property."[41] Missouri also allows real estate to be transferred by affidavit but without a court hearing, although the clerk of the court publishes a notice to creditors, and certifies names of the persons entitled to the described property and attaches it to the affidavit. A certified copy of the affidavit with the attachment is filed in the office of the recorder in each county where real estate is located.

PROBATE: TO AVOID OR NOT TO AVOID

Since probate has significant drawbacks, most people prefer to have their estates pass by holding most of their property in joint tenancy or in a living trust. These are referred to as *will substitutes* because they supersede any provisions in the deceased person's will. Is probate a terrible process to be avoided like the plague? It has been part of our legal system for over a hundred years and must serve a useful purpose or it would be gone by now. Below, we consider probate's major benefits and drawbacks.

The Benefits of Probate

In summary, the major benefits of probate include fairness promoted by court supervision, orderly administration of assets, greater protection from creditors, and some limited income tax savings.

Court supervision. Formal probate requires substantial court supervision, a process that, at its best, promotes fairness. Through the use of petitions, accountings, hearings, and court orders, probate seeks to ensure that asset distribution is fair. No other estate transfer procedure is so controlled by public authorities.

The public-forum nature of probate encourages review and evaluation by numerous observers. Judges and official clerks are called on to approve major estate activities. In addition, other interested private parties such as beneficiaries and creditors have an opportunity to object to perceived inequities in estate administration. For example, they can object to many court rulings, including admission of a certain will to probate, appointment of a certain personal representative, payment of a certain creditor, and distribution of estate assets to a certain individual. They can raise these objections in the probate court itself; the parties need not seek a remedy elsewhere, and they can often do it without hiring a lawyer. In contrast, objections to disposition by joint tenancy or through a living trust require a different, procedurally more complicated, legal action.

Critics of probate contend that the additional degree of equity fostered by probate administration is, at best, minimal. They argue that judges and other public officials too often give only superficial review of proposed actions and rubber-stamp their approval of the conduct of executors. Supporters of probate respond to this criticism saying that judges implicitly and successfully rely on the interested parties, who are formally notified of the proceedings, to speak up in court if they feel they are being treated unfairly. Critics contend, however, that the average interested person would not be aware of the occurrence of many types of subtle wrongdoing.

The claim that probate encourages fairness is also subject to challenge because of the recent trend in the direction of reduced supervision. Also, we saw that UPC states permit the estate's personal representative to select the degree of supervision he or she desires. If "informal probate" is chosen, the estate will receive almost no direct supervision by the court. Thus, in many states, the risk of misadministration in probate is similar to that for trusts because of the opportunity to avoid the public forum. Of course, in UPC states the ability of beneficiaries to request greater formal supervision of the executor at any time during the probate process reduces the risk of mismanagement. Most states permit "summary" probate or allow "claim of right" to transfer small estates. These procedures greatly reduce or completely eliminate court supervision.

Orderly administration of assets. Probate offers orderly administration of estate assets. Supervision by the court and by other public officials ensures that property transfers and title clearance will be done correctly.

Finality to estate settlement. Probate offers distributees protection from creditors of the decedent sooner than other means of transfer. Probate procedures require creditors to file their claims against probate assets within a short time, typically four months, from date of issuance of letters testamentary. Creditors that don't file claims in that time can never collect from probate assets. Nonprobate assets, on the other hand, may only be protected by the state's general limitations period, which can be several years. However, there is a movement among the states to shorten the creditors' claim period for nonprobate estates.

Fairness to creditors. In 1988, the U.S. Supreme Court ruled in *Tulsa Professional Collection Services v. Estate of Pope* that creditors who are "known or reasonably ascertainable" to the personal representative must be given "actual" notice of the limited creditors' claim period, rather than be given just "constructive" notice by publication.[42] Notice by mail is considered acceptable actual notice.

The following is a partial listing of creditors who are usually known or can be reasonably ascertained by the personal representative:

- Hospital where decedent died, all treating physicians, ambulance company and paramedics
- Landlord or mortgage company
- Pool service, gardener, maid, newspaper delivery service
- Installment payment creditor and creditors whose bills arrive in the mail
- Credit card issuers

- Creditors evidenced by "interest deductions" on the decedent's income tax returns, determined from decedent's correspondence, or canceled checks
- Persons given a guarantee by the decedent as the owner of a closely held business

Under *Tulsa*, actual notice need not be given to potential creditors whose claims are a matter of "conjecture," i.e., deduced by surmise or guesswork. An example of a conjectural claim would be that any of a deceased doctor's former patients might eventually assert a malpractice claim against the doctor's estate. The executor does not have to notify all former patients to "submit their claims or lose their right to sue." Indeed, that would likely cause needless problems. The creditors' claim period does not affect the rights of secured creditors to the extent that the debt is covered by collateral.

If there is insurance to cover a claim, the claim is not barred by the short probate creditors' claim period. The estate may be named as a party to the suit, but the real party in interest is the insurance company that will have to pay the claim. Generally, unless the injured party files a creditors' claim within the regular creditors' claim period, state probate statutes limit the recovery to the amount of insurance coverage. There are several reasons why a person might miss the creditors' claim period, yet have a valid claim but for the tortfeasor's death. First, where there is delayed discovery, some states' statutes of limitations do not begin to run until the wrongdoing is or should have been discovered, e.g., negligence by a doctor may not be discovered until long after an operation. Second, where there is delayed injury or damage, the limitations period does not begin to run until the injury or damage actually occurs. For instance, an error in will drafting might prevent an estate from claiming a marital or charitable deduction, yet the error would not cause any damage until the testator's death, which might be years after the will was drafted. Most malpractice insurance is issued on a "claims made" basis, meaning that the insurance covers only errors that occur while the policy is in force and only if a claim is submitted while it is in force. However, when a professional retires, he or she can purchase what is called "tail coverage," which continues to cover later claims for errors made during the period covered by the insurance.

Most people, especially those not likely to be the target of litigation, will find the benefit of the shorter creditors' claim period to be of little value. In view of the fact that probate makes the decedent's assets known to anyone interested enough to "pull the file," many people prefer the more private methods of asset distribution. Individuals who anticipate that there may be hidden or unknown claims that are difficult to identify might prefer the shorter limitations period. For example, professionals such as doctors, lawyers, architects, engineers or accountants are potentially vulnerable to malpractice claims which, if instituted after their death, stand a greater chance of succeeding, partly because the defense's best witness, the decedent, is not available to testify. The shorter probate creditors' claim period decreases this threat but whether it is worth the additional cost is debatable.

In UPC states, estates can have the same claims protection without supervised probate. For example, informal UPC probate offers the four-month creditors' claim period because its provisions allow for the filing of a legal notice to creditors. If the notice is not issued, the UPC imposes a one-year creditors' limitations period, starting at date of death, after which all claims are barred.[43] Certain other forms of summary probate in non-UPC states treat the claims period differently. For example, the four-month probate claim period is not available for a surviving spouse receiving property through California's summary distribution procedure but there is a catchall provision that requires claims against any decedent be asserted within one year of the person's death.[44]

Income tax savings. The probate estate is considered a separate tax entity during its existence, taxable at its own rates. Because it is a separate entity, there is an opportunity for income shifting depending on whether the beneficiary's or the estate's rates are lower. For example, during estate administration, undistributed income earned on estate property will be taxed to the estate rather than to the beneficiaries. This can reduce total income taxes if the estate is in a lower tax bracket than its beneficiaries. However, the advantage has been somewhat undercut by tax reform since 1986, which has generally lowered and compressed the income tax rate brackets for trusts and estates.[45] Indeed, for 2005, estates and nongrantor trusts hit the top marginal rate of 35% once their taxable income is over $9,750, whereas a single individual taxpayer does not hit that top rate until taxable income is over $319,100. In 2005, a trust with taxable income of $30,000 would pay taxes of $9,626 whereas an individual with that much taxable income would pay less than half that at $4,237.50.

The Drawbacks of Probate

Probate has several distinct disadvantages, including complexity, cost, lack of privacy, and delay.

Complexity. Formal probate is a complex process, requiring petitions, accountings, hearings, and other complicated legal procedures. Most laypersons hire a lawyer to meet these requirements. Critics argue that supervised probate is usually an unnecessary, clumsy process offering considerable make-work for the legal profession, especially paralegals and legal secretaries. Others respond that in the many states that allow informal probate procedures, the probate process transfers a decedent's property almost as easily as does a living trust.

Cost. The cost of probate can be high. Usually, the probate administration expenses range between 2% and 10% of the probate estate's gross value. The percentage will likely decrease as the size of the estate increases (especially for those subject to informal UPC administration) because there are certain fixed costs regardless of the size of the estate.

The personal representative's commission usually constitutes the largest probate expense. Of course, a beneficiary of the estate, who serves as personal representative, might waive the commission. The statutes of most states either provide for "reasonable" compensation of the personal representative or a statutory commission based on a percentage of the estate's total value. In general, personal representatives' commissions for formal probate range between 2% and 5% of the gross value.

The next largest probate administration expense is usually the attorney's fee. Most states' statutes do not set attorneys' fees, leaving it to the judge for each case to decide and approve a reasonable fee, whereas other states have a statutory fee set as a percentage of the estate's total value. Where commissions and fees are set as a percentage of an estate's total value, the percentage generally decreases as the size of the estate increases, e.g., it might be 4% of the first $100,000 and 2% of the value above $100,000. In general, attorneys' fees usually range between 2% and 5% of the gross value of the probate estate. Other administration expenses include fiduciary bond fees, appraisers' fees, and court costs, including filing fees.

Probate administration costs will be higher for estates containing real property located in other states. Under what is called *ancillary administration*, that property is probated in the state in which it is located. This usually requires hiring an attorney in the other state to handle the ancillary administration.

Other factors that will affect the level of probate administration costs include the nature of the estate property (e.g., closely held business interests, expensive artwork, etc., versus marketable securities), the complexity of the estate distribution plan, and whether a will contest occurs.

Contrary to popular belief, probate does not increase estate taxes. Indeed, since probate costs are deductible, probate may actually reduce estate taxes by a percentage of the probate costs.

Lack of privacy. Probate is a public process; all probate proceedings are subject to public scrutiny. For example, any person can inspect a decedent's probate file, which will eventually include the decedent's will, the estate inventory and appraisal, any creditors' claims, and the order for final distribution. Those particularly interested in inspecting a file would include survivors who are fighting and members of the press seeking a story about a newsworthy decedent. Commonly cited examples of celebrities receiving considerable publicity which could have been avoided by using trusts include the estates of Amanda Blake, Greta Garbo, Natalie Wood, John Wayne, Darryl Zanuck, and the controversy surrounding the conservatorship for Groucho Marx.

The probate files of most decedents are usually seen only by court officials. Interested parties such as the decedent's relatives and the executor can have the attorney for the estate send them copies of every document that is filed. Many probate attorneys do this as a matter of practice without any request that they do so. Thus most interested parties have no reason to review the court's file unless they suspect that not everything is being sent.

In some situations, a person may actually prefer the lack of privacy inherent in probate. For example, the public aspects of probate might discourage or uncover fraudulent dealings by unscrupulous survivors.

Delay. Even for smaller estates, probate administration takes considerable time, ranging from nine months to several years before final distribution is made. In any particular case, the delay can be quite unpredictable. For example, payment of proceeds of life insurance on the decedent's life to the decedent's testamentary trust will be delayed until the trust takes effect, which usually can be no sooner than the expiration of the creditors' claim period, several months after date of death. Thus, complete, immediate liquidity cannot be provided to the decedent's survivors. Delay can be especially hard on grieving survivors, partly because it can increase or prolong tension and conflict among them. However, preliminary distributions of significant amounts can usually be made earlier if the executor can make a good faith representation that doing so will not jeopardize creditors.

Easier intervention for good or evil. The nature of probate may, in some cases, increase the risk of a will contest which may be settled with a distribution of assets in a manner that conflicts with testator intent. For example, a person named in a prior will might contest the decedent's last will on a technicality or a claim of undue influence. Nonprobate documents of transfer such as a trust are more difficult to contest because execution requirements are less stringent. When there is a probate, making an objection is likely to be relatively easy. Generally, to challenge the actions of a trustee, a disgruntled heir would need to hire an attorney to open court proceedings but with a probate he or she could request to be heard at any noticed hearing or, even in an informal probate, the person could seek a hearing by filing with the court written objections to the personal representative's actions or allegations of problems with the will. Keep in mind that the disgruntled heir might actually be right and stop the personal representative from acting inappropriately.

ALTERNATIVES TO PROBATE

Probate really is a process, not a planning device. Indeed, as explained above, it is the mechanism of transferring property when nothing else takes precedent. It is used whether a will or intestate succession serves as a guide. Other alternatives involve what are referred to as transfers by operation of law, meaning that the title shifts from the decedent without any action on the part of others, including the recipient of that property. Obviously, when compared to probate, these transfers are quicker, cheaper, and to some extent more private e.g., holding property in joint tenancy or tenants by the entirety, establishing POD and TOD accounts will all result in quick transfer of title upon the death of an owner, and transfer is accomplished with little or no fuss. The main two main drawbacks to each of these is that they are asset specific and lack flexibility. By asset specific we mean that each account or security must name a beneficiary or succession of beneficiaries, and are therefore difficult to coordinate with an overall estate plan, especially if long-range planning is desired. In contrast, a will or a living trust can guide the transfer of a whole bundle of assets.

Transfers by Operation of Law

These alternative means of transferring property generally provide clear but rigid disposition. The surviving joint tenant(s) takes outright, pro-rata, the deceased joint tenant's interest, and the last surviving joint tenant has an individual, fee simple interest in the property. Thus, obviously, right of survivorship cannot control disposition of property when the last joint tenant dies.

Direct but inflexible. With any of these alternatives, but especially obvious with joint tenancy, the lack of a survivorship period may make the ultimate beneficiary the luck of the draw, so to speak. With joint tenancy, the last joint tenant has the final say as to what happens to the property. At common law, to acquire sole ownership the survivor had to outlive the other joint tenants for just a few moments. Many states, including UPC states, have a general survivorship requirement of 120 hours that also applies not only to wills but also to trusts, joint tenancy property, TOD securities, and POD accounts.[46] Nevertheless, if a couple holding property in joint tenancy die in an accident with one dying at the scene and the other six days later in the hospital, depending on state law, it is likely that the survivor's family will receive the estate to the exclusion of the other spouse's family. On the other hand, trusts generally have provisions that cover various scenarios, including how to divide property in the event the settlors' deaths occur in close proximity.

POD and TOD accounts (or individual securities, as the case might be) might name beneficiaries in the alternative, just in case the first named beneficiary does not outlive the account owner, but again these have the drawback of being quite specific without any long-range control over the use of the property.

Living trusts also avoid probate but in contrast to the inflexibility of POD securities, TOD accounts, and life insurance, living trusts facilitate long-range planning. This allows for complex planning that utilizes surrogate decision makers, giving them a chance to act upon circumstances as they develop long after the settlor has departed, e.g., suppose one child needs greater medical care than the others, or another child will benefit from post-graduate schooling; the trustee, if authorized, can respond appropriately to the varying needs.

Creditors rights. One potential difficulty in creating joint tenancies is that the property is exposed to the claims of the creditors of the other joint tenant even though the initial owner was merely seeking an inexpensive way to avoid probate. For example, if a parent adds her adult child as a joint tenant on her home and the child is liable for an automobile accident, a judgment against the child might force the partition and sale of the home. A defense to the partition suit might be based on the argument that the joint tenancy was really an informal trust arrangement in which the child had no present interest in the property, but success is uncertain and lawsuits are expensive.

Surrender of control. Another difficulty with creating joint tenancies just to avoid probate is that the initial owner has surrendered, at least partially, control over the property. Suppose a parent, desiring to keep his estate out of probate, transfers his residence into joint tenancy with his adult daughter, and then has a falling out with her. It will be difficult to get title back in his own name; again, there is the argument that this was just an informal trust arrangement. If there are other children, was the father's intention that the daughter would sell the house and share the proceeds with the others? If so, is there evidence of that agreement? The law presumes that everyone who takes title to property understands the significance of how that property is held, including, therefore, that the right of survivorship is the key element of titling property in joint tenancy.

Unlike creating a joint tenancy, the owner of a TOD brokerage account, an individual TOD security, or a POD bank account, neither surrenders control of the property nor has to worry about having creditors of the beneficiary taking the property. However, after the death of the owner, the recipient can be forced to contribute (up to the value of the POD or TOD) to pay creditors, and to satisfy certain family allowances, but only if probate property was insufficient to pay said claims and allowances.[47]

Transfers using Living Trusts

By now you are probably thinking that a course in estate planning could easily be called Trusts 101. For people of even modest wealth, the funded living trust has become the centerpiece of an estate plan. While the settlor is alive, the living trust is usually revocable, which means that its terms are amendable or its assets can be taken out of trust by the settlor. Most settlors name themselves trustee of their living trust and serve as such for as long as they are able to do so. Generally, title reads something like this: "John Grant, as trustee of the John Grant Family Trust dated 2/236/2006" with the date being the day the document was signed.

At the settlor's death, the revocable trust becomes irrevocable and may either terminate, with the corpus distributed to the remaindermen, or continue in existence until a later date. A typical revocable living trust created by a married couple might have all assets placed in one trust, which is revocable by them during their lifetimes. At the first spouse's death, what happens depends on the plan. A commonly used estate plan for smaller estates has the decedent's share of the trust property continue in a revocable trust with the trust corpus belonging entirely to the surviving spouse. The trust property is not subject to probate at either death. At the surviving spouse's death the trust is either terminated and distributed to the children or it is continued for their benefit, at least until they are mature adults with reaching a certain age serving as a convenient proxy for maturity, e.g., the trust terms might require the trust terminate when the youngest child reaches 30 years of age. Other distribution arrangements, particularly those designed to reduce estate tax, are discussed in Chapters 9 and 10.

Taxation of a living trust depends on whether it is revocable. A revocable living trust usually has no transfer or income tax consequences during the settlor's lifetime. A transfer to it does not constitute a taxable gift since the transfer is not complete. And under the grantor trust rules, all income earned by a revocable trust is taxable to the grantor/settlor. In contrast, an irrevocable living trust is usually a separate income tax paying entity; all transfers into it usually constitute completed gifts. Generally, undistributed fiduciary accounting income (FAI) is taxed to the trust, while distributed FAI is taxed to the beneficiaries. Fiduciary income taxes will be covered in Chapter 8.

Funded irrevocable living trusts also avoid probate. They are not as commonly used as the revocable living trust because they usually involve taxable gifts. These trusts are discussed in Chapters 13 and 15 in the context of life insurance planning and gifts in trust designed to leverage the applicable exclusion amount (AEA–the amount that passes free of transfer taxes).

Advantages of the living trust. The advantages of the living trust over other transfer devices are greater assurance of probate avoidance, lower total costs, greater privacy and speed, ability to use the trust as an alternative to a conservatorship of the estate, greater organization, decreased likelihood of litigation, and possibly reduced estate tax.

Probate avoidance. The living trust offers greater certainty that probate will be avoided at the death of the surviving spouse/beneficiary.

> EXAMPLE 4 - 24. Kim and Chris could use a basic will for their simple estates, but they also wish to avoid probate on all their property. Their planner makes it clear to them that joint tenancies will not achieve the latter goal because the surviving joint tenant will wind up owning the property, making it eventually subject to probate. Instead, they execute a living trust, funding the trust with their property. The trust will continue to exist for both their lifetimes. At the survivor's death, the assets will pass from the trust to their designated beneficiaries, free from probate.

The above example was intentionally ambiguous about the individuals' gender and marital status. For a living trust, neither is material; unmarried individuals, including members of the same sex, may legally take title in joint tenancy or co-execute a single trust instrument, or each may hold his or her assets in a separate trust.

Lower total cost than probate. The combined cost of preparation and administration of the living trust is usually significantly less than the combined costs of will preparation and probate. The cost of having a living trust prepared is usually higher than the cost of preparing a will. The trust instrument is usually a more complicated document: its provisions must arrange for the immediate receipt of property, for the management of that property, and for the proper distribution of the property and the trust income for a period that might span several generations. Also, with the living trust, the attorney must still draft a will. As previously discussed, the establishment of the living trust does not totally eliminate the need for a will. Because people sometimes fail to completely fund their trusts, planners provide for disposition of this non-trust property with what is called a *pour-over will*, specifying that any of the testator's assets not in the trust will be distributed, i.e., "poured over," into the trust at the settlor's death. Because it disposes of all property outright to only one party (the trustee), the pour-over will is usually very brief, adding little to the preparation cost of avoiding probate with the living trust.

While the specific cost of preparing the living trust may be higher, the total cost is usually lower due to the relatively high cost of probate administration at death. Compared to probate, administration of a living trust at the settlor's death involves minimal legal work and usually no court appearances. Even if the trust was not fully funded before the settlor's death, depending on the value of the non-trust assets and the scope of the state's informal or summary administration rules, a probate might not be necessary.

Other factors that affect the relative costs of probate versus the living trust include whether the grantor or a family member will serve as trustee or executor, the ability to deduct these costs as an income tax itemized deduction, and the schedule of local court fees and costs.

Greater privacy. A trust instrument is usually private and not subject to public inspection. Although property transfers into and out of a living trust may require examination of the trust instrument by financial and other institutions, the document usually need not be publicly accessible. County recorders may require a filing of the trust in public records, but usually only brief sections of the document need be submitted. In fact, many attorneys in the estate planning process draft a separate short (one or two pages) document called a "trust abstract," a "memorandum of trust," or a "confirmation of trust." This short document is made available to persons or institutions dealing with the trustee, in lieu of the full trust instrument. At a minimum, the abstract will contain sections describing the identity of the trustee and successor trustee, and the trustee powers relevant to investing and to transferring assets. It is formally executed by the settlor and trustee, and their signatures are notarized. In this way critical parts of the trust, including dispositive provisions, may be kept secret.

However, states that impose an inheritance tax may require trustees to file an inventory revealing the nature and value of the trust's assets and the names of its beneficiaries. In addition, if there is litigation, a determined litigant is likely to gain access to the contents of a living trust through discovery.

As mentioned earlier, privacy may be especially desired by wealthy or prominent individuals. They may wish to avoid publicity and inspection by disinherited or contentious survivors who may try to wage a court challenge to a decedent's estate plan.

Quick settlement. Property can usually be transferred out of a trust sooner than out of a probate estate because the transfer process is not subject to supervision and approval by the court. However, failure to perform certain postmortem legal duties (detailed above) can subject the trustee to significant personal liability and can trigger costly and unnecessary litigation. Thus, for example, in those states where creditors' claims can be made against trust assets, the trustee will delay distribution. And for larger trusts that might owe estate tax, the trustee may delay major distributions of trust assets until an estate tax "closing letter" from the Treasury is received. Generally, if there are no audit problems, the closing letter comes within 10 months after the estate tax return is filed.

Speed of disposition of real property located in a different state is more rapid if the property is held in a living trust rather than disposed of by will because ancillary administration is avoided. However, some states require reporting procedures for trusts that are quite similar to the probate administration process.

Alternative to guardianship or conservatorship. A person who becomes physically or mentally incapable of managing assets will need someone to provide that management. Just as a guardianship may have to be established to manage a minor's estate, a guardianship or conservatorship may be necessary to manage the estate of an incapacitated adult. Like probate administration, guardianships and conservatorships are supervised by the court, which usually requires periodic accountings and formal court approval for many acts of asset management.

Used in lieu of a guardianship or conservatorship, the living trust is a good vehicle to avoid the expense, delay and publicity of probate-type administration before the settlor's death. The typical living trust begins with the settlor acting as trustee. Subsequently, a successor trustee takes over when the settlor relinquishes the role, becomes incapacitated, or dies. Thus, the living trust instrument has an additional benefit that is simply not available with a will; it provides for the management of property at the settlor's incapacity. Some commentators consider this the major advantage of the living trust, especially for older people, making the will alternative seriously deficient by comparison.

Another less expensive alternative to the guardianship or conservatorship is the durable power of attorney for financial matters, discussed in Chapter 15, but it does not avoid probate nor does it provide much guidance for the long-term management of assets.

One must get organized. Establishing a living trust requires the person to organize his or her property to create and fund the trust. The actual process of organizing assets increases awareness and enhances efficient personal financial planning.

May reduce litigation. As we have seen, the probate process offers an opportunity for a dissatisfied survivor to initiate a will contest. Such disputes may be minimized with a living trust for two reasons. First, the settlor as the initial beneficiary is able to live with the trust, receiving and making distributions and transferring property to it. These acts may constitute evidence of a well thought-out estate plan. In contrast, a will has little impact on the testator's day-to-day life. Thus, contesting parties may be more successful in showing that the testator's will does not reflect his or her actual intent.

Second, disputes over a person's estate plan may be minimized with a living trust because litigation is more difficult to initiate than simply raising an objection in a probate proceeding. Transfers from a trust generally do not require notice to anyone; probating a will requires notice to interested parties, which may trigger a contest. With probate, a legal process has already been initiated so turning it into a contest is a smaller step than initiating a lawsuit. On the other hand, a trust can be contested on substantially the same grounds as those that are used to contest a will, including fraud, undue influence, lack of capacity and improper execution. Case law generally holds that creating a trust requires a higher mental capacity than is required to create a valid will on the grounds that the trust is in the nature of a complex contract between the settlor and the trustee whereas a will is a single party document. Courts generally require that the settlor have contractual capacity at the time the trust is created. Since contracting requires negotiation between two parties, it is thought to require sharper mental faculties than are needed to execute a will. Whether that is true is questionable, given that little negotiation takes place in the creation of most trusts and the settlor is often the initial trustee.

Other advantages of living trusts. Living trusts are normally simpler to revise than wills. While a codicil to a will requires certain execution formalities (described in Chapter 3), an amendment to a living trust needs no formalities or witnesses, and may be in the settlor's handwriting. However, if the trustee is someone other than the settlor, he or she should at least be notified of the revision, and most attorneys also have the trustee sign and notarize the amendment.

Use of a living trust eliminates any gap in asset management when the settlor dies. While the trustee (or successor trustee) of a living trust is empowered to carry on immediately, no one is authorized to act with regard to probate property until the court appoints a personal representative, at least several days to several weeks after the testator's death. In an emergency, courts will issue temporary letters appointing a personal representative but again, this takes time and money.

Property held in a revocable living trust receives a step-up in basis because it is treated as owned by the grantor and, therefore, it is included in the decedent's gross estate. More on basis issues in Chapter 8.

Disadvantages of the Living Trust. The living trust has several disadvantages, including the burden of funding, possibly greater legal uncertainty, and some minor tax factors.

Funding burden. Establishment of a joint tenancy is a one-step process. The act of creation of the joint interest creates the appropriate title. On the other hand, the establishment of a living trust to avoid probate is a two-step process. First, the trust document is executed by the settlor and the trustee, like a two-party contract. Second, the trust is funded; legal title to the property is transferred from the settlor to the trustee. Some settlors never do the latter because they are unaware that the additional step of funding is necessary. Others are aware of it but simply never get around to doing it. Most find it inconvenient because it requires trips to the bank and to other places where title is officially kept. And people who actively trade their property, such as those involved in frequent real estate deals and securities transactions, may especially dislike the greater complexity inherent in continually keeping property in their name as trustee. However, opening a brokerage account under the trustee's name greatly simplifies the task of keeping track of the trust's investment assets.

Failure to fund the trust will usually result in the settlor's property passing through probate, hopefully guided into the trust by a pour-over will.[48] Most attorneys avoid this undesired outcome by overseeing the initial funding of the living trust rather than leaving the responsibility to the client. This may increase the legal cost of setting up the living trust.

Planners may be able to help their clients who have created living trusts by asking the client's accountant to monitor the funding of the trust. The accountant is asked to pay particular attention to the client's tax-related forms, such as 1099s and K1s, issued by banks, partnerships, S corporations, and other asset account holders, to make sure the trustee is named the owner of the property.

Longer creditors' period. As described earlier, probate offers a shorter creditors' claim period than a living trust. The latter is usually subject to the claims for the regular statute of limitations period, the length of which depends on the nature of the claim. These periods may be from one to three years. However, this disadvantage may be disappearing. Some states have enacted an overall creditors' claim period of one year from date of death. There may be exceptions to the one-year limitation for estates that are subject to some other more specific limitation on creditors' claims, e.g., if there is a probate proceeding, then the shorter provision for probate estates would apply. The one-year statute of limitations applies regardless of the manner in which the decedent held property, and regardless of whether the regular statute of limitations for a particular claim would have ended earlier or later than the one-year period had the person lived.[49]

There is also a trend in state law toward allowing living trusts to take advantage of a shortened creditors' claim period (e.g., four months) if the trustee follows certain notice-to-creditors procedures that are similar to probate proceedings. The law may require the trustee using the shortened claim period to publish a notice in a newspaper of general circulation, to make a reasonable search for creditors, and to give any creditors they locate actual notice of the method to perfect their claims.[50]

Problems with lenders. In some states, if the settlor wishes to refinance property after it has been placed in trust, the lender might require that the trustee transfer title back to the settlor until the refinancing is completed, after which it can again be transferred back to the trustee. As lenders have become more familiar with trusts, fewer are requiring these extra steps, although the settlor is usually required to cosign the loan documents in his or her individual capacity and give written assurance that the trustee has authority to encumber the property.

Greater vigilance in the event of divorce. In states adopting Uniform Probate Code § 2-804(b), divorce or annulment revokes any revocable disposition of property to an ex-spouse or to a relative of an ex-spouse. That section also severs any survivorship interests of the former spouses in property held by them at the time of the divorce, transforming property that they held as joint tenants, tenants by the entirety, and as community property with the right of survivorship into tenancies in common. It also cancels the nomination of an ex-spouse (or the ex-spouse's relatives) for any fiduciary position and cancels any general or limited powers to appoint property. The problem is that there may be non-UPC states that just negate the interest conferred in an unmodified will, leaving intact the ex-spouse's trust and joint tenancy survivorship interests.

CONCLUSION

Obviously, the decision whether to avoid probate is not always a simple one. It requires that each person examine and subjectively weigh the advantages and disadvantages of each, in the context of the laws and procedures of his or her state. There is no correct answer for all situations. In fact, some individuals owning estates may execute a living trust, transfer most of their property into it, and allow the rest to be transferred at death by the probate process, thus obtaining the unique benefits of both arrangements. Many small estates will be most efficiently settled by a combination of a simple will, joint tenancy, and reliance on small estate claiming laws.

The next chapter requires a change of focus, from the qualitative to the quantitative as it focuses on estate tax matters.

QUESTIONS AND PROBLEMS

For some of the problems you will need to consult the UPC or your state's codes. The UPC is on the Teaching Aids disk that comes with the textbook. State codes are available through FindLaw's website by following the appropriate state link through to its statutes <http://www.findlaw.com/11stategov/indexcode.html>.

1. What goals do states try to accomplish through their respective probate codes?

2. The probate process comes in for a fair amount of criticism, however, suppose there was no probate law in the land where Raul died, and his land was in his name alone. His will left everything in equal shares to his three children. How would the children prove that they had a right to own the land? What rights would Raul's unsecured creditors have to his property? How would their debts be satisfied?

3. In what sense is the probate process the mechanism of transfer of last resort? Explain, giving examples.

4. Wesley has just received his lawyer's bill for developing a plan that avoids probate with a living trust. Included is a charge for drafting a will. Did the law firm make a billing mistake?

5. Visit website of The National Conference of Commissioners on Uniform State Laws <http://www.nccusl.org/> and click on "Final Acts & Legislation," then under "Select an Act" scroll down to "PROBATE CODE" click "search" without selecting any state as this will bring up the entire list. Determine whether the following states have adopted the Uniform Probate Code: (a) California, (b) Nevada, (c) North Dakota, and (d) your state of domicile.

6. Consider the relationships between a person and his or her various relatives. For each of the following, state whether the person is an ascendant, a descendant, a collateral relative, or none of the above; and give the degrees

of consanguinity: (a) great-grandfather; (b) husband; (c) first cousin twice removed; (d) grandchild; and (e) nephew.

7. For each of the following pairs, Wanda wants to know who is "closer" to her in relative terms, and the degrees of consanguinity that separate her from each person. Determine who is closer and the number of degrees for her: (a) son and brother, (b) granddaughter and aunt, and (c) grandmother and sister.

8. The late Martha Reddings is survived by her son Andrew, divorced, who has one child in high school, her daughter Jamine, married, but with no children, her daughter Kim, who has two children, one of whom has three children, the other has none; a deceased son, Mark, who left four children, two of whom have two children of their own, another has none, and one deceased child left two children; and her deceased daughter Shirley, who left three children, one of whom has a child, while the other two have none.

   a) Draw a diagram depicting the family tree.

   b) The interest of her issue depends in part on whether her will provides for distribution per stirpes (PS), per capita (PC), or per capita at each generation (PCAEG). For each of the following individuals, determine the fraction of the estate under each alternative:

Possible beneficiaries:	PS	PC	PCAEG
Andrew, Jamine, or Kim			
Mark's spouse			
Each of Mark's living children			
Each of Mark's deceased child's children			
Each of Kim's children			
Each of Shirley's children			
Shirley's grandchild			

9. In problem 8, suppose shortly before her death, Martha married Charlie and tore up her will, planning to replace it, but failing to do so. Her state of domicile had adopted the UPC for common law states (see Exhibit 4-1). How much of her estate, valued at $460,000, would each of the following people receive? Be sure you determine how the spousal share is distributed before you spend time making any other calculations.

Possible heirs	Intestate
Widower Charlie	
Andrew, Jamine, or Kim	
Mark's spouse	
Each of Mark's living children	
Each of Mark's deceased child's children	
Each of Kim's children	
Each of Shirley's children	
Shirley's grandchild	

10. In the prior question, what would Charlie (or his estate) receive if he died shortly after Martha? Why must we pin-down what is meant by "shortly after" in the statement?

11. Describe one characteristic that is common to all three rules of distribution discussed in this chapter.

12. Chester died intestate, survived by his wife, Wanda, and his three children by a prior marriage, Abe, Betty, and Clay. Wanda had no children of her own. Chester's probate estate is valued at $190,000. During his lifetime, Chester had advanced Abe $50,000 and Betty $10,000. Chester memorialized both gifts in a writing that stated the gifts were advancements. Determine how much of the estate would go to each of the four survivors.

13. Repeat the prior problem, changing the facts such that the three children mentioned above are from the couple's marriage, and Wanda has a child, David, from a prior marriage.

14. When he executed his will, Frank and Joan had two young children, Mattie and Ned. Frank's will left half his property to his wife Joan and half to their daughter Mattie. A year after the will was signed, Pam was born into the family. Today, Frank cannot for the life of him figure out why he left half his estate to his little daughter, Mattie, none to his son, and just half to his wife. Frank says he wants to leave all his property (worth $180,000) to Joan when he dies, and if she predeceases him, then to his issue by right of representation. (a) From an estate planning standpoint, what is the first thing

he should do? The second and third things? (b) Apply the UPC to determine how his estate will be shared if he dies without changing the will.

15. Widow Anna died testate. She had three sons and a daughter. Her second son died ten years before her, but his two children have survived. Her daughter died three years ago and left one child. Describe how Anna's property will be distributed to her descendants if her will says "to my issue" by: (1) per capita distribution, (2) per stirpes, and (3) per capita at each generation.

16. Bob died intestate. He owned his home in joint tenancy with close friend John. He was the owner of a car, a racing horse, and a $50,000 savings account. He is survived by his mother, an uncle and two cousins. Given that the UPC is controlling state law, who is entitled to Bob's property?

17. Charlie died intestate. His estate is valued at $400,000. He is survived by his four children, Matt, Chris, Joe and Doug. Five years before Charlie died, he gave stock to Joe valued at $60,000. If this gift is considered an advancement, how much would each of his children receive? If this gift is not considered an advancement, how much would each child receive? What determines whether it was an advancement?

18. Ralph has two children, Betty and Bill. Bill wants to start a company and asks Ralph to give him an advancement of $100,000. Ralph's intent that the gift is an advancement is recorded in writing. What will each child receive if: (a) Ralph died intestate with an estate of $500,000? (b) Ralph died intestate with an estate of $150,000? (c) Ralph died with a valid will that left his estate to his issue by right of representation?

19. Jason's last will was executed on November 17, 1985. It left his entire estate to his wife, Meredith, if she survived him, and, if she did not survive him, then his son Chris, or his issue, would receive 25% and his daughter Doris, or her issue, would receive the other 75% of his estate. It also provided that if either predeceased Jason and left no issue, the other child would receive the entire estate. Jason had a liaison with Jaylene that, in 1997, produced a daughter named Yolanda. Jason died in 2005, survived by his wife, Meredith, and his three children, as well as by Jaylene. The family learned of Yolanda's

existence shortly after Jason's funeral. His estate, all separate property, was worth $600,000. What share of the estate would Meredith receive, and what share for each of the three children?

20. Suppose the same facts as in the prior problem except that Meredith's death in 2004 spared her the shock of learning that Jason had been unfaithful. (a) What would be the shares of the three children? (b) Would it change the outcome if a clause in the 1985 will stated, "anyone not left a part of this estate is hereby intentionally disinherited."

21. Montana, like most states, follows the UPC rule for omitted children that favors only children born after the will is executed, i.e., if the testator leaves nothing to one (or more) of her children, who are alive when she executed her will, the assumption is that she intended to disinherit that child (or those children). However, many states have an important exception to this rule. Visit the website <http://www.elder-law.com/2000/Issue804.html> of Arizona lawyers Fleming & Curti, P. L. C., to answer the following questions: (a) What is Montana's exception to the general rule? (b) What were William Prescott Putnam's two arguments in support of his claim to Gertrude E. Prescott's estate? What evidence did he present to support his arguments? (c) What share of the estate would he have received if successful? (d) How did the court rule? What supported the court's decision?

22. (a) In considering the rights of children who are not left any part of their parent's estate, why do some states allow claims by omitted after-born children (i.e., born after the will was executed) but not by omitted children who were already born when the will was executed? (b) What is the logic behind limiting omitted children born after the will was executed to a share no greater than that of their siblings born when the will was executed?

23. Find, cut out or photocopy (especially if it is not your newspaper), and bring to class a newspaper published "notice" of petition to administer an estate. [You might call a law office to find which local papers are most likely to publish these notices.] What is its purpose?

24. Describe what is meant by "letters" in the probate process. What kinds of

letters are there? How long is this document likely to be?

25. (a) What is meant by "the personal representative of the estate?" In situations where the representative is referred to as "administrator," does that mean the decedent died intestate? Explain. (b) Ordinarily, what must the personal representative accomplish before a judge will permit final distribution under supervised probate?

26. Use South Dakota's probate code (UPC) to answer the following: if a person dies intestate, all other things being equal, what is the priority as to whom the court will choose as administrator?

27. Use California law to decide the issue that follows. Laura died, leaving a valid holographic will that failed to name an executor. The estate is worth approximately $400,000. The will leaves $25,000 to Laura's only daughter, Janet, and the residue is left 40% to grandson Kirk, who is sixteen, and 60% to her nephew Brian. No one contests the validity of the will, nor does anyone claim that there was undue influence. Both Brian and Janet filed petitions to administer the estate. Who is likely to prevail? Explain.

28. Attend a probate hearing. Give the date of attendance, a brief summary of what you observed, and the types of matters considered by the court.

29. (a) What is the purpose of the "Inventory and Appraisement?" (b) What is the purpose of the creditors' claim? Who files it?

30. (a) Using the California Statutory Probate Fee table, determine the attorney's and executor's fees in the following: The decedent had these probate assets: A house worth $900,000 that had a $500,000 mortgage; a car worth $25,000 with a $15,000 lien for a car loan, a brokerage account (stocks and bonds) worth $100,000, and miscellaneous household furniture valued at $25,000. There were various debts that totaled $890, credit card debt of $6,000, miscellaneous probate expenses of $750, and accounting fees of $1,000 for preparing the decedent's last 1040 and the estate 1041. (b) What percentage are the total attorney and executor fees as compared to the gross value of the probate estate? Of the net value of the probable estate?

31. What are the typical costs associated with a probate? How are probate attorney's and executor's fees determined in your state?

32. On November 19, 2005, Alisa was intoxicated when her car clipped a car driven by Bradford, sending his out of control. Alisa, thrown from her car, was killed. Bradford, badly injured, survived. David, after proper published notice to creditors, received his executor letters on January 6, 2006. He mailed a creditors claim form to Bradford's address but it was not submitted to David or to the court within the four month creditors' claim period. On July 13, 2006, Bradford filed suit seeking damages of $750,000 for injuries sustained in the accident. Alisa's auto policy had a $300,000 liability limit.

    Going through Alisa's desk on August 5, 2006, David discovered that Jessica, Alisa's friend living in another town, had lent Alisa $10,000. Although their loan agreement identified Alisa's car as collateral, no lien was filed with the Department of Motor Vehicles. The loan called for a single payment of principle and interest in the amount of $10,800 on September 10, 2006. The damaged car sold for $6,000. Jessica was unaware of Alisa's death until someone told her about it in August.

    Both Bradford and Jessica filed creditors' claims during the last week of August, 2006. Discuss fully the likelihood of success of (a) Bradford's claim, and (b) Jessica's claim.

33. John died intestate, survived by his mother Jan, his wife Alice, and their young daughter, Jenny. His estate consists of the following assets: 1. A home placed in joint tenancy with Jan before he married Alice. 2. Corporate bonds held as community property with Alice. 3. Shares of common XYZ stock held as separate property. 4. A life insurance policy with his friend Carl as the beneficiary. 5. A store owned as tenants in common with Paul, his business associate. 6. A car and a checking account, both in join tenancy with Alice. 7. A pay-on-death savings account naming Jenny as transferee. (a) Which assets are probate estate assets and which ones are nonprobate assets? (b) Who would receive each asset described above? (c) How would the savings account be handled?

34. (a) Who might wish to contest a will by claiming the execution was invalid?

(b) Why is it generally easier to challenge the validity of a will than to challenge the validity of a living trust?

35. Shayna Sapia died domicile in a UPC state. Her close relatives were her mother, her ex-husband, and their two children, Drake Sapia and Jeribeth Peters. Shayna left the following estate:

	Items	Title	Asset FMV
1	Home	Joint tenancy w/ daughter (both contributed equally to the purchase)	$300,000
2	ABC stock	Shayna only	$250,000
3	Big City Muni bonds	POD to son Drake	$275,000
4	Silver Spurs Ranch	Tenant in common w/brother (Shayna owns 40%)	$620,000
5	Riverdale Vacation Cabin	tenancy in the entirety w/ex-husband, did not change title after divorce	$180,000
6	Long Life insurance policy	Shayna as owner, named beneficiaries daughter & son equally	$500,000

a) Determine the probate estate. b) If she died intestate, who would get what? c) If she had a will that left everything to her daughter, who would get what?

36. In the prior problem, suppose Shayna had a testamentary trust that provided that all of her property would be held for her daughter's lifetime benefit, with the remainder to the Lighthouse for the Blind. Her mother, Brandy Kus was named as executor and designated as trustee. (a) What would be held in trust? By what mechanism would it get into trust? (b) Suppose the order for distribution was made on July 10, 2007; how would title to Shayna's interest in Silver Spurs Ranch read once the trust was established? Title to the Muni bonds? Title to the cabin?

37. (a) What is the UPC creditors' claim period? When does it start? (b) What is the creditors' claim period for joint tenancy? (c) For a living trust?

ANSWERS TO QUESTIONS AND PROBLEMS *(odd numbered only)*

1. The probate code seeks to (1) protect both creditor's and the decedent's estate, and (2) assure that the appropriate beneficiaries eventually receive the property.

3. If there is anything else that controls disposition then the assets involved will not be part of the probate estate. For instance, life insurance proceeds are paid directly to the beneficiaries designated, joint tenancy remains with the other joint tenants by operation of law, the trustee of a living trust handles trust assets in accord with the trust document, the IRA and pension benefits go to the alternate beneficiary without involvement of the court.

5. Determine whether the following states have adopted the Uniform Probate Code: a) California–NO; b) Nevada–NO; c) North Dakota–YES; d) Your state of domicile?

7. (a) Son is one degree away while brother is two. (b) Grandchild, grandchild is two degrees away, while aunt is three. (c) Grandparent and sister are both two degrees away.

9. Survivors:	Intestate	Comment
Widower Charlie	$280,000	1st $100k + 1/2 * balance
Andrew, Jamine, and Kim (each share)	$36,000	1/5th the balance
Mark's spouse	$0	none for spouses
Each of Mark's living children	$9,000	1/20th of balance
Each of Mark's deceased child's children	$45,000	1/40th of balance
Each of Kim's children	$0	Kim is alive, so no takers on a lower level.
Each of Shirley's children	$9,000	1/20th of balance
Shirley's grandchild (the grandchildren's parent is still alive and takes the share)	$0	stops at highest living level

11. Under all three rules (per capita, traditional per stirpes, and per capita at each generation per stirpes), the intestate estate is passed to the same descendants. Notice that one inherits only if those above him or her (that is, those in closer relationship) in the line of descent are deceased. Although the same people inherit, the difference in the three rules is found in the amounts allocated to the various descendants.

13. As with 12, start with an enhanced estate of $250,000 but this time Wanda gets $150,000 plus half the balance for a total of $200,000. The children would get $16,666.67 each. Again, Abe's advancement exceeds his share so we leave him out and start over. At the second round, the enhanced estate is $200,000 with Wanda getting $175,000 (i.e., $150,000 + half of $50,000). The balance of $25,000 is split equally. Betty's share is reduced by $10,000 so she gets just $2,500. Clay gets $12,500. The total equals $190,000: $175,000 + $2,500 + $12,500. Note that David does not inherit from Chester but his presence keeps Wanda from getting the entire estate.

15. Per capita distribution: Anna's descendants - two sons and three grandchildren each receive 1/5 of her estate.
    Traditional per stirpes: Each of her two surviving sons receives 1/4 of her property. Each of her deceased second son's children receives 1/8 of her property. The only child of her deceased daughter receives 1/4 of her property.
    Per capita at each generation per stirpes: Each of her two surviving sons receives 1/4 of her property. Each of her three grandchildren receives 1/6 of her property.

17. If the $60,000 gift is considered to be an advancement, Joe would receive $55,000 ($460,000/4 = $115,000, less the $60,000 already received). His siblings would each receive $115,000. If the $60,000 gift is not considered an advancement, each child (including Joe) would receive $100,000.

19. An omitted child takes nothing if the estate is left all to a surviving spouse, see UPC §2-301.

21. This one is too much fun to do on your own so you will have to go to the website for the answers.

23. The notice of death and petition to probate an estate should be available in the legal notices section of most local newspapers. However, some newspapers are more popular than others because of cost. Smaller circulation newspapers that meet the minimum subscription requirements for state or local law regarding legal notices may have more notices published in them than do better-known newspapers with wider circulation.

25. (a) The personal representative of the estate is the person appointed by the probate court to act on behalf of the decedent's estate. He or she is given (pays a couple of bucks, actually) "letters" from the court (certified by the clerk of the court) that verify the person's appointment. This allows the person to represent the estate in the sense of being able to collect assets and pay the debts of the decedent. If the term administrator is used, it means that the person appointed was not named as the representative in the decedent's will. If someone named in the will serves, he or she is called the executor. Someone other than an executor serving may be due to the person dying intestate (hence no will to nominate anyone), or all the persons nominated in the will are unable or unwilling to serve, or the will fails to nominate anyone. If there is a will admitted to probate but someone other than an executor is serving, then the person is called "the administrator with will annexed." (b) Before final distribution is allowed, the personal representative must give a full report and an accounting that shows that all approved debts have been paid and that the estate is ready for final settlement. Generally, that is also the time to request authority to pay the fees of the representative and the attorney.

27. You will find the answers at California Probate Code §§ 8440, 8441, and 8446.

29. (a) Uses of the inventory and appraisement: 1. to establish the assets for which the personal representative is responsible; 2. to describe the estate to all interested parties; 3. to determine the proper bond amount; and 4. possibly to establish estate tax return valuation. (b) Filed by a creditor, the creditor's

claim is the method of formally bringing a claim against the estate to the attention of the personal representative (and/or to the attention of the court).

31. Probate costs usually run between 2 and 10% of the probate estate's gross value. The largest probate expense is usually the personal representative's commission and Chester's fees. Depending on state law, fees are likely to be either set by statute as some decreasing percentage of the estate or are set by the probate judge based upon the time and effort of the attorney and the executor. Even in the latter case, judges will grant more for very large estates than they will allow for small estates.

33. Probate: the stock, the interest in the store, and decedent's half of the community property in those states that require such to be probated.

Non-Probate: all joint tenancy property (home, car, bank account), the TOD account, transfers by contract (life insurance to Carl), and community property going to Alice (bonds) in those states that allow transfers to surviving spouses without requiring a probate.

1. Home: Joint tenancy, to Jan by right of survivorship (title) or operation of law.

2. Corporate bonds: community property, intestate succession favors the surviving spouse when it comes to community property, hence to Alice either by set-aside or by the probate process depending upon state law.

3. Stock: as separate property, depending upon state intestate succession law, Alice would receive either all of the stock or have to share it with their daughter Jenny.

4. Life insurance: Contractual, the named beneficiary, Carl, would receive the proceeds.

5. Store held as tenants in common with Paul: If this is a community property asset, then Alice would receive John's share of the store, but if it was separate property, then she might have to share it with Jenny.

6. Car and checking account, both in joint tenancy with Alice: to Alice as survivor.

7. TOD savings account: to the named transferee, daughter Jenny. Since Jenny is young, there might have to be a guardian of the estate appointed to take title of this asset for the benefit of Jenny. It might also be possible to

have a custodial account established with Alice as the custodian.

35. (a) The gross estate:

1	Home	the half based upon her contribution	$150,000
2	ABC stock	in her name only	$250,000
3	Big City Muni bonds	POD* to son (100% in her estate)	$275,000
4	Silver Spurs Ranch	Tenant in common w/brother (Shayna is 40% owner), i.e., .4 * $620,000	$248,000
5	Riverdale Vacation Cabin	tenancy in the entirety w/ex-husband, this converts to 50-50 tenants in common on the divorce.	$90,000
6	Long Life insurance policy	Shayna as owner, named beneficiaries daughter & son equally (100% included)	$500,000
			$1,513,000

(b) The probate assets:

1	Home	no, joint tenancy	
2	ABC stock	in her name only	$250,000
3	Big City Muni bonds	POD transfers directly to son	
4	Silver Spurs Ranch	tenant in common w/brother (Shayna is 40% owner), i.e., .4 * $620,000	$248,000
5	Riverdale Vacation Cabin	tenancy in the entirety w/ex-husband, this converts to 50-50 tenants in common on the divorce.	$90,000
6	Long Life ins.	paid directly to the named beneficiaries	
		Total	$588,000

(c) Intestate allocation:

1	Home	joint tenancy	to daughter
2	ABC stock	in her name only	half to each child
3	Big City Muni bonds	POD transfers directly to son	son
4	Silver Spurs Ranch	Tenant in common w/brother (Shayna is 40% owner), i.e., .4 * $620,000	half to each child
5	Riverdale Vacation Cabin	tenancy in the entirety w/ex-husband, this converts to 50-50 tenants in common on the divorce.	half of the half to each child.
6	Long Life ins.	paid directly to the named beneficiaries	half to each child

(d) Her daughter would get everything except her son would still receive the POD account and half of the insurance proceeds.

ENDNOTES

1. UPC § 3-1201. Collection of Personal Property by Affidavit.

2. CA Probate Code § 13100.

3. See UPC § 3-1201. [Collection of Personal Property by Affidavit.] and § 3-1203. [Small Estates; Summary Administration Procedure.]

4. UPC § 2-106.

5. UPC § 2-709. Representation; Per Capita at Each Generation; Per Stirpes. See part (b) Representation; Per Capita at Each Generation.

6. UPC § 2-106

7. UPC § 2-302. Omitted Children.

8. UPC § 2-302(c).

9. UPC § 2-114(b).

10. UPC § 2-301. Entitlement of Spouse; Premarital Will.

11. UPC § 2-112. Dower and Curtesy Abolished

12. UPC § 2-203. Composition of the Augmented Estate.

13. UPC § 2-202(b) [Supplemental Elective-Share Amount.]

14. UPC § 2-404 Family allowance.

15. UPC § 2-402.

16. UPC § 3-305.

17. CPC § 8001.

18. CPC § 8000.

19. CPC § 8003.

20. UPC § 3-203. Priority Among Persons Seeking Appointment as Personal Representative.

21. CPC §§ 10400 - 600.

22. CPC § 8481.

23. CPC § 8482.

24. UPC § 3-301 (Informal Probate) and § 3-402 (Formal Probate)

25. CPC § 8110.

26. UPC § 3-706

27. UPC § 3-706. Duty of Personal Representative; Inventory and Appraisement.

28. CPC § 9100.

29. CPC § 9103.

30. CPC § 9201.

31. CPC §§ 11620 - 24.

32. CPC § 11640.

33. CPC §§ 12200 - 252.

34. CPC §§ 12200 - 252.

35. CPC § 10810.

36. CPC § 10800.

37. IPC § 633.197 actually 6% on first $1,000, 4% on the next $4,000. See also IPC §633.199 that allows additional fees for extraordinary services, e.g., real estate sales and tax preparation.

38. UPC § 3-803(a)(1).

39. UPC § 3-1201. Collection of Personal Property by Affidavit.

40. See Alambama Statutes Title 43, § 43-2-692(b)(1) and Wyoming Statutes Title 2, § 2-1-201.

41. Wyoming Statutes Title 2, § 2-1-205.

42. *Tulsa Professional Collection Services v. Estate of Pope* 485 US 478, 108 S.Ct. 1340 (1988).

43. UPC § 3-803. [Limitations on Presentation of Claims.]

44. See California Code of Civil Procedure § 366.2 at California's Website: *<http://www.leginfo.ca.gov/calaw.html>*.

45. See Figure 4-1.

46. UPC § 2-702. Requirement of Survival by 120 hours.

47. Uniform TOD Security Registration Act § 9(c) - (d).

48. *Heggstad v. Heggstad*, 20 Cal. Rptr. 2d 433 (1993).

49. See California Code of Civil Procedure § 366.2 at California's Website: *<http://www.leginfo.ca.gov/calaw.html>*.

50. See California Probate Code §§ 19000-19100 at California's Website: *<http://www.leginfo.ca.gov/calaw.html>*.

CHAPTER 5

The Unified Transfer Tax

OVERVIEW

This chapter is the first of four covering the taxation of wealth transfers. Since wealth is transferred during life and at death, we examine the tax imposed on both types of transfers, i.e., gifts and estates. Given the dramatic change in the law with the passage of the Economic Growth and Tax Relief Reconciliation Act of 2001 (EGTRRA), we will cover the changes that will lead to full repeal of the estate tax in 2010. Individuals may be able to save taxes by transferring wealth to grandchildren or great-grandchildren. However, such transfers may be subject to another transfer tax, the generation-skipping transfer (GST) tax, which will be covered very briefly in this chapter and in more detail in Chapter 17. It is important to understand that these taxes are excise taxes, not property taxes. An *excise tax* is a tax on a transaction. In this case it is levied on the transfer of wealth, with the tax based on the net value of property transferred. We begin with the basics of gift tax and estate tax law. Keep in mind that these two taxes are really part of a unified transfer tax system.

The two taxes are unified in the sense that both use the same tax rate schedule and both tax the net value of the wealth that is transferred. As a general rule, gifts are valued as of the date the gift is given (DOG) and estates as of the date of death (DOD). The tax calculation is done determining a tentative tax based upon the net value of the gift or estate. This tentative tax is derived from the rate table (see Table 1 in Appendix A). To shelter all but the largest estates and gifts from paying a tax the tentative tax is reduced by a unified credit. It is a unified credit in the sense that to the extent it is used on gifts it will not be available to lessen the tax on the donor's estate. Like the rate schedule, the unified credit comes from the Internal Revenue Code (IRC). The unified credit has increased over the years and is slated to continue to increase until 2009. Table 2 in Appendix A (also on the inside front cover) gives the unified credits for the years 1977 through 2009. For the years 2006 through 2008, the estate unified credit is $780,800. If a taxable transfer produces a tentative tax that is equal to, or less than, the available unified credit there will be no tax due. Indeed, a taxable estate of $2,000,000 produces a tentative tax of $780,800. Therefore, if the death occurred in 2006, 2007, or 2008, the tentative tax would exactly match the available unified credit, assuming no prior taxable gifts, and there would be no tax to pay. If the person died in 2007, leaving a taxable estate of $3,000,000, the estate tax would be $450,000. Note that the unified credit covered the first $2,000,000 and the extra $1,000,000 was taxed at the highest marginal rate for the year 2007, i.e., at 45%. The amount that is sheltered by the unified credit is referred to as the applicable exclusion amount (AEA), the term used in the IRC to describe the taxable amount that is sheltered by the unified credit.

Table 2 has separate columns for estate unified credits and gift unified credits, likewise estate AEA and gift AEA columns. Through 2003, estate and gift unified credits for any given year were the same (and hence, so were the AEAs). After 2003, the estate AEA increases periodically whereas the gift AEA remains at $1,000,000. In addition to the AEA as a shelter, for gifts there is an annual exclusion that keeps small gifts from being taxed, indeed, it keeps most gifts from even having to be reported. The annual exclusion is an indexed $10,000 that reached $11,000 in 2002 and is expected to increase to $12,000 in 2006 or 2007. Generally, the annual exclusion is subtracted from the value of the gift before the tentative tax is calculated. In this chapter we will work on understanding these two taxes and how they are related in detail, but for now review these two examples to solidify your understanding of these initial concepts.

EXAMPLE 5 - 1. In 2005, Brandon made a gift of ABC stock to his friend Lolly. The stock was worth $1,811,000 at the time of the gift. The annual exclusion in 2005 is $11,000 per donee so the taxable gift is $1,800,000. Note that the taxable gift falls within the $1,500,000 to $2,000,000 in Table 1. The tentative tax is $690,800, determined by taking $300,000 (the amount above $1,500,000) times 45% (the marginal rate within the bracket) and adding the product to $448,300 (the tentative tax on $1,500,000). From the tentative tax of $690,800 we subtract the gift tax unified credit of $345,800, resulting in $345,000 as the tax that Brandon must pay.

EXAMPLE 5 - 2. Agustin died in 2005, leaving his $3,000,000 taxable estate to his two children. The tentative tax for Austin's estate is $1,250,800 [47% times $1,000,000 that is above $2,000,000, plus the $780,800 tentative tax on $2,000,000]. We subtract from this the 2005 estate unified credit of $555,800 to determine an estate tax of $695,000. Note, that while the estate AEA for 2005 is $1,500,000, that figure does not come into the calculation of the estate tax; it is simply the shelter amount, meaning that a tentative tax on $1,500,000 is equal to the $555,800 unified credit for 2005.

BRIEF HISTORY

There have been four federal taxes that have required some estates to pay taxes based upon the value of wealth transferred at death. All were implemented to provide revenue to finance, or recovery from, military action. The first three did not last very long but the fourth, after almost a century, is still with us.

The first federal estate tax was enacted in 1797 to pay for a naval build-up in anticipation of a possible war with France. The tax, while labeled a "stamp tax" on wills and estates, was really an estate tax levied on the value of the property distributed. The rates were 25 cents on distributions between $50 and $100, 50 cents on the next $400, and $1 on each additional $500.[1] When a treaty with France avoided war, the tax was repealed as of October 1802.[2]

To raise revenue for the Civil War a federal inheritance tax was enacted in 1862. The share of an estate going to ancestors, to issue, or to siblings was 0.75%, to nephews and nieces 1%, to aunts, uncles, and cousins 3%, second cousins 4%, and to even more distant relatives and to unrelated persons 5%. There was a 100% marital deduction, enlightened tax policy that did not become part of the current law until 1982. The inheritance tax was repealed in 1870.[3]

In 1898, to help finance the Spanish-American War, another graduated inheritance tax was passed with a top rate of 15 % on estates over $1,000,000.[4] It was repealed in 1902.[5]

Another war related estate tax was passed by Congress in 1916 as the country prepared for entry into World War I. Initially, after an exemption of $50,000, the rate started at 1% and had a top rate of 10% on estates over $5,000,000.[6] Although modified many times over the years, our current estate tax stems from this 1916 Act. There was no marital deduction, so the tax was applied even if the entire estate went to a surviving spouse. As a tax on transfers at death only, it was relatively easy to circumvent through the use of gifts. In 1924, Congress plugged this loophole by enacting a gift tax. The gift tax was repealed in 1926 and reenacted in 1932. After the war, Congress retained the estate tax but dropped the top rate to 20% in 1926. During the Depression the top rate soared to 70% in 1935. During the World War II, the top rate went even higher–to 77% for taxable estates greater than $10 million.

Since its revenue yield is negligible–generally less than one percent of all federal taxes–the estate tax is thought to be justified, if at all, as a method of redistributing wealth, that is to break up very large estates, thus decreasing the tendency for wealth to be concentrated in the hands of a very small portion of the population.

Prior to the gift tax and estate tax being unified in 1977, there were a number of imperfections in the system that could be exploited to reduce taxes on the transfer of wealth. Because the gift tax rates were only 75% of the estate tax rates, giving large gifts reduced taxes for the very wealthy. For any given size taxable estate, the fact that the decedent had made prior taxable gifts did not increase the decedent's estate tax. Estates of decedents who had made taxable gifts still started at the lowest marginal rates and had the same estate tax exemption as estates of persons who had not made taxable gifts. They were said to "take two trips up the rate ladder" since the gift tax and the estate tax are both progressive. Before the 1977 unification of the estate and gift taxes, there was an annual exclusion of $3,000 per donee, a $30,000 lifetime gift exemption for each donor, and a $60,000 estate exemption, which was undiminished by the decedent's use of the gift exemption. On January 1, 1982, the annual exclusion increased from $3,000 per donee per year to $10,000 per donee per year.

With the Tax Reform Act of 1976[7] a single "unified" rate schedule was adopted, taxing lifetime gifts and transfers at death at the same rate. With the implementation of the "unified" system, the transfer of the estate at death is treated almost as though it were just another gift. Adjusted taxable gifts (i.e., the value of gifts reduced by annual exclusions) serve to boost the donor's taxable estate into its appropriate marginal rate. Furthermore, the donor's post-1976 taxable gifts reduce the amount of unified credit available to shelter transfers at death. The AEA for estates in 1977 was only $120,000 and the top rate for taxable transfers over $5,000,000 was 70%.

In 1981 the Economic Recovery Tax Act[8] dropped the top rate from 70% to 50%, and increases in the unified credit resulted in an AEA of $600,000 by 1987. In 1997, as inflation caused a significant increase in the portion of estates subject to the estate tax, Congress passed the Taxpayer Relief Act[9] which had the AEA increase over the decade, with it topping out at $1,000,000 in 2006. Before that happened, Congress passed the Economic Growth and Tax Relief Reconciliation Act of 2001 (EGTRRA).[10] It provides for periodic reductions in the top marginal rate and dramatic increases in the AEA, finally repealing the tax for calendar year 2010. EGTRRA has a sunset provision that causes the estate and gift tax law to revert back to the 1997 law with a top marginal rate of 55% and an AEA of $1,000,000.[11]

MAJOR CHANGES WITH EGTRRA

The passage of the Economic Growth and Tax Relief Reconciliation Act of 2001 (EGTRRA) made numerous changes to the transfer tax law; indeed it repeals the estate tax altogether, at least for the year 2010. It also repeals the generation-skipping transfer tax for 2010. It phases in lower top marginal rates and increases in steps the amount that can pass estate tax free. Unfortunately, the changes are all temporary.

Complexity Added

For the decade from the passage of EGTRRA in 2001 and the year 2011, estate tax law has become needlessly complex compared to previous years. Over the decade, the top rate declines in increments from 55% in 2001 to 45% in 2009, then is effectively zero in 2010 since there is no estate tax, then it returns to 55% in 2011. The AEA "tax-free" amount is sometimes called the unified credit equivalent, or the credit shelter amount, but since the 1997 Tax Relief Act used the term *applicable exclusion amount* as a proxy for the amount sheltered by the unified credit we will use that term, or the abbreviation AEA, in our discussions.

In 2001, the AEA was $675,000 and was slated to increase to $1,000,000 by 2006, but with the passage of EGTRRA, it jumped to $1,000,000 in 2002 and for estates it continues upward. The estate AEA reaches $2,000,000 in 2006, remains infinite in 2010 (no estate tax), and then drops back to $1,000,000 for 2011 and after. The gift tax AEA remains constant at $1,000,000, even as the estate tax AEA rises. Supposedly, the gift tax AEA will remain at $1,000,000 even if the estate tax repeal is made permanent. For gifts in 2010, the gift tax maximum marginal rate drops to 35% but will revert back to the pre-2002 rates with the top rate being 55% unless the repeal of the estate tax is made permanent, in which case the top gift tax rate is likely to match the top income tax rate.

Uncertainty Added

It is obvious from the preceding discussion that in addition to the added complexity, EGRRTA added uncertainty by repealing the estate tax for just one year, then returning both the estate and gift tax back to what it would have been had the 2001 law never been enacted. The very last section of the EGRRTA provides that

> *All provisions of, and amendments made by, this Act shall not apply—*
> > *(1) to taxable, plan, or limitation years beginning after December 31, 2010, or*
> > *(2) in the case of title V, to estates of decedents dying, gifts made, or generation-skipping transfers, after December 31, 2010.*[12]

Unless changed by another tax act, as of January 1, 2011, it will be as if EGTRRA never happened; the estate tax will return, the AEA for estates will fall back to $1,000,000 (the level it would have reached by 2006 under the pre-EGTRRA law), there will be a top marginal rate of 55% for both gifts and estates, a surcharge of 5% on taxable transfers over $10,000,000, and the GST tax will all reappear. The ETAX2006 spreadsheet program (see page xviii at the beginning of the book) was written with the presumption that prior to 2011, a law will pass making the EGTRRA changes permanent, at least as permanent as such things tend to be.

There is a fair probability that the economic slowdown, coupled with the EGTRRA tax cuts, and likely spending increases (whether for social security, defense, or education) will cause budget deficits to loom large. If that happens, Congress, instead of letting EGTRRA lapse altogether, might hold the AEA at

$3,500,000 (i.e., the 2009 amount) and index it for inflation. A change such as that, combined with planning techniques, would eliminate the transfer tax for all but the wealthiest estates, perhaps only the top one-tenth of one percent (as compared to taxing the top one or two percent in 2001). To make such legislation palatable, Congress might allow closely held businesses to pass tax-free to family members, perhaps with a carryover basis and/or with a recapture provision covering the estate tax saved if the business passes out of family control by sale or gift within a set period of time. It will be interesting to see what happens.

Ground Rules

The sunset provision makes planning difficult, and indeed, makes the subject of estate planning more difficult to learn. In our examples and discussion, rather than switching back and forth from what is and what is likely, we will work with the law as it is, i.e., no estate tax in 2010 and back to the past in 2011, even though we know that one of two things are likely to occur before 2011–either the estate tax will be repealed or the AEA for estates will be set at a level that covers all but a very, very small percentage of estates.

UNIFIED TRANSFER TAX FRAMEWORK

The basic model of the present system is to tax wealth transfers cumulatively, while allowing the donors of gifts and estates modest in size to escape transfer taxes through a combination of annual exclusions (for gifts only) and the unified credit (applicable to both gifts and estates), which corresponds to the AEA discussed earlier. Increases to the unified credit and decreases to the top marginal rates were being phased in even before EGTRRA. Appendix A, Table 1, Federal Unified Transfer-Tax Rates shows the tax rates in effect since 1977. Table 2, Unified Credits (UCr), Applicable Exclusion Amounts (AEA), and the End of the Bubble by Year Since 1977, shows the changing unified credit from 1977 through 2010, the year the repeal of the estate tax is slated to take effect. The latter table also shows the AEA, meaning the amount that passes tax-free because it is covered by the available unified credit. Fear not; while it is a little complicated at first, take this transfer tax business step-by-step, and you will master it. You might want to tag the Appendix A tables and do the calculations yourself for each example. Doing so should facilitate your understanding of this material.

Taxing the Net Value of Wealth Transferred

Although there are many refinements, limitations, definitions, and distinctions, the taxation of wealth transfers is conceptually straightforward. Tax only those transfers that are above a certain threshold in value. The tax is based on the net value of what is being transferred, with the value determined as of the date the transfer is made. The tax rate is progressive (higher values meet higher rates). Certain transfers, such as to a spouse or to charities, are allowed to pass tax free. While the basic premise is that the estate tax is needed to break up large estates, to make it effective there needs to be a gift tax; otherwise the estate tax is easily circumvented.

What is taxed? For gifts this is generally the value of the property transferred. It gets complicated, as we will see in later chapters, when something less than outright transfer is made or when only a fractional interest in property is given. For estates we start with what is called the gross estate, generally being everything the decedent owned but in rare cases, discussed later, it might include things once owned but given away but with the donor-decedent having kept an interest such as the right to receive income. From the gross estate certain deductions are allowed to arrive at the taxable estate. Deductions include the decedent's unpaid debts, expenses of estate administration, and marital and charitable deductions.

Once the taxable estate is determined, a tentative tax is calculated using the unified rate schedule. This is called a tentative tax because it is not the tax that has to be paid, that tax is determined by subtracting the unified credit. This credit is found in Table 2 of Appendix A.

Rate schedule. As a result of the Economic Recovery Tax Act of 1981 (ERTA), revised by the Tax Reform Act of 1984 and the Revenue Act of 1987, rates on taxable transfers in excess of $3 million have decreased periodically. With the addition of EGTRRA, top rates continue downward through the phase-out of the estate tax in 2010. Table 1 in Appendix A shows the federal unified transfer tax rate schedule. It is *unified* in the sense that the same rate schedule is used to calculate the tentative tax on taxable gifts and on taxable estates. The table is divided into 13 parts representing the various periods of decreasing maximum marginal rates from 1977 through the phase-out in 2010. The first part shows the rates for *all* transfer years after 1976 for taxable amounts up to $2 million. The next four parts constitute transition rates that apply to taxable transfers on amounts over $2 million during 1977 - 81, 1982, 1983, and 1984 - 86, a period during which the top rate moved down from a high of 70% to a high of 55%. The next two periods, 1987 - 97 and 1998 - 2001, had the same marginal rates as the immediate prior period but a 5% surcharge (discussed below under the heading, "The Bubble") was added for taxable transfers over $10 million. The next five parts show that the top rate dropped to 50% in 2002 and then decreases by one percentage point each of the next four years before settling at 45% for the last three years of the estate tax. Finally, in 2010 the estate tax is gone and only the gift tax remains with a top marginal rate of 35% for taxable transfers above $500,000.

The federal unified transfer tax rates have been quite progressive with marginal rates ranging from 18% to as high as 77% for pre-1976 taxable estates in excess of $10 million. The pre-1977 gift tax rates and estate tax rates are found in Appendix Tables 4 and 5, respectively. Note that the old gift tax rates were exactly 75% of the old estate tax rate.

A few examples will demonstrate that while the transfer tax rate schedule is unified, the AEA for gifts and estates is not, i.e., post-2003 the AEA remains at $1,000,000 for gifts while it increases over the years for estates.

EXAMPLE 5 - 3. On March 4, 2007, Phyllis gave her two sons an apartment building appraised at $3,524,000. Shortly before April 15, 2008, she filed a gift tax return, Form 709. The two $12,000 annual exclusions reduced the taxable gift to $3,500,000. The tentative tax was $1,455,800 against which she applied her unified credit of $345,800. Along with the return, she mailed a check made out to the Treasury for $1,110,000.

EXAMPLE 5 - 4. As a result of her death on March 4, 2007, Teresa's estate went to her three daughters. The estate had a value of $3,500,000 after subtracting debts and estate expenses. Shortly before December 4, 2007, the executor of her estate filed an estate tax return, Form 706. The taxable estate of $3,500,000 resulted in a tentative tax of $1,455,800 against which was applied a unified credit of $780,800. Along with the return, the executor included a check made out to the Treasury for $675,000. Note that, unlike gifts, there was no per beneficiary exclusion.

The Bubble. Make this paragraph a quick read. For the years 1988 through 2001, the transfer tax law required the recapture of the benefit of the lower marginal rates and the unified credit for large estates. This was accomplished by imposing an additional 5% tax, referred to as a surcharge, on taxable transfers above $10 million, with the surcharge ending when the benefits of the lower rates and the unified credit were recaptured. The range over which the rate jumped from 55% to 60% before dropping back to 55% is referred to as the "bubble." EGTRRA eliminated the surcharge for transfers after December 31, 2001.

Unified credit. In tax law, a *credit* is a dollar-for-dollar reduction in the *tentative tax.* A *deduction* is a dollar-for-dollar reduction from the gross amount to arrive at the amount taxable. A deduction provides only a fractional reduction in the amount of tax. The fraction is determined by the top marginal tax rates applicable to the particular transfer. The unified credit is important in that it comes into play every time there is a taxable transfer, whether by gift or estate. We will cover the state death tax credit very briefly because, while it was once quite important, it was eliminate by EGTRRA for estates of decedents dying after 2004. Since adjusted taxable gifts are added to the taxable estate to calculate the estate tax, a *gift tax payable credit* is allowed to avoid taxing the gift twice. The prior transfer credit and the credit for foreign death taxes only apply to a small portion of estates and not at all to gifts. These two credits will be discussed later.

Prior to 1977 (the first year of the unified transfer tax), a donor was allowed a lifetime exemption (i.e., a deduction) of $30,000 for gifts in excess of the $3,000 per donee annual exclusions; and an estate exemption of $60,000 when the person died. These had the effect of eliminating taxation on modest lifetime gifts and small estates. Using the gift exemption did not reduce the estate exemption. Thus, an estate with a net value of less than $60,000 was tax-free regardless of the amount of lifetime taxable gifts made by the decedent. The Tax Reform Act of 1976 (TRA 76) eliminated the two exemptions and substituted a single *unified credit* applicable to both taxable gifts and taxable estates after 1976. With the new law, the unified credit available at the death of a donor is decreased to the extent that the donor's lifetime gifts used it up.

The unified credit has increased over the years, as shown in Appendix Table 2. After a decade of increases, the period from 1987 through 1997 saw the unified credit remain steady at $192,800. During that period, the credit sheltered $600,000 in net value transferred from gift and estate taxes. With the Taxpayer Relief Act of 1997, the amount that could pass tax-free increased, almost yearly, and was scheduled to reach $1,000,000 in the year 2006; however EGTRRA accelerated and expanded the increase. As the table shows, the estate tax unified credit covers the tentative tax on taxable transfers of $1,000,000 starting in 2002. It eventually shelters taxable estates of $3.5 million in 2009 just before the estate tax is phased out in 2010. As discussed earlier in this chapter, we use AEA as an abbreviation for the taxable amount that can be transferred free of taxes. What really happens is that the transfer generates a tentative tax that is just covered by the unified transfer tax credit.

Table 2 shows the unified credit, the AEA, and the "end of the bubble" since 1977 for both estates and gifts. As stated earlier, the 5% surcharge only applied to taxable transfers above the $10,000,000 level made during 1988-2001. As previously stated, the unified credit for gifts and estates is the same until 2004, at which point the estate tax AEA increases to $1,500,000 (and continues to increase periodically) but the gift tax AEA remains at $1,000,000.

The term *applicable exclusion amount* to describe the tax-free amount can cause confusion since it implies a deduction where none occurs. Better terms would have been either the *credit shelter amount* or the *unified credit equivalent*.[13] The 2007 estate unified credit in the amount of $780,800 shelters $2,000,000 in taxable transfers from estate taxes because the tentative tax on that size transfer is exactly $780,800. For a gift in 2007, the AEA (i.e., the sheltered amount) is $1,000,000 because the tentative tax on that amount is $345,800, exactly matching the unified credit for post-2001 gifts. In doing the calculations, we do not "exclude" the applicable exclusion amount; instead, we determine a tentative tax on the taxable transfer and then apply the appropriate unified credit. We must fall in line and refer to the tax-free transfer amount as the applicable exclusion amount or the AEA, but please, never subtract it when calculating the transfer tax.

EXAMPLE 5 - 5. In 2007, Monica makes a gift of ABC stock worth $842,000 to her friend Pablo. The taxable gift reported is $830,000 which produces a tentative tax of $279,500. This tentative tax is completely covered by Monica's gift tax unified credit of $345,800. Indeed, to the extent that she has used up $279,000 of her unified credit, it will reduce what she can pass tax-free on future gifts and at death.

EXAMPLE 5 - 6. Ann Marie died in 2007, leaving an estate with a value of $842,000 to her children. So long as the gross value of the estate when added to any post-1976 adjusted taxable gifts is less than the $2,000,000 AEA amount for 2007,

Ann Marie's executor does not have to file an estate tax return. Note that assets in the estate still get a step-up in basis even though no return has to be filed (and obviously, no tax is due).

Warning: *Do NOT deduct the applicable exclusion amount. You must subtract the unified credit from the tentative tax for all of these transfer tax calculations. The only appropriate use of the term applicable exclusion amount is in giving general advice to clients, such as "in 2007, the applicable exclusion amount is $1,000,000 for gifts and $2,000,000 for estates." However, less confusion would result by just saying, "The amount that can pass tax-free is $1,000,000 for gifts and $2,000,000 for estates."*

In many situations, the allowable unified credit will be less than the amount in Table 2. The actual amount of the allowable unified credit is the *lesser of either* the unused unified credit in the year of the transfer *or* the amount of the tentative tax. For example, the allowable unified credit for a $250,000 gift made in 2008 (assuming no prior taxable gifts) is $70,800, i.e., the lesser of $345,800, the unified credit available in 2008, and $70,800, the tentative tax on $250,000.

Integration. In wealth transfer taxation, succeeding transfers are unified, in part because they are taxed cumulatively. Under the *cumulative gift doctrine*, all past and present gifts are accumulated; that is, prior taxable gifts are added to current taxable transfers (whether lifetime gifts or the donor's estate at death) to determine the transfer tax base. There is one purpose, and only one purpose, to having adjusted taxable gifts as part of the estate tax calculation, and that is to boost the decedent's estate into higher marginal rates. These are the appropriate marginal rates when the net estate is viewed as just another in a series of transfers.

As we have seen, TRA 76 created the *unified transfer tax*, combining gift and estate taxation into a single tax structure having one rate schedule. However, TRA 76 did not achieve complete unification; for instance, the annual exclusion is available only for lifetime gifts. EGTRRA has widened the gap by locking the gift tax AEA at $1,000,000 while the estate AEA continues to climb. Unification did not produce a tax system that makes planners indifferent as to the timing of transfers; that is, whether one would recommend gifts over holding property until death, or vice versa, depends on the circumstances. For example, lifetime gifts use up less unified credit because of the annual exclusion and future appreciation escapes transfer taxation, but appreciated property transferred at death receives a step-up in basis.

To recapitulate, let us review the points demonstrated in the earlier examples:

First, in calculating the gift tax, one includes in the item called "total prior taxable gifts" all taxable gifts made *since 1932*, the year of enactment of the gift tax. On the other hand, as we have said, in calculating the federal estate tax base, one includes in the item called "adjusted taxable gifts" only the taxable gifts made since January 1, 1977, i.e., since unification.

Second, in the *gift tax* model, the "unused unified credit" is the amount of the current unified credit reduced by the unified credit amount already used up to offset tentative gift taxes on gifts in prior years. It is based on the premise that once the amount of the (lifetime) unified credit is used up, each additional dollar of taxable gift is fully taxable. By way of contrast, in the *estate tax* model, the entire unified credit is subtracted from the tentative tax, because the "gift tax payable" credit for prior gift taxes is limited to the amount of gift taxes that would have been paid on the post-1976 gifts using the rates in effect at the date of death. This means that the gift taxes payable credit might be less than what was actually paid. This occurs where there were pre-1977 taxable gifts that pushed the post-1976 taxable gifts into higher marginal rates, or where very large post-1976 gifts were given at a time when the top marginal rates were higher than those in effect when the donor died. Remember, the top marginal rates for transfers above $2,000,000 have been falling over the years.

For most estates with previous taxable gifts, the gift tax payable credit will equal the gift tax paid because only rarely do donors make taxable gifts large enough to result in an actual tax payment. And the recalculation issue will arise only if the donor made very large gifts both before and after January 1, 1977, or made extremely large gifts that went into marginal rates which were higher than those applied to the donor's estate. Assuming that all taxable gifts by the decedent were post-1976, whether the executor will have to do the recalculation rather than just using the gift taxes paid depends on several things: when the gift(s) were given; the taxable amount; and when the donor died.

For a death in 2001, recalculation was required if the decedent made taxable gifts in excess of $3,000,000 between 1977 and 1984 inclusive, or in excess of $3,500,000 between 1977 and 1983, if the gift pushes the taxable estate above $10,000,000 and into the bubble, i.e., a top rate of 60%. For any death after 2001, any post-1976 taxable gift over $2,000,000 will require a recalculation for estate tax purposes. The ETAX program shows this recalculation as "Gift Tax Payable (estate concept)" in the gift tax portion of the spreadsheet. Compare the entry found there to the amount across from Gift Tax Paid and note that, for recent years, only when the cumulative gifts exceed $2,000,000 is there a difference between the figures and that, when there is a difference, the "payable" amount is always less than the "paid" amount.

In the examples that follow, to simplify, we will assume all of the gifts occurred in the same year, but the result would be the same even if spread over several years, with the year given in the example being the last year of the cumulative gift giving. In each example, to determine the gift tax payable credit, one must use the unified credit in effect when the gift was made but the rate schedule in effect when the donor died.

> EXAMPLE 5 - 7. Donor made taxable gifts of $3,500,000 in 1985 and paid gift taxes of $1,444,000. When Donor died in 2001 her taxable estate was $5,000,000. Since the top rate (i.e., 55%) is the same for transfers in 1985 and in 2001, the gift tax payable and gift taxes paid are the same (i.e., $1,444,000).

> EXAMPLE 5 - 8. Donor made taxable gifts of $3,500,000 in 1983 and paid gift taxes of $1,496,500. When Donor died in 2001 her taxable estate was $5,000,000. Since the top rate in 1983 is higher (i.e., this gift goes into the 57% marginal rate) than the top tax rate in 2001, the gift tax payable (i.e., recalculated using the date-of- death rates) is higher than the gift taxes paid, and the credit is only $1,486,500.

> EXAMPLE 5 - 9. Donor made taxable gifts of $5,000,000 in 1999 and paid gift taxes of $2,179,500. When Donor died in 2004 his taxable estate was $20,000,000. Since the rate applied to the gift in 1999 is higher (i.e., the gift goes through marginal rates of 49%, 53%, and 55%) than the tax rate in effect in 2004 (i.e., a maximum of 48%), the gift tax payable is recalculated using date-of-death rates resulting in a credit that is lower than the $2,009,500 gift taxes actually paid.

Third, the tax on very large estates has decreased over the years. This is because the top marginal rates have decreased and the unified credit has increased. The top marginal rate drops from 70% for estates above $5 million in 1977 to 45% for estates above $2 million in 2007. The unified credit has increased over the years. The only period it remained steady was from 1987 through 1997 when a unified credit of $192,800 covered a taxable transfer of $1 million. The Taxpayer Relief Act of 1997 started it rising, and EGTRRA accelerated the increase through the year 2009 when it is supposed to reach $1,455,800 which translates into an applicable exclusion amount of $3.5 million. EGTRRA clouded the picture with its sunset provision that, after the elimination of the estate tax for the year 2010, restores both the estate and the gift tax to what it would have been had EGTRRA not become law, e.g., a $1 million applicable exclusion amount and a 55% maximum rate.

Fourth, gifts are valued as of the day given and estates are valued as of the day of the decedent's death. However, estates are allowed to elect an alternate valuation date of six months after the date of death, if certain criteria are met. An estate is allowed to make this *alternative valuation election* only if doing so will decrease (1) the gross estate and (2) the estate tax. It must also decrease the GST tax, if said tax is applicable. If the election is made, any property still held by the estate for the full six months is valued as of the six-month date, rather than the date of death; whereas, assets sold, distributed, or otherwise disposed of during the six-month period are valued as of the date each was transferred.[14] The example that follows demonstrates the application of the alternative valuation election.

> EXAMPLE 5 - 10. Wanda died on June 10, 2006, leaving property to her children. Art, her executor, has determined that the estate qualifies for the alternate valuation. Some of the assets included in her estate and their values at different times following her death were as follows:

	FMV on		
Items:	6/10/06	12/10/06	comments:
Home	$200,000	**$210,000**	Distributed 4/20/07, value $215,000.
HighTeck, Inc.	$40,000	**$15,000**	Distributed 4/20/07, value $12,000.
Old Blue, Inc.	$25,000	**$27,000**	Sold on 1/15/07 for $28,000.
BioDice, Inc.	$50,000	$30,000	Sold on 8/12/06 for **$35,000.**
Bond	$10,000	**$10,500**	Distributed 4/20/07, value $10,200.
Utility Inc.	$112,000	$120,000	Distributed 10/31/06, value **$115,000**.

Those items held the six-month period take as their estate tax value the value at the end of that period, hence: the home, High Teck, Inc., Old Blue, and the bond are scheduled on the return at their value on 12/10/06. Within the six-month period BioDice, Inc., was sold and Utility, Inc., was distributed so they take the sale price and distribution value, respectively. Scheduled values (i.e., what will be used on the estate tax return to determine the tax) are shown in bold. Note that, if alternate value is elected, the date-of-death value is not used (unless one sold or distributed the property on that date, an unlikely event) even if it is lower than the value six months later. The scheduled value determines the basis of each asset for income tax purposes.

Where alternate valuation is elected, the alternate values determine the new basis, except as in the case when it is not elected, items that are income in respect to a decedent (IRD) do not get a step-up in basis. IRD includes those items that would have been income to the decedent had he lived, e.g., pension funds, IRA accounts, gain still to be recognized on an installment sell.

The marital deduction. Since 1982, virtually all transfers to a *spouse*, whether made during lifetime or at death, have been tax-free; the amount of the transfer is treated as a "marital" deduction from the total gross estate or gross gifts. A brief history of the gift tax and estate tax marital deductions is described next.

The *gift tax marital deduction* was first enacted in 1948 to equalize tax treatment for married taxpayers in common law and community property states. It allowed a deduction for up to 50% of the value of noncommunity property gifts made to a spouse. TRA 76 changed this limit to 100% of the first $100,000, no deduction for the next $100,000, and 50% for all amounts exceeding $200,000.

The *estate tax marital deduction* was also first enacted in 1948, also to equalize tax treatment across the states. Its amount was limited to one half of the adjusted gross estate. TRA 76 changed this limit to the greater of $250,000 or one half of the adjusted gross estate, subject to further adjustments for any gift tax marital deduction taken and for property held as community property. The *adjusted gross estate* was defined essentially as the decedent's separate property, reduced by deductions for funeral and administration expenses, claims against the estate, and losses during administration.

The *present* 100% "unlimited" gift and estate tax marital deductions became effective in 1982.[15] In 1988 the marital deduction was eliminated for transfers to non-U.S. citizen spouses taking place after November 10, 1988,[16] unless certain arrangements are made, such as placing the transferred property in special trusts called qualified domestic trusts (QDOT's) or the surviving spouse becomes a citizen before the estate tax return is filed (even if filed late).[17] We will cover transfers to non-citizen spouses in more detail later in the book, but for now we will focus on the basics.

EXAMPLE 5 - 11. Last year, Wilder gave property worth $10 million to his wife, Simba, a U.S. citizen. Although Wilder's "gross gift" was $10 million, his taxable gift is reduced to zero by the unlimited marital deduction. Thus, there is no tentative tax.

EXAMPLE 5 - 12. Based on the facts in the prior example, assume instead that Wilder died last year leaving his entire $10 million estate to his wife. His taxable estate and tentative tax are zero, as a result of subtracting the $10 million marital deduction from the $10 million gross estate.

EXAMPLE 5 - 13. On Henry's death in 2004, his will provided that his entire estate worth a net of $10 million goes outright to his wife, Kioko. Although she has lived in the U.S. for over 40 years, Kioko kept her Japanese citizenship and did not become a citizen of the United States. If she does not arrange to have the portion above the AEA placed in a QDOT, the estate will have to pay estate taxes of $4,065,000. Note that Henry's estate has an AEA of $1,500,000; it is only the marital deduction that is lost. So, to avoid the estate tax, Kioko must place assets worth at least $8,500,000 in a QDOT or she must become a U.S. citizen before the estate tax return is filed.

The current unlimited marital deduction will be examined in greater detail in Chapters 9 and 10 when we cover estate planning using multiple trusts.

Unlimited charitable deduction. When determining transfer taxes, there is a 100% deduction for gifts or bequests made to qualified charities. Contrast this with income tax law, which limits the amount that can be deducted based on the type of gift, the nature of the charity (e.g., private foundation versus public charity), and the donor's adjusted gross income. We will reserve for a later discussion the complexities that arise when charitable gifts are made using trust arrangements that benefit both family members and charities.

Calculating the Estate Tax - Basic Model

We start our study of the calculation of the estate tax by considering estates where the decedent did not make any post-1976 taxable gifts and died after 2004 when the state death tax credit is no longer relevant. The steps in making this calculation are shown in Table 5 - 1.

TABLE 5 - 1 Federal Estate Tax (Form 706) Basic Model - **No** Prior Gifts

---

Gross estate	$xxx,xxx
Less: Total deductions	(xx,xxx)
Leaves: Taxable estate	$xxx,xxx
Calculate: Tentative estate tax	$x,xxx,xxx
Less: Unified credit	(xxx,xxx)
Less: Other credits (rare)	(xx,xxx)
Equals: federal estate tax	$xxx,xxx

EXAMPLE 5 - 14. When he died in early 1997, Gregg left his entire estate to his three children. The gross estate was valued at $5,840,000. Total debts were $315,000 and expenses of administration were $55,000. He had made no post-1976 taxable gifts. His estate tax is as follows:

Gross Estate	$5,840,000
- Debts & expenses	($370,000)
= Taxable estate = Estate tax base	$5,470,000
Tentative tax on estate tax base	$2,649,300
- Unified credit	($192,800)
= Federal estate tax (total death taxes for most estates)	$2,456,500

State Death Taxes

Through to 2004, the federal law allowed at least a partial credit for state inheritance or estate taxes.[18] EGTRRA eliminated the credit for deaths after 2004.[19] However, estates that must pay a state death tax are allowed to deduct the amount of the tax from the gross estate in arriving at the taxable estate.[20] Prior to the elimination of this credit, about 33 states had laws whereby the state collected death taxes equal to the federal state death tax credit; this type of state death tax was referred to as a pick-up tax since the state "picked up" the amount that was allowed as a federal credit.

The other 17 states have an inheritance or estate tax separated from the federal taxing scheme and some of the pick-up tax states have switched to an inheritance tax or a state estate tax in the wake of the elimination of the federal credit for state death taxes. The rate schedule for the federal State Death Tax Credit is found in Appendix A, Table 3A and Table 3B. For the next two examples, rather than calculating the state death tax credit, use the ETAX program. For the second problem, for 2005, show the gross estate at $1,550,000 and a deduction of $16,900 for the inheritance taxes.

> EXAMPLE 5 - 15. Craig, a resident of Arizona, died in 2004 leaving his estate to relatives. The taxable estate was valued at $1,550,000. Since Arizona is a pick-up tax state, the total tax is $22,500, the state death tax credit is $16,900 and the federal tax is $5,600. If Craig died in 2005, all else being the same, the tax would still total $22,500 but it would all go to the federal government and none to Arizona.

> EXAMPLE 5 - 16. Similar facts to the last example, Rachel, a resident of Indiana, died in 2004 leaving her estate to relatives. The taxable estate was valued at $1,550,000; however, Indiana has its own inheritance tax. Assume that the inheritance tax was $16,900. The total tax is again $22,500, the state death tax credit is $16,900, the federal tax is $5,600, and the heirs are no worse off than had there been no inheritance tax. On the other hand, if Rachel died in 2005, the estate would owe $16,900 in inheritance taxes. These would be deductible on the estate tax return (taxable estate of $1,533,100 instead of $1,550,000) and the federal tax would be $14,895. Hence the total taxes would be $31,795 instead of $22,500, so the heirs receive almost $9,000 less.

Gift Tax

We start with simple gifts, ones where the donor made no prior taxable gifts, then move to examples where the donor has made prior gifts. Next we go to a simple taxable estate, one where the donor made no prior post-1976 taxable gifts. Finally, we look at an estate where the decedent had made post-1976 taxable gifts.

A copy of the Federal Gift Tax Return, Form 709, is included on the "Teaching Aids" CD ROM that came with this book (see file "Form 709 Gift Tax.pdf"). The return illustrates the gift tax scheme. The *donor* is responsible for filing the return and paying the tax. The return is due on April 15 of the year following the taxable gifts. An extension to file the donor's income tax return acts as an automatic extension (to the same due date) of the donor's gift tax return. If the donor fails to pay the gift tax, the donee is secondarily liable for payment of the tax (up to the value of his or her gift).

Annual exclusion. Any donor can give to anyone (i.e., to any donee) gifts with a value up to $10,000 during any calendar year without reporting it and, of course, without it reducing the donor's unified credit or available AEA. This exclusion from the transfer tax is called the gift tax *annual exclusion*. The $10,000 amount has been indexed for inflation starting for years after 1998, with 1997 being the base year. Since the indexed amount is to be rounded down to the next lower multiple of $1,000, the change for the next several years will occur about every three or four years, assuming inflation remains low.[21] Below is a summary of the changes past and expected.

Changes in the Annual Exclusion

Years	1955 - 81	1982 - 2001	2002 - 05	2006 - 09
Annual exclusion	$3,000	$10,000	$11,000*	$12,000*

* Note: At the time this is being written it is anticipated that the increase to $12,000 is expected to occur in 2006 but it might not happen until 2007. Likewise, the increase to $13,000 is likely to occur in 2010 but, depending on inflation, it could occur the year before or the year after. The examples will assume that the above table is correct. Check the author's website, Sushibrain.com, for updates on indexed figures.

> EXAMPLE 5 - 17. In 2005, Warren gave $30,000 cash to his son, Bob, and a boat valued at $15,000 to his fishing buddy, Bill. Assuming no other deductions, and that Warren made no other gifts that year, his current taxable gifts for the year would equal $23,000. The first portion of Warren's gift tax return would look as follows:
>
> | | |
> |---|---|
> | Total current year's gross gifts | $45,000 |
> | Less: Annual exclusions and deductions | ($22,000) |
> | Equals: Current taxable gifts | $23,000 |

> EXAMPLE 5 - 18. In 2007, Mary gave an apartment building worth $975,000 to her three children as tenants in common. She also gave her brother Frank a used car worth $11,500. She would report gross gifts of $975,000 and taxable gifts, after taking the three annual exclusions, of $939,000. The gift to Frank is not reported since it is below the annual exclusion amount.

To qualify for the annual exclusion, the gift must be one of a *present interest*, meaning that the donee has immediate access to the gift for use and enjoyment.[22] Thus, a gift to an irrevocable trust giving one person a life estate and another the remainder creates two gifts, only one of which qualifies for the annual exclusion. The value of the life estate qualifies for the annual exclusion because it is a gift of a present interest, but the remainder does not qualify because it is a gift of a future interest.

When Congress eliminated the marital deduction for transfers to non-U.S. citizen spouses, it created a special $100,000 annual exclusion for gifts between spouses where the donee is a non-citizen. This is another indexed value, with 1997 as the base year. As of 2005 it reached $117,000. This annual exclusion is in lieu of the regular annual exclusion, i.e., when making a gift to a non-citizen spouse, the donor-spouse uses this special one and does not get to use both.

EXAMPLE 5 - 19. In 2005, Marcus gave stock worth $180,000 to his wife Lorena. He is a citizen of the United States. Lorena is a legal resident but she has kept her Mexican citizenship. Marcus must file a gift tax return, claiming a $117,000 annual exclusion (the indexed amount for 2005), hence the taxable gift is $63,000.

First-time taxable gifts. The steps for calculating the gift tax for a donor who has made no prior taxable gifts are summarized here and in Table 5 - 2). Remember that the annual exclusions is an indexed $10,000 and is available for each donee each calendar year. The deductions are for the marital transfers, charitable transfers, attached mortgages or liens.

TABLE 5 - 2 Federal Gift Tax (Form 709) Basic Model - **No** Prior Gifts

---

Total current year's gross gifts	$xxx,xxx
Less: Annual exclusion(s) and deductions	(xxx,xxx)
Equals: Total taxable gifts	$xxx,xxx
Calculate: Tentative tax on total taxable gifts	$xxx,xxx
Less: unified credit (not to exceed tentative tax)	(xxx,xxx)
Equals: Current gift tax	$xx,xxx

EXAMPLE 5 - 20. In 2006, Gretchen made a gift of GnuCo stock worth $432,000 to her sister, Ophelia. Gretchen had never made a taxable gift before. The tentative tax on a $420,000 taxable gift is $128,600. When $128,600 of Gretchen's unified credit is applied, no gift taxes are due. Remember, a gift tax unified credit of $345,800 is available in 2006.

EXAMPLE 5 - 21. In 2007, Francis made gifts of 1,000 shares of RenCo stock worth $1,850,000. His brother, Peter, received 500 shares and his sister, Patricia, received the other 500 shares. The tentative tax on taxable gifts of $1,826,000 (this time there are two $12,000 annual exclusions) is $702,500 and after application of the $345,800 gift tax unified credit the tax owed is $356,700. To determine the tentative tax, go to Table 1, find the bracket this taxable gift falls within ($1,500,000 to $2,000,000) and multiple the bracket percent (i.e., 45%) times the portion of the taxable gift that exceeds the bottom of the bracket, then add the product to the tentative tax for $1,500,000, hence: 45% * ($1,826,000 - $1,500,000) + $555,800 = $702,500.

EXAMPLE 5 - 22. In 2005, Jessica made a gift of real estate worth $1,783,000 to her friend Jonathan. Jessica had never made a taxable gift before. The tentative tax on a $1,772,000 taxable gift is $678,200. After Jessica's unified credit is applied to the tentative tax, the result is $332,400 tax due, i.e., $678,200 - $345,800 = $332,400. We will continue this example a little later to show how the gift affects Jessica's estate tax.

Gifts with prior taxable gifts. Where there have been prior gifts, the steps for calculating the gift tax for new gifts are as follows (see Table 3): the FMV's for all current period (during calendar year) gifts are determined; the annual exclusions and deductions (marital, charitable, and mortgages or liens attached to the property transferred) are subtracted from the current year's FMV (the gross gifts amount) to arrive at current taxable gifts; the current taxable gifts are added to the taxable gifts for prior years to determine the total taxable gifts; then, using the tax rate table, a tentative tax is calculated for both the prior years' cumulative taxable gifts and the total taxable gifts; from the tentative tax on the total taxable gifts, the tentative tax on prior taxable gifts is subtracted to arrive at the tentative tax on current period taxable gifts; the unused unified credit is determined by subtracting the unified credit used for prior years' post-1976 taxable gifts from the total unified credit allowable for the current year; and, finally, the unused unified credit (the credit still available) is subtracted from the tentative tax for current gifts to determine the gift tax that must be paid.

If the total value of gifts during the year to a particular donee are less than the annual exclusion amount, then those gifts do not need to be reported on the gift tax return (i.e., they will not appear on Form 709). In working problems, students must be careful not to take a full annual exclusion unless the value of the gift exceeds the annual exclusion amount. The best advice is to just ignore those outright gifts to one person where the cumulative value for the year is less than the annual exclusion amount. Of course the preceding advice assumes that the gift is one of a present interest (e.g., an outright gift of property), since there is no annual exclusion available for gifts of a future interest.

TABLE 5 - 3   Federal Gift Tax (Form 709) Overview Model - **With** Prior Gifts

---

Total current year's gross gifts	$xxx,xxx
Less: Annual exclusion(s) and deductions	(xx,xxx)
Equals: Current taxable gifts	$xxx,xxx
Plus: Total prior taxable gifts	xx,xxx
Equals: Total (current and prior) taxable gifts	$xxx,xxx
Calculate: Tentative tax on total taxable gifts	$xxx,xxx
Less: Tentative tax on total prior taxable gifts	(xx,xxx)
Leaves: Tentative tax on current taxable gifts	$xxx,xxx
Less: Unused unified credit (not to exceed tentative tax)	(xx,xxx)
Equals: Current gift tax	$xxx,xxx

For each example below, note that it is the taxable amount of prior gifts (not the gross amount) that boosts the current year's gifts into the appropriate marginal rates. We must also take into account that the earlier taxable gifts used up some (or all) of the unified credit.

EXAMPLE 5 - 23. In 2004, Rosa gave MopCo stock worth $731,000 to her friend, Gerry. The gift tax is calculated as follows:

Total current year's gross gifts	$731,000	
- Annual exclusions	($11,000)	
= Current taxable gifts		$720,000
+ Total prior taxable gifts		$0
= Total taxable gifts		$720,000
Tentative tax on total taxable gifts		$403,200
- Tentative tax on prior taxable gifts		($128,600)
= Tentative tax on current taxable gifts		$274,600
- Unused unified credit [$345,800 - $128,600]		($217,200)
Equals: Current gift tax		$57,400

Generally, it was not necessary to recalculate the tentative tax on the prior taxable gifts since that figure was already available. We have this luxury of just picking up the tentative tax on the prior gifts from the earlier calculation only if the highest marginal rates applicable to the prior gift are the same as would have been applied had the gift been made in the present year. The top marginal rate is decreasing but this affects only taxable gifts that exceed $2,000,000. Where prior period gifts exceed this threshold, it is necessary to recalculate the tentative tax in order to arrive at the correct tentative tax for the current year's taxable gifts.

EXAMPLE 5 - 24. In 2006, Rosa gave gold bars worth $854,000 to George, her favorite former teacher, and bonds worth $980,000 to her friend, Samantha. The gift tax was calculated as follows:

Total current taxable gifts	$1,834,000	
- Annual exclusions	($24,000)	
= Current taxable gifts		$1,810,000
+ Prior period gifts		$720,000
= Total taxable gifts		$2,530,000
Tentative tax on total taxable gifts		$1,024,600
- Tentative tax on prior taxable gifts		($237,200)
= Tentative tax on current taxable gifts		$787,400
- Unused unified credit [$345,800 - $345,800]		$108,600
Equals: Current gift tax		$678,800

In this example, neither the prior taxable gifts nor the tentative tax on prior taxable gifts had to be calculated, since both figures were already available. The prior taxable gifts were the total gifts from the last taxable period reduced by the allowable annual exclusions. The tentative tax was calculated as one of the steps in determining the gift tax for the earlier period. However, see what happens in the next example as the prior period gifts are now over $2,000,000, hence they were taxed at a rate higher than in effect for the present year's gifts.

EXAMPLE 5 - 25. In 2008, Rosa gave her brother Herbert real estate worth $1,258,000. The gift tax is calculated as follows:

Total current taxable gifts	$1,258,000	
- Annual exclusions	($12,000)	
= Current taxable gifts		$1,246,000
+ Prior period gifts		$2,530,000
= Total taxable gifts		$3,776,000
Tentative tax on total taxable gifts		$1,580,000
- Tentative tax on prior taxable gifts		($1,019,300)
= Tentative tax on current taxable gifts		$560,700
- Unused unified credit [$345,800 - $345,800]		$0
Equals: Current gift tax		$560,700

In the above example, the tentative tax on Rosa's prior taxable gifts in 2008 is less than the tentative tax calculated for 2007; this is because the top rate falls from 46% to 45%. Using the ETAX program, put $2,530,000 in as the taxable gifts (without any prior year gifts) and put 2008 in as the year. Note that the tentative tax is $1,019,300. Now change the year to 2006 and the tentative tax is $1,024,600. Consider this–since the entire 2008 current gift of $1,246,000 is being taxed at the top marginal rates (i.e., the prior year taxable gifts exceed $2,000,000), you can take a short cut by just multiplying $1,246,000 by 45% to yield the gift tax of $560,700.

Complex Estate Tax Issues

Estates with prior taxable gifts. Here, we put it all together. The estate tax for an estate with post-1976 taxable gifts is calculated taking those gifts into account (see Table 5 - 4 below). These gifts are referred to as *adjusted taxable gifts*. They are adjusted in the sense that the gross value has been reduced by the annual exclusion and that all gifts that qualified for the marital or charitable deduction are excluded, hence we are only working with the taxable amount. The sole purpose of the adjusted taxable gifts coming into the estate tax equation is to move the decedent's taxable estate up into the appropriate marginal rates. The rates are appropriate in the sense that we now have a unified transfer tax system and the earlier taxable gifts have already occupied the lower marginal rates. Similar to what was done for gifts, start with the gross estate (typically, the FMV of all that the decedent owned at the date of death); subtract debts, expenses, gifts to a spouse or to charities, and other deductions (including any inheritance tax) to arrive at the taxable estate; add the adjusted taxable gifts to determine the total estate tax base; use the tax rate table to determine the tentative tax on the total tax base; from the tentative tax, subtract the gift taxes payable credit for post-1976 gifts (for most estates, the gift taxes payable will be the same as the total gift taxes paid on the post-1976 gifts but keep in mind the decreasing marginal rate problem); subtract the unified credit to arrive at the federal estate tax.

To calculate the gift tax payable credit, one must add all the taxes paid, NOT the tentative tax on those prior gifts. The gift taxes paid (payable) is the amount in excess of the available unified credit. Because the entire prior adjusted taxable gifts (post-1976) are included in the tax base, the full unified credit is used in the calculation.

TABLE 5 - 4 Federal Estate Tax (Form 706) Overview Model - **With** Prior Gifts

---

Gross estate	$xxx,xxx
Less: Total deductions	(xxx,xxx)
Leaves: Taxable estate	xxx,xxx
Plus: Adjusted taxable gifts (post-1976)	xx,xxx
Equals: Estate tax base	$xxx,xxx
Calculate: Tentative estate tax	$xxx,xxx
Less: Gift taxes payable on post-1976 taxable gifts	(xxx,xxx)
Less: Unified credit	(xxx,xxx)
Less: Other credits (rare)	(xx,xxx)
Equals: Federal estate tax	$xxx,xxx

The United States Estate (and Generation-Skipping Transfer) Tax Return, Form 706, is included on the "Teaching Aids" CD ROM (see file "Form 706 Estate Tax.pdf"). The return is commonly referred to as the 706. The due date for the 706 is nine months after the date of death. Hence, the 706 for the estate of a wealthy person who died on May 15th is due February 15th of the following year unless that falls on a holiday or weekend, in which case the return is due on the next business day. We will cover extensions to file and to pay the tax later.

EXAMPLE 5 - 26. Refer back to the gifts given by Jessica in EXAMPLE 5 - 22. Jessica died on March 10, 2009, and left her estate to her four children. Her estate was worth $5,840,000, debts were $315,000, and expenses totaled $55,000. Her estate taxes were due December 10, 2010 (nine months to the day following her death). Taking into account the gift she made in 2005, her estate tax is as follows:

Gross Estate	$5,840,000
- Debts & expenses	($370,000)
- Marital & charitable deductions	$0
= Taxable estate	$5,470,000
+ Adjusted taxable gifts (post-1976)	$1,772,000
= Estate tax base	$7,242,000
Tentative tax on estate tax base	$3,139,700
- Gift tax payable on post-1976 taxable	($332,400)
- Unified credit	($1,455,800)
= Federal Estate Tax	$1,351,500

As was demonstrated with the Rosa gift tax examples, where prior gifts exceed $2,000,000 the tax on the prior gifts must be recalculated. In the present discussion, this means using the rates in effect for the year the donor died. Even if the decedent made taxable gifts that exceeded the gift AEA of $1,000,000, the estate will get the benefit of the higher estate AEA, i.e., if the decedent's adjusted taxable gifts exceed the estate AEA for the year decedent died, the estate tax should equal the top marginal rate for that year times the taxable estate, less the difference between the gift tax AEA and the estate's AEA.

> EXAMPLE 5 - 27. In 2004, Jimmy made a gift of stock worth $4,011,000 to his daughter Claudia. He paid gift taxes of $1,395,000. When he died in 2009, Claudia was the sole heir of his $10,000,000 taxable estate. The tentative tax on the $14,000,000 tax base is $6,180,800. The gift tax payable credit is $1,335,000. This is less than the amount of gift tax actually paid because we must recalculate to come up with what would have been paid using the marginal rates in effect for 2009. Subtracting the gift tax payable credit and the $1,455,800 unified credit results in an estate tax of $3,390,000. We know that the top marginal rate is 45% and the gifts already occupied the lower marginal rates, so why is the estate tax not exactly $4,500,000? Because the estate is getting the benefit of the increased unified credit for estates compared to the gift tax unified credit, i.e., $4,500,000 - ($1,455,800 - $345,800) = $3,390,000.

Other credits. There are four basic estate tax credits: the unified credit, the credit for gift tax payable, the credit for tax on prior transfers, and the credit for foreign death taxes. We have already covered the unified credit and the credit for gift taxes payable; the other two credits just mentioned occur less frequently and are covered briefly at the end of the next chapter. The prior transfer and the foreign death tax credits are introduced in Chapter 6. The prior transfer credit as it relates to life estates is covered in detail in Chapter 10.

FEDERAL GENERATION-SKIPPING TRANSFER TAX

Before EGTRRA, one fundamental policy objective of federal wealth transfer taxation was to tax all individual wealth in excess of a certain amount each time it passed to the next generation.

Only a tax that explicitly addresses the generational relationship between transferor and transferee can consistently tax wealth as it passes to succeeding generations. The GST tax is designed to meet that objective. The GST tax is levied when a transfer is made (by gift or bequest) to a person two or more generations below the donor. Persons in these lower generations are called *skip persons*. Pre-EGTRRA law gave every donor a $1,000,000 GST exemption, so most people have not been too concerned about this tax. EGTRRA makes it even less of a concern as the exemption equals the estate AEA for years 2004 and after, e.g., for a person who dies in 2006 the exemption is $2,000,000.

Gifts covered by the annual exclusion, if made directly to grandchildren (or to any other skip person), are not subject to the GST tax, so they do not use up any of the exemption. There is also a special rule called the predeceased ancestor exception. In general, this rule "moves up" lower generations if the parent in the line of descent dies before the transfer. Generally, the predeceased ancestor exception applies only if the parent was deceased at the time of the transfer or, if the transfer was through a trust, the parent was deceased at the time the trust was first subject to transfer tax. The exception applies to lineal descendants of the transferor and, in some cases, to transfers to collateral heirs. Collateral heirs (nephews/nieces) move up only if the transferor has no living descendants. Where transfers to grandchildren (and to other skip persons) exceed the exemption amount, the tax is horrendous since it is at the highest transfer tax marginal rate (e.g., 46% in 2006 and 45% 2007 to 2009, inclusive) and it is in addition to the gift or estate tax. The GST tax is discussed in more detail in Chapter 17.

ALLOCATION OF DEATH TAXES

Which beneficiaries should bear the burden of death taxes? All of them, or only some? If only some, which ones? If all, should the taxes be shared equally or in proportion to the amount bequeathed? A number of important considerations in determining how to allocate death taxes are examined next.

Statutory Allocation

In the absence of allocation prescribed by the estate plan there are some rules found in federal and state statutes.

Federal law. In the absence of a provision in the will, both federal and state law determine which beneficiaries will share the cost of death taxes. Federal law controls the burden on a few types of assets. The Internal Revenue Code provides that the pro rata share of estate tax on life insurance,[23] property subject to a general power of appointment,[24] QTIP property[25] (usually at the second death), and property included in the gross estate because of a retained interest[26] is payable out of those assets.

State law. Under state law, with regard to all assets owned by the decedent, the old common law rule provided that death taxes were paid from the residuary probate estate. However, most states have changed this rule by enacting an *equitable apportionment statute* that spreads the tax burden proportionately among all of the beneficiaries receiving part of the taxable estate. Thus, even recipients of nonprobate assets, such as property held by the decedent in joint ownership, would owe a portion of the tax. Of course, as a general rule the shares going to charities and spouses do not incur a tax burden, since their distributions are deducted before one arrives at the taxable estate.

Estate Plan Allocations

The estate plan can override these federal and state directives by expressly including a tax clause in the will or trust.

Residuary tax clause. Some attorneys routinely draft wills containing a tax clause embracing the old common law rule: all taxes will be paid out of the residuary estate. Payment of taxes from the residue can speed up the probate process by making it unnecessary to obtain reimbursement from non-residuary and nonprobate beneficiaries. In addition, recipients of specific non-residuary bequests of illiquid assets are not forced to search for the required cash. And paying the taxes out of the residue may be especially helpful if the will specifically bequeaths certain assets over which the testator does not wish the tax burden to fall. For example, if the testator leaves only one relatively illiquid asset, such as a piano, to a particular beneficiary, should that person have to pay any transfer taxes attributable to it? Most people would probably say no unless that beneficiary is known to have considerable wealth, or at least access to a reasonable amount of discretionary liquid assets.

Problems with the residuary tax clause. There are several situations where a residuary tax clause may conflict with the testator's wishes. First, the testator may specifically bequeath an asset such as a closely held business that comprises a very large portion of the entire estate. If the tax clause allocates the entire tax burden to the residue, the effect may be to radically reduce it or eliminate it entirely.

> EXAMPLE 5 - 28. When she died in 2002 Trudy's estate plan left her business to William, her son by her first marriage, and the residue of her estate to Dennis, her current husband. The plan specified that the interest to her son was "free of all estate taxes." The business was appraised at $4 million and the balance of the estate at $3 million. Because the marital share was forced to bear the tax burden, Dennis received only $140,000. Note that this interrelated tax calculation can be demonstrated using ETAX. For the gross estate enter $7 million (i.e., 7000000) and for deductions enter $3 million - B19. The total estate tax is $2,860,000 on a taxable estate of $6,860,000.

Often testators view their residuary legatees as the primary "objects of their bounty" and want them to receive as much wealth as possible. An apportionment tax clause might more closely meet this objective.

Whatever the provisions of state law, the testator should consider including a tax clause in the will or trust for greater certainty. Rarely will the courts override a tax-apportionment clause or if there is none, the application of a statute, even if the outcome seems unfair to some beneficiaries. Consequently, the alternatives should be carefully considered.

IMPERFECT UNIFICATION

Although this chapter introduces the Unified Transfer Tax, there are many ways in which the three taxes (gift, estate, and generation transfer) are not really unified. Indeed, many transfer tax savings techniques take advantage of the fact that our "unified" transfer tax system is less than perfectly unified. To appreciate fully how these strategies work, one should consider how perfect unification might function and how the imperfections inherent in the present system can be exploited to transfer wealth with the least possible transfer tax cost. The following material will first consider what a perfectly unified tax system might be like and contrast it with our present imperfectly unified system. An ongoing example will illustrate the major points.

Perfect unification. With perfect unification of the three transfer taxes, an individual would be *indifferent*, from a total transfer tax planning point of view, as to whether the transfer should be a lifetime gift or a bequest. Under perfect unification, total transfer taxes would be the same whether an individual owned property at death or whether that person gave the property away during life.

To achieve perfect unification of the transfer tax system, all of the following conditions would have to be met:

No special deductions. There would need to be a uniform system of deductions and credits for all gift and estate transfers. Otherwise, individuals would prefer to make that transfer which enjoyed the shelter of higher deductions or credits. As it is now, the annual exclusion favors lifetime gifts because there is no similar exclusion at death. Also, transfers to charity during life result in an income tax deduction (while removing the transferred property from the transfer tax base), but a charitable bequest, while it removes the property from the taxable estate, results in no income tax savings.

Equal applicable exclusion amounts. The AEA should be the same for gifts, estates, and GST.[27] What this really means, of course, is that all three should have the same unified credit. Generally, such has been the case, but with EGTRRA, the AEA for estates increases through repeal in 2010 whereas the gift tax AEA remains at $1,000,000. The GST tax is grafted onto the estate and gift tax in a way that makes it impossible to even think about having a common AEA for it.

Tax all gratuitous transfers at donor's death. All taxes would be levied at the same point in time, namely when the donor died. This avoids the time value of money problem inherent in making gifts large enough to require the payment of gift taxes, and it avoids having the gift taxes paid reduce the tax base. All prior gifts made by the transferor would be added to the transferor's current transfer tax base. No gifts would be excluded, including gifts of very small value (even less than the annual exclusion amount) and gifts made many years ago. The record keeping nightmare that would result will keep this from ever being reality.

All prior gifts would be included in the estate tax base at their *date-of-death value*, not date-of-gift value. Again, the tracking of the transferred property in order to ascertain its date-of-death value would be another nightmare that will keep this from becoming part of the law. However, it would close some loopholes, such as donors greatly diminishing the value of a gift by retaining an interest in the property for a period of years and only counting the value of the remainder interest as a gift. This will be discussed when we consider Grantor Retained Income Trusts in Chapter 12. It might also reduce, if not entirely eliminate, donor's discounting the value of fractional interest gifts, since such gifts would be "merged" when the donor died. This statement will make more sense after we have covered in later chapters the treatment of fractional interests and family limited partnerships.

By not collecting transfer taxes until the donor dies, gift taxes would not be removed from the transfer tax base. As it is now, the time value of money makes gift taxes more expensive than death taxes; however, if the donor lives three years after making the gift that generated the gift tax, the payment of the tax results in a deduction from the estate tax base. Discussed in Chapter 6 is a special rule that requires inclusion in the gross estate all gift taxes paid on gifts made within three years of the donor's death.

Bring the GST tax into line. Only one tax rate schedule should be applied to all transfers treated cumulatively regardless of whether made during life or at death as has been the case since 1977 for estates and gifts but not for the GST tax. Given the purpose of the GST tax and the fact that it applies only to transfers to skip persons, it is hard to imagine how it could be unified with the other two.

Uniform basis rules. The timing of a gratuitous transfer should not affect the basis of the property; either it should remain the same (as is generally the case with gifts) or it should change to its fair market value as of the date of transfer (as is generally the case with transfers at death). As it is now, there are two basic rules, one for gifts and one for estates. If the law changed to just one rule, it would almost have to be for estates to change to the gift tax rule (i.e., a carry-over basis) since it would otherwise be too easy to obtain a step-up in basis if all one had to do was to make a gift of the property. The basis rules are covered in detail in Chapter 8, but it is enough at this time to know that, for most gifts, the donee's basis is the same as whatever the donor's basis was immediately before the gift.

Summarizing, under perfect unification, total transfer taxes would be the same whether an individual retained all property until death or whether he or she had made lifetime gifts. Thus, the present system's failure to completely unify estate and gift taxes can yield substantial transfer tax savings for persons owning medium to larger amounts of wealth. Further discussion of these issues will be deferred to Chapters 11 and 12 where we discuss various lifetime transfers.

CONCLUSION

This chapter has introduced federal wealth transfer taxation, emphasizing the tax calculations. The next two chapters cover the estate and gift taxes with regard to matters that are less quantitative in nature.

QUESTIONS AND PROBLEMS

For these problems use the following annual exclusions: $3,000 for 1977 - 1981; $10,000 for 1982 - 2002; $11,000 for 2002 - 2005; $12,000 for 2006-2008. At the time these problems were written, it was uncertain whether the exclusion would reach $12,000 in 2006 or 2007 but the expectation was by 2006. It is likely to increase to $13,000 by 2009. For problems starting with "Use ETAX," you should use the tax calculation program from the "Teaching Aids" disk that came with this textbook rather than making the calculations yourself. However, being able to do the calculations greatly aids in your understanding of this material, hence do the rest of the tax problems using the tables and a calculator.

1. What kind of tax is the estate tax? Briefly explain how it works.

2. (a) Describe the chronological progression of the amounts of the unified credit. (b) What is the term that, because of the Taxpayer Relief Act of 1997, means the largest amount that can be transferred by gift or through a decedent's estate without generating a transfer tax? (c) In what sense is this term a misnomer?

3. Outline the history of federal wealth transfer taxation with emphasis on the changes that took place in 1977, 1982, 1984, 1998, and 2001.

4. Why would the imposition of an estate tax without an accompanying gift tax be largely ineffective?

5. (a) What is the annual exclusion? (b) Is it available for transfers to non-relatives? (c) When did it increase to $10,000 and what was it immediately

before the increase? (d) Explain indexing for inflation as it relates to the annual exclusion.

6. (a) What is the highest marginal estate tax rate for the years from 2005 through 2009? For the years in question, at what level taxable estate does the highest rate begin? (b) What is the highest it has ever been and at what level taxable estate was it applied?

7. In what sense is the future of the estate and gift tax uncertain beyond the year 2010?

8. We know that "applicable exclusion amount" (AEA) means the amount that can pass estate or gift tax-free. We also know that the amount for gifts is $1 million and as of 2006 is $2 million for estates, yet nowhere in the calculation of either tax is the AEA subtracted. Show, using a $3,000,000 taxable estate for a decedent dying in 2007, how the unified credit is the real source of the tax shelter and how any given unified credit relates to the AEA. Compare to the correct calculation what happens if one subtracts the estate AEA and then applies the marginal rates to the remaining $1,000,000.

9. Susan died in 2005 leaving a taxable estate of exactly $2,000,000. Cathy died in 2007; she also left a taxable estate of $2,000,000. Demonstrate that the estate AEA is really a stand-in for the unified credit using these two estates in your explanation.

10. Describe the unlimited marital deduction. What is the rule for gifts to non-U.S. citizen spouses?

11. In 2004, Tara gave John, her English husband, real estate with an appraised value of $500,000. It was her only taxable gift to him for the year. The next year she gave him stock worth $350,000. How much is reported each year as a taxable gift? [Before answering, check Table 7, Estate Planning Indexed Values, in Appendix A.]

12. Ken died in 2006 leaving a taxable estate (i.e., after all allowable deductions) of $2,960,000. Calculate the estate tax.

13. Sam died in 2006; assuming he made no prior taxable gifts, how large must his estate be before it is subject to the estate tax? How would your answer change if Sam had made a taxable gift of $400,000 in 2003?

14. Marcello died in 2007. His estate went to his two children. The date of death value of the estate was $4,390,000 and allowable deductions (debts, expenses, etc.) were $245,000. Calculate the taxable estate, tentative tax, and the federal estate tax.

15. In the prior problem if Marcello's estate had to pay state inheritance taxes of $130,000 in addition to the $245,000 in debts, expenses, etc., how would that change the amount due?

16. Clarence died in 2006. The date of death value of the estate was $5,930,000 and debts, expenses, etc. were $640,000. His estate was left as follows: $1,500,000 to his wife, $750,000 to United Way, and the residue to his two children by a prior marriage. Calculate the federal estate tax.

17. Brenda died in 2005. The date of death value of the estate was $8,240,000 and debts, expenses, etc. were $436,000. Her estate was left as follows: $2,400,000 to her husband, $500,000 to her university, and the residue to her two children by a prior marriage. The estate also had to pay inheritance taxes of $265,000. Neither the taxes nor the debts, expenses, etc., were charged to bequests going to her husband or to the university. Calculate the federal estate tax.

18. Use the ETAX program: Using as your example a $5,000,000 taxable estate, show how the state death tax credit depends on the year death occurs.

1977	2001	2002	2003	2004	2005

Does it make any difference if the decedent had previously made a $2,500,000 taxable gift?

19. In the past it was said that having a modest state inheritance tax or using the pick-up tax approach did not diminish the amount that beneficiaries of an estate would receive, but that has changed. What is the change? For each of

the following, how did the change affect state revenues and beneficiaries in: (a) states with a pick-up tax; and (b) states with a separate inheritance or estate tax not based on the federal credit?

20. In November of 2005, Ibanez gave his daughter stock worth $940,000. Calculate the adjusted taxable gift, the tentative tax, and the amount of gift tax. What is the due date for filing the return? How would Ibanez get an extension of time in which to file the gift tax return?

21. On June 5, 2006, Rita gave her son stock worth $3,450,000. Calculate the adjusted taxable gift, the tentative tax, and the amount of gift tax. What is the due date for filing the gift tax return?

22. In 2011, Silvia made a gift of stock worth $2,012,000 to her daughter Heather. Assume that the annual exclusion is $12,000. What is the gift tax? [Note that the top rate drops to 35%. At what level will that occur?]

23. Married couple Roy and Ana Marie Gomez are both citizens of the USA. What is the maximum that Roy could give to Ana Marie without paying any gift tax? If he died in 2006, what is the maximum estate he can leave to her without his estate paying any estate tax?

24. In the prior problem, why does it matter whether Ana Marie is a citizen? If Ana Marie is a Mexican national (without dual U.S. citizenship), what would be the maximum outright gift Roy could give in 2005 without using up any unified credit? Maximum before tax would have to be paid?

25. In 2005, Barbara gave her friend, Roger, stock worth $940,000. In 2006, she gave him beach property worth $3,450,000. For the second gift calculate the adjusted taxable gift, the tentative tax, and the amount of gift tax.

26. In 2005, Priscilla gave land worth $1,350,000 to Warren and a yacht worth $160,000 to Michelle. In 2006, she gave stock worth $830,000 to Warren and bonds worth $490,000 to Michelle. Calculate the adjusted taxable gift, the tentative tax on current gifts, and the amount of gift tax for each year.

27. In 2006, Andrew gave land worth $360,000 to Dave, Diane, and Richard. The property was deeded to them as joint tenants. Also in 2006, he gave Josh an airplane worth $450,000. In 2007, he gave Dave, Diane, and Richard $550,000 each. Calculate the adjusted taxable gift, the tentative tax on current gifts, and the amount of gift tax for each year.

28. In 2008, Andrew from the prior problem gave stock worth $1,012,000 to Diane. Use the short-cut method (i.e., taxable gift multiplied by the highest marginal rate) to determine the gift tax.

29. Use ETAX: In 2002, Myra made taxable gifts (i.e., after the annual exclusions) of $2,000,000 and paid gift taxes of $435,000. She died in 2006 leaving a taxable estate (i.e., after all allowable deductions) of $2,960,000. Calculate the estate tax taking the prior gift into account. Compare the resulting tax to the tax in problem 12. Make the following calculation: $2,960,000 * 0.46 - (780,800 - 345,800). What does all of this demonstrate about how the estate tax takes the prior gifts into account?

30. (a) What is the meaning of perfect unification? (b) In what ways is our present unified transfer tax system imperfect? (c) How has EGTRRA made it a little less perfectly unified?

31. Compare the taxes and the net amount going to the children for the following two transfers. Explain the differences. A. In 2007, Sherry makes a gift of stock worth $3,600,000 jointly to her three children. B. The same year, Victor dies leaving his estate worth a net of $3,600,000 to his three children.

32. Use ETAX: In 2002, Evelyn made taxable gifts (i.e., after the annual exclusions) of $4,000,000 and paid gift taxes of $1,430,000. She died in 2006 leaving a taxable estate (i.e., after all allowable deductions) of $2,960,000. Calculate the estate tax taking the prior gift into account. Note that the gift tax payable credit was not the same as the gift tax paid. Compare the result to the taxes determined in problems 12 and 29. Why is the gift tax payable credit the same as the gift tax paid in problem 29 but less than what was paid in this problem? What does this demonstrate about how the estate tax takes the prior gifts into account?

ANSWERS TO QUESTIONS AND PROBLEMS *(odd numbered only)*

1. EGTRRA eliminated the estate tax as of 2010 but included a "sunset" provision that causes the law to disappear by 2011. So unless Congress acts to undo the sunset provision, it will be as if the law was never passed. This would give us an AEA of $1,000,000 and top rates of 55%, with a surcharge for transfers over $10 million. It would also restore the GST tax and the state death tax credit (due to go in 2005). The expectation is that Congress will resolve this before the year 2010.

3. The imposition of a transfer tax at death without an accompanying gift tax would be largely ineffective because very elderly or terminally ill persons could circumvent the tax by making lifetime transfers.

5. (a) The unified credit increased annually from $30,000 in 1977 to $192,800 in 1987. It stayed at that level through 1997. In 1998, it started increasing again and was due to increase to $345,800 in 2006, but EGTRRA accelerated the increase such that the unified credit will be $345,800 in 2002, eventually increasing to $1,455,800.

   (b) The new term is the applicable exclusion amount. The applicable exclusion amount for 2002 is $1,000,000 because the tentative tax on that amount is $345,800, matching the available unified credit for that year.

   (c) The term *applicable exclusion amount* is a misnomer because it implies that the amount is somehow subtracted or not taxed, but technically it is taxed. However, it is covered by the unified credit, therefore amounts less than the applicable exclusion amount will not result in the payment of any transfer taxes.

7. (a) The annual exclusion is an amount that can pass gift tax-free, without using up any of the donor's unified credit. It only applies to gifts of a present interest. [There is one major exception to the present interest requirement. It applies to certain gifts given to benefit minors that meet the requirements of IRC § 2503(c). The exception is discussed later.]

   (b) It is available even for gifts to non-relatives, so be nice to everyone.

   (c) It went from $3,000 in 1981 to $10,000 in 1982.

(d) Indexing means that the $10,000 will increase from time to time, starting in years after 1998, as inflation decreases the purchasing power of the dollar when compared to the base year of 1997. The increases will be in increments of $1,000, with rounding being down to the next lower multiple of $1,000.

9. Computations on a taxable estate of $2 million produce a tentative tax of $780,800. If the death occurred in 2005 when the unified credit is $555,800, the estate would pay taxes of $255,000. If the death occurs in 2007 when the unified credit is $780,800, there is no estate tax to pay. We refer to the amount that is exactly covered by the unified credit as the applicable exclusion amount because an estate of that exact size is excluded from tax due to the unified credit. Of course there is no deduction equal to the AEA.

11. For gifts to a non-citizen spouse, there is a special $100,000 annual exclusion which, due to indexing, was $114,000 in 2004 and $117,000 in 2005. Tara reports $386,000 as a taxable gift for 2004 and $233,000 for 2005.

13. The threshold in 2006 is $2 million. If taxable gifts f $400,000 were made, the threshold would be reduced to $1,600,000.

15. The deductions would increase by $130,000 to $375,000 resulting in an estate tax of $906,750. This is $58,500 less but the estate still comes out behind by $71,500 since it had to pay $130,000 to the state to save $58,500 in federal estate taxes.

17. Taxable estate $4,639,000 (i.e., $8,240,000 - $436,000 - $2,400,000 - $500,000 - $265,000); tentative tax $2,021,130; and estate tax of $1,465,330.

19. The state death tax credit was a dollar-for-dollar credit against the estate tax, therefore so long as the state's death tax was equal or less than the allowable credit, it did not increase the burden on the estate. Indeed, 33 states simply collect the maximum credit (these are called pick-up tax states). In the states with their own separate estate or inheritance tax, if the calculated amount is less than the federal credit allowed, those states have a "soak-up" tax that collects the difference. EGTRRA is decreasing the credit over the period 2002-2004, eliminating it in 2005 (allowing a deduction from the taxable

estate instead). Pick-up tax states will lose all revenue sharing after 2004. The states with their own tax system will lose whatever "soak-up" amount they were collecting under the old law, and the beneficiaries will receive less than they would have under the old system because a deduction will reduce the federal tax much less than would a dollar-for-dollar credit.

21. Adjusted taxable gift of $3,438,000, tentative tax of $1,442,280, less unified credit of $345,800, equals gift tax of $1,096,480. Due: April 15, 2007.

23. No limit for gifts or estates.

25. Adjusted taxable gift of $3,438,000, add adjusted taxable gift of $929,000 for a tax base of $4,367,000, tentative tax of $1,869,620 for total gifts, $318,110 on prior gifts leaves $1,551,510 on current gifts, less unified credit of available of $27,690 (i.e., $345,800 - $318,110) equals gift tax of $1,523,820.

27. 2006: adjusted taxable gifts $762,000 (four annual exclusions); tentative tax $252,980; and gift tax $0.
2007: adjusted taxable gifts $1,614,000; tentative tax $697,020; gift tax $604,200.

29. Estate tax of $926,600 is $485,000 more than without the gifts (see answer to problem 12). Doing the above calculation [i.e., $2,960,000 * 0.46 - (780,800 - 345,800)] results in $926,600 (i.e., the same as the estate tax). This shows us that the gifts used up the lower marginal rates and the estate is moved into the top marginal rate of 46% however the estate is getting the benefit of the $435,000 increase in the unified credit.

31. Even though prior gifts were $4,000,000 instead of $2,000,000, the estate tax remained at $926,600. Although the gift tax paid was $1,430,000, the gift tax payable credit was only $1,355,000 since it had to be recalculated based upon the marginal rates in effect at the time of death. This "correction" is made so that the adjusted taxable gifts just move the estate into the appropriate (i.e., taking cumulative transfers into account) marginal rates without resulting in a refund of previously paid taxes.

ENDNOTES

1. *An Act Laying Duties on stamped Vellum, Parchment, and Paper.* 5th Congress, Sess. 1, Chapter 11. Vol. 1, p. 527. See http://memory.loc.gov/ammem/amlaw/lwsllink.html

2. *An Act to repeal the Internal Taxes.* 7th Congress, Sess. 1, Chapter 19, Vol. 2, p. 148. See http://memory.loc.gov/ammem/amlaw/lwsllink.html

3. 16 Stat. 255-257, Sec. 3.

4. 30 Stat. 464-466.

5. 32 Stat. 97

6. *The Revenue Act of 1916*, 39 Stat. 777-780, 1002.

7. P.L. 94-455.

8. P.L. 97-34.

9. P.L. 105-34

10. P.L. 107-16.

11. The sunset provision was necessary to comply with the Congressional Budget Act of 1974's requirement that revenue changes not create long term budget deficits.

12. *Economic Growth and Tax Relief Reconciliation Act of 2001*, §901. Sunset of Provisions of Act.

13. IRC § 2011. The term "applicable exclusion amount" was added by the Taxpayer Relief Act of 1997.

14. IRC § 2032.

15. Although there is no marital deduction covering outright gifts to a non-citizen spouse, Congress created a special annual exclusion of $100,000 (indexed for inflation) per year.

16. *Technical and Miscellaneous Revnue Act of 1988*, P.L. 100-647.

17. Reg. § 20.2056A-1(b).

18. IRC § 2011(b).

19. IRC § 2011(f).

20. IRC § 2058.

21. IRC § 2503(b)(2).

22. IRC § 2503(b)(1).

23. IRC § 2206.

24. IRC § 2207.

25. IRC § 2207A.

26. IRC § 2207B.

27. From 1/01/1977 through 6/30/1977 the gift tax unified credit was $6,000, for the rest of the year it was $30,000, whereas the estate tax unified credit was $30,000 for the entire year.

CHAPTER 6

The Estate Tax

OVERVIEW

We examine the components of the estate tax in more detail, specifically the gross estate, allowable deductions, and allowable credits. All code sections refer to the Internal Revenue Code (IRC) unless otherwise indicated and are included on the Teaching Aids CD ROM. Generally, there is no need to memorize code section numbers, however some are used by estate planners as shorthand meant to convey a concept, e.g., "a § 2036 problem" with reference to a trust would mean that the settlor had retained certain interests that cause the trust to be included in the settlor's estate. As you begin this study, review Form 706, the U.S. Federal Estate Tax Return, available on the Teaching Aids CD ROM. Our discussion will somewhat follow the organization of the estate tax return.[1] The first page of the tax return walks one through the calculation of the estate tax. The first two lines, the gross estate and allowable deductions, are drawn from the recapitulations that constitute Part five on page three of the return. As discussion begins to focus on a particular code section, take the time to read the code section.

Filing responsibility. In general, a federal estate tax return must be filed for any decedent who was a *citizen* or *resident* of the United States if at the time of death the value of the person's gross estate (regardless of where the property is situated[2]), when added to his or her adjusted taxable gifts, equals or exceeds the estate applicable exclusion amount (AEA) for the year of death.[3] For example, a citizen who dies in 2007, leaving a gross estate of $1,800,000, and who made taxable gifts of $300,000 after 1976, must file a return because the sum exceeds 2007's estate AEA of $2,000,000. Filing is required even if the marital deduction, or debts and expenses, reduces the tax base (i.e., the gross estate plus adjusted taxable gifts less deductions) below the AEA.[4]

Non-citizen, non-residents with property in the U.S. A federal estate tax return must be filed for a decedent *non-citizen, non-resident,* if the person died owning property situated in the United States that was worth more than $60,000.[5] Only the U.S. situs property is taxed,[6] but the estate is entitled to a maximum unified credit of only $13,000.[7] Special rules apply for decedents who are citizens of a U.S. territorial possession, or are U.S. residents but are also citizens of countries having tax treaties with the U.S. Further discussion of estate matters for non-citizen, non-residents is beyond the scope of this text.

Filing the return and paying the tax. The executor is responsible for filing the return and paying the tax.[8] Payment is to the US Treasury. The estate tax return and payment are due nine months to the day after the decedent's death, unless that day is a weekend or a holiday, then they are due the next business day.[9] The return and payment are deemed to be filed or paid on the date of the postmark on the envelope, hence the return is timely filed if postmarked on the due date even if it is received after that date. However, once the return is late, receipt occurs on delivery. An automatic six-month extension of time to file is available by filing Form 4768 so long as the request is made before the due date. Once past the due date, the extension is available only for good cause and one must also explain why the request was not made before the due date.[10] An extension of more than six months might be granted if the executor is abroad.[11] If there is no court-appointed executor (or if he or she fails to pay the tax), persons in actual or constructive possession of any of the decedent's property must file a return, and are liable for the tax to the extent of the value of the property held.[12] This includes surviving joint tenants[13] and the trustee of the decedent's revocable living trust.[14] In Chapter 14, we will discuss extended payment plans for estates with substantial business assets.

Extension to pay tax for reasonable cause. The IRS has discretion under § 6161 to grant a one-year extension to pay the estate tax. This relief is available to any estate on a showing of "reasonable cause." Extensions for good cause can be repeated for a total extended period of 10 years. Be forewarned, the estate must make the first request before the due date of the return, and each subsequent request must be made before the existing extension has expired. If the taxpayer fails to file the request on time, it will be denied no matter how good the reason.

Examples of good cause for extending the time to pay include:

- The estate has illiquid assets or there are liquid assets but they are not yet available to the executor.
- A large part of the estate is in the form of rights to receive payments in the future (royalties, accounts receivable, etc.).
- The estate includes a claim to substantial assets that are being collected through litigation.
- The estate does not have sufficient cash to pay taxes and provide for a family allowance and claims.
- The estate cannot borrow except at rates that would constitute a hardship.

Ordinarily, reasonable cause will not be found merely because liquid assets (e.g., listed securities) must be sold at what the executor considers distressed prices. With an extension to pay, interest will be charged at the late payment rate, however, the interest is deductible on the estate tax return.[15] Generally, to take the interest as a deduction the estate must make a refund claim after the tax and interest are paid.

Deferral of estate tax for a reversion or remainder interest. Section 6163 allows estate tax deferral for that portion of the tax attributed to having a vested reversion or remainder interest included in a decedent's taxable estate. The tax is postponed until six months after the termination of the "precedent" interest, i.e., usually at the death of a beneficiary with a life estate. The termination might occur many years after the decedent's death.

EXAMPLE 6 - 1. When he died, Jake created an irrevocable trust out of a portion of his estate. The trust pays all income to Jake's disabled son, Billy, for his lifetime. Then, the remainder is payable to Jake's daughter, Diane, or to her estate. Diane died in the year 2005. At that time, the trust was worth $500,000, Billy was 80 years old, and the 7520 rate was 6%. The present value of her remainder interest in the trust was $321,980, i.e., $500,000 * 0.64396. Her taxable estate, including the vested remainder, was $3,000,000. The total federal tax on her estate was $695,000, hence her estate was able to defer $74,592, i.e., $695,000 * ($321,980/$3,000,000), until six months after Billy's death. There will be interest to pay on the deferred tax, but it can be claimed as a deduction, thereby reducing the tax.

Penalties and interest. Generally, penalties for not paying taxes when due or failing to file a tax return are the same for income, estate, and gift taxes. The penalty for not paying the tax is equal to ½ % per month, or any portion of a month, times the amount due up to a maximum of 25%, and the penalty for failure to file is 5% per month, or portion thereof, also up to a maximum of 25%. Once the time for filing the return, including any extensions, has passed, mailing the return and the payment does not stop the penalty until the return and payment are actually received. This means that if a return mailed 27 days after the due date arrives at the IRS office four days later, an additional 5% penalty will be due because it is filed in the second month.[16] In circumstances like the one just described, the executor can use one of the private next-day delivery services, and perhaps have the return delivered before the penalty increases. If the return is filed more than 60 days late, then the penalty is not less than the lesser of $100 or 100% of the tax due. The penalty is based upon the net amount due, after taking into account credits and any timely made pre-payments, e.g., payments made with an extension to file request where the taxpayer then failed to file within the time period extended. If the donor files a late return, then only the late filing penalty is assessed for the first five months, i.e., 5% per month rather than 5.5% per month.

> EXAMPLE 6 - 2. Betty died on March 2, 2006. Anthony, as the executor of Betty's estate, estimated the tax owed at $500,000. In the November, he filed Form 4768 asking for a six-month extension to file and a one year extension to pay and included a check in the amount of $500,000 made out to the US Treasury. The due date for filing and paying was December 2, 2006 but the extension gave him until Monday, June 4, 2007, to file and Monday, December 3, 2007 to pay. Unfortunately, Anthony did not file return until January 10, 2008. The return correctly showed the federal tax to be $800,000 and was accompanied by a check for $300,000 to pay what was still owed. The IRS assessed the maximum late filing penalty of 25%, and a late payment penalty for two months (remember, any month or part thereof) of 1%, for total penalties of $78,000.

In addition there are accuracy and fraud penalties. If the failure to file is due to a fraudulent attempt to hide estate assets, the penalty for not filing is 15% per month instead of 5%, up to a maximum of 75% of the tax determined to be due. There is an accuracy penalty that kicks in where the executor tries to reduce taxes by grossly under reporting asset values. If the valuation is 50%, or less, than the correctly determined value, the penalty is 20% of the resulting underpayment of tax. The penalty is increased to 40% of the underpayment if the undervaluation is 25%, or less, of the correctly determined value.[17] The accuracy penalty is not assessed if the underpayment is $5,000 or less.[18]

EXAMPLE 6 - 3. Elroy, a well-known philatelist, died in 2006. Edgar, the only child of Elroy, in his capacity as executor, timely filed the estate tax return, with a taxable estate of $4,000,000 and paid the estate tax of $920,000. Edgar listed the stamp collection at $200,000 but on audit he agreed that the true value was $1,000,000. The additional tax was $368,000 and the accuracy penalty was $147,200, i.e., 40% of the underpayment.

When a payment is paid late, even if an extension of time has been granted, there is interest on the tax due. It is referred to as the interest on underpayment of tax. The rate imposed is the federal short-term rate plus three percentage points.[19] These rates are adjusted quarterly, and in recent years have been fairly low, e.g., 4 to 5% in 2004 and 5 to 6% through the third quarter of 2005.[20]

Deficiency assessment statute of limitations. The statute of limitations for assessing a deficiency for both estate tax returns and gift tax returns is three years from the due date of the return, if the return is timely filed. If it is filed late, then it is three years from the time it is filed.[21] There are exceptions to the three-year rule. If the return under reports the value of the gross estate or the total gifts by more than 25%, the statute of limitations is increased to six years after the return is filed. There is no time limit if the return is not filed or if one is filed with the intent to commit fraud or to willfully evade taxes.[22]

THE GROSS ESTATE

There is no short definition for the term *gross estate*. Of course, it includes all that one owns in the usual sense of ownership but it might include property the decedent did not own. The latter occurs when the decedent had such control over, or a beneficial interest in, the property that inclusion in the estate just seems reasonable, e.g., property held in a revocable trust whereby the trustee holds legal title but the decedent controlled beneficial interests. Indeed, in some circumstances previously transferred property is included for policy reasons, even though the decedent had given up title and control, e.g., life insurance given away within three years of the insured-owner's death is included in the estate.[23] Hopefully, you can see the policy reasons behind that rule.

Before going on to the components of the estate tax, review the summary shown in Table 6-1.

TABLE 6-1 Federal Estate Tax (Form 706) Comprehensive Outline

---

Gross estate (§§ 2031-2045)		$xxx,xxx
Less deductions:		
Debts & expenses (§ 2053)	xx,xxx	
Losses during administration (§ 2054)	xx,xxx	
Charitable bequests (§ 2055)	xx,xxx	
Marital bequests (§§ 2056-2056A)	xx,xxx	(xxx,xxx)
Leaves: Taxable estate (§ 2051)		xxx,xxx
Plus: Adjusted taxable gifts (post-76) (§ 2001)		xx,xxx
Equals: Estate tax base (§ 2001(b)(1)(A) & (B))		$xxx,xxx
Calculate: Tentative tax (§ 2001)		$xxx,xxx
Less Credits:		
Gift taxes payable (post-76) (§ 2001(b)(2))	xx,xxx	
Unified credit (§ 2010)	xx,xxx	
State death tax credit (§ 2011)	xx,xxx	
Prior transfer credit (§ 2013)	xx,xxx	
Other credits (§§ 2014-2015)	xx,xxx	(xxx,xxx)
Equals: Federal estate tax (§ 2001)		$xxx,xxx

Analysis of the components of the gross estate is divided into four parts. The first part covers interests owned at death. The second part covers transfers where the transferor retained an interest or control over beneficial enjoyment of the property transferred. The third part covers the gift tax paid on any gift made within three years of the donor's death.[24] Finally, those few types of transfers made within three years of death that, for policy reasons, must be included in the gross estate even though the decedent-transferor retained neither control nor a beneficial interest in the property.[25]

Basic Interests Owned at Death: §2033

Section 2033 of the Code reads, "The value of the gross estate shall include the value of all property to the extent of the interest therein of the decedent at the time of his death."[26] Common examples are fee simple interests such as ownership of a house, furniture, personal effects, a business, investments, and copyrights. However, the gross estate includes less obvious interests. As a rule, if the decedent created or controlled a beneficial interest in property at death, the interest is probably included.

> EXAMPLE 6 - 4. Decedent died on June 18 owning 100 shares of MOP stock worth $10,000. On May 26, a *dividend* of $1.50 per share was declared payable on June 22 to stockholders of record on June 14. Included in the gross estate will be $10,150, representing the value of the stock plus the dividends declared.

> EXAMPLE 6 - 5. The same facts apply as in the prior example, except that the holder-of-record date was June 19. The dividends are not included in the decedent's gross estate because at the date of death the decedent was not legally entitled to them.

> EXAMPLE 6 - 6. At her death, decedent owned "tax-free" municipal water district bonds. Although income from such bonds is exempt from federal income tax, the value of the bonds (plus the accrued interest on them) is included in her gross estate.

> EXAMPLE 6 - 7. A couple lived and worked in a community property state. Stock was purchased using the wife's wages. They had no agreement or special understanding that the stock would be her separate property. When the husband died, the stock was worth $100,000. Even though it was held in the wife's name, it was community property; therefore, one-half of its value ($50,000) must be included in his gross estate.

Even hard-to-value or speculative assets are included in a decedent's estate.

> EXAMPLE 6 - 8. Movie star Jenny filed a lawsuit against a major studio for breach of contract, seeking $4 million in damages because, according to her claim, it had failed to cast her in a movie that she understood was hers. The movie was a hit, and she sued for a percentage of the gross profits. After the discovery phase of the trial, it looked as though her claim had merit, and the studio started talking seriously about settlement. Unfortunately, Jenny died when her Harley hit a palm tree. The studio is now refusing to settle, so her estate is proceeding to trial. Although the claim is quite speculative, its estimated value is included in her estate.[27]

Chapter 2 covered remainders, life estates, interests for a term of years, and annuities. Such may be included in a decedent's gross estate depending on what the interest is, whether it is vested, or how the interest was created. A remainder is vested if, at the termination of a trust, the property must go to the remainderman or to the remainderman's estate. If the trust is still in existence when the remainderman dies, then the value of the vested remainder is included in his or her estate.

Section 2033 would also cover the present value of a *joint and survivor annuity*, one which continues to be payable in whole or in part to another after the decedent's death, if the decedent purchased the annuity. Its value would be the present discounted value of the survivor's future income payments. Code §2039, covered shortly, specifically calls for the inclusion of such annuities in a decedent's gross estate. Overlapping code sections are not at all unusual. An interest may be included in the gross estate by virtue of a broadly written code section such as §2033 as well as by a more specific section such as §2039 that specifically targets annuities. The overlap is due to an effort by Congress to clarify what property arrangements cause property to be included. A seemingly redundant section may be there to avoid taxpayer suits that raise as an issue whether more general language, such as is found in §2033, was really intended to cover some attenuated property interest such as the possession of a general power of appointment, especially if the power was never exercised.

> EXAMPLE 6 - 9. Jim created an irrevocable trust that gave his daughter Jodi income for her life, after which the corpus would revert to Jim, if living, otherwise to his estate. Jodi was 40 years old and the trust was worth $100,000 when Jim died. His gross estate includes the value of the vested reversionary interest.

Consider the application of transfer tax laws on the estates of people who engage in certain illegal activities as this example is based on a true story.

> EXAMPLE 6 - 10. Decedent died when the plane he was piloting crashed. On board was a load of marijuana and a fair amount of "drug money." His gross estate had to include the cash and the street value of the dope because he had "exclusive possession and control" over both when he died. Further, his estate was not entitled to deduct the value of cash and marijuana forfeited under state drug enforcement laws either as a claim against the estate or as a loss during administration. The courts agreed with the Department of Justice's argument that allowing a deduction would "frustrate the sharply defined state and federal public policy against drug trafficking." Thus, decedent's other assets were used to pay the estate taxes.[28]

Dower and Curtesy Interests: §2034

A dower interest is a surviving wife's life estate in a portion of the real property owned by her deceased husband, and a curtesy interest represents a surviving husband's life estate in a portion of the real property owned by his deceased wife. The extent of these statutory interests varies from state to state. Some states grant surviving spouses dower and curtesy interests as a percentage of the deceased spouse's real and personal property. As we have seen, one purpose of these laws is to prevent a decedent from entirely disinheriting the surviving spouse. Dower or curtesy interests are included in the gross estate of the first spouse to die.[29]

From an estate tax point of view, dower and curtesy interests and community property interests of the surviving spouse have the same effect. Dower and curtesy interests that can be claimed in fee (e.g., a specific percentage of the estate is set aside in fee for the surviving spouse) are included in the gross estate but are fully deductible as interests passing to the surviving spouse. In those states that still define these interests as life estates for the surviving spouse, the property may still qualify for the marital deduction by use of what is called a qualified terminable interest property election.[30] This special election, called a QTIP election, will be covered in Chapters 9 and 10. In community property states, the surviving spouse's half-interest in the community property is excluded from the decedent's gross estate because it does not belong to the decedent spouse. These deducted or excluded marital interests are not taxed at the first spouse's death, but are likely to be taxed when the surviving spouse dies.

Survivorship Annuities: §2039

An annuity is a series of two or more periodic payments, usually received by the annuitant in monthly, quarterly, or annual payments. Annuities are commonly used in retirement planning, often in conjunction with pension and insurance contracts. Ordinarily, an employee-"participant," on retirement, will begin receiving a monthly annuity, possibly for as long as the retiree lives or, perhaps more commonly, for as long as the retiree and the retiree's spouse live. Section 2039 includes in the decedent's gross estate the date-of-death value of an annuity "receivable by any beneficiary by reason of surviving the decedent."

An annuity for the life of the owner of the annuity contract is not part of the person's gross estate under §2039, since the annuity ends with the person's death.

Even if it was considered property owned at death under §2033, the date-of-death value would be zero.

Inclusion in participant's gross estate. Generally, survivorship annuities or "refund annuities" (ones that guarantee a minimum pay back) are fully included in the decedent-participant's gross estate if there is an obligation to continue the payments after the owner of the annuity dies. How much is included and how that amount is calculated depends on several factors. If the decedent retired after 1984 or if the pension plan was not a qualified one, the pension is fully included. If it is fully included, the amount included is either the lump sum amount, if the survivor has the right to take a lump sum, or the present value of the future payments, if the survivor must receive periodic payments. As discussed in Chapter 2, whether one uses Table S or Table B (see Appendix A) depends on whether the payments will continue for the life of the survivor (Table S) or for a fixed number of years (Table B). Prior to 1985, plans that were "qualified" under §401(a) were either partially or fully excluded from the participant's estate. The section is complex, as it details the requirements for plan qualification. The tax advantages of qualified plans are that employer contributions are tax deductible to the employer and are not taxable income to the employee until paid, usually after retirement. In addition, the income earned on contributions is tax-deferred. Generally, non-qualified plans do not receive all of these advantages.

The following summarizes the complex estate inclusion rules for qualified plan annuities:

1. *Fully included annuities.* Regarding any annuity whose payments began after July 17, 1984, or for which prior to that date the decedent had not made an irrevocable election to designate the beneficiaries, the *entire value* of the annuity is included in the gross estate.

2. *Partially excluded annuities.* The estate of retirees who were in pay status (retired and receiving payments) before January 1, 1985, and had made an irrevocable election after December 31, 1982 and before July 18, 1984, as to the form of benefits that would be paid to the beneficiary can exclude up to $100,000 of the combined value of survivorship annuities from qualified plans.

3. *Totally excluded annuities.* The estate of retirees that separated from service prior to January 1, 1983, and who had irrevocably elected the form of benefits before that date, can exclude all of the qualified annuity.

The exclusions just described are available only if the proceeds are not payable to the decedent's estate, and if the decedent could not change the form of benefit. Examples of annuities that qualified for this exclusion include tax-sheltered annuities or tax-deferred annuities (TSAs and TDAs, also called 403(b) plans), individual retirement accounts (IRAs), the "employer's portion" of the pension plans qualified under § 401 and even lump-sum pension payments, provided the beneficiary elects to forego a special 10-year income averaging method available only if the participant-pensioner (i.e., the decedent) was 50 years old before January 1, 1986.[31]

> EXAMPLE 6 - 11. Gaytha retired in 1985. When she died earlier this year, she had three joint and survivor annuities that will continue to make payments to her daughter. There is one from her former employer's qualified retirement plan, one from a tax-sheltered annuity, and another from an individual retirement account. She had started drawing from all three right after her retirement. The value of her gross estate will include the entire value of all three annuities.

> EXAMPLE 6 - 12. During his employment, Stan contributed $25,000 to his qualified pension plan and his employer contributed $75,000. The plan provided Stan and his wife with a joint and survivor annuity on his retirement, which started in 1983. Stan died in 2007, and the value of his spouse's survivorship annuity was $300,000. The amount excluded is the value of the annuity attributable to the employer's contributions up to a maximum of $100,000. The amount attributed to the employer is $225,000 [$300,000*($75,000 / ($100,000))]. Thus the amount excluded is $100,000 and $200,000 is included in his gross estate.

> EXAMPLE 6 - 13. In the example immediately above, had Stan retired before 1983 his estate would have excluded $225,000, the employer's portion. Had he retired after July 17,1984, the entire value would have been included.

In summary, a simple rule applies to decedents who retired after July 17, 1984; the *full* value of all annuities earned through employment or acquired by purchase is included in the decedent's gross estate. For decedents retiring between January 1, 1983, and July 17, 1984, up to $100,000 of the annuity attributed to the employer's contribution is excluded. Finally, for those retiring prior to 1983, the *entire* employer's share of all qualifying retirement annuities is excluded.

Inclusion in gross estate of retiree's spouse. When the participant-retiree's spouse dies first, federal law holds that any pension interest passes 100% to the participant. In other words, the nonparticipant decedent spouse is precluded from making any disposition of the pension.[32] This is true even in community property states.[33]

Joint Tenancy and Tenancy by the Entirety: §2040

Two rules determine the portion of joint tenancy property that must be included in the gross estate when a co-owner dies, the spousal rule and the consideration furnished rule.

Spousal rule: If a married couple are the only joint tenants, when the first spouse dies his or her gross estate must include one-half of the property's fair market value as of the date of death (DOD FMV). The Code refers to spousal joint tenancies and tenancies by the entirety as "qualified joint interests." For these, *one-half* of the total value is included *regardless* of the spouses' original contributions. Prior to 1977, the consideration furnished rule also applied to joint tenancies held by husbands and wives. Surviving spouses in several cases have successfully argued that the old rule still applies where the joint tenancy was created pre-1977.[34] The IRS eventually acquiesced with these decisions.[35] With the property fully included in the first spouse's estate, a full step-up in basis to both halves is obtained. Unless stated otherwise, assume all husband and wife joint tenancies were created after 1976.

> EXAMPLE 6 - 14. At his death in 2006, Joel and his wife Susan held their home in joint tenancy. Susan paid $100,000 when she bought the house in 1980 using her separate funds. It was worth $400,000 when Joel died. Since the house is a *qualified joint interest*, his gross estate will include $200,000. Susan's new basis is half the old basis plus half the date-of-death value, i.e., $250,000.

> EXAMPLE 6 - 15. In the example immediately above, had Susan died first with Joel the survivor, the results would have been exactly the same.

The second rule applicable to all non-qualified joint interests is called the *consideration furnished rule*. With even just one non-spouse as a joint tenant, all interests are non-qualified; e.g., husband, wife, and adult child take title as joint tenants; all are holders of non-qualified interests.

Consideration furnished rule: Include in the decedent owner's estate only that portion of the DOD FMV of the property attributable to that portion of the consideration (money or money's worth) contributed by the decedent. The law starts with the presumption that the decedent co-owner contributed all of the consideration (or was initially the sole owner). To overcome this presumption, the estate has the burden of establishing that the surviving joint tenants contributed to the acquisition of the property. Generally, this is not as difficult as it seems. The IRS is not likely to challenge the contributions where the co-owners, in establishing the joint tenancy, had neither a motive to avoid taxes nor a reason to make gifts to each other, and each of the co-owners had sufficient resources to pay his or her own way.

EXAMPLE 6 - 16. In 1965, two brothers, Jake and Ned, prior to either of them marrying, purchased a fishing cabin on a lake, taking title in joint tenancy. Jake died this year. The records as to how much each paid as a down payment have been lost. But Ned can show that he and his brother were both earning about the same amount of money at the time of the purchase and were both about equally wealthy such that one making a gift to the other would not have made much sense. This would probably be sufficient to establish equal consideration.

EXAMPLE 6 - 17. Similar to the prior example, but change it such that Jake was Ned's father and Jake, although wealthy, already owned his own home whereas Ned was just starting out. Even if Ned claims to have paid an equal share of the purchase price, the circumstances do not support the claim and, without better evidence, it would be difficult to overcome the presumption that Jake furnished all of the consideration. Even a canceled check from Ned payable to the seller of the cabin might not be sufficient evidence, since a gift from Jake of the cash followed by Ned's use of the money as his share of the consideration would be treated as if all the funds came from Jake. Ned needs to establish that his contribution came from a source other than a gift from his father.

A special rule, where a donee (one of the surviving joint tenants) uses funds traceable to a gift from the decedent joint tenant as part of the purchase price, those funds are treated as being part of the donor-joint tenant's consideration rather than that of the donee. Traceable means any capital appreciation in the gift is taken into account, however, income from the gift is not.

EXAMPLE 6 - 18. Calvin gave his daughter Deidre 100 shares of MOP stock worth $50,000. She sold the stock for $70,000 and placed the proceeds of the sale in a bank account in which she already had $30,000. The source of the $30,000 was $10,000 from MOP dividends and $20,000 from money she saved out of her wages. Calvin and Deidre purchased a house for $200,000, each putting up half of the purchase price. Deidre's half share came from the bank account. The house, held in joint tenancy, was worth $300,000 when Calvin died. His estate includes 85% of the DOD FMV, i.e., $255,000. The percentage is calculated by taking Calvin's contribution of $100,000, adding the contribution of Deidre that is traceable to Calvin's gift to her (i.e., $70,000) and dividing the total ($170,000) by the $200,000 purchase price. Note that the capital gain is included in the numerator, but the dividends are not.

Full inclusion in the decedent-donor's estate is preferred when it results in a step-up in basis without an increase in estate taxes.

EXAMPLE 6 - 19. In 2005, Virginia put her home into joint tenancy with her son Scott. At the time of the transfer, the home was worth $400,000. She filed a gift tax return reporting a $190,000 taxable gift. She died in the year 2009 when the house was worth $500,000. The entire $500,000 is included in her estate, and Scott's basis in the house is $500,000. Her other property was worth $75,000 and her estate paid debts and expenses of $30,000, so her taxable estate was just $545,000 and no taxes were owed.

EXAMPLE 6 - 20. At her death, Rose owned a farm worth $100,000 jointly with her brother Tom. The farm was originally acquired for $50,000, with Rose paying $10,000 and Tom paying $40,000. Assuming the contribution of the survivor can be established, under the consideration-furnished test her estate includes only one-fifth of the farm's value, i.e., $20,000 [($10,000/$50,000)*$100,000]. Tom's basis in the farm will be his contribution plus the amount included in Rose's estate, i. e., $60,000 [$40,000 he contributed and $20,000 included in Rose's estate].

EXAMPLE 6 - 21. At her death, Dottie owned $90,000 of ABC common stock jointly with her husband and her son. The survivors know that Dottie actually contributed only $10,000 to the original $50,000 purchase price (and the two of them paid $20,000 each), but they are not sure they can prove it. If they cannot, Dottie's gross estate will include the full $90,000. If they can prove it, her gross estate will include only her proportional share, or $18,000 (i.e., 20%). This is not a qualified joint interest because a non-spouse was a co-owner.

The consideration furnished rule applies only at the death of a co-owner. There is a gift when different amounts of consideration are used to purchase property and the title is taken in joint tenancy because, by property law rules, all joint tenants' interests must be equal. For gift or sale purposes, the "donee" co-owner has a basis in his or her share that is either carry-over or partly carry-over and partly purchase.

EXAMPLE 6 - 22. Edith and June purchased a vacation condominium in South Florida for $100,000, taking title as joint tenants. Edith paid $90,000 and June paid $10,000. Edith made a $40,000 gift [$30,000 taxable] to June since June has a 50% interest. June's basis would be $50,000 [$40,000 carried over with the gift and the other $10,000 is her consideration]. If they later sell the property for $150,000, each would recognize a gain of $25,000. If, instead of selling the property when it was worth $150,000, June made a gift of her half to her son, Tommy, she would report a gift of $75,000 [$65,000 taxable gift] and Tommy would have a carry-over basis of $50,000. This transfer would break the joint tenancy, so Tommy and Edith would be tenants in common, each with a 50% share. Regardless of which one died first, Tommy or Edith, 50% of the value would be included in the person's estate.

For purposes of §2040, "joint interests" encompass only two forms of concurrent ownership: joint tenancy and tenancy by the entirety. In contrast to the complex rules just given, when a person dies holding title to property in tenancy in common or community property, the value that is included in the decedent's gross estate is based on the decedent's proportionate interest in the property.[36]

Power of Appointment: §2041

A power of appointment is a power that allows a person to name someone to receive a beneficial interest in property, even though the person directing the transfer does not own the property. The creator (grantor) of the power is called the donor of the power. The person receiving the power is called the holder or donee. The persons to whom the holder may appoint the property are called the permissible appointees, and if the holder actually appoints property to some of them, they are then appointees. Finally, the persons who receive the property that is not appointed are called the takers by default.

For estate tax purposes, a power of appointment is either a general power or it is a limited (special) power. A *general* power of appointment is defined in the Code as the power of the holder to appoint to the holder, the holder's estate, the holder's creditors, or the creditors of the holder's estate.[37] All other powers are "limited" or "special" powers of appointment. These usually designate as permissible appointees either specific individuals (e.g., the donor gives the holder the power to appoint to the donor's brother Sam or sister Sue) or a class of people (e.g., appoint to any of my issue).

A holder-decedent's gross estate will include the value of any property subject to a *general* power of appointment. It will be included in the gross estate regardless of whether the decedent-holder *exercised* the power at death, or, alternatively, did not exercise it and allowed the power to *lapse* at death. The key is that at the moment of death, the decedent was the holder of a general power.

EXAMPLE 6 - 23. At her death, Carol was trustee of an irrevocable trust created by her Uncle Fred. She had the power to invade the corpus of the trust for the benefit of anyone. The trust named Fred's second cousins, Clarence and Sherrie, as remaindermen in the event Carol failed to appoint all of the corpus. In her will,

Carol appointed her son David to receive the entire corpus. Carol's gross estate will include the entire value of the trust corpus, since it was subject to a general power at her death.

EXAMPLE 6 - 24. The facts are similar to the prior example, except that Carol did not exercise the power at her death. The entire trust corpus is still included in her gross estate even though the power *lapsed* at her death. Note that a proportionate share of the estate taxes would come out of the trust.

EXAMPLE 6 - 25. The facts are similar to the prior example, except that the power to appoint was on behalf of anyone *except* herself, her creditors, her estate, or the creditors of her estate. This is a "limited" power, not a general power, and thus the property is not included in her gross estate whether she appoints to her son or just lets the power lapse. Appointing to her son is not the same as appointing to her estate.

Notice that §2041 focuses on decedent *holders* of general powers, not on the donor or the appointees.

Exceptions. There are two major exceptions to the basic rule that being able to appoint to oneself makes the power a general one. Both exceptions apply in circumstances that so restrict appointment to the holder that Congress, quite rightly, defined them as not being general powers. The first exception applies if the holder's right to benefit is limited to use for "health, education, support or maintenance." This is referred to as a power limited by an *ascertainable standard* exception. The second one applies if the decedent-holder's exercise requires the *approval* of either the creator of the power or an adverse party, hence the *adverse party* exception. An adverse party is "a person having a substantial interest in the property, subject to the power, which is adverse to exercise of the power in favor of the decedent."[38]

EXAMPLE 6 - 26. During his lifetime, the decedent was the income beneficiary of a trust created by his father. The trust gave him the right to invade corpus for reasons of his "health, education, support, or maintenance." Since the power is limited by an *ascertainable standard*, this right to invade is not a general power, and the trust is not included in the decedent's gross estate even if the decedent was the trustee.

EXAMPLE 6 - 27. Same facts as the last example except decedent could invade corpus for reasons of his "health, education, support, maintenance, *or happiness*." The power is not limited by an ascertainable standard; therefore, the invasion right constitutes a general power of appointment, and the entire value of the trust will be included in the decedent's estate even though he never exercised the right to invade.

EXAMPLE 6 - 28. During her lifetime, the decedent was the income beneficiary of a trust established by her grandmother. She could invade corpus for any reason provided she obtained the written approval of her son, the trust's remainderman. Since her son was an *adverse party*, i.e., his remainder interest would be reduced in value if the decedent exercised the power in her own favor, the power is not a general one.

Property subject to a general power of appointment is included in the holder's estate because the power creates rights considered equivalent to ownership. Thus, this estate tax rule makes sense even though under *property law* the holder is not the legal owner of the property. Given that the holder does not have legal title, even if the property subject to a general power is included in the holder's gross estate, it is not included in the holder's probate estate unless the holder appoints it there, an event not likely to happen.

Insurance on Decedent's Life: IRC § 2042

The three circumstances that cause life insurance to be included in the insured's gross estate are: (1) the proceeds are paid to the executor of the decedent's estate, (2) the decedent at death possessed an incident of ownership in the policy, or (3) the decedent transferred an incident of ownership within three years of death.

Receivable by executor. Very seldom is the executor of the decedent's estate named as a beneficiary or alternate beneficiary. This rule applies only if the executor is receiving the proceeds in his capacity as executor, hence if an adult son serves as executor of his mother's estate, and he owned life insurance on her life, his receipt of the proceeds does not result in them being included since he receives them in his individual capacity. On occasion it happens that at the insured's death no named beneficiaries are living and the proceeds are payable to the estate by default. Modern policies generally have a default clause that directs the company to pay the proceeds to the decedent's heirs if the named primary and alternate beneficiaries predecease the insured. The default clauses read something like intestate succession laws, starting with close family members, moving to more remote relatives if no close family members survive, and to the insured's estate only as a last resort.

Decedent possesses incidents of ownership. Policy ownership gives the owner numerous rights including: to assign, to terminate, to borrow against the cash reserves (if any), to name beneficiaries, and to change beneficiaries.

Possession by the decedent of these rights is called *incidents of ownership,* any one of which will result in the proceeds being included in the decedent's estate. The payment of premiums by the insured is not considered an incident of ownership and payment will not by itself cause inclusion. Nonetheless, barring some agreement to the contrary by the married couple, the payment of premiums in a community property state, unless clearly out of separate property funds, may create an incident of ownership. A policy paid from community property funds would be half included in the decedent's gross estate regardless of whether it was issued in the insured spouse's name or the non-insured spouse's name. A written agreement specifying that it is the separate property of one of the spouses should negate the community property presumption.

Life insurance transferred within three years of death. If the insured transferred an interest in the policy within three years of his or her death, both IRC § 2042 and §2035(a) require inclusion of the proceeds in the insured's gross estate. Any time insurance is listed on an estate tax return, the executor must obtain IRS Form 712 from the insurance company, and attach it to the return. The form will show who owned the policy, and if transferred, when and to whom.

> EXAMPLE 6 - 29. On June 12, 2005, Marty transferred a $200,000 policy on his life to his son Joseph. Because the policy was a term policy, its value was under $10,000 and Marty did not have to report it as a gift. On January 1, 2007, Marty died in a car accident. Joseph collected the $200,000. Marty's gross estate must include the $200,000 even though he had no incidents of ownership when he died and there were no strings attached to the transfer.

This IRC section is based on the public policy that life insurance is so closely tied to death, and so dramatically increases in value with the death, it should not escape estate tax if the transfer is motivated by removing the policy from the insured's estate. Rather than creating a difficult to prove or disprove motives test, Congress went with a bright-line rule: a transfer within three years = include (even if death was accidental), and more than three years = don't include.

IRC § 2042 versus §2033. It is important to distinguish between policies on the decedent's life and policies on the lives of others. Policies on the *decedent's life* are covered by IRC § 2042, but what if the decedent owned a policy on the life of another? The policy is included in the decedent's estate under § 2033 as a property interest owned at death. Generally, the value is the cost of replacement rather than the cash surrender value. Cost of replacement is what an insurance company would charge to put the policy in force (with the existing cash surrender value) given the insured's age and health. Where premiums are still being paid on a policy on the life of another, its value is increased by that portion of the premium paid that covers the period extending beyond the owner's death.

> EXAMPLE 6 - 30. Decedent died owning a life insurance policy on his mother with a face value of $60,000. The policy had a value of $14,000 at decedent's death. Although IRC § 2042 does not apply because decedent is not the insured, the decedent's estate must include the $14,000 value under §2033.

> EXAMPLE 6 - 31. When he died, decedent owned a $100,000 life insurance policy on his own life, hence, IRC § 2042 requires the proceeds be included in his gross estate. However, if all premiums had been paid for with community property, it is presumed to be community property and only $50,000 would be included. This result could be overcome if the couple had a written agreement stating that the policy was the separate property of one spouse. Of course, if the surviving spouse is the beneficiary, the 100% marital deduction will keep it out of the taxable estate. Cross-ownership (each spouse owns the policy on the other's life) might be more important where the beneficiary spouse is not a U.S. citizen.

After one spouse dies, if the surviving spouse continues to own a policy on his or her own life, the entire proceeds are included in the surviving insured's estate when he or she dies, regardless of whether community property funds were the original source of the premiums.[39]

So far, we have studied IRC §§ 2033, 2034, 2039, 2040, 2041 and 2042, all of which cover interests owned, held, or controlled by the decedent at death such that the interests are included in the decedent's estate. The next several sections examine codes that result in property being included in the gross estate even though it was no longer owned by the decedent at the time of death. The property is included because the decedent transferred property but kept some interest or control, sometimes just a *little string* attached, such that Congress thought the string justified including the property in the gross estate as if the transfer had not taken place.

Transfers that Haunt the Estate: §§ 2036, 2037, 2038

If a person transfers property and retains an interest in the property, such as the right to control who enjoys it, the retained interest will cause the transferred property to be included in the transferor's gross estate if the retained interest is still present when the transferor dies.[40] This is true even if the retained interest is one that cannot benefit the transferor economically. The interest will also be included if the transferor releases the retained interest within three years of his or her death.[41] Whether a "string" exists at the time of death or the string is snipped within three years of death, it will be as if the decedent never made the transfer, but instead continued to own the property right to the moment of death. Thus, if one of the retained interest code sections applies and the property is pulled back into the gross estate, it will be valued for estate tax purposes at the date-of-death fair market value (DOD FMV) regardless of its earlier gift value. However, if it is drawn into the gross estate, it will not also be treated in the estate tax calculation as an adjusted taxable gift, even though it was a taxable gift when the transfer occurred. The latter sounds bad but is actually good because it keeps the transfer from being taxed twice. Any gift tax paid on the earlier transfer is allowed as a credit even though the earlier gift is not included as an adjusted taxable gift in the calculation of the estate tax. The retained interest code sections are: §2036, Transfers with Retained Life Estate; §2037, Transfers Taking Effect at Death; and §2038, Revocable Transfers.

Characteristics common to all three sections. The three "strings" sections (§§2036, 2037, and 2038) have these characteristics in common:

▶ The transfer was made by the *decedent*.
▶ The transfer was a gift, that is, a transfer "for less than full and adequate consideration in money or money's worth."
▶ The amount included in the gross estate is the value as of the *date of death* (or alternate valuation date), rather than the value at date of transfer.
▶ If the string pertained to only a specific portion of the property transferred, then only that *portion* of the transferred property is included. For example, if the retained control was over one-third of the property, then only one-third of its value is included in the gross estate. However, note that §2036 requires the entire property to be included, even if only the income interest was retained.
▶ A trust is almost always involved.

When the sections overlap, as they often do, the value included in the gross estate is based on whichever section results in the greatest amount included.

Transfer with Retained Life Estate: §2036. A transfer with retained life estate arises when a decedent has made a transfer, by trust or otherwise, for less than full and adequate consideration and has retained either (1) the possession or enjoyment of (or the right to the *income* from) the property transferred, or (2) the right, either alone or in conjunction with any person, to *designate* who will enjoy or possess the property or its income.

Period of retention. In addition to the above retained control, §2036 applies only if the decedent-transferor retained that control for: (1) life, (2) any period that does not in fact end before the decedent's death, or (3) any period not ascertainable without reference to the decedent's death. In the following §2036 examples, assume that decedent D made a lifetime transfer for less than full consideration.

EXAMPLE 6 - 32. At a time when D's vacation home was worth $110,000, D said, while handing over a quit-claim deed, "Son, here's title to my vacation home. It's yours now, but I will expect you to let me use it occasionally." When D died, the home was worth $200,000. The date-of-death value of the home is included in D's gross estate because at the time of D's death, D still retained the *right to enjoy* the property.

EXAMPLE 6 - 33. D transferred property into an irrevocable trust, retaining the right to the income for his lifetime, with the remainder to go to C. The property's value at date of death is included in D's gross estate because D retained the right to the income for his lifetime. Although the remainder value was treated as a taxable gift when the trust was established, it is not an adjusted taxable gift for estate tax purposes since the entire trust has been included in D's gross estate.

EXAMPLE 6 - 34. D transferred property into an irrevocable trust, with income to remain with D for 20 years, after which the trust terminates, with the remainder going to C. Eighteen years after establishing the trust, D died. The property's value is included in D's gross estate because the *period of retention* did not end before D's death. Again, the adjusted taxable gift would be zero insofar as D's estate and this trust are concerned.

EXAMPLE 6 - 35. The facts as in the prior example, except D lived beyond the 20-year term. D's gross estate would not include the trust property. There would be an adjusted taxable gift equal to the remainder value when the trust was funded. That value would boost the rest of D's taxable estate into higher marginal rates.

EXAMPLE 6 - 36. D transferred property into an irrevocable trust, with income to go to D for up to one month before D's death and the remainder going to C. The fair market value of the property as of D's death is included in D's gross estate because the retained period is *not ascertainable without reference* to D's death.

When is a gift complete? Generally, unless the owner releases dominion and control over the property, there is no gift. An outright gift is complete since the donor transfers "dominion and control" immediately to the donee. It is less obvious with gifts in trust where the donor retains some interest. IRC regulations give a number of interesting examples.[42] Bear in mind that a gift may be complete enough to cause a gift tax (generally, the donor released title and control), but still the property is included in the donor's gross estate due to a retained interest. Obviously, if the donor has the right to revoke a gift, then no gift has really occurred, even if the donee has taken possession of the property.

EXAMPLE 6 - 37. Shane created a trust, transferring assets worth $100,000 to the trustee. The trust terms give Richard income for life unless the trust is terminated earlier by Shane. When the trust terminates, whether by Richard's death or Shane's direction, the trust remainder will be distributed to Shane's daughter Catherine. The first year the trustee distributed income of $5,000 to Richard. The second year $6,000 was distributed. At the beginning of the third year, when the trust was worth $120,000, Shane died. No gift occurred when the trust was established and, of course, the trust is included in Shane's estate. While Shane was alive, all trust income (including capital gains) was reported on his income tax return, and the annual distributions were treated as gifts from him to Richard. Given the amounts and Richard's present interest (as each amount was distributed to him), the annual exclusion would have covered the amounts Richard received before Shane's death. Distributions after Shane's death are from an irrevocable trust, hence the trust has income distribution deductions. Richard includes them on his tax returns. The distributions are no longer treated as gifts. Note that while Shane was alive the distributions are from him, not from the trust. From a transfer tax standpoint, only people make gifts, not trusts, not trustees.

When control is retained by the settlor, no gift is deemed to have occurred.[43] This is true even when the terms of the trust make it clear that the settlor cannot benefit in any way from the retained control. Once the control ceases, either by release, death, or by the terms that established the trust, the transfer is complete.

EXAMPLE 6 - 38. Early in 2005, using assets worth $400,000, Abel creates an irrevocable trust for the benefit of Benito and Consuelo with remainder, after they are both deceased, to their children. So long as both are alive, the trustee is given the power to allocate the income between Benito and Consuelo in such proportions as the trustee thinks is appropriate. When one beneficiary dies, the survivor is to receive all income. Abel serves as the initial trustee. During the first year the trust has income of $30,000, which Abel distributes $25,000 to Benito and $5,000 to Consuelo. No gift occurred when the trust was created, even though it was irrevocable. The income is taxed to Abel, and he has made a gift of $25,000

($14,000 taxable) to Benito and $5,000 to Consuelo (not taxable because it is completely covered by the annual exclusion).

EXAMPLE 6 - 39. At a time when the trust was worth $500,000, Abel resigned as trustee, giving the successor trustee a letter (with copies to both beneficiaries) that stated his resignation was irrevocable. At that time, Abel has made a $500,000 gift (both gross and taxable). From that moment on, income was no longer taxed to Abel, and distributions were not considered new gifts but merely distributions of income from the irrevocable trust. Since the trustee can determine how much income each beneficiary will receive, neither Benito nor Consuelo have a present interest in the income stream, hence no annual exclusion is allowed.

EXAMPLE 6 - 40. Suppose that instead of releasing his retained control by resignation, Abel died while still serving as trustee and that the trust assets were valued at $700,000. The $700,000 is included in his gross estate and, from that moment onward, the income distributions would be from the trust, not from Abel (nor from his estate). Distributions would draw out taxable income (which is taxed to the beneficiary receiving it) but the distributions are not considered gifts.

EXAMPLE 6 - 41. Suppose the terms of the trust created by Abel required him to get Benito's approval for anything other than a 50-50% split of the income, otherwise the income had to be divided equally between Benito and Consuelo. The trust's value is still included because Abel retained the right to designate the recipient "alone or *in conjunction with* any other person."

Because these rules are based on transfers with interests retained by the donor, we must bear in mind that a transfer of a community property asset is treated as coming one-half from each spouse.

EXAMPLE 6 - 42. The facts are similar to any of the above examples, except that the transfer was of property held prior to the transfer as community property, 50-50 tenancy in common, or spouses as joint tenancy. Only half the value of the property would be included in the transferor's estate, because only half is traceable to a transfer by the decedent.

EXAMPLE 6 - 43. In 2007, D transferred property into an irrevocable trust funded with assets worth $400,000, retaining one quarter of the income for himself and requiring the distribution of the rest to C. After D's death, C is to receive all of the income and after C's death, the remainder will go to R. For 2007, D must report a completed gift of $300,000, and, assuming C's life estate is worth at least $12,000, the annual exclusion would reduce it to a taxable gift of $288,000. At D's death, only *one quarter* of the trust's value is included in his gross estate since that was the extent of D's §2036 retained interest.

EXAMPLE 6 - 44. D transferred property into an irrevocable trust, authorizing the trustee, a bank, in its sole discretion, to distribute trust income to X or Y in such amounts as the bank trust officer thinks appropriate. D retained the power to replace the bank with another corporate trustee. The value of the property is not included in D's gross estate under §2036 because D's right to replace trustees does not amount to the right by D to change or control the enjoyment of the property. However, the property would be included if D kept the right to appoint *herself* as successor trustee because she would then have retained the ability to control the "enjoyment" of the income.

In the following example, a basic assumption is changed, so that decedent is not the transferor.

EXAMPLE 6 - 45. G transfers property into an irrevocable trust, with income to D for life and remainder to R. The value of the property is not included in D's gross estate under §2036, because D was *not the transferor*. This arrangement is referred to as a bypass trust because the trust assets "bypass" the income beneficiary's estate.

People sometimes engage in transfers designed to appear complete but that involve an implied *understanding* that the transferor has a retained life estate. The IRS has had success in attacking such schemes when they come to light. Consider the following situation in which a court found §2036 to apply to facts that had been structured to appear as a completed sale.

EXAMPLE 6 - 46. Mom, age 82 and in poor health, transferred title to her home to her son and his wife in exchange for $270,000, which was the home's fair market value. The terms of this "sale-leaseback" called for a $20,000 down payment and a five-year mortgage loan of $250,000. Mom immediately forgave the down payment of $10,000 by each of the spouses. In the next two years, in payment of rent, Mom gave son and his wife $10,000 each, and they promptly returned these amounts in payment of the mortgage. Two days after the sale, Mom executed her last will, which contained a provision forgiving any of the remaining debt at the time of her death. The date-of-death value of the home was included in her gross estate under §2036. Circumstances strongly suggested an understanding that decedent was permitted to live in the house until death, which she did, and that none of the consideration offered in exchange was ever really going to be paid. Thus, all consideration was disregarded. The following circumstantial factors, all taken together, indicate a strings-attached transfer: decedent's age and her health concerns, her forgiveness of the mortgage both during her life and by her will, the fact that the rent payments approximated the interest payments on the note, and the fact that the son was the decedent's only heir and the natural object of her bounty.

As a result, Mom was treated as having made a transfer of property for less than full and adequate consideration in which she retained, for a period which did not end before her death, the right to possess or enjoy the property.[44]

Transfers taking effect at death: §2037. A "transfer taking effect at death" will arise when (1) possession or enjoyment of the property through ownership can be obtained only by surviving the decedent and (2) the decedent, at the time of the transfer, retained a reversionary interest, which, at the decedent's death, exceeded five percent of the value of the property. Such reversionary interest is defined as the possibility that the property may return to the decedent or may be subject to a power of disposition by him.

> EXAMPLE 6 - 47. D transfers property into a trust, with income to B for B's life, a reversion to D if he survives B, otherwise the remainder to go to R, or R's estate. Assume that D dies at age 70, predeceasing B, who is then 60 years old. On the date of D's death, the value of the trust property was $1 million and the federal §7520 rate was 8%. Using actuarial tables, it was determined that given D and B's ages, D's contingent reversionary interest (ignoring the fact of his death) was worth more than 5% of the value of the trust. The amount included in D's gross estate is the full value of the trust less the value of B's remaining life estate, i.e., the value of the reversionary interest as though it was vested rather than contingent. Since B is 60 years old and the rate was 8%, the amount included will be the remainder value of $267,940 [.26794 * $1,000,000; see Table S, 8% rate].

In the preceding example, D had a chance of surviving B at D's death, and based on that, a value is calculated for what amounts to a contingent reversion for D. The reader might find this strange given that D, *in fact,* did not outlive B. However, as in certain other valuation situations, this calculation is made without regard to the fact of D's death. Thus, the calculation assumes that, at the moment of D's death, both D and B had average life expectancies for their ages, and that D's reversionary interest was certain rather than contingent.

Revocable transfers: §2038. Although §2038's title is "Revocable Transfers," the section covers much more. Transferred property will be included in the decedent-transferor's estate if, at the time of death, the decedent retained the right to change another's enjoyment of the property. The code section refers to this retained right as one to *alter, amend, revoke, or terminate* the enjoyment of the property transferred. Even without any retained economic interest, almost any retained right to change a beneficiary's interest (or even the timing of enjoyment) will cause the full value of the property to be included in the transferor's estate. Even if the power to revoke requires the consent of another person or persons, whether or not the person has an adverse interest, the existence of the power will cause the property to be included in the settlor's estate.

EXAMPLE 6 - 48. D transferred property into a *revocable living trust*, designed mainly to avoid probate at D's death. D retained the power to revoke the trust. D's gross estate includes the value of this property under §2038.

EXAMPLE 6 - 49. D transferred property into a *revocable living trust*, income to B, remainder to C. D retained the power to revoke the trust but only if C agreed to the revocation. D's gross estate includes the value of this property under §2038.

EXAMPLE 6 - 50. D transferred property into an irrevocable trust that gave B the right to all income. The trust was to last for a term of 20 years, but would terminate earlier in the event of B's death. At such time as the trust terminates, it is to be distributed to B, if living, otherwise, to B's issue. If B leaves no issue, then to C, or C's estate. D retained the right to have the trust terminate earlier than at the end of 20 years if D thought such was in B's best interest. Even though D retained no beneficial interest, the trust property is included in D's gross estate because D retained the power to alter the "enjoyment interests" of others.

Gift causa mortis. An interesting concept developed at common law is called a *gift causa mortis*; literally, a gift caused by death. It is applied when a donor, thinking that death is imminent, gives away personal property with the understanding that if the donor dies the property belongs to the donee, but if the donor survives the property must be returned. Obviously, §2038 applies to gifts *causa mortis*.

EXAMPLE 6 - 51. In 2007, elderly Tom, just before entering the hospital, gave his coin collection (worth $150,000) to Jim, with the understanding that if the heart operation was unsuccessful the collection would be Jim's. Tom died three days after surgery. The collection was included in Tom's estate. Had Tom lived, Jim would have returned the coins and neither the original transfer, nor the return of the coins, would be treated as a gift.

EXAMPLE 6 - 52. In the preceding example, suppose that Tom gave Jim his coin collection to keep no matter what the outcome of the surgery and that Tom died three days after the surgery. The collection would not be included in Tom's estate. Of course, the adjusted taxable gift value ($138,000) would boost his estate into higher marginal rates and the executor of Tom's estate would be responsible for filing a gift tax return showing this gift.

The law gifts causa mortis requires the gift be returned if the donor survives the life-threatening event, even if the donor dies while the donee is still in possession of the property.

> EXAMPLE 6 - 53. Athene was fearful that she would not survive major surgery. She gave Mary, her best friend, her collection of Barbie dolls (valued at $50,000), with the understanding that the dolls would be returned if Athene did not die. The surgery was successful and she made a perfect recovery, but was killed in an automobile accident on the way home from the hospital. Now, Mary admits the agreement, but claims the right to keep the dolls because of Athene's death. With the help of the probate court, Athene's executor will rightfully take possession of the dolls.

Gift Taxes on Transfers Within Three Years of Death: §2035(b)

Since 1977, the Code has included a section that requires inclusion in the gross estate of the gift tax paid by the decedent on *any gift* made within three years of the donor's death. Note that §2035(b) applies only if gift tax is actually paid, i.e., the question is not whether unified credit was used but whether a check was made out to the U.S. Treasury. If a gift results in gift taxes and the donor dies within three years of making the gift, the gift tax paid becomes part of the gross estate, subjecting the gift taxes themselves to the estate tax. Gift taxes owed but unpaid at the time of the donor's death must be paid by the estate, and the amount is treated as a deduction (a debt or tax owed) on the estate tax return; see the third example below.

Grossing up. This inclusion of the gift tax in the gross estate is referred to as "grossing up" the estate; i.e., the estate is being brought up to the level it would have been had the gift tax not been paid. Obviously, there is no refund, this is just for calculation purposes. Keep in mind that the gift is not brought back into the gross estate, just the gift tax.

> EXAMPLE 6 - 54. In 2004, Mack gave Stacy MOP stock worth $2,011,000. Mack paid gift taxes in the amount of $435,000. When Mack died in 2006, his gross estate (not including the gift taxes) was valued at $6,000,000 and his debts and expenses were $1,000,000. Stacy still owned the MOP stock, which had risen in value to $2,500,000. Taking the transfer into account, Mack's gross estate is $6,435,000, his taxable estate is $5,435,000, the adjusted taxable gifts are $2,000,000, and there is a gift tax payable credit of $435,000 (a case where gift tax payable and paid are the same because the gift did not exceed $2,000,000). The estate tax is $2,065,100.

EXAMPLE 6 - 55. Continuing the prior example, had Mack made the gift in 2002 (more than three years before his death), his gross estate would not include the gift taxes and the estate tax would be only $1,865,000. The decrease in taxes is $200,000 which, of course, given that the top marginal rate in 2006 is 46%, happens to be 46% of $435,000. Notice that, regardless of when Mack died, the value of the MOP stock at Mack's death is irrelevant to the estate tax calculation.

EXAMPLE 6 - 56. In 2005, Tamara gave MOP stock, valued at $1,750,000, to her son Kevin. She died in March of 2006, leaving a property worth $7,000,000. The executor of her estate filed the gift tax return and paid $317,550 in gift taxes. Debts and expenses, not counting the gift tax obligation, totaled $500,000. The estate tax return showed a gross estate of $7,317,550 because the gift tax must be included; the deductions are $817,550 because the gift taxes were unpaid, leaving a taxable estate of $6,500,000.

EXAMPLE 6 - 57. Consider the facts of the prior example, holding everything constant except Tamara paid the gift tax shortly before she died. Her estate would be reduced by the tax to $6,682,450. Her gross estate, with the gift tax added back, would be $7,000,000; the $500,000 deduction for debts and expenses would reduce it to $6,500,000. In the prior example, the add back of the tax in effect cancels the deduction with the result that the gift tax is taxed because the money to pay the gift tax is still in her gross estate; in this example it is taxed by adding it back to the gross estate and, since it was paid before she died, there is no related deduction.

The next three examples (and the table that follows them) compare the estate tax results in three situations: 1) where the decedent did not make large taxable gifts, 2) where the decedent made large taxable gifts far enough in advance of his death to avoid grossing up, and 3) where the gift was so close to the donor's death that grossing up is required.

EXAMPLE 6 - 58. In 2008, X died owning property worth $10 million. X's estate paid death taxes of $3,600,000. X's child received $6,400,000.

EXAMPLE 6 - 59. In 2004, Y also owned $10 million, but he gave his child $5 million and paid gift tax of $1,869,720. Y died in 2008 (more than three years after making the gift), still owning $3,130,280 [$10 million - ($5 million gift and gift tax paid)]. Y's estate tax base was $8,119,280, and his death tax was $973,626. Therefore, Y's child received $7,156,654 [the gift plus the estate property less the gift and estate taxes]. Y's child received $756,654 more than X's child. [$7,156,654 - $6,400,000]. The difference is explained partly by the $11,000 gift tax annual exclusion, but mostly by the exclusion from the tax base of the gift taxes paid, diminished somewhat by the fact that the portion of the gift above $2,000,000 was taxed at 48% whereas the top rate for the estate was 45%, i.e., Y's estate saves as follows: 45% * $1,869,720 + 45% * $11,000 - 3% * $2,989,000 = $7,156,654.

EXAMPLE 6 - 60. Same facts as before, except Z died in 2007, within three years of making the gift. The gift tax is included in Z's gross estate, bringing it to $5,000,000 [$3,130,280 owned + $1,869,720 gift taxes] and resulting in an estate tax base of $9,989,000 [$5,000,000 gross estate + $4,989,000 adjusted taxable gift]. The tentative tax of $4,375,850 is reduced by the credit for gift tax payable (only $1,780,050) and the unified credit to result in estate tax of $3,684,720. Thus Z's child received a total of $6,315,280 [$10 million - ($1,869,720 gift tax + $3,684,720 estate tax)], which is 84,720 less than what X's child received. Explain the difference? There are two parts to this puzzl. Z's gift in excess of $2,000,000 is taxed at 48%, whereas had it been taxed in 2008 (or 2007) it would have been taxed at a 45% rate, so there is additional tax of $89,670. This is partially offset by the $11,000 annual exclusion that never is taxed, saving $4,950 (i.e., 45% times $11,000). The $84,720 is the difference between the net to X and Z's respective heirs.

	X	Y	Z
Gross Gifts	N.A.	$5,000,000	$5,000,000
Less annual exclusions, if any	N.A.	($11,000)	($11,000)
Taxable gifts	N.A.	$4,989,000	$4,989,000
Tentative tax (gifts)	N.A.	$2,215,520	$2,215,520
Less unified credit	N.A.	($345,800)	($345,800)
Gift tax	N.A.	$1,869,720	$1,869,720
Taxable estate	$10,000,000	$3,130,280	$5,000,000
Plus adj. taxable gifts, if any	$0	$4,989,000	$4,989,000
Estate tax base	$10,000,000	$8,119,280	$9,989,000
Tentative tax (estate)	$4,380,800	$3,534,476	$4,375,850
Less gift tax payable credit	$0	($1,780,050)	($1,780,050)
Less unified credit	($780,800)	($780,800)	($780,800)
Estate tax	$3,600,000	$973,626	$1,815,000
Total transfer tax (gift+estate) tax)))	$3,600,000	$2,843,346	$3,684,720
Net to the children	$6,400,000	$7,156,654	$6,315,280

Although, as demonstrated above, paying gift taxes might well save overall transfer taxes, most people, even the very wealthy, are unwilling to generate gift taxes, especially given the uncertainty of the future of the estate tax. Other techniques discussed later that reduce the estate without requiring the payment of gift taxes tend to be preferred; such things as zeroed out grantor retained income trusts (GRATs), qualified personal residents trusts (QPRTs), and limited partnerships are discussed in later chapters.

Tax exclusive versus tax inclusive calculations. A different way of describing the grossing up rule is that the gift tax is generally calculated on a tax exclusive basis, i.e., the amount of the gift tax is not included in the base. The taxes paid are not "taxable gifts" even though they are paid by the donor, nor are they part of the transfer tax base, provided the donor lives for another three years after making the gift that generated the gift taxes. On the other hand, the estate tax is calculated on a tax inclusive basis, i.e., the tax is levied on the "taxable estate" out of which the estate tax is paid and the tax itself is not a deduction. Grossing up converts a tax exclusive gift into a tax inclusive one.

Certain Transfers within Three Years of Death: §2035(a)

Section §2035(a) creates a rule that causes certain transferred property to be included in the gross estate even though there is no retained interest when the transferor dies. This three-year rule is subdivided into these two parts: (1) relinquishment or transfer of certain retained interests and (2) the transfer of life insurance.

Limited applicability of the three-year rule. A decedent's gross estate includes the value of property relinquished or given away within three years of his or her death, if that property would have been included in the decedent's gross estate under §§2036, 2037, 2038 (the retained interests sections), or §2042 (the life insurance section) had the decedent kept the interest. Do not apply the rule to any other type of transfer as this three-year rule applies to two, and only two, types of transfers: the *severance of a retained interest* (§§2036, 2037, 2038) or the gift of *life insurance* (§2042).

> EXAMPLE 6 - 61. D transferred property worth $1,000,000 into a trust, with income to S or C for S's life, then remainder to B. D retained the right to allocate the income between the two income beneficiaries. The trust terms also stated that the trustee was to allocate income equally between the two income beneficiaries in any year in which D failed to give written directions concerning the allocation. Because of D's retention of control over the property, no gift is deemed to have occurred. When D died, the trust was worth $1,940,000. D died possessing this right

to "sprinkle" the trust income; therefore, the entire value of the trust property (as of D's DOD) was included in D's gross estate by virtue of both §2036 and §2038.

EXAMPLE 6 - 62. Same as prior example except that in 2005, when the trust was worth $1,900,000, D relinquished his right to make the income allocation by writing a letter to the trustee stating that he irrevocably released his right to allocate the income. This act caused the gift to be complete. Note that the taxable gift is the full $1,900,000, because neither S nor C has an identifiable present interest. D paid gift taxes of $390,000. From that moment onward, D had no retained interest in the trust. However, both §2035(a) and §2035(b) apply if D dies within three years of the relinquishing his retained interest; in which case the property (at the DOD value) and the $390,000 in gift taxes would be included in D's gross estate, with the adjusted taxable gifts being reduced to zero. On the other hand, if D dies more than three years after the relinquishing the retained interest, neither the property nor the gift taxes are included, and the adjusted taxable gifts would be $1,900,000 for estate tax purposes. Either way, the gift tax payable credit of $390,000 would be available.

EXAMPLE 6 - 63. In 2002, D established an irrevocable trust managed by an independent trustee. By the terms of the trust, D retained all income for a period of 5 years, after which the trust terminated with the remainder interest held by D's adult children. D died in 2008; thus the trust had terminated the year before. Because D did not "release" a retained interest, the value of the trust is not included in D's estate even though D died within three years of the trust's termination. The retained interest had simply expired according to the original terms of the trust.

EXAMPLE 6 - 64. D transferred five bonds to C using the state's *Uniform Gift to Minors Act* to appoint herself custodian. D died before C reached the age of majority; therefore, the bonds are included in D's gross estate. Under the *Uniform Act*, D had the ability to liquidate some (or all) of the bonds and to distribute the proceeds to C or apply them for C's benefit. Thus both §§2036 and 2038 apply.

EXAMPLE 6 - 65. Same as prior example, except that shortly before D's death, he turned the bonds over to C because she reached the age at which the law required the custodianship to end (typically at 21 years of age). Even though D died within three years of transferring the bonds, they are not included in D's estate. The transfer was not a "release" of a retained interest, therefore §2035(a) does not apply. D did not release a retained interest, rather it had to end by virtue of the state's UTMA.

Enough release of retained interest stuff, time for a life insurance example.

EXAMPLE 6 - 66. In the year 2005, D assigned his ownership interest in a *life insurance* policy on his life to his cousin Vinney. D died in 2007. The insurance proceeds are included in his gross estate because the transfer occurred within three years of death. Had the transfer not been made, D's gross estate would include the insurance because of §2042. Had he survived more than three years after making the transfer, the gift value of the insurance on the date of transfer less the annual exclusion would enter the estate tax calculation merely as an adjusted taxable gift.

Remember that §2001(b) defines adjusted taxable gifts as post-1976 taxable gifts other than ones included in the gross estate of the donor. Hence where §2035(a) applies (or one of the retained interest sections applies) and the transferred property is brought back into the gross estate, it will not also be an adjusted taxable gift for estate tax purposes. In other words, where the remainder value of a trust, the release of a retained interest, or the transfer of life insurance was treated as a taxable gift but the property subsequently ends up included in the gross estate, the adjusted taxable gift value drops to zero for the calculation of the estate tax.

To avoid the three-year rule, planners make every effort to ensure that a wealthy client never possesses any incident of ownership in a newly issued policy. Thus, the insured can sign a consent to be the insured but he or she should not apply to be the owner. If the policy is owned by the trustee of an irrevocable trust, the insured must not be given any right to change beneficial ownership of the policy, borrow against the policy, change the beneficiary, or in any way influence the trustee as any of these rights would be incidents of ownership, requiring the policy be included in the insured's gross estate.

Finally, the three-year rule of §2035(a) does not apply to *premiums* paid by the insured-transferor, even if paid within three years of death. Therefore, such payments do not cause the insurance to be included in the insured's estate. The premiums themselves may be adjusted taxable gifts if they exceed the annual exclusion amount or are transferred in such a manner that no one has a present interest in them, i.e., to an irrevocable life insurance trust which does not contain a Crummey power. There will be more on life insurance trusts in Chapter 13.

As stated earlier, most transfers are not subject to §2035(a)'s three-year rule. Thus transfers of stocks, bonds, cash, gold, jewelry, land, and other *garden variety* transfers, even if within three years of the transferor's death, are not brought into the gross estate; if over the annual exclusion amount, they are, and remain, simply adjusted taxable gifts. Had the gift not been made, the property, if still owned by the decedent at death, would only be included in the gross estate under §2033, not one of those four sections specified in §2035(a). Thus, outright gifts of property (other than life insurance) are not included in the transferor's gross estate even if made within three years of death. Accordingly, to understand this material fully, the reader must distinguish a single transaction gift from an indirect-strings-attached transfer (almost always through a trust), followed by the transferor eventually relinquishing the retained interest.

> EXAMPLE 6 - 67. In 2007, Leslie gave her son $18,000 in common stock. She died one year later, at which time the stock was worth $200,000. Hey, it was a great investment. Nothing, insofar as this gift is concerned, is included in Leslie's gross estate. It is merely an adjusted taxable gift of $6,000.

The facts in the example immediately above demonstrate that lifetime gifts made shortly before the donor's death, while not included in the gross estate, may still be in the estate tax base as adjusted taxable gifts (i.e., the gift value reduced by annual exclusions) to boost the taxable estate into higher marginal rates. Whether transferred property is included in the *gross estate* or is included in the tax base as an *adjusted taxable gift* is an important distinction. All items in the gross estate are included at their date-of-death value (or their value on the alternate valuation date, if such is elected), whereas adjusted taxable gifts are included in the tax base (but not in the gross estate) at their date-of-gift values reduced by any available annual exclusions.

> EXAMPLE 6 - 68. Continuing the prior example, assume that Leslie transferred a life insurance policy (face value $200,000) on her life instead of transferring stock. At the time of the transfer, the policy's value for gift tax purposes was $18,000. If Leslie died more than three years after the transfer, the proceeds would not be in the gross estate and the adjusted taxable gifts would include the $6,000 (i.e., the $18,000 value reduced by the annual exclusion). On the other hand, if Leslie died within three years of the transfer, the gross estate would include the $200,000 *face value* and the adjusted taxable gifts would be zero insofar as this gift is concerned.

Congress singled out life insurance because of its unique characteristic of suddenly, and radically, increasing in value when the insured dies, a feature that strongly motivates taxpayers to avoid subjecting that increase to transfer taxes. In the absence of §2035(a), a deathbed gift of a policy on the life of the donor could cause a quick, relatively large avoidance of estate tax, at little or no gift tax cost. For example, without §2035(a), a deathbed gift of a $1 million term policy might avoid estate tax on the entire face value with no gift tax consequences.

Comparing powers of appointment to retained interests. Consider that almost any retained interest by the settlor (trustor) of a trust results in the inclusion of the trust in the settlor's estate regardless of how meager the retained interest was, whereas a power can be very broad and, so long as it is not a general power, the property subject to the power is not in the holder's estate. So, when trying to determine whether a trust that is connected in some way to a decedent should be included in the decedent's estate, it is helpful to use a decision table, whereby one starts by determining whether the interest is a retained power or a power of appointment. You might find it helpful to diagram the decision table that follows.

1. Did the decedent create or fund the trust? If no, go to #5, if yes, go to #2.
2. Did the decedent retain an interest in the trust that either gave the decedent an economic benefit or the ability to control enjoyment? If no, then it is not in the decedent's estate. If yes, go to #3.
3. Did the decedent release the retained interest? If no, it is in the decedent's estate. If yes, go to #4.
4. Was the release within three years of decedent's death? If yes, the property is in the decedent's gross estate at the date-of-death value. If no, it is not in the gross estate, but it is an adjusted taxable gift.
5. Did someone give the decedent a power to appoint property such that the decedent would be considered the holder of a power? If no, then the trust property is not in the decedent's estate. If yes, go on to #6.
6. Could the decedent at any time have appointed the property to decedent's self, decedent's creditors, decedent's estate, or the creditors of the estate? If yes, it was a general power; go on to #7. If no, it was a limited power, and as such it is not included in the gross estate nor is it an adjusted taxable gift.
7. Was the general power still there when the holder died? If yes, the property subject to the power (whether exercised or lapsed) is included in the holder's estate. If no, go on to #8 if it lapsed during the holder's lifetime, go to #9 if it was exercised during life, or go back to #2 if the power was released by the holder (the release makes the "holder" a settlor as to the portion of trust that could have been claimed).
8. Was the general power greater than the greater of $5,000 or 5% of the trust (i.e., a 5 & 5 power)? If no, it is not in the gross estate, only because it was not in effect when the holder died. If it did exceed the 5 & 5 limits before it lapsed *and* the holder continued to have an interest in the trust, go back to #1 [the lapsed % that exceeded 5% (or $5,000 if greater) is probably included as a retained interest]. If yes, but the holder had no continuing interest in the

trust after the lapse, nothing is included, but the lapsed % that exceeded 5% (or $5,000) is an adjusted taxable gift.

9. When the general power was exercised, was the property given to the decedent or the decedent's creditors, or did the decedent exercise the power in favor of someone else? If exercised in the holder's favor, then there is no taxable gift (but presumably the property increased the holder's estate). If exercised in favor of someone else (i.e., "trustee, please give $25,000 to my friend Betty"), it would be treated as a gift from the holder, and, if over the annual exclusion amount, it would be treated as an adjusted taxable gift.

Use the decision table as you work through these examples (assume all trusts are irrevocable unless otherwise stated).

EXAMPLE 6 - 69. Sandra created an irrevocable trust for her brother Duane. Duane received all income each year, and he could appoint up to 5% of the corpus of the trust to whomever he might choose each year. Duane's children were the remaindermen. When he died, the trust was valued at $1,000,000 and he had never exercised the power. Because this is a general power, even though it lapses unexercised, $50,000 [5%*$1,000,000] is included in his gross estate. Note that the $50,000 remains in the trust (it is not part of Duane's probate estate). The trustee of the trust will have any of Duane's estate taxes attributed to the inclusion of the $50,000 (i.e., the pro rata amount of this trust portion compared to the rest of Duane's taxable estate), unless his estate plan calls for some special allocation of the estate taxes.

EXAMPLE 6 - 70. David created a trust for Keith. The trustee could distribute as much of the income or trust as the trustee thought would be good for Keith. The trustee never exercised the special power other than to give Keith income from time to time. The trust gave Keith the unrestricted power to appoint up to 25% of the corpus at his death through specific mention of the power in his will. Lillian, or her estate, was the remainderman. Keith died with a will that made no mention of the trust. The trust was worth $1,000,000 when Keith died. Since this is a general power, Keith's estate will include $250,000 [25% * $1,000,000] even though the power was restricted to exercise at death and Keith let it lapse without exercise.

EXAMPLE 6 - 71. Curtis created a trust to benefit Donna for life, with remainder to her children. Roberta was the initial trustee, with Koala National Bank as the successor trustee. The trustee had the power to appoint as much of the trust to Donna as the trustee thought was needed to keep Donna happy. The power was never exercised and the trust was worth $1,000,000 when Donna died. Since Donna was neither a holder nor the settlor, none of the trust is included in her estate. What if Roberta dies before Donna–is any of the trust included in her estate? No, Roberta is a holder, but a holder of a limited power. And Curtis? Nothing is in his estate; he created the trust, but he did not retain any interest.

EXAMPLE 6 - 72. The same facts apply as in the prior example, except Curtis retained the right to appoint himself trustee. The entire trust would be included in his estate, since he retained the power to determine who would enjoy the property even though he could not benefit himself.

EXAMPLE 6 - 73. At a time when the 7520 rate for valuing split-interest gifts was 12%, Melinda, aged 65, established an irrevocable trust funded with all her worldly possessions and investments worth $1,000,000. The independent trustee was to pay her income for life with the remainder paid to her friend Dianne. The value of the gift (the remainder) using Table S was $226,950. Since this was a gift of a future interest, there was no annual exclusion. When Melinda died six years later, the trust was worth $1,125,000 and the full amount had to be included in her estate. The adjusted taxable gift for estate tax calculation drops to zero because property that is drawn back into the gross estate is not also counted as an adjusted taxable gift.

EXAMPLE 6 - 74. In 1997, 80-year-old Alejandro established an irrevocable trust funded with investments worth $750,000 (just a small portion of his vast wealth). The independent trustee was to pay income to such individuals as Alejandro each year directed. In any year Alejandro failed to direct the trustee, the income had to be accumulated. At the end of 10 years, the trust was to terminate and the remainder was to be paid to Alejandro's sister Irene, or to her issue. Even though the settlor did not retain any economic interest, the retention of control causes this to be an incomplete gift, hence nothing, not even a remainder interest, is treated as a gift. When Alejandro died in 2005, the trust was worth $1,375,000. This is the value included in his gross estate. In 2007, the trust terminated and the property, then worth $1,500,000 was distributed to Irene. No new gift or transfer taxes occur as a result of this termination.

EXAMPLE 6 - 75. Suppose, in the preceding example, Alejandro died two years after the trust terminated. The results would be quite different. With the termination of the trust, his right to direct income ceased and a gift of $1,500,000 was complete. Alejandro would have paid gift taxes of $204,840 on the gift (Irene is the donee, so there is an annual exclusion of $12,000). The trust would not be included in his gross estate because he did not have any retained interests when he died. What about the fact that the retained interest ceased within three years of his death? It would not be a "release" of a retained interest since the interest merely ended as per the terms of the original trust, therefore §2035(a) does not apply. However, §2035(b) does apply and the $204,840 must be included in his gross estate. Of course, since the trust property itself is not included in the gross estate, an adjusted taxable gift in the amount of $1,488,000 and a $204,840 gift tax payable credit are part of the estate tax calculation.

For the next four alternative examples, the common facts are as follows: Melanie created an irrevocable trust with assets worth $750,000. The trust required income be distributed to Carol or Sean in such amounts as Melanie allocates each year. Any year she fails to advise the trustee on the allocation, and after her death as well, the income must be divided equally between Carol and Sean. After an income beneficiaries dies, the income must be paid to the sole survivor; and after both die, the trust must terminate and be distributed to Ruben, or to his estate. Because of Melanie's retained control, no taxable transfer of the corpus occurs until her right to allocate income ends. Until then, she will be taxed on the income and each distribution to Carol or Sean must be treated as if it was a gift directly from her.

EXAMPLE 6 - 76. Suppose two years after establishing the trust, Melanie died and the trust was worth $1,180,000. Her estate would include the date-of-death amount, not because she died within three years of establishing the trust, but because she retained a §2036 interest.

EXAMPLE 6 - 77. Suppose that Melanie died seven years after establishing the trust. The trust was then worth $1,585,000. The date-of-death amount is included; again, this is a retained interest and inclusion has nothing to do with a three-year rule.

EXAMPLE 6 - 78. Suppose instead that in 2004, when the trust was worth $2,100,000, Melanie released her right to decide who gets the income (i.e., she wrote a letter to the trustee stating that she irrevocably gives up her right to make any further income allocations). In 2006, almost two years later, she died. At that time the trust was worth $2,250,000. The release was a taxable gift, resulting in her payment of gift taxes in the amount of $472,440 (assuming two $11,000 annual exclusions). Because of §2035(a), her gross estate includes the date-of-death value of the trust, i.e., $2,250,000, and because her gift was within three years of her death, the $472,440 is also included in her gross estate. Her adjusted taxable gifts are zero and a gift taxes paid credit of $472,440 is available.

EXAMPLE 6 - 79. Change the facts; suppose Melanie released her right to allocate income in 2004, as in the last example, when the trust was worth $2,100,000, and died in the year 2008, when the trust was worth $2,375,000. Nothing insofar as this trust is concerned is in her gross estate since her death was more than three years after she released her retained interest. When she released the right to allocate income, there was a taxable gift ($2,078,000) that resulted in gift tax of $472,440. Her estate reports $2,078,000 as an adjusted taxable gift but can only claim a gift tax payable credit of $470,880 since the estate tax marginal rate is lower than was the gift tax marginal rate and the gift is not included in the gross estate.

RULES

THE CONNECTION BETWEEN GIFTS & THE DONOR'S ESTATE

These **rules** should help you understand how post-1976 gifts relate to the donor's estate:

One: Generally, gifts given are simply "adjusted taxable gifts" to the extent such gifts exceed the annual exclusion. §2001(b)(2).

Two: Gift taxes paid (or payable) are generally allowed as a credit against the tentative tax to offset the fact that the adjusted taxable gifts are used to boost the estate into its appropriate marginal rate. §2001(b)(2).

Three: Gift taxes paid on <u>any</u> gift made within three years of death are added to the gross estate. §2035(b). [This is referred to as "grossing up" the estate.]

Four: Retained interests in transfers (usually transfers in trust) will cause the property transferred to be included in the transferor's estate as though the transfer never took place. §§2036 - 2038.

Five: There are only three exceptions to rule number one:

a. Transfers of an interest in **life insurance** within three years of death will result in the date-of-death value being included in the transferor's estate. §2035(a).

b. The **release** of a **retained** interest within three years of death will result in the date-of-death value of the trust assets being included in the settlor's estate as though no release occurred. §2035(a).

c. Where an interest that was given away on the creation of a joint tenancy is included in a deceased joint tenant's estate because of the "consideration furnished test," it will be included at the date-of-death value. §2040.

Notes to rules four and five: If a transferred property ends up in the gross estate, it will **not** also be an adjusted taxable gift for *estate* tax purposes. If transferred property is in the gross estate, it must be valued as of the date of death **not** the date of the gift. Finally, if gift taxes were paid and the property ends up in the gross estate, the estate is still entitled to a credit against the estate tax for those gift taxes.

Part-Sale, Part-Gift Transfers: §2043

Some people wrongly believe that a transfer is not a gift if the transferor receives any consideration in exchange. They think that a small token from the donee shelters the transaction from gift taxation. The correct result is that unless the transaction is at arm's length, a gift occurs measured by the *difference* between the respective values of the consideration exchanged.

Where IRC § 2035(a) (the three-year rule), §§ 2036-2038 (retained interests), or § 2041 (a general power of appointment) result in property sold as part of a bargain sale to be included in the seller's gross estate, §2043 provides that the date-of-death value of the property is reduced by a "consideration offset." This means that the estate must include the value at its date-of-death fair market value, but can subtract the value of the consideration received.

> EXAMPLE 6 - 80. D "sold" his son his $20,000 vacation home, reserving the right to use the home from time to time. D was "paid" 200 shares of very speculative stock then worth just $1,000. When D died, the stock was worth $17,000 and the vacation home was worth $30,000. His gross estate will include the date-of-death value of the home [i.e., $30,000], less only the $1,000 received as consideration. The post-gift appreciation on both the stock received (because D owns it) and the vacation home (because of the retained interest) are in D's estate. Note that there is no three-year rule involved here.

The example immediately above illustrates relatively uncommon estate-planning transfers. Most bargain-sale-type transfers are treated differently because they generally do not include a retained interest or a general power of appointment. Therefore, since the transferred property is not included in the gross estate, the §2043 offset rule does not apply. However, a simple bargain sale will be included in the *estate tax base* as an adjusted taxable gift equal to the original gross gift value, less both the annual exclusion(s) and the consideration received by the donor.

> EXAMPLE 6 - 81. In 2005, Jessie "sold" a parcel of land to her son Charles for a mere $200 even though they both knew it was worth $50,000. This sale is not subject to a retained interest or a general power of appointment, therefore §2043 does not apply. Jessie will be treated as having made a gross gift of $49,800 and a taxable gift of $38,800. If Jessie dies before 2010, the $38,800 will show up as an adjusted taxable gift that will boost her estate into higher marginal rates.

It should be kept in mind that §2043 applies only to transfers included in the gross estate under §§ 2035(a), 2036-2038, or 2041. Section 2043 does not specifically mention §2042 (life insurance), but §2035(a) does. So, if life insurance is "sold," other than in an arm's length transaction within three years of the insured's death, §2043 will apply.

EXAMPLE 6 - 82. Four years before he died, Max sold Rita a $100,000 face-value policy on his life. At the time, they both knew that it had a gift value of $1,800 but Max charged Rita just $500. Since more than three years have passed, his gross estate does not include this policy. However, the transfer-for-value rule will render the proceeds in excess of the purchase price taxable as income to Rita.

EXAMPLE 6 - 83. Based on the facts in the prior example, if Max died within three years of the "sale," his estate would be increased by $99,500, i.e., a $500 offset is allowed based on §2043 which makes a reference to §2035(a) (three year rule) that, in turn, makes a reference to §2042 (life insurance).

ESTATE TAX DEDUCTIONS

Estate tax deductions include funeral expenses, expenses in administering the estate, claims against the estate, debts of the decedent, losses incurred during estate administration,[45] charitable bequests,[46] and the marital deduction.[47] In this section, we will introduce the marital deduction and charitable deduction, both of which are developed in detail in later chapters.

Marital Deduction: §2056

In calculating the taxable estate, the gross estate may be reduced by the value of any qualifying interest in property passing from the decedent to the surviving spouse. Thus, essentially an "unlimited" amount of property passing to the surviving spouse can avoid estate taxation, provided that certain requirements are met.

Requirements for the marital deduction. Subject to several exceptions, a property transfer to a spouse will qualify for the unlimited marital deduction if it meets the following three requirements:

1. *Included in decedent's gross estate.* The property must be *included* in the decedent's gross estate.

2. *Passes to the surviving spouse.* The property must actually *pass* to the surviving spouse.

3. *Not a terminable interest.* To qualify for the marital deduction, the interest passing to the surviving spouse cannot be a terminable interest.

To qualify for the full marital deduction, most estate plans require taxes and expenses be paid from property *not* qualifying for the marital deduction. An additional problem of paying estate taxes out of the marital share is the need to make interrelated computations, i.e., in order to calculate the amount of the marital deduction, one needs to know the amount of the tax; however, in order to calculate the tax, the amount of the marital deduction must be calculated.

> EXAMPLE 6 - 84. When Orca died in 2005, she left an estate with a net value of $5 million. Her will left a pecuniary bequest of $2 million to Walter, her son by a prior marriage, and the residue to her husband Martin. Unfortunately for Martin, she used a will form that had the clause "all estate taxes shall be paid from the residue of my estate." Because the tax on the transfer to Walter reduces Martin's interest in the estate, it also reduces the marital deduction, which in turn further increases the tax, etc., with the final result that the tax is $424,528 and Martin receives just $2,575,528. If the tax was charged to Walter's share, the marital deduction would be $3,000,000 and the tax would drop to $225,000.

You can work the above example using ETAX: put 5000000 in as the "gross estate" and +3000000-b21 in the "deductions" cell.[48]

A *terminable interest*, defined in §2056(b)(1), is one that *might* terminate on the happening of some event or contingency or on the failure of some event or contingency. The terminable interest rule was created to ensure that property owned by a married couple is taxed in at least one of the spouses' estates. There are exceptions to the rule, each of which is intended to facilitate legitimate estate planning goals yet assure that the property will eventually be taxed in one of the spouses estates. Without these rules, property could qualify for the marital deduction in the estate of the first spouse and never show up in the estate of the surviving spouse.

> EXAMPLE 6 - 85. In his will, Bruno transfers property into a trust, with income to his wife for her life, then remainder to his child. The value of the life interest to the wife will not qualify for the marital deduction because it will "terminate ... on the occurrence of an event...." The event that causes termination of her interest is her death. In general, unless a special election is made, a *life estate interest* passing to a surviving spouse does not qualify for the marital deduction. The special election is described below.

Because of the way the code section defines a terminable interest, a transfer to a surviving spouse will not be considered a terminable one if no other person will possess or enjoy any part of the property after the interest passing to the surviving spouse terminates.

EXAMPLE 6 - 86. At her death, Mrs. Carrie, an inventor, was receiving annual payments from several companies using one of her patented ideas. Her husband received her entire estate, including the patent rights (good for 20 years when first issued) that still had 14 years left. The value of the patent is included in Mrs. Carrie's estate and it qualifies for a marital deduction because *no other person* will enjoy any part of the property after the patent is finished.

Exceptions to the terminable interest rule. There are several exceptions to the terminable interest rule that will be covered in detail in the chapter that introduces estate plans for wealthy couples. We will just introduce three of the major ones here.

Short survivorship clauses. First, the rule will not be violated if decedent-testator conditions a spousal bequest on surviving no more than *six months* after the decedent's death.[49] Thus, the survival clauses specifying "30 days" or "four months" are regularly included in the wills and do create terminable interests, but the exception allows them to qualify for the marital deduction provided the spouse lives long enough for the interest to vest. Some states, such as California, have enacted *marital deduction saving* statutes for those wills and trusts that show a clear intention to qualify for the marital deduction but which, due to poor drafting, include a survivorship period in excess of six months. The statutes reduce the survivorship period to six months. Other statutes provide a more generic solution, such as declaring void any provision that would cause the loss of the marital deduction whenever it is clear from the estate plan that the availability of the deduction was intended.[50] Unfortunately, judicial reaction to these statutes has been less than enthusiastically supportive.

Life estate coupled with a general power of appointment. Second, a transfer in which the surviving spouse receives a life estate in all of the income, payable at least annually, plus a *general power of appointment*, exercisable during life and/or at death (usually accomplished through language in the holder's will), is allowed to qualify for the marital deduction.[51] This arrangement is used in what is called a *general power of appointment trust*, a type of marital trust covered in Chapters 9 and 10 as part of our discussion of estate planning for wealthy couples.

The Qualified Terminable Interest Property (QTIP) Election. Third, if the surviving spouse is given a life estate in a portion of the decedent's estate, the executor can elect to claim a marital deduction on that portion of the estate. The property must be *qualified terminable interest property* (QTIP) meaning that it meets certain Code requirements; most importantly the surviving spouse must have a life estate in the property.[52] Making the QTIP election requires a trade-off; the property that qualifies for the marital deduction because of the election must be included in the surviving spouse's estate when he or she dies.[53] A further discussion of this important estate planning tool is postponed until we study estate plans for wealthy couples in Chapters 9 and 10.

Special rules for transfers to a non-U.S. citizen spouse. Property passing at death to a non-U.S. citizen *surviving spouse* does not qualify for the marital deduction unless it is placed in a *qualified domestic trust* (QDOT). The QDOT does not have to be established before the first spouse dies, indeed it does not have to have been part of the couple's estate plan, i.e., the survivor is allowed to create (and fund) the QDOT. The surviving spouse receives the income for her lifetime. The QDOT assets are subject to the estate tax (based on the first spouse to die's estate) when the surviving spouse dies or when corpus is transferred to her free of trust. There is an exception that allows distributions to the surviving spouse for emergencies without the distribution triggering a transfer tax. The marital deduction is also allowed if the surviving spouse becomes a U.S. citizen before the estate tax return is filed (even if filed late).[54] The rationale for requiring the creation of this trust is to ensure collection of the estate tax on the death of a surviving spouse who might otherwise remove the wealth from the United States.

Charitable Deduction: §2055

The charitable deduction is evidence of Congressional encouragement of philanthropy. Compared to the various rules limiting the amount of deduction for income taxes, the charitable deduction is quite simple insofar as the transfer tax system is concerned. Outright transfers to qualified charities (most U.S.-based religious organizations, publicly funded educational institutions, organizations for the disabled, for health research, etc.) are 100% deductible for both estate and gift tax purposes. For gifts, the deduction is based on the value of the gift at the moment of transfer. For a bequest, it is the value of the property at the date of death or the alternate valuation date if such is elected.

EXAMPLE 6 - 87. True story: David Marine had been a doctor. At the time of his death in 1984, he had accumulated considerable wealth, but had very few friends and no close relatives. His executors were given the limited power to appoint his estate to such "persons who have contributed to my well-being or who have been otherwise helpful to me during my lifetime...." The bequest to any one of these persons was limited to no more than one percent of his estate, with a provision that it "may be considerably less." The residue of the estate was left in equal shares to Princeton University and Johns Hopkins University. The net estate was worth $2,130,081, of which the executors appointed $10,000 to Dr. Marine's housekeeper and another $15,000 to a friend of his. The balance of the estate was divided between the two universities and the executor claimed a $2,105,081 charitable deduction. The IRS successfully challenged the deduction on the grounds that at the time of the doctor's death, the amount that would eventually go to the universities was unascertainable. The court stated that, although the amount of each bequest was limited to one percent of the corpus, since "the number of such bequests was unlimited and a standard for determining the amount of a bequest was uncertain, the amount of the charitable bequest could not be ascertained at the time of death and the deduction was not available."[55] The tax on a taxable estate of $2,130,081 in 1984 was $748,240.

EXAMPLE 6 - 88. Another true story, this one with a happier ending: Anne Scheiber died on January 9, 1995, at the age of 101. She had worked for the IRS. Her salary was just $3,150 per year when she retired in 1943. In 1944, she used her life savings of $5,000 to open an investment account. By living frugally, investing, and reinvesting, her stock and bond investments had grown to over $20 million when she died. Except for $50,000 that went to a niece, the balance of her estate (more than $22 million by the time it was distributed) went to Yeshiva University, a small co-ed university in New York City. The bequest specified that it be used for women's scholarships. The estate paid no estate taxes.

If a bequest is left to the discretion of the executor (or of a beneficiary), then no estate tax deduction will be allowed even if the person decides to leave a portion of the estate to a charity. Thus, precatory words (i.e., an earnest request) in a will such as, "I leave $100,000 to Reverend Teagarden in the hope he will use it for the ministry of the Church," do not result in a charitable deduction.

Transfers made to charities through the use of trusts must meet certain requirements specified in Code §2055. The special requirements for charitable giving through the use of trusts are designed to give reasonable assurance that the charity will actually receive a benefit that is reasonably close to the amount of tax deduction allowed, whether the deduction is an income tax deduction in the case of lifetime gifts or an estate tax deduction for transfers that take place at the death of the donor. Additional material on charitable gifts and the charitable deduction is found in later chapters.

Expenses, Debts, and Taxes: §2053

In determining the gross estate, a deduction is allowed for certain expenses, debts, and taxes. Generally, expenses associated with transferring the estate are deductible. These include executor and trustee's commissions (i.e., fees), attorney and accountant's fees. Reasonable expenses incurred in connection with the burial of the decedent are also deductible, e.g., for funeral services, burial lot, tombstone, and/or cremation.

Deductible debts would include credit card balances, unpaid utility bills, and most mortgages, liens, and promissory note obligations. Mortgages and liens are deductible in full if they are secured by property included in the estate and they are recourse obligations. Recourse debt means that if the property securing the obligation had to be sold so the creditor could collect the debt and the sale proceeds were insufficient, the other assets of the estate would have to be used to pay the deficiency. With non-recourse debt, the creditor looks only to the asset for payment, and if there is a deficiency the creditor has no further recourse. With non-recourse debt, the deduction is limited to the value of the security. A debt voluntarily incurred is deductible only if the liability was created in exchange for an adequate and full consideration in money or money's worth.[56] Hence, the balance on a promissory note that was signed when the decedent borrowed money is fully deductible. On the other hand, if the decedent signed a note promising to pay his daughter $5,000 upon her graduation, that debt is not deductible even if the daughter graduated before decedent died; although the promise might be legally binding, there is no exchange for money or money's worth.

Claims against the estate, such as for torts (e.g., negligently causing injury, slander, and assault), are deductible. Taxes that are deductible include income taxes on the decedent's final returns, accrued property taxes on property included in the gross estate, unpaid gift taxes, and, since 2005, state inheritance or estate taxes. The federal estate tax is not deductible. Note that property taxes that accrue after the decedent's death may be deductible as an expense of administering the estate but fiduciary income taxes are not deductible.

Losses: 2054

Akin to the casualty loss deduction allowed for determining taxable income, estates are allowed a deduction from the gross estate for "losses incurred during the settlement of the estates arising from fires, storms, shipwrecks, or other casualties, or from theft, when such losses are not compensated for by insurance or otherwise."[57] Even though the estate is still open, no deduction is allowed if the damage, destruction, or theft occurs after the property is distributed to a beneficiary. If the estate claims an income tax casualty loss, it cannot deduct the same loss for estate tax purposes.[58]

ESTATE TAX CREDITS

As mentioned in the last chapter, there are five main estate tax credits: the unified credit, credit for state death taxes, credit for gift taxes payable, credit for tax on prior transfers, and the credit for foreign death taxes. Since the unified credit and the state death tax credit were covered in the last chapter, the following material discusses only the other three. Each of these credits represents Congress's attempt to take the sting out of the fact that some transfers may be taxed twice.

Credit/Offset for Gift Taxes Paid or Payable

To help prevent double taxation, the unified transfer tax system allows some level of offset for gift taxes on all gifts included in the decedent's estate tax base. Without this offset, the estate tax would be calculated on all accumulated transfers whether at death or as gifts, unfairly disregarding the fact that a transfer tax had already been paid on some of them. The law allows offsets for two different categories of gift taxes: those paid on pre-1977 gifts, and those paid on post-1976 gifts.

Credit for gift taxes on pre-1977 gifts. The credit for gift tax on pre-1977 gifts shows up on line 17, page one, of the estate tax return. The amount of the credit is limited to the lesser of the gift tax or the estate tax on the property that is included in the estate.[59] One might wonder why there would be a credit for gift taxes on pre-1977 gifts given that only post-1976 gifts are included as adjusted taxable gifts in calculating the estate tax. Well, it is possible to have a pre-1977 gift pulled back into the donor's gross estate if the gift had a retained interest attached such that §2036, §2037, or §2038 applies, or if the donor-decedent had made a pre-1977 transfer with a retained interest and relinquished the interest within three years of death such that §2035(a) applies.

> EXAMPLE 6 - 89. In 1975, decedent, then age 50, created an irrevocable trust, funding it with $2 million in property. Under the terms of the trust, income was payable to the decedent for life, with remainder to his descendants. Decedent paid a gift tax of $235,118 on the gift of the *remainder* interest. If decedent dies today, his gross estate will include today's value of the entire trust corpus, under §2036. A credit for gift tax paid will be allowed based on the lesser of the gift tax paid in 1975 that is attributable to the gift (pro rata share if more than one gift that year), or the amount of estate tax attributed to having the trust included in his taxable estate (i.e., the pro rata share of the federal estate tax attributable to including the trust in the taxable estate). Obviously, as we move further from 1976 the likelihood of a post-1976 trust being included in a decedent's estate decreases and the importance of this credit diminishes, especially since the credit applies only if the establishment of the trust by the decedent resulted in a gift tax.

Credit for gift taxes paid or payable on post-1976 gifts. It should be clear that two categories of post-1976 gifts are included in the decedent's estate tax base. First, as with pre-1977 gifts described in the previous section, post-1976 gifts that fall within the grasp of §§ 2036, 2037, 2038, or 2035(a) are included in the transferor's gross estate. Although the Code does not specifically address a credit for the gift tax paid in situations where previously taxed gifts are pulled back into the gross estate, it stands to reason that a credit must be allowed for the full amount actually paid (not some recalculated "payable" amount) since the transferred property is drawn back into the gross estate at its date-of-death value. Second, adjusted taxable gifts (post-1976 gifts that are not in the gross estate) are added to the estate tax base. Again, to prevent double taxation, the law allows an offset to the tentative tax for gift taxes paid on these gifts.[60] This offset is calculated by determining the amount that would have been "payable" had the tax rates in effect at the decedent's death been applicable at the time of the gift. The gift tax paid may be more than the payable amount if the decedent made taxable gifts both pre-1977 and post-1976, since the earlier gifts pushed the later gifts into higher tax brackets but are not included as adjusted taxable gifts for present estate tax calculations. As discussed in detail in Chapter 5, the gift tax payable credit will be less than the gift taxes paid if the marginal rates applied to the gift were higher than those in effect at the time of the donor's death. Although the code section does not refer to this offset as a "credit," it has the effect of reducing the tentative tax dollar for dollar to an amount called the "gross estate tax," and it clearly is a credit. This credit is placed on line seven of page one of Form 706.

The Prior Transfer Credit: §2013

It seems inequitable to tax property twice on those occasions when it passes swiftly through two estates such that the second owner only had a limited opportunity to enjoy the inherited property. Congress obviously agrees. It has given relief in the form of a prior transfer credit (PTC) if the two deaths occur within 10 years of each other.[61]

Background on the PTC. As originally enacted, double taxation was avoided by allowing a deduction in the second estate equal to the value of property traceable to the first estate.[62] The relief was available only if the two deaths occurred within five years of one another and the old law required the executor claiming the deduction to trace the property from the first estate into the second. If the inherited property was sold and the proceeds were commingled with other funds out of which both investments and consumables were purchased, it was difficult (sometimes impossible) to trace the property. There was a fair amount of litigation between estates and the IRS over the tracing issue.

The PTC today. Present law allows a tax credit where property is included in the transferor's taxable estate and the transferee dies within 10 years of the transferor. The inherited property does not have to be found in the transferee's estate, hence tracing is no longer necessary. Since the credit is intended to reduce the unfairness of taxing property that passes quickly through two estates, a time factor affects the amount of the credit available, decreasing the maximum available by 20% two years after the transferor's death and another 20% for each additional two-year period until the credit disappears altogether at the end of 10 years. Actually, the credit is available even if the transferee dies two years before the transferor, but the circumstances, involving vested remainder interests, are so rare that they will not be covered. The credit, before applying the time factor, is based on the amount of additional tax the inclusion of the transferred property generates in each estate. Since this is relief from double taxation, the credit is equal to the lesser of the two amounts.

The above overview greatly simplifies the law. The actual calculation is a three-step process. In the explanation that follows, D1 represents the first decedent and D2 the second decedent (the recipient of property from D1's estate).

Credit Limit One. Limit one is the portion of the federal estate tax which bears the same ratio to D1's estate tax as the transferred property bears to D1's taxable estate.

$$CL1 = \frac{adjusted\ value\ of\ transferred\ property}{adjusted\ value\ of\ D1's\ taxable\ estate} * D1's\ federal\ estate\ tax$$

Credit Limit Two. Compute the increase in estate tax at D2's death caused by inclusion of the net value of the transferred property. The net value is the value of the transferred property reduced by all death taxes (federal and state) attributed to it at D1's death. The federal estate tax is determined with the net value of the property included, then again with it excluded, with the difference between the two amounts being credit limit two.[63]

Federal tax on D2's taxable estate (including transferred property)	xxxx
Federal tax on D2's reduced estate (reduced by the adjusted value of the transferred property)	(xxxx)
Credit Limit Two	xxx

Time Factor. The prior transfer credit is the *lesser of* limit one and limit two, times the appropriate time factor percentage based on how many years D2 lived after D1 died.

Years	1 - 2	3 - 4	5 - 6	7 - 8	9 - 10
Percentage	100%	80%	60%	40%	20%

An extended prior transfer credit example. As we go through each of the three prior transfer credit (PTC) steps, we will start each with some general comments. For limit one, the numerator is the value of the transferred property, adjusted by deducting liens, mortgages, and the transferred property's proportionate share of federal and state death taxes. The denominator is D1's taxable estate, adjusted by deducting all death taxes. If the net value of the property (property less liens and mortgages) is used in this step of the calculation, and all death taxes are allocated pro rata, there is no need to make any adjustments for the taxes since the adjusted values (above and below the line) will be in the same ratio as the unadjusted values. If the property in D2's estate is the result of a bequest made "free of estate tax," which probably means the residue of the estate paid the death taxes, the transferred property's value (the numerator) would not be adjusted for taxes but the taxable estate (the denominator) would have to be reduced by all death taxes.

The federal estate tax is adjusted only if one of two very rare events occurs; either a credit for gift taxes was allowed for D1's estate under §2012 (pre-1977 transfers with a retained interest) or if D1's estate also benefited from a prior transfer credit. For most PTC computations, no adjustments need to be made to the denominator to adjust the value of D1's taxable estate, other than for death taxes, and (as pointed out earlier) even then an adjustment is not necessary for the numerator or the denominator if the death taxes were proportionately assessed. The significance of this is that limit one is almost always simply the portion of D1's federal estate tax allocated to the property left to D2, i.e., if D2 received one-fourth of D1's estate, limit one is one-fourth of D1's estate tax. Use the ETAX program to follow along with these examples.

> EXAMPLE 6 - 90. D1 died February 15, 2004, leaving a taxable estate of $6,000,000. Each of D1's children received one-third of the estate. The total D1 estate taxes were $2,145,000. D1's state was a pickup tax state, so it collected an amount equal to the federal state death tax credit ($127,700), and the balance of $2,017,300 went to the Federal Treasury. D1's son, D2, died March 28, 2008, leaving a taxable estate of $5,000,000. In D1's estate the death taxes were allocated pro rata. Credit limit one is calculated as follows:

$$CL1 = \frac{\$2,000,000}{\$6,000,000} * \$2,017,300 = \$672,433$$

Notice that D2 received one-third of the estate and limit one is one-third of D1's federal estate tax. Remember, the assets transferred need not be part of D2's estate, so no tracing of assets is required. The theory is, that if the property had been sold, and the proceeds consumed, the money from the sale allowed D2 to retain other property that is taxed in D2's estate. The value of D2's estate is not used in calculating credit limit one.

There are three steps to calculating credit limit two. These steps determine that part of D2's federal tax that is attributable to the property D2 received from D1. The calculation is done by figuring the federal estate tax both with the net value of the transferred property included, and again with it excluded, with the difference being the additional tax attributed to the inherited property. First, determine the federal amount that would have been paid on D2's taxable estate, i.e., reduce the tentative tax by the unified credit and the state death tax credit. For estates after 2004 there is no state death tax credit so the calculation is simpler. Second, determine the federal estate tax on D2's estate with the net value of the transferred property removed. We call this D2's *reduced* taxable estate. To arrive at D2's reduced taxable estate, one must subtract from D2's taxable estate the net value of the property transferred from D1's estate. To determine the net value of the transferred property, subtract from the value of the property transferred its *share* of *all* death taxes (yes, including state death taxes, if any) and any debts, liens, or other obligations that reduced the value of the property when it was transferred from D1 to D2. Generally, we will ignore debts and the like, and just work with net values.

Continuing with this example, credit limit two is calculated as follows:

Federal estate tax on D2's $5,000,000 taxable estate	$1,350,000
Less federal estate tax on D2's reduced taxable estate.	
This is the tax on $3,715,000, i.e.,	
$5,000,000 - (1/3 * ($6,000,000 - $2,145,000))	(771,750)
Credit limit two	$578,250

The figure $1,350,000 is the federal estate tax on an estate of $5,000,000 after subtracting the unified credit for 2007 of $780,800 from the tentative tax. The calculation (1/3 * ($6,000,000 - ($2,145,000)) is the net value of the property transferred, that is, one-third of D1's estate adjusted for its pro rata share of *all* death taxes. The figure $771,750 is the federal tax on D2's reduced taxable estate of $3,715,000.

To finish this example, the time factor adjustment must be made. Since D2 died just a little over four years after D1's death, the allowable credit is 60% of the lesser of the two credit limits. Therefore:

$$60\% * \text{ the lesser of } \begin{cases} \textit{limit one: } \$672,433 \\ \textit{limit two: } \$578,250 \end{cases} = \$346,950$$

The two-year brackets start with the date of D1's death and end at midnight of each two year anniversary (two, four, six, etc.), e.g., if D1 died in the morning of August 10, 2005 and D2 in the afternoon of August 10, 2007, the two deaths are within the first two-year time frame, and a PTC time factor of 100% applies.

The chapter on advanced marital deduction and bypass trust planning discusses how the PTC is combined with marital deduction trusts to reduce taxes, even where no transfer of corpus takes place. Chapter 17 covers this combination in greater detail.

Credit for Foreign Death Taxes

A credit is allowed for most, but not all, foreign death taxes paid on property that is (a) included in the U.S. gross estate, and (b) situated in that foreign country. Similar to the PTC, the amount of credit allowed is the lower of the amount of tax the property generates in the U.S. versus the amount it generates in the foreign country.[64] A detailed explanation of this credit is beyond the scope of this text.

Adjustment to the Unified Credit for Certain Pre-1977 Gifts

When members of Congress were working on the massive overhaul of the estate and gift tax laws in 1976, there was concern that when wealthy individuals got wind of the changes, specifically the replacement of the lifetime $30,000 per donor gift exemption with a unified credit, many would make large gifts to use up any unused exemption, with the idea that they would start fresh with the brand new unified credit. This would give them an advantage over those who did not move quickly to use up their unused exemption, so Congress added a special adjustment for those donors who used up any gift exemption during the closing months of 1976. Those donors must reduce their unified credit by 20% times the amount of exemption used for gifts made during the time period September 9, 1976, and December 31, 1976.[65]

EXAMPLE 6 - 91. On November 11, 1976, Graham made a gift of $50,000 worth of MOP stock to his daughter Alison. Previously, he had never made a gift above the annual exclusion amount. From the gross gift of $50,000 was subtracted the $3,000 annual exclusion and the $30,000 lifetime gift exemption to arrive at a taxable gift of $17,000. Because the use of the lifetime exemption fell within the "adjustment" time period, he must reduce his unified credit by $6,000 [20% * $30,000]. Hence, if he died in 2007 his unified credit would be $772,800 instead of $780,800.

CONCLUSION

This chapter has examined the principal items found on the estate tax return, including components of the gross estate, estate tax deductions, and estate tax credits. The next chapter examines the components of the gift tax return, and covers basis rules as they relate to gifts and estates.

QUESTIONS AND PROBLEMS - Use the ETAX program to do the problems that require calculation of estate or gift taxes. If an annual exclusion is available, use the following amounts: $3,000 for 1977 - 1981; $10,000 for 1982 - 2002; $11,000 for 2002 - 2005; and $12,000 for 2006-2008.

1. Dana died on June 12, 2007, leaving his entire estate to his children. (a) If he had made no taxable gifts during his lifetime, what would his gross estate have to be worth before his executor would be required to file an estate tax return? (b) How would your answer to "a" change if he had made taxable gifts of $75,000 in 1970, $120,000 in 1980, and $40,000 in 1995?

2. Samuel, a single man, died in 2007. (a) The trustee of his probate-avoiding trust held assets worth $3,500,000 and the only other significant asset was a Transfer on Death brokerage account worth $120,000 that was collected by his sister, the designated transferee, shortly after his death. Who would be responsible for filing the estate tax return? When would the return be due? What extensions for filing and paying are possible? (b) Who would be liable for paying the tax if the trustee distributed the trust to Samuel's issue (the remaindermen) without filing a return or paying the tax?

3. Given the facts for each estate, decide whether an estate tax return needs to be filed.

died	taxable gifts post-1976	gross estate	additional information	file?	comments (why/why not, etc.)
2003	$300,000	$900,000	estate left to D's adult children		
2005	$300,000	$1,400,000	$500,000 of the estate went to surviving spouse (S2).		
2007	$0	$2,700,000	debts exceeded $600,000		
2009	$900,000	$2,000,000	estate left half to D's adult children & half to D's alma mater.		
2010	$250,000	$850,000	$500,000 of the estate was a life insurance policy paid to D's children.		
2011	$0	$1,300,000	$100,000 to charity, debts were $50,000, residue left to D's adult children.		

4. Shauna created an irrevocable trust that gave Brandon income for life with a vested remainder for Ralph. When Ralph died in 2006, the trust was worth $1,000,000 and Brandon was still spry at the age of 80. (a) Given a 7520 rate of 6% what portion of this trust is included in Ralph's estate? (b) Ralph's taxable estate, including the remainder value of the trust, is $3,400,000. What is the estate tax and how much of it can be postponed using §6163? When must the postponed portion have to be paid?

5. What is the maximum time the executor can postpone paying estate taxes based on good cause? In so as far as timing the request, what is the key thing to remember?

6. When Mary died, her son Charlie was entitled to receive annuity payments of $2,500 per month for 15 years. The §7520 rate used for valuing annuities

was 8%. Use Table K to adjust for the fact that the payments are made monthly.

7. When Sally died, her son Frank was entitled to receive annuity payments of $1,400 per month for 10 years. The §7520 rate used for valuing annuities was 6%. Use Table K to adjust for the fact that the payments are made monthly.

8. After Dudley died in November of 2003 his pension from TooMuch, Inc., continued at $1,250/month for the life of Rose Marie, his 75 year-old ex-wife. They were divorced in 1995. For the month Dudley died the rate in effect for valuing annuities was 6%. Show how the amount included in Dudley's estate is dependent on when he started collecting his pension (the rules are a little more complex, but we can use "retirement status" as a shorthand for this). Determine the amount included in his gross estate assuming he retired in May of--

   a) 1980
   b) 1983
   c) 1990

9. When Connie died, her 80-year-old husband was entitled to receive a survivor's pension of $600 per month for his lifetime from a fully qualified plan (his employer had made all contributions). The §7520 rate used for valuing annuities was 10%. Determine how much is included in his estate if Connie retired in (a) 1986; (b) 1983; or (c) 1980. Use Table K to adjust for the fact that the payments are made monthly.

10. When Jack died, his 65-year-old wife was entitled to receive a survivor's pension of $3,800 per month for her lifetime from a fully qualified plan (his employer had made all contributions). The §7520 rate used for valuing annuities was 6%. Determine how much is included in his estate if Jack retired in (a) 1986; (b) 1983; or (c) 1980. Use Table K to adjust for the fact that the payments are made monthly.

11. When Morton died in 2007, he left his estate to his three children. He left stock worth $1,560,000, a home worth $345,000, a car worth $9,000, home furnishings worth $23,000, and a bank account with $3,500 in it. The total of

his debts and expenses was $45,000. He also had a $200,000 life insurance policy on his life that was paid to his three children and a life insurance policy on his mother (alive and well, thank you). The policy on his mother was valued at $25,000 and had a face value of $150,000. A mountain cabin worth $150,000 was held in joint tenancy with his brother John. They bought the cabin for only $30,000 years ago with John paying $20,000 and Morton paying $10,000. Calculate: (a) the gross estate, (b) the taxable estate, (c) the probate estate, (d) the total death taxes, (e) the state death tax credit, and (f) the federal estate tax.

12. (a) What is a general power? (b) What is the significant tax difference between a general power and a limited one? (c) When will a power to appoint to one's self not be a general power?

13. At his death, decedent-trustee was the holder of a power of appointment over property held in a trust created by his rich uncle. Determine whether any portion of the trust principal is included in decedent's gross estate given each of the following alternative trustee powers. If a power is exercised in favor of someone other than the holder, state the gift and estate tax consequences that follow.

   a. The unrestricted power to appoint property to his surviving descendants by specific mention of the power in his will. Decedent appointed the entire corpus to his son.
   b. Same as part a, except decedent did not appoint property to anyone at his death.
   c. The power to appoint property to himself for "health" reasons.
   d. The power to appoint property to himself, but only with the approval of his son, who is also the remainderman.

14. Herbert established an irrevocable trust to benefit his second wife, Judy, for her lifetime. Judy received all of the income for her lifetime and at her death the trust terminates and is distributed to Herbert's two children from his first marriage. The trust is worth $1,000,000 at all times relevant here. Determine how much of the trust would be included in Judy's estate when she dies given the following alternatives:

a) Judy served as trustee of the trust and could withdraw corpus if she needed it for her health, education, support, or maintenance.

b) Judy served as trustee of the trust and could withdraw corpus if she needed it for her health, education, support, or pleasure.

c) Starlight National Trust, Inc., served as trustee of the trust and could distribute corpus to her if the trust officers thought that she needed additional wealth for her health, education, support, or pleasure but they couldn't be compelled to do so.

15. Whether a trust is included in a person's estate might depend on whether the decedent retained an interest or created a power to appoint, and if the latter whether a general one or a limited one. For each of the following, assume that the trust was worth $2,010,000 when established in 2002, and $2,300,000 when D died. For each case: (i) state whether a gift tax was paid, and if so approximately how much; (ii) explain why D's interest, if any, is a retained interest, a general or limited power, or something else; (iii) state what is included in D's gross estate; and (iv) give the estate's adjusted taxable gift.

a) D established the trust to take care of her brother, Charlie, who had been injured in a car accident. At Charlie's death the trust would terminate and go to his children. The trustee was Skylight National Trust, Inc. D died two years after establishing the trust.

b) Same as prior, but the trust document gave D the power to require the Trust to hold back income or, if D thought it was needed, to distribute corpus to Charlie.

c) D's father established the trust to take care of D's brother. The trust document gave D the power to require the Trust to hold back income or, if D thought it was needed, to distribute corpus to Charlie. D died five years after the trust was established.

16. At her death, decedent-trustee was the holder of a power of appointment over property held in a trust created by her rich aunt. Determine whether any portion of the trust principal is included in decedent's gross estate given each of the following alternative trustee powers. If a power is exercised in favor of someone other than the holder, state the gift and estate tax consequences that follow.

a. The unrestricted power to appoint property to herself or her descendants. By her will she appointed property to her son.
b. Same as part b, except decedent did not appoint to anyone at her death.
c. The power to appoint property to herself for her "comfort."
d. The power to appoint property to herself, but only with the approval of her son, who was also the remainderman.

17. Under IRC § 2036, two very different circumstances will cause a trust to be included in the settlor's estate. (a) Describe the one in which the settlor retains an economic benefit. (b) Describe the one in which the settlor does not retain an economic benefit.

18. When she died, Roxanna was serving as the trustee of an irrevocable trust with assets valued at $700,000. The trust allowed her to distribute corpus or income to her children or the children of her sister Laurie. For each of the following alternatives, determine whether the trust is included in her estate: (a) The trust had been established by the Roxanna's mother many years before. (b) The trust had been established by Laurie, many years before, and at the same time, Roxanna had established and funded a similar trust with Laurie as trustee. (c) Roxanna had established the trust, but kept no economic benefit for herself. (d) Ten years ago, Roxanna's rich uncle had established the trust at his death. Initially, Roxanna was both trustee and a permissible appointee, but a couple of years later, she irrevocably released the right to appoint to herself. She never appointed trust property to herself before or after the release.

19. In 2003, Isidro established an irrevocable trust with one million dollars worth of assets. The §7520 rate was 6% when the trust was established The trust was to last for ten years and income had to be distributed to Rudy and/or Veronica, or the survivor of the two of them. After ten years or the earlier death of both income beneficiaries, the trust would terminate and go per capita at each generation to the two beneficiaries' issue. The trustee was Starlight National Trust, Inc., and it had full management powers, except that Isidro could direct the proportion of the total income Rudy and Veronica would get each year. If he failed to give directions in this regard by January 20th of each year, the trustee had to decide based upon the beneficiaries' needs how much to distribute to each of them.

a) Was there a taxable gift when the trust was established? Explain.

b) In the third year of the trust, Isidro directed the trustee to distribute 40% of the income to Rudy and the rest to Veronica. Did this create a gift? Assume for the sake of making your answer clear that the income for the year was $50,000.

c) In year four, when the trust was worth $1.1 million, Isidro wrote the trustee a letter wherein he gave up "now and forever" the right to allocate the income. The following year when the trust was worth $1.2 million, Isidro died. (i) Did the letter create a taxable gift? Explain. If there is a gift, would annual exclusions be allowed? Why or why not?

d) Assume the same facts as in the preceding problem but that Isidro died four years after writing the letter; again assume the trust was then worth $1.2 million. Insofar as this trust is concerned, state (i) the amount included in Isidro's estate and (ii) the adjusted taxable gift for estate tax purposes.

20. Use the language of the IRC to describe the three common retained powers or rights that cause a trust or bank account to be included in a decedent's gross estate under IRC § 2038. Identify three common estate planning arrangements to which this code section would be applied, e.g., a type of trust or account.

21. In 2003, Valeri gave Melvin stock worth $2,511,000. When she died the stock, still owned by Melvin, was worth $3 million. The property Valeri owned at death had a net value of $5 million. For each of the following alternatives what is: (i) the gift tax; (ii) the amount included in Valeri's gross estate; (iii) the adjusted taxable gift; and (iv) the gift tax payable credit?
a) Valeri died in 2005.
b) Valeri died in 2007.

22. In 2002, Glenn gave Carlene land worth $1,711,000 and paid gift tax of $300,000. When he died the land, still owned by Carlene, was worth $2 million. The property Glenn owned at death had a net value of $4 million. For each of the following alternatives what is: (i) the amount included in Glenn's gross estate; (ii) the adjusted taxable gift; and (iii) the gift tax payable credit?
a) Glenn died in 2003.
b) Glenn died in 2006.

23. True or false: A gift of life insurance within three years of the insured-donor's death is the ONLY circumstance where an outright gift (i.e., one with no strings attached) is included in the gross estate of the donor.

24. Why is it important to distinguish between assets previously given away that are nevertheless included in the gross estate versus transfers that are part of the tax base but only as adjusted taxable gifts?

25. When Rick died in 2007, he was the insured for a life insurance policy with a face value (proceeds at death) of $500,000. His daughter Ellen was named as the sole beneficiary. (i) How much would be included in his gross estate and (ii) what, if any, would be the adjusted taxable gift for estate tax purposes, given the following alternative facts:
a) Rick was the owner of the policy but the proceeds were paid directly to Ellen.
b) Rick transferred the policy to Ellen in 2002. He filed a gift tax return correctly reporting its gift value as $45,000 (taxable gift value of $35,000).
c) Rick transferred the policy to Ellen in 2005. He filed a gift tax return correctly reporting its gift value as $45,000 (taxable gift value of $35,000).
d) In 2005, Ellen purchased the policy on Rick's life. At all times she was the sole owner and beneficiary.

26. Insofar as large taxable gifts are concerned, what is included in the gross estate of the donor depends on (1) how long before the donor's death the gift occurred; (2) whether gift tax actually had to be paid; and (3) whether the kind of gift falls into one of the special exceptions, i.e., is insurance on the donor's life or the release of a retained interest. Consider the different outcomes where Karen gives Tommy property that increases in value from the time she makes the gift in 2004 and when she dies. For each of the following determine (i) the amount included in Karen's estate and (ii)the adjusted taxable gift for estate tax purposes.
a) The property was a $500,000 face amount insurance policy on Karen's life that had a value for gift purposes of $50,000. Karen died in 2006.
b) Same as the prior case but Karen died in 2008.
c) The property was LARC stock worth $3,010,000 that increased in value to $5 million when she died in 2006. Karen paid the gift taxes of $915,000.
d) Same as the prior case but Karen died in 2008.

27. Gary transferred property worth $60,000 to his sister Pamela. Because of the unified credit, Gary paid no gift taxes when he made the transfer. When Gary died, the property was worth $100,000. For each case, state (insofar as the transfer goes) what is (i) in his gross estate; and (ii) the adjusted taxable gift for estate tax purposes.
   a. Gary transferred stock two years before he died.
   b. Gary transferred stock four years before he died.
   c. Gary transferred life insurance ($60,000 was its gift value) two years before he died. Pamela collected the $100,000 proceeds.
   d. Gary transferred life insurance ($60,000 was its gift value) four years before he died. Pamela collected the $100,000 proceeds.

28. Craig left his $14,000,000 estate to his wife, Rebecca. There were debts and expenses of $500,000. Craig and Rebecca were both U.S. citizens and residents. (a) What is Craig's gross estate? (b) His taxable estate? (c) How would your answers change if Craig was not a U.S. citizen but Rebecca is? (d) If Craig was a citizen but Rebecca is not?

29. When she died in 2005, Florence left her net estate (after debts and expenses) of $3,000,000 to her husband, Juan Carlos. They were both residents of the United States for most of their adult lives. How much estate tax would be paid given each of the following circumstances? (assume no QDOT and no post-death change of citizenship) (a) Both were U.S. citizens. (b) Florence was a U.S. citizen and Juan Carlos is a citizen of Mexico. (c) Florence was a citizen of Mexico and Juan Carlos is a U.S. citizen. (d) Both were citizens of Mexico and permanent legal residents of the U.S.

30. Guy created a revocable probate-avoidance trust. On his death in 2007, the trust (worth $4.3 million) gave 50% of the corpus to the university where he received his bachelor's degree and 50% to United Way. A life insurance policy that he owned paid out $3,000,000 to a favorite niece. Debts and expenses totaled $250,000. Unfortunately, the trust included a clause that required the trustee to pay all death taxes out of trust assets. Use ETAX to determine Guy's (a) taxable estate and (b) total estate tax. [Set deductions as +4300000+250000-b19 and remember to include the life insurance as part of the gross estate. The reason for the minus sign before "b19" is that the estate tax is reducing the charitable deduction.]

31. When Kristen died in 2007, her will specified that her entire estate was to go to her university, a bequest that qualifies for a charitable deduction. Her probate estate was valued at $3,800,000. There were no debts and the total expenses associated with transferring her estate came to $50,000. Her will had a clause that required all death taxes from probate and non-probate assets to be paid from the residue of her probate estate. The only asset outside the trust was a Transfer on Death brokerage account with assets worth $3,500,000 that were transferred to her brother Bill. The executor of Kristen's estate tried to get Bill to disclaim the benefit of having the estate pay the estate taxes on his share of the estate, but he refused. Use ETAX to determine the (a) taxable estate and (b) estate tax. [Set deductions as +3800000+50,000-b19 and remember to include the brokerage account as part of the gross estate.] (c) What amount is received by the university and by Bill? (c) How much would each receive had Bill disclaimed the tax payment benefit?

32. Review the estate tax return (the 706) to answer the following questions:
    (a) On what line of page one does one report adjusted taxable gifts? Identify by letter the schedule where one reports gift taxes paid on gifts made within three years of death. Where does the gift taxes payable credit appear?
    (b) On page three, where does one report total charitable gifts? Identify by letter the schedule where one gives the details of charitable gifts. How does the IRS know whether estate taxes were charged to charitable gifts?
    (c) Identify the line on page three where the total for transfers with a retained interest appears and by letter the schedule where the details for such transfers are listed.
    (d) Identify the line on page three where the total for the marital deduction appears and by letter the schedule where the details for the marital deduction are listed. Review that schedule to explain how one makes a QTIP election. Where is information about the surviving spouse's citizenship reported?

33. In 2001, when he was 60 years old, Settlor Sam created an irrevocable trust, funding it with property worth $7 million. The trustee was Maximo Independent Trust Company. Sam's niece, or her estate, was named as the remainderman. For each independent variation, "a" through "d," calculate: (i) the gross gift; (ii) the taxable gift; (iii) the gift tax paid, (iv) the amount of the trust included in Sam's gross estate; (v) the adjusted taxable gift; and, (vi) the amount of gift tax credit allowed and whether it is it payable or paid.

a. Sam retained a life estate in the trust. At the time of funding, the 7520 rate for split interest gifts (i.e., for valuing remainders, etc.) was 6%. He died in 2006. The trust was then worth $8,000,000.

b. Sam retained no economic interests in the trust, but the terms of the trust gave him the right to allocate income between his brothers Daniel and James. If he failed to allocate (whether due to inaction or his own prior death), then the trustee was to distribute the income equally, and once one brother died, the surviving brother was to receive all of the income each year. Sam died in 2006 without ever directing the trustee as to how to allocate. Both brothers survived him and the trust was worth $8,000,000.

c. Same facts as the prior scenario, except in 2002 Sam sent the trustee a letter stating that he forever released his right to make the allocation. The trust was worth $7,200,000 when Sam released this right. When he died in 2006, the trust was worth $8,000,000.

d. Same facts as "c" except the release occurred in 2005 when the trust was worth $7,600,000. It was worth $8,000,000 when Sam died in 2006.

e. Under what circumstances would the gift taxes paid by Sam be included in his gross estate? Is this a special rule that relates only to transfers into trust?

34. Dudley Donor made a taxable gift of $4 million in 1997, paying taxes of $1,648,000. He died in 2005 leaving a taxable estate of $10 million. (a) What is the gift tax payable credit? (To check the ETAX gift tax payable amount you could use a calculator to figure the gift tax on $4 million using the 1997 unified credit and the 2005 marginal rates) (b) What is the estate tax? (c) Since the estate is in the top marginal rate of 47% (the gift having used up the lower rates) why is the tax not exactly $4.7 million?

35. When Adam died on May 5, 2005, his taxable estate in the amount of $4,500,000 was left equally to his three children. Adam's estate paid federal estate tax of $1,400,000. When Adam's oldest child, Stacey, died on July 4, 2007, her taxable estate of $5,600,000 was left to her two children. Stacey's estate tax without the application of the PTC would have been $1,620,000. Calculate the following: (a) limit one; (b) limit two; (c) the PTC; and (d) the estate tax after applying the PTC.

36. When Sara died on August 12, 2003, her taxable estate in the amount of $3,400,000 was left to her only son, Jake. Sara's estate paid total death taxes of $1,121,000, of which $109,800 went to the state and $1,011,200 went to the federal government. When Jake died on February 8, 2005, most of his $4,700,000 taxable estate could be traced to the estate that he had inherited from his mother. The federal estate tax on his estate without application of the PTC would have been $1,494,000. Calculate the following: (a) limit one; (b) limit two; (c) the PTC; and (d) the federal estate tax after applying the PTC.

37. In December of 1976, Martin gave each of his daughters POP stock worth $25,000. Each gift qualified for the $3,000 annual exclusion and he applied his $30,000 lifetime exemption to reduce the gift taxes. He made no post-1976 taxable gifts. When he died in 2007, his taxable estate was $4,000,000. How much did the 1976 gifts increase his estate tax as compared to what it would have been had he made the gifts in the first half of 1976?

38. In October of 1976, Sally gave her son TOP stock worth $18,000. The gift qualified for the $3,000 annual exclusion and she applied part of her $30,000 lifetime exemption to avoid any gift taxes. She made no post-1976 taxable gifts. When she died in 2007, her taxable estate was $3,500,000. How much did the 1976 gifts increase her estate tax as compared to what it would have been had she not made the gifts?

ANSWERS TO QUESTIONS AND PROBLEMS *(odd numbered only)*

1. Dana's estate: (a) The gross estate plus post-1976 taxable gifts would have to exceed the AEA for the year of death. Given that there were no gifts and the AEA for 2007 is $2,000,000, that is the threshold. (b) Only the post-1976 gifts are added to determine the threshold, so $1,840,000 [$2,000,000 - $120,000 - $40,000]. Ignore the 1970 gift.

3. The basic rule is that an estate tax return must be filed if the adjusted taxable gifts (post-1976) and the gross estate combined exceed the estate AEA; a return must be filed even if deductions drop it below the AEA.

died	taxable gifts post-1976	gross estate	additional information	file ?	comments (why/why not, etc.)
2003	$300,000	$900,000	estate left to D's adult children	yes	*AEA = $1 million, gifts + estate is greater than that.*
2005	$300,000	$1,400,000	$500,000 of the estate went to surviving spouse (S2).	yes	*over the AEA even if taxable is under $1.5 million*
2007	$0	$2,700,000	debts exceeded $600,000	yes	*over the AEA even if taxable is under $2 million*
2009	$900,000	$2,000,000	estate left half to D's adult children & half to D's alma mater.	no	*total gifts plus gross estate is less than $3.5 million AEA*

2010	$250,000	$850,000	$500,000 of the estate was a life insurance policy paid to D's children.	no	*supposed to be no estate tax in 2010*
2011	$0	$1,300,000	$100,000 to charity, debts were $50,000, residue left to D's adult children.	yes	*gross estate is over the $1 million AEA (on the doubtful assumption of no change in the law*

5. Up to ten years but each request must be made timely and are grant for just one year at a time, i.e., the first one before the return is due (within nine months after the decedent's death) and each subsequent one before the prior year's extension is up.

7. Sally (Table B 6%): $12*1,400*7.3601*1.0272 = \$127,013$

9. Connie (Table S 10%): (a) all: $12*600*4.9061*1.045 = \$36,913$ (b) none, it is less than $100,000; (c) none, regardless of value

11. Morton's estate: comments - On the mountain cabin, use the consideration furnished rule (hence 10k/30k times $150k).

Item	(a) Gross estate	(c) Probate estate
stock	$1,560,000	$1,560,000
home	$345,000	$345,000
car	$9,000	$9,000
home furn	$23,000	$23,000
bank account	$3,500	$3,500
life ins.	$200,000	
life ins. (mom)	$25,000	$25,000
cabin	$50,000	
total	$2,215,500	$1,965,500
Less debts & expenses	($45,000)	
(b) taxable estate	$2,170,500	

(d) total tax: $518,545; (e) state death tax credit: $56,220; and
(f) federal tax: $462,325.

13. The powers receive the following treatment:
    a. Limited not included, exercise does not matter.
    b. Limited not included whether exercised or not.
    c. Limited by an ascertainable standard, the H in HSEM.
    d. Not included, the adverse interest exception.

15. (a) i) complete gift, hence $435,000 gift tax on $2 million; ii) it does not
    appear that D retained any interest; iii) hence only the gift tax would be
    included in D's gross estate; and iv) the adjusted taxable gift would be either
    $2,010,000 or $2,000,000 depending upon whether Charlie had a present
    interest that would have qualified the transfer for one annual exclusion.
    (b) i) no gift tax would be paid since this is considered an incomplete gift, D
    has not released dominion and control over the enjoyment of the gift; ii) the
    power to determine when the trust beneficiary will enjoy the transferred
    property is a retained interest under §2036 and 2038; iii) the retained interest
    causes the DOD value to be included, e.g., the full 2.3 million; and iv) there
    is no adjusted taxable gift since no lifetime gift occurred.
    (c) i) gift tax would have been paid by D's father but not by D; ii) D didn't
    create the interest and it can't benefit him so D holds a limited power of
    appointment; iii) limited powers are not included in the holder's estate, hence
    nothing is included; and iv) no adjusted taxable gift for D's estate.

17. (a) A retained life estate. (b) Retained power to decide who (other than the
    settlor) enjoys the income or the property.

19. (a) No, Isidro has retained too much control over the enjoyment of the
    property for it to be considered a completed gift.
    (b) Isidro is getting taxed on all of the trust income due to his retained
    interest. This year Isidro has made two gifts, $20,000 to Rudy ($8,000
    taxable) and $30,000 to Veronica ($18,000 taxable).
    (c) (i) Yes, when the retained control is released it is treated as a gift of $1.1
    million. There is no annual exclusion since neither Rudy nor Veronica has a
    present interest even after the release by Isidro of his retained interest because

neither can be certain that he or she will receive anything (even if it is certain that one of them will). (ii) Since the release and the gift tax liability occur within 3 years of his death, the DOD value of the trust is included, plus any gift tax paid is included in the gross estate and it should get a credit for the gift tax.

(d) i) None, having made it more than 3 years from the release of the retained interest, neither the trust nor the gift tax is included. ii) The adjusted taxable gift would be the $1.1 million value on the date of the release. As stated above there would be no annual exclusion since no one had a present interest in the trust.

21. [Note, this is stock, no 3 year rule here other than for the gift tax. The gift tax payable credit drops because the top marginal rate is lower in 2005 and lower still in 2007.]

a) Valeri died in 2005. i) $680,000; ii) $680,000; iii) $2,500,000; and, iv) $670,000.

b) Valeri died in 2007. i) $680,000; ii) 0; iii) $2,500,000 iv) $660,000.

23. True, although students of estate planning keep trying to add others.

25. (a) i) Since he owned the policy at his death 100% included even though not part of his probate estate it is in his gross estate, i.e., $500,000 included. ii) no gift in this alternative.

(b) i) zero included since the policy was transferred more than 3 years before Rick's death; and ii) $35,000 adjusted taxable gift.

(c) i) the $500,000 date of death value is included due to the §2035(b) 3 year rule that applies to life insurance; and ii) the adjusted taxable gift drops to zero since one doesn't count the same asset twice.

(d) i) zero included (Rich never owned the policy); and ii) no taxable gift.

27. (a) GE zero; Adj.TxG $50,000. Stock, no three-year rule.

(b) GE zero; Adj.TxG $50,000.

(c) GE $100,000; Adj.TxG zero. Life insurance, special three-year rule.

(d) GE zero; Adj.TxG $50,000. Life insurance beyond the three-year reach.

29. (a) Zero estate tax, 100% marital deduction. (b) $695,000 estate taxes, no marital deduction. (c) Zero estate tax, 100% marital deduction. (d) $695,000 estate taxes, no marital deduction.

31. Kristen's estate: (a) gross estate: $5.5 million [$3.8 million + $1.7 million]; deductions $3,333,333 [$3.8 million + $50,000 - b19]; (b) estate tax $516,667. (c) Since the deductions and taxes come from the university's share, it receives $3,800,000 - ($50,000 + $516,667) = $3,233,333, and Bill receives the full TOD account, worth $1,700,000, free of tax. (d) The university's share would still be charged with the $50,000 debts and expenses, but not the taxes, hence: $3,800,000 - $50,000 = $3,750,000; Bill would receive $1,700,000 - $277,500 = $1,422,500 (Note, taxes drop because the charitable deduction is not burdened with any tax).

33. (a) (i) gift? .35033 * $7,000,000 = $2,452,310, (ii) taxable gift? Same, no annual exclusion because gift is one of a future interest; (iii) gift tax paid? $781,882 (iv) Trust in the estate? $8,000,000 date-of-death value - retained interest; (v) adjusted taxable gift? Zero, transferred property is in the gross estate; (vi) gift tax payable credit? Actual amount paid because date-of-death value is included, i.e., $781,882.
(b) (i) gift? No gift, he retained control until he died. (ii) taxable gift? Zero, no gift. (iii) gift tax paid? Zero, no gift. (iv) trust in the estate? $8,000,000. (v) adjusted taxable gift? No. (vi) gift tax payable credit? No.
(c) (i) gift? No gift until control is relinquished. Release in 2002, gift $7,200,000 (ii) taxable gift? Income interest of each brother exceeds the annual exclusion, hence $7,180,000. (iii) gift tax paid? $3,020,000. (iv) Trust in the estate? No, the retained interest was released more than three years before Sam's death. (v) adjusted taxable gift? As in "ii" $7,180,000. (vi) gift tax payable credit? Only $2,817,800. (Rates are lower in 2006 than they were in 2002.)
(d) (i) gift? No gift until control is relinquished. This occurred in 2005. $7,600,000. (ii) taxable gift? $7,580,000. Two annual exclusions (see "c ii"). (iii) gift tax paid? $3,057,600. (iv) Trust in the estate? Yes, at full date-of-death value ($8 million) § 2035(a) 3-year rule for released retained interests. The gift taxes paid must also be included. (v) adjusted taxable gift? Zero (whole trust is in the gross estate). (vi) gift tax payable credit? Should be the tax actually paid ($3,057,600).

(e) Only if Sam died within three years of making a gift that triggers the actual payment of gift tax. This is not a special rule; any gift, whether in trust or not and whether life insurance, diamonds, land, stocks or bonds, or whatever, is governed by this rule. If taxes are paid and death occurs within three years of the gift, the gift taxes are part of the gross estate.

35. Calculating the PTC:
   (a) limit one: $1,400,000/3 = $466,667
   (b) limit two:

FET on D2's taxable estate of $5,600,000	$1,620,000
Less FET on D2's reduced taxable estate: i.e., $5,600,000 - (4,500,000 - 1,400,000)/3). This gives a reduced estate of $4,104,667. The federal tax on this is	($947,100)
The difference is limit two	$672,900

time factor: *Since Stacey died just over two years after her father the factor is 80%, applied to the lower of the limits: 80% * $466,667 = $373,334.*

(c) Tax on a $5,600,000 estate	$1,620,000
Prior transfer tax credit	($373,334)
Federal tax	$246,666

37. The gifts used up some of Martin's unified credit. The reduction is 20% times the gift exemption used on gifts made in 1976 after September 8th (see IRC § 2010(b)). Since the entire $30,000 gift exemption was applied to the two gifts, the unified credit is reduced by $6,000 to $774,800 and the estate tax is $906,000 instead of $900,000.

ENDNOTES

1. The file name is Form 706 Estate Tax.pdf.

2. IRC § 2031(a).

3. IRC § 6018(a)(1).

4. Reg. § 20.2053-7, Deduction for unpaid mortgages.

5. IRC § 6018(a)(2).

6. IRC § 2103.

7. IRC § 2102(c)(1).

8. IRC § 2002; *Fleming v. Commissioner*, No. 90-2576, 7th Cir. 1992.

9. IRC §§ 6075, 2203, 6018(a).

10. Reg. § 25.6081-1(c).

11. IRC § 6081(a), see also Reg. § 25.6081-1.

12. IRC §§ 2002 & 2203, also see IRC §§ 6018(a), § 20.618-2.

13. *Estate of Guide v. Commissioner*, 69 T.C. 811 (1978).

14. LR 8335033.

15. *Estate of Bahr v. Commissioner*, 68 T. C. 74 (1977), acq. 1978-1 C.B. 1

16. IRC § 7502(a), Reg. 301.7502-1(c)(1).

17. IRC § 6662(a), IRC § 6662(h).

18. IRC § 6662(g)(2).

19. IRC § 6621(a)(2).

20. To find recent rates, go to http://www.irs.gov/newsroom/ and search for "interest rate underpayment".

21. IRC § 6501(a).

22. Exceptions to the three-year rule, generally, see IRC § 6501(c), and the 25% under reporting penalty, see § 6501(e).

23. IRC § 2035(a).

24. The Taxpayer Relief Act rearranged IRC §2035; old § 2035(c) is now § 2035(b).

25. Pre- TRA '97 IRC § 2035(d)(2) is now § 2035(a).

26. IRC § 2033.

27. *Davis*, T.C. Memo 1993-155.

28. TAM 9207004.

29. IRC § 2034.

30. IRC § 2056(b)(7).

31. See IRC § 1401(a) of P.L. 104-88.

32. 1984 Retirement Equity Act, P.L. 98-397.

33. *Boggs v. Boggs*, 117 S.Ct. 1754, 138 L.Ed. 2d 45 (1997).

34. See *Gallenstein* 975 F. 2d 286 (CA6, 1992) affg. 68 AFTR 2d 91-5721.

35. IRB 2001-42, Oct. 15, 2001.

36. IRC § 2033.

37. IRC § 2041(b)(1).

38. IRC § 2041(b)(1)(C)(ii).

39. *Estate of Cavenaugh*, 100 TC, CCH ¶12,927 (1993).

40. IRC §§ 2036, 2037, and 2038.

41. IRC § 2035(a).

42. Reg. § 20.2511-2.

43. Reg. 25.2511-2(c) and (f).

44. *Maxwell*, 3 F. 3d. 591, affirming 98 T.C. 594 (1992).

45. IRC § 2054.

46. IRC § 2055.

47. IRC § 2056.

48. Make sure your spreadsheet iterations are set high enough. For Excel follow this path: tools, options, calculations, then check iterations and them set at 40.

49. IRC § 2056(b)(3)(A).

50. E.g., CA Probate Code § 21525.

51. IRC § 2056(b)(5).

52. IRC § 2056(b)(7).

53. IRC § 2044.

54. IRC § 2056A(a).

55. *Estate of Marine*, 990 F2d 136 (4th Cir. 1993).

56. Reg. § 20.2053-4.

57. IRC § 2054.

58. Reg. 20.2054-1.

59. IRC § 2012.

60. IRC § 2001(b)(2).

61. IRC § 2013.

62. IRC § 812(c) of the 1939 Code.

63. Reg. § 20-2013-3.

64. IRC § 2014.

65. IRC § 2010(b).

CHAPTER 7

The Gift Tax

OVERVIEW

Chapter 5 introduced the gift tax, showing how it is calculated and how it is unified with the estate tax. Chapter 6 amplified the estate tax. This chapter dose the same for the gift tax, looking at qualitative matters, such as the requirements for a valid gift, types of taxable gifts, how gifts qualify for the annual exclusion, and how certain specific transfers are (or are not) subject to gift tax. The reader is encouraged to review both the overview of the gift tax scheme found in Tables 5-1 and 5-2 of Chapter 5, plus the United States Gift Tax Return, Form 709, found on the "Teaching Aids" CD ROM (see file "Form 709 Gift Tax.pdf").

FEDERAL GIFT TAX

Estate planners use the word "gift" in different ways. Most people think of gifts as gratuitous lifetime transfers, but estate planners define gifts as "completed property transfers in exchange for less than full and adequate consideration." This definition is broad enough to include transfers at death. Thus, it is correct to say, "...in his will he gave the grand piano to his daughter." However, to avoid the necessity of always using the modifier "lifetime," all references to gifts in this chapter, and the ones that follow, will mean lifetime gifts unless the context clearly indicates otherwise.

Requirements for a Valid Gift: Influence of Local and Federal Law

Whether a transfer is treated as a gift is important for two reasons in estate planning. First, it will influence the respective property rights of the parties. Second, it will determine whether a taxable event has occurred. In deciding these issues, two different sets of rules must be examined: local property law and federal gift tax law.

Local property law. To be valid under local property law, a gift must ordinarily meet four requirements:

1. The donor must be capable of transferring property.
2. The donee must be capable of receiving and possessing the property.
3. There must be delivery to, and some form of acceptance by, the donee or the donee's agent.
4. Finally, under local law, a valid gift ordinarily requires donative intent on the part of the donor.

Federal gift tax law. To be subject to taxation under federal gift tax law, a gift must meet all of the above local property law requirements, subject to two major federal modifications:

1. Federal tax regulations explicitly state that donative intent is not required for a transfer to be subject to gift tax. Although not required for a gift, the existence of donative intent would be strong evidence that a gift had actually been made.
2. Under the unique language of federal law, the gift tax applies only to completed gifts, which arise when "...the donor has so parted with dominion and control as to leave him no power to change its disposition, whether for his own benefit or for the benefit of another..."[1]

Ordinarily, completed gifts are made either outright or in trust. *Outright transfers* made beyond the donor's dominion and control are virtually always complete for gift tax purposes. Transfers in trust, on the other hand, may be complete, incomplete, or partially incomplete. An example of a complete transfer in trust is a transfer to an irrevocable trust with no retained interests or controls; the entire transfer is subject to gift taxation. An example of an incomplete transfer in trust is a transfer to a typical revocable trust; it is not at all subject to gift taxation because the trustor has retained the power to demand return of the trust property. An example of a partially incomplete transfer in trust is one to an irrevocable trust in which the trustor has retained only the right to the income (but not control of it) but not to the remainder; thus there is a complete gift of the remainder interest. Or, the trustor could give away the income interest for a period of time with the corpus reverting to the trustor when the time is up, e.g., another is given the income for 10 years after which the trust terminates and the corpus is returned to the trustor or to the trustor's estate. Thus, for transfers in trust in which more than one property interest is created, gift tax law requires that each interest be examined independently to determine whether a completed gift of that interest has been made.

Both federal tax law and local property law influence gift taxation. Summarizing, the relationship between federal law and local law with regard to the requirements for a valid gift may be stated as follows: Local law dictates whether a transfer of property rights has in fact been made, irrespective of taxability. On the other hand, federal tax law, in conjunction with local law, specifies whether a gift is subject to taxation. Federal law also spells out rules, discussed later in this chapter, relating to the taxation of specific types of gifts, such as those in connection with powers of appointment, life insurance, joint ownership, and disclaimers.

Aspects of Taxable Gifts

Who is subject to gift tax? The federal gift tax law applies to all individual United States citizens or residents regardless of where the property is located and regardless of whether the transfer is direct or indirect, real or personal, tangible or intangible. It also applies to nonresident aliens but only with regard to transfers of real property and tangible personal property situated within the United States.[2]

Valuation. The value of the gift for tax purposes is its fair market value at the date of the gift. Any consideration received in exchange is subtracted in determining the gross value of the gift.

EXAMPLE 7 - 1. In 2007, Sally "sells" an automobile worth $25,000 to her son Mark for $1. She has made a gross gift in the amount of $24,999 and must report (after applying a $12,000 annual exclusion) a taxable gift of $12,999.

Basis. The next chapter will cover income tax matters related to gifts and estates, including how the recipient of transferred property determines his or her basis in it. Basis is used to determine gain or loss when property is sold. Usually it is determined by the price one pays to acquire property, but what happens when it is acquired by gift or inheritance? Generally, gifts have a carry-over basis, meaning that the donee's basis is the same as what the donor's basis was before the transfer, and estate property receives a new basis equal to its fair market value on the date of the decedent owner's death. The exceptions to these two rules are covered in the next chapter.

Measuring the consideration received in exchange. To be recognized, consideration received in exchange must be measurable in money or money's worth. If it is not reducible to money or money's worth, it will be disregarded.

> EXAMPLE 7 - 2. Gertrude tells her daughter Alice that her kindness over the past years has been priceless. Gertrude promises Alice that if she continues being so kind she will transfer her $250,000 Duesenberg automobile to her on her next birthday. When Alice's birthday arrives, the card from Gertrude contains the title and keys to the Duesenberg. Even if Alice's sweet attention is worth more than money can buy, it is not considered an exchange in money or money's worth. Therefore, Gertrude has made a taxable gift.

The above example illustrates a situation where a gift is subject to gift taxation despite the fact that local law may view the exchange of consideration to be equal, and donative intent, therefore, to be nonexistent.

Fortunately, in the case of property settlements between divorcing spouses, federal law no longer requires a determination of the total value of the consideration exchanged by each spouse. Transfers of property subject to a written divorce or separation agreement are deemed to be made for full and adequate consideration even when it is clear that the "exchange" is not for money or money's worth.[3]

Gifts versus sales. With sales between related parties, IRS agents may contend that a gift rather than a sale has been made. However, sales between unrelated parties are presumed not to be gifts.

> EXAMPLE 7 - 3. Herb, owner of a retail drugstore, sold his aging delivery pickup truck to Karl, a stranger, who read about the truck in the classified section of the newspaper. Karl paid Herb $4,200 and promptly took out a similar ad and sold the

truck three days later for $6,700. Herb made a bad bargain, but not a gift, because the truck was sold in an arms-length transaction.

Filing and Payment Requirements

Due date and extensions. In general, a gift tax return is due when the donor's income tax return is due (or if the donor is not required to file an income tax return, then when it would have been due had the donor been so required). Usually, this means April 15 of the year following the gift. An extension to file one's income tax return is also an automatic extension to file one's gift tax return. A gift tax return must be filed by any donor who in any calendar year gives:

- more than the annual exclusion amount (i.e., $10,000, indexed) to any donee (other than to a spouse or charity), or
- a gift of a future interest regardless of how small the value, or
- total gifts exceeding $100,000 (indexed) to a non-citizen spouse, or
- a gift for which both spouses want to elect gift splitting even if after the split each gift is less than the annual exclusion amount.

Who files? Generally, it is the donor's responsibility to file the tax return. Only people file gift tax returns. For example, if a partnership or a corporation makes a gift, the individual partners or stockholders are considered the donors, hence required to file the return and pay the tax. If the trustee of a revocable living trust makes a gift subject to taxation, it is either the grantor or the holder of a power of appointment who is treated as the donor depending on the circumstances. If a donor dies before filing a return, the donor's executor must file for the deceased person.

Who pays? The donor is responsible for paying the gift tax;[4] the donee is not subject to either gift tax or income tax on the gift.[5] However, there is transferee liability if the donor fails to pay the tax. This means that any donee can be forced to pay the gift tax, up to the value of the gift received, if the donor fails to pay.

Penalties. The penalties for not filing the gift tax return and/or not paying the gift tax are the same as those discussed in the last chapter related to the estate tax. Likewise, refer back to the discussion in the last chapter of the accuracy and fraud penalties as the rules for these penalties are the same whether for estates, gifts, or income tax.

Net gifts. Some donors, however, might wish to make a *net gift*; that is, to arrange in advance for the donee to be responsible for paying the gift tax. The Supreme Court has ruled such a transaction to be part sale, part gift, causing the donor to realize taxable income to the extent that the gift tax paid by the donee exceeds the donor's adjusted basis.[6] However, other advantages may still make the net gift attractive.

> EXAMPLE 7 - 4. In 2007, Vera transferred her horse ranch, valued at $5,000,000, to her daughter Felicity with the understanding that Felicity would pay the gift taxes. Given an annual exclusion of $12,000, the net gift value is $3,760,690 and Felicity paid gift taxes of $1,227,310. Note that these three numbers add to $5 million.

Use the ETAX program to verify the calculations in the last example. In cell D7 enter: +5000000-12000-D18. Since this is an interrelated calculation you should hit recalculate (key F9) several times to assure the correct result, i.e., continue to recalculate until the "gift tax paid" figure remains constant.

Deductible Gifts

Two types of gifts are fully deductible, and three are completely excluded from being treated as gifts, with the end result (whether deducted or excluded) that they are not treated as taxable gifts.

Charitable gifts. First, gifts to qualified charities are fully deductible.[7] Owners of "qualified works of art" can loan them to a charity without the loan being treated as a taxable gift, provided the use of the work by the charity is related to its charitable purpose (e.g., an art museum receiving a Van Gogh on loan will put it on display rather than hang it in the director's private study).[8] Generally, gifts to charity also produce an income tax deduction, but only up to certain percentages of adjusted gross income. Chapter 14 will discuss strategies for charitable gifts.

Gifts between spouses. Second, under the unlimited marital deduction, gifts to a U.S. citizen spouse are fully deductible, provided that they are not terminable interests.[9] However, even terminable interest gifts might qualify for the marital deduction by using a gift qualified terminable interest property (QTIP) election.[10] We will get into an analysis of terminable interests and the estate tax marital deduction in Chapters 9 and 10.

Since 1988, only the first $100,000 (indexed) per year in gifts to a non-U.S. citizen spouse escapes gift taxation.[11] Thus, gifts above $100,000 per year to a non-U.S. citizen spouse use up unified credit and may even generate a gift tax.

Gifts for tuition and medical care. Third and fourth, qualified payments in any amount made directly to an educational institution for tuition, and payments in any amount made directly to a provider of medical care on behalf of any individual are fully excluded from being taxable gifts. Two things to emphasize here: the transfers must be directly to the providers, and not to the individuals themselves, and the person benefiting from the payments does not have to be related to the donor.[12]

Gifts to political organizations. Fifth, gifts are not taxable if made to a "political organization (within the meaning of section 527(e)(1)) for the use of such organization."[13]

Gift Tax Annual Exclusion

Most gifts neither generate a gift tax nor need to even be reported. Obviously the transfer tax system is concerned with major shifts of wealth, not with small gifts typically associated with birthdays, Christmas, Chanukah, weddings, friendship, and such. The indexed annual exclusion of $10,000 keeps modest gifts from being taxed; of course modest is relative given that most people neither give nor get gifts approaching the annual exclusion. Note that the donor and donee do not have to be related and that gifts to the same donee are cumulated for the calendar year. As discussed earlier, the annual exclusion reached $11,000 in 2002 and is likely to be $12,000 by 2006. The main requirement for obtaining the annual exclusion is that the donee have an immediate *present interest* when the donor completes the gift.[14] *Present interest gifts* are ones where the "enjoyment" of the gift can start immediately, whereas future interest gifts have some condition attached that causes some delay in the donee's possession and enjoyment of the transferred property.

EXAMPLE 7-5. In 2007, widow Sanderson gave her daughter Polly three corporate bonds valued at $10,000 each. Even though Polly will not collect the par value until maturity, and even though the periodic interest income is payable in the future, the gift is of a present interest and qualifies for the annual exclusion. Widow Sanderson did not place any restriction on Polly's right to enjoy the bonds and Polly could sell them immediately if she wished to do so. Assuming that she made no other gifts to Polly during the year, the taxable gift is $18,000 [$30,000 - $12,000].

Congress in 1932 chose to deny the annual exclusion for gifts of future interests for three reasons: (1) future interests may be difficult to value; (2) the number of donees of a future interest is often indeterminable at the date of gift; and (3) future interests are sometimes created to avoid taxes.

Gifts in trust. Most problems regarding future interest gifts arise in the context of trusts.

> EXAMPLE 7 - 6. In 2007, widow Sanderson transferred bonds worth $30,000 to an irrevocable trust, whereby the trustee could give the bonds to Polly whenever the trustee thought it appropriate to do so, but, at the very latest, to transfer them to her on her 25th birthday. The gift is reportable for the year the bonds are transferred into the trust, and is a $30,000 taxable gift of a future interest. It will not qualify for the annual exclusion because, by the terms of the transfer, Polly does not have the right to immediate possession and enjoyment. The result remains the same even if the trustee quickly transfers one or more of the bonds to Polly.

No annual exclusion means, of course, that absent any other deductions, the gift will be entirely taxable, such that part or all of the donor's unified credit will have to be used. Further, at the donor's death, the value of the taxable gift is added to the estate tax base, which may push the donor's estate into a higher marginal rate. Thus, the donor may prefer a disposition that is at least partly sheltered by the annual exclusion.

> EXAMPLE 7 - 7. Altering the facts of the prior example a little bit, assume that when the trust was created in 2007, instead of being allowed to accumulate the income, the trustee was required to pay all income at least annually to Polly, an adult, with the remainder going to Richard at the end of a 10-year term. On creation of the trust, two interests arose: a present interest in the income for 10 years and a remainder interest. At 10 percent, the present value of an income interest for a 10-year period equals .614457 times the value of the bonds. The product of 0.614457 * $30,000 is $18,434, which represents the portion of the gift that is considered a present interest qualifying for the annual exclusion up to a maximum for any one donee of $12,000. Hence, the total taxable gift equals $18,000 [$30,000-$12,000]. Note that the amount subtracted from the gross value of the gift is the lesser of the present interest (here $18,434) or the annual exclusion, i.e., that year's $10,000 indexed amount.

> EXAMPLE 7 - 8. Suppose Polly's mother placed bonds worth just $15,000 into the 10-year trust; the present interest would be $9,217 [0.614457 * $15,000] and the taxable gift would be $5,873 [$15,000 - $9,217].

A few exceptions to the present interest rule. There are few exceptions to the rule that there must be a present interest before a gift qualifies for the annual exclusion, and one is found in IRC §2503(c). The annual exclusion is allowed for gifts placed in trust (these are referred to as 2503(c) trusts) for the benefit of a person who is under age 21, even though the beneficiary does not have a present interest. Special "529 saving plans" for higher education allow the creation of savings accounts to meet future educational needs, usually for children or grandchildren, without the beneficiary having a present interest. These two planning tools (and others), designed to give financial and educational help to younger family members, are covered in Chapter 11.

Gift Splitting

Gift splitting treats a gift of the property owned by one spouse as if it were made one-half by each spouse. It is conceptually similar to federal spousal income splitting on a joint income tax return; indeed, both were first added to the tax code in 1948 as part of a restructuring that attempted to put common law states on par with the community property states. Also added at that time was the initial marital deduction (equal to 50% of the adjusted gross estate) and the provision that stepped-up both halves of community property even though only one half was included in a decedent spouse's estate.[15]

Under federal gift tax law, a spouse may *split a gift* by making an election, with the consent of the non-donor spouse, on the gift tax return. If the election is made, a gift by the donor spouse of his or her own property is treated as if made one-half by each of them.[16] According to the regulations, the election must cover all gifts that were made during the year to third parties by either spouse. The election allows a married person the benefit of two annual exclusions (and two unified credits, if needed) to cover what is really just one gift.

EXAMPLE 7 - 9. In 2005, Johnna Lynn gives $50,000 of her own money to her nephew. Assuming no other gifts and no gift splitting, her taxable gift, after the annual exclusion, is $39,000. Thus, she must use up $7,980 of her unified credit. Alternatively, she can split this gift, if her husband Fred is willing; each is then considered to have made a gross gift of $25,000. After each donor's annual exclusion, the taxable gift is $14,000 and (assuming no prior taxable gifts) each will use up $2,600 of their unified credit. Johnna Lynn and Fred must both file gift tax returns.

To make the split gift election, the consent of the non-donor spouse is required on the donor spouse's return. If, after the split, the values exceed the annual exclusion, two gift tax returns (one by each spouse) must be filed whereas, only the donor spouse needs to file a gift tax return if the split brings the gifts down to or below the annual exclusion.

> EXAMPLE 7 - 10. Billy and Millie are married parents. In 2006, Millie gave $24,000 of her property to their son. Assuming no other gifts, if the couple agree to gift splitting, only Millie will be required to file a gift tax return; Billy's consent will appear on Millie's return. (Assumes $12,000 annual exclusion for 2006.)

Gift splitting is needed only if the property that is given was owned by just one spouse, since their co-owned property is, by its nature, already "split," generally making the election unnecessary. This is especially true of community property, which is always owned in equal shares (i.e., 50% each) by the spouses.

> EXAMPLE 7 - 11. In the prior example, had the $24,000 been community property, jointly held property, or an in-common interest in property (here assume 50%-50%), the gift would be considered as made one-half by each spouse. Since the value of each spouse's half interest is covered by the annual exclusion, neither spouse would need to file a gift tax return.

> EXAMPLE 7 - 12. If, in 2006, a couple gave their nephew property worth $28,000 that had been held in joint tenancy, each spouse would have made a gross gift of $14,000 and a taxable gift of $2,000 (assuming $12,000 as the annual exclusion). Again, there is no need for gift splitting, and each spouse must file a gift tax return because each gift exceeds the annual exclusion.

Somewhat oddly, if a split gift results in the payment of a gift tax and the donor-spouse dies within three years of the gift, the entire gift tax paid, not just the one-half, is grossed up in the donor's gross estate.[17]

> EXAMPLE 7 - 13. In 2007, from his property, Charles gave $150,000 to the couple's son and stock worth $150,000 to their daughter. Charles's wife, Susan, gave $9,000 of her property to their son. The effects on reportable gross gifts, annual exclusions, and taxable gifts of the decision whether to split the gifts or not is shown in the table below. If no split gift election is made, Susan will not have to file a Form 709, since her gift is covered by the annual exclusion. If gift splitting is elected, the taxable amount on both returns will be identical.

	Without Gift Splitting		With Gift Splitting	
	Charles'	Susan's	Charles'	Susan's
	Form 709	Form 709	Form 709	Form 709
Gross Gifts:		(not filed)		
To Son	$150,000	$9,000	$79,500	$79,500
To Daughter	$150,000	$0	$75,000	$75,000
Total per return	$300,000	$9,000	$154,500	$154,500
Total per family	$309,000		$309,000	
Exclusions:				
Gift to Son	$12,000	$9,000	$12,000	$12,000
Gift to Daughter	$12,000	$0	$12,000	$12,000
Total per return	$24,000	$9,000	$24,000	$24,000
Total per family	$31,000		$48,000	
Total per return	$276,000	$0	$130,500	$130,500
Total per family	$276,000		$261,000	

Electing gift splitting reduces the family taxable gifts by $15,000 [$276,000 - $261,000]. The reduction is the result of the additional $15,000 in total family annual exclusions, since with the election Susan is allowed $24,000, rather than just $9,000. Gift splitting can mean lower gift taxes, or, as in this example, it may just result in using up less of the parents' total unified credit.

In summary, gift splitting can lower gift taxes because it permits the use of two full annual exclusions per donee, even though just one gift is given and, for large gifts, both spouses' unified credits are used.

Powers of Appointment

General power holders and taxable events. As with the estate tax, only general powers are subject to gift tax, and, if there is a gift, it is treated as having come from the donee-holder.[18] Of course, when the general power was first created, the donor of the power (if created by gift) or the donor's estate (if created at death by will or trust) may have paid transfer taxes, unless the transfer was not subject to tax because of the annual exclusion, a marital deduction, or the application of the unified credit. For instance, if a donor placed property in an irrevocable trust that gives the income beneficiary a general power over 25% of the trust corpus, it would be the entire property placed in trust that would be the gift, not just the 25% subject to the general power. As was discussed in conjunction with the estate tax, a general power is defined in § 2514 (c)[19] as one that the holder can use to benefit the holder, the holder's creditors, the holder's estate, or the creditors of the holder's estate.

Three events during the holder's lifetime can trigger gift tax to the holder of a general power of appointment: exercise by the holder in favor of someone else, release by the holder, or lapse of the holder's right to exercise or release the power. Where the holder exercises the power in his or her own favor, no gift occurs.

EXAMPLE 7 - 14. Carla's estate plan called for the creation of two trusts at her death. Trust A was called the marital trust and it gave her husband Ian income for life and a power to appoint the entire corpus to whomever he wished upon his death, with the corpus going to their three children if Ian fails to exercise this general power. According to the terms of the estate plan, Trust A was to be funded with so much of Carla's estate as exceeds the applicable exclusion amount and Trust B was to be funded with assets equal to the applicable exclusion amount. For Trust B Ian was given a life estate and had a general power to appoint up to 5% of the trust each year to anyone. At Ian's death, the power lapses and the trust will be distributed to the couple's three children. Because Carla's total net estate was worth $940,000 when she died in 2003, only Trust B was funded (i.e., the $940,000 estate went into Trust B) and there was no Trust A. Ian's 5% withdrawal right created a marital deduction of $47,000 and the taxable estate was $893,000. Trust B is considered to have been taxed even though the tentative tax was less than Carla's unified credit, so no estate tax was actually paid.

EXAMPLE 7 - 15. In 2003, the trust was worth $1,160,000 when Ian asked the trustee to distribute corpus worth $25,000 to him. Since this was less than 5% of the value of the trust, the trustee obliged and, since the distribution was to Ian, the holder of the general power, no gift was made.

EXAMPLE 7 - 16. In 2004, the trust was worth $1,280,000 when Ian asked the trustee to distribute corpus worth $70,000 to Judith. The trustee pointed out that this exceeded his 5% power, so Ian told him to give her the maximum this year and the balance in 2004. The trustee gave Judith $64,000 in 2003 and another $6,000 in January of 2004. Both transfers are treated as gifts directly from Ian. Since the annual exclusion was $11,000 for those two years (due to indexing), only $53,000 of the first gift, and none of the second gift, was taxable.

EXAMPLE 7 - 17. In 2005, the trust was worth $1,220,000 when Ian asked the trustee to distribute corpus worth $30,000 to his alma mater, Midwestern State University. Since this gift was within the 5% limit even when combined with the gift earlier that year to Judith, the trustee obliged and Ian was able to claim a charitable deduction on his income tax return for the amount of the gift. Note that, to the extent the trust had distributable net income for the year, it will claim a deduction for the income distributed at his request and he will have to report the income on his return.

EXAMPLE 7 - 18. In 2006, the trust was worth $1,350,000 when Ian died. He had not exercised his 5% power that year. His estate must show on schedule H of the estate tax return $67,500 attributable to this general power. If Ian's estate is large enough that estate tax is owed, the trust would have to pay its proportionate share of the estate tax (i.e., $67,500 over the taxable estate times the estate taxes).

In the above examples, we used a general power equal to 5% of the value of the trust for good reason. It is very common to find trusts that give a holder a general power that is limited to exactly that percentage because of a special code section that we discuss next.

Lapse powers and the 5 & 5 exception. The general rule is that the lapse of a general power is treated as a transfer from the holder to whomever is the taker by default. However, §2514(e) creates an exception that allows the lapse of certain general powers to occur during the life of the holder without the lapse being deemed a taxable gift. The exception applies to the lapse during the holder's lifetime of a power, but only to the extent that what could have been transferred (but for the lapse) did not exceed the greater of $5,000 or 5% of the value of the property out of which appointment would have been satisfied. Powers that are drafted to make use of this exception are referred to as "5 & 5" powers, and they permit the holder to appoint property from a trust up to the greater of $5,000 or 5% of the value of the trust corpus. Usually the right is given such that it can be exercised annually and the failure to exercise the right in any year will not increase the dollar amount or the percentage for the next year. In other words, it is a noncumulative, annually lapsing power (or right).

Lapsing powers are often placed in irrevocable trusts created for the benefit of minors in order to obtain the annual exclusion for the parent-donor. The power of the child to withdraw an amount each time the parents add to the trust creates a present interest for the child-donee even though the power to withdraw lapses after a short period of time, as set forth in the trust, and even though there is a strong expectation that the child will not exercise the right to withdraw. This demand right is referred to as a "Crummey demand right" or as a "Crummey power." Trusts for this type of provision are called *Crummey Trusts,* and when established for minor children, they may be called *Minors' Demand Trusts.*

EXAMPLE 7 - 19. Grantor has set up a minors' demand trust for three grandchildren. Each grandchild can claim up to the lesser of one-third of the amount transferred into the trust that year or the annual exclusion amount. If a grandchild does not demand his or her share, the right to claim the gift lapses at the close of the year (with demand rights for gifts made late in the year extended to a minimum of 30 days). If no demand is made during the demand period, the transfer is locked into the corpus and, by other trust terms, it stays there until the youngest of the three grandchildren reaches age 30. If a grandchild dies before termination of the trust, his or her share goes to the other grandchildren who survive. If initially the trust is funded with less than $15,000 and none of the beneficiaries demand their share, no gift from the beneficiaries is deemed to have been made as a result of the lapses because of the §2514(e) exception. Without this exception, there would be the smallest of gifts, i.e., each beneficiary would be making a contingent future interest gift to the other two. The value of each gift is discounted because it is a future interest gift and discounted further since its value is based on the very low probability that he or she (each grandchild-donor) might not survive until the youngest reaches age 30. If the youngest grandchild lives to age 30, all three of them will take their one-third interest in the trust corpus.

EXAMPLE 7 - 20. If the initial transfer was $24,000, then each child would be deemed to have made a transfer to the extent his or her share lapsed and exceeded the "5 & 5" limits. Thus, each grandchild would be deemed to have transferred $3,000 to the trust. Since there are two other grandchildren who will be the remaindermen if a grandchild dies, each grandchild will be deemed to have made a gift of a contingent future interest that vests when the youngest child reaches age 30. The value of the gift from each grandchild can be determined actuarially. For each child, it would be based on the probability of that grandchild dying before the termination of the trust. Obviously, the gift is very small in value considering the unlikelihood of the event that would cause the gift to vest in the other children (the death of a child before the youngest turns 30) and the fact that the gift is one of a future interest, since enjoyment is postponed until the termination of the trust. Because the gift is one of a future interest, no annual exclusion is available and a gift tax return would have to be filed for each grandchild. If each grandchild is one year old at the time of the transfer ($3,000 from each child), the probability for each child of dying before age 30 is about 2% (see Table 90CM in the Appendix to compare the number alive at age one to the number alive at age 30) and the present value factor for the gift using an 8% rate is .099377 (Table B, remainder after 30 years), hence the value of the gift is approximately six dollars.

The adverse result of creating lapsing powers of appointment in excess of the "5 & 5" limit is not the gift tax generated, since the gift value is usually extremely small, but rather the retained life estate implications. If a beneficiary has a retained life estate in any property that the beneficiary has previously transferred, whether into trust or otherwise, §2036 causes the transferred property to be included in his or her estate at death. The Regulations make it clear that the lapsing of powers that exceed the 5% limit are simply accumulated.[20] There is no attempt to apply sophisticated mathematics to take into account the fact that each subsequent release of a power includes a release of a portion of the trust previously released. The mathematics are kept simple, but this works against the taxpayer (the holder of a power greater than 5%, who lets it lapse) in that it causes greater inclusion in the estate of a beneficiary-holder who dies before the trust terminates.

To further clarify, the "5 & 5" exception does not apply to lapses that take place at the death of the holder. Hence, a noncumulative annually lapsing power to claim up to 5% of the corpus of a trust each year that was not exercised during the holder's last year of life would cause inclusion in the holder's estate of 5% times the date-of-death value of the trust (or $5,000 if such was greater).

> EXAMPLE 7 - 21. When Benny's father died in 2003, his estate plan established a trust that gave Benny income for life and a noncumulative, annually lapsing general power of appointment over a portion of the trust. At Benny's death, the trust terminated and the remaining corpus went to Benny's sister, Rachael. At all times relevant to this example, the value of the trust remained constant at $1,000,000. Benny died in 2007, never having exercised the power. If the power was exercisable over 5% of the trust, then 5% ($50,000) of the trust value would be included in Benny's estate. None of the lifetime lapses of the power were deemed to be transfers.

> EXAMPLE 7 - 22. If the power had been over 8% of the trust (instead of 5%), then for the years 2003, 2004, 2005, and 2006 each lapse would be treated as though 3% (that which exceeded 5%) was transferred by Benny to the trust, with Benny retaining a life estate in the transfers. Section 2036 would cause 12% of the trust to be included in Benny's estate and, since Benny died with an unexercised general power over 8% of the trust, §2041 causes the inclusion of another 8%. Thus, a total of 20% of the value of the trust would be included in Benny's estate.

Ascertainable standard, adverse party exceptions. Similar to estate tax law, a power of appointment to name oneself, one's creditors, one's estate, or the creditors of one's estate is not treated as a general power if the power is subject to an ascertainable standard of health, education, maintenance, or support, or if it is exercisable only in conjunction with either the creator of the power or an adverse party.[21] Ascertainable standard language is commonly used in trust instruments to give flexibility, yet keep the trust out of the holder's estate; it also keeps the lapse of such power from being treated as a gift from the holder. There should not be a gift if one of these powers is exercised in favor of the holder.

Life Insurance

A taxable gift of life insurance can arise either during the insured's lifetime or at the insured's death.

Assignments. During the insured's lifetime, an assignment of ownership rights in the policy may constitute a taxable gift equal to the value of the rights assigned. Ordinarily, the owner assigns all of his or her rights to a policy, and the gift is the value of the policy at that time.

> EXAMPLE 7 - 23. Joe assigns his life insurance policy to his son. The policy has a face value of $600,000 and a value for gift tax purposes of $87,000. Joe has made a present interest gross gift of $87,000 and a taxable gift of $77,000.

In contrast to the assignment of ownership interests, the owner's simple act of naming a beneficiary does not constitute a taxable gift since no property rights are transferred; the named beneficiary has a "mere expectancy," contingent on the owner's keeping the policy in force and not changing the beneficiary designation.

The unholy trinity. A taxable gift of life insurance can arise at an insured's death. This will occur when the insured, owner, and beneficiary are all different parties. Sometimes this arrangement is referred to as the "unholy trinity."

> EXAMPLE 7 - 24. Madeline uses her own separate funds to purchase a $100,000 life insurance policy on her husband Dave's life, naming their son Bret as the beneficiary. On Dave's death, Madeline will have made a $100,000 gift to Bret. A better way to handle this is to transfer the policy to Bret while Dave is still alive.

> EXAMPLE 7 - 25. Changing the facts in the preceding example, assume that Dave purchased and owned the policy until his death, paying the premiums entirely with community property funds. At Dave's death, Madeline will have made a $50,000 gift to Bret, reflecting her one-half interest in the proceeds. Madeline may be able to claim half of the proceeds, if she can show that she was unaware of the policy's existence or that she was unaware that her husband had named someone other than herself as beneficiary.

In the above example, the other $50,000 is includable in Dave's gross estate under §2042. Can you see why? It is because Dave's community property interest is a 50% ownership in the policy. Estate planners typically avoid this tax trap by having the beneficiary also be the owner any time someone other than the insured owns the policy.

Gifts Into Joint Tenancy

Ordinarily, gifts are made when the owner of property transfers his or her entire interest to the donee. Sometimes, however, a donor transfers only a partial interest, as when a donor transfers his or her property into joint tenancy with others.

General rule. The actual moment that a gift occurs when there is a change of title from solely owned into joint tenancy depends on the nature of the property. In general, ownership and possession of most types of property are considered transferred when documents evidencing a transfer of title are executed and delivered or recorded. Where there are co-owners, the donee need not physically take possession of the document of title but need only acknowledge acceptance of the gift. Thus, a gift usually arises when the donor adds the donee's name to property already owned by the donor or includes the donee's name on the title of newly acquired property. The value of the gift will be the net value of the property interest transferred at the time of the gift.

> EXAMPLE 7 - 26. Uncle Charlie bought an automobile for $30,000, paying cash, and taking title in joint tenancy with his nephew Brad. Charlie has made a gift of $15,000 to Brad in the year of purchase.

> EXAMPLE 7 - 27. Changing the facts in the prior example just a bit, assume that Charlie bought the car two years ago for $48,000, taking title in his own name. This year, when the car is worth $30,000, Charlie instructs the motor vehicle bureau to change the title to read: "Charlie Jones and Brad Smith, as joint tenants." This year, Charlie has made a gift to Brad of $15,000.

> EXAMPLE 7 - 28. This year, Clive purchased a building for $150,000, taking title in joint tenancy with his five adult sons. This year, Clive has made a gift of $25,000 to each son.

Two exceptions. There are two principal exceptions to the rule that the inclusion of others as co-tenants for less than full consideration results in an immediate gift. First, in the case of a joint tenancy bank account, in most states a gift arises on the withdrawal of funds by the donee, not on the creation of the jointly held bank account. Second, where title is taken in the conjunctive, e.g., Mary Smith or Sara Smith, with one of the parties paying more than half of the consideration, no gift takes place until the property is sold or redeemed. No immediate gift takes place because the donor has retained control over the account or bond, since he or she can withdraw all of the funds or cash in the bonds without the aid of the donee joint tenant. Compare that situation to a transfer of real estate into joint tenancy; once the deed is recorded (or delivered to the donee), the original owner cannot unilaterally recover what he or she has given away, i.e., control of that portion has been lost. This is also true of corporate stocks or bonds. Once the transfer agent has changed title into joint tenancy, the original owner cannot unilaterally change it back into just his or her name without the cooperation of the transferees or a certified death certificate showing them to be deceased.

> EXAMPLE 7 - 29. On June 1 of last year, Rochelle deposited $40,000 in a savings account held jointly with her son Conrad. He withdrew $6,800 on February 1 of this year. Rochelle made a gift to Conrad, but not until February 1 of this year. It was covered by the annual exclusion.

> EXAMPLE 7 - 30. Lionel purchased a $20,000 EE savings bond years ago, taking title with his son Patrick as joint tenants. At the bond's maturity next month, if Lionel redeems the bond, there will be no gift. If Patrick redeems it, Lionel will have made a gift of $20,000. If they split the proceeds, Lionel's gift to Patrick of $10,000 will be covered by the annual exclusion.

Disclaimers

The prior examples assumed that the donees accepted the gifts as given. Suppose that for some reason the intended donee does not want to accept a substantial gift made under a will, trust instrument, or other document. Obviously, if one accepts a gift or bequest and then transfers the property to another, it will trigger a transfer tax unless the transfer is sheltered by the annual exclusion or a charitable or marital deduction. To avoid creating a taxable transfer, a donee might wish to refuse the gift. Section 2518 allows the donee to "disclaim" a gift in such a way that it will be as though the gift was never made and, in the case of a bequest, as though disclaimant predeceased the decedent-donor. In order to disclaim and have this favorable result, referred to as *making a tax effective disclaimer*, i.e., the disclaimer does not generate a taxable transfer, the following requirements must be met:

1. The refusal is "an irrevocable and unqualified refusal...to accept" the interest.
2. The refusal is made in writing.
3. The refusal is made within nine months after the later of:
    a) the date on which the transfer creating the interest was made, or
    b) the day on which the person disclaiming reaches age 21.

4. The donee (i.e., the disclaimant) did not accept any interest in the benefits.
5. And, as a result of the refusal, the interest passes (without the disclaiming person's direction) to someone else.

With regard to the fourth requirement, acts indicating "acceptance" include using the property, accepting dividends, interest, or rents from the property, and directing others to act with regard to the property. However, acceptance will not be found in cases where the disclaimant merely accepted title to property or merely because title vested immediately in the disclaimant on death of the decedent, as in the case of survivorship under joint tenancy. Benefits received by a person under 21 years of age are disregarded.[22]

Section 2518(b)(4)(A) creates a special privilege for the spouse of a donor or decedent. He/she may disclaim and still retain benefits in the disclaimed property. This is used in estate plans that call for property disclaimed by the surviving spouse to be placed in a trust that gives her (the disclaimant) a life estate and/or the power to withdraw limited by an ascertainable standard.

Meeting all of these requirements is particularly important because failure to meet any one could result in two completed transfers subject to taxation.

EXAMPLE 7 - 31. Gaylord gives his adult son Daniel his vacation bungalow on the lake, completing the necessary transfer of title. After spending a weekend there, Daniel decides that he hates fishing and can't stand the mosquitoes, so he transfers title back to Gaylord. Daniel's act is not a valid disclaimer because he had already accepted a benefit. Therefore, two gifts occurred, first the one by Gaylord and then the gift by Daniel.

EXAMPLE 7 - 32. During their life, husband and wife owned their home in joint tenancy. Within nine months of husband's death, wife acts to disclaim her survivorship interest. Her disclaimer is not invalid merely because her survivorship interest vested immediately at his death and she continued to live in the house and pay all expenses and related taxes prior to making the disclaimer, provided that while husband was alive the tenancy could be unilaterally partitioned.[23] The reason the use does not disqualify the disclaimer is that her interest prior to his death was an undivided one, meaning that she supposedly had full use of the property even before he died. We might reach a different conclusion if it was rental property and she was collecting half the rent before he died and then all of the rent after his death.

EXAMPLE 7 - 33. Mildred died, disposing of her entire $1.8 million estate by will. It read, "to my husband, Henry, if living, and, if not, then to our children." Within the nine months following Mildred's death, Henry, before receiving any interest or benefit in the property, presented a written refusal of "so much of Mildred's estate as equals the applicable exclusion amount" to the executor of her estate. Henry has made a valid disclaimer, and he will not be considered to have ever owned that portion of the property. The disclaimed property will now pass by the terms of the will to the children. This will use Mildred's unified credit and reduce Henry's taxable estate.

The present law allowing tax effective disclaimers is generally seen as a valuable method for correcting inefficient transfers in wills and trust instruments.[24] Chapter 12 will discuss estate plans that use disclaimers to add flexibility to estate plans.

Miscellaneous Gift Tax Issues

Reciprocal gifts. Donors who get together on a scheme to use reciprocal gifts in order to gain additional annual exclusions may find their actions subject to IRS scrutiny. The argument will be that substance should prevail over form.

EXAMPLE 7 - 34. In 2007, hoping to take advantage of the annual exclusion, Mr. Garbanzo gives $12,000 to his son and $12,000 to Mrs. Ceci's daughter. At about the same time, Mrs. Ceci gives $12,000 to her daughter and $12,000 to Mr. Garbanzo's son. The IRS will treat the "mirror image" transfers as if they were made to each donor's own child. Thus, each parent will be treated as having made a $24,000 gross gift to his own child.[25]

Multiple taxation of transfers. Certain transfers may be subject to both gift tax and estate tax.

EXAMPLE 7 - 35. Pope, age 55, transfers $100,000 in property into an irrevocable trust with an independent trustee. He retains a life estate in the income and names his nephew as the remainderman. At the time the § 7520 rate was 8%. Pope has made a completed gross gift this year of $21,166, the current value of the remainder (based on Table B 8%, i.e., 0.21166 * $100,000). As a gift of a future interest, it does not qualify for the annual exclusion. At Pope's death, the date-of-death value of the entire trust corpus is included in his gross estate under IRC § 2036(a). The adjusted taxable gift is reduced to zero, and a credit for any gift tax paid is allowed to prevent double taxation. Of course, if Pope's taxable gifts never exceeded the AEA, no gift taxes will be paid during his lifetime.

Where transferred property comes back into the gross estate because of a string being attached (IRC §§ 2036-2038) or because the transfer falls under one of the

§ 2035(a) exceptions (transfer of life insurance or the severing of a string), the earlier gift will not be considered an adjusted taxable gift for purposes of calculating the donee's estate tax. The last sentence of § 2001(b) defines "adjusted taxable gifts" as being post-1976 taxable gifts "other than gifts which are includible in the gross estate of the decedent." It would seem appropriate that the gift tax actually paid (rather than the gift tax payable credit) would be applied against the estate tax whenever the property that generated the gift tax is pulled back into the gross estate. In these situations the gift tax paid should be viewed as an advanced payment of the estate tax.

CONCLUSION

This chapter has focused on certain qualitative aspects of the federal gift tax. The next chapter will present a brief overview of the federal income tax issues as they relate to trusts and estates.

QUESTIONS AND PROBLEMS - Use the ETAX program to do the problems that require calculation of estate or gift taxes. If an annual exclusion is available, use the following amounts: $3,000 for 1977 - 1981; $10,000 for 1982 - 2002; $11,000 for 2002 - 2005; and $12,000 for 2006-2008.

1. On January 2, 2002, Corinne bought shares of LARC stock for $250,000. On November 4, 2005, she gave her brother, Eugene, the shares then worth $550,000. Corinne had never before given a gift that exceeded the annual exclusion amount. On the last trading day of the year 2004, the stock was worth $750,000. At the close of April 15, 2007, the stock had dropped back to $600,000. (a) What value is reported on the gift tax return? What is the taxable amount? (b) When is the return due?

2. How would your answers to the questions in the prior problem change if Eugene was Corinne's husband instead of her brother?

3. How would your answers to questions in the prior problem change if, although Connie's husband Eugene is legally living in the U.S., he is not a citizen?

4. Lisa created a revocable trust in the 1970s, transferring in land that turned out to hold substantial oil and gas reserves. Skylark National Trust, Inc., serves as the trustee of the trust, managing trust assets worth over $25 million at the beginning of 2006. During that year, at Lisa's written request, the trustee gave assets worth a total of $6 million to her three children. (a) How much gift tax would be owed? (b) Who must file the return and when would it be due? (c) How would one obtain an extension to file the return?

5. In 2006, Mike made a gift to his friend Laurent of stock worth slightly more than $1.5 million. However, just a few weeks later, Mike left the U.S. and went to Europe to, as he put it, "lead the life of a free spirit." What burden does this place on Laurent?

6. In 2007, Olan gave David ABC stock worth $2,542,000 on condition that David pay the gift tax that results from the transfer. (a) What is the gift tax that must be paid? In the ETAX cell for "Current year taxable gifts" put the following: "+2542000-12000-D18". (b) What would the tax be without this net gift arrangement?

7. In 2006, Lois transferred $25,000 to an irrevocable trust that is required to distribute all income annually to her son, age 55, for his life; the remainder will be distributed outright to his issue. Assuming a 6% federal rate, calculate Lois's present interest and the taxable gift.

8. In 2007, Avery transferred $50,000 into an irrevocable trust. His daughter, Dayna, is to receive all of the income from the trust for five years, followed by his daughter, Sandra, receiving the income for the next five years, after which the trust terminates and is distributed to his son, Walter. Assuming a federal rate of 4%, calculate Avery's present interest and the taxable gift.

9. For each of the following independent alternatives, determine whether the transfer in 2007 of $50,000 worth of ABC stock qualifies for the annual exclusion in order to determine the taxable gift amount. If a §7520 rate is needed to determine the value of the present interest use 6%.
   (a) Gerry transferred the stock to Joan and Steve as joint tenants.

(b) Jaime transferred the stock to an irrevocable trust that gives Polly income for five years, then the income interest shifts to Tracy for five years, after which the trust terminates and the trust assets are distributed to Anna.

(c) Same as the prior problem but the trust terms require the trustee to retain the stock for a period of two years and the ABC company is a non-dividend paying closely held business.

(d) Paula transfers the stock to an irrevocable trust. The independent trustee is required to distribute, in such proportion as the trustee deems appropriate, all income at least annually to Fred (age 50) and Susan (age 55) for their lifetimes. After both are deceased the trust terminates and will be distributed to their issue.

10. (a) Where on the 709 does a donor indicate that she is making a § 2513 split gift election with her spouse? (b) Where does the non-donor husband sign, showing his consent? (c) Where does the "split" take place on the donee spouse's return? (d) Where does the non-donee spouse's return account for half of the gifts made by donee spouse?

11. Both Edward and Mindy Esker have children by prior marriages. For the most part they have avoided commingling their respective properties. In 2007, Edward gave each of his three children property worth $442,000, i.e., $1,326,000 total, and Mindy gave each of her two children property worth $442,000, i.e., $884,000 total. (a) How much would they each pay in gift tax if they do not split the gifts? (b) How much would they pay if they make a split gift election? (c) What alternatives would you suggest for allocating the gift tax if they do split the gifts?

12. In 2007, Brenda gave her daughter Susan MOP stock worth $2,740,000. Because she did not want to pay gift taxes, she asked her husband, Fred, to split the gift. (a) What is the taxable gift and the gift tax that Brenda reports if she alone files a return? (b) If they split the gift, what is the taxable gift each reports and the gift tax? (c) How much is saved by splitting the gift?

13. In 2007, John gave ABC stock worth $1,600,000 to his daughter Marlene. John and his wife, Lola, are thinking about splitting the gift. (a) What is the taxable gift and the gift tax that John reports if he alone files a return? (b) If they split the gift, what is the taxable gift each reports and the gift tax? (c) How

much is saved by splitting the gift? (d) Summarize how gift splitting saves gift taxes.

14. Kenneth created an irrevocable trust, transferring assets worth $1 million to an independent trustee. The trust was to help various family members, but specifically excluded helping Kenneth and his wife. Eventually, the trust was to terminate and be distributed to several individuals and their families. Part of the trust read as follows, "Kenneth reserves the right to distribute up to 10% of the trust each year to such of his issue as he thinks need help to pursue additional education or for support." When he died, the trust was worth $1.5 million. He had never exercised the right to distribute a portion of the trust. Explain how much, if any, of this trust is included in his estate. Be sure to focus on the difference between retained interests and limited powers of appointment.

15. Crystal established a trust for the benefit of Arthur, during his lifetime, with remainder to Sarah on Arthur's death. Arthur was 50 years old when the trust was established. The terms of the trust give Arthur the noncumulative right to demand up to 5% from the trust in any year. In years 1, 2, 3, 5, and 6, he did not exercise the right. In year 4, he took out the maximum allowed. The trust was worth exactly $1,000,000 at all times relevant here, i.e., with appreciation in the remaining assets, the trust quickly returned to $1,000,000 after any withdrawal of corpus and such was its value in the 6th year when Arthur died.
(a) In the first year the power lapsed, what was the gift to Sarah?
(b) How much of this trust would be included in Arthur's estate?
(c) If the demand right had been the greater of 7% or $7,000, what would be the gift to Sarah in the first year? Would a gift tax return have to be filed?
(d) If the demand right had been the greater of 7% or $7,000, how much would be included in Arthur's estate? Why does the adjusted taxable gift drop to zero?

16. James established a trust (worth exactly $1,000,000 at all times relevant here) for the benefit of Judith during her lifetime with the remainder to Lisa. Judith was 70 years old when the trust was established. In addition to all income, Judith was given the noncumulative right to demand each year up to 5% of the trust's value. Over the years, Judith did the following: year 1 demanded and received the full amount allowed; year 4 demanded and received 3% of the

trust; year 5 demanded and received 2%; and in both years 6 and 7 demanded and received 5%. In all other years she asked for nothing over and above the income. With appreciation in the remaining assets, the trust quickly returned to $1,000,000, which was its value in the 8th year when Judith died.

(a) Explain, without doing the math, how the gift to Lisa would be calculated for year two (i.e., when the power lapsed), but for the 5 & 5 exception.

(b) How much of this trust would be included in Judith's estate?

(c) If the demand right had been the greater of 8% or $8,000, again without doing the math, explain how one would calculate the value of the fifth-year gift to Lisa? If the calculated value was $9,000, would a gift tax return have to be filed?

(d) If the demand right had been the greater of 8% or $8,000, how much would be included in Judith's estate?

17. Ralph established a trust in 1985 that gave Linda income for life, remainder to Linda's three children. Explain the effect on Linda's estate at her death of each clause (considered independently) if such is part of the trust:

 (a) The trustee is given absolute discretion to transfer the principal of the trust to Linda, if doing so would be in her best interest.

 (b) Linda is given the power to appoint, by direct reference to this power in her will, the remainder of the trust among her children in such portion as she deems appropriate.

 (c) Linda is given the right to invade the corpus up to a maximum of 3% of the trust in any one year. This right shall be noncumulative.

 (d) Linda is given the power to invade the corpus of the trust, up to the whole amount, if such be necessary for her health, education, maintenance, or support.

18. Martin established a trust to take care of his mentally disabled son, Charlie. The trust document gave Martin's daughter, Diane, the power to require the Trustee to hold back income or, if Diane thought it was needed, to distribute income and corpus to Charlie or for Charlie's benefit. Diane died five years after the trust was established. The trust was worth $2,000,000 when established in 2002 and $2,300,000 when Diane died. For each alternative case: (i) explain the nature of Diane's interest; and (ii) state what, if anything, is included in Diane's gross estate.

(a) The trust document also gave Diane the right to demand for her own benefit up to 10% of the corpus of the trust if such was needed for Diane's health, education, maintenance or support. Diane never made the demand.

(b) In addition to the power to benefit Charlie, the trust gave Diane the right to demand for her own benefit up to 4% of the value of the trust each year. Diane never made the demand.

(c) Same as "b" except the demand right was up to 8%.

19. Abraham established an irrevocable trust to benefit his second wife, Hannah, for her lifetime. Hannah received all of the income for her lifetime and at her death the trust terminates and is distributed to Abraham's two children from his first marriage. The trust is worth $1,000,000 at all times relevant here. Determine how much of the trust would be included in Hannah's estate when she dies given the following alternatives:

(a) Starlight National Trust, Inc., served as trustee but Hannah had the right to demand up to 5% of the corpus of the trust each year without having to justify why she wanted it. She never made such a demand and the right lapsed when she died.

(b) Same as the previous situation but shortly before she died she had the 5% withdrawn and gave it to her church to satisfy a pledge she had made in support of a church building project.

(c) Starlight National Trust, Inc., served as trustee but Hannah had the right to demand up to 7% of the corpus of the trust each year without having to justify why she wanted it. During the 11th year of the trust's existence Hannah died without ever making any demands to withdraw corpus.

(d) Same as "c" but in year four she demanded and received 3% of the trust's corpus.

20. Frank purchased a $280,000 life insurance policy on his own life. A year later, when it had a value for gift purposes of $25,000, he assigned the policy to his son, Sam. A few months after making this gift, Frank died. Frank's wife had always been the named beneficiary and Sam failed to change the beneficiary designation. (a) Explain the estate tax consequences. Does the marital deduction come into play? (b) Explain all gift tax consequences.

21. Grant owned a $500,000 life insurance policy on his life. For gift purposes it was worth $50,000. For each alternative case: (i) Is there a taxable gift, and if

so, how much? (ii) What amount is included in Grant's gross estate? (iii) What is the adjusted taxable gift?

  (a) Grant named his daughter Gina the beneficiary in 2000 and he died in 2008.

  (b) Grant gave his daughter the policy in 2004, she named herself the beneficiary, and he died in 2006.

  (c) Same as prior problem but Grant died in 2008.

22. Carolina owned a $500,000 life insurance policy on her life. For gift purposes it was worth $50,000. Her son, Ernesto, and daughter, Erin, were named beneficiaries. In 2005, Carolina transferred the policy to her son. When she died in 2007, Ernesto and Erin each collected $250,000. (a) Was there a taxable gift when the policy was transferred, and if so, how much? (b) What amount is included in Carolina's gross estate? (c) What is the adjusted taxable gift? (d) Did the payment of the proceeds result in another taxable gift? Explain.

23. In 2005, Vera transferred LARC stock that she had purchased for $60,000 into joint tenancy with her son, Wilbur, at a time when the stock was worth $100,000. In 2007, they sold the stock for $150,000 and each kept $75,000. (a) When and in what amount was the gift? (b) How much gain should each report?

24. In 2004, Bonnie opened a $70,000 joint bank account in her and her son Gerardo's names. In 2005, Gerardo withdrew $30,000 to pay his credit card debt. In 2007, they both withdrew $6,000 to take a trip through Europe. In 2008, Bonnie closed out the account by removing the remaining funds. Discuss by year whether gifts occur.

25. Insofar as timing goes, what do a qualified disclaimer and an estate tax return have in common? How are they different?

26. On January 1, 2006, Clarisa died, leaving an estate valued at $800,000. Her will left the entire estate to her children, William and Michelle. Walter, her financial advisor, served as executor. William has four adult children and Michelle has two. For each alternative that follows, (i) determine the transfer tax consequences of the action described and (ii) who gets what.

(a) On June 9, 2006, William wrote a letter to Walter stating that he (William) disclaimed his interest in his mother's estate.

(b) Same facts as in the prior problem except the letter also requested that the one-fourth share that would otherwise pass to William's son, Greg, be transferred to the trustee of Greg's special needs trust rather than go outright to Greg.

(c) On August 12, 2006, Michelle wrote a letter stating that she (Michelle) disclaimed 40% of her inheritance.

(d) Same facts as in the prior problem but the letter was dated December 12, 2006.

27. When Noah died on November 10, 2006, his estate was worth $2,500,000. Noah left his estate to his wife, Claudia, with the provision in his will that any amount she disclaimed would go into a trust that would give her income for life with the remainder to their issue per capita at each generation. Claudia was in very, very poor health and had her own estate worth over $1,000,000. (a) Can Claudia make a qualified disclaimer? If so, how and when must she do it? (b) Must she give up the right to the income on what she disclaims in order to make the disclaimer a qualified one? (c) Will the trust that results from a disclaimer be included in Claudia's estate?

28. Tony's eyesight became so weak that he could no longer drive his car, so he let Larry, a neighbor in his teens who helped him with shopping, drive it. After a while, the car was parked at Larry's house. Both Tony and Larry kept a set of keys. At Tony's 80th birthday party, in front of several guests, he told Larry that the car was his. He asked his caretaker to find the title slip so he could sign the car over to Larry, but the slip could not be located. Tony died two weeks after the party. The slip was located in his safe deposit box and the second set of keys found on his dresser. Tony's executor wants to sell the car as part of the estate, and has offered it to Larry at low Blue Book of $23,000, but Larry says the car already belongs to him. What supports the executor's position? Larry's position? What additional facts might support one position or the other?

29. Brooke established an irrevocable trust with assets worth $5,000,000. Skylark National Trust, Inc., serves as independent trustee. Arthur and Janet are the income beneficiaries and at their deaths, the trust terminates and is distributed

to Janet's issue per capita at each generation. Brooke retained the right, personal to himself, to have the Trustee apportion the income between the two beneficiaries with the trust having a default provision that the income be split equally each year that Brooke is silent as to the division. One provision requires all income to be distributed each year and another that once one beneficiary dies all of the income must be distributed to the survivor. (a) Given that Brooke cannot benefit himself, his estate, his creditors, or the creditors of his estate, was there a completed gift when the trust was established? (b) Would there be a gift if Brooke gave up the right to allocate income? (c) If Brooke dies before the death of either income beneficiary, would the trust be in his estate? Explain. (d) If Janet or Arthur died before Brooke, would the death cause a completed gift?

30. During the last 10 years of her life, Loraine, a widow, undertook each of the following independent transactions. For each one, explain whether or not it is considered a taxable gift.

(a) Purchased a life insurance policy on her life, naming her son beneficiary.

(b) Transferred title to her personal residence to her daughter and continued to live there, rent-free, for two years, at that time she moved out and formally relinquished all rights to the property.

(c) Funded a revocable living trust.

(d) Funded an irrevocable living trust, under which her daughter was the sole beneficiary.

(e) Purchased some land, taking title in the names of herself and her son as joint tenants. Loraine paid $90,000 of the $100,000 purchase price, and son paid $10,000.

(f) Purchased common stock, taking title in the names of herself and her husband as joint tenants.

(g) Purchased life insurance on the life of her uncle, naming her daughter beneficiary. Two years later, uncle died and daughter was paid the proceeds.

(h) Paid $21,000 in tuition and $8,000 in room, board, and other fees each year for five years for her son's college education.

(i) Opened a joint checking account with her daughter, depositing $26,000 of her own funds.

ANSWERS TO THE QUESTIONS AND PROBLEMS *(odd numbered only)*

1. Reporting Corinne's gifts: (a) Gift returns use the date of gift value, i.e., $550,000 (adjusted amount would be $539,000). (b) The return is due on April 15, 2006.

3. Gift to non-citizen husband Eugene: (a) Again, the value is as of the date of gift, i.e., $550,000. For gifts to non-U.S. spouses the annual exclusion is $100,000 (indexed $117,000 for 2005), hence the taxable gift is $450,000 (indexed $443,000). (b) Still due on the 15th of April 2005.

5. Covering the tax on Mike's gift: Because of transferee liability, Laurent would have to pay the gift tax (slightly more than $200,000). Note, this is not a net gift situation since Mike and Laurent did not agree in advance that Laurent would pay the gift taxes.

7. Present interest: $25,000 x .71075 = $17,769. The present interest exceeds the annual exclusion amount; hence the full $12,000 reduces the taxable gift to $13,000.

9. Alternative scenarios each involving a transfer in 2007 of $50,000 worth of ABC stock:

    (a) to Joan and Steve as joint tenants. There would be two annual exclusions, so the taxable amount would be $26,000 (annual exclusion of $12,000 per donee).

    (b) to an irrevocable trust that gives Olan income for five years, then to Tracy for five years, terminates with distribution to Anna. The first five years' income stream is a present interest but not the next one or the remainder. The present interest has a value of $12,637, i.e., 0.252742 * $50,000. The taxable gift is $38,000 [$50,000 - $12,000].

    (c) Same as "b" but the trustee must retain the non-dividend paying stock for two years: The two year delay in any possible income for Olan means that no one has a present interest, hence no annual exclusion and all $50,000 is a taxable gift.

    (d) to an irrevocable trust, independent trustee allocates and distributes income to Fred and Susan. Since neither beneficiary has a present interest there is no annual exclusion and the taxable gift is $50,000.

11. Eskers' split gifts to children by prior marriages: (a) If they don't split, then Edward has taxable gifts of $1,290,000 and pays $119,700 and Mindy has $860,000 and pays no gift taxes. (b) By splitting each will have made taxable gifts of $1,075,000 and must pay gift taxes of $30,750. The total gift tax of $61,500 is $58,200 less than by not splitting. (c) Given that Mindy would not have paid any tax but for the election, it would seem fair for Edward to pay all of the tax. Consider that Mindy has also used up AEA that might have reduced her estate taxes.

13. John's gift splitting: (a) Without splitting: taxable gift $1,588,000 and tax of $249,600. (b) Each reports half: two taxable gifts of $788,000 result in no taxes (the gifts drop below gift AEA). (c) Taxes saved: $249,600.

15. (a) No gift taxes are generated because the gift (the lapse of the right to withdraw $50,000) is covered by the 5 & 5 exception.

(b) The 5 & 5 exception does not apply to lapses at death; therefore, $50,000 would be included in Arthur's estate. Note: nothing is actually taken out of the trust due to this inclusion in Arthur's estate; it is included for calculation purposes only. Any estate tax attributed to this inclusion is charged to the trust.

(c) Each year that a lapse occurred (years 1, 2, 3, and 5) due to a year ending without a withdrawal, a gift occurred of the amount not sheltered by the 5 & 5 exception. Thus for each of those years, a gift of a remainder interest in $20,000 must be reported. In the first year, for example, if the federal rate for future interest gifts was 8%, the gift would be: 0.16388 * $20,000 = $3,328 [Table S (8%), 50 year old, remainder factor]. Each year that a lapse occurred, a gift tax return would have been required since the amounts over 5% would be deemed gifts of future interests (no annual exclusion), discounted because of Arthur's retained life estate.

(d) For each year a right to withdraw lapsed at the end of a year, it would be as if Arthur had transferred 2% of the corpus into trust and retained a life estate in the property transferred. Lifetime lapses occurred four years (years 1, 2, 3, and 5), thus for these years 8% of the trust is included. In the last year, the entire 7% lapse is included because there is no 5% shelter for lapses at death. So the total of 15% times the value of the trust at his death is included in his estate. The adjusted taxable gifts become zero, even though gift tax returns were filed, because adjusted taxable gifts do not include gifts that end up in the donor's gross estate.

17. (a) The trustee is the holder of a limited power and this trust is not included in Linda's estate. (b) Linda is the holder of a limited power, and nothing is included whether or not she exercises the power. (c) This is a general power, and 3% of the trust's value on her death will be included in her estate, assuming she did not exercise the power that last year. If she did exercise it to the full 3%, then none of the trust would be included. The property taken out, if any, would be in her estate unless she gave it away or consumed it. (d) This is a power limited by an ascertainable standard as such is defined in IRC § 2041 and is therefore considered a limited power, therefore, nothing is included.

19. Abraham's irrevocable trust giving a life estate to his second wife, Hannah, with various alternative provisions:

     a) Starlight National Trust, Inc., as trustee, Hannah's 5% demand right: $50,000, i.e., 5% of the trust is subject to her general power at the time of her death.

     b) Same but the 5% withdrawn and given to church: None, assuming she died in the same year as making the withdrawal as she had no withdrawal right at the time she died. However, if she withdrew the money in late December and she died after a new right started in January, then $50,000.

     c) Unused 7% demand right over the 11 years: Included $250,000. Each year that a lapse occurred she made a 2% gift of the remainder interest into a trust in which she held a life estate, hence for 10 years she increased inclusion in her estate by 2% per year, plus the full 5% in the year of her death for a total of 25%.

     d) Same as "c" but in year four she demanded 3% of the corpus: $230,000. The year she made the withdrawal dropped the lapse amount below 5% which means it was covered by the §2041 5&5 safe harbor rule. So now there are 9 lapses at 2% (only that above the 5% is treated as a transfer with a retained interest), plus the 5% year of death lapse for a total of 23%.

21. Grant's $500,000 life insurance and asking about (i) taxable gift, (ii) the gross estate, and (iii) the adjusted taxable gift.

     (a) Daughter Gina named the beneficiary in 2000: (i) No lifetime transfer, so no gift. (ii) Since he had an incident of ownership when he died, the entire $500,000 proceeds amount is in his gross estate even though the payment is made directly to Gina. (iii) No gift hence no taxable gift.

(b) Daughter given the policy in 2004, names herself beneficiary, and he died in 2006. (i) Gift was $50,000 but the annual exclusion reduces the taxable gift to $40,000. (ii) The §2035(a) rule pulls life insurance into the insured's estate if he/she transfers the policy within 3 years of his/her death; hence the $500,000 proceeds amount is included. (iii) Where the transferred property ends up in the gross estate, the adjusted taxable gift for said property drops to zero.

(c) Same as prior problem but Grant died in 2008. (i) Again, gift of $50,000 of which $39,000 is taxable. (ii) Because Grant lives more than 3 years after making the gift, the policy is not in his gross estate. (iii) The adjusted taxable gift is $39,000.

23. In 2005, Vera transferred $100,000 LARC stock (basis $60,000) into joint tenancy with her son, Wilbur, at a time when the stock was worth $100,000. In 2007, they sold the stock for $150,000 and each kept $75,000. (a)The gift? (b) The gain? (a) Gift occurred when the joint tenancy was created since Vera could not unilaterally "withdraw" the stock. Gift of $50,000 and taxable gift of $39,000. (b) For gift purposes there is a COB, hence each recognizes a gain of $45,000, i.e., $75,000 - $30,000.

25. There is a "nine months" connection. A disclaimer must be made within nine months of an interest being created; hence for an inheritance it generally starts with the death of the person leaving his or her estate. The estate tax return must be filed within nine months of the death. The difference is that one can get an extension to file an estate tax return but one cannot get an extension to make a disclaimer.

27. Claudia and disclaiming Noah's estate: (a) How and when to disclaim. (b) Her right to the income and having a qualified disclaimer. (c) The trust and her estate.

(a) Yes, she must follow the rules set forth in §2518, e.g., make it in writing to the executor of Noah's estate, deliver it within 9 months of Noah's death, etc. (b) She can keep the income interest. Part of 2518 says the interest can qualify if "as a result of such refusal, the interest passes without any direction on the part of the person making the disclaimer and passes either- (A) to the spouse of the decedent,..." This taken to mean that a surviving spouse can still have an interest without the disclaimer being an unqualified one. (c) Not unless

Noah's executor makes a QTIP election (introduced in Chapter 6). Claudia will not be considered to have created the trust and she will not have a power of appointment over it, so there is neither a retained interest nor a power that would cause the interest to be included in her estate.

29. Brooke's retained interest in the trust he established: (a) The gift is incomplete because Brooke did not give up "dominion and control" of the enjoyment of the income. (b) Yes, if the release of the right is done in a manner that makes it irrevocable then the gift becomes complete. (c) Yes, the retained interest causes it to be included. (d) Yes, the death of either would result in Brooke losing the ability to alter enjoyment, i.e., dominion and control would end. Note, this would not be a release of a retained interest (it would just end) hence there would not be a three year inclusion period to worry about.

ENDNOTES

1. Reg. § 25.2511-2(b).

2. IRC § 2501(a)(2), §2511(a).

3. IRC § 2516.

4. IRC § 2502(c).

5. IRC § 102(a).

6. *Diedrich* 457 U.S. 191 (1982).

7. IRC § 2522(a).

8. IRC § 2503(g).

9. IRC § 2523.

10. IRC § 2056(b)(7).

11. IRC § 2523(i).

12. IRC § 2503(e).

13. IRC § 2501(a)(5).

14. IRC § 2503(b).

15. The Revenue Act of 1948.

16. IRC § 2513.

17. TAM 9128009; §2035(b).

18. IRC § 2514(b).

19. IRC § 2514 parallels estate related IRC § 2041

20. IRC § 2514(e), Reg. 25.2514-3(c)(4), see also Reg. § 20.2041-3(d)(5), Reg. § 20.2041-3(d)(4).

21. IRC § 2514(c)(1) and (c)(3)

22. Reg. § 25.2518-2(3).

23. Reg. § 25.2518-2 (d)(1); LR 9135043; LR 9135044; TAM 9208003.

24. Reg. § 25.2518-1(b).

25. TAM 88717003.

CHAPTER 8

Income Tax: Gifts, Estates, and Trusts

OVERVIEW

This chapter covers income tax basics as they relate to gifts, estates, and trusts. We start with the various rules that govern how basis is determined for property received as a gift or from a decedent's estate. How property was titled may determine the new basis for surviving co-owners. Much of the chapter is devoted to fiduciary income tax, i.e., the taxation of trusts, estates, and their beneficiaries. The net income received by trusts and estates generally finds its way to beneficiaries. Whether it is taxed to the fiduciary entity (i.e., the trust or estate) or to a beneficiary depends on the nature of the income, the timing of distributions, and elections made by the fiduciary's personal representative.

BASIS RULES

The manner in which one acquires property determines the owner's initial basis in the property. Basis is important for two reasons: 1) basis is the starting point for determining depreciation for depreciable property; and, 2) on sale, it is the difference between the price (net amount realized) and the adjusted basis that determines the amount of gain or loss for income tax purposes.

Gain and loss. The gain or loss realized from the sale of property is calculated by subtracting an asset's adjusted basis from the amount realized:

Gain or Loss = Amount Realized - Adjusted Basis

EXAMPLE 8 - 1. Candice owns 100 shares of MOP common stock purchased several years ago for $13,000 (hence, her adjusted basis in the stock). If she sells the shares for $16,000, net of selling commissions, her realized gain is $3,000. On the other hand, if the stock is sold for $11,000, she has a realized loss of $2,000.

Amount realized is defined as the fair market value of all money or property received, less selling expenses such as commissions.

EXAMPLE 8 - 2. In the prior example, the sales proceeds could have been in the form of cash or in kind. Alternatively, the buyer could have canceled an existing debt owed by the seller. Hence, if the buyer paid $6,000 cash, assigned title to his automobile (valued at $8,000), and also tore up a $2,000 IOU owed by the seller to the buyer, the total amount realized is still $16,000.

Adjusted basis is the taxpayer's "initial basis" as "adjusted" by certain increases or decreases. The initial basis for an asset that is purchased is its cost. Adjustments to basis include items that reduce basis, such as allowance for depreciation, depletion, and obsolescence that reduce the taxpayer's taxes. The basis in stock may be decreased by non-taxable distributions. The most common adjustment that increases basis is for capital expenditures that improve property.

EXAMPLE 8 - 3. In the earlier example, the adjusted basis of $13,000 was probably the original purchase price of the stock, including any trading commission or other fee. However, had the asset been a machine used in the taxpayer's business, adjusted basis would likely reflect its current book (depreciated) value, including all capital improvements made subsequent to its acquisition. Hence, the $13,000 adjusted basis for a machine could, for example, be the net result of a $27,000 original purchase price, less $17,000 in accumulated depreciation, plus $3,000 in capital improvements.

Recapture of depreciation, which arises when a depreciable business asset is sold for greater than its adjusted basis, is beyond the scope of this text other than to say that a portion of the gain (the depreciation recaptured) may be taxed as ordinary income or in the case of depreciated real estate at a special 25% rate rather than at the more favorable capital gains rate.

Intangible assets (stocks, bonds, etc.) and personal use assets (one's home, the family car, etc.) cannot be depreciated. Therefore fewer adjustments to basis are likely with these types of assets than are likely with tangible business-use assets.

Holding period. A gain or a loss can be either short-term or long-term, depending on the length of the holding period. The holding period is how long the asset was held by the seller and, in the case of property acquired by gift, by prior owners too. A gain or a loss is *short-term* if the holding period is not more than one year; it is *long-term* if the property is held more than one year. Inherited property is automatically considered long-term property. In determining the holding period, a donee gets to include the donor's holding period, e.g., if the donor held the property for eight months, the donee will need to hold it just four more months for it to be long-term property. If a taxpayer has both long-term and short-term sales during the year, they are reported separately and each type is netted separately to determine whether there is a gain or a loss. The net gain on the sale of appreciated short-term investments is taxed as ordinary income, whereas the net gain on the sale of long-term investments is taxed at the lower capital gains rate. Presently, the maximum capital gains rate for individuals (estates and trusts, too) is 15% (5% for taxpayers in the 10% or 15% bracket). The capital gains rate also applies to dividends received from domestic corporations and qualifying foreign corporations, as well as to corporate dividends passed through to investors by a mutual fund or other investment company. The 5% rate drops to zero for the year 2008. The capital gains treatment for dividends ends (unless the law is extended) December 31, 2008.

Realized versus recognized gains and losses. A gain or loss is *realized* when the basic transaction, typically a sale, has occurred. On the other hand, a gain or loss is *recognized* when the taxpayer reports the gain or loss on a tax return. Recognition will commonly occur either because tax law requires recognition in that year or because the taxpayer elects a code-permitted option to defer the tax to a later time. Common examples of gains or losses that may be recognized in tax years after the year of realization include installment sales,[1] tax-deferred exchanges of like-kind property,[2] involuntary conversion[3] (e.g., destruction of a warehouse by fire with insurance proceeds used to purchase a replacement warehouse), and certain capital transactions between corporations and their shareholders. Generally, the rate in effect when the gain is recognized is the rate that is applied. For instance, the long-term capital gain portion of current payments for an installment sale will benefit from the current lower maximum rate even if the sale took place in a year when the maximum rate was higher, e.g., it would be only 15% for payments received this year even though the rate was 28% when the property was sold.

Property Acquired by Gift

As described above, the initial basis for property acquired by purchase is its cost, which is later adjusted by such items as depreciation and capital improvements, if any. In this section, we will cover the somewhat more complex rules for determining the basis of property acquired by gift. Generally, in determining whether the donee's gain or loss is short-term or long-term, the length of the donor's holding period is added or "tacked on" to the length of the donee's holding period.[4] The exception is: if the donee must use the FMV at the time of gift as his or her basis, then the holding period starts the day after the gift is made.

Value equaling or exceeding donor's basis. A simple rule applies for gift property whose date-of-gift value is equal to or greater than the donor's adjusted basis at the date of gift: the donee's basis will equal the amount of the donor's adjusted basis (herein, we will just use "basis") at the date of the gift. This is called the donee's *carryover basis* (COB for short).

> EXAMPLE 8 - 4. Ten years ago, donor purchased common stock for $10,000. Two years ago, donor gave donee the stock when it was worth $11,500. This year, donee sold the stock for $14,500. Since date-of-gift value was greater than donor's basis, donee has realized a gain of $4,500, the difference between the amount realized ($14,500) and donee's COB basis ($10,000).

> EXAMPLE 8 - 5. As in the prior example, except that donee sold the stock for $7,000. Since date-of-gift value is greater than donor's basis, donee's basis is still $10,000. Therefore, donee has realized a loss of $3,000, the difference between the amount realized and donee's COB.

Value less than donor's basis. If a donee receives property with a date-of-gift value that is less than the donor's basis, then for purposes of calculating a loss only, the donee's basis will be date-of-gift value. For purposes of calculating a gain, though, the COB rule applies, i.e., the donee's basis is the donor's basis at the date of the gift.

> EXAMPLE 8 - 6. Donor acquired property several years ago for $6,000. Last year, when it was worth $4,200, donor gave it to donee, who this year sold it for $3,600. Since date-of-gift value is less than donor's old basis, donee's basis for loss is the $4,200 date-of-gift value, and hence donee has realized a loss of only $600.

In effect, the donee is not permitted to recognize the portion of the loss resulting from the property's decline in value while owned by the donor.

> EXAMPLE 8 - 7. As in the prior example, except that donee sold the property for $7,100. Although date-of-gift value is less than donor's basis, donee's basis for gain is the donor's basis at the date of the gift. In this case, donee's basis is $6,000, and donee has therefore realized a gain of $1,100.

Occasionally, gift property having a date-of-gift value less than the donor's basis is sold by the donee for an amount that is less than donor's basis but more than date-of-gift value. In this case, the donee realizes neither gain nor loss.

> EXAMPLE 8 - 8. Several years ago, donor acquired an asset for $2,000 and later gave it to donee when it was worth $1,450. If donee sells the asset for $1,800, no gain or loss will be realized. Since date-of-gift value ($1,450) is less than donor's basis at the date of the gift ($2,000), for purposes of calculating a loss, donee's basis will be the date-of-gift value. There is no loss because the amount realized is greater than donee's basis (i.e., $1,800 minus $1,450 is not negative). On the other hand, for purposes of calculating a gain, donee's basis will be donor's basis at the date of the gift ($2,000).

Gift tax might increase basis. If the donor pays gift tax on the gift, a portion of that tax is added to the donor's adjusted basis at the date of the gift to determine the donee's new basis. The amount added is that portion of the tax attributable to appreciation. Appreciation is considered to be the difference between the FMV on the date of gift and the property's basis. Hence:

New Basis = Old Basis + ((FMV Gift - Old Basis)/ FMV Gift)) * Gift Tax

EXAMPLE 8 - 9. In 2007, donor gave stock, purchased 20 years ago for $400,000, to donee. The stock was worth $1,712,000 at the time of the gift. Donor paid gift taxes in the amount of $300,000. Donee's new basis equals $629,907, i.e., $400,000 + $300,000 * ($1,712,000 - $400,000) / $1,712,000.

Summary for gifts and basis. For most gifts, the donee's basis for calculating a potential gain is just a carryover of the donor's pre-gift basis. There are two special rules: one for a gift of property that has a fair market value less that the donor's basis on the date of the gift and another where the donor has to pay gift taxes. Where the gift value is lower than the donor's basis, the donee's basis for calculating a loss is the date-of-gift value and for gain it is the carryover basis, with sales in between resulting in no gain or loss. Where the donor pays gift taxes, the donee gets a partial step-up in basis. The increase is the portion of the gift tax that is attributed to the net appreciation of the gift. "Net appreciation" is the value of the gift less the donor's pre-gift basis. The product of the net appreciation divided by the full value of the gift times the gift taxes is added to the carryover basis to arrive at the donee's new basis.

Property Passing Through an Estate

As a general rule, the basis of property in the hands of a person acquiring the property from a decedent is the fair market value of the property at the date of the decedent's death.[5] This is true whether the person received the property by bequest, devise or intestate succession, or as a surviving joint tenant.

Notice that the change in the basis of property acquired by another's death can be a "step-up" or "step-down" in the basis depending on whether the decedent's pre-death basis was lower or higher than the value at death. However, common usage is to refer to this change at death as a *step-up* in basis. Where special elections apply such as the alternate valuation date election of §2032 or the special use election of §2032A, the value as shown on the estate tax return determines the basis. To simplify our discussion, the "date-of-death" (DOD) value should be understood to include the alternate valuation or special use valuation, if such are applicable.

If an estate tax return (Form 706) is filed, there is a rebuttable presumption that the Form 706 values are correct.[6] The change in basis occurs whether or not there is a tax, and, indeed, even if no return is filed. Thus, when a person dies, even if he or she leaves a very modest estate, the property in the estate will have a change in basis to the date-of-death value.

Holding period. The holding period for property acquired from a decedent is long-term, regardless of the actual holding period. Thus, a decedent could have purchased the asset shortly before death and the devisee could have sold it shortly after death, and any gain or loss will be long-term.

Property owned by the decedent alone. Generally, property owned solely by a decedent receives a full step-up in basis for the person who acquires it.

> EXAMPLE 8 - 10. Peter held onto land that he had purchased for $500 in 1934 until his death in 2006, when it passed on to his son Frank. At Peter's death the property was worth $640,000. Peter's total estate was worth only $1,300,000, so there was no need to file an estate tax return. Frank kept the property for six months, and then sold it for $675,000. Frank has a realized long-term capital gain of $35,000, the gain being the difference between the sale price and the value established at Peter's death. Since it was acquired from a decedent, the holding period for the property is long-term.

An exception: The rubber band rule of §1014(e). Internal Revenue Code §1014(e) provides that where a person gives away "appreciated property" and then inherits the property from the donee within one year of the original gift (i.e., it comes bouncing back as if it had a rubber band attached when it was given), the adjusted basis of the property to the donor will be the donee-decedent's adjusted basis immediately before the donee-decedent's death. Appreciated property means property worth more at the time of the gift than its basis. Since the donee had a carryover basis, the donor will also get the property back with the basis unchanged.

> EXAMPLE 8 - 11. Walter gives Kerri, his terminally ill wife, title to land that Walter purchased many years ago for $400. The property has a value on the day of the gift of $90,000. Kerri, who died two months later, devised the land back to Walter, who then sold it for $95,000. Because the property was appreciated at the time Walter gave it to his wife and she died within one year of the gift, Walter realizes a gain of $94,600 on the sale, not just $5,000.

Hence, there is an advantage to gifting low-basis property, in the case of a donor-devisee, if the donee-decedent lives at least one year after the date of gift. This strategy will work even if the original donor is not the spouse of the decedent, but the original gift will use some of the donor's applicable exclusion amount if it is not covered by the annual exclusion. Section 1014(e) does not apply if the donee-decedent leaves the property to someone other than the original donor or the donor's spouse.

EGTRRA repealed § 1014(e) for post-2009 deaths, replacing it with a new IRC § 1022. This section denies a basis increase for property acquired by gift within three years of death. The only exception is property acquired by gift from a spouse so long as the donor spouse did not acquire the property by gift. Thus it appears that after 2009, a spouse can gain an increased basis in appreciated property by giving it to a dying spouse who then leaves it back to the donor. This benefit may not have been intended by Congress, so watch for this apparent loop-hole to be plugged. Of course this change too will sunset with the rest of EGTRRA unless Congress extends it before 2011.

Basis After the Death of a Co-owner

If, at death, the decedent was one of several owners sharing title to property, usually only the decedent's share is stepped-up. The factor that determines whether any surviving co-owner can also enjoy a step-up in basis for his or her share depends on how title is held. In general, the surviving co-owner's share does not receive a step-up in basis unless the asset is either owned as community property or for some reason the survivor's share was included in the deceased co-owner's gross estate.

Community property. The new basis is the FMV at the date of death for both halves of the community property even though only one-half is included in the decedent spouse's estate. This is referred to as a full step-up in basis.

Joint tenancy. What is included in the decedent estate and the surviving co-owner's new basis will follow one of two rules that depend on the relationship between the decedent and the surviving co-owners.

Husband and wife rule. Where the only joint tenants (or tenants by the entirety) are husband and wife, then half of the FMV at the date of death is included in the decedent's estate and the surviving spouse's new basis will equal half the total pre-death basis and half the FMV at the date of death.

$$\text{New Basis} = (\text{DOD FMV} + \text{Old Basis}) / 2$$

Where joint tenancy property was purchased prior to 1977, the surviving spouse can use the consideration furnished rule instead of the husband and wife rule. This will be advantageous if the decedent spouse contributed more than half of the purchase price and the property appreciated in value prior to his or her death.[7] It appears that the IRS accepts the husband and wife rule even for pre-1977 properties unless the surviving spouse brings up the date-of-purchase issue. Obviously, the further we move away from 1976 the less often this will become an issue.

Consideration furnished rule. Where the joint tenants include nonspouses, the rule is that the decedent's gross estate includes that portion of the property as the decedent's share of the consideration bears to the total consideration (i.e., the price paid for the property). Decedent's consideration includes any gifts given to other joint tenants and any share acquired by the prior death of a co-owner.

Include = (Decedent's Consideration / Total Consideration) * FMV DOD

The new basis for each surviving co-owner's interest is his or her old basis plus an increase by the amount included in the decedent's estate split equally among the surviving joint tenants. The examples that follow demonstrate both rules.

EXAMPLE 8 - 12. In 1990, Ricky and Victoria, husband and wife, owned common stock as joint tenants. She paid $50,000 and he paid $110,000 of the original $160,000 purchase price. When Ricky died in 2006, the stock was worth $220,000. Four months later, Victoria sold the stock for $290,000. The consideration each paid is irrelevant and Victoria's basis is equal to half the old basis plus half the fair market value at Ricky's death; hence, her realized gain is $100,000 [$290,000 - ($160,000 + $220,000)/2].

EXAMPLE 8 - 13. Same facts as in the prior example, except Ricky and Victoria bought the stock as joint tenants in 1976. Even though they are married, because this joint tenancy was created before 1977, Victoria can use the consideration paid rule to determine her basis. Included in Ricky's estate is $151,250 [$220,000 * ($110,000/$160,000)]. Victoria's basis is equal to the amount she paid plus the amount included in Ricky's estate, hence, her realized gain is $88,750 [$290,000 - ($151,250 + $50,000)].

Consider the very different outcome for community property.

EXAMPLE 8 - 14. Same facts as in the prior example, except that at Ricky's death, they owned the stock as community property. Once again half would be included in Ricky's estate but Victoria's basis would be the FMV DOD amount of $220,000, and her gain would be only $70,000.

Thus, ordinarily community property states have a decided advantage over common law states with regard to basis adjustments at death. Couples residing in community property states should hold appreciated property as community property. On the other hand, if the property has decreased in value, community property will receive a full step-down in basis at the first death and some other form of title might be preferred.

A number of community property states (e.g., California, Nevada and Wisconsin) have adopted legislation creating "community property with the right of survivorship." There is concern that the IRS will challenge attempts to apply the step-up for both halves, seeking instead to have this hybrid treated for basis purposes under the rules for husband and wife joint tenants.

EXAMPLE 8 - 15. Years ago, brothers Steve and Stan purchased stock for $10,000, taking title as joint tenants. Steve paid $6,000 and Stan paid $4,000 toward the purchase. At Steve's death the stock was worth $20,000. Included in Steve's gross estate is 60% of the stock's value because that corresponds to his share of the consideration paid for the stock, even though property law recognized that he owned 50% of the stock immediately before death. Stan's new basis would be $16,000, which is $12,000 (the amount included in Steve's estate) plus Stan's $4,000 basis in his pre-death interest in the property.

EXAMPLE 8 - 16. Three friends purchased a vacation cabin in 1986. Abe paid $20,000, Betty paid $30,000, and Cathy paid $50,000 of the $100,000 purchase price. In 1996, when the cabin was worth $160,000, Abe died. His estate included 20% of the DOD FMV, i.e. 20% * $160,000 = $32,000. Betty's new basis in her 50% interest in the cabin became $46,000 (½ * $32,000 + her original consideration of $30,000) and Cathy's new basis is $66,000 (½ * $32,000 + her original consideration of $50,000).

EXAMPLE 8 - 17. Continuing from the last example, in 2006, Cathy died, leaving Betty as the sole surviving joint tenant. The cabin was then worth $224,000. The amount included in Cathy's gross estate is based on her portion ($66,000) of the combined (hers and Betty's) pre-death bases of $112,000. Therefore, included in her estate is $132,000 (($66,000 / $112,000) * $224,000), and Betty's new basis would be $178,000 (the $132,000 included in Cathy's estate plus Betty's old basis of $46,000).

It should be noted that a gift from one prospective co-joint tenant to another is treated as consideration from the donor, not the donee.

> EXAMPLE 8 - 18. Martin gave his son, Andy, $50,000 shortly before they purchased a vacation condo for $150,000. Martin paid $100,000 on the purchase and Andy paid $50,000. When Martin died, the condo was valued at $200,000, all of which had to be included in his estate because Andy's contribution was traceable to Martin's gift.

Tenants in common. Tenancy in common is the preferred form of co-ownership for nonrelatives. It does not have the survivorship feature found in joint tenancy, thus the co-owners control the disposition of their respective shares. Unlike joint tenancy, tenants in common can have unequal undivided shares, meaning that you could have one owner owning 20%, another owning 30%, and the third owning 50%. When a tenant in common owner dies, his or her share of the total FMV DOD of the property is included in the decedent's gross estate. The disposition of a deceased tenant in common's interest depends on the decedent's will or, if there is no will, intestate succession laws.

> EXAMPLE 8 - 19. Friends Arthur, Tony, and Maria purchased property as tenants in common. Of the $100,000 purchase price, Arthur paid $50,000 and took a 50% interest, Tony paid $30,000 and took a 30% interest, and Maria paid $20,000 and took a 20% interest. Years later when Tony died, the property was worth $250,000 and his estate included $75,000 since he owned a 30% interest. If Tony left his interest to his widow Nancy, her basis would be $75,000. If he instead left his interest to co-owner Maria, her total basis in the 50% interest she would then own would be $95,000 ($75,000 + her $20,000 contribution).

As demonstrated in the preceding example, property law recognizes unequal shares where property is held by the owners as tenants in common. Obviously, how one holds title to co-owned property determines what the surviving co-owners' basis will be if one of the owners dies.

FIDUCIARY INCOME TAX

Subchapter J of the IRC covers the income taxation of fiduciary entities, i.e., estates and trusts. In this chapter, the tax rules discussed are for irrevocable trusts since revocable trusts, such as probate avoidance trusts where the settlors serve as trustees, are not treated as separate tax entities. Unlike partnerships and S Corporations, a fiduciary entity can be both a separate taxpayer and a flow-through entity. The character of all income, deductions and credits is determined at the entity level. Net taxable income is allocated to the beneficiaries based on entity distributions and distributable net income. To the extent taxable income is allocated to the beneficiaries, the beneficiaries pay tax on the income, while the entity pays taxes on the net taxable income retained. The primary goal of Subchapter J is the proper allocation of the net taxable income thereby limiting purely tax-motivated allocations.

Computing Net Taxable Income

Both estates and trusts use individual income tax rules in the computation of net taxable income. Unless an exception is made in the IRC or regulations, all income, deductions and credits are characterized by a fiduciary entity using the same rules individuals use to classify their income, deductions and credits. On Form 1041, "adjusted total income" is the entity's net taxable income for the year, taking into account the entity's income and deductions for the tax year. Adjusted total income is then allocated between the entity and its beneficiaries based on distributable net income and the entity's distributions.

Accounting method and tax year. Fiduciary entities can select any accounting method available to individuals. Most entities will choose a cash-based accounting method, since most entities keep their books on a cash-based system. IRC Section 644 requires most trusts to use a calendar year. Estates can elect any tax year that ends on the last day of any month that is not more than 12 months from the date of death. Beneficiaries must include in income any net taxable income allocated from the fiduciary entity in their tax year which includes the entity's tax year-end.

> EXAMPLE 8 - 20. If Joe died on June 12, 2005, the executor could elect to end the estate's tax year at the end of any month from June 30, 2005 to May 31, 2006. If Joe's executor elected April 30, 2006 as the estate's year-end, any taxable income earned prior to that date and distributed to the estate's beneficiaries would be taxed in the beneficiaries' 2006 tax year, even if the

distribution to the beneficiaries was made in 2005, because all distributions are treated as though they were made on the last day of the estate's tax year.

Where a revocable trust is part of an estate plan, upon the death of the settlor or of a beneficiary, if the trust is in the decedent's gross estate, then the trustee, in conjunction with the executor (if any), can elect to have the trust taxed as part (all) of the decedent's estate for income tax purposes.[8] By making this election, the trustee can select a fiscal year-end. If no estate tax return is required, a trust that makes this election can keep its fiscal year for two years after the decedent's death. If a return must be filed, the trust can use its fiscal year-end only until six months after the date of the final determination of the estate tax liability after which it must switch to a calendar year-end.

Income and deductions. Since fiduciary entities are taxed similarly to individuals (less personal exemption and standard deduction) many of the benefits and burdens that apply to individuals when they compute their taxes apply to fiduciary entities. Estates and trusts qualify for the special tax rates that apply to qualified dividends and capital gains for individuals. Passive activity rules are applicable as well. Whether an activity is passive is determined by the involvement of the fiduciary in the activity. Miscellaneous itemized deductions must be reduced by 2% of the entity's adjusted gross income. As a special exception for fiduciary entities, expenses incurred in the administration of an estate or trust which would not have been incurred if the property were not held in the trust or estate are not subject to the 2% floor.[9]

Most estate expenses are classified as either transmission (i.e., transfer of assets), management, or income expenses. Transmission and management expenses can be deducted for either estate tax or income tax purposes. An estate is assumed to take these expenses for estate tax purposes unless the executor makes an irrevocable election on the estate's income tax return to deduct these expenses for income tax purposes. By making the election, these expenses cannot be deducted on the estate tax return. Income expenses cannot be deducted for estate tax purposes, since these expenses relate to income earned after death.

While most of the individual tax rules apply to fiduciary entities, there are some modifications. To the extent the entity has tax-exempt income, all expenses incurred to create the exempt income, and a portion of the entity's indirect expenses, are not deductible. A fiduciary entity cannot elect to expense certain depreciable business assets, e.g., an IRC §179 election is not available. An entity can take a deduction for all taxable income allocated to a charitable beneficiary, regardless of its adjusted gross income. A portion of every type of income (taxable and exempt) included in accounting income, or Distributable Net Income, must be allocated to a charitable beneficiary, which causes the entity's charitable deduction to be less than its actual distribution to the charity.

Distributable Net Income and the Income Distribution Deduction

Once the fiduciary has computed adjusted total income, the fiduciary must determine how much of the adjusted total income is allocated to the beneficiaries. The Income Distribution Deduction is the portion of adjusted total income allocated to the non-charitable beneficiaries. Computation of the Income Distribution Deduction begins with determining Distributable Net Income (DNI). DNI is an IRC concept that places a ceiling on how much taxable income can be allocated to the non-charitable beneficiaries. Unless taxable income is included in DNI, it cannot be allocated to the beneficiaries.

Distributable Net Income. DNI can never be negative, so if adjusted total income is negative, the entity most likely will not have DNI. Unless DNI exists, no taxable income is allocated to the beneficiaries. Starting with adjusted total income, the fiduciary computes DNI. Net tax-exempt income is added to adjusted total income. Net exempt income is computed by subtracting from gross exempt income all direct and indirect exempt expenses. Net capital losses never reduce DNI, so if the entity has a net capital loss for the year, the net capital loss is added back. Net capital gains are included in DNI when: (1) net capital gains are included in accounting income, (2) they occur in the entity's final tax year, and (3) the net capital gains are actually distributed to the beneficiaries. Normally, net capital gains are included in corpus for accounting purposes with the consequence that, except in the final year, capital gains are generally taxed to the fiduciary entity. When the fiduciary makes a corpus distribution, the character of the distribution is not defined. Unless the fiduciary makes some entry in the accounting records that the corpus distribution included capital gains, capital gains will not be included in DNI except in the final year. The sum of adjusted total income, net exempt income, and net capital gains equals DNI.

The 65-day rule. The trustee or executor can elect to treat all or part of the distributions made within 65 days after the end of the trust's or estate's year as made in the current year.[10] The election is filed with the current-year's tax return. To the extent a distribution from the following year is included in the current year, it is excluded from the following year, i.e., just a portion of those distributions might be pulled into the current year. Only amounts necessary to remove any remaining current-year's DNI can be distributed under the 65-day rule.[11]

> EXAMPLE 8 - 21. In year 1, Trust B had DNI of $60,000 but only made distributions to beneficiaries of $50,000. During February of year 2, another $15,000 was distributed to beneficiaries. The trustee elected to treat $7,000 of the $15,000 as having been distributed in year 1, hence the distribution deduction was $57,000, leaving just $3,000 as trust taxable income. The beneficiaries will receive Schedule K-1s showing how they are to report the $57,000 that is allocated to them. The remaining $8,000 from the February distributions is part of the distribution deduction for year 2.

Simple trusts. The IRC establishes two types of trusts for calculating the income distribution deduction. Sections 651-652 are used to compute the distribution deduction for simple trusts and §§ 661-663 are used to compute the deduction for complex trusts. The terms "simple" and "complex" are not found in the Code, but are used throughout the regulations. The definition of a trust can change from year to year; however, in its final year, because corpus is distributed, it will always be complex.

Section 651 defines a simple trust as a trust that:
1. is required to distribute all of its trust accounting income (TAI) currently,
2. has no distributions used for charitable purposes, and
3. allows no distributions in excess of TAI for the year.

The trust document determines if the first two requirements are met.[12] If the document requires the trustee to distribute all the current-year's TAI, the beneficiaries are deemed to have received the TAI for taxation purposes, whether it is actually distributed or not. If the document does not require all the TAI to be distributed currently, the trust cannot be classified as a simple trust, even if the trust actually distributes all of its TAI for the year. TAI is the dollar amount of the income that, according to the terms of the trust, the trustee is required or allowed to distribute to the income beneficiaries. Even if the trustee is required to distribute all income to the beneficiaries, they will get more or less depending on how the trust document defines income. For instance they get more if income includes short term capital gains and less if a reserve for depreciation must be established. On the other hand, DNI is a tax computation that is not at all based on what the beneficiaries might or might not receive from the trust.

A simple trust is limited in the type of distributions it can make. If the trust could have made a distribution that would qualify for a charitable deduction, the trust cannot be classified as a simple trust, even if no charitable distributions are actually made.[13] Further, if the trust makes distributions greater than TAI, it cannot be a simple trust. Although corpus distributions are allowed under the trust document, the trust will be a simple trust, unless distributions greater than current-year's TAI are actually made. In years the trust does not make any corpus distributions, it will be a simple trust, and in years it makes a corpus distribution it will be a complex trust.

A simple trust is allowed a deduction for the TAI distributed, limited by DNI.[14] The deduction is reduced by any amount not included in gross income less any applicable expenses, e.g., the deduction is reduced by the amount of tax-exempt income, net of related expenses, included in TAI.

Complex trusts. If a trust does not meet the definition of a simple trust, it is a complex trust. The income distribution deduction for complex trusts and all estates is determined under §§ 661-663. A trust that can accumulate income, make charitable contributions or makes a corpus distribution will be a complex trust. Since a trust must distribute all remaining corpus in its final year, it will always be a complex trust in its final year. The main difference between the computation of the income distribution deduction for simple and complex trusts is the use of a tier system for complex trusts. The tier system results in a greater amount of DNI being allocated to beneficiaries who receive required TAI distributions.

Exemptions. A fiduciary entity is not allowed a standard deduction, however, IRC § 642(b) allows an exemption depending on the nature of the entity; estates have a $600 exemption, simple trusts have a $300 exemption, and all other trusts have a $100 exemption.

Distributions. For tax purposes, a fiduciary entity makes two types of distributions: Tier I and Tier II. Tier I distributions are mandatory distributions of accounting income. Normally, estates do not have mandatory distributions, so generally only trusts have Tier I distributions. Although the trust does not have to actually distribute the Tier I income by year-end, for tax purposes, the distribution is deemed made on December 31st even if it is not actually distributed during the year. Generally, Tier II distributions are discretionary distributions of income or corpus made during the year.

Distributions excluded from income. Where the distribution is a specific sum of money or of specific property under the terms of the governing instrument, e.g., the trust or the will, the beneficiary does not have any taxable income and the entity has no distribution deduction, since this type of distribution does not qualify for the distribution deduction. If a specific sum of money, to qualify for non-tax treatment, it must be paid in three installments or less.[15] The beneficiary's basis is the entity's basis.[16] The entity's holding period is tacked onto the beneficiary's holding period, however if the property received a step-up in basis (i.e., was not IRD) as a result of being included in the decedent's estate, it is considered to be held long-term for capital gain purposes.[17]

Income Distribution Deduction. The Income Distribution Deduction is the amount of taxable income included in DNI allocated to the non-charitable beneficiaries. When the entity makes a Tier I and/or Tier II distribution, DNI must be allocated to the beneficiaries. If total Tier I and Tier II distributions exceed DNI, all of the entity's DNI is allocated to the beneficiaries, and the entity deducts the entire amount of taxable income included in DNI. If total Tier I and Tier II distributions are less than DNI, the sum of Tier I and Tier II distributions equals the amount of DNI allocated to the beneficiaries. In this case, only a proportionate amount of the taxable income included in DNI is allocated to the beneficiaries and it is the proportionate amount that can be deducted. The entity is taxed on taxable DNI not allocated to beneficiaries and on any taxable income not included in DNI (e.g., capital gains).

Allocation of DNI amongst beneficiaries. When allocating DNI, the fiduciary cannot allocate a specific type of income to certain beneficiaries. A beneficiary receives a proportionate share of every type of income, taxable and exempt, included in DNI. DNI is allocated first to beneficiaries who receive Tier I distributions. If total Tier I distributions exceed DNI, only beneficiaries who receive Tier I distributions receive DNI. When DNI exceeds total Tier I distributions, the excess DNI is allocated to the beneficiaries who receive Tier II distributions. When Tier I or Tier II distributions are allocated to multiple beneficiaries, each beneficiary receives a percentage of the DNI allocated to the tier distribution based on the beneficiaries' percentage of that particular tier distribution.

EXAMPLE 8 - 22. Bill and Sue were the beneficiaries of an irrevocable trust created when their father died. The trustee was required to distribute $20,000 each year to Bill, and could make additional discretionary distributions to Bill and Sue. During the year, the trust had DNI of $50,000, and the trustee distributed $35,000 to Bill and $40,000 to Sue for a total of $75,000. Of the $50,000 DNI, $20,000 is allocated to Bill as a Tier I distribution. This leaves $30,000 DNI to be allocated between Bill and Sue based upon their respective Tier II distributions. Bill received $15,000 as a Tier II distribution so he is allocated $8,182 additional DNI ($30,000 * $15,000/$55,000) giving him a total DNI allocation of $28,182. Sue received a Tier II distribution of $40,000, so $21,818 of the DNI ($30,000 *$40,000/$55,000) is allocated to her.

Income in Respect of a Decedent and the Estate Tax Deduction

When computing the estate tax, the gross estate includes all assets owned by the decedent at death under accrual accounting principles. This means that the gross estate includes income earned by the decedent that was not reported on his or her last income tax return. For cash-based taxpayers, only income received before death is included on the decedent's final income tax return. Income realized (i.e., earned) before death but collected after death is income in respect of a decedent (IRD).[18]

Income in Respect of a Decedent. IRD has a zero basis for income tax purposes, so when it is collected, the recipient must pay income taxes on the IRD. The character of IRD reported by the estate or beneficiary is the same as if the income had been collected by the decedent while alive. If an estate receives the IRD, it must include it in income; however, if a beneficiary receives the IRD directly, the beneficiary is taxed on it.

EXAMPLE 8 - 23. Joan was employed by Big Time Corporation on the day she died. She had worked for ten days since her last paycheck. Although she had earned her salary before she died, her wages were paid after death under Big Time's normal payment schedule. The earned wages are included in Joan's gross estate under accrual accounting principles, but the earned wages are not included on her final individual income tax return, since Joan was not in actual or constructive receipt of the wages at her death. Whoever collects Joan's final wages will include the wages in ordinary income just like Joan would have had Joan collected the wages before she died.

IRD includes any realized income not collected on or before death. Examples of IRD include:

- Accrued wages, salaries, fees and renewal commissions, such as life insurance commissions, that are unpaid as of the date of death.
- Accounts receivable of a cash method proprietorship or partnership.
- Unreported gross profit on an existing installment obligation.
- Uncollected proceeds on a completed sales transaction.
- Accrued interest income on Series EE or Series I U.S. savings bonds.
- Accrued benefits within a traditional IRA, qualified retirement plan, or other tax-deferred retirement plan account.
- Deferred income within an annuity.

Deductions in respect of a decedent. Accrued expenses owed by the decedent at death are classified as debts for estate tax purposes and are deductible in computing the taxable estate. Certain accrued expenses can be deducted for income tax purposes, also. These expenses were owed at death, but not deductible on the decedent's final income tax return, because they were not paid until after death. These accrued expenses, known as deductions in respect of a decedent are limited to:

- Business expenses - Section 162
- Interest deductions - Section 163
- Deduction for taxes - Section 164
- Expenses to produce income - Section 212
- Depletion deduction - Section 611
- Foreign tax credit - Section 27

Medical expenses, alimony, capital losses, net operating losses and charitable contributions are not deductions in respect of a decedent.[19]

Estate tax deduction. IRD is taxed for both estate tax and income tax purposes. To reduce the tax burden, the recipient of IRD can take an income tax deduction for that portion of the federal estate taxes attributed to including IRD in the gross estate.[20] Further, an income tax deduction is allowed for generation skipping transfer taxes ascribed to IRD items included in a taxable termination or direct skip caused by the transferor's death.

The deduction is allowed in the year IRD is included in income. To compute the deduction, all items treated as IRD in the gross estate are aggregated. The total is reduced by all DRD to arrive at a net value. Once the net value is determined, estate taxes are recomputed by excluding the net value from the gross estate. The marital and charitable deductions must be adjusted to reflect the elimination of the net IRD values. If a specific bequest of IRD is made to a surviving spouse or a charity, the deduction is eliminated. Any credits taken must be reduced by the exclusion of the net IRD value. The difference between the original estate tax and the recomputed estate tax is the IRD deduction. The deduction is allocated among the various IRD items and the IRD recipients. A deduction can be claimed even if the estates taxes have not been fully paid. The deduction is claimed, for the year the IRD is received, on the recipient's Schedule A and is not subject to the 2% floor on itemized deductions. The estate tax does not have to be paid before a recipient of IRD claims an IRD deduction.

EXAMPLE 8 - 24. Roberta's estate is the beneficiary of her IRA. At her death in 2006, the IRA, valued at $2,000,000, was part of her $5,000,000 taxable estate. With the IRA, the estate tax was $1,380,000, and without the IRA, the tax would have been $460,000. As the IRA is collected by the estate, the estate's taxable income is allowed a deduction of $920,000, that being the estate tax attributable to the IRA (an item of IRD) being included in the taxable estate.

EXAMPLE 8 - 25. Dan was entitled to salary of $5,000, dividends of $3,750 and rental income of $1,250 at his death. Dan owed real estate taxes of $2,500 on his rental property. Sue, his widoe, inherited the stock portfolio, his daughter, Jane, was entitled to the real estate, and the salary was collected by the executor of his estate. Sue inherited half of Dan's estate and the estate tax marginal rate is 45% (remember the IRD deduction is determined as coming out of the top portion of the decedent's taxable estate). The marginal rate is applied to the net IRD of $7,500 ($10,000 less $2,500) less the net IRD deemed allocated to the marital deduction ($3,750 not subject to the estate tax because of the marital deduction). The $1,688 deduction 45% * ($7,500 - $3,750) is allocated as follows:

	IRD Received	Percentage	Deduction
Estate	$5,000	50.0%	$844
Sue	$3,750	37.5%	$633
Jane	$1,250	12.5%	$211
Total	$10,000	100.0%	$1,688

Tax Rates and Filing Requirements

Generally, the personal representative for the fiduciary entity, i.e., the trust or estate, is responsible for filing the federal income tax returns if income exceeds certain thresholds. A state fiduciary return is likely as well, unless the estate or trust's situs is in a state without an income tax.

Fiduciary tax rates. Trusts and estates have their own tax rates. Notice how little taxable income is required for an estate or trust to take it into the highest tax bracket. Rates shown in the table below are those in effect for the year 2005.

TABLE 8-1 Federal Income Tax Rates: Estates and Trusts - **2005**

Taxable Income Over	But not over	Base amount	+ percent	On excess over
$0	$2,000	$0	15%	$0
$2,000	$4,700	$300	25%	$2,000
$4,700	$7,150	$975	28%	$4,700
$7,150	$9,750	$1,661	33%	$7,150
$9,750	----	$2,519	35%	$9,750

Filing requirements. Generally, a decedent's estate must file a fiduciary income tax return, Form 1041, if: (a) the estate has annual gross income of $600 or more, or (b) the estate has a beneficiary who is a nonresident alien. A trust must file a Form 1041 if it has: (a) any taxable income, or (b) gross income of $600 or more, or (c) a beneficiary who is a nonresident alien. Most revocable trusts are not separate tax entities and the settlor-trustee continues to file a 1040 as though the trust did not exist.

The return is due by the 15th of the fourth month following the entity's year-end and is filed with the Service center for the region in which the fiduciary resides or has its principal place of business. An extension can be obtained by filing Form 8736 for trusts and Form 2758 for estates. Additional time is obtained by filing Form 8800.

Form 56, Notice Concerning Fiduciary Relationship, should be filed when the trust or estate is created. Form SS-4 must be filed to obtain the fiduciary entity's employer identification number, i.e., the tax identification number used for income tax reporting, regardless of whether the fiduciary entity has employees. If the trust is a revocable trust and the settlor-trustee continues to file a 1040, no new tax identification number is needed as he or she will continue to use his or her social security number for all investment accounts.

THE EFFECT OF TRANSFERS AND DISTRIBUTIONS

In this section, we consider the income tax implications of making asset transfers to and from estates, trusts, and beneficiaries. Generally, non-cash distributions (in-kind distributions) are subject to the same rules as cash distributions. The beneficiaries must treat distributions of property as income received if DNI is allocated to the distribution. This results in the beneficiaries having to pay tax, though they might not have the cash. Further, the type of income that comprises DNI determines the taxability of the distribution, not the type of property received as a distribution.

General Rule for Property Transfers

If the transfer of property is not considered a sale by the fiduciary entity (i.e., neither a § 643(e)(3) election nor a pecuniary bequest), the basis of the property in the hands of the beneficiary is the entity's adjusted basis in the property immediately before distribution.[21] The beneficiary can tack the entity's holding period to his holding period. The entity can only consider the lesser of the property's basis or its FMV when computing the income distribution deduction. This can result in the beneficiary having a basis greater than the taxable income received from the trust or estate.

Distributions Treated as Sales

Some distributions are treated as though the trust or estate sold the property to the beneficiary who receives it. This generally results in the entity recognizing a gain or loss, and the beneficiary having a basis in the property equal to its FMV on the day of distribution.

Electing to treat a distribution as a sale. In certain situations, the fiduciary entity can elect to treat a distribution of property as a sale; this is referred to as making a § 643(e)(3) election. Generally, a beneficiary's basis in property received as a distribution equals the entity's basis immediately before distribution, adjusted for any gain or loss recognized by the entity.

Generally, where the entity does not recognize a gain or loss on the distribution, its basis is used to determine the beneficiary's basis and the beneficiary can tack on the entity's holding period. If a § 643(e)(3) election is made, the entity can consider the FMV of the property when computing the income distribution deduction and the beneficiary will have a basis equal to the FMV.

EXAMPLE 8 - 26. Trust B has DNI of $50,000. Trust B distributes stock valued at $50,000 to Mona. The trust's adjusted basis in the stock is $10,000. Effect of *no election*: (1) No gain on transfer; (2) DNI is reduced by $10,000, so the trust pays tax on the $40,000 retained DNI; and (3) Mona has income of $10,000 and her basis is $10,000. If the *election is made*: (a) trust has a gain of $40,000 (note, the gain does not increase DNI); (b) the distribution deduction is increased to $50,000; and (c) Mona has income of $50,000 and her basis in the stock is $50,000.

Transfers of property to satisfy a pecuniary bequest. A capital gain or loss is recognized when a trust or estate transfers property to satisfy a pecuniary gift, bequest, or claim, which is defined as a required distribution of a specific sum of money or specific property. The gain or loss is determined by the difference between the FMV of the property on the date of transfer and the entity's basis in the property. The entity is considered to have distributed cash and the beneficiary to have turned around and bought the property.[22] If the distribution does not meet the requirements of § 663(a), the gain might be included in any DNI allocation, subjecting the beneficiary to taxation. If the distribution does meet the requirements of § 663(a), or the gain cannot be included in DNI, the entity must pay taxes on the gain without any distribution deduction. The beneficiary's basis is the FMV of the property at the time of distribution and he must begin a new holding period. The distribution deduction equals the FMV of the property, providing sufficient DNI exists.

EXAMPLE 8 - 27. Norm's will requires a $10,000 distribution to Keith. Instead of distributing cash, the executor distributes stock valued at $10,000. The estate's basis in the stock is $7,000. The estate must report a $3,000 long-term gain on its Form 1041, but can include the full $10,000 when computing the income distribution deduction. Since Keith is treated as having purchased the stock, his basis in the stock is $10,000 and he must hold the stock for 12 months before being eligible for long-term gain treatment on sale. Unless this distribution was made in the estate's final year the estate must pay taxes on the gain, since it cannot be included in DNI.

EXAMPLE 8 - 28. Norm's estate has estate accounting income (EAI) of $15,000. The executor decides to distribute a car valued at $15,000, instead of cash, to Ann. Since EAI is not a pecuniary bequest, no sale occurs, unless § 643(e)(3) is elected. If the car's basis is $9,000, Ann's basis is $9,000 and she can tack the estate's holding period to hers on any future sale. When computing the income distribution deduction, the executor must use $9,000.

Transfers of Passive Activities

There are some fairly specific rules concerning transfers of passive activity investments between the grantor/decedent and the fiduciary entity and between the fiduciary entity and the beneficiaries. These rules are in addition to the rules that apply to in-kind property distributions.

Lifetime transfers from a grantor to a trust. If a grantor has any suspended losses when he or she transfers the investment to a trust, the losses are added to the basis. While the grantor is treated as disposing of the asset, according to the passive activity rules, he or she cannot recognize any of the suspended losses on his or her personal return.[23]

EXAMPLE 8 - 29. Harry owned an office building. His basis in the building was $100,000 and he had $20,000 in suspended losses. After he transferred the building to an irrevocable trust, its basis in the building was $120,000. However, the trust cannot use the increase in basis other than to lower capital gains when the building is eventually sold, i.e., it cannot increase the deduction for depreciation above what Harry would have been allowed had he kept the building. By making the transfer, Harry can never use the suspended losses to reduce his own taxable income, now or in the future.

Transfers from a decedent to his or her estate. The death of a person is treated as a distribution of his or her entire interest in all things owned, so on the decedent's final return suspended losses, reduced by any increase in basis, are used to reduce other income. The increase in basis referred to in the last sentence is the difference in the decedent's basis in the property and its fair market value at the date of death.[24] Only when the suspended losses exceed the increase in basis can they be deducted on the decedent's final return.[25]

EXAMPLE 8 - 30. Mary died on November 12, 2006. Her basis in a partnership was $20,000. The FMV of the partnership interest was $50,000. Mary had $100,000 of suspended losses. On Mary's final return, $70,000 of the losses may be deducted. ($50,000 - $20,000 = $30,000; $100,000 - $30,000 = $70,000)

EXAMPLE 8 - 31. Martin died on December 31, 2007. His basis in a partnership was $200,000. The FMV of the partnership interest was $30,000. His suspended losses totaled $150,000. None of the suspended losses will be recognized on Martin's final Form 1040 and the estate's basis will be $30,000. Since the increase in basis, $230,000, exceeded the total suspended losses, neither Martin nor the estate can deduct the losses.

Transfers from trust/estate to a beneficiary. Transfers of passive activities to a beneficiary are treated in the same manner as transfers from a grantor to a trust. Any suspended losses incurred by the entity are added to the basis and the entity is prevented from using the losses in the future.[26] If the distribution of a passive activity by the executor of a decedent's estate is considered a sale, e.g., a distribution of property rather than cash to satisfy a pecuniary bequest,[27] the estate can use the suspended losses on Form 1041. The related party rules of § 267 prevent a trustee from utilizing the suspended losses by making a similar "sale" distribution.[28]

INCOME DISTRIBUTION DEDUCTION AND THE TAXATION OF BENEFICIARIES

As said earlier in the chapter, the main focus of Subchapter J is to allocate taxable income between the fiduciary entity and the beneficiaries. The trust or estate receives a deduction based on the taxable income distributed to the beneficiaries during the year. The deductible amount is computed on Schedule B, Form 1041 and recorded on Line 18, Form 1041. Since a fiduciary entity can distribute income and corpus, depending on the terms of the fiduciary document, an amount called distributable net income (DNI) must be calculated.[29] DNI limits the amount of taxable income allocated to the beneficiaries. Any amount distributed greater than DNI will be considered either undistributed net income (UNI) or corpus.

Taxation of Beneficiaries

According to Regulation § 1.652(b)-3, the character of the income and deductions:

> *... shall have the same character in the hands of the beneficiary as in the hands of the estate or trust. For this purpose, the amounts shall be treated as consisting of the same proportion of each class of items entering into the computation of DNI as the total of each class bears to the total DNI of the estate or trust unless the terms of the governing instrument specifically allocate different classes of income to different beneficiaries.*

The composition of DNI determines the type of income distributed and taxed to the beneficiaries. If 80% of DNI is taxable income and 20% is tax-exempt interest, then 80% of the DNI allocated to the beneficiaries will be taxable income. The other 20% will be tax-exempt interest. As a general rule, the fiduciary is not allowed to "pick and choose" how to allocate the types of income amongst the beneficiaries.

Schedule K-1. The fiduciary records on Schedule K-1 the amounts taxable to the beneficiaries. The K-1 is shown on a net basis. Any amounts recorded on the schedule are net of any expenses, so the beneficiaries report the net effect of any allocation only. Only net income can be allocated to the beneficiaries, except in the final year, when losses can be allocated to the corpus beneficiaries. Negative numbers are not shown on the Schedule K-1, except in the final year.

Unless a specific allocation in the fiduciary document prescribes otherwise, a charity-beneficiary is deemed to receive some of each type of income included in DNI.[30] This rule prevents an improper shifting of taxable income to a charity or tax-free municipal bond income to a high tax bracket beneficiary.

Special allocations. Sometimes the fiduciary document provides for a specific allocation of income to certain beneficiaries. These specific allocations can take many forms.

EXAMPLE 8 - 32. Trust X is to distribute all the income from an apartment house to Sam. This is a specific allocation allowed under the Regulations;

therefore, Sam is taxed on any taxable income attributable to the apartment house. Sam's distribution is solely dependent on that specific type of income.

EXAMPLE 8 - 33. Trust X is to distribute $10,000 to Kathy, to be paid from tax-exempt income to the extent possible and the rest from taxable income. This would not be recognized as a specific allocation, so Kathy is allocated some of each type of income included in DNI, even if the fiduciary actually pays the $10,000 entirely from tax-exempt income. Kathy's distribution is fixed whatever the amount of tax-exempt income earned by the entity, so the only effect of the allocation is an attempt to apportion more of the tax-exempt income to her, which is not allowed under the code.

EXAMPLE 8 - 34. Trust X is to distribute one-half of the tax-exempt interest to Anita. This is an allowable specific allocation, since Anita's distribution is determined solely by the amount of tax-exempt interest earned by the trust.

For a specific allocation, such as the one in the prior example, to be effective in allocating the entity's DNI, the document must not give the trustee any discretion in how the allocation is made. The special allocation rule applies to charitable distributions also. In drafting, if the grantor wants a certain beneficiary to receive a specific type of income, he or she can include a provision in the fiduciary document requiring the fiduciary to allocate that type of income to the beneficiary; however, he or she must make sure to draft the provision to comply with the requirements of the code. Specific allocations will be given effect in the allocation of DNI from a fiduciary entity, providing they have an economic impact independent of the income tax consequences.[31]

Excess deductions. In years when interest, taxes, and administrative expenses exceed income, the entity has excess deductions. Since these expenses cannot be included in a net operating loss (NOL) under § 172 and cannot be allocated to the beneficiaries, the entity has wasted excess deductions, because they are lost forever. Only in the final tax-year can the entity allocate these excess deductions to the beneficiaries. The beneficiaries may take the allocated deductions as miscellaneous itemized deductions on their personal returns. If the beneficiary does not itemize, or if the 2% AGI floor is too great, the beneficiary will not be able to utilize these deductions.

THE KIDDIE TAX

In trying to save income taxes by shifting income to trusts or to family members in lower income brackets, there are a few hurdles to overcome. As mentioned above, trusts have compressed income tax brackets such that the top marginal rate is reached at about taxable income of $10,000. Tax on trust income can be shifted to beneficiaries by giving them withdrawal rights (similar to Crummey powers) to all taxable income. They will be treated as receiving the income even if it is not demanded, i.e., as if taken and then given back to the trustee. However, if the beneficiary is under the age of 14, this might not save any income tax. All unearned income of children under age 14 in excess of a threshold amount is taxed at the parents' marginal rate. This special treatment is referred to as the "kiddie tax."[32]

The threshold amount was originally $1,000 but, due to indexing, it climbed to $1,600 in 2004 (and has remained at that level at least through 2005, see the Table of Indexed Values in Appendix A.) Of that amount, half is a standard deduction for a taxpayer claimed as a dependent by another (e.g., a child claimed as a dependent by her parents) and the next $800 is taxed at the child's base rate (10% in 2005).[33] No adjustment is made until the Consumer Price Index (CPI) moves the base value up at least $50 (indeed, unless the change lands right on a multiple of $50, the indexed amount is rounded down to the next lower $50).

A separate return can be filed for the child using IRS Form 8615. For convenience, the parents' return may include the income of a child under 14 if the child has only dividend and interest income totaling no more than $8,000 in 2005 (started as an indexed $5,000). "Piggyback" reporting on the parents' return (by attaching Form 8814) has some drawbacks. The child cannot take advantage of certain other deductions, such as charitable donations or the standard deduction for being blind. Also, using the parents' return increases their adjusted gross income, which raises the threshold amount used to determine cutbacks in itemized deductions and personal exemptions.

The source of the child's unearned income is immaterial; excess unearned income is taxed at the parents' rate even though they were not the original source of the property producing that income.

EXAMPLE 8 - 35. In 2005, Dale and Josette's joint taxable income is $360,000, putting them in the top income tax marginal rate of 35%. Their 12-year-old daughter Lara has $3,500 in unearned income, including $1,550 in dividends from stock received as a gift from Dale's parents, and $1,950 in interest from a bank savings account which originated from earned income when Lara was a newspaper delivery girl. Dale and Josette elect to report Lara's income on a separate return. Of the first $1,600 of unearned income, $800 will be tax-free, and $800 will be taxed at 10%. The $1,900 balance (i.e., $3,500 - $1,600) is taxed at the parents' marginal rate of 35%. Her total tax is $745, i.e., 10% * $800 + 35% * $1,900.

EXAMPLE 8 - 36. Continuing the prior examples, if Lara had turned 14 in 2005, her tax would drop to $270, since the first $800 would not be taxed, and the balance of $2,700 would be taxed at the 10% rate. This is a savings of $475 when compared to the kiddie tax result.

The kiddie tax moves the federal government a step closer toward taxing the family as a single economic unit.

CONCLUSION

When it comes to basis, the treatment for assets acquired from a decedent is very different than for those acquired by gift. While estate assets generally receive a step-up in basis to the date-of-death value such is not always the case, e.g., the executor may be able to elect alternate valuation with most assets then having a basis based on value six months after death, or the property might be IRD in which case there is no change in basis. With most gifts there is a carry over basis, meaning the donee's basis is the same as what the donor's basis was, but not always, e.g., for selling at a loss, it may be reduced to the value of the gift if the basis is higher than the gift value.

Trusts and estates are taxed like individuals in many respects but also have some pass-through characteristics. The primary purpose of Subchapter J is to allocate income and expenses between the fiduciary entity and the beneficiaries. Knowing the fiduciary document, state law, and fiduciary accounting is important to the successful completion of a fiduciary tax return. There are two primary parts to preparing a fiduciary income tax return: computing adjusted total income, and allocating the income and deductions between the entity and the beneficiaries, which requires determining DNI and the income distribution deduction.

For any given level of taxable income, trusts and estates generally pay income taxes at a higher level than do individuals since the fiduciary rates are compressed. This is one reason that personal representatives of these fiduciary entities usually distribute most of the income to beneficiaries each year.

In the next several chapters we will consider estate planning that is done for wealthy families in order to reduce the estate tax. Subsequent chapters will discuss how lifetime gifts play into the mix of tools used to reduce transfer taxes.

QUESTIONS AND PROBLEMS

1. In 1995, Renee purchased MOP stock for $120,000. In 2005, she made a gift of the MOP stock to her daughter Bianca. Renee reported the gift as $481,000 (the stock's value), claimed the annual exclusion of $11,000. Because of prior gifts, Renee paid gift taxes of $220,900. When Renee died in 2007, the MOP stock, then worth $522,000, was still owned by Bianca. What is Bianca's basis in the stock? Explain.

2. After making big money in Texas oil, Lucky Nick purchased property on the bay front, paying $1,000,000 in cash. In 2007, when the property was valued at $2,512,000, Nick gave it to his favorite niece, Susan. Nick paid gift taxes in the amount of $660,000. (a) What was Nick's original basis in the property? (b) What is Susan's new basis? (c) What would Susan's basis have been if she had inherited the property due to Nick's death in 2007, rather than receiving it as a gift?

3. In 2006, Stacey gave stock worth $5,012,000 to her brother Mitchell. The annual exclusion reduced the taxable gift to $5 million and Stacey paid gift taxes of $1,815,000. Stacey had purchased the stock in 1994 for $2,000,000. (a) What is Mitchell's basis in the stock? (b) Had Stacey died in 2006, leaving the stock to Mitchell, what would his basis be?

4. In 2005 Wallace bought LARC stock for $90,000. In 2007, when the stock was worth $120,000, he gave it to Karen. For each of the following, state how much gain or loss Karen reports.
   (a) Wallace paid no gift tax. Karen sells it for $80,000.
   (b) Wallace paid no gift tax. Karen sells it for $170,000.
   (c) Because of prior gifts, Wallace paid gift tax of $40,000. Karen sells it for $170,000.

5. In 2005 Alicia bought ABC stock for $180,000. In 2007, when the stock was worth $140,000, she gave it to Russell. No gift tax was paid. For each of the following state how much gain or loss Russell must report when he sells the stock.
   (a) Russell sold the stock for $150,000.
   (b) Russell sold the stock for $200,000.
   (c) Russell sold the stock for $120,000.

6. Priscilla bought LARC stock for $50,000. On March 15, 2004, she gave her ailing father, Raul, the stock then worth $95,000. For each alternative case: (i) state the amount included in Raul's estate, and (ii) the beneficiary's basis in the stock after Raul's death.
   (a) Raul died on February 10, 2005. The stock was valued at $110,000. Priscilla inherited the stock.
   (b) Same as prior problem, but Raul died on April 15, 2005.
   (c) Raul died on February 10, 2005. The stock was valued at $110,000. Priscilla's son, Glenn, inherited the stock.

7. Hubert died February 2, 2007. He left RIP stock to Heather. He bought the RIP stock for $75,000 on December 12, 2006 but it was worth just $60,000 when he died. Heather sold the stock for $72,000 on June 14, 2007. Explain your answers: (a) How much gain or loss would Heather report? (b) Would her gain/loss be long-term or short-term?

8. Abigail died January 10, 2006. Her estate included MOP stock that she bought on November 9, 2005 for $45,000. The value of the stock was $62,000 on her date of death. The estate sold the stock for $66,000 on

March 3, 2006. Explain your answers: (a) How much gain would the estate report? (b) Would the gain be long-term or short-term?

9. When Emilio (E) died his estate included the property shown in the following table. His entire estate went to his daughter Rosa (R). What is Rosa's basis in the properties?

Property	Emilio's basis	FMV	Rosa's basis	comments/what rule?
Residence	$120,000	$450,000		
stock in E's IRA	$0	$40,000		
stock E bought but put in joint tenancy w/R	$50,000	$30,000		
timeshare E's name alone	$20,000	$5,000		

10. When Brandon died his estate went to his sister, Gwen. The estate was well under the applicable exclusion amount. Included in the estate were the following three assets: a house purchased for $200,000 valued at $450,000, an IRA account worth $56,000, funded by Brandon with pre-tax dollars, and a $90,000 note, balance $60,000, secured by a duplex that Brandon sold several years ago. Brandon reported the gain on the sale of the duplex using the installment method. His basis in the duplex was $40,000; he sold it for $100,000, taking $10,000 down and the note for $90,000. What is Gwen's basis in (i) the house; (ii) the IRA; and (iii) the note?

11. Martha inherited real estate from her mother. It was valued at $120,000 in her mother's estate. Eventually, Martha transferred the property to herself and James as co-owners. It was valued at $480,000 when Martha died and

her entire estate was left to James. (i) How much is included in Martha's estate and (ii) what is the new basis for James given the facts in each of the following alternatives:

(a) They were brother and sister. She gave James a 30% tenants in common interest and kept the other 70%.

(b) They were brother and sister. She transferred the property into joint tenancy with just the two of them on title.

(c) They were husband and wife (no, not brother and sister—these are just hypothetical alternatives). She transferred the property into joint tenancy with just the two of them on title.

(d) They were husband and wife. She transferred the property into community property.

12. Colleen and Thomas bought a home for $100,000 for use as their residence. Colleen paid $70,000 of the $100,000 purchase price and Thomas paid the rest. It was valued at $400,000 when Colleen died. Her estate was left to Thomas. (i) How much is included in Colleen's estate and (ii) what is the new basis for Thomas given the facts in each of the following alternatives: (a) As brother and sister, they took title as tenants in common with Colleen having a 70% interest and Thomas a 30%. (b) As brother and sister, they took title in joint tenancy. (c) They were husband and wife, and they took title in joint tenancy. (d) They were husband and wife, and they took title as community property.

13. John and Mary Smith live in a community property state. They own shares of MOP common stock as joint tenants. They purchased the stock in 1985 for $250,000, with John paying $225,000 and Mary $25,000. John died recently. At the time of his death, the stock was worth $1,000,000. Consider the following basis issues: (a) According to the general rule, how much of the stock's value is included in John's estate? What is Mary's basis in the stock? (b) Was it a good idea to hold the stock as joint tenants? Given their domicile, how should title have been held? Why?

14. In the prior problem, suppose John and Mary had purchased the stock in 1970; what argument would Mary use to obtain a higher basis? What would that basis be?

15. Brothers Brooks, Jason, and Shad purchased vacant land for $100,000, taking title as joint tenants. Although they planned to develop the property they did not make any improvements. They paid the following amounts toward the purchase price: Brooks $50,000, Jason $30,000, and Shad $20,000. Determine the amount included in the decedent's estate and each survivor's basis given the following information: (a) Brooks died and the FMV of the property was $200,000. (b) Several years later, Jason died leaving just Shad as the owner. The FMV of the property was $240,000.

16. Family members Dawn, Victor, and Linda purchased vacant land for $100,000 planning to develop it. They took title as joint tenants. They did not make any improvements to the property. They paid the following amounts toward the purchase price: Dawn $50,000, Victor $30,000, and Linda $20,000. Determine the amount included in the decedent's estate and each survivor's basis given the following information: (a) Victor died and the FMV of the property was $200,000. (b) Several years later, Linda died leaving just Dawn as the owner. The FMV of the property was $240,000.

17. Carmen died March 29, 2006. Her estate is left to her two sons. The probate estate receives net income of $4,000 each month. Her executor makes distributions of $9,000 on July 10, 2006 to each son and another $5,000 to each son on January 12, 2007. (a) What is the end date for the longest tax year her executor can elect? What is the end date for the shortest? (b) Suppose her executor chooses a January 31 year-end; in which of their tax years do Carmen's sons report these two distributions (both sons use a calendar year-end)?

18. Karl and Joyce Hooper had an ABC trust plan that converted their single family trust into three trusts when Karl died on February 10, 2005. The A Trust received all of Joyce's property and was revocable by her. The B and C Trusts, funded solely out of Karl's estate, were irrevocable. The B Trust received assets equal in value to $2,000,000 (the AEA amount), and Trust C received the rest of his estate valued at $1,500,000. Trust B was a sprinkling trust with Joyce and the couple's three children as permissible income beneficiaries. All of the income of Trust C had to be distributed

to Joyce for her lifetime. An estate tax return (showing no tax due) was filed on November 10, 2005 and a final determination "closing letter" dated August 16, 2006, accepting the return as filed was received on August 23, 2006. (Details on this kind of planning are found in Chapter 9.) (a) Which of these three trusts can have a fiscal year-end? Explain. (b) Classify each trust as simple or complex. (c) If the trustee chooses a January 31 year-end, when must the trust(s) switch to a calendar year-end? What factors will influence the trustee as to when (what month to end the fiscal year) to switch to a calendar year-end?

19. When Tim died on November 19, 2005, his inter vivos trust became irrevocable. His three adult children are the income beneficiaries as well as the remaindermen, with trust termination required in the year 2015 when the youngest child reaches age 35. The trustee has discretion on income distributions. The trustee chose a December 31 year-end and made no distributions in 2005. In 2006, the trust had DNI of $30,000 but made distributions to the children of only $7,000 each. On March 2, 2007, the trustee distributed $2,000 to each child and made no additional distributions until June of 2007. For 2007, the trust had DNI of $40,000 and the trustee distributed to the children a total of $36,000 (including the March distributions). There were no distributions in the first three months of 2008. The trust had no tax-exempt income. Explain your answers: (a) Is this a simple or complex trust? (b) For 2006, given the option of using the 65-day rule, what is the range of taxable income? (c) If the trustee elected to increase the distribution deduction to the maximum allowed for 2006, what would be the trust's taxable income for 2007?

20. Sylvia's probate avoidance trust became irrevocable when she died on April 20, 2006. Pelican Bank and Trust took over as successor trustee. The remaindermen were her brother Allen and sister Donna, both high tax-bracket taxpayers. The main assets of the trust were Sylvia's house (DOD value $250,000), personal effects, a checking account (about $6,000), and a savings account (about $14,000). In May 2006, the trustee received $8,000 by closing Sylvia's traditional IRA (zero basis). There was no significant source of trust income. The home was sold in July of 2006 for $275,000 after expenses (commissions, escrow fees, title insurance, etc.).

In August (shortly after the sale of the house), the trustee distributed $5,000 to Allen and $5,000 to Donna. The trust was terminated and all assets distributed in January of 2007. Explain your answers: (a) Can the trustee choose a fiscal year-end? Should it? (b) Who will be taxed on the IRA? (c) Who will be taxed on the capital gains from the sale of the home?

21. The irrevocable trust established at Marty's death requires the trustee to pay Marty's widow, Kelly, $15,000 each year. The trustee is given discretion to pay additional amounts to his widow or to his two children, Brian and Leonard. During year one, the trust had DNI of $25,000 of which $5,000 was tax exempt income. The trustee distributed $15,000 to Kelly and $8,000 to each child. Can the tax exempt income be allocated to Kelly's distribution? How would this year's distributions to the three beneficiaries be taxed?

22. Continuing with Marty's trust from the prior question, we move to year two. At Kelly's request, the trustee switched to growth stocks and made no distributions to her (contrary to the trust's terms). The trust had DNI of $12,000 all from leasing pasture land to farmers for grazing their sheep. The trustee withheld distributions to Kelly and distributed $7,000 to each child. What are the income tax consequences of the trustee's actions?

23. Phyllis died in 2007, leaving a taxable estate of $5,000,000 to her two children. Her daughter Alice was the recipient of Phyllis's $1,000,000 IRA (all IRD) and $1,500,000 in non-IRD property. Her son Tony received the $2,500,000 balance of the estate property. There were no DRD deductions. Alice elected to take the IRA distributions over her life expectancy. During 2008, Alice withdrew $100,000 from the IRA. (a) Use ETAX (or your knowledge of the top marginal rates) to determine the deduction for estate tax attributable to IRD. (b) How much of the 2008 IRA withdrawal was taxable to Alice after applying the estate tax IRD deduction?

24. When Leon died in 2007, his estate was left to his three children, Emma, Judy, and Vickie. Included in the estate were two IRAs, one for $30,000, left to Emma and another for $10,000, left to Vickie. There was a $2,000 item of DRD. (a) Given that the estate was in the top marginal rate (all taxable estate after 2005 will be in the top marginal rate), what is the total deduction for estate tax attributable to IRD? How is it allocated? (b) Judy and Vickie both took the option that allowed them to make withdrawals from their respective inherited IRAs over a five year period. In 2008, Emma withdrew $18,000 from her IRA. How much was taxable after applying the deduction? (c) In 2009, Vickie, seeing that her IRA was declining in value, choose to take the entire $8,000 balance as her first and only withdrawal. What was her taxable amount?

25. Agustin's will left $45,000 to his sister Kim, and the balance of his estate to his two children, Eric and Myrna. Included in his estate was an installment note related to a parcel of land (his basis $10,000) he had sold for $50,000. He had taken $20,000 down and carried the balance represented by an interest-only five-year note. At his death the note still had a $30,000 balance and two years until it came due. With the blessing of all beneficiaries (including Kim), the executor distributed the note to Kim along with $15,000 to satisfy her bequest. (a) Since most property passing from a decedent receives a step-up in basis, why does the transaction described trigger a tax? (b) When is the gain recognized and who is taxed?

26. In the prior problem, change the facts such that during the estate's first year it had DNI of $60,000, and the executor did the following: paid cash of $45,000 to Kim, cash of $24,000 paid half to Eric and half to Myrna, plus distributed the note to them as tenants in common. (a) What is the estate's distribution deduction? How much DNI is drawn out by the distribution made to Kim? (b) When is the gain on the note recognized and by whom? What is Eric and Myrna's basis in their respective half-interests in the note?

27. As part of his estate plan to reduce his taxable estate, Katie's grandfather has been making gifts under the annual exclusion amount into a custodial account. Although the account's tax ID number is Katie's social security number, her mother Sharon serves as the custodian. In 2006, Katie's grandfather was in the 35% tax bracket and Sharon was in the 25% tax bracket. The account had interest income of $2,900. Katie had no other income of her own. (a) What determines whether the so-called kiddie tax is applicable? (b) If it is applicable, how is the $2,900 taxed?

28. In the year 2000, when Gordon was just four years old, his grandmother established a custodial account for his benefit as part of her estate planning. When the custodial account was established, Gordon's parents as custodians, were advised to invest in growth stocks that produce no dividends. Gordon's parents are high tax bracket taxpayers. (a) What probably prompted the advice to invest in non-dividend producing stock? Why might investing in a more balanced portfolio (i.e., one with dividend paying stocks as well as growth stocks) be less costly now than when the account was established? Is this decrease in tax cost temporary? (b) Vis-a-vis this account, why is the year 2009 significant? What about 2010?

ANSWERS TO THE QUESTIONS AND PROBLEMS *(odd numbered only)*

1. Bianca's basis: $120,000 + $220,900 * ($481,000 - $120,000)/$481,000) = $285,790. Note, the stock is NOT included in Renee's estate even though the gift was within three years of her death. The gift taxes would be included but that does not change how the stock's basis is determined.

3. Stacey's gifts, Mitchell's basis: (a) basis: $2,000,000 + $1,815,000 * ($3,012,000/$5,012,000) = $3,090,738. (b) FMV at date of death, $5,012,000.

5. Alicia's gift of ABC stock (basis $180,000) to Russell:
(a) Russell sold the stock for $150,000. *This is the special case where on the date of the gift the FMV is less than the basis so when the sale is in between there is no gain or loss, i.e., $180,000>$150,000>$140,000, so no gain or loss.*
(b) Russell sold the stock for $200,000. *The sale is above the donor's basis, so use the higher of the basis or FMV, and the gain is $20,000.*
(c) Russell sold the stock for $120,000. *The sale is below the date of gift FMV, so use that as the basis for determining a loss, i.e., $120,000 - $140,000 = -20,000 as a loss.*

7. Hubert left RIP stock (decline in basis, i.e., step-down at DOD) to Heather:(a) Property received from a decedent (unless it is IRD) receives a new basis equal to its DOD FMV. This true even when there is a decrease in value. Hence, the gain is $12,000. (b) Property received from a decedent's estate is automatically long-term even though total holding period is less than one year.

9. Various property from Emilio to his daughter Rosa:

	Emilio's		Rosa's	
Property	basis	FMV	basis	comments/what rule?
Residence	$120,000	$450,000	$450,000	DOD FMV rule basis

stock in E's IRA	$0	$40,000	$0	IRD, no increase in basis
stock jt w/R	$50,000	$30,000	$30,000	contribution rule, hence 100% included in E's estate and DOD FMV basis rule
timeshare	$20,000	$5,000	$5,000	DOD FMV rule basis, just goes to show that it isn't always a step-up in basis.

11. Martha and James, change in basis for co-owned.

(a) They were brother and sister. She gave James a 30% tenants in common interest and kept the other 70%. *i) Include 70%, i.e., 70% * $480,000 = $336,000. James has a COB of $36,000 [30%*$120,000] plus the amount included in Martha's estate: $336,000 + $36,000 = $372,000.*

(b) They were brother and sister. She transferred the property into joint tenancy with just the two of them on title. *i.) Since we use the consideration furnished rule, 100% included: $480,000, and ii) James has a basis of $480,000.*

(c) They were husband and wife (no, not brother and sister—these are just hypothetical alternatives). She transferred the property into joint tenancy with just the two of them on title. *Husband and wife, half step-up rule applies: i) half is included: $240,000, and ii) ½ * ($120,000 + $480,000) = $300,000.*

(d) They were husband and wife. She transferred the property into community property. *Community property rule includes only half but the new basis applies the FMV at death to both halves: i) half is included: $240,000, but ii) new basis is $480,000.*

13. Mary and John's jointly owned property: (a) General rule for spouses is the half step-up: ½ * ($250,000 + $1,000,000) = $625,000. (b) No, holding it as community property would have allowed a full step-up in basis to $1,000,000.

15. Brothers Brooks, Jason, and Shad's vacant land: Include half of the DOD FMV in Brook's estate. Allocate that $100,000 to the other two owners (half each) and add their respective considerations to arrive at their new basis, e.g., Jason's basis = $1/2 * $100,000 + $30,000 = $80,000 and Shad's basis = $1/2 * $100,000 + $20,000 = $70,000 . Repeat the process when Jason dies, e.g., include $80,000 * $240,000/$150,000 = $128,000; Shad's basis is his post-Brook basis of $70,000 plus the amount included in Jason's estate ($128,000) resulting in a new basis of $198,000.

17. Carmen's tax years: (a) The estate can have a fiscal year-end that ends on the last day of a month that is not more than one year after Carmen's date of death. Hence, the longest is February 28, 2007 and the shortest is March 31, 2006. (b) All income distributions, to the extent they are taxable, are reported as if made on the last day of the fiduciary entity's tax year, hence both sons report $14,000 on their respective 1040s for 2007.

19. Tim's trust, distributions, the 65-day rule: (a) Because the trustee has discretion on distributing income, it is considered a complex trust. (b) The 65-day rule allows the trust to allocate distributions that occur within 65 days of the trust's year-end as though they were distributed before the close of the year. If no election is made, the trust will have taxable income of $9,000, i.e., $30,000 - $21,000. If all the income distributed in the first 65 days is allocated to 2006, then the taxable income is $3,000 since the distribution deduction would increase by the $6,000 distributed within 65 days of the year-end. (c) Since the $6,000 distributed in March was counted as a 2006 distribution, it does not reduce DNI for 2007, hence the taxable income is $10,000, DNI of $40,000 less $30,000.

21. Marty's trust with mandatory distributions to Kelly: Generally, barring specific allocations in the governing document (i.e., rental income to a particular beneficiary), all distributions share proportionately in the various types of income. This means that the tax exempt income cannot be allocated to Kelly even if she is in a high tax bracket and the kids are in a low one. Since the $15,000 distribution to Kelly is mandatory, it is a Tier I distribution and first draws out income with the balance of the DNI allocated in proportion to what each distributee received. The result is that

Kelly received $15,000, of which $3,000 is tax exempt, and each child received $5,000 of which $1,000 is exempt.

23. Estate of Phyllis, IRA as IRD, and the estate tax IRD deduction: (a) The estate tax is calculated both with and without the net IRD. The difference is the IRD deduction. Since the IRD is $1,000,000 all taxed at the top marginal rate of 45%, the deduction (all allocated to Alice) is $450,000. (b) Since she withdrew $100,000 (i.e., 10% of the total), she can claim 10% of the deduction in 2008, i.e., $45,000, leaving $55,000 taxable.

25. Agustin's estate, distribution to satisfy a pecuniary bequest: (a) The gain inherent in an installment sale note is IRD because it was gain realized by the decedent but not yet recognized for tax purposes. Since Kim is entitled to cash in the amount of $45,000, taking the note in partial satisfaction is treated as though Kim purchased the note from the estate. This means that Kim's basis in the note is $30,000 and she will recognize interest income when she is paid interest but there will be no capital gain when the note is paid off. The estate, on the other hand, must recognize gain from the sale of the note. Its basis in the note is the same as was Agustin's, i.e., $6,000 (20% times $30,000, based on a ratio of basis to sale price of $10,000:$50,000). This results in a gain of $24,000. (b) The gain is recognized when the note is distributed to Kim in partial satisfaction of her pecuniary bequest. The estate recognizes the gain and will pay the capital gains tax unless the transaction occurs in the estate's final year. If the transaction occurs in the estate's final year, the gain will be reported on the estate's 1041, allocated to the beneficiaries on the K-1s, and be taxed on their respective 1040s.

27. The kiddie tax and selection of the marginal rates (parents' not the grandparents'): (a) Unearned income (above a fairly low threshold) is taxed at a child's parents' (or guardian's) highest marginal rate until the year in which the child turns 14. (b) The first $800 for a dependent is tax-free, the next $800 is taxed at the lowest marginal rate, i.e., 10%, and above that at the parents' rate. Although the grandparent made the gift, it is the parents' top rate that determines the child's tax, hence the balance of $1,300 (i.e., $2,900 - $1,600) is taxed at the parents' 25% rate.

ENDNOTES

1. IRC § 453.

2. IRC § 1031.

3. IRC § 1033.

4. IRC § 1223(2).

5. IRC § 1014(a).

6. Rev. Rul. 54-97, 1954-1 C.B. 113.

7. Gallenstein V. U.S. (6th Cir. 1992) 975 F. 2d 286.

8. IRC § 645.

9. IRC § 643(e)(1).

10. IRC § 663(b).

11. TRA'97 (Pub. L. 105-34, IRC § 1306(a)) amending § 663(b).

12. IRC § 643(b).

13. Reg. § 1.651(a)-4.

14. IRC §§ 651(a) and (b).

15. IRC § 663(a)(1).

16. IRC § 1014.

17. IRC § 1223(11)

18. IRC § 691.

19. Reg. §§ 1.691(b)-1 and 1.691(c)-1.

20. IRC § 691(c).

21. IRC § 643(e)(1).

22. Rev. Rul. 67-74, 1967-1 CB 194 and Regs. § 1.651(a)-2(b).

23. IRC § 469(j)(6).

24. IRC § 1014.

25. IRC § 469(g)(2).

26. IRC § 469(j)(12).

27. Reg. § 1.1014-4.

28. See endnote 12, *supra*.

29. IRC § 643(a) defines DNI.

30. Reg. § 1.662(b)-2.

31. Reg § 1.652(b)-2.

32. IRC § 63(c)(5), §1(g)(7)(B)(i).

33. IRC § 63(c)(5) and IRC § 1(g)(7)(B)(i).

CHAPTER 9

Common Estate Plans: Bypass and Marital Trusts

OVERVIEW

This chapter demonstrates how bypass planning and the marital deduction are used by wealthy couples to reduce estate taxes. More advanced applications of these techniques, including use of the prior transfer credit, special estate plans, and trusts that obtain the marital deduction for non-U.S. spouses are covered in the next chapter.

As discussed previously, the estate tax might be eliminated for the estates of decedents who die after 2009. For deaths before then, most estates will avoid estate tax because of the substantial increase in the applicable exclusion amount (AEA), e.g., $2,000,000 passes tax-free in the years 2006 through 2008, and the amount jumps to $3.5 million in 2009. Hence, married couples with fairly large estates will be able to pass them to their heirs free of estate taxes by doing a little bit of estate planning.[1] Indeed, since the passage of the Economic Growth and Tax Relief Reconciliation Act of 2001 (EGTRRA) much of estate planning has focused on postponing taxes, if at all possible, with the hope that at least one spouse lives to 2010 or beyond, and the estate tax repeal is made permanent.

EXAMPLE 9 - 1. In 2007, an elderly couple together own property with a net worth about equal to the AEA, i.e., about $2,000,000. Without any estate planning, other than simple wills, it is likely that their children will eventually receive their estate free of tax, regardless of how ownership of the property was originally divided between the spouses, and no matter which spouse dies first. This is true because the AEA will be increasing over the next several years, so it is likely that their combined estates will remain tax-free. If the value exceeds the AEA, then tax savings could be accomplished with a little more planning. This might include gifts to reduce their estate and/or the use of multiple trusts so as to use both spouses' unified credits. Most planners expect that by 2011 the law will change with either the permanent repeal of the estate tax or the estate AEA set above $3,000,000 with some increases based on indexing.

Minimizing estate taxes is a concern mainly for families whose taxable estates are expected to exceed the AEA at the second spouse's death, where that second death is expected to occur before the repeal of the estate tax has been completed. With lifetime gifts within the annual exclusion amount and various estate tax deductions (such as administration expenses and debts), gross estates over the AEA will be transferred tax-free if the gifts and deductions reduce it to the AEA or less. Thus, our focus is on those married couples whose estate *tax base* significantly exceeds the AEA.

EXAMPLE 9 - 2. At the time of her death in 2007, Ellen's gross estate was $2,075,000; debts were $120,000; administration expenses were $50,000. Lifetime taxable gifts totaled $70,000 (i.e., gifts less any annual exclusions). Her taxable estate was $1,905,000 and the estate tax base was $1,975,000. Thus, there would be no estate tax because the estate tax base does not exceed $2,000,000, the estate AEA for 2007.

EXAMPLE 9 - 3. Joshua died in 2004, leaving his half of their community property to his wife, Mary. Neither owned significant separate property and the community property was worth $1,500,000 at that time. Because of good investment advice from an estate planner (I think he said, "put it in real estate"), Mary's net estate was worth $2,500,000 when she died in 2006. Her estate passed to her two grown children, but not until after $230,000 in estate tax was paid. Had Joshua's half of the community property been placed in a bypass trust that benefited Mary for her lifetime and then passed on to the children, no taxes would have been owed. Indeed, if Mary had lived to 2009, the increased AEA of $3,500,000 would have made this a no-tax estate.

ABBREVIATIONS, SIMPLIFICATIONS, AND ASSUMPTIONS

In this chapter, the term "transfer" refers to lifetime gifts and transfers at death. Unless stated otherwise, we will assume that any lifetime gifts were less than the annual exclusion amount. To simplify discussion, figures for estates will be net values (i.e., all deductions, except the marital deduction, have already been taken).

In the discussions that follow, we will generally refer to the "first spouse to die" and the "second spouse to die" as S1 and S2, respectively. As a practical matter, wives outlive their husbands by an average of almost 10 years; hence it is not unusual in estate planning discussions to refer to S1 as the husband and S2 as the wife. From a tax standpoint, the crucial factor is not whether the husband or the wife dies first, but what property each owns when S1 dies and the structure of their estate plan. For example, the order of death might have very significant implications if one spouse is working and the other is not, or if there is a great disparity in their incomes or in their individual net wealth.

Starting in 1988, the marital deduction was eliminated for property going to any non-U.S. citizen spouse unless certain requirements are met to give some assurance that the property transferred stays in the U.S. where it is likely to be taxed as it passes to the next generation. Because there is a different marital deduction structure for non-citizen spouses, our examples are for U.S. citizens. Planning for the non-citizen spouse is discussed briefly in Chapter 10.

THE MARITAL DEDUCTION

Subject to certain requirements which we will discuss later, today's gift and estate tax law allows a 100% marital deduction for transfers between spouses. The law allows one spouse to transfer any amount of property to the other spouse without gift or estate taxes. It has not always been that way.

The History of the Marital Deduction

It is helpful to understand the history of the marital deduction before getting into an extended discussion of the basic estate plans. As hard as it is to believe, there was no marital deduction until several years after World War II. Then, for almost 30 years, the marital deduction for property passing from one spouse to the other was limited to 50% of the net value of S1's estate. Only since 1982 has the 100% marital deduction been part of the law.

The first marital deduction applied to estates of decedents dying after April 2, 1948. It set the maximum marital deduction at 50% of S1's adjusted gross estate (AGE), i.e., S1's gross estate less the deductions allowed for expenses, indebtedness, taxes, and losses[2]. Of course the maximum marital deduction was achieved only if at least half the estate was left to S2, since the marital deduction claimed could not exceed the value of the property passing from S1 to S2.

The purpose of the marital deduction was to eliminate disparate treatment originating from differences in the two systems of state property laws. Some states, for example California and Texas, are community property states that trace their property law to early Roman law. In a community property state, each spouse owns half of all property acquired by the labor of either spouse while married and domiciled in a community property state. Other states, such as Kansas and New York, are common law states that trace their property law to early English law. In common law states the husband generally held title to all property acquired during the marriage. Husbands tend to die before their wives, thus, before the change in 1948, for any given amount of combined wealth, a family in a common law state was likely to pay a higher estate tax when the first spouse died than would have been paid had the family resided in a community property state.

Years	Maximum Marital Deduction
1917 - 1947	► no marital deduction allowed
1948 - 1976	► 50% of AGE, except no marital deduction for community property.
1977-1981	► Greater of { 50% of AGE or $250,000
1982 to present	► 100% of amount S1 ----> S2 with no limit.

During the early period from 1948 through 1981, the marital deduction was designed such that if the husband died first the resulting taxable estate would probably be the same regardless of the couple's domicile. No marital deduction was allowed for S1's half interest in community property since allowing a marital deduction for community property would have resulted in a "quartering" of the estate, which would have perpetuated the inequality between the two property law systems.

> EXAMPLE 9 - 4. Guilliano died in 1960, while residing in Kentucky. He left his estate to his wife, Cheryl. During the entire marriage they lived in Kentucky and acquired property with a net worth of $1,000,000. Because Kentucky is a common law state, 100% of the property was included in Guilliano's gross estate. The marital deduction removed half, leaving $500,000. The $60,000 death tax exemption reduced the taxable estate to $440,000. If Guilliano had lived and died in Texas, a community property state, the $1,000,000 would have been community property. Only his half would have been included in his estate. There would have been no marital deduction, and after the exemption, the taxable estate would have been $440,000, the same result as in Kentucky.

Of course, there were still inequalities. For instance, if a person died domiciled in a common law state and owned very little property, it was unlikely that there would be an estate tax even if the surviving spouse was already wealthy. In a community property state, if the wealth was acquired while the couple was married, then half of the property would be included in the estate of the first spouse to die, and since no marital deduction was allowed for community property, it would be subject to tax. Under current law, with the 100% marital deduction, it makes little sense to continue to allow a full step-up for community property. Indeed, in the future, Congress might decide to change that by allowing only a half step-up for community property, much like the treatment presently given to husband-wife joint tenancies.

From 1977 through 1981, the law allowed a marital deduction equal to the greater of 50% of the adjusted taxable estate or $250,000. For estates in excess of $500,000, the maximum was 50% of the adjusted gross estate (just as it would have been pre-1977) but for estates under $500,000 the greater amount was obviously $250,000. Thus, for estates between $250,000 and $500,000 the marital deduction was $250,000 and for estates below $250,000 it became a 100% marital deduction. To keep community property states on par with common law states, Congress allowed a marital deduction for small estates that included community property to assure that the estate received at least the $250,000 minimum marital deduction.

The Terminable Interest Rule

When the marital deduction first became part of the law, any transfer to a surviving spouse of what is called a *terminable interest* failed to qualify for the marital deduction.[3] A transfer is a terminable interest if the interest transferred to S2 ends at, or before, S2's death or on the happening of some event, i.e., S2's remarriage. The reason for this limitation on the marital deduction is that to do otherwise might allow most estates, even those of the wealthy, to completely escape taxation. This would occur because the marital deduction would reduce or eliminate tax at S1's death on property that would later skip S2's estate (and, therefore, would escape the estate tax) when S2 died because S2 did not own the property. The most commonly encountered terminable interest is a trust created by S1 that, at his death, reserves a life estate for S2 with the remainder to the couple's children. S2's interest is a terminable interest because her only interest in the property will terminate at her death and the "enjoyment" of the property will pass to the children.

The rule. For purposes of the marital deduction, a *terminable interest*[4] is defined as a property interest with these three characteristics:

- It is subject to some future absolute or *contingent* termination of S2's interest.
- The possibility of termination was created by S1 and, if it occurs, there will be a shift in the interest.
- Some other person or entity (other than S2 or her estate) will possess or own the property.

Application of the rule. The question is not whether a termination must occur, but whether, viewed as of the moment of S1's death, a termination *might* occur. Thus, the second and third requirements of the rule exclude situations where the terminable nature was not created by S1, including those unique property interests that simply end by their very nature. Thus, a bequest conditioned on the surviving spouse living for nine months beyond S1's death is a terminable interest, even if she does survive. An ownership interest for a period of years granted to S1 by a third party could be left to S2 for the remainder of the term, and it would not be a terminable interest. Likewise, a lease or a patent will terminate but the interest of S1 does not shift to someone else.

> EXAMPLE 9 - 5. Mark's will stated: "I leave the residue of my estate to my wife, Gloria, provided she survives to the close of probate, and if she does not so survive then it shall be divided among my issue by right of representation." His $3,000,000

estate was transferred by probate to Gloria within a mere five months of his death. Nevertheless, the bequest does not qualify for the marital deduction since Gloria *might* have died before the close of the probate, in which case her interest would have terminated. He created the terminable character of the interest. The interest might have gone to Mark's issue, who then would have enjoyed the property. Because it meets the three elements of the rule, it is a terminable interest and no marital deduction is allowed even though Gloria received the property and it is likely to be in her estate when she dies.

EXAMPLE 9 - 6. When Lori died, she left her patent for turning base metals into gold to her husband Earl. The patent still had 11 years to run. Even though a patent by its very nature must terminate, the interest does not shift to someone else. Furthermore, it is not considered a terminable interest because even though Lori invented the process and obtained the patent, she did not create the termination. Therefore, the value of the patent qualifies for the marital deduction.

EXAMPLE 9 - 7. Selina owned a strip mall. She did not own the land, but was the lessee under what was originally a 99-year land-lease. At the time of her death the land-lease still had 63 years remaining. Even though the mall was built on leased land, Selina's interest was very valuable. (It is not uncommon to find commercial property on leased land. At the end of the lease, the land, together with any structures, reverts to the lessor.) When she died, she left her entire estate to her husband, Duane. Since Selina never owned any more than a leasehold, the shift in interest back to the lessor at the end of the lease is not one that she created. Thus, the value of her interest in the leasehold qualifies for the marital deduction. If, however, she had left the mall to Duane for 10 years, and then to her son for the balance of the lease, it would have been a terminable interest and not even the value of the lease for the period that Duane would have it qualifies for the deduction.

Reason for the rule. Consider what would happen if the law allowed a marital deduction for a terminable interest, such as a life estate for a surviving spouse, without requiring inclusion of the terminable interest property in S2's estate. The value of the property would be split into two parts, the life estate and the remainder interest. There is no denying that a life estate can be a valuable interest and that the interest can be valued using actuarial methods.

When the interest is created at S1's death, a marital deduction based on a life estate might swallow up most of the value of the transfer, leaving very little (i.e., just the remainder interest) subject to the transfer tax. The tentative tax on this might be covered by S1's unified credit. Since the beneficiary of a life estate is not treated as a transferor when the life estate terminates at the beneficiary's death, none of the property subject to the life estate would be included in S2's estate.

> EXAMPLE 9 - 8. Suppose the law did allow a marital deduction based on the value of a life estate (remember, this is not the law) and that S1 died in 2002, leaving S2 a life estate in a trust worth $3,000,000. If S2 was 60 years old and the federal rate for split interests was 8%, the value of S2's life estate is 0.73206 * $3,000,000 = $2,196,180 (the value of the remainder is $803,820). The tentative tax on a $803,820 taxable estate is $269,290, which is covered by S1's $345,800 unified credit; hence, no tax would be due at S1's death. Then if S2 passes away in 2007 and the trust property is worth $4,000,000, it would be transferred to S1's children tax-free since there is nothing to include in S2's estate. Note that a $4 million estate in 2007 would pay a tax of $900,000.

Terminable Interest Rule Exceptions

Why have exceptions to the terminable interest rule? The law creates a number of exceptions to the terminable interest rule, each of which allows the marital deduction even though the interest is technically a terminable interest. Congress certainly did not want a loophole that would allow large estates to avoid estate taxes, however, there are policy and/or practical reasons for each of the exceptions. Additionally, all of the exceptions are ones in which the property qualifying for the marital deduction is ultimately included in S2's estate, unless S2 consumes it or gives it away. If S2 gives it away in large chunks (greater than the annual exclusion), her gifts may use up her unified credit.

Six months or common disaster rule: IRC § 2056(b)(3). Almost from the start of the marital deduction and its related terminable interest rule, Congress created an exception to the rule for "six months or common disaster" survivorship clauses, so long as S2 survived long enough to satisfy the contingency and receive the property. Typically, these clauses make a bequest contingent on the beneficiary actually outliving the decedent by six months or some period shorter than six months. The law also allows the marital deduction for a marital bequest conditioned on S2 surviving a common accident. A "common disaster" clause might state, "if my wife and I are injured in the same accident, and I die, I leave her my estate provided she eventually recovers from said accident." Even though recovery might take longer than six months, this bequest would qualify for the marital deduction so long as recovery did occur.

Therefore, a survivorship clause, as part of the decedent's will or living trust, can be part of the estate plan, and a marital deduction will be allowed provided the survivor actually survives to receive the property.[5]

A survivorship clause may be specific, relating just to certain bequests, or it may cover all beneficiaries, e.g., *"For purposes of this Will, a beneficiary shall not be deemed to have survived me if that beneficiary dies within six months of my death."*

The clause avoids a double probate in situations where the beneficiary does not live long enough to really use the bequest. It also allows the testator to determine the alternate beneficiary of the bequest, rather than allowing it to be governed by the disposition of the beneficiary's estate. Without a survivorship clause the property goes into the beneficiary's estate even if the beneficiary lives just a moment longer than the testator.

Whether a bequest is a terminable interest is determined as of the death of S1; it does not depend on whether the interest in fact terminates. Therefore, without the IRC § 2056(b)(3) exception, no marital deduction would be allowed for estates that actually passed to the surviving spouse if the bequest was subject to a survivorship clause.

Qualified terminable interest property (QTIP): IRC § 2056(b)(7). There are valid estate planning reasons for creating terminable interests whereby a surviving spouse is given income from a decedent spouse's estate for life, and yet the surviving spouse is given little or no control over the ultimate disposition of the property. With the population living longer, and with the high rate of divorce, marriages with one or both spouses having children by prior marriages are quite common. It is natural that a person with considerable wealth entering into a second (or third) marriage would want to take care of the new spouse, yet also desire to assure that his or her wealth does not go to the new spouse's family after both are deceased.

Prior to 1982, the maximum marital deduction for a large estate was equal to 50% of the estate's net value. To qualify for the marital deduction, the surviving spouse had to receive the property, or at least be given a general power of appointment over it. To obtain the maximum marital deduction, at least half of S1's estate had to be transferred to the surviving spouse. Thus, S1 was forced to choose between obtaining the maximum marital deduction and losing control over who would ultimately own the property, or retaining control and giving up the marital deduction. Fortunately, the qualified terminal interest property (QTIP) election allows a marital deduction without forcing S1 to give up control as to who ultimately receives his property.

Under the prior law (i.e., before we had the 100% marital deduction), leaving more than half of S1's estate to S2 did not increase the marital deduction for large estates, therefore, the most common plan left S2 only so much of S1's estate as qualified for the marital deduction. This could be either outright or in a trust that gave S2 a life estate and a general power to appoint the corpus.[6] The rest of S1's estate was transferred to a bypass trust, usually (but not in all cases) one giving the income from that trust to the surviving spouse for her life, with the remainder going to S1's family after her death. This arrangement did not sacrifice estate tax dollars on the first death and avoided having the corpus of the bypass trust included in S2's estate.

Without a new exception to the terminable interest rule, the change allowing a 100% marital deduction for transfers after 1981 would have created a dilemma for every couple who had kept their wealth separate because they had children by prior marriages. They would have been forced to choose between providing for the surviving spouse or assuring that their estates passed to their own children. The planner would have been forced to either transfer control of everything in excess of the AEA to the surviving spouse or pay an estate tax on the first death.

Fortunately, an option known as the QTIP election was added to the law.[7] This election allows the executor of S1's estate to obtain a marital deduction for what is called " Terminable Interest Property," referred to by the acronym QTIP. To qualify for this election, the terminable interest property must meet these requirements:

- The surviving spouse must receive all income from the property for life. Note that the right to use property is generally considered the same as receiving the income; hence a home may be part of the QTIP property.
- The right to the income cannot be contingent.
- During the surviving spouse's life, the property cannot be appointed to anyone other than to the surviving spouse.[8]

The executor must make an election to claim the marital deduction for the QTIP property when S1's estate tax return is filed. The law allows the executor to make the QTIP election on less than 100% of the terminable interest property. This is done by electing to QTIP a fraction of the property. Thus, if the terminable interest property is in the form of a trust with a life estate for the surviving spouse, remainder to their children, and the trust is funded with property exceeding the AEA, the executor might elect to QTIP only that portion of the trust that exceeds the value of the AEA.

There is no free lunch. The fraction of the QTIP property that receives a marital deduction at S1's death must be included in S2's estate at the time of S2's death.[9] Hence, the choice in making a QTIP election is how much of the terminable interest property to tax at S1's death versus how much to tax at S2's death. Of course, with EGTRRA some estates will completely avoid tax by making the QTIP election to postpone all taxes until the second death provided S2 lives to 2010 and Congress passes additional legislation to avoid the 2011 sunset provision that would repeal the repeal.[10]

> EXAMPLE 9 - 9. Fernando died in 2002 leaving his entire estate, $3,127,452, less debts and expenses of $197,420, in an irrevocable trust for his wife, Arcela. She was given a life estate and a limited power to appoint corpus at her death among their three children. Arcela had a modest estate of her own. Since the executor of Fernando's estate wanted to postpone all taxes until after Arcela's death, he QTIPed that portion that exceeded the AEA estate, i.e., that numerator is the amount by which the estate exceeds the AEA. Since the net value of the trust is $2,930,032, the QTIP fraction is:
>
> $$\frac{\$2{,}930{,}032 - \$1{,}000{,}000}{\$2{,}930{,}032}$$
>
> When this fraction is multiplied by the net value of the trust, the marital deduction is $1,930,032, resulting in a taxable estate of exactly $1,000,000.

The QTIP fraction serves a dual role; it determines how much of the QTIP property qualifies for the marital deduction on the first death and, more importantly, it determines how much of that property (valued at the second death) must be included in S2's estate.

> EXAMPLE 9 - 10. When Arcela died in 2006, the trust Fernando had established for her had grown from its initial worth to $3,954,372, with debts of $420,870 resulting in a net value of $3,533,502. Arcela had her own property worth $780,450 with debts and expenses that totaled $110,400, for a net value of $670,050. She too left her estate to their children. In determining her taxable estate, her executor would have to add to what she owned the portion of the trust that had previously been QTIPed:
>
> $$\frac{1{,}930{,}032}{2{,}930{,}032} * \$3{,}533{,}502 = \$2{,}327{,}542$$

Adding this amount to $670,050 results in a taxable estate of $2,997,592, which, in 2006, would result in an estate tax of $458,892.

The QTIP fraction equation given above uses S1's AEA and defers all taxes to the second death. The AEA in the formula must be adjusted to take into account any use of the unified credit elsewhere, either because S1 made taxable gifts during life or left part of the estate to someone other than the surviving spouse. Such transfers use up unified credit (unless to a charity). Hence, the AEA in the numerator should equal the AEA that remains available.

EXAMPLE 9 - 11. Suppose Fernando also owned a $250,000 life insurance policy that named his daughter by a prior marriage as the beneficiary. Now his gross estate would be $3,377,452. The net value after debts and expenses would be $3,180,032 [$250,000 life insurance plus the $2,930,032 in the trust]. The life insurance would use $250,000 of the AEA; hence, the QTIP fraction in the above example would be ($2,930,032 - $750,000) divided by $2,930,032. The portion of the QTIP property elected for the marital deduction would be equal to $2,180,032. Thus, after the marital deduction, the taxable estate would again be $1,000,000, comprising the $250,000 life insurance policy and the $750,000 portion of the QTIP property that was not covered by the marital deduction. [$3,377,452 - $197,420 -$2,180,032 = $1,000,000]

Of course, 100% of the QTIP property in the above example could have for the marital deduction, but electing to QTIP 100% of the trust would have reduced S1's taxable estate below the AEA, thus wasting part of S1's unified credit and needlessly increasing the amount of the property that could eventually be included in S2's estate.

If the second death is likely to occur before the estate tax is completely repealed, it might be advantageous to generate a tax on the first estate by using a QTIP fraction less than that necessary to defer all taxes. For instance, if S1 died in 2006, leaving QTIP property worth $8,000,000 in trust for S2, and S2 has no estate of her own, it might be advantageous to QTIP half of the $8,000,000 trust instead of just three-quarters of it. By doing so, instead of postponing the tax, just the half qualifies for the marital deduction, leaving a taxable estate of $4,000,000. On S2's death, half of the trust will be included in her estate. Since the top marginal rate starts at a taxable estate of $2,000,000 and the estate AEA in 2006 is $2,000,000, there is no tax saving by running twice up the "rate ladder," however, as will be discussed in the next chapter, generating a tax in both estates sometimes allows the second estate to use a prior transfer credit, further reducing the total estate taxes.[11]

General power of appointment exception: IRC § 2056(b)(5). A power to appoint property is the right to tell the owner of the property to transfer it to someone else. Powers of appointment were discussed in greater detail earlier in the book. As a reminder, the Code defines a general power as "a power which is exercisable in favor of the decedent, his estate, his creditors, or the creditors of his estate. . . ."[12]

> EXAMPLE 9 - 12. Fred creates an irrevocable trust for Gerry's benefit. The terms of the trust provide Gerry with all the income from the trust and give her the right, when she reaches 25, to have the trustee terminate the trust and transfer all assets to anyone that Gerry designates (including herself). From the moment Gerry reaches age 25, she has a general power of appointment.

The holder of a general power must include in his or her estate the value of property that could have been transferred by the exercise of a general power of appointment, regardless of whether it is ever exercised. It is enough that it merely could have been exercised. Limited powers do not result in inclusion of the property in the estate of the holder, provided the holder of the power did not create the power. Where the holder also created the power, the Internal Revenue Code treats it as a retained interest rather than as a power to appoint.

A marital deduction is allowed for property passing in trust from S1 to S2, provided S2 is given income for life in the property and has a general power of appointment over the property exercisable during life and/or at death.[13] Since S2 is a holder of a general power, the property will be included in S2's estate, or if she appoints it during her lifetime to someone else, it will be a gift from her to that person. Thus, although a transfer into a general power of appointment trust technically creates a terminable interest, it is allowed to qualify for the marital deduction because (unless consumed) it will eventually be either given away by S2 or included in S2's estate. Since Congress is allowing a marital deduction based on S2 receiving a life estate, the trust must either require the trustee to make the trust assets productive, or state law must give S2 the power to require the trustee to make them productive (most states have such laws). If the trust document gives the trustee absolute investment power, especially if it includes a statement allowing investment in unproductive assets, the marital deduction may not be available even though S2 is given a life estate.[14]

EXAMPLE 9 - 13. On her death, Geraldine creates a trust for her husband, Bob. It is funded with assets having a net value of $2,950,714. Bob is given a life estate in the trust and the power to appoint the corpus at his death to whomever he chooses. The trust provides that this power is exercisable only by specific reference to it in his will and, if he fails to exercise the power, the property is to be distributed to their issue. The trust will qualify for the marital deduction because of § 2056(b)(5). Therefore, although it is in Geraldine's gross estate, it is not in her taxable estate. Of course, when Bob dies, because the power is a general one, the entire trust will be included in his gross estate whether or not he exercises the power.

EXAMPLE 9 - 14. Upon his death in 2007, Gerry's estate plan creates a trust to benefit his wife, Betty. It is funded with property worth $3,000,000. The terms of the trust give Betty a life estate and the power to appoint the corpus to any of their five children when she dies. If she does not appoint the corpus, it will be distributed by per capita at each generation. Because Betty only has a limited power of appointment, § 2056(b)(5) does not apply, and there is no automatic marital deduction. Assuming no QTIP (discussed later) election is made, the trust will be taxed at Gerry's death (resulting in estate taxes of $435,000), but no additional taxes will be owed vis-a-vis this trust when it terminates. The latter is true no matter how much the trust has grown, and no matter whether Betty exercises or fails to exercise her limited power to change the remainder interests of the children.

Pensions for the benefit of S2: IRC § 2056(b)(7)(C). If an annuity included in S1's estate is payable to S2 alone during S2's life, the QTIP election is automatic unless the executor of S1's estate affirmatively elects to have the annuity taxed in S1's estate. Electing to have it taxed will avoid having any value that remains at S2's death taxed as part of S2's estate, whereas allowing the automatic QTIP causes that value to be included in S2's estate.

Charitable Remainder Trusts following S2's interest: IRC § 2056 (b)(8). Property transferred to a charitable remainder trust,[15] that has the surviving spouse as its only non-charitable beneficiary, qualifies for the marital deduction, even though it is a terminable interest. This is a special rule and no QTIP election is necessary. The surviving spouse's interest does not have to be a life estate; it can be for a term, so long as it does not exceed 20 years.[16] The value of the income interest qualifies for a marital deduction and the value of the remainder qualifies for the charitable deduction. Since S2 did not create the trust and there is no QTIP election, there is no new gift at the end of a trust for a term of years, likewise, the trust is not included in S2's estate even if she has a life estate; hence there is no additional charitable deduction for her or her estate. If the executor is in doubt as to whether a lifetime trust is a " charitable" remainder trust, he or she should make a protective QTIP election, i.e., list it as part of the QTIP property on Schedule M of the 706. It would then qualify for the marital deduction and be included in S2's estate but qualify for a charitable deduction.

THE BASIC ESTATE PLANNING PATTERNS

Planning to minimize the estate tax with the marital deduction and the bypass arrangement generally involves some variation of one of three basic planning options. They are the *100% marital deduction*, the *AB Trust*, and the *ABC Trust*. These options do not depict precise will or trust arrangements; instead they trace the overall flow of property after S1's death. Our concern is with the timing of estate tax payments, the amount of those taxes, and which spouse (S1 or S2) controls who will eventually receive the property. First, we will take up the simplest plan, where S1 transfers all his estate to S2. Next, we will cover the bypass trust because it is common to almost all multiple trust plans. Then we will take a look at the basic multiple trust plans, before going back to the QTIP election and how it is used in conjunction with the ABC Trust plan.

Planning Option 1: the 100 Percent Marital Deduction

Often the unlimited marital deduction provides a simple and practical estate planning strategy. It entirely shelters all property S1 transfers to S2 from gift tax and estate tax. In the simple 100% marital deduction strategy, S1 leaves all property to the surviving spouse. The transfer is protected from transfer tax by the 100% marital deduction. Outright transfers by S1 to S2 that qualify for the 100% marital deduction include: gifts, transfers by will, transfers by right of survivorship when title is held solely by the spouses in joint tenancy or tenancy by the entirety, and insurance on S1's life payable to S2. Transfers in trust for the benefit of S2 qualify too if they meet certain criteria.

EXAMPLE 9 - 15. Tom and Gerri each have estates of $840,000. At her death in 2005, Gerri leaves her entire estate to Tom by a simple will. There is no estate tax because the estate is sheltered by the 100% marital deduction. At Tom's death in

2007, the combined estate worth $1,940,000 is left to their children. There is no estate tax because of his available AEA (i.e., up to $2,000,000 passes tax-free).

Advantages. The attractiveness of the 100% marital deduction strategy is its simplicity. It is very easy to understand and inexpensive to establish. More elaborate estate planning may not be necessary for clients whose combined estates are less than one AEA. Even with estates above the estate AEA, some couples may not be concerned about whether taxes, e.g., where the couple leaves no issue or they plan to leave a large enough portion of their estate to charities such that at the second death the taxable estate will be less than the AEA.

Of course, these simple plans give S2 total dispositive control over all of the couple's property. This may be an advantage or a disadvantage, depending on the circumstances. S2 will receive full ownership of the property, a fee simple interest. S2 can use it, consume it, gift it, or sell it. When she dies, she can give what is left to whomever she chooses, and in such manner as she chooses.

Not all marital deduction plans confer full dispositive control to S2. S1 may retain dispositive control by placing the property in a trust known as a QTIP trust. These are most commonly found in multiple trust plans such as the one known as the ABC trust. Indeed, a QTIP trust can be used alone where S1 wants dispositive control but sees no need for multiple trusts. Patience, we will get to this soon.

Disadvantages. The 100% marital deduction that transfers all control to S2 has several significant drawbacks for large estates.

Might result in higher total estate tax. Assuming the second death will occur before 2010 (or an estate tax is retained after 2009), the first drawback for wealthy couples is a higher total estate tax due to two factors. First, each spouse has the protection of the unified credit, but when S1 gives his entire estate to S2, his unified credit is unused. Unless S2 consumes or gives away S1's property using the annual exclusion or charitable gifts, it will become part of S2's transfer tax base, subject to either gift tax or estate tax to the extent that the combined value exceeds S2's AEA. Second, S2's estate might benefit from a prior transfer credit that will not be available if S1's estate avoids estate tax by using the marital deduction.

EXAMPLE 9 - 16. S1 and S2 had an estate of $7 million, with each owning one-half. They have simple wills leaving property to one another, or to the children if the other is deceased. At S1's death in 2004, there is no estate tax because the entire

$3.5 million sheltered by the marital deduction passes to S2 tax-free. If S2 dies in the year 2006, having neither transferred nor consumed the property, a $7 million taxable estate will result in estate taxes of $2,300,000. If the estates were split such that each was a taxable estates $3.5 million, first death in 2004 and second in 2006, the respective tax would be $945,000 and $690,000, for combined estate taxes of $1,635,000 (even less if a prior transfer credit is available to reduce the tax at the second death; this is a matter discussed in Chapter 12).

The simple 100% marital deduction planning is said to have the effect of "overqualifying" or "overusing" the marital deduction, which results in the "loading up" of the taxable estate of S2, and subjecting a greater amount of the couple's wealth to tax at the second death than would occur with a more complex plan. In summary, two negative results can occur as a result of pouring the first estate into the second: S1's unified credit is wasted and S2's estate loses the possibility of using a prior transfer credit to reduce estate taxes. Nevertheless, as we approach 2010, executors for S1's estate will be inclined to postpone taxes by whatever means are available if there is a fair probability that S2 will outlive the estate tax or at least be able to utilize a substantially higher AEA than presently available.

May not avoid probate. If a couple uses simple wills to carry out their 100% marital deduction planning, or if they hold everything in joint tenancy, there will be a probate, at least at the second death. Some states do not require a probate for property left from one spouse to the other. Of course, the use of living trusts as part of the estate plan overcomes this problem.

Not available for property to non-citizen spouse. The marital deduction only applies to property left to citizen spouses. The property of U.S. citizens and non-citizens permanently resident in the U.S. is subject to estate taxation anywhere in the world. The property of a non-citizen, non-resident is subject to estate tax only if the property is located in the U.S. Because a non-citizen spouse could take the property and leave the country (preventing estate taxation at S2's death), the marital deduction does not apply to property left to a non-citizen spouse, even if she is a permanent resident, unless a special trust (with a U.S. trustee) is used or the spouse becomes a citizen before the estate tax return is filed. More on this in the next chapter.

Bypass Planning

The common theme of most bypass planning is the division of S1's estate into a bypass portion and a marital deduction portion. The bypass portion is transferred in a way that bypasses S2's estate. It is important to note that the bypass portion is considered to be "taxed" at the first death even if the use of S1's unified credit results in no tax being due. The marital deduction portion is transferred to S2 in a way that qualifies it for the marital deduction. Bypass planning thus avoids the two major problems with simple marital deduction planning since it makes use of S1's unified credit and it potentially saves S2's estate taxes by using a prior transfer credit.

There are many variations on the bypass planning theme, including the way the bypass property is transferred (whether outright or in trust), the number of trusts used and their characteristics, the proportion of S1's property in the bypass portion, and whether it will equal the AEA (so no tax will actually be paid) or exceed it (and cause some tax at the first death). Usually, the bypass portion is eventually transferred to the couple's children, but there are many other possibilities. Remember, it is called bypass planning because it bypasses S2's estate (or some other income beneficiary's estate) for tax purposes. It is taxed in S1's estate whether taxes are paid or not, e.g., the tentative tax may be fully absorbed by S1's unified credit.

Outright bypass. The simplest form of bypass is the outright bypass where the AEA is left directly to someone other than S2.

> EXAMPLE 9 - 17. Herbert had an estate worth $3,500,000 when he died in 2005. To his daughter, Denise, he left property worth $1,500,000 protected from tax by his unified credit, and to his wife, Wilma, he left property worth $2,000,000 protected from tax by the marital deduction. When Wilma died in 2006, she left to Denise an estate valued at $2,300,000 partially protected by her AEA. The estate tax was $138,000. If Herbert had left the entire $3,500,000 estate to Wilma, it would have been protected at his death by the marital deduction, but at Wilma's death, her estate would have greatly exceeded her AEA. Assuming modest growth, an estate of $3,800,000 would produce a tax of $828,000.

Control issues. The couple might have strong reservations about the bypass plan if, at S1's death, it caused an immediate, outright transfer to the children. The children may be too young to be responsible for the property. S2 may need either the income from the property, or the property itself, for support. S2 might prefer to retain control over the management of those assets ultimately intended for the children. These are common and legitimate objections to the use of an immediate, outright transfer to the children to create a bypass. Fortunately, the bypass can be arranged (and these objections overcome) by using trusts.

Recall that by limiting the powers given to the beneficiary of a life estate, the trust is excluded from the holder's gross estate. The beneficiary can have the right to take the income and a power of appointment that does not rise to the level of a general power of appointment, such as the right to take principal measured by the "ascertainable standard."

Generally, bypass property is taxed at the time it is initially transferred for the benefit of the income beneficiary, but not again when the income beneficiary dies. The amount transferred in this fashion might be equal to the AEA, i.e., just enough to create a tentative tax equal to the unified credit. Thus, although technically the transfer is taxed, the donor, or in the case of a bequest, the decedent's estate, does not have to pay any transfer tax.

For most of our discussion we will assume that the income beneficiary in question is S2, and that the bypass property is a bypass trust established by S1. We make this assumption because it is the most frequently encountered bypass arrangement, but there are other possibilities. The bypass plan works because the transfer of an amount sufficient to use S1's unified credit to someone other than S2 can be arranged to conform to both spouses' overall estate planning objectives.

In a typical bypass trust, the children of the marriage are the ultimate beneficiaries, or remaindermen. Neither spouse is likely to object to the children as the remaindermen of the bypass trust created at S1's death, since in all likelihood, both spouses expect their combined estates to eventually go to their children. S2 usually has the income from the bypass property as well as access to the principal for purposes of health, education, support or maintenance, without the property being included in her estate.

Multiple Trusts in Estate Planning

Each of the three plans (including the 100% marital deduction plan discussed earlier) can be set up with a will or a trust instrument. Due to the costs and lack of privacy associated with probate, most wealthy couples that spend the time, energy, and money to have one of these more complex estate plans written choose the living trust over the testamentary trust (although either will accomplish the tax savings discussed in this chapter). For the most part, we will assume a living trust for these multi-trust plans. The documents that implement a multi-trust estate plan are usually separated into three phases. The first phase can be described as the family trust phase. There is usually only one trust in this phase, although each spouse may have a separate trust, especially if they have estates quite unequal in value or if they have children by prior marriages. The couple's property is transferred to the trustee while the trustors are alive; hence it is called a "living" trust or an "inter vivos" trust. Most married couples serve as the initial trustees of their family trust, and they reserve the power to revoke or amend it.

The second phase starts at the death of one of the spouses, who we refer to as S1. The family trust is divided into multiple trusts after the S1 dies. The multiple trusts are funded from the family trust. It is not known which spouse will be the first to die at the time the plan is drafted; hence the distribution of assets into the various trusts is based on the order of the two deaths. Generally, in these complex estate plans, Trust A receives all of S2's property. Sometimes, some of S1's property goes into Trust A too, depending on the size of S1's estate and the type of estate plan. Trust B is funded from S1's estate. Whether Trust B receives all of S1's estate, or only part of it, depends on the size of S1's estate and the type of estate plan. If there is a Trust C, it too will be funded from S1's estate. The funding of these trusts is fixed by the plan, and the trustee generally has very little flexibility to change the plan. After S1's death, Trusts B and C become irrevocable. S2 can control the distribution of assets only according to the terms of those trusts, e.g., she may or may not be given a limited power to appoint corpus when she dies or she may have a power to withdraw corpus that is limited to an ascertainable standard. Usually, these plans allow S2 to amend (or even revoke) Trust A, since corpus is principally from S2's property.

The third phase commences with S2's death. Unless her death occurs very shortly after S1's death, the different trusts should already be funded. The executor, filing the estate tax return, notes which trusts (or portions thereof) are included in S2's estate. After paying the estate tax, the trustee distributes the remaining trust property outright to the children if they have reached the age specified in the trust document, commonly 25, 30, or 35. On the other hand, if the children are much younger, then the two trusts (AB plan) or three trusts (ABC plan) are likely to be merged into a single "pot trust" (perhaps "children's trust" is a better name) until the children reach the age specified in the trust, at which time the trust is subdivided into equal shares for the children. Up until the time it is subdivided, the entire trust estate is available to meet the needs of any and all of the children. The name "pot trust" is derived from the fact that all needs are met from the same "pot" rather than being charged to each individual child's share based on such child's needs and usage. The subdivision (creating separate trusts) is usually specified as when either the youngest reaches a certain age (e.g., 21) or when the oldest reaches some age, although the trust can simply set a specific date after which division should be made, such as, "as soon after January 1, 2015, as the division can be accomplished."

Sometimes a testamentary trust arrangement is used for these complex estate plans, although it is becoming less common than using a living trust. The testamentary trust is a lengthy will that incorporates a trust. With the testamentary trust, there is a probate after the testator dies. At the conclusion of the probate, the trust is funded by a court order, which incorporates into the order the will's trust language. The order directs the distribution of the probate property to the trustee, who is charged with managing the trust estate in keeping with the terms of the trust. There may be several trusts depending on the specific estate plan. Once the probate is completed and the trust or trusts are funded, the process is just like plans that start with an inter vivos family trust.

When you work with these complex estate plans, at the first death start by determining the property (and its value) included in S1's estate to arrive at S1's gross estate (net estate before the marital deduction if the values given are net values). At the same time, you will determine the value of S2's estate as it is at S1's death. The next step is to review their estate plan to determine how the property is to be allocated to each of the trusts. At the second death, the trusts are already funded; therefore, after determining the net value of each trust, the task is merely to determine what portion of each trust is included in S2's estate. The portion included may depend on the trust's characteristics (e.g., S2's general power to appoint the corpus of Trust A means that it is always included) or it may depend on what was done at S1's death (e.g., whether a QTIP election was, or was not, made on a terminable interest trust).

Definitions. In the discussions that follow, we will be using the shorthand terms "AB Trust" and "ABC Trust." These terms are frequently used as shorthand designations, and effectively convey the general pattern of an estate plan to people who work in this field. The following names are frequently used for these trusts, but there are many other possibilities:

- Trust A is likely to be called the Survivor's Trust, the Marital Trust, or the General Power of Appointment Trust.
- Trust B is likely to be called the Bypass Trust, the Applicable Exclusion Trust, the AEA Trust, the Credit Shelter Trust, or the Nonmarital Trust.
- Trust C is likely to be called the QTIP Trust, the QTIP Marital Trust, or even Trust Q.

Depending on the plan and how Trusts B and C are defined, either may be called the Residuary Trust. Thus, if in an ABC Trust plan Trust B is defined in terms of the amount necessary to use the available unified credit (i.e., the AEA for S1) and the residue of S1's estate flows into Trust C, the latter may be called the Residuary Trust. On the other hand, if Trust C is defined as the minimum amount that, when qualified for the marital deduction, will reduce S1's taxable estate to the AEA, with the balance flowing into Trust B, then it is Trust B that may be called the Residuary Trust.

Planning Option 2: the AB Trust

With the AB Trust plan, the "B" Trust is the bypass component and the "A" Trust is the surviving spouse's trust. The two components are structured and funded so as to leave the maximum amount possible to the surviving spouse while still utilizing both spouses' unified credits. Payment of transfer taxes is deferred until S2's death. For large estates, whichever spouse lives longest will ultimately control who receives the bulk of the couple's estate. Only Trust B, the AEA trust, has the remainder interest fixed by S1 at S1's death. This plan makes sense for wealthy couples whose children are solely from their present marriage since the plan may give S2 ultimate control over the greater portion of the couple's combined estate.

> EXAMPLE 9 - 18. The combined value of Hal and Wanda's property at S1's death in 2006 is $5,000,000. So long as both of them have estates that exceed the AEA amount, it does not matter whether Hal or Wanda dies first because Trust B, the trust that initially holds the AEA, receives assets from S1's estate with a net value of $2,000,000 and the balance of the estate, in the amount of $3,000,000, goes into Trust A. Trust B would have the remaindermen irrevocably designated (probably

the couple's children), while Trust A would be subject to the control of S2. There is no requirement that the couple's children ultimately receive the property from Trust A. If S2 remarries, or for any reason decides they are not deserving, she can change the remaindermen for that trust. Because it is not part of S2's estate, Trust B will not be taxed again at S2's death even if it then exceeds the AEA. The terms of the plan could add flexibility by giving S2 a limited power over Trust B, e.g., perhaps giving her the power to change the shares of the children or to give some of the corpus to specifically named charities.

The character of Trust A. Trust A receives all of S2's property, plus all of S1's property that exceeds S1's available AEA. S1's unified credit is applied against taxable transfers up to the AEA. These taxable transfers include property going into Trust B, property going to people other than S2, and S1's lifetime post-1976 taxable gifts. To obtain the marital deduction at S1's death for property transferred from S1's estate into Trust A, the trust must have two characteristics: (1) S2 must receive all the income for life, paid at least annually; and (2) S2 must be given a general power of appointment exercisable during life and/or at her death. Of course, if S2 has a general power to appoint exercisable during her entire lifetime, she also has income for life even if the trust is silent in that regard.

The character of Trust B. The funding for Trust B is usually defined in terms of S1's available AEA. It usually receives exactly enough of S1's estate to cause a tentative tax equal to S1's "available" unified credit. What is available starts with the AEA for the year S1 died and is reduced by the value of property passing to someone other than S2 and any post-1976 taxable gifts. Methods for achieving the right amount of funding are described at the end of this chapter under the heading "Allocating Assets to the Trusts." For most estates, the initial value of Trust B will be the AEA since this will cause a tentative tax equal to the unified credit available in the year of S1's death. The tentative tax is then canceled out by S1's unified credit.

Since the purpose of this trust is to use S1's unified credit and avoid inclusion in S2's estate, any characteristics that would cause inclusion (such as giving S2 a general power of appointment over trust corpus) must be avoided. The marital deduction is not sought for Trust B, so while most of the time S2 is given all of Trust B's income for her lifetime, such is not required. The terms could call for sprinkling the income among S2 and the children, or it could even allow the trustee to accumulate income or distribute corpus to persons other than S2. A general power to appoint would cause inclusion in S2's estate, so it is to be avoided. However, S2 may be given a power to invade the corpus limited by ascertainable standards or S2 may be given a limited power to allocate the remainder. A limited power, in those plans using one, is likely to be limited to the couple's children and/or specific charities, adding flexibility to the plan within limits, without causing the trust property to be included in S2's estate.

AB Trust plan's benefits. The AB Trust plan provides the opportunity for S2 to manage the assets from both estates, enjoy all of the income, and have access to all of the principal, i.e., even Trust B corpus can be reached if the trust includes a power to withdraw limited by an ascertainable standard. In the event both spouses die while their children are young, the plan allows disbursement to the children to be delayed until they are old enough to manage the property. Along with the general power that S2 has over Trust A, additional flexibility can be obtained by giving S2 a limited power to change the distribution plan for Trust B. The plan uses S1's unified credit to decrease overall taxes; and the marital deduction to delay taxation until the second death. The following example compares the estate taxes using the unlimited marital deduction with the result of using an AB Trust plan.

EXAMPLE 9 - 19. S1 dies in the year 2004 (when the AEA is $1,500,000) and S2 dies in the year 2007 (when the AEA is $2,000,000). All of the estate, with a net value of $8,000,000, belongs to S1 and poor S2 owns nothing. In an AB Trust plan, even though S2 has no assets, the plan calls for S2's property to go into Trust A since, before either spouse dies, no one can be certain which spouse will be S1 or S2, or whether a spouse with little property might acquire a substantial estate before S1's death.

	100% Marital Deduction		AB Trust	
	S1 dies 2004	S2 dies 2007	S1 dies 2004	S2 dies 2007
GE	$8,000,000	$8,000,000	$8,000,000	$6,500,000
MD	$8,000,000)	$0	($6,500,000)	$0
TE	$0	$8,000,000	$1,500,000	$6,500,000
TT	$0	$3,480,800	$555,800	$2,805,800
UC	$0	($780,800)	($555,800)	($780,800)
ET	$0	$2,700,000	$0	$2,025,000

A tax savings of $675,000 results. This is partly due to $1,500,000 being "taxed" at S1's death even though no tax is paid. The reason that the tax savings is more than the $555,800 unified credit used at S1's death is that the $1,500,000 held in Trust B would have been taxed in S2's estate at her estate's highest marginal rates, i.e., those between $6,500,000 and $8,000,000. Avoiding those higher marginal rates results in an additional $119,200 saved. Of course, if Trust B grew in value between the two deaths, even more is sheltered since a bypass trust is not taxed at S2's death, regardless of its value at that time.

EXAMPLE 9 - 20. This example is similar to the last example except both spouses have community property and separate property. To allow easier comparison between the examples, the total net value will stay at $8,000,000, and the plans and timing of the two deaths will remain the same. S1 has separate property worth $3,350,000, S2 has separate property worth $2,700,000, and they own community property worth $1,950,000.

	100% Marital Deduction		AB Trust	
	S1 dies 2004	S2 dies 2007	S1 dies 2004	S2 dies 2007
GE	$4,325,000	$8,000,000	$4,325,000	$6,500,000
MD	($4,325,000)	0	($2,825,000)	$0
TE	0	$8,000,000	$1,500,000	$6,500,000
TT	0	$3,480,800	$555,800	$2,805,800
UC	0	($780,800)	($555,800)	($780,800)
ET	0	$2,700,000	$0	$2,025,000

Notice the gross estate at S1's death is the same for both plans. S1's estate consisted of separate property plus one-half of the community property, i.e., $3,350,000 + 50% * $1,950,000 = $4,325,000. Of course, our assumption, made for the sake of simplicity, that the values remain the same between S1's death and S2's death is unrealistic. The use of S1's unified credit is not being postponed until S2's death, since Trust B is actually taxed at S1's death but the tentative tax is completely covered by S1's unified credit. Trust B is not taxed at S2's death because it entirely bypasses S2's estate.

If either spouse is uncomfortable with the control given to S2 by the AB Trust plan, they should consider the ABC Trust plan which reduces the amount of property over which S2 exercises ultimate control, yet still allows estate taxes to be postponed until the second death.

Planning Option 3: the ABC Trust

The ABC Trust plan is like the AB Trust plan except that S1's net estate in excess of the AEA goes into Trust C instead of passing to Trust A. The terms of Trust C qualify it for the marital deduction through the QTIP election, thus making it possible to defer all estate taxes until the second death. One of the real advantages of this plan, when compared to the AB Trust, is that S1's estate in excess of the AEA goes into Trust C, which cannot be changed by S2. Since Trusts B and C are irrevocable, S1 can rest in peace knowing that the remaindermen for these two trusts are fixed. S2 may be given the power, limited by an ascertainable standard relating to health, education, support, or maintenance, to invade the corpus of Trusts B and C. This invasion right can even be limited such that it only becomes available to S2 when Trust A has less than a certain value remaining, e.g., only if Trust A is worth less than the AEA. S1 can also give S2 a limited power of appointment, perhaps exercisable only by will, over Trusts B and C. Remember, neither a limited power to appoint, nor a power to invade limited by an ascertainable standard, will cause inclusion of the property in the holder's estate. Even though S2 is given these powers, it is S1 who defines their limits.

The character of Trust A. Trust A in an ABC Trust plan is likely to have the same characteristics as Trust A in an AB Trust plan. It receives property equal in value to all of S2's separate property and her one-half interest in community property. S2 is given a general power to appoint the corpus of this trust or to revoke it. Unless property actually passes from S1's estate into Trust A, there is no marital deduction for property in this trust because it will hold property that already belongs to S2. It is not unusual for S1's plan to leave some property, such as all the tangible personal property, to S2's Trust A. The transfer of such property into Trust A would automatically qualify for the marital deduction. Of course, there is also an automatic marital deduction for property (such as cars and the household bank account) held in joint tenancy by the couple. S2 might transfer these items to Trust A so they are part of the overall estate plan and will avoid probate at her death.

The character of Trust B. Trust B will have the same characteristics as Trust B in the AB Trust plan, including being defined in terms of S1's available AEA. Thus, in most instances the value of the trust will initially be S1's available AEA (e.g., $2,000,000 in 2006). The "available AEA" language allows the estate plan to make the most of the increased bypass opportunity. This is a bypass trust in that it will be taxed at S1's death and escape tax (regardless of its growth) at S2's death. Again, the trust can be a sprinkling trust without harming the planning objectives but quite commonly S2 is given all trust income for her lifetime. As will be discussed in the next chapter, giving S2 income for life (also referred to as a life estate) in this trust under certain circumstances allows S2's estate to claim a larger prior transfer tax credit than would be available if it was designed as a sprinkling trust.

The character of Trust C. Trust C is a QTIP trust. As such it must meet all IRC § 2056(b)(7)'s QTIP requirements[17] to ensure that a marital deduction is available should S1's executor decide that it is in the estate's best interest to claim one. The requirements are that S2 must receive income for life, and no one can hold a power to appoint the trust property to anyone other than S2 during her lifetime. This trust usually receives that portion of S1's estate that exceeds the AEA. When a QTIP election is made for Trust C, the executor of S1's estate is claiming a marital deduction and, in effect, making a pact with the IRS that the property will eventually be subject to transfer tax triggered by S2 making a gift of her interest in the trust or by her death.[18] If the QTIP election is not made, Trust C will be taxed at S1's death and will not be taxed again when S2 dies even though S2 enjoys a life estate. Thus, Trust C is a marital deduction trust if the election is made and a bypass trust if it is not.

According to the Regulations, the qualifying income interest for S2 is satisfied if she is given "substantially that degree of beneficial enjoyment of the trust property during her life which the principles of the law of trusts accord to a person who is unqualifiedly designated as the life beneficiary of a trust."[19] This means that she can compel the trustee to make unproductive assets productive, she receives the income from investment property, and she has the use of any tangible property that is part of this trust (such as the home and its contents). She may place income from the trust in her personal accounts or in her Trust A accounts.

Generally, S2 must withdraw the income from Trust C as leaving it in is treated as a gift from her into a trust over which she has a retained life estate, creating a § 2036 retained life estate problem. Of course this is only a problem if the QTIP election is not made since, if it is made over the whole trust, the trust will be included in S2's estate anyway.[20]

The QTIP election is made on S1's 706 return (i.e., the U.S. Federal Estate Tax Return). Once the election is made (or not made) on a return and the time for filing the estate tax return has passed, the executor cannot change the decision. Fortunately, the QTIP election can be made even on a late filed return.

Trust C cannot be a sprinkling trust since S2 must receive all income from the trust for life. The income must be distributed at least annually, and S2 must have the right to require the trustee to change unproductive assets (ones that produce little or no income) into reasonably productive income producing assets. Even if some required terms are not in the trust, state law often remedies the deficiency, e.g., if in the context of the overall estate plan it appears a trust was supposed to qualify for the QTIP election the law might supply missing elements such as requiring trustees to distribute income at least annually or give surviving spouses the right to force trustees to make unproductive assets productive. These statutes satisfy the QTIP requirements even if the trust instrument is silent on the timing of income distributions, or if at the time of S1's death, a significant portion of the trust estate is made up of unproductive assets (such as undeveloped land) and the trust terms say nothing about the trustee being obligated to make them productive. Note, as long as S2 has the right to require unproductive assets be made productive, the trustee need not make the assets more productive for the QTIP election to be made. Of course, if S2 makes the request, the trustee must comply with the request and seek a higher return on unproductive assets.

S2 can be given a power to invade corpus, limited by an ascertainable standard. She can also have a limited power to appoint corpus so long as it is exercisable only at her death. The limited power to appoint is usually limited to allocation among the couple's children and, perhaps, specific charities.

The trust instrument can also add flexibility by giving S2 a 5 & 5 power; however, S1 would be giving up some certainty as to who will ultimately receive the corpus. If one of the reasons for choosing the ABC plan was to assure that S1's property would go to S1's children by a prior marriage, a 5 & 5 power might not be desirable since each exercise by S2 takes property out of the trust.

WORKING WITH THE QTIP ELECTION

When a QTIP election is available after S1's death, the executor must determine how much of the QTIP property to QTIP, i.e., the optimal portion of S1's estate to have taxable at S1's death. Subtracting that optimal amount from S1's total estate gives the marital deduction desired. The marital deduction is obtained by making a QTIP election of part (or all) of the QTIP property. If the document allows a division of the QTIP trust into two or more trusts, one of which the executor (the trustee) elects to completely QTIP and the other for which no election is made (let's call them Trust CQ and Trust CNQ, respectively), some additional planning opportunities exist. With the division, the trustee can "spend down" Trust CQ if S2 needs to use corpus. Since a QTIPed trust is in S2's estate, reducing a Trust CQ is better than reducing a single partially QTIPed Trust C since, in the later case, any reduction to the trust would reduce pro rata both the QTIP and the non-QTIP portion of the trust. However, if the document is silent as to the trustee's power to create separate trusts, the Regulations require that the QTIP election be for a specific portion (i.e., on a fractional basis) of the full value of the trust. A fraction is created with the QTIP marital deduction amount as the numerator and entire value of the QTIP property as the denominator. This is the fraction of the QTIP property that is protected by the marital deduction at S1's death. This fraction also determines how much of the QTIP property will be taxed at S2's death. To determine the taxable part at S2's death, the value of the QTIP property at S2's death is multiplied by the QTIP fraction. Before applying this to specific estate plans let us break this process down into six steps.

Determining and Using the QTIP Fraction - A Step by Step Approach

Step 1. Determine the desired taxable estate for S1: Usually, the executor wants to postpone all taxes to the second death, but still use S1's unified credit. This means using the marital deduction to bring the taxable estate to the AEA, e.g, $2,000,000 in the year 2006. However, if generating some taxes at the first death saves taxes in the long run, it might be advantageous to bring the taxable estate to some higher value. This might be accomplished by not QTIPing all of the QTIP property.

Step 2. Determine the QTIP marital deduction (QTIP MD), i.e., the amount of marital deduction necessary to arrive at the desired taxable estate: Total S1's Estate − S1's Desired Taxable Estate = MD amount. If the marital deduction is only by way of a QTIP election, this will also be the QTIP MD amount. If some property passes to S2 immediately by joint tenancy, through life insurance, or by being transferred from S1's estate into a trust that S2 controls (e.g., Trust A), such will qualify for an automatic marital deduction (automatic MD). The automatic MD must be subtracted from the MD amount to arrive at the appropriate QTIP MD.

Step 3. Determine the value of the QTIP property: This is the property, almost always a trust, that meets the QTIP code requirements (§ 2056(b)(7)) and to which the QTIP election will be applied to give us the QTIP MD. Which trust is the QTIP property depends on the particular estate plan, e.g., with the ABC plan it is the value of Trust C, usually S1's estate less the AEA (the AEA having been transferred into Trust B). Generically, we will refer to it as the QTIP Trust.

Step 4. The fraction: Create a fraction with the QTIP MD (from Step 2) over the QTIP property (from Step 3) to arrive at the QTIP fraction.

$$\frac{QTIP\ MD}{QTIP\ Trust} = QTIP\ Fraction$$

Step 5. S1's taxable estate: S1's taxable estate is S1's total estate less any automatic MD and less QTIP MD, determined by multiplying the QTIP fraction times the value of the QTIP property. Check your calculation; the result should match the desired taxable estate (from Step 1).

$$S1's\ Taxable\ Est. = Total\ Est. - automatic\ MD - (\frac{QTIP\ MD}{QTIP\ Trust} * QTIP\ Trust)$$

Step 6. S2's taxable estate: At S2's death, to determine S2's total estate, the QTIP property (*as it is then valued*) is multiplied by the QTIP fraction to determine the amount of the QTIP property (e.g., that portion of Trust C) that is included in S2's estate. This in turn is added to the rest of S2's estate (generally Trust A).

$$S2's\ Taxable\ Est. = Trust\ A + (\frac{QTIP\ MD}{QTIP\ Trust\ [@S1'sDOD]} * QTIP\ Trust\ [@S2'sDOD])$$

If the trust document allows the trustee to divide Trust C into Trust CQ (portion of Trust C that is QTIPed) and Trust CNQ (that portion not QTIPed), there are a few changes to the steps. One would still go through steps 1 - 2 as before, then at step 3, Trust CQ would be allocated the QTIP marital deduction amount and Trust CNQ the balance of S1's property. The fractions at step 5 would be 100% (1/1) for Trust CQ and zero for Trust CNQ. Finally, step 6 would have S2's estate equal all of S2's property plus all of Trust CQ. Since Trusts B and CNQ are fully included in S1's taxable estate, they are both bypass trusts and, as such, are not included in S2's estate.

Step by Step: Applied to the ABC Trust Plan

The extended example set that follows is designed to increase your understanding of the QTIP election. Using a modern ABC plan, the example compares the result of death taxes for a 100% QTIP election to what happens where there is no QTIP election. Later, we will explore what happens when S1's executor makes a partial QTIP election where the trustee does not have authority to divide Trust C into separate trusts. For examples in this chapter, we will ignore the prior transfer credit, as it will be covered in connection with multiple trust plans in the next chapter. We will assume that Trust C meets all of the QTIP requirements. The assumption is also made that S2 does not remarry; therefore, there is no marital deduction for S2's estate. To simplify these examples, all figures are given net of debts and expenses, and the values of the trusts increase modestly each year during the 10 years between the two deaths. The assumption that the two deaths occur 10 years apart avoids having to tackle the prior transfer credit as part of the example.

Step 1. Determine the desired taxable estate for S1, e.g., equal to the AEA so as to postpone all taxes, or have S1 and S2's estates equal as of S1's death, or some dollar amount as determined by the executor to be optimal in reducing overall taxes for the two estates.

Step 2. Total Estate – Desired Taxable Estate = QTIP MD amount.

Step 3. Trust C is the QTIP property, defined as being S1's estate in excess of the AEA (Trust B):

S1's Total Estate – Trust B = Trust C

Step 4. Create a fraction with the QTIP MD amount (Step 2) over the QTIP property (Trust C) to arrive at the QTIP fraction:

$$\frac{QTIP\ MD}{Trust\ C} = QTIP\ Fraction$$

Step 5. S1's taxable estate is S1's total estate less the product of the QTIP Trust and the QTIP fraction. The result should match the desired taxable estate (from Step 1).

$$S1's\ Taxable\ estate = Total\ estate - (\frac{QTIP\ MD}{Trust\ C} * Trust\ C)$$

Step 6. At S2's death, the amount *then* in Trust C is multiplied by the QTIP fraction in order to determine the amount of Trust C included in S2's estate. Add that amount to the rest of S2's estate (e.g., Trust A) to determine S2's total estate.

$$S2's\ Taxable\ Est. = Trust\ A + (\frac{QTIP\ MD}{Trust\ C\ [@S1'sDOD]} * Trust\ C\ [@S2'sDOD])$$

An extended example. Facts for this extended set: Henry (S1) and Wilma (S2) lived, and died, in a community property state. Their estate plan was an ABC Trust plan as described above. When Henry died in 2002, they owned property valued as follows:

S1's separate property	$1,500,000
Their community property	$1,800,000
S2's separate property	$2,000,000
Total	$5,300,000

Note: If Henry and Wilma lived in a common law state, the outcome would be the same if we equally divide the community property between them:

S1's separate property	$2,400,000
S2's separate property	$2,900,000
Total	$5,300,000

In fact, the property laws for common law and community property states result in ownership rights for each spouse that largely depend on how the spouses acquired their property.

After Henry's death the trusts were funded with assets having a net value as shown here:

Trust A	$2,900,000
Trust B	$1,000,000
Trust C	$1,400,000
Total	$5,300,000

The values of the trusts at Wilma's death in 2007 will be given in Step 6.

QTIP to postpone estate taxes. The executor of Henry's estate elects to postpone all taxes until Wilma's death but desires to use Henry's unified credit. Given that he died in 2002, the optimal taxable estate is equal to the AEA, i.e., $1,000,000.

Step 1. The desired taxable estate for S1 = $1,000,000.

Step 2. $2,400,000 - $1,000,000 = $1,400,000

Step 3. The QTIP property: S1's Total Estate – Trust B = Trust C.

$2,400,000 - $1,000,000 = $1,400,000

Step 4. Create a fraction with the QTIP marital deduction amount from Step 2 divided by the Trust C amount from Step 3 to arrive at the QTIP fraction.

$$\frac{\$1,400,000}{\$1,400,000} = 100\%$$

Step 5. S1's taxable estate is S1's total estate less the product of Trust C and the QTIP fraction:

$$S1's\ Taxable\ Estate = \$2,400,000 - ((\frac{\$1,400,000}{\$1,400,000}) * \$1,400,000)$$
$$= \$1,000,000$$

Step 6. At S2's death in the year 2007, the amount *then* in Trust C is multiplied by the QTIP fraction to determine the amount of Trust C that must be included in S2's estate. Add that amount to Trust A to determine S2's total estate. Assume that in the five years the values for the three trusts increased to the following:

Trust A		$3,400,000
Trust B		$1,350,000
Trust C		$1,650,000
	Total	$6,400,000

Note: The entire amount of Trust C, valued at S2's death, is included in S2's estate since *all* of Trust C was QTIPed. S2's estate is:

$$\$3,400,000 \text{ [Trust A]} + \$1,650,000 \text{ [Trust C]} = \$5,050,000$$

Trust A was not part of Henry's taxable estate because it contained only Wilma's property. Trusts B and C combined equal Henry's gross estate because all of Henry's property is allocated to these two trusts. Regardless of whether a QTIP election is made, the value of Trust B will be taxed as part of Henry's estate, although with a 100% QTIP of Trust C there will be no tax due, since the unified credit will match the tentative tax generated by Trust B. While Trust C's value is always part of the *gross* estate, it need not be taxed if the QTIP election is made to cover the entire trust, because it then is protected by the marital deduction and will be taxed in S2's estate.

When Wilma dies, there are several reasons why Trust A is included in her estate. She holds a general power over it, that would cause inclusion of any property transferred to it by Henry; and she transferred her own property to it, retaining the right to revoke the transfer. Trust B is excluded from Wilma's estate because it is a bypass trust. Wilma did not fund Trust B, therefore, she could not have a retained interest in it; nor did she hold a general power of appointment over it. Trust C is included in her estate only because of the QTIP election after Henry's death. This was a trade-off: it allowed Trust C to escape tax when Henry died, so it had to be included in her estate when Wilma died.

Notice that the QTIP election, or the failure to elect, does not change the amount of property going into each trust. Of course, if no QTIP election is made, then taxes must be paid from Trusts B and C at S1's death, since the value is in excess of the AEA.

No QTIP marital deduction claimed. Change the facts. Suppose the executor of Henry's estate decided that it was best NOT to postpone any taxes on Henry's share of the property, and therefore, elected NOT to make a QTIP election. This means the desired taxable estate equals all of Henry's property, i.e., $2,400,000. Even though it's obvious that the amounts going into Trusts B and C (all of Henry's estate) will be the amount taxed at his death, and Wilma's property (all of Trust A) will be the only property taxed at her death, the steps are set forth here to make it apparent that we are following the same format, an important lesson before we start working on partial QTIP elections.

Step 1. The Desired Taxable Estate for S1 = $2,400,000.

Step 2. Total Estate – Desired Taxable Estate = QTIP Election amount.

$$\$2,400,000 - \$2,400,000 = \$0$$

Step 3. Trust C is the QTIP property.

$$\text{S1's Total Estate} - \text{Trust B} = \text{Trust C} = \$1,400,000$$

Step 4. Create a fraction with the QTIP MD from Step 2 over Trust C (Step 3) to determine the QTIP fraction.

$$\frac{\$0}{\$1,400,000} = zero$$

Step 5. $S1's\ Taxable\ estate\ =\ Total\ estate\ -\ (\frac{QTIP\ MD}{Trust\ C} * Trust\ C)$

$$S1's\ Taxable\ Estate\ =\ \$2,400,000\ -\ ((\frac{\$0}{\$1,400,000}) * \$1,400,000)$$

$$=\ \$2,400,000$$

Step 6. In this case, since none of Trust C was QTIPed, S2's estate is just $3,400,000 [The value of Trust A only].

In all of these plans Trust A is included in S2's estate because it holds S2's property and, as to any property that flows into Trust A from S1's estate, S2 holds a general power of appointment over this trust. Where S1's executor forgoes the QTIP election, Trust C is taxed at S1's death and then escapes tax at S2's death. Trust B is not included in S2's estate because it is a bypass trust, already taxed in S1's taxable estate, but bypassing the estate of S2. When possible, Trust B is funded with property expected to appreciate because it escapes tax at S2's death, even if its value greatly exceeds the AEA for that year.

Optimal Allocation: the Partial QTIP Election

Trust C has the chameleon character of being like a marital deduction trust if the QTIP election is made, or a bypass trust if the QTIP election is not made. However, the law permits flexibility by allowing partial QTIP elections. This allows a portion of the QTIP trust (Trust C in the ABC plan) to qualify for the marital deduction at S1's death. When the executor of S1's estate makes such an election, a portion of the QTIP trust, the QTIP fraction portion, acts like a marital trust and the rest of the trust acts like a bypass trust. The QTIP election portion of Trust C escapes taxes at S1's death because of the marital deduction, but that same fraction of the QTIP trust, valued at S2's death, is included in S2's estate when S2 dies. The non-QTIP election portion is taxed at S1's death but not at S2's death.

A partial QTIP may be desirable to lower the overall estate taxes by taking advantage of lower marginal rates in both estates and by utilizing the prior transfer credit (discussed in conjunction with the marital deduction in the next chapter). Generally, executors choose to postpone all taxes until S2's death, even though the absolute amount of total taxes paid will almost always be greater when this is done. Given the time value of money, postponing taxes makes sense rather than paying taxes at the first death. Besides, if taxes are paid at the first death, they are paid out of property intended to produce income for the surviving spouse; whereas postponing the taxes takes them out of the property going to the children (or others, if there are no children).

The picture changes dramatically if it is known at the time S1's estate tax return is being prepared that S2 is quite certain to die soon. In that case, paying taxes on each estate, rather than just at S2's death, will not only use both estates' unified credits but S2's estate will be able to use a prior transfer credit that substantially reduces taxes on the second death. When considering the prior transfer credit (PTC), the optimal allocation between the two taxable estates depends on such factors as the age of S2 at the time of S1's death, the federal rate for valuing split interests, the size of the combined estates, and how long S2 outlives S1. Generally, the lower the federal rate, the older the surviving spouse, and the larger the estate, the higher the percentage that should be allocated to S1's taxable estate as compared to S2's. For instance, if the first death occurs in 2005 when the §7520 rate is 6%, S2 is 70 years old, dies about a year and a half after S1, and the combined estate value is $10,000,000 at the time of S1's death, the tax bill is lowest if $7,500,000 is taxed in S1's estate and only $2,500,000 is taxed in S2's estate. Under the circumstance just described, if all taxes are deferred until the second death, whether through a QTIP or regular marital deduction, with only the AEA being sheltered at S1's death, the estate taxes would be about $1,000,000 more than they would be with the optimal allocation.

Several competing factors must be considered when deciding the appropriate QTIP fraction. One consideration is the time value of money. If the deaths are not expected to occur close together, taxes paid a long time in the future are less burdensome than taxes paid today. However, if the property appreciates substantially between the deaths, the total tax bill will be higher. If property is appreciating very rapidly, sometimes it makes sense to get the tax paid sooner on a smaller amount. Another consideration is the prior transfer credit that substantially reduces taxes at the second death, but only if the deaths are close together in time. One must also consider the relative size of the two estates. A QTIP election can only shift the taxable estate in S2's direction, so optimization by QTIP election works only when S1's estate is larger than S2's, and only if it is large enough to equal the optimal S1 taxable estate.

Where the second death is likely to occur within a few years after the first death, and the estates have a combined value in excess of two AEAs, the optimal allocation usually has S1's taxable estate slightly larger than that of S2, thus when the two estates are about equal in size, or when S2 has the larger estate, there should be no QTIP election because doing so would only further increase S2's taxable estate.

Since deductions other than the marital deduction are generally beyond the executor's control, the focus in the examples to follow is on the marital deduction that can be increased or decreased depending on the QTIP fraction. For simplicity, we will continue to ignore the other deductions.

Partial QTIP election examples. While it seems more complex, the process for calculating estates with a partial QTIP election is the same process discussed earlier for the "all or nothing" QTIP elections. Where it was "all," the QTIP fraction was equal to one[21] and where it was "nothing," it was equal to zero.[22]

Choosing a specific taxable estate at S1's death. If Trust C qualifies for the QTIP election, S1's executor can choose any size taxable estate from a low of the AEA amount (Trust B) to all of S2's estate (Trust C plus Trust B).

EXAMPLE 9 - 21. Sam has an estate of $5 million and his wife Susan has an estate of $1.7 million. His executor elects to have $4,100,000 taxed at Sam's death in 2004. The value of the three trusts at Sam's death would be: Trust A, $1,700,000; Trust B, $1,500,000; and Trust C, $3,500,000.

Step 1. Sam's desired taxable estate is $4,100,000.

Step 2. Sam's Total Estate – Desired Taxable Estate = QTIP MD

$$\$5,000,000 - \$4,100,000 = \$900,000.$$

Step 3. Trust C is the QTIP property: $3,500,000.

Step 4. $\dfrac{QTIP\ MD}{Trust\ C} = \dfrac{\$900,000}{\$3,500,000} = QTIP\ Fraction$

Step 5. *Sam's Taxable estate = Sam's Total Estate* $- (\dfrac{QTIP\ MD}{Trust\ C} * Trust\ C)$

$$\$5,000,000 - (\frac{\$900,000}{\$3,500,000} * \$3,500,000) = \$4,100,000$$

Step 6. By Susan's death in 2006, Trust A grew to $2,300,000, Trust B grew to $1,900,000; and Trust C grew to $4,200,000. The portion of Trust C included in her estate is:

$$\frac{\$900,000}{\$3,500,000} * \$4,200,000 = \$1,080,000$$

When added to Trust A, her total estate is $3,380,000 [$2,300,000 + $1,080,000]. Notice that Trust B is not taxed at Susan's death, even though it exceeded the AEA for the year of her death.

QTIP to equalize estates. If a PTC is likely for S2's estate, equalizing the two taxable estates at the first death will come pretty close to saving as much tax as will be saved with an optimal allocation. The example that follows assumes that the executor seeks to have both taxable estates equal as of S1's death. Equalizing the estates uses the six-step process that we have used previously. If S1's estate is larger than S2's, the two are averaged and the average is the desired taxable estate for Step 1.

EXAMPLE 9-22. Using the facts from the prior Sam and Susan example, suppose Susan is in extremely poor health at Sam's death and, therefore, the executor chooses to equalize the estates.

Step 1. Sam's desired taxable estate:

$$\textit{Average:} \quad \$5,000,000 + \$1,700,000 = \frac{\$6,700,000}{2} = \$3,350,000$$

Step 2. Sam's Total Estate − Desired Taxable Estate = QTIP MD:

$$\$5,000,000 - \$3,350,000 = \$1,650,000.$$

Step 3. Trust C = $3,500,000.

Step 4. $$\frac{QTIP\ MD}{Trust\ C} = \frac{\$1,650,000}{\$3,500,000} = QTIP\ Fraction$$

Step 5. $$Sam's\ Taxable\ estate = Sam's\ Total\ estate - (\frac{QTIP\ MD}{Trust\ C} * Trust\ C)$$

$$\$3,350,000 = \$5,000,000 - (\frac{\$1,650,000}{\$3,500,000} * \$3,500,000)$$

Step 6. Suppose at Susan's death Trust A has grown to $2,300,000, but because taxes were paid out of Trust B and C, they were $1,560,000 and $3,800,000, respectively. The portion of Trust C that would be included in her estate would be:

$$\frac{\$1,650,000}{\$3,500,000} * \$3,800,000 = \$1,791,429$$

Susan's estate would be $4,091,429 [Trust A $2,300,000 + Trust C $1,791,429].

There is a shortcut to equalize the estates that reaches the same result. S2's estate is subtracted from S1's estate and half the difference is the amount of the QTIP election (Step 2). Here is the shortcut, using Sam and Susan's estate from the above example:

$$\frac{Sam's\ estate\ -\ Susan's\ estate}{2} = QTIP\ MD$$

$$\frac{\$5,000,000\ -\ \$1,700,000}{2} = \$1,650,000$$

Notice that this is the same result as Step 2.

ALLOCATING ASSETS TO THE TRUSTS

Estate planning involves planning for an uncertain future. The planner and client must guess how much and what kind of property will be in the estate. They must also guess whether the intended beneficiaries will be alive, and what their circumstances will be at the time the estate is distributed. Because of this uncertainty, planning documents are drafted to deal with uncertainty. Two drafting techniques for structuring disposition clauses in wills or trusts are pecuniary bequests and fractional share bequests.

A *pecuniary bequest* passes property to various shares such that the value of the assets adds up to the dollar value needed to satisfy the pecuniary bequest. For example, the clause funding Trust B might read: *"assets equal in dollar value to the amount that will generate a tentative tax exactly equal to S1's available unified credit, and all assets above that amount are given to the trustee of Trust A."*

Or, the marital bequest going to Trust A of an AB trust plan (or Trust C, in an ABC trust plan) could be defined in dollars: *"assets equal in dollar amount to the marital deduction necessary to reduce S1's taxable estate such that it generates a tentative tax exactly equal to S1's available unified credit are allocated to Trust A, all other assets are allocated to Trust B."*

Using a *fractional share bequest*, both bypass and marital shares will receive a fractional interest in each and every asset in the estate: *"Trust C shall consist of the smallest fractional share of S1's estate that, when added to all other interests in property that pass from S1 to S2, and qualify for the marital deduction, will eliminate, or reduce to the maximum possible extent, any estate tax. The balance of S1's estate shall be allocated to Trust B."* The factors involved in deciding which type of provision to use are beyond the scope of this text.

CONCLUSION

In this chapter we have seen how estate taxes are saved by using both spouses' unified credit and using the QTIP election to allocate the combined estates in a way that produces, or at least attempts to produce, the lowest overall estate tax. To some extent, the uncertainty of the future of the estate tax pushes executors in the direction of postponing estate taxes whenever possible in the hope that the tax will either go away or the AEA amount will increase so dramatically that little, if any, tax will ever be paid. The next chapter discusses additional estate plans for wealthy couples. For the most part, these will be variations on the theme already established, namely utilizing both unified credits and taking advantage of the marital deduction by making optimal QTIP elections. We will also discuss how trusts and the QTIP election can be used in conjunction with the prior transfer credit to dramatically reduce estate taxes in some fairly common circumstances.

QUESTIONS AND PROBLEMS - Use the ETAX program to do the problems that require calculation of estate or gift taxes. If an annual exclusion is available, use the following amounts: $3,000 for 1977 - 1981; $10,000 for 1982 - 2002; $11,000 for 2002 - 2005; and $12,000 for 2006-2008.

1. In 2007, what is the largest estate size that an *individual* can transfer, estate tax-free, with a *simple will* to (a) a spouse; (b) anyone else? Explain, and state any assumptions made.

2. (a) In 2007, what is the largest net estate that a *husband and wife* can transfer to their children, estate tax-free, with *simple wills*? (b) Does it make any difference how much is owned by each spouse? Explain.

3. The marital deduction has changed dramatically over the years. For each case calculate the marital deduction and the taxable estate on the assumption that the entire estate was left to S2. The year shown is the year S1 died.

year	S1's net estate	marital deduction	taxable estate
1940	$800,000		
1960	$800,000		
1980	$400,000		
1980	*$200,000		
2000	$2,000,000		

*S1's ½ of the community property

4. For each case calculate S2's share, the marital deduction, and the taxable estate on the assumption that S1's estate was left 75% to S2 and 25% to S1's children. The year shown is the year S1 died.

year	S1's net estate	S2's share	marital deduction	taxable estate
1940	$800,000			
1960	$800,000			
1980	$400,000			
1980	*$200,000			
2000	$2,000,000			

*S1's ½ of the community property

5. Briefly state the reason for the terminable interest rule. Then explain why Congress allows each of the following exceptions to the rule:
   (a) The six months survivorship clause.
   (b) The transfer to a general power of appointment trust.
   (c) The transfer to a QTIP trust, with a QTIP election.
   (d) The pension to the surviving spouse automatic QTIP election.
   (e) Income for S2 for ten years with remainder to a qualified charity.

6. S1 has left his estate to S2 but with the condition stated. For each case determine: (i) whether the bequest is a terminal interest ("T") or not ("NT"), (ii) whether it qualifies for the marital deduction (yes/no); and (iii) if yes, whether it is because of an exception to the terminal interest rule. Explain.

	condition placed on the bequest	T/NT	yes/no	section/explanation
(a)	"provided that S2 survives until our youngest child is 18" [at the time the youngest child turns 18 in two months]			
(b)	same as "a" except the child was already 20 when S1 died.			
(c)	same as "a" but elsewhere in the trust it is written, "This trust is intended to qualify for the marital deduction."			

7. S1 has left his estate to S2 but with the condition stated. For each case determine: (i) whether the bequest is a terminal interest ("T") or not ("NT"), (ii) whether it qualifies for the marital deduction (yes/no); and (iii) if yes, whether it is because of an exception to the terminal interest rule. Explain.

	condition placed on the bequest	T/NT	yes/no	explanation
(a)	"in trust, with S2 to receive income each year equal to 6% of the value of the trust, upon her death the trust is to be distributed to State University."			

(b)	"in trust, with all income to S2 for her lifetime, then to S1's children. The trustee has the absolute final say in the selection of investments."			
(c)	same as "b" but elsewhere in the trust it is written, "This trust is intended to qualify for the marital deduction."			

8. Explain why each of the following bequests to a surviving spouse would or would not qualify for a marital deduction:

(a) A bequest of a sum, not to exceed $100,000, that she could use to purchase a residence, provided she relinquish her dower (life estate) rights to decedent's home. She did relinquish the right within two months of S1's death, and the executor immediately paid $100,000 towards her purchase of a $160,000 home.

(b) Decedent's will gave S2 the right to elect either a life estate in S1's home or to take $100,000 outright. She chose the $100,000.

(c) Decedent's living trust left his entire estate in trust for S2. She had a power to appoint, at her death, the trust, to anyone, including to her own estate. The remainder went to their children if she did not exercise the power to appoint. The trustee could accumulate income if such was not needed for S2's reasonable support and maintenance. The trust had a corpus valued at $950,000. Decedent's pour-over will left his property, in trust, to the trustee of his living trust. They also held $300,000 in a joint bank account; the source of this money was an inheritance from the decedent's parents. Consider both the trust, specifically § 2056(b)(5), and the bank account, § 2040. With the latter, what effect does the pour-over will have?

(d) When he died in 2005, Decedent left his entire $2,500,000 estate to his only son, with a provision that if his son died it would go to his son's issue by right of representation. Because of a pre-nuptial agreement, S2 could not claim a dower interest. The son, who had no issue, disclaimed so much of the estate as exceeded the AEA, by writing a letter to S1's executor stating, "My father should not have disinherited my mother. I hereby refuse to accept any of my father's estate that is in excess of the AEA and I assign that excess to my mother." The probate court accepted this as a valid assignment of the son's interest in the probate property that exceeded $1,000,000 in value and, at the conclusion of the probate, ordered the excess ($500,000) distributed to S2. Review IRC § 2518 to determine whether this qualifies as a tax effective disclaimer and therefore qualifies for the marital deduction. Would your answer change if the son had issue at the time of his father's death and when he wrote the letter to the executor?

9. Explain why each of the following would or would not qualify for the QTIP election.
(a) An estate plan drafted in 1976, created at S1's death in 2006 a trust holding S1's entire estate worth a net of $2,500,000. The trust required that all income be distributed at least annually to S2. After S2's death the property was to be distributed to the couple's issue by right of representation. The independent trustee was given the power to distribute corpus to S2, if the trustee thought the income was insufficient for her happiness.
(b) The same facts as in "a" except the trustee could also distribute funds to pay medical bills or educational expenses of the couple's children.
(c) The couple's estate plan was an ABC Trust plan. Decedent's estate had a net worth of $4,000,000 consisting mainly of undeveloped land. Terms of the trust, that also applied to Trust C, said that the trustee would not be liable for failing to diversify investments, or for continuing to hold property that was in trust at the time of the settlor's death, or for failing to make such property productive. In giving an answer, you should consider both how this "absolution from liability" clause might be interpreted and state marital deduction-savings statutes that might help. A weaseling answer would be good.
(d) The couple had an ABC Trust plan. S1's estate was worth $4,000,000 and S2's estate was worth about the same. Although Trust C had a provision giving S2 income for life, it also said that, in the event S2 became mentally incompetent, the trustee could directly pay S2's bills for living expenses and accumulate any funds not needed. The executor of S1's estate QTIPed all of Trust C. S2 died 11 months after S1's death. S1's executor has filed an amended 706 that states the QTIP was claimed in error because Trust C could not qualify for the QTIP election. The executor attached a check for the estate tax. Was the executor right? What benefits are sought by the executor?

10. For the 100% marital deduction describe (a) the major advantages and (b) the major disadvantages.

11. Assuming a wealthy couple had a simple 100% marital deduction plan when S1 died, explain how each of the following defer or reduce the estate tax for S2: (a) remarriage; (b) consumption; or (c) gifts. (d) Explain the drawbacks to each of these estate planning devices.

12. (a) In 2007, what is the largest net estate that a husband and wife can transfer to their children, estate tax-free, with an AEA bypass plan? (b) Does it make any difference how much is owned by each spouse? Explain.

13. In multi-trust estate plans, why is Trust A often called the survivor's trust?

14. In multi-trust plans, when and why is Trust B likely to be called the credit shelter trust? Under what circumstances are taxes likely to be paid from it? Why is it unlikely that taxes will be paid from it at S2's death, even if it exceeds the AEA for that year?

15. In ABC Trust plans, Trust B funding is likely to be defined as "an amount that uses up the available unified credit" rather than in specific dollar terms. Use the changes made by EGTRRA and the possibility of taxable gifts to explain why it is defined in this manner.

16. One spouse has considerable wealth and the other very modest wealth.
(a) Why is an AEA bypass plan a "hit or miss" arrangement?
(b) What is the minimum amount of property that each spouse must own to assure a bypass plan will work?
(c) What change could the couple make that would remove the "hit and miss" aspect of the plan?
(d) Regarding the change in part c, how much should be involved?
(e) What factors help determine whether a bypass should entail an outright transfer or a transfer into trust? Is estate tax savings a factor? Why or why not?

17. (a) What is the purpose of the QTIP election? Identify three estate planning benefits accomplished by its use. (b) In what sense is the QTIP election a "trade-off"? What must S1's executor consider? What factors favor one choice over the other?

18. In an ABC plan, what problem is created if S2 is given a power over Trust C to invade corpus for "health, education, maintenance, support, or happiness"? Is it a serious problem if S1's executor intends to QTIP Trust C? If the executor wants to preserve the QTIP option during a six-month extension period for filing the estate tax return, the executor should recommend S2 take what course of action?

19. In an ABC plan, what determines whether it is Trust C or Trust B that is likely to be named the Residuary Trust?

20. Complete the six steps discussed in the chapter. When S1 died in 2006, the couple had an ABC estate plan and his executor wants to equalize the two taxable estates. As part of step one note the values of the three trusts. S1 had separate property of $5,340,000, their community property was worth $1,650,000, and S2's separate property was worth $1,824,000. When S1 died S2 was in very poor health and died in 2007. At the time of her death, the value of the trusts were: Trust A = $2,755,000; Trust B = $1,890,000; and Trust C = $3,950,000.

21. When S1 died in 2005 the couple had an AB estate plan with property as shown:

At S1's death:		(a) Show the value of S1's estate.
S1's SP	$4,000,000	(b) Show the value of each trust after S1's death.
their CP	$800,000	(c) What is S2's taxable estate if at her death in
S2's SP	$1,600,000	2007 the trusts have the following values:
		A $4,700,000 and B $1,700,000.
		(d) How much estate tax is saved by using the AB trust when compared to leaving all the property outright to S2?

22. When S1 died in 2005 the couple had an AB estate plan with property as shown:

At S1's death:		(a) Show the value of S1's estate.
S1's SP	$1,600,000	(b) Show the value of each trust after S1's death.
their CP	$800,000	(c) What is S2's taxable estate if at her death in 2007 the trusts
S2's SP	$4,000,000	have the following values: A $4,700,000 and B $1,700,000.

(d) Compare this problem with the prior problem. In the prior problem the wealthy spouse died first whereas this time the less wealthy one died first, yet the taxable estates remain the same. Explain.

23. When S1 died in 2005 the couple had an ABC estate plan with property as shown below. At S1's death his executor elected to QTIP all of Trust C.

At S1's death:		(a) Show the value of S1's estate.
S1's SP	$5,000,000	(b) Show the value of each trust after S1's death.
their CP	$1,200,000	(c) What is S2's taxable estate if at her death in 2007 the trusts have the following values:
S2's SP	$1,600,000	A $2,400,000, B $1,600,000, and C $4,428,000.

(d) Calculate the estate tax.
(e) Calculate the tax owed had all the property been left outright to S2 and show the savings.

24. Same as in the prior problem except S1's executor did not make a QTIP election. Assume that "c" still correctly states the values of the trusts at S2's death in 2007.
(a) What is S1's taxable estate?
(b) How much tax would be owed at his death?
(c) What is the tax at S1's death?
(d) What is the tax at S2's death and the total taxes for both estates?

25. Same as in the prior problem except S1's executor desired a taxable estate equal to one-half of the couple's combined wealth. Assume that "c" still correctly states the values of the trusts at S2's death in 2007.
(a) What QTIP fraction would accomplish this?

(b) Show how the fraction is applied to Trust C to arrive at S1's desired taxable estate.

(c) What is the tax at S1's death?

(d) What is the tax at S2's death and the total taxes for both estates?

26. Same as in the prior problem except 1's executor desired a taxable estate equal to $2,340,000. Assume that "c" still correctly states the values of the trusts at S2's death in 2007.

(a) What QTIP fraction would accomplish this?

(b) Show how the fraction is applied to Trust C to arrive at S1's desired taxable estate.

(c) What is the tax at S1's death?

(d) What is the tax at S2's death and the total taxes for both estates?

27. For the prior set of problems, given S1's estate, what is the lowest taxable estate that S1's executor would choose? The highest taxable estate that could be chosen? Explain.

28. When S1 died in 2005, the couple had an ABC estate plan. At S1's death his executor elected to QTIP all of Trust C. At S1's death:

At S1's death:	
S1's SP	$7,000,000
S2's SP	$3,800,000

(a) Show the value of S1's estate.

(b) Show the value of each trust after S1's death.

(c) What is S2's taxable estate if at her death in 2007 the trusts have the following values: A $4,200,000, B $1,300,000, and C $6,500,000.

(d) Calculate the estate tax.

(e) Calculate the tax owed had all the property been left outright to S2 and show the savings.

29. Same as in the prior problem but S1's executor did not make a QTIP election. Assume that "c" correctly states the values of the trusts at S2's death in 2007.

(a) What is S1's taxable estate?

(b) What is the tax at S1's death?

(c) What is the tax at S2's death?

(d) What is the total tax for both estates?

30. Same as in the prior problem but S1's executor desired a taxable estate equal to $4,300,000.
    (a) What QTIP fraction would accomplish this?
    (b) What is the tax at S1's death?
    (c) What is the tax at S2's death?
    (d) What is the total tax for both estates?

31. In 2000, Robert made a $410,000 gift to his son Max. When he died in 2006, his entire estate, net value of $4,500,000, was placed in an irrevocable trust for his wife, Anna, with the remainder to Max. Anna was given a life estate and the right to withdraw corpus based on the ascertainable standard related to health, education, support, or maintenance. The executor of Robert's estate QTIPed the portion of the trust that exceeded the available exclusion amount. When Anna died in 2007, the trust had grown to $5,000,000. Anna had little property of her own. (a) What trust or trusts (A, B, C, etc.) is Robert's trust most like? (b) Determine how much of this trust must be included in Anna's estate.

32. Carol died in 2003, leaving an estate worth $2,800,000 net of debts and expenses. Her estate plan established a single irrevocable trust for her husband, Bob, with the remainder going to her two children by a prior marriage. Bob's estate plan leaves his estate to a federally recognized charity. The executor would like to postpone all taxes until after the death of Bob. (a) What is the QTIP fraction that accomplishes postponement without wasting any of Carol's AEA? (b) If Bob died in 2006, calculate the trust value that would produce a taxable estate that equals the applicable exclusion amount.

ANSWERS TO THE QUESTIONS AND PROBLEMS *(odd numbered only)*

1. Estate size: (a) a spouse - no limit if S2 is a U.S. citizen, otherwise, only the AEA, e.g., $2,000,000 if S1 died in 2007. The decedent still has the use of a unified credit even if S2 is not a citizen; (b) Others? Explain. The AEA for the year of death, e.g., $2,000,000 for deaths in 2007. This is reduced by any AEA used up during life due to post-76 taxable gifts. There is no limit if the giving is to a charity.

3. Marital deduction over the years, entire estate to S2:

year	S1's net estate	marital deduction	taxable estate
1940	$800,000	zero	$800,000
1960	$800,000	*$400,000*	*$400,000*
1980	$400,000	*$250,000*	*$150,000*
1980	*$200,000	*$50,000*	*$150,000*
2000	$2,000,000	*$2,000,000*	*$2,000,000*

   *S1's ½ of the community property

5. No marital deduction is allowed unless S2's interest is vested. Congress was concerned that a marital deduction might be allowed even though the transfer did not benefit the surviving spouse and that the property might then pass to someone else without being taxed. (a) The six months survivorship clause. If S2 makes it, the property is in S2's estate. If S2 does not make it, then no MD. (b) The transfer to a general power of appointment trust. The GPA causes the trust to be included in S2's estate. (c) The transfer to a QTIP trust, with a QTIP election. If no election is made, no MD. If it is made, then the QTIP portion is taxed at S2's death. (d) The pension to the surviving spouse automatic QTIP election. The surviving spouse collects the pension for his or her life, and the PV of the remaining payments are included in S2's estate when S2 dies. (e) Income for a term for S2, with remainder to a charity exception. The only beneficiaries are S2 and ultimately the charity.

7. Conditional bequests and the marital deduction:

	condition placed on the bequest	T/NT	yes/no	section/explanation
(a)	"in trust, with S2 to receive income each year equal to 6% of the value of the trust, upon her death the trust is to be distributed to State University."	T	yes	*annuity with remainder to a charity §2056(b)(8)*
(b)	"in trust, with all income to S2 for her lifetime, then to S1's children. The trustee has the absolute final say in the selection of investments."	T	no	*the trustee can invest in nonproductive assets thereby taking away S2's income for life*
(c)	same as "b" but elsewhere in the trust it is written, "This trust is intended to qualify for the marital deduction."	T	prob-ably	*This should make §2056(b)(7) available since the trustee could be forced to invest in income producing assets*

9. Qualifying for the QTIP election: (a) Even pre-QTIP law trusts can qualify for the QTIP election, provided they meet the QTIP requirements; this one does. Note that the power to distribute to S2 does not create any problem; a QTIP trust cannot allow distributions to anyone other than S2 during S2's lifetime.

(b) For the reasons given for "a" the possibility of appointment to someone other than S2 causes the trust to not qualify. Perhaps all of the children will make a tax effective disclaimer (see § 2518) of this potential benefit, in which case it would qualify.

(c) If the language is interpreted to mean that the trustees need not invest in productive property even if S2 so requests; then S2 is deprived of an income interest, and a QTIP election is not available. If the language merely protects the trustee from liability in the event the value of the property goes down (or fails to keep up with other reasonable investments), even though prudence would have suggested diversification, the QTIP should be available. Many states have laws that give the surviving spouse the right to compel the trustee to make the property productive in the absence of language to the contrary in the trust document. Those states that have such laws generally compel interpretation of vague language, such as discussed here, in such a way as to obtain the marital deduction if it is clear from the overall estate plan that such was the intent of the estate plan. Since this language is applied to Trust C, a trust intended to qualify for the marital deduction, the clause would be given the interpretation that S2 could compel the trustee to make the property productive, e.g., develop it or sell it and re-invest in income earning investments.

(d) Probably so. S2 did not have a vested life estate since, under some circumstances, the trustee had authority to accumulate income. The executor seeks to undo the QTIP and pay some taxes on S1's death (in light of S2's death so soon), thereby using the lower rates of S1's estate and setting S2's estate up for the benefit of a prior transfer credit.

11. (a) Remarriage: another marital deduction, including possibly using a lifetime QTIP gift, if the new spouse is old and poor. (b) Consumption: spend it and it is not there for the taxman. (c) Gifts: using annual exclusion and/or unified credit of the survivor gets some portion of the estate transferred tax-free (annual exclusion amounts) and any future appreciation avoids tax. (d) Explain the drawbacks to each of these estate planning devices. It's obvious, but still worth thinking about. Remarriage: S2 might disinherit the children of the first marriage, or at least make them wait until the new spouse dies before they come into their inheritance. Consumption: Unless it is spent on the kids, they hate to see too much of that wealth disappear. Generally, no one likes to see his or her wealth decrease. Gifts: parallel comments as to consumption.

13. It generally is funded with S2's property, and even if some of the corpus has as its source property from S1, S2 has a general power of appointment over the trust. Indeed, in many estate plans she can revoke the trust, withdrawing all corpus.

15. Even with plans that have Trust B as an AEA shelter trust, it might be more or less than the AEA that existed when the estate plan was drafted. The TRA '97 has greatly increased the AEA. By using language that funds the trust based on available unified credit, the documents do not have to be changed whenever Congress increases the unified credit. If the settlor has made taxable gifts post-76, some of the unified credit will have been used up. Likewise, if some of S1's estate is left to someone other than to S2 or to a charity, that bequest will use up unified credit, thus reducing Trust B.

17. It allows the excess of S1's estate over his or her exclusion amount to: 1. qualify for the marital deduction, 2. provide support for the surviving spouse through a life estate, while 3. allowing S1 to maintain control over who will ultimately receive the corpus of his/her (trust C) estate. (b) The executor of S1's estate must decide between paying the taxes at the first death and paying them when S2 dies. The executor must consider the time value of money (which favors paying the taxes later) and whether it is worth it to use S1's lower marginal rates and perhaps gaining a PTC for S2 (these two require paying taxes early, i.e., after S1's death). Finally, the likelihood that estate tax will be reduced or eliminated would suggest postponing the taxes.

19. Trust C is called the Residuary Trust if Trust B is defined in pecuniary terms so as to match the applicable exclusion amount, because the residue of S1's estate after funding Trust B flows into Trust C. If the amount going to Trust C is defined as the minimum marital deduction amount necessary to avoid death taxes, then Trust B will be the residuary trust.

21. (a) ½ S1 SP + ½ CP = $4,400,000
(b) A $4,900,000 B $1,500,000
(c) Just trust A, i.e., $4,700,000.
(d) Assuming the total value was $6,400,000, tax saved is at the top marginal rate for 2007, i.e., $1,700,000 * 45% = $765,000

23. (a) ½ S1 SP + ½ CP = $5,600,000.
(b) Tr A $2,200,000; Tr B $1,500,000; Tr C $4,100,000. Note, B + C = S1's taxable estate.
(c) Tr A + Tr C = $6,828,000

(d) $2,172,600

(e) Assuming the total value is 8,428,000, the estate tax is $2,892,600.

25. (a) Desired taxable estate is $3,900,000. QTIP fraction = $1,700,000/$4,100,000

(b) $5,600,000 - ($1,700,000/$4,100,000) * $4,100,000 = $3,900,000

(c) Tax on $3,900,000 for 2005 is $1,118,000

(d) S2's estate is Tr A + QTIP fraction * Tr C = $2,400,000 + ($1,700,000/$4,100,000) * $4,428,000 = $4,236,000. Tax on this is $1,006,200. Total taxes: $2,124,200.

27. The lowest would be equal to the AEA for 2005, i.e., $1,500,000, since there is no reason to waste S1's unified credit. The highest would be $5,600,000 where one would not make a QTIP election. The latter makes little sense because estate tax would be lessened by QTIPing to equalize the estates (especially since S1's estate is considerably larger than S2's estate) or QTIPing to postpone all tax until after S2's death.

29. (a) $7,000,000 (what he owned with no marital deduction)

(b) Tax on $7 million in 2005: $2,575,000

(c) Tr A only, so tax on $4,200,000 in 2007: $990,000

(d) $3,565,000.

31. (a) It is most like a combined BC Trust in that it both utilizes Robert's remaining AEA [i.e., Trust B] and qualifies for the QTIP [i.e., Trust C]. (b) To avoid tax the taxable estate had to be equal to the available AEA, i.e., $2,000,000 - $400,000 = $1,600,000. Hence, $4,500,000 - $1,600,000 gives $2,900,000 as the marital deduction. The QTIP fraction = $2,900,000/$4,500,000. This fraction times the DOD value of $5,000,000 equals $3,222,222.

ENDNOTES

1. IRC § 2010.

2. IRC §§ 2053 and 2054.

3. IRC § 812(e)(1)(B) of the 1939 Code.

4. IRC§ 2056(b)(1).

5. IRC § 2056(b)(3).

6. IRC § 2056(b)(5).

7. IRC § 2056(b)(7).

8. IRC § 2056(b)(7)(B).

9. IRC § 2044.

10. *Economic Growth and Tax Relief Reconciliation Act of 2001*, §901. Sunset of Provisions of Act.

11. IRC § 2013 and Reg. § 20.2013 - 4, Example (2).

12. IRC § 2041(b)(1)

13. IRC § 2056(b)(5).

14. Reg. § 20.2056(b)-5(f)(5)

15. IRC § 664.

16. Reg. § 20.2056(b)-8(2)

17. IRC § 2036(b)(7).

18. IRC § 2044.

19. Reg. § 20.2056(b)-(7)(d)(2) by reference back to quoted language of Reg. § 20.2056(b)-5f.

20. IRC § 2044.

21. $\dfrac{Trust\ C}{Trust\ C} = 1$

22. $\dfrac{0}{Trust\ C} = 0$

CHAPTER 10

Advanced Bypass and Marital Trusts

OVERVIEW

This chapter continues the discussion of marital deduction and bypass planning, starting with variations on the basic trust plans described in the last chapter, followed by a review of a couple older plans seen now only in estate planning museums. The prior transfer tax credit's rather surprising application to bypass trusts is explained. The chapter concludes with a discussion of estate planning for wealthy couples where one spouse (or both) is not a citizen of the U.S.

VARIATIONS ON A THEME

There are variations on the AB Trust and the ABC Trust plans that may better suit certain families, yet use both unified credits and, like the ABC plan, keep the option at the first death of paying estate taxes or deferring them to the second death. Recent variations, developed in response to the Economic Growth and Tax Relief Reconciliation Act of 2001 (EGTRRA), take into account the increasing applicable exclusion amount (AEA) that shelters ever larger estates and the eventual elimination of the estate tax.

THE AsuperB TRUST PLAN

The AsuperB Trust plan has Trust A defined as all S2's property and Trust B defined as all S1's property. It is simpler than the ABC plan as there is one less trust, and given the absence of any reference to a separate applicable exclusion amount trust (AEA trust), it may be more readily understood by clients. The AB Trust plan takes an automatic marital deduction for the property in excess of the AEA because that excess is transferred from S1's estate into Trust A; however, the AsuperB plan allows the executor of S1's estate to decide (via QTIP) whether to pay taxes at the first death or to postpone them until the second death.

Trust B must have all the QTIP attributes that allow a QTIP election if it is desired, i.e., mainly income for life for S2 and no power to appoint to anyone other than S2 during S2's lifetime. Of course utilization of S1's unified credit is important so, even if one wished to pay no taxes, the executor would use that QTIP fraction for Trust B that would reduce S1's taxable estate to the available AEA. Once again, the six-step process is used, starting with determining the optimal taxable estate at S1's death.

> EXAMPLE 10 - 1. When S1 died in the year 2002, the couple's AsuperB Trust plan gave S2 a life estate in Trust B, plus a power to withdraw corpus that was limited to an ascertainable standard. At S2's death, Trust B property is distributed to S1's children by a prior marriage. Trust A is revocable by S2, and her children by a prior marriage are the remaindermen. Their combined net worth was $3,877,250, of which S1's property, worth $2,843,760, was allocated to Trust superB, and S2's property, worth $1,033,490, was allocated to Trust A. To postpone all taxes until S2's death, the executor of S1's estate wants to QTIP Trust B to bring S1's taxable estate to $1,000,000.
>
> Step 1. The desired taxable estate for S1 = $1,000,000.
>
> Step 2. Determine the QTIP MD: Total estate – Desired taxable estate = QTIP MD.
> $$\$2,843,760 - \$1,000,000 = \$1,843,760$$
>
> Step 3. For the AsuperB plan there is no separate AEA trust, therefore Trust B is the QTIP property, i.e., S1's estate = Trust B (the superB) = the QTIP property = $2,843,760.

Step 4. Create a fraction with the QTIP MD (Step 2) over the QTIP property (Trust superB) to arrive at the QTIP fraction.

$$\frac{QTIP\ MD}{Trust\ B} = \frac{\$1,843,760}{\$2,843,760} = QTIP\ Fraction$$

Step 5. S1's taxable estate is S1's total estate less the product of the QTIP property and the QTIP fraction.

$$S2\text{'s taxable estate} = Trust\ A + (\frac{QTIP\ MD}{Trust\ B} * Trust\ B)$$

Therefore, S1's TxE = $2,843,760 - $1,843,760 = $1,000,000.

Step 6. Assume that S2 dies in 2007, and that Trust A is then worth $1,137,642 and Trust B is then worth $3,117,970. At S2's death, the total estate is equal to all of Trust A plus the QTIP fraction multiplied by the amount then in Trust B.

$$S1\text{'s taxable estate} = total\ estate - (\frac{QTIP\ MD}{Trust\ B} * Trust\ B)$$

S2's taxable estate is:

$$S2\text{'s TxE} = \$1,137,642 + \frac{\$1,843,760}{\$2,843,760} * \$3,117,970$$

$$= \$3,159,187$$

Of course, S1's executor can make a partial QTIP that equalizes the estates if that produces a better result than either making a partial QTIP to defer all taxes or making no QTIP election (resulting in a tax on all of Trust B). If S1's executor was very certain that S2 was going to die shortly after S1 (or if S2 had already died when S1's executor was preparing the estate tax return) the QTIP might be made to equalize the two estates.

EXAMPLE 10 - 2: Using the same values from the previous example, equal estates at S1's death would be:

Step 1. Start by dividing the total of both estates by two:

$$\frac{S1\text{'s E} + S2\text{'s E}}{2} = \frac{\$2,843,760 + \$1,033,490}{2} = \$1,938,625$$

Step 2. Determine the QTIP MD: Total estate – Desired taxable estate = QTIP MD amount = $2,843,760 - $1,938,625 = $905,135

Step 3. Trust B is the QTIP property, i.e., S1's estate = Trust B (the superB) = the QTIP property = $2,843,760.

Step 4. Create a fraction with the QTIP MD (Step 2) over the QTIP property (Trust superB) to arrive at the QTIP fraction.

$$\frac{\$905,135}{\$2,843,760} = QTIP\ Fraction$$

Step 5. S1's taxable estate is S1's total estate less the product of Trust B and the QTIP fraction.

$$S1's\ taxable\ estate = \$2,843,760 - (\frac{\$905,135}{\$2,843,760} * \$2,843,760)$$

$$= \$2,843,760 - \$905,135 = \$1,938,625$$

Step 6. S2's estate includes all Trust A, plus the QTIP fraction times Trust B (valued at S2's death):

$$S2's\ TxE. = \$1,137,642 + \frac{\$905,135}{\$2,843,760} * \$3,117,970 = \$2,130,055$$

There are several reasons a couple might prefer the AsuperB plan over the AB plan. S1 may not want to have property in excess of the AEA pass into S2's control, as must happen with the AB plan, yet their total estate might be just approaching, or be just slightly greater than, the AEA. For a couple in that situation, an ABC plan, with the complicating factor of the third trust, might be overplanning. For instance, if S1 died with an ABC estate plan in 2006, leaving a net estate worth $2,075,000, Trust B would be funded with assets worth $2,000,000 and Trust C with assets worth a mere $75,000; both trusts would have to file state and federal income tax returns each year, and the trustees would have to maintain separate accounts for each trust. With the AsuperB plan, Trust B would be funded with assets worth $2,075,000 and there would be no Trust C. If the executor chose to postpone estate taxes, the QTIP fraction would be $75,000/$2,075,000. For an elderly couple whose combined estate is over one AEA but less than two AEAs, given that there is a high probability that S2's estate will be under the ever increasing AEA, the simpler but equally effective AsuperB plan might be preferred to the ABC plan. If, at S1's death, the superB Trust is slightly, or even greatly, above the AEA, a partial QTIP can be used to defer taxes.

Even for large estates there is at least one advantage in the AsuperB as compared to the ABC Trust, but it comes with a trade-off. The funding provisions of most ABC plans define either the B Trust or the C Trust as a pecuniary bequest, e.g., "After the death of the first Settlor, the trustee shall allocate to Trust B property equal in value to that amount which will be needed to increase the taxable estate to the largest amount that will not result in a federal estate tax being imposed on the deceased Settlor's estate after allowing for available unified credit." The "equal in amount" language translates into dollar terms, e.g. $2,000,000 if the first death occurs in 2006; therefore it is a pecuniary bequest. Where, as usually happens, it takes months, and occasionally years, for the trustee to allocate the assets in the family trust (or for the probate estate to obtain an order for distribution) to the separate trusts, the values are likely to be very different from those at the date of death. Where a pecuniary bequest is funded with assets that have appreciated in value, the difference between the basis (the date-of-death value or alternative date value) and the fair market value on the date of funding is a capital gain to the family trust (or to the probate estate) making the transfer. Since the gain occurs when the family trust (or probate estate) is terminating, the gain is passed on to the pecuniary trust, which must then pay taxes on the gain. Of course, the trust would then have a basis in those assets equal to their fair market value at the time of funding. If property used to fund the trust has decreased in value between S1's death and funding, no loss is recognized because the family trust and the pecuniary trust (B or C) are considered related parties. The superB Trust avoids the problem of gain recognition because it is not defined in pecuniary terms but rather in terms of "all S1's property."

Many plans using multiple trusts give all tangible personal property (cars, furniture, etc.) to S2 or to the trustee of S2's Trust A. Since such property is not investment property, it might be best to allow S2 to control those assets without any need to account for them to the remaindermen.

THE AB WITH DISCLAIMER TO C TRUST PLAN

A wealthy couple with a long and trusting marriage, with no children by prior marriages, might prefer that the first to die transfer his or her entire estate to the survivor; trusting the survivor to eventually take care of the children and the grandchildren. Nevertheless, they would most likely want to at least use the shelter of a bypass trust to utilize S1's AEA, thus the AB Trust plan would seem ideal, but it has drawbacks. Because the marital deduction is automatic for property transferred from S1's estate into Trust A, the AB plan does not allow sophisticated postmortem planning, such as the equalization of estates or some other apportionment between the two taxable estates, whereas the AB with disclaimer into C Trust plan (ABdC) does allow the postmortem manipulation of relative size of the two taxable estates. This plan begins by defining Trust B as the AEA trust, with S1's estate in excess of the AEA left to the trustee of Trust A (who also holds S2's property). So far this sounds just like the modern AB Trust plan, however this one adds a provision that any of S1's property in excess of the AEA that is disclaimed by S2 will be transferred to Trust C, a QTIP trust.

A disclaimer is tax effective (or "qualified") if it is done so that the disclaimant (S2) is not treated as having made a taxable gift. In general, to be tax effective, the person making the disclaimer must act within nine months of the interest's creation, he or she cannot "direct" to whom the property goes, nor can he or she receive any benefit from the property disclaimed. IRC § 2518(b)(4)(A) creates an exception to the "no-benefit" rule and allows an interest disclaimed that passes "to the spouse of the decedent" to qualify as a tax effective disclaimer. Thus, the surviving spouse (S2) can receive income from the disclaimer trust (Trust C), can be given a 5 & 5 power, or can be the holder of a power to withdraw that is limited by an ascertainable standard. None of these "benefits" cause a disclaimer by a surviving spouse to be treated as a taxable gift. Furthermore, none of the benefits will cause the disclaimer trust to be included in S2's estate. However, a 5 & 5 power will cause the inclusion in S2's estate of that small portion of the trust that could have been withdrawn just before her death had she exercised the power.

Since the disclaimant cannot direct where the disclaimed property goes, this Trust C, unlike the one in the ABC plan, must not give S2 even a limited power to appoint the property. Remember, for the typical ABC Trust, flexibility is enhanced by giving S2 a limited power to appoint Trust C corpus at her death.

The disclaimer is most likely to be used where, due to S2's poor health or extreme old age, S2 is not likely to live for very long after S1's death. Since the decision to disclaim is not made until after S1's death, the assessment of S2's health is not to be made until that time. However, § 2518 requires that the decision of whether to disclaim must be made within nine months immediately following S1's death.

EXAMPLE 10 - 3. When S1 died in 2005, the couple had an ABdC Trust. It gave S2 a life estate in Trust B, plus a power to withdraw corpus limited to an ascertainable standard, and she was given a limited power to appoint Trust B corpus among their children. In the absence of exercise of the power the remainder would be distributed to their issue. Trust A was revocable by S2, and, to the extent she does not appoint it, the remainder also goes to their issue. Their combined net worth was $5,831,010, with S1's property worth $4,360,790 and S2's property worth $1,470,220. No disclaimer was made. Trust B received $1,500,000 from S1's estate, and the rest, plus all S2's property, was added to Trust A, giving it a value of $4,331,010. Since the property in excess of the AEA went to Trust A, the estate automatically received a $2,860,790 marital deduction, thereby reducing S1's taxable estate to $1,500,000.

EXAMPLE 10 - 4. Suppose, after S1's death in 2005, it was determined that S2 was in very poor health and was not likely to live more than two or three years. With this prospect, S2 disclaimed all S1's estate in excess of the AEA with the result that it went into Trust C instead of into Trust A. The three trusts are valued as follows: Trust A $1,470,220; Trust B $1,500,000; and Trust C $2,860,790. S1's executor could then QTIP 100% of Trust C to postpone all taxes until after S2's death, but doing so would create very unequal estates. This would be foolish, given that avoiding the tax at S1's death loses the prospect of obtaining a prior transfer credit for S2's estate. Therefore, the executor of S1's estate would QTIP Trust C so as to equalize the two estates. (You should be able to identify the six-step process even though some steps are combined.)

$$\frac{S1's\,E + S2's\,E}{2} = \frac{\$4,360,790 + \$1,470,220}{2} = \$2,915,505$$

The QTIP election necessary to reduce S1's estate from $4,360,790 to $2,915,505 is:

$$QTIP\ MD = \frac{\$1,445,285}{\$2,860,790} * \$2,860,790 = \$1,445,285$$

Therefore, taxable estates as of S1's death are:

$$S1'sE = \$4,360,790 - \$1,445,285 = 2,915,505\ and$$
$$S2'sE = \$1,470,220 + \frac{\$1,445,285}{\$2,860,790} * \$2,860,790 = \$2,915,505$$

With the ABdC plan the equalization (or some other allocation between the two estates) can be accomplished by S2 (or S2's executor) making a partial disclaimer sufficient to equalize the two estates and S1's executor forgoing the QTIP election. Using this approach, Trust B plus Trust C equals S1's desired taxable estate and Trust C is the amount that must be disclaimed to arrive at the desired estate. Hence, simple algebra gives us:

Disclaimed amount = Trust C

Trust C = desired taxable estate - Trust B

EXAMPLE 10 - 5. S2's executor in the preceding example could simply disclaim that portion of S1's estate that would result in the two estates being equal in value as of S1's death. The desired estate equals $2,915,505. Since Trust B will equal the AEA for 2005, i.e., $1,500,000, Trust C must equal $1,415,505, which is the amount that must be disclaimed by S2. Trust A is worth $2,915,505 [$1,470,220 + $1,445,285)], Trust B is worth $1,500,000, and Trust C is worth $1,415,505 [$4,360,790 - $1,445,285 - $1,500,000].

Although the above example equalizes the estates, any allocation can be achieved with the one constraint that Trusts B and C cannot exceed S1's estate. If S1's estate is smaller than the desired taxable estate, S2 (or her executor) should disclaim all S1's estate because doing so will result in S1's estate being as close to the desired estate as possible. Given that the top marginal rate is reached at a taxable estate of $2,000,000, there is no reason to have S1's taxable estate above that level, if the sole purpose is to utilize lower marginal rates. Since, after 2005, the estate AEA is $2,000,000 or more, the only reason to generate a tax in S1's estate will be to obtain a prior transfer credit (PTC) for S2's estate. As will be explained later in the chapter, a PTC based upon S2's life estate in trusts created by S1 is available only if she outlives him by a year and, since the PTC phases out, less than ten years.

EXAMPLE 10 - 6. S1 and S2 had an ABdC estate plan. When S1 died in September of 2005, his estate was worth $6,100,000. S2 died in August of 2006, leaving an estate of $1,900,000. Although no PTC was available, in order to use the lower marginal rates available to S1's estate, the executor of S2's estate considered disclaiming $500,000 of S1's estate. With the disclaimer, S1's taxable estate is exactly $2,000,000 and S2's is approximately $6,000,000. Without the disclaimer they are $1,500,000 and $6,500,000, respectively. Comparing the two outcomes, only $5,000 is saved by the disclaimer but this does not take into account the opportunity loss of having to pay $225,000 eight months earlier than if all taxes are postponed until nine months after S2's death. With this information, S2's executor decides not to disclaim any of S1's estate. With S1's estate at $1,500,000 and S2's at $6,500,000 the estate tax was $2,070,000. Use the ETAX program to verify these results.

EXAMPLE 10 - 7. In the prior example, if S2 died in October of 2006 a PTC would be available; hence S1 and S2 had an ABdC estate plan. In order to use the PTC, the executor of S2's estate must use a disclaimer (done within nine months of S1's death) to generate an estate tax for S1's estate. To create two equal estates, the executor would disclaim $2,500,000 which would go into Trust C, Trust B would receive the AEA amount of $1,500,000, and Trust A the balance of $4,000,000. S1's estate would pay estate taxes of $1,165,000 on a taxable estate of $4,000,000. If the federal rate for valuing life estates was 6% and S2 was 75 when S1 died, the estate tax on her estate (Trust A) would be $920,000 reduced by a PTC of $505,715 to $414,285. Hence, the total tax for the two estates is $1,579,285 compared to $2,070,000 if the taxes had been postponed. The precise calculation of the PTC is explained as part of the problems at the end of the chapter.

A tax effective disclaimer must be delivered to S1's executor within nine months after S1's death, therefore, if S2's state of health is uncertain as that deadline approaches, S2 can make a disclaimer, and the decision as to whether Trust C should be QTIPed can be delayed a further six months by obtaining an extension to file the estate tax return, together with an extension to pay the tax. S2's poor health, and the need for additional time to assess the wisdom of making the QTIP election, is sufficient justification for the six-month extension. Six months is the longest allowed extension for filing the estate tax return if the executor is within the country.[1] Although it is possible to make a QTIP election on a late filed return, the penalties for late filing (if one decides to generate a tax at S1's death) might outweigh any benefits derived by splitting the tax between the two estates.

Choosing between the ABC plan and the ABdC plan is like choosing between varieties of apples rather than between apples and oranges. The main difference being that with the ABdC plan S2 decides whether to take control of S1's estate that exceeds the AEA, whereas S2 has no such option with the ABC plan. Although a limited power may be part of the ABC plan for both Trusts B and C, it can only be used with Trust B in the ABdC plan. Also, the ABdC Trust is a much more complicated plan to explain to clients. In those situations where a tax should be generated at the first death, it may be more difficult to carry out with the disclaimer plan if S2 is in poor health, whereas, with the ABC plan, it is S1's executor who makes the QTIP election.

For large estates using the ABC plan, where taxes might be saved by making a partial QTIP election but, because of the time value of money, the executor is leaning toward deferring the taxes until the second death, the executor is always well advised to obtain the six-month extension to allow the longest possible time to evaluate S2's health before making (or foregoing) the QTIP election. With the ABdC, the disclaimer must be made within nine months of S1's death or it is not tax effective, so it is not possible to get an extra six months to "wait and see." True, with an ABdC plan, S2 can always make a disclaimer that would accomplish the optimal split between the two taxable estates, and the executor of S1's estate could then wait until the six-month extension period is almost up to file the return, making or not making the QTIP election at that time (depending on S2's health), but that is a much more complicated way to create an ABC plan. Besides, as stated earlier, the ABdC plan must have a more restrictive Trust C, i.e., S2 must be denied a limited power of appointment. Furthermore, S2 might be too ill to make a disclaimer, a circumstance that might indicate that generating a tax in S1's estate would be wise. A court is likely to rule that the right to disclaim is personal to S2, so long as she is alive and might not allow a conservator to make a disclaimer on her behalf, whereas the decision to make a QTIP election rests with S1's executor. If S2 is nominated as executor of S1's estate but is too ill to serve, the alternate executor would be in a position to make the appropriate QTIP election with the regular ABC Trust plan.

A durable power of attorney, discussed later in this book, could be written for S2 with enough specificity to allow the holder of the power to make a disclaimer if S2 is too ill to do it herself. Unless there is specific language authorizing the agent to make a disclaimer, it might not withstand a challenge by the IRS that it was revocable by S2, if she were to regain her health. Of course, if S2 dies before the nine months are up, S2's executor can make the disclaimer, assuming he or she can be appointed by a court in time. Given that S2 is dead, the probate court is not likely to object to a disclaimer that is made to save death taxes, especially if the remaindermen of all trusts are the same people.

THE A WITH DISCLAIMER TO B TRUST PLAN

As the AEA increases, more wealthy couples are finding that one AEA is sufficient to cover their wealth. Furthermore, if they believe that one or both of them will outlive the estate tax, they may be less inclined to worry about sheltering a portion of the estate at the first death. Therefore, rather than having an AB or ABdC trust arrangement they are selecting a plan that at the first death has S1's property transferred to Trust A but gives S2 the option of sending it to a disclaimer Trust B if S2 so chooses, i.e., an A with a disclaimer to B Trust plan, or AdB Trust. Note that the AdB Trust should be used only if both spouses are comfortable with S2 having ultimate control over the estate, hence one would expect selection of this plan by couples with children from their present marriage only, especially if the marriage is a long one. It is less likely to appeal if there are children by prior marriages, the marriage has been short, or there is quite a disparity in the wealth brought to the marriage.

Trust A has the characteristics of the other A trusts we have discussed, e.g., a life estate for S2 and a general power to appoint the trust corpus. Trust B can have the characteristics of almost any of the B trusts we have discussed, depending on what the couple wants to accomplish. However, just as with the ABdC plan, S2 must not be given even a limited power over the disclaimer trust as such destroys the tax effectiveness of the disclaimer. Generally the couple seeks to maintain the option of using S1's AEA and the lower marginal rates in both estates in the event both die before 2010. Whether Trust B should have QTIP characteristics or be a sprinkling trust depends on the circumstances. In many cases it will not matter. If both deaths occurred because of an accident, one could create taxable estates about equal in value by having S2's executor disclaim property. Obviously if S2's estate is larger than S1's, the executor should disclaim all S1's property. If S2's estate is smaller than S1's, the executor should disclaim just enough to make them equal. If after the disclaimer both trusts are worth less than the AEA, a Trust B that does not qualify for the QTIP election makes no difference since no additional marital deduction is necessary to avoid tax at the first death. The main reason one might want a Trust B that qualifies for the QTIP is that disclaimers must be made within nine months of the first death, whereas a QTIP can be made on an extended return filed six months later.

> EXAMPLE 10 - 8. When S1 died in 2005, the couple had an AdB estate plan. S1's estate was worth $2.8 million and S2's $1.4 million. Although she felt well, S2 was 90 years old so she decided to disclaim so much of S1's estate as exceeded his AEA. The $1.5 million that went into Trust B used S1's unified credit, hence no tax was paid. Without the disclaimer, S1's AEA would have been wasted. Trust A, initially valued at $2.7 million, might escape taxation if S2 survives to 2009.

EXAMPLE 10 - 9. When S1 died in 2006, the couple had an AdB estate plan. S1's estate was worth $1,600,000 and S2's $1,800,000. Because she was in poor health, S2 decided to disclaim all S1's estate. Trust A, initially valued at $1,800,000, is less likely to grow above one AEA before S2 dies. Also, less will be subject to tax if she lives beyond 2010 and the AEA actually falls back to $1,000,000.

Giving a disclaimer Trust B the characteristics of the superB trust previously described, e.g., a life estate for S2, might make it possible to claim a prior transfer tax credit on S2's tax return. Maintaining this option is important if the combined estates are significantly greater than two AEAs and if either spouse is very elderly or in poor health as a PTC might greatly reduce S2's estate tax.

EXAMPLE 10 - 10. When S1 died in May of 2005, the couple had an AdB estate plan. The Trust B gave all income to S2 for her lifetime. S1's estate was worth $5.6 million and S2's $1.4 million. S2 was 80 years old and in questionable health so S1's executor encouraged her to disclaim $3.5 million of S1's estate, resulting in both trusts being equal to $3.5 million. The executor obtained a six-month extension to file the return. When S2 died in July of 2006, the executor of S1's estate filed the return without making a QTIP election. Because the PTC was available for S2's estate, the tax on the two taxable estates of almost equal size was much less than would have been paid had everything been taxed in S2's estate or had the executor QTIPed S1's estate down to the AEA.

GIFT QTIP TRUSTS

Although most of our examples, and most real-life QTIP trusts, concern decedent's estates, the QTIP election is also available for lifetime transfers.[2] The trust must have the QTIP characteristics discussed in chapter 9, mainly a life estate for the donee spouse and the interest cannot be contingent. The donor spouse makes the QTIP election on a gift tax return that describes the trust as the gift. A gift QTIP trust could be used by a wealthy spouse who wants to bring the value of his or her spouse's estate up to at least the AEA. The use of the QTIP trust allows the wealthier spouse to keep the property in his or her family, whereas an outright gift surrenders control of the property. Of course, to use the less wealthy spouse's unified credit, the wealthy spouse must be willing to part with some property even if the other spouse (the donee spouse) dies first.

EXAMPLE 10 - 11. Eighty-year-old Ellen had a net worth of $6,500,000 when, after 10 years of widowhood, she married Frank, a kindly gentleman of modest means. Ellen wants to take care of Frank, should she die before him. She was also willing to have a significant portion of her estate go immediately to her children if Frank died before her. Therefore, in 2005, she established a lifetime QTIP trust. The trust was funded with stocks and bonds worth $1,700,000. The terms of the trust give Frank a life estate, and, if Frank died first, her children would receive only so much of the corpus as equals the AEA available for Frank's estate (taking into account his own property and any taxable gifts he might have made), the balance of the trust would revert back to Ellen, if she is still alive, otherwise, it will go to her children. Ellen filed a gift tax return and elected to QTIP all of the trust.

EXAMPLE 10 - 12. When Frank died in 2007, the QTIP trust had a net worth of $1,850,000 and his own property had a net worth of $300,000, for a total of $2,150,000. Frank's family received his property, and Ellen received $150,000 from the trust, which was just enough to bring Frank's taxable estate down to the AEA level for 2007 (i.e., down to $2,000,000). The balance of the trust (i.e., $1,700,000) went to her children. The tentative tax on Frank's estate equaled $780,800, which was completely covered by his unified credit.

The wealthy spouse establishing a gift QTIP trust must part with control of the assets in that trust. Since the donee spouse's interest cannot be contingent, the trust will continue even if the couple divorce. It might be wise, from the standpoint of the donor spouse, to have the estate planning documents include a postnuptial agreement that takes the QTIP trust income into account.

THE PRIOR TRANSFER CREDIT AND BYPASS TRUSTS

Illogical though it might be, the prior transfer credit (PTC) is available for an interest in a life estate (as in Chapter 6, when this PTC topic was introduced, we will sometimes refer to the first to die as D1 and the second to die as D2).[3] What is deemed to have been transferred from D1 to D2 is the value of the life estate measured as of the date of D1's death. Valuation is based on the life table factors published by the Treasury even though, due to the PTC time factor (i.e., there is no credit 10 years after the first death), this credit would seldom be available to anyone who lived the life expectancy implicit in the table.

EXAMPLE 10 -13. On October 4, 2005, when D died, her net estate, worth $3,500,000 went into a trust, with income for life to B (age 60), and a vested remainder for R (age 40) followed B's life estate. D's estate paid estate taxes of $930,000 to the federal government. B died on December 10, 2007, leaving an estate with a net value of $4,200,000 to three nephews. The trust established by D was distributed to R a few months after B's death. Although the trust's value was then in excess of $3 million, it is not included in B's estate, yet the estate is entitled to a PTC.

PTC Step 1. The value of the property "transferred" to B before adjustment for taxes is the value of B's life estate. The federal rate for valuing split-interest gifts for the month of October, 2005, was 4%,[4] therefore, the life estate factor for a 60-year-old income beneficiary was .50856, and the value of the property deemed to be transferred is $1,779,960. Limit one is:

$$LT1 = \frac{\$1,779,960}{\$3,500,000} * \$930,000 = \$472,961$$

Of course, the fraction reduces to the life estate factor since we used the factor in the first place to arrive at the value of the life estate. Therefore, limit one in this case can be calculated by multiplying the factor times the federal tax, as follows:

LT1 = .50856 * $930,000 = $472,961.

PTC Step 2. The tax on B's $3,200,000 taxable estate without a PTC is $990,000. To determine the second limit, the federal tax on the reduced estate must be calculated and subtracted from the federal tax on B's taxable estate. The reduced estate is $4,200,000 less the amount deemed transferred and subtracted from the federal tax on B's taxable estate net of its share of the total death taxes:

Federal estate tax on B's $4,200,000 taxable estate	$990,000
Less federal estate tax B's reduced estate of $2,893,001, i.e., $4,200,000 - .50856 * ($3,500,000 - $930,000)	(401,850)
Credit limit two	$588,150

Remember, the amounts shown as federal estate tax, $990,000 for the full estate and $401,850 for the reduced estate, are the federal estate tax, i.e., the tentative tax reduced by the unified credit on taxable estates of $4,200,000 and $2,893,001, respectively. To arrive at the reduced taxable estate, B's taxable estate is reduced by the net value of what was deemed transferred to B, i.e., the value of B's life estate in the B and C trusts, after S1's death taxes have been subtracted, i.e., 0.50856 * ($3,500,000 - $930,000).

PTC Step 3. Since B died more than two years, but less than four years, after D, the time factor is 80% and the actual PTC is:

$$80\% * \text{ the lesser of } \begin{cases} \textit{limit one}: \$472,961 \\ \textit{limit two}: \$588,150 \end{cases} = \$378,369$$

Therefore, B's estate pays taxes as follows:

Federal estate tax before PTC	$990,000
less prior transfer credit	($378,369)
Federal estate tax	$611,631

If the remainderman dies after the income beneficiary, but still within 10 years of the settlor (D1), there will also be a PTC for the remainderman's estate based on the remainder value at D1's death of the remainderman's interest. If the remainder is vested, and the remainderman dies before the income beneficiary, the remainderman-decedent's interest is included in the remainderman's estate. This value is based on the beneficiary's age (B's age), the value of the trust, and the federal split-interest rate (i.e., the §7520 rate) at that time. R in the above example would become D2 for the purpose of computing the PTC for his estate. Obviously, the income beneficiary will be older than he or she was when the trust was established, therefore the remainder factor (from Table S) is likely to be higher; however, this depends on the § 7520 rate at R's death. Thus, the amount included in R's estate insofar as the trust is concerned would be the remainder factor (based on B's age) times the trust's value as of R's death. These changes are taken into account when calculating the value of the remainder in R's (D2) gross estate, but in calculating the value of what was transferred for determining PTC limit two, one must continue to use the value of the remainder as of D1's death. Remember, any change in value insofar as the property transferred is concerned is irrelevant to the PTC calculation. What is deemed to have transferred is based on the values at D1's death, and that is the value used in calculating R's reduced estate. To the extent the value of a trust (or a vested remainder in a trust) is part of D2's estate, the value is as of D2's death.

THE PRIOR TRANSFER CREDIT AND THE QTIP ELECTION

The PTC has its greatest estate planning potential when used in conjunction with the ABC, AsuperB, or ABdC estate plans, because the partial QTIP election gives S1's executor some control in the allocation of the couple's total estate between the two taxable estates. For large estates, if the surviving spouse is diagnosed as terminally ill before S1's estate tax return is filed, it may be better to make either no QTIP election or only a partial QTIP election, so that some taxes are generated in the first estate, which in turn will generate a PTC for the second estate. The optimal QTIP election is one where the QTIP fraction used is one that will best utilize lower marginal tax rates for both estates and the PTC for S2's estate in such a way that the greatest amount possible passes to the children. This is demonstrated in the example set that follows. Keep in mind that the maximum extension to file is six months; therefore, the maximum period after S1's death to assess S2's health is 15 months.

FACTS FOR THE EXAMPLE SET: At the time of S1's death on January 11, 2005, S1 and S2 have property worth $8,500,000, S1 owns separate property worth $6,000,000, and S2 owns separate property worth $2,500,000. Their estate plan is an ABC Trust plan, with S2 given a life estate in Trusts B and C. S1 dies at age 75 and S2 is 60 years old. The federal rate for valuing split-interest gifts for January of 2005 is 4%. The net value going in each trust is: Trust A $2,500,000; Trust B $1,500,000; and Trust C $4,500,000. S2 is in extremely poor health.

EXAMPLE 10 -14. S1's executor very diligently assembles the information and valuations necessary to file the estate tax return by its due date of October 11, 2005. He elects to QTIP all of Trust C so as not to pay any tax. Unfortunately, S2 dies March 27, 2006. The assets in the three trusts increased in value by 5%; as a result, the three trusts are worth: Trust A $2,625,000; Trust B $1,575,000; and Trust C $4,725,000, for a total value of $8,925,000. S2's taxable estate is the combined value of Trusts A and C ($7,350,000), so, although this strategy results in zero taxes at S1's death, S2's executor pays $2,461,000 for her estate. The net amount going to the children is the total of the three trusts less the tax:

$$\$8,925,000 - \$2,461,000 = \$6,464,000$$

EXAMPLE 10-15. In this alternative version, S1's executor is very cautious. She diligently assembles the information and valuations necessary to file the estate tax return by its due date but she obtains an extension to file and to pay until April 11, 2006, intending to re-assess S2's health as that later date approaches. S2's death makes re-assessment unnecessary.

As in the prior example, the assets in the three trusts increase in value by 5%. S1's executor does a partial QTIP election, even though it means Trusts B and C have to pay estate taxes about a year earlier than if the taxes were postponed until after S2's death, and some interest has to be paid for the six-month extension period. It helps that the interest amount for both the federal and state death taxes is deductible on S1's return. Since she had obtained an extension to file and to pay, no penalties are assessed.

To work through to the amount paid at each death we follow the six-step QTIP calculations (combining some of the steps in the interest of brevity). At Step 5, we calculate S1's taxes. Note, we will charge the tax prorata to Trusts B and C before we increase the value by 5% (obviously a simplification since the tax is not paid until the return is filed). As another simplification, interest is not taken here as a deduction although in a real situation it would be. Step 6 is followed by the three-step PTC calculation for S2's estate to determine S2's taxes. From the value of the three trusts at S2's death, having already subtracted the taxes at the first death we now subtract the taxes at S2's death to determine the net amount going to the children. Finally, we compare this alternative to the net amount using the 100% QTIP alternative.

Step 1. By trial and error the executor determined that a very good result is accomplished when S1's taxable estate equals $4,700,000 (about 55% of the combined estates).

Step 2. The marital deduction necessary to achieve the desired taxable estate:

$$\$6,000,000 - \$4,700,000 = MD = \$1,300,000$$

Step 3. Trust C is the QTIP property, therefore the QTIP fraction is:

$$\$1,300,000/\$4,500,000$$

Steps 4 and 5. S1's taxable estate equals S1's estate less the marital deduction that results from the QTIP election. Therefore, S1's taxable estate is:

$$\$6,000,000 - \$1,300,000 = \$4,700,000$$

This results in federal taxes of $1,494,000. These are charged to trusts B and C in direct proportion to their values, hence 1/4th to Trust B and 3/4ths to Trust C, leaving a net in each trust of: A $2,500,000; B $1,126,500; and C $3,379,500.

Step 6. S2's estate equals Trust A plus the QTIP fraction times Trust C's value at that time. All three trusts increase by 5% to values as follows: A $2,625,000; B $1,182,825; and C $3,548,475. Therefore, S2's taxable estate is:

$2,625,000 + ($1,300,000/$4,500,000) * $3,548,475 = $3,650,115.

Having determined S2's taxable estate, we turn our attention to calculating the PTC and the estate taxes.

PTC Step 1. Limit one: Using a federal rate of 4% and given that S2 was 60 years old when S1 died, the factor for computing her life estate value is .50856.

.50856 * $1,494,000 = $759,789

PTC Step 2. Limit two: The total taxes on an estate of $3,650,115 before taking the PTC is $759,053 federal tax.

Federal estate tax on $3,650,115	$759,053
Less tax on S2's reduced taxable estate of $1,259,883	
i.e., $3,650,115 - .50856 * ($6,000,000 - $1,300,000)	(_____$0)
Credit limit two	$759,053

Again, a reminder that the amounts used to arrive at limit two are the federal taxes on S2's taxable estate and on S2's reduced taxable estate, each calculated taking both the unified credit and, if applicable, any state death taxes into account. Because the reduced taxable estate is less than the AEA for 2006 the tax on it is zero and limit two is the tax on the full estate.

PTC Step 3. Since S1 and S2 died within two years of each other the time factor is 100%. We use the lower of the two limits, hence the PTC is:

$$100\% * the\ lesser\ of \begin{cases} limit\ one: \$759,789 \\ limit\ two: \$759,053 \end{cases} = \$759,053$$

Therefore, S2's estate pays taxes as follows:

Death taxes before PTC	$759,053
less prior transfer credit	($759,053)
Federal estate tax	$0

In other words, the PTC has eliminated estate taxes for S2's estate. Compare the value going to the children using the optimal QTIP election with what was previously calculated. By postponing all taxes until the second death, the value to the children was $6,464,000, whereas with the optimal QTIP election the amount is the value of the trusts, $7,356,300. The optimal QTIP results in $892,300 [$7,356,300 - $6,464,000] more to the children than with the 100% QTIP election.

This potential savings that comes from using the PTC with multiple trust plans is obviously just as important as the utilization of both unified credits. It results from the phantom transfer from S1's estate to S2, (the fact that an estate is allowed a PTC based on the hypothetical value of S2's life estate) even though, due to S2's death, very little is actually transferred. Of course it is limited in usefulness to those times when the two deaths are close enough in time to use the PTC. The optimal QTIP fraction depends on the following factors:

- the federal rate for valuing split interests such as life estates
- the age of S2
- the combined value of the couple's estates
- whether S1's estate equals (or exceeds) the amount necessary to make the optimal mix

Given the multiple factors (age, § 7520 rate, values, increasing AEA) and the fact that only a portion of S1's estate is deemed to have been transferred, the optimal QTIP fraction tends to be one that taxes more of the combined total in S1's estate. Indeed, in the above example the optimal QTIP fraction had about 55% of the combined estate taxed in S1's estate. The exact ratio can be determined by trial and error - or by using a computer program. Even for very large estates, a QTIP election that equalizes the two estates generally produces results fairly close to those achieved by the optimal QTIP election, and certainly very superior to the 100% QTIP alternative.

NONCITIZEN SURVIVING SPOUSE: THE QDOT TRUST

Generally, all property passing outright to a surviving spouse qualifies for the marital deduction, however, with the Technical and Miscellaneous Revenue

Act of 1988 (TAMRA), Congress removed benefit of the marital deduction for property transferred after November 10, 1988, to a non-U.S. citizen spouse.[5] There are several ways that the marital deduction can be salvaged. One, if S2 becomes a U.S. citizen before the estate tax return is filed and provided that she has remained a resident of the U.S. at all times following S1's death, property passing to her will qualify for the marital deduction.[6] Two, S1's property can be placed in a "qualified domestic trust"[7] (QDOT) that gives some assurance that the property will eventually be taxed in the U.S. The intent of the law is to ensure the eventual collection of estate tax on marital deduction property given to a spouse who may have less secure ties with the U.S. than are thought to exist for most citizens.

The requirements for a QDOT to qualify for the marital deduction are set forth in IRC § 2056A. At least one of the trustees of a QDOT must be a U.S. citizen or domestic corporation. The Secretary of the Treasury is given authority to write regulations to assure the collection of the tax on distributions from these trusts. Those regulations require that the trustee keep sufficient assets within the U.S. to assure payment of the tax or that the trustee have a minimum net worth to assure the payment.[8] The third requirement is that S1's executor must elect to have the marital deduction apply to the trust. Note, the election can be made even on a late filed return, so long as it is not more than one year late.[9]

Estate tax is imposed (once S1's unified credit is exhausted) on any corpus distributed prior to the spouse's death, and on the value of the corpus remaining at the spouse's death (or sooner, if the trust ceases to qualify as a QDOT). However, distribution of income, and distribution of principal on account of "hardship," are exempt from the tax.[10] The tax is the amount that would have been imposed, after all credits, had the property subject to the tax been included in S1's taxable estate.

EXAMPLE 10 - 16. When S1 died in 2005, his estate worth $4 million was left entirely to S2, a resident of the U.S. for 50 years, but still a citizen of Canada. Within a few months after her husband's death, S2's lawyers created a QDOT into which she transferred assets worth $2.5 million. When she filed the estate tax return she elected to have the QDOT qualify for the marital deduction, hence the taxable estate was $1.5 million. By using S1's AEA no estate tax was owed.

EXAMPLE 10 - 17. In 2007, S2 died and the QDOT was worth $3 million. S2's estate was worth $500,000 and owed no estate tax. Assuming no taxable distributions, the tax is based on S1's taxable estate, adding the $1.5 million taxed in 2005 to the $3 million DOT results in a taxable estate of $4.5 million. The tax relates back to S1's estate; hence the tax is $1,400,000.

Note that the QDOT is taxed in S1's estate in a manner similar to the gift tax calculation in the sense that distributions and the final termination move into higher marginal rates but, unfortunately, the estate does not get to take advantage of the increase in the unified credit between the time of S1's death and S2's death. Compare this to the QTIP election that tosses a portion of S1's estate into S2's. If one had a choice, sometimes a QTIP will reduce the taxes more than a QDOT because the QTIP uses some of S2's unified credit, e.g., in the example above had the trust been a QTIP, the taxable estate at S2's death would have been $3.5 million and the tax $675,000. If both estates are substantial, i.e., each considerably larger than the AEA, the QTIP does a slightly better job than the QDOT since it will take advantage of the phase in of lower marginal rates, e.g., in the last example, if S2's estate was worth $4 million instead of half a million, a QTIP would add the $3 million to it, resulting in a taxable estate of $7 million (tax of $2,250,000–remember $1,500,000 was sheltered in 2005); whereas a QDOT would result in two taxable estates, S1's at $4.5 million (tax of $1,400,000 based on 2005's rates and unified credit) and S2's at $4 million (tax of $900,000 using 2007's rates and unified credit).

The trust need not have been created by the decedent prior to death; either the executor or the surviving spouse may create the QDOT prior to the due date of S1's estate tax return (including extensions). For a QDOT created after S1's death, the surviving spouse must irrevocably assign property that she would have otherwise received from S1 to the trust before the due date of the return.[11]

The surviving noncitizen spouse's choice of whether to transfer S1's property into a QDOT may be based on the decision to defer or to equalize their estates. If S2 creates and funds a QDOT, S1's estate will get a marital deduction for the property, but the property will be subject to estate tax at S2's death (or earlier, if trust property is transferred to S2 during her lifetime). Alternatively, if S2 accepts the property without transferring it to a QDOT, the property will be subject to S1 estate taxation immediately, but may avoid estate tax later to the extent S2 can convert the property into "non-U.S. situs" assets. Some noncitizen S2s may prefer to pay the tax up front, then take the property and disappear. The AEA still shelters some (or all) of S1's estate, even if the estate is left to a noncitizen spouse. Furthermore, property that would have qualified for a marital deduction but for the fact that S2 was not a citizen will qualify for a prior transfer credit (PTC) if her estate is taxed in the U.S. at her death. This credit is calculated without being diminished by the usual PTC time factor (i.e., the decrease in the PTC by 20% every two years following S1's death does not apply here).[12]

QDOTs post-EGTRRA. The repeal of the estate tax will keep the property going to a noncitizen spouse from being taxed if S1 dies after 2009. Indeed, there will be no tax on the property in the QDOT if S2 dies after 2009. However, distributions of corpus from a QDOT before 2021 will be subject to the QDOT tax on distributions if S2 is still alive. Apparently this 10-year delay in eliminating the estate tax on these distributions is a safeguard in case the repeal of the estate tax is not made permanent.

ESTATE PLANNING USING TRUSTS

From an estate planning standpoint, almost anything that can be described in words, with or without examples, that one can get a trustee to agree to carry out, can be accomplished through the use of trusts, so long as it is legal and not against public policy. Any of the plans discussed here can be accomplished by a testamentary trust just as well as through a living trust with the exception of avoiding probate at the first death. With a testamentary trust the funding process at the first death is the probate court's order for distribution.

State death tax. For the most part, we have ignored the influence of state death taxes. Generally, their effect is relatively small compared to the impact of the federal tax. Prior to the federal state death tax credit being phased out (2001-2004), about half of the states had adopted what was called a pickup tax as their only death tax, that is, an amount exactly equal to the federal credit for state death taxes. Consequently, in the pickup tax states, no additional taxes were paid as a result of the state death tax. With the elimination of the federal credit as of 2005, many of those states were left without an estate tax although some have adopted some form of death tax. States that impose an inheritance tax usually charge more when the estate goes to distant relatives or to non-family members than is charged if it goes to close relatives. As of

2005, state death taxes are allowed as a deduction from the gross estate in calculating the federal estate tax.

Revocable living trust or testamentary trust. The main advantage to the living trust is that it avoids probate of the settlor's assets to the extent they are held in trust at the time of the settlor's death. The testamentary trust is funded through the probate process and does have the advantage that in most states the probate process considerably shortens the period during which creditors can assert their claims.

Married couples, one trust or two? A one trust document plan for both spouses, called a *joint spousal grantor trust*, will work as long as the assets of each spouse are carefully identified and distinguished. It does not have the gift tax danger and dispositive restrictions of the joint and mutual will, which generally becomes irrevocable as to all probate assets at the first spouse's death. In contrast, the joint trust usually keeps the surviving spouse in control of the trust that holds her property (e.g., Trust A) and only the trust holding the deceased spouse's property (e.g., Trust B) is irrevocable.

If commingling of assets is a significant concern, each spouse can execute his or her own living trust document. Another reason for two trusts is that a poorly drafted joint spousal grantor trust document could give rise to estate or gift tax consequences for wealthier clients, particularly when the spouses fund the trust with different amounts of individually owned property. For example, the spouse contributing the greater amount may be deemed to have made a gift that may be taxable, if the terms of the trust do not qualify it for the marital deduction. The latter is not likely to occur with a well drafted joint trust because they are usually revocable so long as both spouses are alive, and the portions that are irrevocable after the first death are designed to either use the unified credit or to qualify for the marital deduction.

Civil unions and non-traditional marriages. For tax purposes, the federal government does not recognize the legal status of civil unions (e.g., Vermont and California) or of marriages between same sex couples even if the marriage is recognized by state law (e.g., Massachusetts) or foreign countries (e.g., Belgium, Canada, Netherlands, and Spain). Obviously, estate planning is still important to these couples, perhaps more so in the area of specifying an agent for healthcare and financial matters in the event one of them becomes incapacitated. An advanced care directive gives the designated agent the authority to step in, whereas, without a document, in states that do not sanction these unions, medical personnel and managers at financial institutions might look to the closest kin of an incapacitated person for guidance. Even in those states that have not sanctioned these unions, private institutions, such as hospitals and banks, might formulate their own policy of recognition if there is documentation that the incapacitated person intended the relationship to be a marriage or civil union.

As for using trusts, obviously, no marital deduction is available, so creating a separate QTIP trust as in an ABC trust arrangement makes little sense. Nevertheless, the first spouse (or partner) to die can maintain ultimate control over his or her estate and estate taxes can be saved at the second death by utilizing an arrangement similar to the AsuperB plan. Depending on the degree to which the couple has merged their property, they are likely to either each create a separate trust or they might create a single trust that becomes two trusts at the first death. The main benefit of trust planning, from a tax standpoint, is that the property does not merge at the first death into one estate controlled by the survivor, nevertheless, he or she gets the benefit of a life estate without the property being taxed when the survivor dies. Furthermore, each person designates the remaindermen who will receive his or her trust estate when the survivor dies. This might be the person's family, own set of friends, or favorite charities. Since a QTIP is not in order, the trust for the survivor can have contingencies that cause the survivor's interest to end before his or her death. Perhaps the settlor's trusted relatives are willing to hold a limited power to appoint the corpus or terminate the trust early based upon a set of guidelines drawn up by the settlor, e.g., the trust might terminate if the survivor becomes very wealthy, is so incapacitated that the trust is of no benefit, or is in prison.

Debts and expenses. Of course, any estate will have deductible debts and expenses, which will alter the calculations. Expenses in administering a decedent's probate estate typically range between 5 and 10% of the total estate, whereas expenses to transfer (or allocate) assets vis-a-vis a decedent-settlor's funded living trust are likely to be less than 2%. Ordinarily, estate planners handle debts and expenses in the following manner: Regarding debts, in performing the calculations, planners use net worth as the value of the estate property; regarding expenses, planners either estimate the expenses or simply ignore them because they are not likely to have a significant influence on the choice of estate plans. Given the complexity of multiple trust plans, most planners want to keep the calculations used as examples as simple as possible without misleading the client. A gift of this book is a good idea.

PLANNING IN THE ERA OF UNCERTAINTY

EGTRRA has created difficulty in planning, most glaringly because the sunset provision creates uncertainty as to whether repeal is for real. Even if one assumes that repeal will take place, the lag between the legislation and repeal coupled with the new basis rules creates another dilemma. Planners are used to the trade-off between saving taxes by sheltering some of S1's estate in a bypass trust and forgoing a second stepped-up basis for those assets when S2 dies. With the QTIP trust the trade-off came in the form of avoiding taxes at the first death but getting a stepped-up basis at the second death or paying the taxes at the first death and forgoing the stepped-up basis at the second. Assuming repeal becomes permanent, if S2 dies after 2009, property in any previously created bypass trust (e.g., Trust B) or QTIP trust (e.g., Trust C) will not receive a step-up in basis. Although these trusts no longer serve the purpose for which they were designed (avoiding or postponing estate tax), by not being included in S2's estate they lose the opportunity to have a new basis. This is also true of GST exemption trusts designed to confer benefits to several generations without triggering the generation-skipping (GST) tax. With repeal the shelter is no longer needed, and the benefit of basis step-up is lost. There may be little that can be done with existing bypass and GST exemption trusts as they are likely to be irrevocable. It will be interesting to see whether courts will allow some of those trusts to be terminated after 2009 on the grounds that they have ceased to serve their original purpose.

With trusts that are still amendable planners may wish to put in a provision that gives the remaindermen the authority to appoint the assets of the bypass trust and the QTIP trust to the surviving spouse. In situations where the remaindermen were S2's issue and they felt fairly confident that the estate would eventually come to them, they could exercise the power in favor of S2, thereby having the assets receive a stepped-up basis on her death.

In the past, the credit shelter trust (i.e., Trust B) has been defined such that it shelters an amount equal to S1's available AEA, thus keeping pace with Congress's propensity to increase the amount from time to time. When these plans were drafted it was prudent for the wealthy to shelter the maximum that could be sheltered. In 2010 the AEA becomes in effect infinite and S1's entire estate is likely to be controlled by the credit shelter trust. Indeed, great distortion of the estate plan may result. A very wealthy person with children by a prior marriage may have designed a plan whereby his or her issue receive the maximum amount that does not generate a tax (presently the AEA) and the balance is placed in a QTIP trust to take care of S2 for life. After 2009, that plan would result in the issue receiving the entire estate. Plans need to be revised such that the settlor's goals are reached regardless of whether repeal takes place.

Given the uncertainty and the need to retain maximum flexibility to change estate plans based on what future legislation holds, couples should also consider adding to their durable powers specific clauses that allow their agents to amend the trust. Many states prohibit an agent from changing an estate plan unless the authority to do so is written into the durable power. Perhaps there should be constraints placed on the agent; however, many constraints are likely to hinder taking advantage of changes in the law. Any constraint that would keep S2 from having control of property will almost certainly result in it not being eligible for an increase in basis when S2 dies. Perhaps a more flexible solution would be to name as co-agents the principal's spouse and one or more of the principal's children.

CONCLUSION

This chapter continued the discussion of the sophisticated estate plans that have been used to reduce the estate tax. The importance of the prior transfer credit used in conjunction with the QTIP election was explained. In the next couple of chapters we will consider how gift giving is also used to reduce transfer taxes.

QUESTIONS AND PROBLEMS

Use the ETAX program to do the problems that require calculation of estate or gift taxes. If an annual exclusion is available, use the following amounts: $3,000 for 1977 - 1981; $10,000 for 1982 - 2002; $11,000 for 2002 - 2005; and $12,000 for 2006-2008.

1. When S1 died in 2005 the couple had an AsuperB estate plan. The executor of S1's estate QTIPed Trust B to postpone all taxes but fully utilize S1's unified credit.

   Holdings when S1 died:

   S1's SP $4,800,000
   their CP $3,460,000
   S2's SP   none

   (a) What is the value of S1's estate and the value of each trust?
   (b) What is the QTIP fraction?
   (c) What is S2's taxable estate if, at her death in 2007, the trusts have the following values: A $2,100,000 and B $6,800,000.
   (d) If S1 died in 2006 would the value of the trusts change? of the QTIP fraction?

2. From the prior problem, answer "b" and "c" given that S1's executor used a QTIP election to produce a taxable estate of $5 million.

3. When S1 died in 2006 the couple had an AsuperB estate plan. The executor of S1's estate QTIPed Trust B to result in a taxable estate of $3,500,000.

   Holdings when S1 died:

   S1's SP $6,600,000
   S2's SP $2,300,000

   (a) What is the value of S1's estate and the value of each trust?
   (b) What is the QTIP fraction?
   (c) What is S2's taxable estate if, at her death in 2007, the trusts have the following values: A $2,400,000 and B $7,200,000.
   (d) If S1 died in 2009 would the value of the trusts change? of the QTIP fraction? Explain.

4. If in the prior problem the couple had an A disclaimer to a B Trust (AdB) plan, how much would S2 have had to disclaim to result in a taxable estate of $3,500,000 at S1's death? What then would be the value of each trust?

5. Trust B in the ABdC Trust plan is usually funded with assets that have a value equal to the AEA at S1's death. (a) What two circumstances would result in it being funded at less than the AEA? (b) Identify two ways in which Trust B in the AsuperB Trust plan differs from the one in the ABC Trust plan. (c) Compare how the marital deduction is achieved in the AB trust plan versus in the AsuperB trust plan.

6. When S1 died in 2007 the couple had an ABdC estate plan. At S1's death, S2 disclaimed so much of S1's estate as to equalize their estates based upon the values at his death. No QTIP election was made.

    Holdings when S1 died:

S1's SP	$8,000,000
their CP	$4,500,000
S2's SP	$2,600,000

    (a) What would have been the value of each trust without a disclaimer?
    (b) Show the value of each trust after S1's death taking into account S2's disclaimer. What is S1's taxable estate?
    (c) What is S2's taxable estate if, at her death in 2009, the trusts have the following values: A $7,600,000, B $2,500,000, and C $5,900,000.

7. Use the information from the prior problem, and add as a new fact that S1 made post-1976 taxable gifts in the amount of $700,000 to answer these questions. (a) What would be the value of each trust? (b) Would S2 need to make a disclaimer to postpone taxes to S2's death? Explain. (c) How much would S2 have to disclaim to result in S1's taxable estate being equal to $6,000,000? Explain.

8. When S1 died in 2007 the couple had an ABdC estate plan. At S1's death, S2 disclaimed so much of S1's estate as to result in a taxable estate of $7,250,000 without a QTIP election.

Holdings when S1 died:

S1's SP $9,000,000
their CP $2,200,000
S2's SP $1,400,000

(a) What would have been the value of each trust without a disclaimer?

(b) Show the value of each trust after taking into account S2's disclaimer.

(c) What is S2's taxable estate if at her death in 2008 the trusts have the following values: A $5,450,000, B $2,060,000, and C $5,400,000.

9. In the prior problem, suppose that after the disclaimer S2's health greatly improved, so S1's executor decided to make a QTIP election to postpone all taxes. For both the disclaimer and the QTIP election explain how, where, and when each would be done.

10. Continuing from the prior problem, instead of postponing all taxes, what QTIP fraction applied to Trust C results in a taxable estate of $5 million? Explain.

11. When S1 died in 2007 the couple had an AdBC estate plan. At S1's death, S2 disclaimed so much of S1's estate as to result in a taxable estate of $7,000,000 without a QTIP election.

Holdings when S1 died:

S1's SP $9,600,000
S2's SP $3,400,000

(a) What would have been the value of each trust without a disclaimer?

(b) Show the value of each trust after taking into account S2's disclaimer.

(c) What is S2's taxable estate if at her death in 2008 the trusts have the following values: A $5,800,000, B $2,300,000, and C $5,100,000.

12. Use the information from the prior problem, add as a new fact that S1 made post-1976 taxable gifts in the amount of $600,000 to answer again questions "a" and "b."

13. Lynda and Clyde Hoggert have three adult children from their present marriage and Clyde has a daughter from a prior marriage. When they started inquiring about estate plans in 2006, their estate's net value was between four and five million dollars. (a) What would draw them towards the AsuperB estate plan rather than an AdB? (b) Under what circumstances might they prefer the AdB plan? (c) Why might they prefer the ABdCplan?

14. Betty and Steven Jacks have four adult children all from their present marriage. In 2006 the Jacks, with an estate worth approximately $2.5 million, started inquiring about having an estate plan done. (a) What circumstances would draw them towards the AdB estate plan? (b) Under what circumstances might they prefer the AsuperB Trust plan rather than an ABC plan or an AdB plan?

15. Lisa and Forest Mills' children, all from their present marriage, are adults. Forest received a substantial inheritance when his parents passed away. Invested in his name alone, it is now worth about $4,000,000. (a) What estate planning challenge does this very unequal division of wealth create? (b) What might Forest do to improve the estate tax planning aspect? (c) How does the stability of their marriage enter into the decision-making?

16. Where on the gift tax return does the donor list the gift of a QTIP trust? How does the donor then indicate that he or she is making a QTIP election covering the QTIP trust?

17. S1 died February 28, 2005, survived by 80-year-old S2. The §7520 rate was 4%. They had an ABC estate plan. At S1's death their holdings had the following net value:

S1's separate	$6,400,000
community property	$3,000,000

S2's separate $1,800,000
            Total value $11,200,000

(a) Determine as of S1's death: (i) S1's estate; (ii) the value of Trusts A, B, and C; (iii) the QTIP fraction necessary to equalize the two estates at $5,600,000; and (iv) the estate tax.

S2 died November 9, 2007, and the trusts had the following values:

  Trust A: $3,500,000   Trust B: $1,600,000   Trust C: $6,800,000

(b) Given the above values for the three trusts: (i) show how one arrives at $5,943,750 as S2's taxable estate; and (ii) use ETAX to determine the federal estate tax without the PTC.
(c) Determine credit limit one.
(d) Determine: (i) S2's reduced taxable estate; and (ii) credit limit two.
(e) Determine: (i) the PTC after adjusting for time; and (ii) the estate tax.

18. S1 died June 7, 2005, survived by 60-year-old S2. The §7520 rate was 10%. They had an ABC estate plan. At S1's death their holdings had the following net value:

                S1's separate $9,350,000
                S2's separate $2,400,000
                    Total value $11,750,000

(a) Determine as of S1's death: (i) the value of Trusts A, B, and C; (ii) the QTIP fraction that resulted in S1's taxable estate being $7,300,000; and (iii) the estate tax.

S2 died May 12, 2007, and the trusts had the following values:

  Trust A: $2,600,000   Trust B: $1,550,000   Trust C: $8,220,000

(b) Given the values for the three trusts: (i) show how one arrives at $4,746,624 as S2's taxable estate; and (ii) use ETAX to determine the federal estate tax without the PTC.
(c) Determine credit limit one.
(d) Determine: (i) S2's reduced taxable estate; and (ii) credit limit two.
(e) Determine: (i) the PTC after adjusting for time; and (ii) the estate tax.

19. S1 died January 9, 2005, survived by 65-year-old S2. The §7520 rate was 8%. They had an AsuperB estate plan. At S1's death their holdings had the following net value:

S1's separate	$14,840,000
S2's separate	$1,400,000
Total value	$16,240,000

(a) Determine as of S1's death: (i) the value of Trusts A and B; (ii) the QTIP fraction necessary to bring S1's estate to $8,120,000; and (iii) the estate tax.

S2 died March 21, 2009, and the trusts had the following values:

Trust A	$1,600,000
Trust B	$16,450,000

(b) Given the for the two trusts: (i) show how one arrives at $9,049,057 as S2's taxable estate; and (ii) use ETAX to determine the federal estate tax without the PTC.
(c) Determine credit limit one.
(d) Determine: (i) S2's reduced taxable estate; and (ii) credit limit two.
(e) Determine: (i) the PTC after adjusting for time; and (ii) the estate tax.

20. S1 died on April 12, 2005, survived by 70-year-old S2. The §7520 rate was 6%. They had an AsuperB estate plan. At S1's death their holdings had the following net value:

S1's separate	$7,200,000
community property	$1,420,000
S2's separate	$0
Total value	$8,620,000

(a) Determine as of S1's death: (i) S1's estate; (ii) the value of Trusts A and B; (iii) the QTIP fraction necessary to bring S1's estate to $4,000,000; and (iv) the estate tax.

S2 died on March 6, 2007, and the trusts have the following values:

Trust A	$740,000
Trust B	$8,300,000

(b) Given the above values for the two trusts: (i) show how one arrives at $4,842,781 as S2's taxable estate; and (ii) the estate tax without the PTC. (c) Determine credit limit one. (d) Determine: (i) S2's reduced taxable estate; and (ii) credit limit two. (e) Determine: (i) the PTC after adjusting for time; and (ii) the estate tax.

21. Lucia, a citizen of the USA, has a separate estate of $3.3 million and her husband, Fortino, a citizen of Italy, has a separate estate of $7.5 million. Permanent residents of the USA for the last 50 years, they are not only very elderly but in poor health. (a) If Lucia died in 2006, what is the approximate estate tax, assuming everything is left to Fortino? Is there any point to having a QDOT? If a QDOT is used, what amount should be placed in it? Would an ABC Trust plan be in order? (b) If Fortino died in 2006, what is the approximate estate tax assuming everything is left to Lucia and no QDOT is used? Is a QDOT needed to avoid estate taxes?

22. Consider the facts of the prior problem and assume Fortino died in 2006, Lucia died 2007, and the estate values did not change. Answer the following questions without calculating the prior transfer credit: (a) Fortino's estate plan placed all his property in a trust that gave Lucia a life estate. If his executor made a QTIP election to equalize the two estates, what is the approximate estate tax at each death before the application of any PTC? (b) Which estate might benefit from a prior transfer credit? What determines whether it is available? (c) Does the trust Fortino created have to meet QDOT rules? Explain.

23. Amy and Dave Beasley have three adult children, all from their present marriage. Most of their combined wealth of $4 million comes from the inheritance that Dave received when his parents passed away. They have an ABC estate plan with the income from all three trusts going to the survivor (of course the survivor has full control over Trust A). The Beasleys have a very stable marriage but Amy has had serious gambling addiction problems as has the couple's youngest child, Walter. (a) What planning problems does Amy's gambling addiction present? What estate planning techniques might be partial solutions to protecting Amy's long-term financial well-being? (b) How might Walter's eventual share of the estate be handled differently than that given to the other two children?

ANSWERS TO THE QUESTIONS AND PROBLEMS *(odd numbered only)*

1. AsuperB estate plan with community property, QTIP to postpone:
   (a) S1's estate is half of community property plus all S1's separate property for a total of $6,530,000. Trust A $1,730,000 and Trust B $6,530,000.
   (b) The AEA = $2 million, so $5,030,000/$6,530,000.
   (c) All of Tr A plus fraction times Tr B: $2,100,000 + ($5,030,000/$6,530,000) * $6,800,000 = $7,337,979.
   (d) No and yes. Second part: The AEA = $2 million, so $4,530,000/$6,530,000.

3. AsuperB QTIPed down to $3,500,000:
   (a) S1's estate = $6.6 million. Trust A $2,300,000 (all of S2's property) and Trust B $6,600,000 (all of S1's property).
   (b) The desired taxable estate is $3.5 million, so the QTIP fraction has as the numerator the amount of marital deduction needed to bring S1's taxable estate down to the desired estate: $6,600,000 - $3,500,000 = $3,100,000. The denominator is the QTIP property, i.e., Trust B, therefore the fraction is $3,100,000/$6,600,000.
   (c) S2's estate equals Tr A + the fraction times Tr B: $2,400,000 + ($3,100,000/$6,600,000) * $7,200,000 = $5,781,818.
   (d) The trusts would be the same (the estate plan hasn't changed) and, since the desired taxable estate is still $3.5 million, the fraction also stays the same.

5. Comparing trust plans:
   (a) Trust B might be funded with assets less than the AEA because of prior transfers (gifts), transfers to someone other than S2 (e.g., life insurance to a child), or S1's estate might be smaller than the AEA.
   (b) 1. In AsuperB the B trust may be greater than the AEA amount whereas in an ABC plan it is defined as being equal to the available AEA. 2. With the AsuperB, trust B is likely to be just partially QTIPed whereas with the ABC trust plan it is Trust C that is QTIPed and Trust B not at all.
   (c) The AB automatically uses the marital deduction for property in excess of the AEA, whereas with an AsuperB trust plan the executor has the opportunity to QTIP or not QTIP Trust B.

7. Continue prior problem with a taxable gift of $700,000:
   (a) Tr B would be reduced by the taxable gifts since they used up some of S1's AEA amount, hence: Tr A $13,800,000 and Tr B $1,300,000.
   (b) No disclaimer would be needed since the amount of S1's estate above the available AEA already flows into Trust A and qualifies for the marital deduction.
   (c) Since Trust B and C combined will equal the desired taxable estate and we have already determined that Trust B will be $1,300,000, Trust C must equal $4,300,000.

9. Prior problem, change of mind, QTIP to postpone all taxes:
   The goal is to have S1's taxable estate equal the AEA amount. Since the disclaimer created a Trust C worth $5,250,000 it would have to be fully QTIPed to bring the taxable estate down to $2 million (i.e., Trust B). The disclaimer had to be completed within 9 months of S1's death. The QTIP election is made on the estate tax return. With an extension to file, the return could be filed as much as 15 months after S1's death.

11. An AdBC Trust disclaimed to a taxable estate of $7,000,000:
    (a) There would be no Trusts B and C, just Trust A with a value of $13,000,000.
    (b) The disclaimer must equal the desired taxable estate, i.e., $7 million. It first fills up Trust B to the AEA level and the rest goes into Trust C, therefore, Tr A $6,000,000, Tr B $2,000,000, and Tr C $5,000,000.
    (c) Since no QTIP election, only Trust A is in S2's estate, i.e., $5,800,000.

13. Estate planning taking into account Clyde's daughter by a prior marriage:
    (a) S1 may not want his or her property greater than the AEA to pass into S2's ultimate control hence the advantage of AsuperB. Also, the combined estates slightly exceed 2 current AEA amounts so it's "easier" to bet that S2 will live long enough so that her estate will not have to actually pay any estate tax so long as the two estates aren't combined and given the likelihood that the AEA for estates will be increased by Congress. Clyde might worry that Lynda would disinherit his daughter from his earlier marriage.
    (b) Where neither spouse minds that whoever lives the longest will have full control over the entire estate. This might even be the situation if Clyde

has had little contact with his daughter from the prior marriage and does not plan to leave her anything even if he is the surviving spouse.

(c) The ABdC might make sense if they really think that the estate AEA might go back to just $1,000,000 after 2010. Or they might write the trust such that if Clyde dies first, Trust B provides a share for his daughter that is equal to some percentage (e.g., 20% or whatever other percentage Lynda and Clyde are comfortable with) of the overall estate as measured when Lynda dies. Lynda couldn't change it after Clyde's death.

15. Estate planning given the Mills' unequal wealth:

(a) If Lisa dies first, her estate might not be enough to fully utilize her unified credit (i.e., if it is under the AEA amount in the year she dies, the B trust in an ABC or AB plan would be under funded). This might result in estate tax at Forest's death.

(b) For tax purposes he may give his wife enough of his estate that they are about equal so as to be able to use up both of the AEA amounts regardless of who dies first. If this is done it will lighten the tax burden. Indeed, this could be done by using a lifetime QTIP trust that would be included in Lisa's estate if she dies first but would not give her control over the trust corpus.

(c) The stability of the marriage is a huge question. One would not want to transfer assets to Lisa if Forest thinks divorce is likely or if he thinks that she will squander away the property. Even placing the assets in a QTIP trust has some danger. Since the trust must be irrevocable and can't be contingent on their remaining married, if they divorce, she will continue to receive the income from the trust. Just because it might make tax sense to "share the wealth" it might not be a wise move if the marriage is not stable.

17. PTC problem with an ABC Trust:

(a) (i) S1's estate = $7,900,000; (ii) Tr A $3,300,000, Tr B $1,500,000, and Tr C $6,400,000; (iii) QTIP fraction = $2,300,000/$6,400,000; and (iv) federal tax of $1,917,000.

(b) (i) S2's estate equals Tr A plus QTIP fraction times Tr C: $3,500,000 + ($2,300,000/$6,400,000) * $6,800,000 = $5,943,750; and (ii) the tax is $1,774,688.

(c) Life estate factor for an 80 year old at a 4% rate is 0.25253, hence limit one is 0.25253 * $1,917,000 = $484,100.

(d) (i) Reduced taxable estate: $5,943,750 - .25253 * ($7,900,000 - $1,917,000) = $4,432,863; and (ii) credit limit two is $1,774,688 - $1,094,788 = $679,900. Note, $1,094,688 is the federal tax on the reduced taxable estate.

(e) Lower of the two limits times a time factor of 80%: 80% * $484,100 = $387,280. Tax: $1,774,688 - $387,280 = $1,387,408.

19. PTC problem with an AsuperB Trust:

(a) (i) Tr A $1,400,000 and Tr B $14,840,000; (ii) $6,720/$14,840,000; and (iii) $3,101,400.

(b) (i) Tr A = QTIP fraction * Tr C: $1,600,000 + ($6,720/$14,840,000) * $16,450,000 = $9,049,057; and (ii) $2,497,076.

(c) factor * federal tax: 0.66792 * $3,101,400 = $2,071,487.

(d) (i) $9,049,057 - 0.66792 * ($14,840,000 - $3,101,400) = $1,208,611; and (ii) zero tax on the reduced taxable estate, hence limit two is $2,497,076.

(e) (i) lower of the two, more than four years, hence: 60% * $2,071,487 = $1,242,892; and (ii) $2,497,076 - $1,242,892 = $1,254,184.

21. Using a QDOT:

(a) She would have her entire estate taxed with no MD since her husband is not a citizen of the U.S., hence a tax of $460,000. A QDOT would allow for a marital deduction. The amount to postpone all taxes would be the amount above Lucia's available AEA, e.g., here $1,700,000. Unless Trust C is fashioned to be a QDOT, an ABC Trust would not serve much purpose since a regular C trust would not qualify for the marital deduction. If it is designed to be a QDOT, then it makes good sense in that Lucia's unified credit is used (Trust B) and a marital deduction is available (Trust C-DOT) and she selects the remaindermen of both trusts.

(b) There is a marital deduction without using a QDOT since the estate goes to a citizen spouse. The citizenship of the decedent spouse does not effect the marital deduction. An ABC trust makes sense as it allows Fortino to control the ultimate disposition of his estate and still use his unified credit.

23. Addiction problems seem to be hereditary, trusts might help:

(a) You don't want Amy to have unlimited access to corpus, or possibly even the ability to have unrestricted income. Amy should not serve as a trustee; there should be an independent trustee making the decisions. This is where putting an ascertainable standard in place would allow the trustee to make the tough decisions all the way around.

(b) A higher minimum age for distribution could help give Walter more time to "recover" from his addiction problem before being able to access corpus without restriction. Or his share could stay in trust for his lifetime, with remainder to his issue or given to the Beasley's other children if Walter leaves no issue.

ENDNOTES

1. IRC § 6081.

2. IRC § 2523(f).

3. The reader may wish to review the basic prior transfer credit material presented in Chapter 6 before tackling this material.

4. The 7520 rate for October 2005 was not available when this example was written.

5. IRC § 2056(d).

6. IRC § 2056(d)(4).

7. IRC § 2056(d)(2)(A).

8. Reg. § 26.2056A-2(d).

9. Reg.§ 20.2056A-3(a).

10. Reg. § 20.2056A-2(d).

11. IRC § 2056(d)(2)(B).

12. IRC § 2056(d)(3).

CHAPTER 11

Gift Planning Fundamentals

OVERVIEW

The last two chapters focused on property transfers at death. This chapter covers some of the estate planning techniques used in giving gifts. Lifetime transfers take many forms and are made for many reasons to family, friends, and charities. They are made outright or to a fiduciary, such as a trustee or custodian. They are completed transfers, such as bargain sales and outright gifts; or they are incomplete, as in trust with a retained interest. Some are transfers of the donor's entire interest in property or it might be a partial interest, such as income from the property for a period of time.

Keep in mind two important principles. First, different types of transfers are designed to accomplish different types of goals. Second, the less complete the transfer, the more probable the asset will be part of the donor's estate and the less likely the transfer will achieve desired tax goals. This may be problematic if the donor wants to retain some control over the transferred property. By definition, every transfer of property rights requires the relinquishment of some control. Gifts mean loss of access, control, and flexibility; individuals who are reluctant to give this up are likely to feel uncomfortable with a gift-giving program as part of their estate plan no matter what the magnitude of the financial rewards might be. Planners should be sensitive to this issue.

To minimize loss of access, control, and flexibility, some individuals may contemplate gifts to family members who secretly agree to always make the assets available to the donor. This arrangement is a retained interest which, if it came to light after the donor died, would cause the property to be included in the donor's estate. There are other problems with this arrangement: First, the donees may have a "change in attitude," and dispose of the gift asset or refuse to share it or return it. Second, the gift assets are subject to the claims of the donee's creditors.

Assuming the donor and the donee are capable persons, a gift is complete for tax purposes when the donor surrenders dominion and control by making delivery of an interest in property to a donee who accepts the gift. Either party might be incapable of making a gift due to being such a young age or suffering from a mental disability that he or she does not appreciate the act of parting with or accepting title to property.

EXAMPLE 11 - 1. Eleven-year-old Millie tells five-year-old Anne that they will always be best friends if Anne will give Millie her xyz. If Anne parts with the xyz, her parents can get it back for her since Anne is too young to appreciate the nature of making a gift.

However, the donor may not wish to bestow the degree of control that occurs with an outright gift, e.g., a person might wish to help a grandchild with college expenses, but may be reluctant to make an outright gift. The usual alternative to an outright gift is a transfer to a fiduciary, who is responsible for managing the property and distributing its income and principal in accordance with the conditions contained in the underlying document or established by local law. Significant gifts for minors are especially likely to be in the name of a fiduciary, such as a custodian or a trustee. Gifts to adult donees are usually outright but may also be made in trust.

IMPACT OF EGTRRA

Gifts may be used somewhat less in the post-EGTRRA era for two reasons. First, with the estate tax decreasing and possibly disappearing, there will be less need for all types of tax reduction devices. Some of the estate planning techniques for married couples, and for passing wealth to the next generation, make sense only if one assumes both spouses are likely to die before 2010 or that the estate AEA will fall back to $1,000,000 in 2011 due to EGTRRA's sunset provision. For most couples, at least one of them will be alive after 2009 and it is more probable than not that the AEA will increase to at least $3,500,00 or that the estate tax repeal will be made permanent. Second, one response to the uncertainty is to use devices that keep options open for adapting to potential tax law changes. People may defer making gifts, instead adopting a wait-and-see approach. Gifts are not a good match for an environment where options need to be kept open. Outright gifts are not possible to undo and incomplete gifts generally do not avoid the donor's estate.

NON-TAX MOTIVES FOR MAKING GIFTS

There are many non-tax motivations that encourage people to make gifts, such as the desire by parents or grandparents to provide for an expensive education, to help children finance a home or an automobile, to help establish or expand a business, to encourage a child to work in the parent's business, to help a child who has experienced a significant loss or who is unemployed, to care for elderly parents, and the simple desire to witness a donee's enjoyment of the benefits that a gift can bring. Individuals will be most willing to make gifts for the tax advantages to be described next when they are also motivated by one or more of these non-tax objectives.

TAX CONSIDERATIONS IN MAKING GIFTS

One should consider the death tax and income tax advantages and disadvantages of making gifts.

Tax Advantages of Gifting

Gifts are commonly made to save federal and state death taxes, generation-skipping transfer (GST) tax, and federal, state, and local income taxes. In the examples that follow, look for two common tax threads. First, some gifts have no gift tax cost. Second, even if a gift tax is incurred, gifts may still be desirable because they have the potential of reducing total transfer taxes and income taxes.

Estate tax and GST tax advantages. Estate tax and GST tax advantages include the ability to reduce or freeze the taxable estate in three ways: using the shelter of the annual exclusion and the unified credit, removing the money paid as gift tax from the transfer tax base, and excluding post-gift appreciation.

Shelter of annual exclusion and unified credit. Most people about to embark on a program of gifting will be able to transfer a significant portion of their estate, free of gift tax, death tax, and GST tax. The gift tax and GST tax annual exclusions enable a donor to give, free of tax, $10,000 (indexed) per donee per year. The annual exclusion increased to $11,000 as of 2002, and as previously stated, it is anticipated that it will increase to $12,000 starting in 2006 but the increase might not happen until 2007. Likewise, the increase to $13,000 is likely to occur in 2010 but, depending on inflation, it could occur the year before or the year after. For our purposes we will use $12,000 for examples occurring 2006 through 2009, and $13,000 for gifts in the years 2010 through 2013. A married couple can give $24,000 per donee in 2007, splitting the gift if the property belonged to just one spouse.

> EXAMPLE 11 - 2. In making a gift in 2007, Marlene wishes to give maximum equal amounts of her own property to her three children and three grandchildren. She can give each of the six donees $12,000 gift tax and GST tax free, for a total tax-free transfer of $72,000. If her husband will join in gift splitting, that figure doubles to $144,000.

During each calendar year, so long as the donor limits the gifts given to each donee to the annual exclusion amount, there is no need to file a gift tax return. Of course, splitting the gift requires a gift tax return by the donor spouse. If the gifts after being split fall below the annual exclusion, then only the donor spouse needs to file, otherwise, both must file.

Generalizing from these examples, the total number of annual exclusions available over time equals the number of donors times the number of donees times the number of years of gifting. As indexing increases the annual exclusion, more can be given without using up any unified credit. It appears that the gift tax will remain after 2009 whether the EGTRRA changes are made permanent or are repealed.

Actually, a donor can give a much larger amount, gift tax (and GST tax) free if the donor is willing to use up some unified credit (and, if applicable, the GST exemption). Thus, a couple with five donees who start an aggressive gift-giving program in 2006 could give $2,480,000 over five years completely gift tax free. Of course, the couple would use up all of their respective $1 million gift exclusions. If they both died before 2010, their estates would be able to use any increase in the AEA (i.e., above $1 million) to shelter part of their estates.

Significant gifts can be made to skip persons by applying the donor's GST exemption to the transfers. As a result of EGTRRA the GST exemption increased in 2004 to equal the estate AEA for the year of transfer, e.g., $2 million in years 2006 through 2008. Gifts under the annual exclusion amount do not use up any of the donor's GST exemption. The GST tax is to end in 2010, but as with the estate tax, planners must be concerned about the sunset provision that completely revives the GST tax in 2011, coupled with a reversion back to an indexed exemption that will be around $1.3 million by then. Additional information on the GST tax is included in Chapter 17.

Summarizing, making annual exclusion gifts, gifts sheltered by the unified credit, and gifts sheltered by the GST exemption enable individuals to substantially reduce their gross estate without having to pay gift taxes or the GST tax. Current gift planning is clouded by the uncertainty of what will happen to the estate tax and the GST tax after 2010.

Removing the gift tax from the transfer tax base. The second advantage of gifting is the ability to exclude the amount of any gift tax paid on gifts given more than three years before death from the gross estate and thus the death and GST tax. Unlike the estate tax, the gift tax is calculated on a tax-exclusive basis.

Of course one must weigh the possible benefit (i.e., that gift taxes are a deduction from the transfer tax base) with the fact that if the donor lives to 2010, the estate tax may be gone or the estate AEA increased such that most wealthy couples will not have to pay an estate tax so long as they have an estate plan like the ones discussed in the last two chapters.

Removing post-gift appreciation. The third tax advantage of gifting is the ability to exclude post-gift appreciation of the gifted property from future estate tax and GST tax. Gifts accomplish this tax saving in two different ways. First, gifting will freeze estate tax values by limiting the estate tax value of the transferred asset to its adjusted gift value. Second, gifting can leverage the use of exclusions and exemptions because post-gift appreciation also escapes transfer taxes. The following example illustrates the usefulness of freezing and leveraging techniques.

EXAMPLE 11 - 3. In 2005, Eighty-two-year-old Jeanne's estate consists of $3 million in bonds and $1 million in common stock. Able to live well on the bond income, Jeanne gifts the stock to an irrevocable trust that pays the income to her three children for their lives with the remainder going to her grandchildren. Jeanne allocates $1 million of her GST exemption to this transfer. In this simple but effective estate freeze, Jeanne has virtually ensured that she will die with an estate tax base at about $4 million (assets owned at death plus adjusted taxable gifts), no matter how much the values of the stocks rise. And Jeanne has leveraged the use of her GST exemption. For example, if the stock is eventually worth $4 million when it passes to the grandchildren, each $1 in current GST exemption will have sheltered $4 from GST tax. Of course if it passes to the grandchildren after 2009 it might pass GST tax-free anyway.

For the next several years, the very wealthy have an interesting choice, a tradeoff between GST tax and basis step-up. In 2006, by making gifts, a donor will be able to shelter $2 million from the GST tax but only $1 million from gift taxes (an exclusion-exemption gap). If one creates a GST tax trust, whether by gift or at death, and shelters it by application of the exemption, future transfer estate taxes might be saved on terminations or distributions to skip persons that occur before 2010 but the cost of doing so is paying a gift tax on property that might have escaped all transfer taxes. The benefit is uncertain due to the sunset provision of EGTRRA and the likelihood that Congress will dramatically change the transfer tax within the near future.

Income tax advantages. The making of gifts offers some income tax advantages, including the shifting of income.

Shifting income. Gifts can result in some income shifting. After a completed gift, the donee is taxed on the income generated by the property. Generally, the donee is in a lower marginal income tax bracket than the donor. Rather than making annual gifts to a relative to help with living expenses, it might be wise to transfer income producing assets, especially if the property is likely to return to the donor when the donee dies.

> EXAMPLE 11 - 4. Each year, Aaron and his wife, Sue, made gifts of approximately $20,000 to Aaron's mother, Cynthia, to supplement her income from some savings accounts and Social Security. Since they were in a combined state and federal income tax bracket of 45%, they decided to transfer $300,000 in assets to Cynthia, with the understanding that at her death she would leave the property to them. If the property produces $20,000 that is taxed at a combined 15% bracket, the tax saved by the extended family is $6,000 ($20,000 * (45%-15%)) per year. Of course the transfer was a taxable gift, but given the increase in the estate AEA, they are less concerned about using up some of their own and Cynthia's estate is not large enough to generate an estate tax.

Tax Disadvantages of Gifting

There are several tax disadvantages to large lifetime gifts, including prepaying the transfer tax, perhaps paying a transfer tax that would never have to be paid if the estate AEA continues to rise or the estate tax repeal is made permanent, and the possible loss of the step-up in basis.

Prepaying the transfer tax. A large gift can result in a gift tax liability that must be paid by April 15 of the following year, thereby reducing the donor's available funds for investment. Nonetheless, prepayment of the transfer tax is justifiable if it has the effect of substantially reducing the donor's estate tax. This will happen if the gift property appreciates greatly before the donor's death or if it appreciates modestly and the donor can avoid grossing up by surviving at least three years after making the gift. On the other hand, gifting property and prepaying the transfer tax may have little benefit if the property declines in value and/or the donor dies within three years of making the gift, and/or if the donor lives beyond 2009 and repeal of the estate tax holds or the estate AEA is dramatically increased. Then, transfer taxes will have been paid that would have been avoided if the property had been kept. The donee probably has a lower basis in the property than had it been included in the donor's estate. Thus, to assess the likelihood of financial benefits resulting from a large gift, the planner should consider factors such as the life expectancy of the donor, the expected appreciation potential of the property, the different basis rules, the potential time of death relative to tax rule changes, and the utility of the property to the donor and donee.

Limited but real–the three year rule. We mentioned in the preceding discussion that if a gift is made within three years of death, § 2035(b) requires the gift tax paid to be included in the donor's gross estate under the "gross-up" rule. In addition to this adverse consequence, recall from the discussion of the retained interest rules that the entire date-of-death value of the gift property is included in the donor's gross estate if §§ 2036, 2037, or 2038 apply, or if an incident of ownership in life insurance was retained (§ 2042) at the date of death. Section 2035(a) causes inclusion if the decedent transferred (released) a retained interest or an incident of ownership in life insurance on the donor's life within three years of death.

In summary, if the transfers are within three years, the death occurs before 2009, and § 2035(a) and § 2035(b) apply, all advantages of gifting are lost, even the benefit of the annual exclusion. If this occurs, the only positive thing is that appreciated property will receive a step-up in basis.

Gifts complete but still included in the donor's estate. If it is later determined that a gift was not complete, the date-of-death value of the property is included in the donor's gross estate even if the donor reported it as a gift. The estate will receive a credit for the gift taxes paid, but from a transfer tax perspective the gift will be considered as not having been made.

EXAMPLE 11 - 5. Carmen transferred title to her house to her sons, but continued to live in the house rent free. Her sons had their own homes. It should not be too difficult to establish that there was an understanding that she retained the right to live there. This would cause the value of the house to be included in her estate.[1]

EXAMPLE 11 - 6. Dan created an irrevocable trust, giving the trustee discretion to determine how much income to distribute each year to Dan's children. Dan also reserved the right to replace the trustee. Because the terms of the trust were silent as to whether Dan could replace the trustee with himself, it is likely that he has a retained interest.[2]

EXAMPLE 11 - 7. On her deathbed, decedent made a gift by writing a check on her bank account. She died a day before the check was cashed. Because she had the power to revoke the gift by stopping payment on the check, the gift was considered to be incomplete (a § 2038 revocable transfer) and the amount of the check was included in her gross estate.[3]

Loss of step-up in basis. A major tax disadvantage of making lifetime gifts is the loss in the step-up in basis that would have been received on appreciated property had it been retained by the donor until death. This is a drawback for a donee who wishes to sell the appreciated property. It is also a drawback if the property is depreciable, since a step-up at death allows the person inheriting the property to start over again with depreciation.

EXAMPLE 11 - 8. Granny has always wanted to do something nice for her adult grandson. She gives him rental real property that she acquired in the 1920's. Grandson has a low carry over, fully depreciated, basis whereas there would have been a step-up in basis if Granny held on to the property until her death.

Net gifts may result in capital gains to the donor. Very rarely, a taxable gain for the donor results when a net gift arrangement is used. This is where the donee agrees to pay the gift tax thus reducing the value of the gift, which in turn reduces the gift tax. A net gift results in a taxable gain to the donor only if the gift tax paid by the donee exceeds the donor's basis in the property. Several factors combine to make your chance of coming in contact with a net gift that produces a capital gain about the same as being struck by lightning on a sunny day. These factors include the increased size of the AEA, the reluctance of even the wealthy to make taxable gifts so large as to require the actual payment of gift tax, and the pending elimination of the estate tax.

> EXAMPLE 11 - 9. During the summer of 2006, Harold gave his son Julian closely held MOP stock worth $1,712,000 on condition that Julian pay the gift tax. Harold's basis in the stock was $140,000 so, when Julian paid the gift tax of $300,000 it created a taxable gain of $160,000 for Harold.

SELECTING PROPERTY TO GIVE AWAY

In giving, the donor usually has a wide selection of assets from which to choose. From an estate planning perspective, some assets make better gifts than others. The following constitutes a basic set of guidelines for selecting gift property. As the examples will illustrate, the choice of the best asset will usually depend on the specific family situation.

Basis Considerations

A person who has decided to make gifts for estate planning reasons will want to consider the basis of various assets since the basis will partially determine whether a particular asset is a good candidate to select as a gift. Other factors enter into the decision, such as whether the donee will sell the asset to raise his or her income level and whether the donor will sell assets he or she has kept in order to make up for income lost as a result of giving away an income producing asset.

Gifting high-basis assets. If the donee is likely to sell the asset soon after receiving it, other things being equal, a high-basis asset makes a better gift than a low-basis asset. As we have seen, the general rule is that the donee retains the donor's basis. A sale by the donee at a price above this basis results in a taxable gain. The higher the basis, the lower the taxable gain.

> EXAMPLE 11 - 10. Donor wishes to give donee $100,000 in marketable securities. Donor owns stock A, now worth $100,000, which she purchased two years ago for $95,000, and stock B, also worth $100,000, which was acquired 15 years ago for $20,000. The donee plans to sell the stock he receives when it reaches $110,000 in value. The donee will realize a gain of only $15,000 on the sale of stock A but a

gain of $90,000 on the sale of stock B. Needless to say, the donee would prefer to receive stock A.

Although a high-basis asset usually makes a good gift from an income tax point of view, it will make an unattractive gift if its basis is higher than its date-of-gift value. Property in which the owner has an unrealized loss is not a good asset to give because the donee, on selling it, will not be able to recognize that loss. A better strategy would be for the donor to sell the property, realize the loss, and then give the cash to the donee.

Gifting low-basis assets. In some circumstances, giving low-basis assets makes sense. For example, if for liquidity or other reasons a donor plans to sell a retained asset at the time of giving another asset, he or she should consider gifting a lower-basis asset and selling the higher-basis asset in order to personally incur a lower tax outlay. This strategy is especially productive if the donee is in a lower tax bracket or has no immediate plans to sell the property received as a gift. Gain realized on later sale by the donee will at least be deferred and may be totally eliminated, if the donee dies before the asset is sold. Keep in mind the rubber band rule, discussed previously, whereby appreciated property that returns to the donor as a result of the donee's death has a carry-over basis. The adjusted basis to the surviving donor is the same as the donee-decedent's adjusted basis immediately before he or she died. Post-2009, the rubber band rule will be replaced with a carry-over rule for any gift property received within three years of death except for gifts received from a spouse.

Assets having sentimental or utilitarian value are more likely to be kept by a donee. If a gift is going to be kept by the donee, basis considerations are less relevant.

Post-gift Appreciation

The person considering gifts should consider growth assets, i.e., assets expected to appreciate substantially, rather than assets whose value is likely to remain stable or fall. Some assets have greater appreciation potential than others. Assets such as life insurance and equity interests in either a closely held business or real estate (in a good location) are likely growth prospects, while assets such as patent and royalty rights, which have values that usually decline over time, often do not make good gift assets. Cash and cash equivalents are also less desirable, because their values do not rise. In general, from a transfer-tax point of view, assets having a combined low gift tax value and potentially high estate tax value make the best gifts.

For the very elderly and/or very ill, for the next several years estate tax reduction might remain a major goal. Of course, if the donor outlives the estate tax, there will be regret that the assets were given away (assuming appreciation really does take place—ah for a crystal ball) as the opportunity to receive a step-up in basis will have been lost. The carry-over basis that is supposed to take effect in 2010 (if the law for that year becomes permanent) will not reach most estates since it does not apply to estates under $1.3 million or a much higher threshold if the estate is left to a surviving spouse.

Opportunity shifting. Opportunity shifting is the transfer of a potentially highly appreciating asset before its value is objectively ascertainable. For example, a businessperson may recognize the potential of a profitable commercial enterprise before it blossoms into a verifiably valuable opportunity. By transferring ownership during a venture's early stages, a donor can shift value to a donee with minimal transfer tax cost and before the income the venture generates is attributable to the donor.

> EXAMPLE 11 - 11. Scott, the owner of a successful computer component firm, has just established a new corporation to pursue the viability of a recently developed engineering idea. The new firm is capitalized at $150,000, and Scott gives his daughter, Jenna, 30% of the stock and his son, Rielly, another 30%. If the idea proves to be successful, each child's share could be worth millions yet the gift was under the annual exclusion amount. To avoid having the valuation challenged later, Scott attached a well-documented appraisal of the stock to the gift tax return.

This example demonstrates that it is advantageous to transfer interests in a new enterprise before the value of the enterprise has manifested itself. Similar techniques can be arranged for almost any asset that is expected to appreciate in value. Good hunches by knowledgeable people are the major sources of intra-family opportunity shifting.

Administration Problems

Assets that are likely to create problems in estate administration may make good gifts. For example, art works, especially those currently worth less than the annual gift tax exclusion, may not need to be valued if transferred by lifetime gift. They could create valuation disputes, a potentially higher estate tax, and additional costs of valuation if transferred at death. A business included in the decedent's estate may cause a conflict between the executor (charged with safeguarding assets) and the heirs, especially if some heirs are running the business and others are not. If some heirs take hard-to-value assets, e.g., a business, as their part of the estate, they may be in conflict with others who take assets with a readily ascertained value, e.g., stock traded on an exchange or cash. Heirs taking the hard-to-value assets may argue for a value lower than what the other family members think is reasonable.

Qualifying the Donor's Estate for Tax Relief

Some provisions of the IRC give estate tax relief to a decedent's estate if the decedent's business is more than a certain percentage of the estate. Giving away nonbusiness property may increase the percentage of the estate considered business property to gain these advantages. Or the owner might sell some nonbusiness assets and use the proceeds to improve the business property, thus increasing the business portion. Discussed in greater detail in Chapter 14, what follows are some of these relief sections:

1. **§ 303** - This section allows the estate to pay death taxes, funeral bills, and administrative expenses, with cash from a closely held corporation provided the corporation stock is valued at 35% or more of the decedent's adjusted gross estate (AGE). The corporation can buy back stock from the decedent's estate with the transaction being treated as a capital transaction instead of a dividend distribution. Since the stock held by the estate will have received a step-up in basis due to the owner's death, there should be very little, if any, capital gain.[4]

2. **§ 2032A** - This section allows the real estate used in a closely held business to be reduced by up to $750,000 (indexed) based on its special use valuation.

The decedent's special use real estate must equal or exceed 25% of the decedent's AGE and the real estate combined with the rest of the special use business must equal or exceed 50% of the AGE.[5]

3. **§ 6166** - This section allows estate tax payment over 14 years (with a favorable late payment interest charge on the deferred tax) provided the business is equal to or greater than 35% of AGE.[6]

For individuals with business interests that do not meet the percentage requirements, gifts of nonbusiness assets will increase the business percentage. However, IRC § 2035(c)(1) requires that the percentage requirements for § 303 and § 2032A be met with any transfers within three years added back into the gross estate. Section 2035(c)(2) also requires that the § 6166 threshold of 35% for the business interest be met both with and without adding back into the gross estate any gifts made within three years of decedent's death. Note that this "add back" is done to determine whether the estate still meets the percentage thresholds; it does not mean that the gifts are actually added into the gross estate for tax purposes.

EXAMPLE 11 - 12. Farmer Brown had the following assets immediately before and after he gave away his XYZ stock to his three children:

Items	FMV pre-gift	2032A %	FMV post-gift	2032A %
Stock	$1,500,000		given away	
Other Property	$1,100,000		$1,100,000	
Farmland	$1,400,000	32.6%	$1,400,000	50.0%
Farm Equipment	$300,000	7.0%	$300,000	10.7%
Total Farm	**$1,700,000**	**39.5%**	**$1,700,000**	**60.7%**
Total	$4,300,000		$2,800,000	

To qualify for § 2032A, the business land must equal 25% or more of AGE, and the land and other business property (tractors, etc.) must equal 50% or more of AGE. The gift accomplishes this, provided the thresholds are still met when he dies.

EXAMPLE 11 - 13. Farmer Brown dies after making the gift of stock. The stock has increased in value to $1,600,000 and the other items (still owned by him when he died) have the values shown in the table:

Items	FMV @ Death less than 3 Yrs.	2032A %	FMV @ Death more than 3 Yrs.	2032A %
Stock	$1,600,000		given away	
Other Property	$1,300,000		$1,300,000	
Farmland	$1,480,000	32.0%	$1,480,000	48.8%
Farm Equipment	$250,000	5.4%	$250,000	8.3%
Total Farm	**$1,730,000**	**37.4%**	**$1,730,000**	**57.1%**
Total	$4,630,000		$3,030,000	

If his death was just short of three years after making the gift, the land percentage is met (i.e, 32% > 25%), but the total special use business percentage is not met (i.e., 37.4% < 50%), and special use is not available. If his death is just beyond the three-year reach of § 2035(c)(1), then the gift is not added back to determine § 2032A, and the two § 2032A percentage limits are exceeded (i.e., 48.8% > 25% and 57.1% > 50%).

Notice that the 35% threshold for § 6166 (drawn-out payment schedule) is met both with and without the gift. Therefore the § 6166 election is available regardless of whether the death was just under or just over three years after the gift. One final comment: even if farmer Brown died within three years of the gift, the stock's appreciation is NOT being taxed, nor is the annual exclusion lost. The gift of the stock is still an adjusted taxable gift of $1,470,000 (three kids, three annual exclusions). It is not part of the gross estate. It is brought back merely to test whether the elections (§§ 303, 2032A, and 6166) are available.

Miscellaneous tax factors. Because parents are likely to be in higher tax brackets than their children, they might not qualify for tax benefits that are available to their children. Yet the children might not be in a financial position to take advantage of the tax benefits, especially those involving retirement planning. As a general rule, given the effect of tax-free compounding of income-earning pension-like accounts, the earlier they are established the greater the likelihood that the value will be significant when the person retires. In the early years, working young adults, especially if married and raising young children, might want to establish a 401k or 403(b) account but find it difficult to do so and still meet living expenses. Parents might agree to annual gifts provided the money is placed in some sort of tax-deferred account that includes at least some of the child's own funds. Obviously, some arrangements, such as 403(b) accounts for government or charity employees, require a wage reduction agreement between the employee and the employer, with direct payments made by the employer to the fund trustee. In such cases, the parents' gifts will be made directly to the child to make up for the income that is being placed in the account.

> EXAMPLE 11 - 14. Because of their high income, the Piatts are not qualified to contribute before-tax dollars to an Individual Retirement Account (IRA). Their adult son, John, is qualified, but he cannot afford to make the contributions. John enters into an informal agreement with his parents, who will give him $1,500 a year, to help contribute $2,000 to his own IRA. This arrangement is to continue indefinitely, so long as John adds $500 and does not make any premature withdrawals. Each year, John will save hundreds of dollars in income tax by taking the IRA deduction. The Piatts have the satisfaction of knowing that they have increased his financial security.

As a result of the kiddie tax, generous parents may wish to transfer to their young children property that does not generate taxable income, at least not until the children reach age 14. Possible assets include U.S. government EE bonds, municipal bonds, interests in land, a closely held business, and growth stocks. In many situations, the parent can then determine the timing of the tax "hit" by choosing which year to liquidate the assets and realize the likely gain. It should be mentioned that the popular U.S. Government EE savings bonds are not transferable. An outright gift of them is considered a redemption. However, there is no restriction on an owner adding co-owners.

GIFTS FROM ONE SPOUSE TO THE OTHER

Earlier chapters examined in some detail marital deduction techniques designed to minimize, or at least postpone, the estate tax for a married couple. Where one spouse is much wealthier than the other and the less wealthy spouse dies first, estate taxes might be saved by means of a program of inter-spousal gifts coupled with bypass planning. The goal is to make sure two AEAs are used instead of using just the wealthy spouse's AEA.

EGTRRA's impact. EGTRRA creates the risk of adverse effects with this technique. If at the time of the second death there is no estate tax or the AEA is so high that there would have been no taxes owed even without a bypass trust, then the use of the trust has no estate tax benefit at the second death but has the negative effect of precluding basis step-up because the trust is not included in the estate. Indeed if the changes become permanent, QTIP trusts, regardless of whether an election was made, will not be included in the survivor's estate after 2009 because the law states, in regard to trust property, "The decedent shall be treated as owning property transferred by the decedent during life to a qualified revocable trust . . . "[7] The QTIP trust fails to meet the criterion on two counts; it is not created by the surviving spouse and it is not revocable.

It is likely that ABC Trust plans will be amended to give the surviving spouse a springing general power over trust C that is triggered by the estate tax being repealed during the surviving spouse's lifetime. If there are no children by prior marriages, it might make sense to have Trusts B and C pour over to Trust A as of such time that the estate tax repeal is made permanent. Drafting should address the very real risk that Congress may not allow the repeal to take place, instead substituting a high AEA. Less likely, but still a risk is that Congress could allow the sunset provision to actually take place. Another risk, harder to draft around, is that one Congress makes the repeal of the estate tax "permanent" followed by another Congress that brings it back. What happens to the plans that allowed the estate to merge based upon the repeal?

Risks. Even if both deaths are likely to happen before 2010, the wealthier spouse may have some reservations about making a sizable gift to his or her spouse. First, for the transfer to be complete, the donor spouse must be willing to surrender complete dominion and control to his or her spouse. Planners should consider the possibility of future marital strife and its effect on the overall plan. The donor might regret that the gift was ever made. Further, even if the spouses are happily married, the wealthier spouse may still be reluctant to relinquish control over so much wealth. As a possible solution, the donor spouse can create a lifetime-funded QTIP trust, hence the donor spouse controls who will eventually receive the corpus. There could even be a provision that if the donee spouse dies first, the trust property reverts to the donor spouse. With that provision, if the estate tax is still around when the beneficiary of the QTIP trust dies, the donor spouse could disclaim an amount equal to the deceased spouse's AEA (thus utilizing her unified credit). If she dies after 2009 (and the estate tax is really gone), the surviving spouse can accept the reversion of the property without negative consequences.

Gifts to reduce income taxes. Ordinarily, there is no lifetime income tax advantage to inter-spousal gifts. As we have seen, the joint income tax return, filed by the overwhelming majority of spouses, has the effect of combining spousal income and produces one tax, no matter which spouse earned the income.

However, a completed gift from one spouse to the other can save income taxes if the donee spouse dies first, and the donor later sells it at a gain. The tax-saving results from the opportunity to experience a step-up in basis before sale and was illustrated earlier. Of course one must avoid §1014(e)'s rubber band rule providing that if one gives appreciated property and the donee bequeaths it back within one year, there is no step-up in basis.

> EXAMPLE 11 - 15. Bob gave his wife stock that he had bought for $6,000. It was worth $50,000 when he gave it to her. She died seven months later, leaving the stock, then worth $55,000, to Bob. He was unable to obtain a step-up in basis due to the restriction in Code Section 1014(e). However, had his wife lived longer than one year, Bob's basis would have been $55,000 (assuming that as the date-of-death value), because of the resulting step-up in basis.

> EXAMPLE 11 - 16. In the prior example, had Bob's wife bequeathed the property to her bypass trust for Bob's benefit, § 1014(e) would not apply because the property would pass to a different party (the trustee) and not back to the donor-spouse. Thus, a step-up would have been available even if the donee spouse had not lived one year after the gift had been made.

Couples using gift strategies, such as those in the examples, will save estate tax and income tax. In community property states, of course, since the surviving spouse receives a step-up in basis at S1's death for all community property owned, this gifting strategy need only be considered for separate property.

GIFTS TO CHILDREN

Gifts to minor children are unique because of the manner by which their transfer is usually arranged. Gifts of significant value are usually not made outright to minors but through a fiduciary in a custodianship or a trust. Parents who are trying to find ways to pay for their children's college expenses may wish to transfer assets to the children to reduce the income tax bite. This might be done by using a custodial brokerage account. While the child is under age 14, to avoid the kiddie tax, they might invest in growth stock that does not pay dividends. Once the child is over 14 years of age they may wish to change to a more balanced approach and might even consider a mutual fund that tracks one of the broader indexes, e.g., Standard and Poor's 500 or the Russell 2000.

In addition, income tax laws may help them to acquire certain investments to finance college expenses without transferring assets and at no tax cost. They should consider qualified U.S. Saving Bonds, Hope Scholarship Credits, Lifetime Learning Credits, Educational IRA's, Section 529 Qualified State Tuition Programs and private Section 529 Savings Plans. Because of their relative importance, we will discuss 529 Savings Plans separately.

Some higher education funding plans have phase-out provisions that decrease or remove the benefit for high income individuals. For instance, interest on certain U.S. Savings Bonds (e.g., series EE) purchased and owned by one or both parents themselves (or by the student, if at least 24 years old) are not subject to income tax if redeemed to pay tuition and fees. However, this interest exclusion is subject to phase-out based on the taxpayer's "modified adjusted gross income" in the year the bonds are cashed. The phase-out brackets are indexed for inflation. In 2005, the phase-out for single and head of household taxpayers starts at $61,200 and is complete at $76,200, and for joint return filers it starts at $91,850 and ends at $121,850. For this particular purpose the Code defines modified adjusted gross income as adjusted gross income without regard to §§ 911, 931 or 933 (foreign income exclusions), and after application of § 86 (taxable social security income), § 219 (retirement contribution deductions), and § 469 (limit on deductibility of passive losses).

General Observations.

Outright gifts transfer the greatest amount of control to the donee, invite the least amount of challenge from the IRS, and are the least complicated to make. But an outright gift to a person, whether a minor or an adult, will only work satisfactorily when the donee has sufficient maturity to rationally possess, conserve, and enjoy the gift property. In other circumstances, the transfer should be made to a fiduciary. Many states have statutes that require gifts, above some set value, given to a minor be held for the minor by a fiduciary.

Objectives. The transfer to a fiduciary should be arranged to achieve the same tax advantages (use of the annual exclusion and shifting of income) as are available with an outright gift. It should protect the donee from the risks of his or her own immaturity and comply with any restrictions that state law places on the ownership and use of property by minors.

Before examining types of fiduciary gifts that meet these objectives, recall that if income from a gift is used to discharge the obligation of support of the donor-parent, that income will be taxable to the parent.[8]

> EXAMPLE 11 - 17. Dad gives 14-year-old Junior $500 so that Junior can purchase lunches during his freshman year in high school. Junior deposits the money in his own savings account, subsequently withdrawing interest as well as principal to buy the lunches. The interest income will be taxable to Dad as income used in discharge of a support obligation.

This rule applies even if the source of the income is not from the parents, e.g., income from a trust established by the beneficiary's grandparents. Thus, in order to enjoy the full tax advantages of a completed gift to a minor, income from the gift must not be used to discharge support obligations. Ordinarily, parents are not obligated to support their adult children, so the issue does not usually apply to adult donees. However, there are exceptions. In some states, including Illinois and New Jersey, judges in divorce cases have imposed the duty of support for higher education for adult children. However, several factors limit the application of this exception. In 1992, Pennsylvania's Supreme Court ruled that divorcing parents would no longer be so obligated, reasoning that children become adults at age 18 and that the state's legislature had not explicitly addressed the issue. No court has required parents in an intact family to pay for an adult child's higher education.[9]

Transfer tax considerations. If the donor serves as the custodian or trustee, then establishing the account or funding the trust is probably an incomplete gift since the donor continues to exercise dominion and control over it. Hence, if avoiding estate tax is one of the goals of making these transfers to benefit young family members, one must be mindful that allowing the donor to retain control of the property will cause its inclusion in the donor's gross estate. The underlying Code provisions have been covered in Chapter 6, specifically, § 2036 transfers with retained life estate, and § 2038 revocable or amendable transfers.

One other possible problem with a gift not being complete is that the donor does not take advantage of the annual exclusion until the gift does become complete. This can cause unintended gift tax problems.

EXAMPLE 11 - 18. When his son, Francisco, was 10 years old, Javier established a custodial brokerage account for him. Javier served as custodian of the account under his state's Uniform Transfer to Minors Act. Each year he added an amount just below the annual exclusion amount. In 2007, Francisco turned 21 and Javier transfer the account, then worth $120,000, to him. The $108,000 in excess of the annual exclusion is a taxable gift. Had someone else served as custodian, the annual transfers would have been complete and the final liquidation of the account would not be a taxable transfer. Whether this could be accomplished by having Javier's wife serve as custodian is an open question.

To make the gift complete and to assure that it is not in the parent-donor's estate requires an independent custodian or trustee. Inclusion in the parent-custodian or parent-trustee's estate will not occur if the grandparents make the gift. However, there may then be a GST tax issue if the gift exceeds the annual exclusion amount. Be aware of the possible problem but also recognize that with the GST exemption equal to the estate AEA, e.g., $2,000,000 in 2006, this not a problem you are likely to encounter. On the other hand, if the parents are the donors, the grandparents can serve as custodians or trustees without either of the aforementioned problems, since there would be neither a retained interest nor a generation skip. Given that most of these transfers are completed, i.e., in the hands of the children, by the time the beneficiary is in his or her mid-twenties, the grandparents are likely to live long enough to see the task through, however alternates should be selected, other than the child's parents, just in case.

The kiddie tax. As discussed in greater detail in Chapter 8, all unearned income of children under age 14 in excess of a statutory amount is taxed at the child's parents' marginal rate. This special treatment is referred to as the "kiddie tax" and is applied if either parent is alive at the end of the tax year. This special treatment ends for the tax year in which the child turns 14. Until the child reaches that age, the kiddie tax makes shifting income to the child a difficult or at least a very complicated endeavor.

Custodial Gifts

Custodial gifts are easy to establish at a bank, savings and loan, or stock brokerage. The institution should have its own forms and have staff familiar with setting up the account. Usually, the minor's social security number is used for the account. One should remember, however, that the establishment of the account is a completed gift, at least from a property point of view, meaning that the donor has no right to take back the gift, although he or she can use it (spend it) for the benefit of the minor.

Uniform Gifts to Minors Act. The Uniform Gifts to Minors Act (UGMA), adopted in one form or other in all states, allows a relatively simple method of making fiduciary gifts to minors. No court supervision is required. The gift property is transferred in the name of someone, acting "as custodian for (minor's name) under the (state name) Uniform Gift to Minors Act." This title serves to "incorporate by reference" all of the provisions of that act, including broad investment powers under the "prudent person" standard, and the ability of the custodian to spend property on behalf of the minor without a court order. Further, a bond need not be given and, unless the donor or donee requests them, accountings are not necessary.

Permissible gift property under UGMA includes securities, cash, life insurance, and annuities, but there is legislative movement by several states to greatly expand this list. In most UGMA states, real property cannot be held in custodial form.

Uniform Transfers to Minors Act. In 1983 the National Conference on Uniform Laws adopted the Uniform Transfers to Minors Act (UTMA), designed to replace the UGMA. Major changes include the following:

1. It allows any property interests to be transferred, including real estate, partnership interests, patents, royalty interests, and intellectual property.
2. It allows custodial gifts at death by permitting a fiduciary (executor or trustee) to establish a custodianship if authorized in a governing will or trust.
3. It authorizes transfers to a custodian from persons other than the transferor who are obligated to the minor (examples of situations include a personal injury recovery, life insurance proceeds payable to a minor beneficiary, and a joint bank account of which the minor is a surviving cotenant).
4. It allows a transferor to nominate a custodian to receive property in the future.

As of mid-2005, all states except South Carolina and Vermont had adopted UTMA (Vermont's legislature was considering it), and most have done so without significant alterations. UTMA, like the UGMA before it, as a default position has distribution to the minor at age 21. States can modify that to the age of majority (i.e., age 18) or some other age. California uses 21 as the default age but allows a donor to specify an older age (up to a maximum age of 25).[10]

Evaluation of custodial gifts. A custodial gift can avoid the time and expense involved in establishing a trust. It is considered a completed gift that qualifies for the annual exclusion. Although a custodianship is like a trust in many ways, it is more restrictive for the following reasons:

- A custodial gift may be created for only one person; a trust can provide for multiple beneficiaries, with unequal distributions among them.
- A custodianship is not a separate legal entity; all income is taxable to the minor. In contrast, an irrevocable trust is a separate taxpayer, enabling one additional "run up the rate ladder."
- Because the law gives the custodian the power to distribute income or principal to the minor, if the donor serves as the custodian and predeceases the minor, §§ 2036 and 2038 bring the custodial property into the custodian's gross estate. This is not a problem if someone other than the donor serves as custodian or as trustee.
- Donees usually must receive custodial property outright by age 21; trust beneficiaries' distributions of principal may be delayed to a later age.
- Finally, a custodianship does not have spendthrift provisions.

UTMA provides that custodial property may not be used to satisfy any obligation of support for the minor, such as an obligation stemming from a divorce decree. Thus, custodial gifts if properly structured can achieve essentially all of the tax advantages of completed outright transfers.

Gifts in Trust that Benefit Minors

Although custodial gifts are usually an improvement over substantial outright gifts to minors, there are serious drawbacks as described above. They usually terminate at or shortly after the donee's age of majority, at which time the donee enjoys fee simple ownership of the property. They may restrict the type of property that may be given under the laws of some states. They are also inflexible in that the controlling state law usually cannot be modified by private document. The presence of these and other drawbacks lead many donors to use irrevocable trusts for gifts to minors or not make the gift at all.

In structuring gifts in trust for the benefit of minors, planners usually seek to obtain all of the tax benefits available to outright gifts. The four major tax objectives are:

1. Using the annual gift tax exclusion and the unified credit to avoid gift taxes,
2. Excluding the gift from the donor's gross estate,
3. Excluding all post-gift appreciation in the value of the gift property from the donor's estate tax base, and
4. Shifting the taxable income earned on the gift property to the trust or to the donee.

An irrevocable trust may also have the non-tax advantage of insulating the gift property from the parents' creditors and, in some cases, even from the child's creditors. Drafting an irrevocable trust takes great care because the nature of such transfers seems to invite scrutiny by the IRS. For example, the donor may wish to act as trustee and to restrict the minor child's enjoyment of the trust principal and income for some period of time. These requirements reflect the donor's desire to retain a considerable degree of control over the gift property. The problem is that a very fine line exists between harmless controls and controls that the IRS deems to be retained interests by the donor.

To qualify for the annual exclusion, the donee must be given a present interest, an unrestricted right to the immediate use, possession, or enjoyment of the property or the income from the property. There are methods of obtaining the annual exclusion without really giving a minor control of the property transferred in trust. These exceptions to the present interest requirement are IRC § 2503(c), and two planning devices sanctioned by the courts, even if not loved by the IRS. The three alternatives are called the 2503(c) Trust, the Crummey Trust, and the Mandatory Income Trust.

2503(c) Trust. Under § 2503(c), a gift in trust is not considered a gift of a future interest (even though it really is one) if three conditions are met.

First, the trust must provide that the property and income may be expended by or for the benefit of the donee before the donee attains age 21.[11] This requirement creates the same potential retained interest problem (§§ 2036-2038) for grantors wishing to be trustees as it does for custodial gifts. Second, any portion of the property not so expended must pass to the donee at age 21. Third, if the donee dies before age 21, the property must be either payable to the donee's estate or the donee must hold a general power of appointment over the property. This is met even if the general power is exercisable only through the donee's will, and the trust contains a clause making siblings the takers by default. In most states, a minor is not legally competent to execute a will, so in the event of the death of the minor, the trust property would most likely go to his or her siblings.

The 2503(c) exception was created to allow parents to make gifts that take advantage of the annual exclusion without giving their young children actual control of the property given. The § 2503(c) trustee need not distribute the corpus when the beneficiary reaches age 21, as long as the beneficiary can request complete distribution at age 21 and the beneficiary is so informed.[12]

The Crummey Trusts. Crummey is the name of a taxpayer who succeeded in federal court in getting an annual exclusion by establishing a trust containing withdrawal rights for the benefit of minor children.[13] The typical Crummey Trust clause provides that the child has the right to withdraw, for a brief period (30 to 90 days) as set in the trust document, after each transfer of property into the trust, the lesser of the amount of the available annual exclusion or the value of the gift property transferred. Since the child has the right to withdraw that amount, the gift is considered a gift of a present interest satisfying the § 2503(b) present interest requirement and the donor receives an annual exclusion for the gift. To be effective, the child must be given actual notice of the withdrawal right.

Use of a Crummey power can result in undesired gift tax and income tax consequences. A beneficiary's failure to exercise a Crummey power in a given year may mean that the beneficiary has made a taxable gift by permitting a general power of appointment to lapse.[14]

The taxable gift value will be very small since only the amount that goes to someone other than the person who let the withdrawal right lapse is considered a gift, and even that must be discounted since it is a future interest. Furthermore, if the person who let the withdrawal right lapse eventually receives the corpus of the trust, the gift will not be an adjusted taxable gift since the transfer (a contingent remainder) has reverted to the beneficiary.[15] The latter situation is the usual case, since the beneficiary with the withdrawal right is usually also the remainderman, especially for minors' trusts.

Given the extremely small gift tax value and the likelihood that the transfer would not enter into the estate tax calculation most planners ignore this tax consequence. Some avoid the problem by limiting the annual withdrawal right to the lesser of the annual exclusion or the 5 and 5 limits, i.e., the greater of $5,000 or 5%, or by giving the beneficiary a general testamentary power of appointment over the trust principal.

The gift tax value would be the amount that the value permitted to lapse exceeded the greater of $5,000 or 5% of the aggregate value of the property from which the exercise of the power could be satisfied. For example, suppose $120,000 was contributed as an initial gift in trust, with a child of the trustors having a $20,000 demand right that lapses 90 days after each addition. When the demand right lapses unexercised, the amount that $20,000 exceeds the greater of $5,000 or 5% of $120,000 (i.e., $14,000) is treated as a future interest gift to the remaindermen. Since it is a future interest, it would be discounted, making the actual gift much less than $14,000; however, as a gift of a future interest, it will not qualify for the annual exclusion.

Mandatory Income Trust (MIT). A trust that requires mandatory distribution of income annually to the minor, either outright or to a custodial account established for the minor's benefit, as the way of entitling the donor to the annual exclusion is called a mandatory income trust. The gift is considered as comprising two parts, the income interest and the remainder or reversion interest. Tax law considers the former to be a present interest qualifying for the annual exclusion and the latter to be a future interest that does not so qualify. The alternative fractions making up the gift are derived from Tables S or B, depending on the nature of the income interest.

EXAMPLE 11 - 19. Gerry transferred $100,000 into an irrevocable trust established for his friend, Betty, giving her income for life with the corpus to revert to Gerry, or to his issue, after Betty's death. Betty just turned 85 years old and the rate for valuing split interest gifts was 8%. Therefore, the factor would be 0.34614. This means that $34,614 represents the value of the income interest qualifying for the annual exclusion. Since the present value exceeds $10,000 the full annual exclusion is allowed.

Because IRC § 2503(b) requires the donee to have a present interest in order for a gift to qualify for the annual exclusion, and because this trust makes use of the present interest value of the income stream to satisfy that requirement, it is called a § 2503(b) Trust by some estate planners. This is an unfortunate choice of terms since many other trusts qualify for the annual exclusion by creating a present interest, e.g., Crummey trusts, wherein the demand right satisfies that requirement. We will use MIT instead of § 2503(b), but be aware that the latter is still in common use.

Comparison of the three trusts. MITs and § 2503(c) Trusts have become less attractive since the Crummey decision. Prior to Crummey, planners had to choose between an arrangement requiring annual distribution of all trust income to the minor [satisfying IRC § 2503(b)] or one effectively requiring distribution of the entire trust corpus at age 21 [satisfying IRC § 2503(c)]. Although some planners favored the MIT for larger gifts, the choice was not enthusiastic, partly because the value of the income interest qualifying for the annual exclusion had to be discounted. The Crummey provision solved this dilemma by enabling the donor to give the child the right to demand a modest amount from the trust annually, without handing income or principal over at age 21. Usually the child understands that there is much to lose by exercising the demand right. The parent might simply refuse to make any more gifts into the trust or withhold a greater inheritance later because of the child's demonstrated immaturity. However, the IRS takes the position that the child's power of withdrawal cannot be illusory, as it would be if there was an "understanding" or "agreement" not to exercise it.[16]

Income taxation has recently become a more important factor in choosing a minor's trust. The short tax rate "ladder" for trusts (e.g., in 2003 a trust or an estate hits the 38.6% marginal rate at taxable income above $9,350) encourages people to seek to avoid trust taxation of income. A newly created Crummey-type trust may be able to avoid taxation at the trust level by giving the Crummey power holder a general power of appointment over trust income as it is earned, causing it to be taxed to the holder even if the income is not withdrawn.

A ninth Circuit Court decision, the *Cristofani*[17] case, made Crummey powers even more attractive by sanctioning annual exclusions for the trustor's grandchildren who were given a 15-day $10,000 demand right. The significance was that the grandchildren were only contingent beneficiaries of the trust principal because they stood to receive principal distributions only if their parents predeceased the termination of the trust. In *Cristofani*, the IRS unsuccessfully argued that it was so unlikely that the grandchildren would receive the principal, there was "no imaginable reason" why the grandchildren would not exercise their withdrawal rights unless there was, in fact, a prior understanding that they would not do so. Hence, it was argued that they really had no present interests in the transfers. The court rejected this implied agreement argument, ruling that the test of a Crummey power is the legal right of the beneficiary to demand the property, not the likelihood of actually receiving the property. The IRS may continue to litigate the court's broad interpretation of *Crummey* in situations similar to *Cristofani*, but only in cases arising outside the Federal 9th Circuit.

> EXAMPLE 11 - 20. Christopher resides in the 9th Circuit. He creates an irrevocable trust to last for 10 years. The trust provides for distribution of the remainder to his two children, if surviving. A predeceased child's share shall go to his or her issue. One child has three children and the other has two, for a total of five grandchildren. All seven beneficiaries are given Crummey demand powers. Beginning this year, Christopher can fund the trust annually with $70,000 in property, entirely sheltered by seven annual exclusions even though the trust corpus will most likely go just to the two children.

Qualified Tuition Programs

In 1996, Congress authorized "qualified tuition programs" that have as their purpose meeting the qualified higher education expenses of the designated beneficiary of the account. These programs are known as "529 savings plans" after the IRC section that establishes the rules for these accounts. They have pretty much replaced other higher education funding strategies such as trusts or custodial accounts for minors. With custodial accounts and trusts for minors, the parents have the challenge of filing income tax returns for the child and, if a trust is involved, fiduciary returns. There is also the problem that taxes are paid at the parent's rate if the child is under the age of 14. With a custodial account, the custodian must transfer it to the child at the end of the maximum holding period as established by state law. This is usually set at age 21, although some states set an older age. This means that if the child does not attend higher education, he or she will get a windfall that probably was not contemplated by the parents when they established the custodial account. With the 529 plans, the contributor (usually the parent or grandparent) maintains control. The contributor can even take back the funds, but the income accumulated in the account must not only be included in the contributor's gross income for the year of withdrawal, but it is also subject to a 10% penalty. On the other hand, the contributor, instead of liquidating the account, can simply change beneficiary to a person related to the old beneficiary without the adverse tax consequences.

The qualified tuition plans must be sponsored by a state, its agency, or an eligible educational institution. Most of these plans are managed on behalf of the state or educational institution by well-known financial institutions such as Fidelity, Vanguard, Smith-Barney, etc. Only cash can be contributed to the account, so parents who wish to use an already established custodial mutual fund account, or other investment account, would have to liquidate it first. Each account must be accounted separately for each beneficiary, and the parents cannot manage or direct the investments. To prevent abuse of the accounts, there are limits placed on the amount that can be contributed such that they do not exceed that which is necessary to provide for the beneficiary's qualified higher education expenses.

Benefits for contributors. The account's income and capital gains are not taxed to the contributor or the beneficiary. Even though the designated beneficiary has no present interest, the contributor is allowed an annual exclusion. Indeed, if a contributor's contribution in the year exceeds the annual exclusion, the contributor can elect to use his or her annual exclusions for the following four years (hence, five years in all). If the contributor dies with any advanced use of the annual exclusion still on the books, so to speak, the estate must include such in the contributor's estate.

> EXAMPLE 11 - 21. In 2005, Myrtle established through State University a 529 savings account to benefit her grandson Billy. She wanted to fund it as fully as possible without using up any of her AEA. She put in $55,000 and elected to use her annual exclusion for the years 2005 through 2009. In 2006, after the annual exclusion increased to $12,000, she added another $16,000, again electing to use the annual exclusion four years out (i.e., 2010) and the extra $1,000 for the years 2006 through 2009. When Myrtle died in 2007, her estate had to include $36,000, i.e., the amount she sheltered by using annual exclusions for the years 2008, 2009, and 2010.

The contributor does not have to be related to the beneficiary and there are no restrictions based on the contributor's income. One can establish an account for oneself, allowing the investments to grow cash free. If not all of the money was used for one's own education, one could change the designated beneficiary to a child (separate accounts if more than one child). Of course, this would be a gift since the child is in a younger generation, but the annual exclusion rules discussed above should apply.

Tax benefit for beneficiaries. Distributions used to pay qualified higher education expenses are not included in the beneficiary's gross income. Qualified higher education expenses include: tuition, fees, books, supplies, equipment required for the enrollment, expenses for special needs services in the case of a special needs student-beneficiary, and, within limits, the room and board of a student who is at least half-time. If the beneficiary dies, what is left in the account is not includible in his or her estate unless for some reason it is distributed to his or her estate, which is not a likely event.

Special rules. The contributor can change beneficiaries so long as the new beneficiary is a member of the family of the old beneficiary. Note, these are members of the old beneficiary, not of the contributor, but this may not be a problem since in most cases the contributor is the parent of the old beneficiary, hence his or her siblings are eligible replacements, as are cousins, nephews, and nieces. Warning, if a custodial account is used to fund the 529 savings account, the parent (former custodian-contributor) has no right to change the beneficiary since establishing a custodial account gives the child equitable title to the property even though the parent holds legal title. A distribution to a beneficiary is not treated as a gift, nor is a change in beneficiary a gift unless the new beneficiary is a generation below the generation of the old beneficiary (as such would be determined for generation skipping purposes).[18]

CONCLUSION

This chapter has looked at some of the fundamental ways that gifts are used in estate planning. It also considered the challenge presented by the uncertain future of the estate tax. The benefits and drawback of making gifts within the family were discussed. While many higher education planning strategies, such as custodial gifts and trusts for the benefit of minors, were reviewed, we finished with an explanation of 529 Savings Plans since these seem to have made the others almost obsolete.

QUESTIONS AND PROBLEMS

1. What types of people are most likely to make significant gifts? What is likely to be their motivation?

2. (a) What is the approximate net worth (1) a single person or (2) a married couple should have before considering significant gifts of $10,000 or more in order to save estate tax? Explain your answer. (b) What factors other than wealth should be considered? (c) How will EGRRTA change the way the very wealthy think about making gifts? How has the law made it more difficult to plan?

3. In 2006, Carrie, a rich 93-year-old widow who has never made taxable gifts before, wants to begin a program of lifetime gifting. (a) How much can she give to her four children in the next three years (2006, 2007, and 2008), without paying any gift tax, but completely using her AEA? Show how you arrive at the total of these transfers. (b) If she dies in 2009, what size taxable estate would generate an estate tax? Explain.

4. What is meant by "grossing-up" in relation to the estate and gift tax?

5. Internal Revenue Code §2035(c) imposes a three year rule when the executor of the estate of a deceased business owner seeks to have the estate qualify for one or more of the special tax saving provisions that are available to business owners' estates. Explain using an example.

6. What is considered the major income tax disadvantage of giving a gift of appreciated property compared to holding the same property until the owner's death and then leaving it to the intended donee? Explain

7. Summarize the major tax disadvantages to making gifts, especially ones large enough that gift tax must be paid.

8. This chapter discussed how net gifts might be used to reduce taxes. In what rare circumstances does a net gift of low basis property result in an income tax liability for the donor? Explain using these facts as an example: In 2006,

Charlie gives his daughter ABC stock worth $3 million with the agreement that she will pay the gift tax. Charlie's basis in the stock is $50,000.

9. "High-basis assets make better gifts." From an income tax point of view, is this statement true, false, or uncertain?

10. Explain why, in some situations, giving high-basis assets rather than low-basis assets makes sense and, in other situations, giving low-basis assets rather than high-basis assets makes the most sense.

11. Joe, age 30, owns LARC stock worth $80,000. His basis in the stock is $20,000. Joe gifts the stock to his very ill father (Joe is an only child) with the expectation that his dad will leave the stock to him, thereby substantially increasing the basis in the stock. What might go wrong with Joe's coarse little plan?

12. Auntie Em owns three empty lots in Kansas. To decrease her large estate, Auntie Em wants to give one, and only one, of the lots to her niece, Dorothy. It is understood that Dorothy will sell the lot once it is hers. When Auntie Em dies her estate will go to Dorothy. (a) Based upon the following information, which lot would you recommend be given to Dorothy? (b) What are your thoughts on giving Lot C to Dorothy?

	Lot A	Lot B	Lot C
FMV	$6000	$6000	$6000
Basis	$5000	$2000	$8000

13. Under what circumstances might an interspousal gift save estate tax?

14. What are four major tax objectives in structuring gifts in trust for the benefit of minors?

15. Will the funds held in an UTMA account be included in the donor's gross estate if the donor is the custodian of the account? Explain.

16. Explain the public policy reason for dispensing with the present interest requirement for trusts that satisfy § 2503(c). Is there any other code section that allows an annual exclusion without the donee receiving a present interest?

17. What key clause makes a trust a "Crummey Trust" and what purpose does the clause serve?

18. For a large gift to benefit a minor, why might a MIT be preferred to a Section 2503(c) Trust?

19. Compared to gifts using a trust, what are the drawbacks and benefits of using UTMA custodial accounts?

20. In saving for university, what are the advantages of a parent establishing a 529 Savings Plan instead of opening a UTMA custodial brokerage account for a ten-year-old son or daughter?

21. In 2006, Walter established a 529 Savings Plan for his nine-year-old daughter, Zoie. Over several years he put in the maximum that the law allowed without using up any of his AEA. He made no other gifts to her (what, not even a birthday present?). What amount did he put into the account each year for 2006, 2007, and 2008?

22. Julia has TREX common stock that she bought several years ago for $5,000. It is now worth $30,000. She wants to establish a 529 Savings Plan for her son, Tyrone. Can she fund it with the stock and thereby avoid recognition of the capital gains? Explain.

ANSWERS TO THE QUESTIONS AND PROBLEMS *(odd numbered only)*

1. Attributes of individuals most willing to make sizeable gifts: Wealthy, older, generous, owning rapidly appreciating assets and an expectation that he or she would not live to 2010, or that the estate tax will still be around even after 2009. Motivated by a desire to help other family members (or charity) and possibly to reduce estate taxes.

3. (a) In 2006, Carrie could give each child $12,000 covered by the annual exclusion and another $250,000 sheltered by the unified credit. This would be a total of $1,048,000. Because the AEA for gifts, unlike the AEA for estates that increases each year and then disappears, remains at $1 million so each year for the period 2003-2009 she can only give $12,000 for each child, i.e., just $44,000 in 2007 and 2008, hence the grand total is $1,144,000 [$1,000,000 + 3 * $48,000]. (b) Because her gifts used up $1,000,000 of the AEA and the 2009 AEA for estates is $3,500,000, there will be estate tax if her taxable estate exceeds $2,500,000.

5. IRC §2035(c)(1) requires that the percentage requirements for §303 (35%) and §2032A (25% & 50%) be met with any transfers made within 3 years added back into the gross estate. Section 2035(c)(2) requires that for §6166 the business meet the 35% threshold with and without gifts made within three years of the decedent's death. Example, suppose Builder Brian's construction company is worth 32% of his $5,000,000 estate; if he can increase the value of the business or decrease the nonbusiness side such that the business is equal to 35% it qualifies for the long-term payment of estate taxes. If he gives away $150,000 in nonbusiness assets, the estate would qualify but only if he lives three years after the gift, since it will be added back to the nonbusiness side when the percent is calculated. A better idea would be to purchase business assets worth $150,000, using nonbusiness funds as this would bring the percentage to the threshold and there is no three year rule to worry about.

7. Major tax disadvantages to gifting:
   (a) Time value of money is a drawback to prepaying the gift tax. Also, given the larger estate AEA, a tax might be paid that would never have been paid had the property been held until the owner died.
   (b) Possible adverse § 2035 consequences with certain transfers or the gift is ruled incomplete.
   (c) Loss of step-up in basis

9. Uncertain. A high basis makes a better gift only if one or more of the three assumptions below can be made:
   (a) The basis does not exceed the current value of the gift. Otherwise, the donor should realize the loss him/herself. If the donor does not realize the loss, no one else will.
   (b) The donee is likely to sell the gift asset before his/her death. Or, if it is a depreciable asset, the donee is in a position to use the depreciation deduction.
   (c) The donor, for other reasons, is not left in the position of having to sell another asset with a lower basis.

11. His father must live one year after the transfer, otherwise he will retain his original basis. His dad might meet someone and leave the stock to her.

13. An inter-spousal gift can save estate tax when the wealthier spouse transfers enough property to the poorer spouse, who dies first, so that the bypass share can be fully funded. This will save taxes only if both spouses die before 2010. The wealthy spouse should at least consider a gift QTIP Trust.

15. Because the custodian has the power to distribute income or principal to the minor the custodian has "control over enjoyment" if the custodian was also the transferor, then §2036 and §2038 apply.

17. The typical Crummey Trust clause provides that the child has the right to withdraw, for a brief period (30 to 90 days) as set in the trust document, the lesser of the amount of the available annual exclusion or the value of the gift property transferred, after each transfer of property into the trust. The clause creates a present interest for the holder of the withdrawal right and, according

to §2503(b), a present interest is required to qualify a gift for the annual exclusion.

19. In most states that have adopted the UTMA, property must be relinquished to the child when he or she turns whatever the maximum age allowed by that state's UTMA. The maximum age in most states is 21 although some allow it to be set older. By using a trust (other than 2503(c)), the term may extend well past age 21. The remainderman of the trust does not have to be the initial beneficiary, i.e., an educational trust established with a Crummey provision could shift the interests over time to several family members.

21. Forward use of the annual exclusion would allow the following cash contributions to a 529 Savings Plan:
In 2006, $12,000 * 5 years = $60,0000.
In 2007, $12,000 (for 2011).
In 2008, $12,000 (for 2012).

ENDNOTES

1. IRC § 2036.

2. IRC § 2036.

3. IRC § 2038.

4. IRC § 303.

5. IRC § 2032A.

6. IRC § 6166.

7. IRC § 1022(d)(1)(B)(ii).

8. IRC § 677(b).

9. Wall Street Journal, November 19, 1992, p. B1.

10. California Probate Code §3920.5.

11. Controls over the expenditures can disallow the annual exclusion. *Illinois National Bank of Springfield v. U.S.* 756 F.Supp. 1117 (1991).

12. LR 8507017.

13. *Crummey v. Commissioner*, 397 F.2d 82 (9 Cir. 1968).

14. IRC § 2514(e).

15. IRC § 2001(b).

16. Rev. Rul. 81-7, 1981-1 CB 474.

17. *Estate of Maria Cristofani* 97 TC 74 (1991).

18. IRC § 529(b)(5) . For determining generations see IRC §2651

CHAPTER 12

Planning Lifetime Transfers

OVERVIEW

Clients may find it hard to accept planning that includes making significant gifts for several reasons. It can reduce wealth and make the donor feel financially insecure. It also means giving up ownership of selected property, a difficult step for many donors. They may also be concerned that transferring wealth, especially to a young person, will destroy the recipient's initiative.

This chapter explores intrafamily arrangements where some consideration is received for the gift or where the donor retains an interest in the transferred property. The chapter will also cover lifetime charitable transfers, including ones allowing the donor to increase income and receive an income tax deduction.

INTRAFAMILY TRANSFERS FOR CONSIDERATION

Topics covered here have the transferor receiving *consideration*--taking something of economic value for something given up–that may also involve a gift. Sometimes there is no recognizable gift, rather one family member helps another by structuring a deal on favorable terms that would not be available elsewhere. This discussion centers on lifetime intrafamily transfers that are complete and do not involve using trustees or fiduciaries.

Intrafamily Loan

A loan between family members is a simple method of transferring assets in exchange for consideration. Often, the financial benefits of an intrafamily loan are worth the financial and emotional risks.

Ordinary loan. Loans work best when market borrowing rates are high compared to investing rates of return, e.g., if short-term borrowing rates are around 9% and one-year certificates of deposit earn about 3.5%, a one-year loan of $10,000 at 6% could save the borrower $300, and net the lender an extra $250. Long-term loans would probably save less per year because rate differentials generally are not nearly as pronounced. However, one of the major advantages of intrafamily home mortgages is the ability to avoid up-front points, application fees, and the long loan processing time typically encountered with commercial lenders. Most importantly, relatives are more willing to make loans to other family members in situations that would cause commercial lenders to pale.

Financial risks. Lending within the family may make the loan payments difficult to collect, resulting in family friction if the borrower runs into financial difficulty. The loan should be secured as if it were an arm's length transaction. If the loan is used as a down payment on real estate, the lender should be given a second trust deed. Security documents must be properly filed to ensure the lender's priority over other creditors. Taking these precautions makes it more likely the lender would receive payment if the borrower has to file for bankruptcy. The risk of unexpected taxation is discussed below.

Nonfinancial risk. An intrafamily loan may cause jealousies and antagonisms. A child with financial troubles may receive more parental help than siblings. The parents may have made loans not really expecting to collect on them. Indeed, the transactions may have been structured as loans rather than as gifts to save face for the borrower, yet other children may be upset by the failure of the borrower to repay the loans. The arrangement may be seen as punishing those who are financially successful. The grumbling is often heard after the death of the parents as the children deal with dividing up the estate.

Income taxation. Interest paid by the borrower is, of course, taxable income to the lender. Interest is not tax deductible to the borrower unless the loan is secured by a principal or secondary residence, incurred in connection with a trade or business, or related to an investment.[1] If the loan is in default, the lender will not be able to deduct the loss unless a businesslike effort is made to collect it.

Furthermore, in the event the loan is not paid, the discharge of the indebtedness is income for the borrower unless he or she is insolvent or the debt is discharged in bankruptcy.[2]

Gift taxation. No gift will result if the borrower's note reflects an arm's length transaction. Thus, there must be provision for repayment and the interest rate charged must be reasonable. The lender may elect to forgive loan payments under the shelter of the annual exclusion. However, if the IRS can establish that a prior agreement had been made to forgive all payments, it will contend that the entire loan constituted an immediate gift. To avoid this result, a lender might accept each payment, and later gift a somewhat different amount back to the borrower. So long as there is no prearrangement this should also avoid the problem of the borrower having to report the cancellation of the debt as income.

Estate taxation. The value of a note is included in the lender-decedent's gross estate at death.[3] If taken as part of an arm's length transaction, a note in an estate is valued at its fair market value, which is generally less than the outstanding balance. Its value depends on many factors such as how well the note is secured, the financial health of the debtor, and the note's interest rate. Where the debtor is a family member, the note must be included in the estate at the date-of-death balance. To do otherwise would open the door to manipulation of the value of decedents' estates.

Gift-type loans. The income and gift tax effects discussed above assume a true loan, one that does not have a gift element. In other words, the borrower exchanges full consideration in the form of a note that, when issued, has a present value equal to the amount borrowed.

Other intrafamily loans entail additional tax risks. Individuals may wish to charge no interest, or an interest rate that is below market rates. These "gift loans" may subject the lender to income and/or gift taxation.

Income taxation. In subjecting these loans to income tax, the law assumes a fiction: that the forgone interest was paid by the borrower and then the lender gave the money back.[4] Thus, the lender must report the imputed interest payments as income. Whether a loan is "below market" depends on whether the lender charged a rate at least equal to the applicable federal rate (AFR), as described in § 1274(d) and published by the U.S. Treasury each month.

There are two exceptions to the imputed interest rules. First, they do not apply to loans up to $10,000 used to purchase property that does not produce income, e.g., an automobile. Second, they do not apply to loans up to $100,000 if the borrower's net investment income is less than $1,000. This might work well for investment-poor students needing large amounts to fund educational expenses or for a child needing the money for a down payment on a house. If the loan is up to $100,000 and the borrower's net investment income exceeds the $1,000 limit, the interest that must be reported is the lesser of the borrower's investment income or the imputed AFR amount.

Gift taxation. If the loan rate is below the market, the lender will be treated as having made a gift. If the loan is a term loan with a specified maturity, the value of the gift is the difference between the amount loaned and the discounted present value of the note. If the loan is a demand loan with no specified maturity and the lender has the right to demand full repayment at any time, the lender will be treated as having made an annual gift of the imputed interest for the portion of the year the loan was outstanding, less the amount of interest actually received. Unless the loan is really substantial, well above $100,000, the annual exclusion should cover the imputed gift and the lender will not need to file a gift tax return.

Properly structured, intrafamily loans can benefit both lender and borrower. Both should understand the terms and put them in writing.

Sales Within the Family

A person might sell to another family member property at its fair market value, or at considerably less than its fair market value. Either way, the seller might want to spread out gain recognition by treating the transaction as an installment sale.

Ordinary sale. Under certain circumstances, an ordinary sale is beneficial to both family members. The owner of property may truly wish to sell at a fair price, but would prefer to keep the asset in the family. The buyer will be spared the effort and expense of looking for similar property, and commission costs are avoided. As in any sale, there may be income tax consequences to the seller. Careful records should be kept, since intrafamily sales might receive greater IRS scrutiny than a sale between unrelated parties, especially if the transaction is sizable. The buyer, of course, must acquire the cash needed for the purchase. The tax code does not allow loss recognition on sales between related parties.[5] However, the loss that was disallowed may shelter some of the buyer's gain when he or she sells the property.

EXAMPLE 12 - 1. Renee sells a lot with a $100,000 basis to her son Tad for $90,000. She cannot claim the $10,000 loss even if the sale price was at fair market value. Later Tad sells the lot to a developer for $130,000. Although his gain is $40,000, he only has to recognize $30,000 since he can deduct his mother's disallowed loss.

Bargain sale. If a person has mixed motives, wanting to give an asset to a family member but wanting some money in return, a bargain sale is one way. In a bargain sale, the owner sells the asset for an amount less than fair market value. The difference between the consideration received and the value of the asset is a gift to the buyer-donee for transfer tax. For income tax, the seller would recognize a gain to the extent the consideration received exceeds the basis. The buyer-donee's basis is the greater of the donor's carry-over basis or the amount paid.[6]

EXAMPLE 12 - 2. Roxanne owns property with a basis of $90,000 and a current value of $240,000. She sells it to her son for $110,000. Roxanne's taxable gain is $20,000, the difference between $110,000 and her $90,000 basis. Son's new basis is $110,000, his purchase price. Roxanne has also made a gift of $130,000, the difference between the FMV of the property and the consideration paid to her.

Sometimes a donor may intend a true tax-free gift but may find it will be treated as a bargain sale.

EXAMPLE 12 - 3. George borrows money from a bank to purchase a building. After claiming depreciation on the property for a number of years, he "gives" the property to his daughter, who assumes the debt. The transaction will be treated as a bargain sale, and if his adjusted basis is less than the outstanding debt he will recognize a gain. George will be deemed to have received consideration in the amount of the debt assumed.[7]

As a compromise between a gift and a sale, the bargain sale can be arranged to reflect the person's degree of generosity.

Installment sale. Instead of selling the asset to a family member for immediate cash, the owner could take an installment note. The buyer agrees to make periodic payments of principal and interest, at a fair market rate of interest. This is seller financing, and the seller is said to take back paper, by receiving a note instead of cash. An installment sale can defer income tax on some or all capital gain while keeping post-sale appreciation out of the seller's gross estate.

Income taxation. Under the income tax installment sales rules, the seller may spread recognition of the gain over the collection period.[8] Each year's interest is ordinary income. Each year's principal is return of capital and capital gain in the same proportion as the sale. Although it is presumed that the seller will use the installment method to recognize gain, the seller can make an election to recognize the entire gain in the year of sale. That might make good sense if the seller has offsetting capital losses for the year. There are restrictions on deferral of gain on an installment sale of certain trade or business inventory.[9] Losses are never reported on an installment basis.

> EXAMPLE 12 - 4. Julie, a widow, sells her rental house to her daughter, Martha, for $80,000, payable with a down payment of $10,000. Interest is payable monthly, and principal will be payable in five equal annual $14,000 payments. Julie's current adjusted basis in the house is $20,000. Her gross profit is $60,000, and each year she will recognize a capital gain of 75% or $60,000/$80,000 of the principal amount received. Thus, in the year of sale, her reportable gain is $7,500 of the $10,000 received. In each of the succeeding five years, she will report a gain of $10,500 (i.e., 75% * $14,000).

Interest paid is fully deductible by the buyer if it is some type of qualified interest such as business interest, investment interest offset by investment income, or interest on a debt secured by a primary or secondary residence.

At least two different events will trigger an immediate recognition of part or all of the remaining gain to the seller. If the seller sells or "otherwise disposes" of the installment note, or if the seller cancels the note, then he or she will have to recognize the remaining gain from the original transaction. Gain recognition is also triggered if the buyer of the property is a related party who resells the property within two years of the purchase.[10]

Generally, the buyer's basis in the property is the purchase price. However, the death of a seller who holds an installment note does not cause a step-up in the basis of the note because the unrecognized gain is considered income in respect of a decedent.[11] The estate, and the heir who eventually receives it, continue to report installment gain the same way as the seller.

Gift taxation. If the installment transaction is a bona fide sale for full and adequate consideration, there are no gift tax consequences. Lack of full consideration occurs when the interest rate in the note is too low.

EXAMPLE 12 - 5. Continuing with the above example, assume the installment note specifies an interest rate of 10%, which is equal to the current applicable federal rate (AFR). Since the rules for installment sales under § 7520(a)(2) require a minimum rate of 120% of the current AFR to avoid the inference of a gift, the present value of the sum of all principal and interest payments, discounted at 12%, will be less than $80,000, the current value of the house. Thus, Julie will be treated as having made a gift to Martha of the difference. For a small loan, the annual exclusion will cover the gift.

A parent may wish to forgive one or more of the purchaser's future payments. In the usual case, only the amount forgiven constitutes a taxable gift in the year forgiven, and it qualifies for the annual exclusion.

EXAMPLE 12 - 6. If Martha uses the money to buy a car and Julie forgives a $14,000 annual payment, Julie has made a gift of that amount. After the annual exclusion, Julie's taxable gift is $4,000. If Julie were married and split the gift with her husband, it would be zero. However, from an income tax standpoint, Julie will be treated as though she received the payment and then returned it to her daughter.

The IRS quite correctly maintains that if the seller, at the time of the sale, had an understanding with the buyer that the seller would not collect on the note, then the entire value of the property is a taxable gift. However, an IRS challenge has rarely prevailed where the note has been correctly drafted and properly secured.

Estate taxation. Ordinarily, when the holder of an installment note dies, only the present value of the installment note is included in his or her gross estate.

EXAMPLE 12 - 7. If Julie dies just before the fourth payment is due, her gross estate will include the discounted value of the note. Of course, Julie's gross estate will also include any proceeds from receipt of earlier payments from her daughter, to the extent retained by Julie, or any assets she purchased with those proceeds. However, her gross estate will not include the value of the rental house sold.

If the seller made a partial gift and took back paper secured by the property transferred, and died before the note was paid off, the date-of-death value of the property sold would be included in the seller's gross estate less the actual consideration paid.[12] This arrangement would be considered a transfer for less than full and adequate consideration, with a retained income interest.

Since family transactions are often scrutinized more carefully by the IRS, the owner should be strongly advised to determine the value of the asset by qualified appraisal and to use an adequate rate of interest.

Handling installment notes as part of a decedent's estate. An installment note owned by a decedent does not get a step-up in basis. The unrecognized gain is income in respect of a decedent (IRD), discussed extensively in Chapter 8. The gain is recognized as the principle installments are collected. Generally, mere distribution of an installment note will not cause the gain to be recognized, however, if the estate (or beneficiary) sells the note, then the gain will be recognized. If the note is used to satisfy a pecuniary bequest, i.e., one stated in dollar terms, it will be treated as if the note was sold and the estate will recognize the gain and the beneficiary will be treated as having bought the note, hence he or she will have a basis in the note different from what the decedent had. A note that is left to a specific beneficiary can be distributed to that beneficiary without triggering the recognition of gain, but of course the beneficiary will recognize the gain as the note is paid down. A note that is part of the residue of an estate (or trust) distributed pro rata to the residuary beneficiaries does not trigger gain, however, a non-pro rata distribution will trigger gain, but not to the estate as one might expect. Instead, it is treated as if those who gave up an interest in the note had sold their interests to those who took more than a pro rata share of the note.

When dealing with installment notes, one must determine the "gross profit ratio" (GPR) for the sale. The GPR, often expressed as a percentage, is the expected profit divided by the contract price. The gain recognized (i.e., the portion taxed) each year is the GPR multiplied by the principal payments received during the year. To understand this in the context of estates, one must also realize that the installment note has a basis that allows the owner (initially the seller) to recapture his or her capital investment without it being treated as a gain. The basis of the note is the flip side of the GPR, hence if the GPR is 25%, the basis of the note must be 75% of its outstanding balance, and each payment on principal will be 25% taxed and 75% will be a return of capital that reduces the note's basis. Handling installment notes as part of an estate is another case where examples demonstrate better than mere words can explain.

EXAMPLE 12 - 8. In year one, David sold for $1,000,000 land that he had purchased for $600,000. He took a down payment of $240,000 from Ian, the buyer, and an installment note for the $760,000 balance. The note required principal payments of $76,000 for ten years with payments of principal and interest starting the following year. The GPR was 40% so, the first year, David recognized a gain, attributable to the down payment, of $96,000. In the second year he recognized a gain of $30,400. David died the following year before receiving that year's payment so the note had at that time an outstanding balance of $684,000 (i.e., $800,000 -

$76,000) and a basis of $410,400 (i.e., 60% * $684,000). David's two children, Abe and Betty, inherited his estate. The executor collected the next payment and the estate recognized a gain of $30,400. The note was then distributed to Abe and Betty, who collected the remaining eight payments, each time reporting a gain of $15,200 on their respective half. Notice that over time, the entire $400,000 gain has been recognized as follows: David $126,400, the estate $30,400, Abe $121,600, and Betty $121,600.

EXAMPLE 12 - 9. Consider what would happen if instead of distributing the note to Abe and Betty, the executor before collecting any payments sold the note to Martha for a discounted price of $615,600 (i.e., 90% of its $684,000 balance). The estate has a basis in the note of $410,400 (i.e., 60% * $684,000), therefore the gain on the sale is $205,200, that being the difference between the selling price and the basis. Because the total collected in connection with selling the land is $931,600 instead of $1,000,000, the total gain recognized is $331,600 instead of $400,000. The gain has been recognized as follows: David $126,400 and the estate $205,200.

EXAMPLE 12 - 10. Another alternative using David's note: Suppose, instead of selling the note to a third party, Betty alone took the note and Abe took other estate property to make up releasing his interest in it. The executor distributed the note to Betty who then collects the nine remaining payments. When the note was distributed to Betty, it had an outstanding balance of $684,000 and a basis of $410,400. Abe was deemed to have sold his half interest in the note to Betty, hence he must report a gain of $136,800, i.e., 50% * ($684,000 - $410,400). Betty's basis in the note is $547,200, i.e., her basis of $205,200 in the half of the note she inherited and $342,000 that she used to acquire Abe's half interest in the note. Since Betty's basis in the note is 80% of its value, 20% of each payment she collects is recognized gain, hence she recognizes $15,200 on each receipt, i.e., 20% *76,000. The entire $400,000 gain is recognized as follows: David $126,400, Abe $136,800 (all at once), and Betty $136,800 (over time).

Self-canceling installment notes. The seller may seek to avoid inclusion of the value of the note in his or her gross estate by incorporating a self-canceling provision, specifying that no further payments will be made after his or her death. Since the initial value of a *self-canceling installment note* (called a "SCIN") is less than one whose payments cannot be prematurely canceled, the buyer will have to give additional consideration, usually in the form of a higher principal amount or a higher interest rate.[13] And, of course, the older the individual, the greater the additional consideration. Otherwise, the IRS could assert the existence of a gift element in the transaction, again creating the risk of § 2036(a) application.

> EXAMPLE 12 - 11. Marty, age 53, sells property, currently worth $100,000, to Barbara. Marty agrees to take a 20-year self-canceling installment note of $114,156. The likelihood of Marty dying before reaching age 73 is .283116 [1 minus (65,154/90,885], see Table 90CM. Since he might die the next day or live more than 20 years, they agree to additional consideration of $14,156 as reflected in the note.

Case law is that the value of the canceled SCIN is not includable in the gross estate so long as the buyer and seller are not related parties.[14] However, there are several other tax consequences. At the note-holder's death, cancellation of the remaining payments triggers recognition of the rest of the gain; and it must be reported on the estate's income tax return.[15] The gain will be income in respect of a decedent. No income tax deduction for its proportionate share of the estate tax is available because the note is not in the decedent's gross estate. Because the tax on this gain is recognized by the estate, it is not a debt at the time of death and therefore is not deductible from the gross estate.

The SCIN represents aggressive planning and should be used only when the individual is willing to risk potentially greater income tax exposure. Intrafamily sales, whether of the ordinary, bargain, or installment variety, are significant value-shifting devices. The sale can freeze a portion of the person's estate, since post-sale appreciation will belong to the new owner, who may have a much longer life expectancy and a smaller estate.

Private Annuity

A private annuity is the exchange of an asset for the unsecured promise of another person (usually a family member) that he or she will pay an annuity for the life of the transferor. The recipient of the annuity payments is called an annuitant and the person making the payments is called an obligor. It is similar to a commercial annuity purchased from a financial institution.

> EXAMPLE 12 - 12. Parker, age 65 and in poor health, agrees to transfer a $100,000 asset ($20,000 basis) to his son, under a private annuity arrangement when the federal rate for valuing annuities is 10%. Based on Table S (10%), Parker should receive $13,725 a year for life (i.e., $100,000/7.2860).

The private annuity generates periodic income for the annuitant and can exclude the transferred property from the gross estate. The gift and estate tax treatment of a private annuity is fairly simple but when it comes to income tax things get a little complex for both the annuitant (person receiving the payments) and the obligor (person required to make the payments).

Gift taxation. There is no taxable gift since the value of the property transferred must equal the present value of the annuity. If the annuitant had a greater than 50% probability of living more than one year (or did live 18 months or more) from when the private annuity was established, the IRS accepts the use of the actuarial tables to value the private annuity.[16] If a gift element is present, the major risk is that it will be deemed a transfer for less than money's worth with a retained interest, resulting in the date-of-death value of the asset being included in the annuitant's estate.[17]

Income taxation. No gain is immediately recognizable on the creation of a private annuity because the amount realized is not considered immediately ascertainable. Thus, as with the installment sale, gain is reported as the annuity payments are received. But unlike the installment sale, taxability of the payments is governed by the annuity rules of IRC § 72. Each year's payments are split into the three parts described below.

One part is the return of the annuitant's basis, called the *investment in the contract*. This is the amount the annuitant should get back tax free if he or she lives. The tax free recovery is spread over the average life expectancy for someone the annuitant's age. The tax-free amount of each payment is found by multiplying the payment by the *exclusion ratio*. The ratio is the investment in the contract divided by the *expected return* which is the required annuity payment times the annuitant's life expectancy. The life expectancy is obtained from the mortality table found in IRS Reg. § 1.72-9.

The second part is the proportional return of any gain in the asset at the time of the contract, and is taxed as capital gain. The gain is calculated by dividing the total gain by the life expectancy at the beginning of the contract. That amount is recognized each year until the annuitant reaches the original life expectancy.

The third part is the balance of the payment after the investment in the contract and the gain are removed. It is taxed as ordinary income. After the annuitant reaches the original life expectancy, and all the investment in the contract and gains have been paid, the payments are entirely ordinary income. If the annuitant dies before reaching the life expectancy, the unrecovered basis is deductible as a loss.

EXAMPLE 12 - 13. Continuing the prior example: Parker's tax-free portion of the payment is $1,000, which is the product of an annual payment, $13,725, and the exclusion ratio, of .07121. This ratio is calculated by dividing the investment in the contract (i.e., the $20,000 he paid) by his expected total return on the contract, $274,500 (i.e., the annual payment of $13,725 times Parker's 20-year life expectancy). Parker will be required to report $4,000 as gain, or one twentieth of his $80,000 total gain in each of the first 20 years. Thus, for the first 20 years, of the entire $13,725 payment, Parker will take $1,000 tax free, and report $4,000 as taxable gain, and $8,725 as ordinary income. If Parker outlives his 20-year life expectancy all subsequent payments are ordinary income. If he dies within 20 years, gain reporting stops and he will receive a loss deduction on his final income tax return for the unrecovered basis.

Estate taxation. When the annuitant dies, none of the transferred property is included in the estate tax base if there was no retained interest in the property transferred. The original exchange, if done properly, is considered a sale of the property for its full worth. As with any life estate, the lifetime annuity terminates at the death of the annuitant.

EXAMPLE 12 - 14. Continuing the example above, if Parker lives for two years, his son will have paid less than $30,000 for an asset worth $100,000. Parker's gross estate will not include the $100,000 asset.

If the original transaction is ruled a gift because the annuity is worth less than the property transferred, the annuitant's gross estate includes the entire date-of-death value of the property, reduced by the payments actually received, as an IRC § 2036(a) transfer with a retained life estate. That would destroy the tax benefit of the transaction. That danger can be reduced by securing a qualified professional appraisal. Some experts suggest incorporating a provision in the annuity contract for a "valuation readjustment" or "savings" clause. The clause would require the purchaser to pay additional consideration if the IRS determines the property was undervalued. However, the IRS has attacked these clauses arguing that, as completed gifts, the transactions cannot be altered, and they are contrary to public policy since the revaluation is triggered only if the parties get caught.

Advantages and disadvantages. For estate taxes, the private annuity is better than an installment sale, giving complete exclusion of the asset from the annuitant's estate. The private annuity is most likely to succeed when the annuitant is unhealthy and expected to die much sooner than average expectancy tables based on census data would suggest. Obviously an early departure lets the obligor off after making relatively modest total repayments to the annuitant.

There are some major drawbacks to using private annuities. The private annuity arrangements cannot be secured by the property transferred. Using the property as security will include the property in the annuitant's gross estate as a retained interest.[18] This may increase the risk of not being repaid--a major problem for an annuitant who depends on the payments for support. From the obligor's perspective there is the problem that no part of the annuity payment is deductible.[19] Finally, as a planning device intended to remove value from the annuitant's estate, there is a risk that he or she may live much longer than expected resulting in a larger estate than might have been if the asset had just been kept.

> EXAMPLE 12 - 15. Continuing the example above, if, instead of dying young, Parker regains his health and lives 20 years, his son will have paid more than $274,000 for an asset worth $100,000. Parker's gross estate may have to include this amount (which is nearly three times the value of the asset transferred), and any resulting income, if he does not consume or gift these receipts during his lifetime.

Since the private annuity can accomplish significant estate freezing without gift tax consequences, it can be a very attractive transaction if the parties are willing to assume the risks. As we have seen, it works best when the person wants to save estate tax, is not expected to live more than a few years, has a significant cash flow need, and trusts the obligor to make the payments as promised. These characteristics are rare, even among the wealthy.

INCOMPLETE INTRAFAMILY TRANSFERS

This section briefly covers three currently used incomplete intrafamily transfers: the intentionally defective irrevocable trust, gift-leaseback, and the grantor retained income trust.

Intentionally Defective Irrevocable Trust

When a person wishes to make gifts to significantly reduce estate tax, has little interest in shifting income, and wishes to retain some control over the transferred assets, the planner may recommend an intentionally defective irrevocable trust (IDIT). The different tax rules about retained powers in §§ 2036 - 2038 (estate tax) and §§ 671-677 (*grantor trust* income tax rules) mean transfers to an IDIT are complete for federal estate and gift tax but incomplete for income tax. Thus, the trust corpus is a complete gift, not included in the grantor's gross estate, but all trust income is taxable to the grantor because the trust provides for grantor retained powers uniquely proscribed by the grantor trust rules. This offers an opportunity to save estate tax, at no gift tax cost, since income tax paid by the grantor on the beneficiary's trust income reduces the grantor's estate.

> EXAMPLE 12 - 16. Maxwell transfers $685,000 to an IDIT for the benefit of his adult son, Kirk. Since Maxwell has made no prior taxable gifts, he can totally shelter the current gift from gift taxation with the annual exclusion and unified credit. Required to distribute all income to Kirk annually, the trustee distributes $50,000 income in the first year. Maxwell must pay an additional $17,500 income tax, based on his 35% combined marginal rate. Maxwell has effectively transferred an additional $17,500 for the benefit of his son, free of gift tax. Each succeeding year he will pay the income tax again, effectively transferring more.

Powers that the grantor may retain to control an IDIT include acting as trustee and having the grantor's spouse as one of the trust beneficiaries. As trustee, the grantor can have the powers to invest, to allocate receipts between income and principal, to vote shares of stock held in the trust, and to distribute income or principal to trust beneficiaries for such reasons as "sickness," "emergency," or "disability." Naming the spouse as a beneficiary enables the grantor to retain indirect access to the trust. Of course, any distributions to the spouse could increase the spouse's estate, which may run contrary to the estate tax goals of the trust, and there is a risk that the IRS may treat the payment of income taxes by the grantor as a gift.

Gift Leaseback

When a business-owning parent wishes to establish a gift program but is held back for lack of available assets, he or she might find the answer in a gift-leaseback arrangement. As its name suggests, the parent gives a business asset outright or in trust to a lower-bracket family member and leases the asset back for use in the business. The parent is able to continue using the asset, can take a deduction for the lease payment, and can still enjoy all the other advantages inherent in gifting.

The ability to deduct the lease payments under a gift-leaseback depends in part on the location of the person's business and in part on how carefully the arrangement is structured. In some circuits, the Federal appellate courts have disallowed the deduction, while other circuits have allowed it as a legitimate business expense. Even in circuits that allow the deduction, the transaction must be properly structured. Some requirements for success include having a legitimate business purpose, charging a reasonable lease payment, having a written and enforceable lease, and, if the gift is in trust, naming an independent trustee who is not subservient to the donor.

Grantor Retained Interest Trusts

A dollar given in the far future is worth a lot less than a dollar given today. Estate planners use this fundamental financial fact to leverage the AEA. By establishing a grantor retained interest trust (GRIT), wealth can be transferred to the next generation with the taxable gift being just a fraction of the property's value. The basic plan is to establish an irrevocable trust with substantial assets with the grantor (settlor) retaining the income interest for a term of years. Since the income interest is retained, the only gift is the value of the remainder interest. In most cases, one would expect the remaindermen to be the grantor's children, however when children (or any other lineal descendants) are the remaindermen special rules, discussed below, apply so these first examples will assume the remainderman is a friend of the grantor. We use Table B to value a remainder. If the grantor's retained interest is stated in terms such as "all the income from the trust," to determine the value of the remainder, we multiply the remainder factor (REM column) for the given 7520 rate and term of years times the value of the property transferred into trust. If the grantor's retained interest is in the form of an annuity, we determine the value of the retained interest by multiplying the annuity factor (the "A" column) times the annual payment and subtract the product from the value of the property transferred into trust. In our examples we will assume the income is paid annually, with the first starting at the end of the first year, however, if the payment schedule is other than annual, Table K is used to adjust the value.

To maximize the amount transferred one might seek to have the remainder value be fairly close to the gift AEA of $1,000,000. The amount that will accomplish this depends upon the 7520 rate and the term of years. We can reduce the remainder value further by putting in a contingent reversion, but we will hold off on that for the moment. Since the 7520 rate is beyond the grantor's control, that leaves in play only the term of the trust and the amount he or she is willing to put into the trust. Given that at the end of the trust term the property is transferred to the remaindermen, this is planning that will be done only by those wealthy enough to part with a substantial portion of their wealth.

> EXAMPLE 12 - 17. When he was sixty, Myron established a GRIT to last for 10 years with his friend Felicita as the remainderman. The § 7520 rate was 6% when the trust was funded. It was his desire to have the remainder value approximate $1,000,000, and since the remainder value for 6% and a term of 10 years is .558395, he determined the maximum he could put in without going over the gift AEA was $1,790,847 so he funded just below that at $1,750,000.

Note that determining the maximum value that can be placed in the trust without causing the gift to exceed the gift AEA is simple algebra, since X*factor = desired value, solve for X. Here, the factor and the desired value are known, so the math is: X = $1,000,000/.558395 = $1,790,847. Keep in mind that there is no annual exclusion because the gift is one of a future interest. Of course the goal is to maximize the transfer while keeping the taxable gift under the gift AEA. If a contingent reversion is added as a provision in the trust the value to the remaindermen is decreased, hence the value of the gift is decreased. The language might be something like, "In the event the settlor dies before the end of trust's 10-year term, the trust corpus shall revert to the settlor."

The probability that the settlor will survive the term, and hence the remaindermen will receive the property, decreases as the settlor's age increases and the term increases. Since it is the value of the remainder that is the gift, this probability needs to be quantified. We can do that by using Table 90 CM at the end of Appendix A. Out of 100,000 people born at time zero, there are "x" number of people who reach age one, fewer, age two, etc., and using the Table we can quantify the probability of a person alive at a given age living to some later age by dividing the number alive for the later age by the number in the earlier age group, e.g., the number alive at age 60 is 85,537 and at age 70 is 71,357, hence the probability of someone in the first group being in the second is 71,357/85,537 or a little over 84% (in doing the calculations, use the fraction rather than rounding off). To determine the maximum to place in a trust that includes a contingent remainder, we determine the amount as before then divided by the fraction that represents the settlor's probability of surviving the term. Of course when one divides by a fraction one multiplies the denominator and divides by the numerator, i.e., one flips the fraction over.

> EXAMPLE 12 - 18. Continuing with the last example: Since Myron was 60 when he established the 10-year GRIT, if the trust includes a contingent reversion in the event he dies during its term, it increases the maximum value that can be placed in trust and have the remainder value under the AEA. The value previously determined was $1,790,847, so taking the probability of survival into account multiply that value times 85,537, and divide the product by 71,357 to arrive at $2,146,723. What is this number? It is the exact dollar value of assets that a 60-year-old settlor could use to fund a 10-year GRIT (with a contingent reversion and a 7520 rate of 6%) so as to result in a remainder value of exactly $1,000,000.

Often, we start with the value of the property to be placed in trust as well as the length of time the trust will last and must determine the value of the gift, i.e., the remainder value. The first paragraph of this section gave the basics; if there is a contingent reversion, then just multiply by the survival probability fraction. One type of GRIT that allows us to use the general valuation rules just discussed is called a Qualified Personal Residence Trust (QPRT, pronounced as if spelt "quepert"). This will be covered a little later, but for now just say that it involves transferring one's home to a trust, retaining the right to live there for a term of years, after which the remaindermen own the home.

> EXAMPLE 12 - 19. When Stuart was 70, he established a QPRT for a term of five years with his children as remaindermen. The home was worth $1,400,000 and the 7520 rate was 4%. He reported a taxable gift of $974,796 determined as follows: $1,400,000 * .821927 * 60,449/71,357, this being, respectively, the trust's initial property value, the 7520 factor from Table B, and the survival fraction determined using Table 90 CM.

Since the settlor has a retained interest, if he or she dies before the trust terminates, the trust property is included in his or her estate at its date-of-death value. So while the goal is to move wealth to the next generation at a reduced transfer tax value, it might not work out as planned but the downside is hardly worse than if no transfer had been made. If the trust is pulled into the grantor's gross estate, the adjusted taxable gift drops to zero because § 2001(b) defines "adjusted taxable gifts" as all post-1976 taxable gifts except for those "that are includable in the gross estate." This means that properly structured GRITs carry very little downside risk other than the attorneys' fees in establishing them and the accountants' fees in maintaining them.

Abuses and antifreeze legislation. During the 1970s and 1980s GRITs were hailed as a great way to avoid estate taxes. One way to really maximize the transfer of wealth was to create a trust along the lines stated above, value the trust by using Treasury tables that assume a specific rate of return will be paid to the grantor, then have the trustee make investments that focus on growth and produce little or no income. The wealthy grantor-parent could do without the income, and the strategy increased the likelihood that the remaindermen-younger generation would receive substantially more than it would with a more balanced investment mix. Remember, there is no new gift when the trust terminates regardless of the growth in value of the trust assets.

In 1990, Congress passed legislation to stop this perceived abuse. Chapter 14, Special Valuation Rules (IRC §§ 2701-2704), was added to the Internal Revenue Code. New section 2702, Special Valuation Rules in Case of Transfers in Trust, took aim at GRITs. This is a complex area, so we won't cover all of the nuances but the material and examples contained here will give you a good grasp of the fundamentals. The legislation starts with the premise that if a retained interest is uncertain should be give zero value. The new legislation, which in addition to trusts, also sought to stop certain valuation abuses involving business entities (material covered in Chapter 14), is referred to as "antifreeze" legislation by many commentators. Not to quibble, but they should have called it "antileverage" legislation since it sought to stem practice of using the gift AEA to shelter transfers that were expected to greatly exceed the AEA amount, not merely because future appreciation escapes transfer taxes (that is considered a freeze) but the transfer itself is greatly discounted as a future interest.

Not all GRITs are subject to the antifreeze rules. The rules apply only if the remaindermen are members of the grantor's family as such is defined in the code.[20] Generally, family members are the grantor's siblings, ancestors, lineal descendants, and their respective spouses. Also included as family members are the grantor's spouse and the spouse's ancestors, lineal descendants, and their respective spouses. So what relatives are excluded? Nephews, nieces, and cousins are left out, so are aunts and uncles. Any non-relative can be a remainderman without application of the antifreeze rules. For our discussion, we will use the term "family member" to mean those subject to the antifreeze rules and we will lump other family members, e.g., nephews and cousins, in with "friends."

Working with GRITs. If the rules apply, then the retained interest must be a "qualified interest" to be given any value other than zero. A qualified interest is one that is certain, such as a fixed annuity payable at least annually. Whereas, the interest "all income" payable at least annually to the grantor is not a qualified interest because the amount is uncertain, dependent upon what investments the trustee chooses. Requiring fixed payments effectively curtails the abuse of valuing the remainder as if substantial trust income was going to be paid to the grantor, while all along knowing the trustee would invest for growth without income. So, if remaindermen are family members, a fixed annuity will be valued and subtracted from the value of the trust property to arrive at the value of the gift. Some leveraging will result, but there is likely to be an inverse correlation between the annuity level and the value of the corpus that is eventually distributed to the remaindermen, e.g., the higher the annuity, the lower the gift but also expect the remaindermen to receive less than if the annuity is set low. When the fixed income is stated in terms of a dollar amount paid annually, the GRIT is referred to as grantor retained annuity trusts (GRAT). Sometimes the fixed income is stated as being a fixed percentage of the value of the trust corpus, determined initially by the value of the property used to fund the trust, then revalued each year (usually as of January 1st); these are called grantor retained unitrusts (GRUT).

As mentioned before, Congress excluded from the antifreeze rules QPRTs. The main rule is that the property funding the trust must be the grantor's residence or vacation home. There are special rules, beyond the scope of this text, that limit what else can be included (e.g., a limited amount of cash) and there are requirements that the trust convert to a GRAT or GRUT if the home is sold and not replaced by another home within two years. Since the antifreeze rules do not apply to QPRTs, it does not matter that the remaindermen are the grantor's family members, e.g., his or her children, and it does not matter that no income is paid to the grantor; it is enough that he or she has the right to reside in the home for the duration of the trust.

Consider the antifreeze rules and the treatment of a contingent reversion; since the reversion might or might not happen, it is given a zero value if the antifreeze rules apply. If they don't apply, then we can take the possibility that the grantor might die during the term into account and reduce the remainder value by the survival fraction. In the GRIT Summary Table, "100%" represents the initial value of property transferred into trust, "REM" means the gift value is based on

GRIT Summary Table						
	GRIT (all income)		GRAT/GRUT (income fixed)		QPRT (residence)	
Remaindermen	Friend	Family	Friend	Family	Friend	Family
Gift Value	REM	100%	100%-A	100%-A	REM	REM
CR discount?	yes	NA	yes	no	yes	yes

the remainder factor taken from Table B, "100%-A" means the gift value is the value of the property less the value of the annuity (determined using A column of Table B), and "CR discount?" asks whether a contingent reversion can be used to decrease the gift value. The examples that follow should help clarify these rules.

> EXAMPLE 12 - 20. When Don was 65, he established a 15-year GRIT, retaining all income for the term and with his cousin Alice named as the remaindermen. If he dies during the term, the trust corpus reverts to the trustee of his probate avoidance trust. The initial trust property is worth $2,500,000 and the 7520 rate is 8%. He must report a taxable gift of $466,645, determined as follows: $1,800,000 * .315242 * 47,084/79,519.

> EXAMPLE 12 - 21. Same facts as in the prior example, except Don's daughter Marie is named as the remainderman instead of cousin Alice. The retained interest is not a qualified one, hence it is given a zero valuation and the gift is the entire $2,500,000.

> EXAMPLE 12 - 22. When Becky was 70, she established a 10-year GRAT with her nephew Marcus as remainderman. The trust requires the trustee pay her an annuity of $94,000 at the end of each year. If she dies before the trust term is up, the trust assets revert to her estate. The property has an initial worth of $1,800,000 and the 7520 rate is 4%. She must report a taxable gift of $692,325 determined as follows: $1,800,000 - 6.7101 * $94,000 * 47,084/71,357.

EXAMPLE 12 - 23. Same facts as in the prior example, except Becky's son Carlos is named as the remainderman instead of nephew Marcus. The antifreeze rules apply, and while the retained income interest is a qualified one that can be valued, the contingent reversion is not, so it receives a zero value. The value of the gift is $1,169,251 determined as follows: $1,800,000 - 6.7101 * $94,000.

EXAMPLE 12 - 24. When Kimberly was 80, she established a five-year QPRT with her nephew Neil as remainderman. If she dies before the trust term is up, the trust assets revert to her estate. The house was worth $2,000,000 and the 7520 rate is 8%. Since this is a QPRT the antifreeze rules do not apply and she reports a taxable gift of $918,449, determined as follows: $2,000,000 * .680583 * 31,770/47,084.

EXAMPLE 12 - 25. Same facts as in the prior example, except Kimberly's son James is named as the remainderman. With a QPRT is does not matter who is the remainderman, the antifreeze rules do not apply, hence, the result is the same, i.e., the gift is the discounted remainder valued of $918,449.

Zeroed-out GRATs. We have noted that one can manipulate the term of the trust and the annuity amount to arrive at a desired remainder value. For the very wealthy the desired value might be zero, which has lead to what is called the "zeroed-out GRAT." Note that with a zeroed-out GRAT, not only is there is no gift tax, the grantor does not use up any unified credit. These were much the rage at estate planning seminars in the early 1990s, including excitement about one and two-year term zeroed-out GRATs (yes, the retained income amounts were huge). In 1999, Audrey Walton funded two GRAT with more than $100 million in Wal-Mart stock. Each two-year GRAT was set up so that in the event of her death the annuity from the trust would continue to be paid to her estate for the remainder of the two years. The present value of the combined annuity payments almost equaled the value of the assets transferred into the GRAT, which meant that the trusts were "zeroed-out" in the sense that for gift tax purposes the remainder was worth almost nothing. In this high-profile case, the Tax Court agreed with Walton's attorneys that the actuarial value of the remainder in the trust was effectively zero. In November 2003, the IRS acknowledged the Tax Court's ruling. Today it is possible to create a tax-free GRAT if the remainder interest is zeroed out over a fixed term. A trust payable for a fixed term that includes the grantor's estate as alternate payee if necessary to complete the term is nicknamed a "Walton GRAT."[21]

While Audrey Walton's trusts successfully avoided gift taxes they were not otherwise successful in that the value of the Wal-Mart stock went down and the trustee had to return all of the trust assets to Audrey Walton in order to make the required annuity payments. However, had the value of the stock increased by 50% during the two years, Audrey's daughters would have each received almost $50 million free of gift taxes. Furthermore, since she receives the stock back, she can repeat the process over and over again, meeting with success when the stock value increases during the term, and without any real loss when the value goes down or stays level.

The Impact of EGTRRA on GRIT planning. EGTRRA has had a major impact in this area of planning, throwing estate freezing techniques involving retained interest trusts into turmoil and possibly making them obsolete. If one truly believes that the estate tax will be permanently repealed in 2009, there is no reason to create a GRIT of any sort with a term that would go beyond then. The sole purpose of this kind of planning is to leverage the AEA, and the biggest fear has always been the estate tax, not the gift tax. We control gifts, deciding when and whether, but have no such choice with death. It is conceivable that wealthy individuals will continue to use GRITs to leverage the $1 million gift tax AEA, but to what purpose? To enrich children and grandchildren beyond what can be accomplished using the annual exclusion and the $1 million AEA to cover outright gifts? Perhaps. The concern is, of course, the uncertainty of whether the estate tax will be repealed, the estate AEA drop back to $1,000,000, or be increased dramatically. GRITs remain a viable hedge for the pessimists (realists?) who fear that the sunset provision really means what it says, and that the estate tax will resurrect in all its glory on January 1, 2011.

PLANNING CHARITABLE GIFTS

Transfers to charity, whether lifetime or at death, are supported by several provisions of the Internal Revenue Code that allow generous deductions on a contributor's income tax, gift tax, and estate tax returns. Lifetime charitable transfers are the primary focus of this section because they have significant income tax advantages over charitable transfers at death, and they often are more complex and need greater elaboration. Lifetime gifts to charity are of two types, outright gifts or split-interest gifts.

At the outset, it should be noted that charitable gifts may result in a net decrease in a client's wealth. Thus, the client will usually need to possess a charitable motive to feel comfortable about making such transfers. The material presented below describes some ways to minimize the decline in family wealth resulting from charitable donations.

Tax Consequences

To qualify for an itemized charitable income tax deduction, the donee charity must meet the requirements under the Code.[22] In addition, the Code contains complex limitations on the amount of charitable contributions deductible from income by an individual in a tax year. There are limitations on both the total amount deductible for all charitable gifts and on the specific amount deductible for any particular gift.

Deductibility. Total deductible charitable contributions may not exceed 50% of a taxpayer's "contribution base" (CB), an amount that is approximately equal to adjusted gross income.[23] However, there are some major exceptions with regard to this 50% limitation. Taxpayers are limited to 30% of the CB for contributions to private foundations. In addition, deductible limits for both public charities and private foundations are reduced to 30% and 20%, respectively, for contributions of most kinds of "capital gain property."[24] Contributions in excess of these limits may be carried over for five years.[25] To further complicate matters, since 1991, charitable deductions for high-income taxpayers are subject to a 3% overall floor as an itemized deduction.

> EXAMPLE 12 - 26. Fanny Superstar, a prominent singer, just donated her $15 million Malibu estate to charity. This year she earned $20 million in income. She can deduct $5.4 million, which is $6 million (30% * $20 million) reduced by the 3% floor (3% * 20 million). She can carry over the remaining $9 million ($15 million - $6 million) to later years. Assuming that her income remains about the same for the next three years and that her combined marginal tax rate is 50%, Fanny should save approximately $2.7 million in each of the first and second years, and $1.2 million in the third year, for a total income tax savings of about $6.6 million.

The amount deductible from adjusted gross income for any particular charitable gift is usually its fair market value, subject to the total annual limitations outlined above. However, there are two important exceptions for noncash gifts. First, if sale of the property would have resulted in ordinary income or in short-term capital gain, the asset is called "ordinary income property," and the donor is limited to deducting the adjusted basis of the property, with a 50% CB limit.

Second, if the property would have resulted in a long-term capital gain had it been sold instead of donated, it is called "capital gain property," and one of three alternative tax consequences will occur. If the property is tangible personalty given to a public charity, which uses it in its activities, then the fair market value is deductible (with a 30% CB limit). If, on the other hand, the charity is a private foundation, or if it is a public charity that cannot use the donated property in its activities, then the amount deductible is limited to the donor's basis, with a CB limit of 50% for donations to public charities and a 30% limit for donations to private charities. An example of a "related use" is placing a donated painting on a wall of the donee art museum or the donee university. An example of an unrelated use would be the storage of the painting in the institution's basement or the immediate sale of the painting. Finally, if the donation to a public charity qualifies for a deduction based on its fair market value, but with a 30% CB limitation, the taxpayer can elect to use the property's basis as the deduction and raise the CB limit to 50%.[26]

Any charitable contributions of $250 or more must be substantiated contemporaneously in writing by the donee charity. The writing should state the amount of cash donated, a description (but not necessarily the value) of the property, and a good faith estimate of the value of any property it provided in consideration for the donation.[27] In addition, a donor of property exceeding $5,000 in value is required to obtain a "qualified appraisal" and supply additional information detailing the transaction.

This summary of the annual limitations has been a short overview. Individuals wishing to make large contributions should consult a tax adviser specializing in this area.

Outright Gifts to Charity

Several planning strategies evolve from the tax rules just discussed.

Income tax consequences. In many cases, contributing capital gain property to a public charity is more advantageous than contributing cash.

EXAMPLE 12 - 27. Jeff, who is in the 35% combined (i.e., state and federal) ordinary income tax bracket and a 22% combined capital gains tax bracket, wishes to contribute $5,000 to his favorite public charity. Jeff could give an original oil painting, acquired for $1,000 and now worth $5,000, or he could sell the painting and donate the cash proceeds. If Jeff contributes the painting, his after-tax cost will be $3,250 which is the $5,000 value of the painting, less the $1,750 tax savings from the deduction. Alternatively, if Jeff sells the painting and still donates the full $5,000, his after-tax cost will be $4,130, which is the $5,000 donated cash, plus the $880 tax on the gain ($4,000 * 22%), minus the $1,750 tax saving from the deduction.

Owners of nonmarketable property that they wish to sell may consider making a bargain sale of the property to charity. The income tax consequences of a bargain sale to charity are not the same as a bargain sale to a private individual. With the related party bargain sale, no loss can be recognized and a gain is recognized only if the bargain price exceeds the seller-donor's basis. But for a bargain sale to a charity, the transaction is treated as though it is two transactions in one: a sale and a gift. The old basis is allocated to each part in direct proportion to the part's value when compared to the whole. Thus, where B represents the old basis, B_g represents the portion of the basis allocated to the gift and B_s represents the basis allocated to the sale, G stands for the value of the gift, which is the difference between the amount paid (S for sale) by the charity and the fair market value (FMV) of the property transferred to the charity at a bargain price.

$$B_g = (G/FMV)*B$$
$$B_s = (S/FMV)*B$$
$$Gain = S - B_s$$

EXAMPLE 12 - 28. This year, Margaret transferred title to her vacant city lot worth $500,000 to her church in exchange for its promise to pay her $150,000. The lot was valued at $100,000 when she inherited it from her mother. Margaret plans to purchase a $500,000 life insurance policy so her son will not be too disappointed about her transferring the lot. Margaret's gain:

Gain = $150,000 - ($150,000/$500,000)*$100,000 = $120,000

Of course Margaret will have a charitable deduction of $350,000, the difference between the FMV and the amount paid to Margaret. If Margaret has modest income, she and the church might wish to structure this as an installment sale whereby the church pays the price in installments. The portion of the charitable deduction that exceeds the contribution base limits can be carried forward for five years, and installment reporting avoids bunching up the capital gain in the first year.

As in a private sale, an outright gift of mortgaged property to charity is treated as a bargain sale, resulting in taxable gain to the donor. However, the bargain sale may be a simple way to sell assets with a limited market, such as an interest in a closely held business.

Gift tax consequences. Similar to the unlimited marital deduction, an unlimited gift tax deduction is allowed for the present value of gifts to qualifying charities.[28] The rules covering the charitable deduction no longer require that a gift tax return be filed, even if the gifts exceed the annual exclusion amount.

Estate tax consequences. Similar to lifetime inter-spousal gifts, lifetime gifts to charity are not included in the donor's estate tax base. They are not includable in the gross estate because they are not owned by the decedent at death, nor are they adjusted taxable gifts.

Outright bequests to charity are totally deductible from the gross estate.[29] Thus, a multimillionaire could give all (or all but the AEA) of his or her entire estate to charity and ensure total avoidance of the estate tax. Of course, he or she could also accomplish this goal by making a series of lifetime charitable transfers. In fact, lifetime charitable transfers are preferable to donations at death, as the next example illustrates.

EXAMPLE 12 - 29. Sampson wishes to make an outright gift of $100,000 to his church, which has been a source of continuous spiritual support to him and his family for many years. Sampson's estate planner recommends a lifetime transfer over a similar transfer at death, reasoning as follows: If Sampson donates the property at his death, his gross estate will be reduced by the amount of the gift, but he will enjoy no income tax benefit.[30] Alternatively, if Sampson makes the gift during his lifetime (even a deathbed gift), not only will his gross estate and estate tax base be lower by the date-of-death value of the gift property, but Sampson will also be able to save income taxes by deducting some or all of the value of the gift from his income.

Other Charitable Giving Strategies

Other strategies include inter-spousal transfers, redemption bailout of corporate stock, gifts of life insurance, and the gift annuity.

Inter-spousal transfers. If a person insists on making a testamentary bequest to charity, the planner might urge the person to consider making an outright gift to the surviving spouse, who could then donate the property to charity. While the estate tax consequences are the same, the income tax results will improve, since S2 will be able to enjoy a charitable income tax deduction. Of course, S2, as fee simple recipient of the property, might decide not to make the donation. Placing the property in a QTIP trust, with the charity named as the remainderman, will ensure receipt by the charity, but not until after S2's death, thus there would be no income tax advantage.

Redemption bailout of corporate stock. A person owning stock in a closely held corporation may wish to gift some stock to a charity which will later tender the stock for redemption by the corporation. Advantages include saving income tax, "bailing out" corporate earnings and profits without incurring dividend income, helping younger family shareholders concentrate their ownership, and enabling the charity to receive cash. This arrangement should be undertaken with great caution, however, and may be challenged if the IRS believes it can prove the existence of an "understanding" between donor and charity that the charity would surrender the shares for redemption. In that case, the donor would be forced to incur a taxable gain.

Gift of life insurance. Lifetime gifts to charity of life insurance policies are popular. The insured can transfer an existing policy to charity, or the person can purchase a new policy naming the charity as beneficiary and assigning to the charity all ownership rights in the policy. The insured may agree to continue to pay the premiums. The person should be able to take income tax and gift tax charitable deductions for the policy's terminal value at the date of the gift (or adjusted basis, if less, in the case of income tax) and take additional income tax deductions as premiums are paid.

Gifts of Split Interests

Despite the added income tax advantage of lifetime charitable gifts, even individuals with strong charitable motives are sometimes reluctant to make outright gifts to charity because they are not willing to relinquish total control of an asset. For example, they may be relying on an asset as a source of income or enjoyment, or they may have been planning to pass the asset to their children.

They may be more willing to make a split-interest gift in which the charity is given a vested future interest in property. The donor may accomplish several objectives such as increasing income while generating an income tax deduction and possibly reducing estate taxes.

A split-interest arrangement divides the asset into two separate property interests, the income interest and the remainder interest. Usually the owner retains the right to the income and gives the remainder interest to a charity. However, if the income is not needed, the owner can give the income interest for a period of time to a charity and give the remainder to someone else.

Donating a remainder interest. Three devices recognized by tax law are commonly used by individuals to retain an income interest in an asset and give the remainder interest to charity. Two of them, broadly called *charitable remainder trusts*, are the annuity trust and the unitrust. The third is called the *pooled income fund*. For each, the charity receives an irrevocable (vested) remainder interest in the asset. These 'strings-attached' arrangements will cause the date-of-death value of the property to be included in the donor's gross estate,[31] but an equal charitable deduction will reduce the taxable amount to zero.[32]

Charitable remainder annuity trust. With a *charitable remainder annuity trust* (CRAT), the person receives annuity income equal to at least 5% of the original value of the assets transferred into trust, payable at least annually, usually for life. The value of the deductible interest is calculated from IRS valuation Table S.

> EXAMPLE 12 - 30. Carrie, age 75, creates a CRAT, funding the trust with $100,000 in appreciated securities. The trust provides for a 5% annual payment to Carrie for her life. When the trust was funded the § 7520 rate was 10%. The value of the retained income interest is $28,939 [5.7877 * $5,000]. Therefore, the charity's interest (and Carrie's deduction) is $71,062, i.e., the difference between the total value of the property and the value of the retained income interest.

Charitable remainder unitrust. The charitable remainder unitrust (CRUT) is much like the CRAT, except that the annual income depends on a fixed percentage of the current fair market value of the assets in the trust, redetermined annually. Thus, the amount of the annual income paid to the person will vary (hopefully upward) from year to year.[33]

The CRUT can provide for the income to be the lesser of the unitrust amount or the amount actually earned on the trust property, with any deficiencies payable in later years when earnings are higher. Thus, the owner of a rapidly appreciating, low-dividend-paying corporation can contribute stock to a CRUT and enjoy a large stream of income years later, after retirement, when the stock starts paying dividends. This "net income with make-up" unitrust (NIMCRUT) represents risky planning because the IRS has challenged these arrangements.

Calculation of the remainder interest for a CRUT is complex and beyond the scope of this text. Most charities have access to computer programs that will "run the numbers" without cost for prospective donors.

At their best, charitable remainder trusts offer to an individual the advantages of higher cash flow during lifetime, lower investment risk, and greater portfolio diversification. At their worst, they can be a confusing financial burden. In one case a $25 million estate lost an $18 million deduction because its charitable trust was not in the form of an annuity trust, a unitrust, or a pooled income fund.[34] Although the IRS regulations are exceedingly complex, requiring the drafting of long and technical documents, the Treasury has issued safe harbor sample documents which may be suitable for most peoples' needs. However, this is an area where very experienced counsel is needed.

Disillusioned clients will become more prevalent if financial planners continue to aggressively promote these trusts primarily as a means of increasing retirement income and avoiding capital gains tax. Advertisements appear in newspapers with the main pitch being "stop paying unnecessary taxes" with little or no mention that a sizable charitable contribution is required. If you have clients interested in using charitable trusts as part of their estate plan, you should consider associating with an expert who is experienced in these complex matters. The charities themselves often have lists of estate planners who are conversant with establishing charitable trusts.

Pooled income fund. A pooled income fund is an investment fund created and maintained by a charity that "pools" property from many similar contributors instead of requiring each donor to create their own separate trust. Thus, the donor is spared the expense of planning and drafting a trust, an arrangement that would be uneconomic when the charitable donation is relatively small (e.g., $10,000 to $100,000).

Many pooled income funds limit donations to cash and cash equivalents. The pooled income fund ordinarily provides that the charity will pay to the grantor an income for life and, if desired, for the life of the grantor's spouse, based on the rate of return actually earned by the fund as a whole. At their death, the property passes to the charity. Valuation of the charitable deduction is calculated using Treasury tables available from the IRS.

Comparison of the three techniques. All three techniques have the advantages of providing an income for life, reducing estate tax, and obtaining a relatively immediate income tax deduction. The CRAT may appeal to individuals who desire the certainty of a fixed income, even in a declining market. The CRUT may be preferred by those willing to risk fluctuating income for the opportunity of realizing higher income payments. Thus, the CRUT can offer a hedge against inflation. Assets in a CRUT do require an annual valuation, a possible extra trust cost. Most of the larger charities and most colleges and universities have established pooled income funds. The pooled income fund may be preferred by those who would like to avoid having to establish and maintain a trust. Pooled income funds are not permitted to invest in tax-exempt securities.[35]

Charitable lead trust. Instead of contributing a remainder interest, a person can donate an asset's income interest for a period of years to charity, with the remainder interest then passing to a private party (reverting to either the grantor or spouse, or passing to another person, such as a child or grandchild). The person or the person's estate will receive an income tax deduction for the value of the income interest, based on Treasury valuation tables. To get the charitable deduction, the trust must be set up as a grantor trust, making the income taxable to the grantor,[36] unless the trust is established at the grantor's death. Thus, charitable lead trusts are often designed to take effect after the person's death.

In a manner similar to a zeroed-out GRAT, a charitable lead trust (CLT) may be structured to generate a charitable deduction equal to almost 100% of the current value of property transferred by way of the trust. If done successfully, the value of the remainder interest (probably given to the settlor's children) will approximate zero, resulting in very little use of the settlor's unified credit. Further, nothing (or very little) is included in the individual's taxable estate. In calculating the value, the executor is allowed to use the 7520 rate for the month the decedent died or either of the prior two months. For a CLT the lowest rate produces the lowest remainder interest, hence the highest charitable deduction. Either the person will not own the property at death (because it was a lifetime charitable gift), or, if this is done as part of a testamentary plan, the estate will be entitled to a charitable deduction that offsets most of the value of the property going into the CLT. The goal is for the property to not only benefit the charity for a period of years, but to grow in value so the remaindermen eventually receive a sizable distribution at the end of the term, all without incurring transfer taxes on the donated property. As the examples below show, success of the CLT depends on the actual rate of future asset appreciation.

> EXAMPLE 12 - 31. Reed creates a lifetime CLT, funding it with $100,000 in stock of his closely held corporation. The trust is obligated to pay a "guaranteed annuity" of $11,750, or 11.75% of the initial value of the corpus annually to the charity for a period of 20 years. Then, the trust will terminate and the remaining corpus, if any, will be distributed outright to Reed's surviving children and grandchildren. Assuming a 10% discount rate, the IRS Table annuity factor is 8.5136. The value of the charity's 20-year income interest is $100,034.80, the product of $11,750 and 8.5136. Reed's deduction is limited to $100,000, the value of the property. Since the value of the present income interest is higher than the value of the property, the value of the remainder interest is zero, which means that Reed has made no taxable gift.

> EXAMPLE 12 - 32. Continuing the example immediately above, assume 20 years have passed. The closely held stock in the trust has returned much more than 11.75% and its annual income has been more than enough to pay the annuity. As a result, its current value is $800,000. The stock will pass outright to Reed's descendants completely transfer-tax-free.

> EXAMPLE 12 - 33. Altering the projected outcome in the example above, assume again that 20 years have passed, but the closely held stock has earned only a 10% annual average rate of return, forcing the trustee to use trust corpus to satisfy the $11,750 annual distribution requirement. By the end of the trust's term, its corpus will have been distributed to the charity and there will be nothing left for the remaindermen.

The outcomes in the two preceding examples represent two extremes. For most individuals, the results will be somewhere in between. The gift tax value of the remainder will not be zero, which means the grantor will have to partially use up his or her unified credit on a future interest gift that does not qualify for the annual exclusion. In addition, at the end of the trust term, with prudent investing, the corpus will probably have appreciated somewhat.

When the former first lady Jackie Kennedy Onassis died May, 19, 1994, her will, signed March 22, 1994, directed the residue of her estate be used to fund a charitable lead trust to favor charities to be selected by the trustees. The trust, to be named the "J Foundation," would pay the charities an amount equal to 8% of the trust's initial net value each year, with the payments made quarterly.

Apparently the trust was never funded, perhaps because funding was contingent on her two children making disclaimers that were not made. It has been estimated that her estate was worth about $200 million. Had the trust received half of that, the present value of the 24-year income interest would have been slightly more than $99 million; this amount would have qualified as a charitable deduction, leaving less than $1 million of the $100 million to be taxed. Given that the estate was in the highest estate tax bracket, this planning would have reduced the tax on that portion of her estate from $55 million to about $500,000. The calculation is explained in the following example.

> EXAMPLE 12 - 34. At his death in May of 1994, Charlie's estate plan established a charitable lead trust with a 24-year term. The trust received assets worth $100,000,000. The trust must pay the charity quarterly payments of $2,000,000. The § 7520 rate for May of 1994 was 7.8%; it was 7.0% and 6.4% for April and March, respectively. The executor used the 6.4% rate to calculate the value of the charities' lead interest. The 24-year annuity factor for 6.4% is 12.0995 and the adjustment for quarterly payments is 1.0237, hence the lead interest value is $8,000,000 * 12.0995 * 1.0237 = $99,090,065. If the 7520 rate used was 7.8%, the lead interest value is $88,121,247 [$8,000,000 * 10.7068 * 1.0288]. Thus for a CLT, the lower the rate, the better the charitable deduction.

The CLT works best for wealthy, estate-tax-avoiding individuals who can afford to forego substantial income for a period of time. The remaindermen will be most pleased if the trust assets appreciate greatly during the trust's term and still manage to generate sufficient income to meet the required payout.

CONCLUSION

This chapter has focused on various nongift, lifetime intrafamily transfers and charitable gifts that really work. The techniques not only reduce taxes, but they also help other members of the person's family and/or they help charities by providing funds that allow them to carry out their charitable purposes. It is often a win-win situation. Some of the techniques allow both families and charities to increase their wealth.

QUESTIONS AND PROBLEMS

1. Why are many planning-minded persons disinclined to make significant gifts even when they could afford to do so?

2. How can a bargain sale add flexibility to gift planning?

3. John has a vintage Corvette that he bought in 1969 for $4,000. Today, it is worth $40,000. He would like to give it to his son to enjoy, but he also wants his son to pay something for it on the theory that he will appreciate the car more than if he were just given the car. Therefore, John sells the car to his son for $12,000. John is not sure how to treat the sale. How would you advise him?

4. Jaime owned a condo that he bought in 1979 for $40,000. When it had a fair market value of $300,000, he sold it to his son for only half of its fair market value, or $150,000. What is Jaime's taxable gain, and what is his son's new basis in the condo? If Jaime's basis was $200,000, what is his son's basis in the condo?

5. Scarlet sold a horse to her friend Butler for $50,000. Butler agreed to pay Scarlet $10,000 per year on principal, plus interest, for the next five years. Scarlet received the horse two years ago from her father. At the time, he filed a gift tax return showing the worth of the horse (before the annual exclusion) to be $30,000, based on appraisals, and he reported a basis of $15,000. (a) How much gain must Scarlet recognize in year one? (b) Of the total annual payment, how would you describe the portion of the payment that is not gain?

6. Summarize the major advantages and disadvantages of the private annuity.

7. Compare the income, gift, and estate tax aspects of the installment sale and the private annuity.

8. In March of year one, Darcie sold land for $500,000. Her basis was $340,000. Accepting a down payment of $90,000, she took back an installment note of

$410,00. She agreed to ten payments of $41,000 each, with the first one three months after the escrow closes and subsequent payments due on June 15th of each year until paid. Darcie collected the first four payments before she died. Her executor collected one payment before distributing the note to the three children, Arnold, Bobbie, and Charles, as tenants in common. They collected the final five payments. (a) What is the GR and the note's basis percentage? (b) Construct a table that shows by year (rows) the following (columns): recipient, principal received, gain recognized, note balance (after the payment), basis in the note. (c) State how much gain was recognized by Darcie, by the estate, and by each of her three children. Does the total gain recognized square with the $160,000 that should be reported?

9. In the prior problem, suppose the executor of Darcie's estate, after collecting one payment, sold the note for $184,500, discounted from its balance of $205,000. From the date of the sale of the land through the sale of the note, what is the gain or loss recognized, and by whom? Why isn't the total gain $160,000?

10. Going back to the initial facts concerning Darcie's land sale, suppose shortly after collecting the year five payment, the executor, pursuant to an agreement with the children, distributed the note to Charlie, who collected the remaining five payments. Arnold and Bobbie took other estate assets to make up for their interest in the note. (a) How much gain would Darcie report? When? (b) How much gain would the estate report? When? (c) How much gain do each of the three children report? When? (d) Does the total gain recognized square with the $160,000 that should be reported?

11. Under what circumstances will a gift-leaseback work well?

12. When are the trust antifreeze rules of §2702 applicable?

13. List the exceptions to the trust antifreeze rules of §2702.

14. A very wealthy person is considering establishing an irrevocable trust, keeping an interest for 10 years and then letting the trust terminate in favor of her s issue. She understands that this will leverage her AEA. Explain why

a contingent reversionary interest decreases the value of the remainder interest in a QPRT but not in an otherwise qualified GRAT.

15. Eduardo established a $5 million GRIT. The terms of the trust gave Eduardo income for 10 years. If Eduardo died during the term of the trust, the corpus reverted to his revocable probate avoidance trust. When the trust was established, Eduardo was 65 and the federal interest rate for valuing transfers was 8%. (a) If the contingent remainderman was Eduardo's nephew, Ricky, what is the value of the gift? (b) If the contingent remainderman is Eduardo's son, Carlos, what is the value? Why the difference? (c) If Eduardo died in year two when the trust was worth $5,500,000, how much would be included in his estate? Does your answer depend upon whether the remainderman was the nephew or the son? Explain.

16. When he was 80 years old, Brian established a three-year GRAT, funding it with assets worth $1,000,000. Income payments are made at the end of each year. Deborah is the remainderman. For each alternative, determine the value of the gift. Explain your answer and show any calculations. (a) Deborah is his daughter, he retained the right to all income, and the § 7520 rate was 8%. (b) Same as "a" except Deborah is his niece. (c) Deborah is his daughter, he retained income of $80,000 per year, and the § 7520 rate was 8%.

17. When she was 70 years old, Patricia established a five-year GRAT, funding it with assets worth $500,000. Income payments are made at the end of each year. Patricia retained a contingent reversion that returns all trust assets to her estate if she dies before the trust terminates. Craig is the remainderman. For each alternative determine the value of the gift. Explain your answer and show any calculations. (a) Craig is her son, Patricia retained the right to all income, and the § 7520 rate was 12%. (b) Same as "a" except Craig is her nephew. (c) Craig is her son, she retained income of $60,000 per year, and the § 7520 rate was 8%.

18. When he was 75 years old, Eulalio established a four-year QPRT, funding it with his home worth $1,000,000. Maria is the remainderman. If Eulalio died before the trust terminated the corpus reverts to his estate. For each

alternative determine the value of the gift. Explain your answer and show any calculations. (a) Maria is his daughter and the § 7520 rate was 6%. (b) Would your answer change if Maria was his niece? (c) Maria is his daughter and the § 7520 rate was 12%.

19. When she was 90 years old, Cynthia established a five-year QPRT, her home worth $500,000. Cynthia retained a contingent reversion that returns all trust assets to her estate if she dies before the trust terminates. Ralph is the remainderman. For each alternative determine the value of the gift. Explain your answer and show any calculations. (a) Ralph is her son and the § 7520 rate was 12%. (b) Same as "a" except Ralph is her nephew. (c) Continue from "b," Cynthia died in 2008, the trust had not terminated, and the house was worth $550,000. What value insofar as this QPRT is included in her gross estate and what is the adjusted taxable gift?

20. Compare the advantages of the CRAT, the CRUT, and the Pooled Income Fund.

21. Explain the terms and add some detail to the following comment: Gifts to pooled income funds have many of the advantages of CRUTs and CRATs with much less expense to the donor.

22. Use the table that follows to compare the advantages of various lifetime transfers. In each box, place the number that you think describes how well that transfer accomplishes each goal, using the following rating system: 3 = excellent, 2 = good, 1 = fair, and 0 = poor. Use a range if the outcome is uncertain and be prepared to explain why you choose a number or a range.

TABLE 14-1	Comparative Advantages of Lifetime Transfers									
Types of Transfers	Goals									
	Ability to Retain		Ability to Avoid		Step-up in Basis	Shift income	Estate Tax Base		Avoid Probate	Low risk of IRS attack
	Control	Income	Income Tax	Gift tax			Reduce	Freeze		
Annual exclusion gifts										
Large out-right gifts										
Ordinary sale										
Bargain Sale										
Installment sale										
Private annuity										
Gift-lease back										
Grantor retained income trust (GRIT)										
Irrevocable Life Insurance Trust										

ANSWERS TO THE QUESTIONS AND PROBLEMS *(odd numbered only)*

1. Planning-minded persons are often unwilling to make outright gifts because they do not want to relinquish: 1) dominion and control over assets; and 2) income earned from the assets. Also, they might not want to spoil the recipient.

3. John's bargain sale of his Corvette.
   The transaction would be considered a bargain sale (i.e. the consideration received is less than the fair market value). John would recognize a taxable gain of $8,000, which equals the consideration paid to him less his basis in the vehicle ($12,000-$4,000). In addition, John has made a $28,000 gift to his son ($40,000-$12,000 annual exclusion). The son's basis in the Corvette would be equal to the purchase price of $12,000.

5. Scarlet's sale of her horse to Butler:
   (a) Scarlet must recognize $7,000 of gain in year one (($50,000 – 15,000)/$50,000) * $10,000 [carry-over basis)
   (b) The remaining portion, $3,000, is non-taxable return of capital and the rest is interest income.

7. Comparing installment sales to private annuities:
   Installment sale
   Income taxation: Under the income tax installment sales rules, the seller may spread recognition of the gain over the collection period. The seller can also make an election to recognize the entire gain in the year of sale. If the installment method is used, the gain is recognized in proportion to the amount of each payment of principal.
   Gift taxation: If the installment transaction is a bona fide sale for full and adequate consideration, there are no gift tax consequences to the lender.
   Estate taxation: Ordinarily, when the holder of an installment note dies, only the present value of the installment note is included in his or her gross estate. If the seller made a partial gift and took back paper secured by the property transferred, and died before the note is paid off, the date-of-death value of the property sold would be included in the seller's gross estate less only the actual consideration paid.
   Private annuity

Gift taxation: There is no taxable gift as long as the value of the property transferred equals the discounted present value of the annuity promised.
Income taxation: No gain is immediately recognizable upon creation of a private annuity. Gain is reported as the annuity payments are received.
Estate taxation: When the annuitant died, none of the transferred property is included in his or her estate tax base. However, if the original transaction were to be ruled a gift because the value of the annuity promised the annuitant is less than the value of the property transferred, the annuitant's gross estate will include the entire date-of-death value of that property, reduced only by the payments actually received.

9. Another Darcie question, with the executor selling the note:
As before, Darcie would recognize gain of $81,280 (i.e., 32% times the $90,000 down payment and four payments of $41,000). The estate would recognize gain of $13,120 on the payment collected (32% of $41,000). The sale of the note for $184,500 when its basis was $139,400 produces a gain of $45,100. The total gain, Darcie's and the estate's combined, is $126,380 rather than $160,000. The difference of $20,600 is the amount the executor discounted the note, i.e., $205,000 - $184,400 = $20,600. Consider, the person who bought the note has a basis in it of $184,400 and will recognize the $20,600 as the note is paid off.

11. A gift-leaseback will work well for a business-owning individual who wishes to shift income to a lower bracket family member and has business assets that can be transferred.

13. §2702 does not apply
To retained interests in a personal residence,
To trusts where the remaindermen are not the settlor's issue or ascendants, spouse, or siblings (nephews/nieces are ok).

15. Eduardo's 10-year GRIT:
(a) 0.463193 * $5,000,000 = $2,315,965; $2,315,965 * 60,449/79,519 = $1,760,557
(b) $5,000,000. There is no evidence of fixed payments; therefore, the zero exclusion rule applies.

(c) DOD FMV = \$5,500,000; it doesn't matter, in both cases the DOD FMV is included, and in both cases the adjusted taxable gift (\$1,760,557 and \$5,000,000) goes to zero because the transfer is fully included in Eduardo's estate.

17. Patricia's five-year GRAT:
(a) Because the remainderman, a son, is a "member of the transferor family" and the retained interest is not a qualified one, it is given a zero value; hence the gift is the full \$500,000. Obviously, the contingent reversion is not a qualified interest and therefore must be given no value. (b) A nephew is not a member of the family, hence this is a common law GRIT (i.e., the antifreeze sections do not apply). Use Table B: 0.567427 * \$500,000 = \$283,714. Also, because this is a common law GRIT, the gift is reduced further by the contingent reversion: \$283,714 * 60,449/71,357 = \$240,344. (c) This is a qualified GRAT: \$1,000,000 - 3.9927 * \$60,000 = \$260,438. Since the antifreeze rules apply, no value is assigned to the contingent remainder, hence \$260,438 is the gift.

19. Cynthia's five-year QPRT:
(a) Because this is a QPRT it does not come within the purview of the antifreeze sections and we treat it as a common law GRIT. Use Table B. 0.567427 * \$500,000 = \$283,714 and adjust for the contingency: \$283,714 * 6,282/17,046 = \$104,558. (b) Same answer; since this is a QPRT it does not matter what the relationship is between settlor and remainderman. (c) The date-of-death value is included, i.e., \$550,000 and the adjusted taxable gift is zero to avoid counting the same asset twice.

21. Evaluate a comment about trusts and pooled arrangements: True, all three provide income for life, a current tax deduction based upon the remainder value of the contribution, and a decrease in the estate tax. A savings occurs because there is no trust to draft and no additional tax returns to file, hence lesser fees to attorneys and accountants, but the donor has less investment control.

ENDNOTES

1. IRC § 163.

2. IRC § 61(a)(12).

3. IRC § 2033.

4. IRC § 7872(a)(1).

5. IRC § 267.

6. Reg. 1.1015-4(a)(1).

7. *Juden*, 89-1 USTC 9142; 63 ¶ AFTR 2d 89-595 (ECA-8, 1989).

8. IRC § 453.

9. IRC §§ 453(b)(2) & 453(l).

10. IRC § 453(e)(1).

11. Income in respect of a decedent (IRD) is discussed in Chapter 7.

12. IRC § 2043.

13. For an example of a successful SCIN involving a $12 million note, see *Wilson*, TCM 1992-480.

14. *Estate of Moss,* 74 TC 1239 (1980).

15. *Frane v. Commr,* 998 F. 2d 567 (CCA-8, 1993) in part reversing *Estate of Frane,* 98 TC 26 (1992); IRC § 691(a)(5).

16. Reg. § 25.7520-3(b)(3).

17. IRC § 2036(a).

18. IRC § 2036. See also *Bell Estate v. Commr,* 60 TC 469 (1973).

19. IRC § 453(b)(1); *Rye v. United States,* 92-1 USTC ¶50,186.

20. IRC § 2702(e) incorporating § 2704(c)(e)

21. Audrey Walton is the ex-wife of Sam Walton's brother, Bud Walton, a co-founder of Wal-Mart. See *Walton v. Commissioner* 119 T. C. 589 (2000), acq. in result, Notice 2003-72, 2003-2 C. B. 964, 2003-44 IRB

22. IRC § 170(c).

23. IRC § 170(b)(1)(F).

24. IRC § 170(b).

25. See IRC §§ 170(b)(1)(B), 170(b)(1)(C), 170(b)(1)(D), & 170(d)(1)(A).

26. IRC § 170(b)(1)(C).

27. IRC § 170(f)(8).

28. IRC § 2522(a).

29. IRC § 2055(a).

30. *U.S. Trust Co. v. U.S.*, 803 F. 2d 1363 (CCA-5, 1986).

31. IRC § 2036(a).

32. IRC § 2055.

33. Valuation of unitrust interests are calculated based on the § 7520 applicable federal rate, released monthly by the IRS, along with unitrust valuation factors derived from the Treasury department's *Actuarial Values-- Beta Volume* (IRS Pub. 1458), available from the U.S. Government Printing Office on the web at http://bookstore.gpo.gov/index.html

34. *E. La Meres Estate*, TC CCH 12,880.

35. IRC § 642(c)(5)(C).

36. Attaining grantor trust status without subjecting the corpus to estate taxation under IRC §§ 2036-2038 can be a challenge, see LR 9224029 and LR 9247024.

CHAPTER 13

The Role of Life Insurance in Estate Planning

OVERVIEW

This chapter will explore the role of insurance in estate planning. First, we will survey the various types of insurance policies commonly used.[1] Next, we will review the major concepts in the income, gift, and estate taxation of insurance. Finally, we will examine insurance related planning techniques frequently used to provide needed liquidity. Death may trigger a need for liquidity; directly related expenses include federal and state death taxes, expenses of estate (probate and/or trust) administration, payments to lawyers, executors, accountants, appraisers, and trustees. There may be debts and claims against the decedent's estate including last illness and funeral expenses.

Funds may be needed during the readjustment period as the surviving family members struggle to rearrange their lives. Perhaps the greatest need is for money to support surviving dependents. How much is needed depends on who (and how many) are dependent. For children, there is a need for food, shelter, and education that may continue for many years. For a disabled dependent, the time frame may be measured by the person's life expectancy. Life insurance is the only investment one can make that assures an instant estate of some significance.

LIFE INSURANCE CONTRACTS

Life insurance has several uses, but in estate planning, its major purpose is to provide funds to cover cash needs arising at a person's death. For some estates it is the major source of needed liquidity. A life insurance policy is a contract. If the insured owns the contract but is not the beneficiary, it is in a special category of bilateral contract referred to as a third-party beneficiary contract, distinguished from other bilateral contracts by the fact that the two parties to the contract intend to benefit a third party. An example would be where a parent purchases life insurance on her life, owns the policy, and names her child as the beneficiary. The parent and the insurance company are the parties to the contract and the child is the third-party beneficiary. For most contracts only the parties to the contract can enforce it, but with a third-party contract the beneficiary can also enforce it.

If the beneficiary purchases the policy, it is a standard bilateral contract, e.g., the child purchases a policy on the parent's life with the child as both owner and beneficiary of the policy. The amount that the insurance company pays when the insured dies is called the *face value* or the *policy proceeds*. The owner may be the *insured*, i.e., the person whose death is a condition precedent to the insurance company's obligation to pay. Someone other than the insured may be the owner, such as the beneficiary or the trustee of a life insurance trust. The owner designates the *beneficiary*, i.e., the person who receives the proceeds when the insured dies. The owner can cancel the policy, borrow money from the insurance company if the policy has cash reserves, assign the policy (i.e., transfer title to someone else as a gift or for money), and change the beneficiary designation.

Life insurance is not technically a property that transfers by operation of law since it requires the action of the insurance company (i.e., it will verify the death of the insured before it issues a check), nevertheless, it shares many of the characteristics of such properties. It has named beneficiaries, generally with alternates, its disposition is quick, and usually very straightforward, not necessarily a bad thing, but somewhat limiting from an estate planning standpoint. If paid into a trust, then much more long-term control and management can be accomplished, but this has more to do with trusts than the character of life insurance. Unless life insurance was used as collateral for a loan, or the owner has borrowed against the policy, the proceeds are not subject to the insured's creditors.

TYPES OF LIFE INSURANCE

It seems as though there are an endless variety of insurance policies sold in the United States today. There are policies called level term, decreasing term, mortgage payment insurance, whole life, variable life, etc. However, most are variations of one of two basic life insurance products: term insurance or cash value insurance. Cash value is also called permanent or whole life insurance.

Term. The simplest form of insurance is a one-year policy whose premium is based on the likelihood of death in that year. If the insured dies, the beneficiary is paid the face value. If the insured does not die, the company owes nothing and the contract terminates. This is the essence of term insurance: whether the company is financially obligated to pay depends solely on whether the insured dies during the contract period.

Most term insurance is renewable. The company is obligated to sell another year's insurance at a previously agreed-on price, at the option of the policy owner. Evidence of insurability, such as a physical exam, cannot now be required. Most term policies are renewable to some maximum age set by the company, e.g., age 70 or 75. The increasing periodic premium, or cost of annually renewable term insurance policies, rises annually with increasing age, reflecting the increased likelihood of death. Other term insurance policies have premiums that remain constant for five, 10, or 20 years, and then rise to a new plateau for another similar period. These are called "five-year level term" or "10-year level term" depending on the period during which the premiums stay the same. With most term insurance contracts, the premiums are guaranteed for one, five, or 10 years. Thereafter, premiums can be raised but not above some stated maximum. Regardless of how often the premium rises, all term insurance is characterized by periodic increases in the premiums and by the fact that the company will not offer the insurance coverage beyond some maximum age.

Cash value. In contrast to term insurance, cash value insurance has a constant ("level") periodic premium. It also has certainty. When a cash value insurance contract ends, either because the insured dies or because the policy owner no longer wants coverage, the company will be obligated to pay a predetermined amount of money. If the insured dies, the company will pay the face value. If the owner surrenders a cash value policy before the insured's death, the company will be obligated to pay an amount called the *cash surrender value*.

Cash value insurance originated as a solution to a problem inherent in term insurance. Many years ago, when term insurance was just about the only policy sold, policy owners frequently terminated their insurance as it became more and more expensive with the advancing age of the insured. To retain policyholders, companies started offering cash value insurance, charging a constant premium. Evidence shows that such policies are not as likely to be canceled by policyholders, despite advancing age. The earlier years' premiums are more than the company actuarially needs to fund death and other claims, and the later years' premiums are less than the company needs. The extra premium in the early years enables the company to accumulate an actuarial reserve. Typically, the owner may borrow, pledge, or in the event of surrender prior to the insured's death, receive the cash surrender value outright.

Cash value policy premiums usually are three to five times the initial premium charged for an annually renewable term policy for a given policyholder. Over time, the annual term policy premiums will increase to exceed the annual premiums on the cash value policy. For cash value policies, the guaranteed cash surrender values are listed, year by year, in the policy itself.

EXAMPLE 13 - 1. Audrey, an insurance salesperson, offers Gerard, age 45, a choice of two policies, each having a face value of $100,000. First, she describes a cash value whole life policy, sold by the ABC Co., which has a level annual premium of $2,700. Its cash surrender value at the end of the fifth policy year will be $7,500. At the end of the 20th policy year, the cash surrender value will be $43,500. Audrey then describes an annually renewable term policy that is guaranteed renewable to age 75. The policy, sold by the XYZ Co., has premiums for the first five years of $500, $550, $610, $680, and $750. If Gerard keeps the policy long enough, the premiums will be more than $3,000 per year by the time he reaches age 70.

Policies mature. All cash value policies have a maturity date at which, if the insured reaches it alive, the face value will be paid. A whole life cash value policy has a maturity date that extends beyond the "whole life" of most insureds, typically the insured's 95th or 100th birthday.

EXAMPLE 13 - 2. In the prior example, if Gerard purchases the whole life policy and keeps it in force, ABC will send him a check for $100,000 if he lives to be 100. Of course, if he does not live to be 100, the company will send his beneficiaries the $100,000.

Universal life. During periods of high interest rates, traditional cash value policies, such as whole life, tend to lose their allure because the guaranteed cash value growth rate is quite low in comparison to the returns available on other short-term, interest-sensitive investments. People considering insurance tend to be more attracted to term insurance, with the idea that the money saved from the much lower initial premiums will be invested elsewhere to earn higher yields. In response, the insurance industry developed a product called universal life insurance, which is a form of cash value insurance that offers the policyholder greater flexibility and, sometimes, greater investment yield. It offers greater flexibility because the policyholder is permitted to vary the amount of the face value and the premium payments to meet changing financial conditions.

Variable universal life can offer a greater investment yield because the policy owner selects from an array of portfolios (similar to a mutual fund family) managed by the insurance company for the investment of his or her excess premiums. The portfolios of nonvariable universal life typically hold debt instruments of shorter duration than do portfolios of whole life policies. As such, in periods of high interest rates these universal life portfolios also offer greater investment yields than do whole life portfolios. With either variable or nonvariable universal life, the insurance company (and the policyholder) hopes that the underlying portfolios will outperform the typical whole life guaranteed rate. If successful, some of the additional value is used to pay for additional insurance coverage, additional cash value, and/or reduced premiums. The typical universal life policy offers a low guaranteed rate of appreciation, commonly 4%, with the provision that a higher rate will be earned if the investments are more profitable.

Universal life insurance has been criticized as too complex compared to whole life and term insurance and because its flexibility makes it difficult to make cost comparisons when considering its purchase.

Split-dollar arrangements. A split-dollar arrangement is most commonly found as a nonqualified employee fringe benefit. It is a unique method of paying cash value insurance premiums rather than a different type of insurance. In the typical plan, the employer pays the insurer a portion of the premium equal to the lesser of the total premium or the increase in the cash value. The employee pays the balance of the premium. When the insured dies or when the policy is surrendered, the employer receives an amount equal to the premiums it paid. The remainder is paid to the beneficiary (if the insured dies) or the policy owner (if surrendered). Split-dollar insurance enables the employee to purchase cash value insurance at lower cost than if purchased individually.

TAXATION OF LIFE INSURANCE

Life insurance receives favorable income tax treatment in two major areas: generally, neither the cash value accumulation nor the policy proceeds are subject to income taxation.

Income tax. As a general rule, increases in cash value are not subject to income taxation.[2] However, if a cash value policy is surrendered, any excess of the amount realized over the total premiums paid (i.e., the owner's adjusted basis) is included in the owner's gross income. Loans from the cash buildup in a policy are not taxable either unless the amount withdrawn exceeds the amount paid into the policy.

IRC § 7702 was enacted to plug a loophole whereby insurance companies were selling single premium life insurance policies or modified endowment contracts (with very little life insurance protection) as tax-free investment vehicles rather than as life insurance. As defined in § 7702(A), a modified endowment contract is a life insurance policy entered into after June 20, 1988, that fails the "seven pay test." Failure occurs any time the cumulative premiums paid into the policy in the first seven years exceed the total of net level premiums which would have been sufficient to provide a paid-up policy, based on the initial death benefit, after seven annual payments.

The effect of a policy failing the test in § 7702 and being classified as a modified endowment contract is that withdrawals and distributions, even as loans, are treated as taxable income to the extent of any cash value accumulation, and is subject to an additional 10% income tax unless the owner is more than 59½, disabled, or receiving the payment as part of a series of equal annuity payments for life.

Life insurance proceeds paid because of the insured's death are generally excluded from gross income.[3] However, if a policy is transferred for valuable consideration, then the proceeds are included in the gross income of the transferee, less the price and premiums paid. This is called the *transfer for value* rule. It does not apply to transfers for value to the following parties:

- The insured (or to a grantor trust of the insured)[4]
- A partner of the insured
- A partnership in which the insured is a partner
- A corporation in which the insured is a shareholder or officer
- A transferee whose basis will be determined by reference to the transferor's basis (i.e., the donee of a gift of the policy)[5]

EXAMPLE 13 - 3. For more than 15 years, Terry was the owner of a $10,000 face value insurance policy on his life. Last year, he gave the policy to his beneficiary-son, Ralph, who began to pay the premiums. Terry died last month. No portion of the proceeds will be includable in Ralph's gross income because Ralph did not buy the policy.

EXAMPLE 13 - 4. Sherman borrowed $100,000 from Polly, pledging his $500,000 cash value policy as collateral. The insurance company was informed of the loan, and was irrevocably instructed to, in the event of Sherman's death, pay off the loan and pay the balance to Sherman's daughter, Tina. Additional instructions assigned the policy to Polly in the event Sherman failed to make scheduled loan payments. Unfortunately for Tina, Sherman failed to make any of the required payments so Polly exercised her right to acquire title to the policy, and immediately named herself beneficiary. Business is business. To keep the policy in force, she made $5,000 in premium payments before Sherman died. Included in her gross income is the $395,000 difference between the $500,000 payout and her $105,000 basis in the policy.

EXAMPLE 13 - 5. Ulysses and Zeno are business partners. For years, each owned an insurance policy on his own life. Now, their attorney is drafting a "cross-purchase business buyout" contract, and the partners have agreed to exchange policies, with some cash also included as part of the transaction. Thus, Ulysses will become owner and beneficiary of the policy on the life of Zeno, and Zeno will become owner and beneficiary of the policy on the life of Ulysses. On the death of either partner, no part of the proceeds will be includable in the other's gross income.

The above example illustrates the use of existing insurance policies to fund a business buyout agreement.

Gift tax. There are two common situations where insurance is subject to gift tax. First, a taxable gift may arise when the owner assigns ownership of the policy to another person without receiving consideration in return. Ordinarily, the gift of an insurance policy will qualify for the annual exclusion, unless it is made to an irrevocable trust. Even then, if a beneficiary of the trust is given a Crummey demand power, the annual exclusion is available. Second, a taxable gift of the policy proceeds may arise when the insured dies. If the insured, owner, and beneficiary are all different parties, the proceeds are considered a gift from the policy owner to the beneficiary. The effect of this rule is that planners recommend that if someone other than the insured will own the policy, he or she should also be named as the beneficiary.

Estate tax. Life insurance is most commonly included in a decedent's federal estate tax base under §§ 2001, 2033, 2035(a), or 2042. Under § 2001, the decedent's adjusted taxable gifts include the date-of-gift value less the annual exclusion for any life insurance policy the decedent transferred after 1976 and more than three years before death. Under § 2033 (property owned at death), the value of the decedent's date-of-death ownership interest in a life insurance policy on the life of someone other than the decedent will be included in the decedent's gross estate. Under § 2035(a), the proceeds of a life insurance policy on the life of the decedent will be included in the decedent's gross estate if the decedent made a transfer of any incidents of ownership in the policy within three years of death. Under § 2042, proceeds of a policy on the life of the decedent are includable in the decedent's gross estate if, at the insured's death, either the proceeds were receivable by the decedent's executor or the decedent possessed any incidents of ownership in the policy.

LIFE INSURANCE PLANNING

Life insurance is used in liquidity planning to meet cash needs while minimizing income, gift, and estate tax, and other costs. To do this efficiently, we must choose the most appropriate insured, owner, and beneficiary for each life insurance policy.

Selecting the insured. The life of each spouse whose death is expected to trigger a cash need should be insured sufficiently to meet the cash need. For smaller estates, there will typically be a need for cash at the death of either or both spouses based upon replacing their financial or service contribution to the family.

For larger estates, we have seen that effective planning (with the use of the marital deduction trust and the credit shelter bypass trust) usually eliminates the need to pay estate tax at the death of the first spouse (S1), but it creates a relatively large need at the surviving spouse's death (S2). Thus, ordinarily, little or no insurance is required on S1's life to pay estate tax. The real insurance need will be on S2's life. However, some insurance may be needed at S1's death to meet nontax needs, such as to cover last expenses, readjustment, and cash requirements during the dependency period. As with smaller estates, there may be a need to replace the financial or service contribution to the family. This will be particularly important for parents with substantial earned income who are supporting younger children.

Since most couples do not know whether the husband or the wife will be the surviving spouse, both may need to be insured. Several commonly used purchase arrangements are discussed next.

1. *Full coverage for both spouses.* One simple but costly plan is to insure both spouses for the full amount of protection needed at the surviving spouse's death. Because of needless extra cost, this plan is seldom recommended.

2. *Minimal coverage for both spouses.* An alternative method of insuring the spouses is to purchase a small amount of insurance on both spouses which, on the death of either, can be used to purchase a "fully paid-up" larger policy on the life of the survivor. This has the advantage of eliminating the cash flow drain on the surviving spouse to pay the premium.

3. *Second-to-die insurance.* Both spouses could purchase *second-to-die insurance*, also called *survivorship life insurance*. Both spouses are insured in one policy, but the contract requires payment when the second death occurs. This alternative saves premium dollars in two ways: First, only one policy is purchased. Second, the contingency insured against is more remote in time than that insured against under a single-life policy, consequently, the premiums are lower than a similar policy on either spouse's life. Even though one spouse may be uninsurable, a second-to-die policy should still be available since the medical underwriting standards are eased as long as one spouse is healthy.

4. *Full coverage for wife only.* Another alternative is to insure only the wife, assuming she has the longer life expectancy. If she survives her husband, the contract becomes a de facto second-to-die policy. If she predeceases him, the proceeds could be invested or partly used to buy a paid-up policy on his life to pay the estate tax at his death. The cost of insuring only the wife is likely to be more expensive than a second-to-die policy.

Selecting the owner and beneficiary. Selecting the owner and beneficiary for a married couple with a smaller estate is simple since no transfer taxes are expected if the net value of the combined estates (with the insurance included) is less than the AEA. Each spouse may own policies on his or her own life with the proceeds payable to the other. The contingent beneficiary could be the couple's children, if sufficiently mature, or could be the trustee of the couple's probate-avoidance living trust.

When transfer tax costs are a concern, more thought must be given to selecting owners and beneficiaries. Naming one or the other spouse as owner or beneficiary will not minimize transfer costs. It will usually subject the proceeds to a transfer tax, probate administration, or both, depending on which spouse dies first. Consider the complicated tax and probate consequences for each alternative.

First, if the insured spouse dies first and is the owner, the proceeds will be includable in his or her gross estate under § 2042. If the proceeds qualify for the marital deduction, avoiding taxation at the first death, whatever proceeds remain will be included in the gross estate and taxed at the second death. If the insured spouse dies second and is the owner, then the proceeds will be included in his or her gross estate with no marital deduction available.

Second, if the insured spouse dies first and the noninsured spouse is the owner and beneficiary, then the proceeds that remain will be included in the gross estate at the second death. If the noninsured spouse is named owner and someone else is the beneficiary, when the proceeds are paid, the owner-spouse will have made a taxable gift to the beneficiary. Thus, the noninsured spouse should not be named either owner or beneficiary if the surviving spouse's estate is likely to exceed the AEA.

In planning for wealthy couples, two important conclusions can be drawn from the above. First, naming either spouse as owner or beneficiary of a policy on the life of a spouse will subject the proceeds to transfer taxation at least at the second death. Thus, to minimize transfer taxes, neither spouse should be designated owner or beneficiary of an insurance policy on the life of the other. Second, since a taxable gift will occur whenever the insured, owner, and beneficiary are different parties, whoever is selected should be named both owner and beneficiary, to avoid gift tax consequences.

Instead of a spouse, one of the couple's children could be named owner and beneficiary. The child could be requested to use the proceeds to provide liquidity to the estate on the death of the insured. This alternative will work best when the child is sufficiently mature to handle the responsibility. Nonetheless, there will always be risks. The child may permit the policy to lapse. Or the child, having received the policy proceeds on the death of the insured parent, may be unwilling to provide the funding needed by the estate. Once the child receives the proceeds, any gratuitous transfer of funds to the estate will receive standard taxable gift treatment unless the child is the sole beneficiary of the estate. To avoid making a gift, the child could purchase estate assets or lend money to the estate.

IRREVOCABLE LIFE INSURANCE TRUSTS

For wealthy individuals and couples, where estate taxes are a concern, the irrevocable life insurance trust (ILIT) is generally recommended.

Basic structure. The person to be insured creates and transfers funds into the ILIT and selects an independent trustee. The trustee then uses the funds to obtain insurance on the trustor's life, naming the trustee as the owner and beneficiary of the policy. The trust must be irrevocable or § 2038 would draw the trust (i.e., the insurance proceeds) into the trustor's estate. The trustor must not be named a trust beneficiary, because of possible § 2036(a) problems; since the uninsured spouse is usually one of the beneficiaries of an ILIT, he or she should not be a trustor.

Most ILITs are drafted with clauses that give Crummey demand rights to the children and even to the grandchildren. These clauses are inserted to create the necessary present interest so that the annual exclusion may shelter the funds the insured gives the trustee to pay the premiums. Because the holders of the powers must be given a reasonable time in which to exercise their demand rights, the trustee must receive the funds far enough in advance of the premium due date to give the holders notice and have the demand period expire before the payment must be made. The demand period (typically 30 or 60 days) must be stated in the ILIT as part of the Crummey provision.

On the death of the insured, the trustee collects the proceeds and follows the terms of the trust document. Generally, the trustee is authorized to lend the proceeds to the insured's estate and to purchase assets from the estate. If the insured is S1, then the trust corpus usually continues to provide benefits to S2 in the form of a bypass trust. At the death of S2, the trust is again authorized to lend cash to the S2 estate and to purchase estate assets. The trust could then be terminated, with the corpus payable to the children. Alternatively, the trust could be continued, distributing income to the children until they reach a specified age, or to the grandchildren until they reach a specified age.

Purpose driven. If an ILIT is to be used as a source of cash to pay estate taxes, it is important to choose a type of policy that will be there when estate taxes are due or at least covers the period until estate tax is repealed. Term insurance becomes increasingly expensive as the insured gets older and may not even be available beyond a certain age (i.e., most insurance companies do not write term policies for people over the age of 75).

A married couple has two choices. First, if the sole purpose is to pay estate taxes at the second death, then a second-to-die policy is the least expensive of the cash value policies. With a sophisticated estate plan incorporating bypass and marital trusts, the taxes are most likely to be postponed until the second death.

A potentially more complex situation occurs rarely when S2 is dying at the time of S1's death and the executor wants to generate a tax at S1's death. Will use of a second-to-die policy cause hardship or force the executor to postpone the taxes to the second death even though it means more overall estate taxes? The answer is no. Section 6161 allows executors to postpone payment of the estate tax for reasonable cause. Thus the executor of S1's estate would not be forced to sell assets but would file the return, report the estate taxes owed, and request a one-year extension with an explanation as to why cash is presently unavailable.

Second, for a younger, less wealthy couple, the purpose is likely to provide funds to replace the financial contribution of the deceased spouse. Term insurance may be the better choice. The income earners (one or both) should be separately insured taking into account the amount of insurance needed to replace the insured's earning capacity. For any given family wealth level (until we reach the very wealthy), a young couple with dependent children will need greater amounts of insurance than an older couple with grown children. Term insurance allows them the most insurance for their premium dollars. If the couple can afford additional insurance and is concerned about covering estate taxes in the event both die young, then they should consider a second ILIT to purchase a second-to-die policy.

Who should pay the premiums on the trust-owned policy? One alternative is to fund the trust with sufficient income-earning assets to enable the trust to pay them. The grantor trust rules will make that income taxable to the grantor (trustor) rather than the trust.[6] A preferred alternative is for the trustor to make annual gifts to the trust to pay the premiums. In community property states, the insured spouse should make the periodic gifts from his or her separate property to keep the proceeds out of the estate of the noninsured beneficiary spouse. A

Crummey demand right held by the insured's children will make the gifts to the ILIT qualify for the annual exclusion.

Expected ILIT results. For a married couple with an estate that exceeds the AEA, the ILIT achieves all of the following goals:

1. Excludes the insurance proceeds from income taxation and from the taxable estates of both spouses and, perhaps, the children.
2. Excludes the insurance proceeds from the probate estates of both spouses.
3. The annual exclusion can shelter gifts to the trust of the policy and money to pay premiums.
4. Ensures that a responsible party will provide the needed post-death liquidity.
5. Makes the proceeds available to the surviving spouse for health or certain other reasons.

A single person can also use an ILIT to achieve similar tax and nontax goals. Generally, the remaindermen, even contingent remaindermen, are named as holders of the Crummey right to withdraw.

EXAMPLE 13 - 6. Marshal and Deanna Wotton were married and living in California when, as part of a plan to pay for estate taxes, they had an ILIT created. If she outlived him, the ILIT gave Deanna a life estate starting with Marshal's death. The trustee purchased a $4,000,000 policy on Marshal's life. Pursuant to a written agreement, they opened "his" and "her" checking accounts, each designated as the respective owner's separate property. Marshal used some of the funds in his account to send sufficient funds to the trustee to cover the premiums. A clause in the trust required the trustee to notify the Wotton's three children that they had 45 days to withdraw one-third of the funds each time they were placed in the trust. The demand right was limited to the lesser of one-third of the money placed in the trust that year or that year's annual exclusion amount reduced by any gifts made directly to the child. When Marshal died, the trustee collected the proceeds, invested them and paid Deanna the income. When she died several years later, the trustee distributed the trust to the three children. They used it to pay the estate taxes. The proceeds were not included in Marshal's or Deanna's estates. It is not in Marshal's estate because, while he made transfers of cash, he did not transfer life insurance and he did not retain any interests in the trust. It is not in Deanna's estate because, while she had an interest, it was not a retained one since she did not make any transfers to the trust. The purchase of the policy by the trustee avoids the three-year rule applicable when an insured transfers his or her interest in a policy.

> EXAMPLE 13 - 7. In the prior example, if Marshal and Deanna used a joint checking account to send money to the trustee, there is a strong argument that, at Deanna's death, half of the value of the trust is included in her estate. The argument goes as follows: the funds used to maintain the trust were from community property, hence half hers, with the result that even if Marshal wrote the checks to the trustee, Deanna made a transfer and kept a retained interest, namely her right to a life estate. This negative result reaches only half of the trust corpus since, although Marshal contributed to the purchase of the policy, he did not have a retained interest.

Tax issues. For income tax, an ILIT will not ordinarily fall within the grasp of § 2036 (retained life estate). However, because they are not direct skips, annual exclusion transfers into the trust will not insulate the corpus from GST tax. Thus, planners may elect to allocate some of the GST exemption to such transfers, anticipating that the premature death of a child may give rise to a taxable distribution or a taxable termination.

Excluding the insurance proceeds from the gross estate of a decedent has the additional benefit of avoiding transferee liability for payment of the estate tax. In one unusual case, the decedent died possessing incidents of ownership in a $50,000 life insurance policy. The IRS was unable to collect $62,378 in estate tax from the decedent's assets, which were then owned by his nonresident alien widow, living in Venezuela. However, the insurance beneficiary, a U.S. citizen, was held liable for $50,000 of the taxes.[7]

If an existing policy is transferred to the trust, the trustor-insured must live three years after the policy is transferred to ensure that § 2035's three-year rule for life insurance transfers does not apply. Whenever possible, the policy should be purchased by the trustee to avoid the three-year rule. If the insured transfers an existing policy, the annual exclusion will not apply unless the trust gives the beneficiaries a Crummey invasion power.

The trust can include a contingent marital deduction clause, so that if the three-year rule causes the proceeds to be included in the insured's gross estate, then the trust is required to pay the widow income for life payable at least annually. This clause would allow a QTIP election and the resulting marital deduction would avoid estate taxes. Of course, a QTIP election will cause the trust to be included in S2's estate. On the other hand, if the insured lives longer than three years, the ILIT avoids both estates, the contingent income clause that would have mandated income payments solely to S2 becomes meaningless, and the trust can be a sprinkling trust that distributes income to the children as well as to S2.

If each spouse is an insured, then two trusts will have to be established, with each trust owning one policy. These trusts must be drafted very carefully to avoid § 2036(a) problems.

If the trust is required to use insurance proceeds to pay the decedent's estate debts, including taxes, the proceeds will be includable in the decedent's gross estate under § 2042. Instead, the trust should give the trustee permission to lend the proceeds to the estate or to purchase estate assets, thus facilitating the payment of the estate tax without causing the proceeds to be part of the gross estate.

Although GST tax rules prevent annual exclusion gifts to a single trust for the benefit of both nonskip and skip persons from also being sheltered from the GST tax, planners achieve complete shelter from GST tax in one of two ways. Either they create one trust and use the trustor's GST exemption to shelter these gifts, or they create two trusts, one for the benefit of only nonskip persons (e.g. spouse and children) and the other for the benefit of only skip persons (grandchildren, etc.).[8]

Trustee selection. An insured spouse who is also the trustor should not be named the trustee since this could constitute an incident of ownership in the policy. The other spouse could be named the trustee without this adverse result.

Some corporate trustees are reluctant to become trustees of an insurance trust prior to the insured's death if the trust is otherwise unfunded. Even if it is funded, the advent of higher-risk, higher-return life insurance policies and growing insurance company insolvency problems have made trustees concerned about possible liability if expected policy death benefits are not paid or if the policy turns out to be relatively uncompetitive. In addition, an ILIT may not be profitable for a corporate trustee even after the proceeds are received, particularly if they must be allocated in one of two ways: proceeds immediately distributed to trust beneficiaries, or used to acquire closely held business stock, a difficult asset to manage.

To overcome the liability concerns and encourage a fiduciary to act as trustee of a life insurance trust, the trust may include language that exculpates the trustee from liability in connection with holding the life insurance policy. The trust must make it clear that the trustee is released from liability for investing only in life insurance since the failure to diversify investments violates the prudent investor rule. The trust can indemnify the trustee, i.e., reimburse the trustee for any expenses, including attorneys' fees, that might arise from a challenge by the remainderman. Exculpatory clauses are enforced by the courts, but are strictly construed against the trustee. They offer no protection from acts of "bad faith," "reckless indifference," "gross negligence," or "willful misconduct."

Finally, the planner can arrange for an individual, such as a family friend, to act as initial trustee, with the corporate fiduciary succeeding as trustee only after the insured(s) has died and the proceeds have been paid. Of course, the family friend should also have the benefit of the exculpatory clauses just discussed.

LIFE INSURANCE CASH ADVANCES AND VIATICAL SETTLEMENTS

Accelerated death benefit. The Health Insurance Portability and Accountability Act, signed into law in August of 1996, allows people diagnosed with a terminal illness to "cash in" their life insurance early without having to pay income tax on the proceeds. These funds are available either directly from the insurance company, provided the policy has an accelerated death benefit (ADB) provision, or from an outside company that offers what is called a viatical settlement. The ADB is either part of the original insurance contract or added later as a rider. The insurance company agrees to pay the proceeds at a discount from the face value of the policy. The fewer months the insured is expected to live, the lower the discount. Generally, the remaining amount will be paid when the insured dies.

EXAMPLE 13 - 8. Karen had a terminal illness that was likely to result in death within 12 months. The company that issued her $400,000 insurance policy had added an ABD rider several years ago. Upon verification of her life expectancy, the company paid her 45% of the insurance amount (i.e., $180,000). When she died eight months later, the balance of $220,000 was paid to her daughter as the designated beneficiary.

Viatical settlements. A viatical settlement is an agreement between a company representing a group of investors and an individual with a projected life expectancy of less than 48 months due to a terminal illness. The insured who enters into one of these contracts is called the *viator* and the company is called a *viatical company* or, if an individual, a *viatical investor*. After the death of the viator, the investor's share of the insurance proceeds are included in his or her gross income under the transfer for value rule.

Under the 1996 Act, in order for the ADB or the viatical settlement to be income tax-free for the viator, a physician must certify that the insured has a physical condition that can reasonably be expected to result in death within 24 months from the date of certification. Most ADB clauses set a maximum life expectancy that is considerably shorter (e.g., just 12 months or even as short as six months). Viatical companies generally seek contracts where death is expected to occur within 24 months. They may enter contracts where the life expectancy is longer, but the favorable income tax treatment for the viator would not be available.

> EXAMPLE 13 - 9. Karol has an advanced case of AIDS that has failed to respond favorably to any of the recent treatments. She decides that she would like to take her three children to visit their grandparents in Amsterdam. Her funds are extremely limited, so she contacts a viatical company to see if there is an interest in her $300,000 term policy. At the company's request, her doctor furnishes a complete medical report and signs a certificate that gives his opinion that Karol's life expectancy is between 12 and 18 months. The company agrees to pay $200,000 immediately, with an additional sum payable to her children. The additional amount is $50,000 if she dies in the first month after the settlement, reduced by two thousand dollars for each additional month, or portion of a month, that she lives beyond the first month.

Comparing insurance advances and viatical settlements. The insured may use the ADB or viatical proceeds in any way he or she desires. Given the substantial discounts, most people will not use an ADB clause or enter into a viatical settlement if there are other reasonable sources of funds. Hence, it is likely that the funds will be used to pay for medical treatment or special nursing care where no other reasonable source of payment is available, but the law does not require that the money be so used. Indeed, the insured could use the funds for one last glorious trip to a place he or she always wanted to visit. For investors, they should be warned that this is a mostly unregulated area. See the excellent article, "Viatical Settlements: Myths & Misconceptions," by JJ MacNab, Insurance Analyst, at <http://deathandtaxes.com/viatical.htm>. Ohio's disclosure requirements for viatical investment companies seeking to do business in that state can be found at <http://www. viatical.org/Disclosure/Ohio_dis.htm>.

Federal law gives favorable treatment for persons who are "chronically ill" and can benefit from an ADB payment or a viatical settlement, however the proceeds are tax-free only if used for "costs incurred by the payee . . . for qualified long-term care services" where such care is not covered by insurance or otherwise subject to reimbursement.

CONCLUSION

Life insurance has a very important place in estate planning. For families in the early stages of building a secure financial base, often with both spouses working and with young children, there is no other way to assure an instant estate in the event that one spouse dies. For families with substantial financial wealth, the purpose of buying life insurance might be to avoid the forced sale of assets to pay estate tax or to give additional comfort to the surviving spouse by paying off mortgages or other debt. As we saw, for the very wealthy, trust planning is needed to keep life insurance from being included in the insured's taxable estate.

The next chapter covers estate planning solutions to the problems faced by owners of closely held businesses. Often the business is a significant portion of the owner's estate, complications arise in how to fairly divided up the estate, especially where some family members participate in the business and others do not. There are steps the owner can take to reduce the transfer tax burden. The financial planner can help the owner design an estate plan to maximizes the likelihood that the owner's estate will qualify for one or more of the many IRC sections that give estate tax relief.

QUESTIONS AND PROBLEMS

1. (a) What traits distinguish cash value insurance from term insurance? (b) Universal life insurance from other types of cash value insurance?

2. Is life insurance ever subject to income taxation? Explain.

3. Explain the two primary ways life insurance is subject to gift taxation.

4. Max and Minnie are friends. Max loaned Minnie $50,000, taking back an assignment of her paid-up $300,000 face value insurance policy as security for the loan. They agreed that he would not file the assignment with the insurance company so long as she repaid the loan within six months. When she failed to repay anything on the loan, Max sent the company the paper work that resulted in the policy being transferred to him. Two years later, Minnie died (hey, natural causes) and Max collected the $300,000. Would the policy be in Minnie's estate? Would the proceeds be taxable to Max?

5. Steve was in very poor health when he borrowed $25,000 from Foxtail Lending, Inc., (Foxtail) using his $100,000 life insurance policy as collateral. He could have cashed in the policy but would have received only $7,000 as cash surrender value. By their agreement, Foxtail was made beneficiary and held the policy and a conditional assignment of its title, i.e., in the event of Steve's default on the loan Foxtail was authorized to change title to its name. So long as Steve made his loan and premium payments (handled by Foxtail) the policy remained in Steve's name and in the event of his death proceeds in excess of those needed to pay off the loan were to go equally to Steve's two children. In the event of default, Foxtail would own the policy and could cash it in or keep it and eventually collect the proceeds. The insurance company was notified of the loan and instructed not to change the beneficiary unless said request was joined by Foxtail. After making some payments, Steve defaulted on the loan and Foxtail had title changed to show it as owner. The balance of the loan at default was $20,000 and Foxtail paid another $5,000 to keep the insurance in force until Steve died. What gain must Foxtail recognize? This is an example of what income tax rule?

6. Life insurance can be subject to estate taxation under §§ 2001, 2033, 2042, and 2035(a). Briefly explain the application of each.

7. April, age 40, is a recently divorced single mother of two young children. She is not on friendly terms with her ex-husband who, in her opinion, is a "selfish spendthrift." April owns few assets and asks your estate planning advice to help achieve her goal of financial security for her children.

8. Sixty-year-old Adrian has an estate worth $3,500,000 with a significant part being very illiquid real estate. He wishes to pass the assets to his 40-year-old nephew, Clark. Adrian has heard about using insurance to pay estate taxes, and being in good health, he plans to purchase a $500,000 life insurance policy naming his estate the beneficiary. What advice would you give to Adrian regarding his decision? Would you advise term or whole life? Check with an insurance agent to see what each would cost. For the term policy use a 10-year level term. (State your source and the name of the insurance company.)

9. In each case, would it make sense to purchase insurance? If so, for what purpose and what kind? Who should be the owner and who the insured? Assume for couples that the household wealth is $500,000 and for singles it is $250,000. Estate plans for couples are simple wills with estate left first to spouse, then to children, and if no children or spouse, to parents. For singles it is first to children, if any, otherwise to parents.
(a) Spouses in their 30s, husband working, wife at home with two young children.
(b) Spouses in their 30s, both working, no children.
(c) Spouses in their 50s, both working, children are self-supporting adults living elsewhere.
(d) Single adult, no children.
(e) Single parent of one six-year-old child.
(f) Retired couple, self-supporting adult children living elsewhere.

10. Answer the prior question assuming a $6 million estate for couples and half that for singles. Couples have ABC trust plans and singles have simple wills as described above. In each case would it matter how liquid the estate?

11. Selecting Life Insurance: For each of the following state whether whole life insurance or term insurance is most appropriate, who should be the insured, the owner, and for each response explain why.
(a) A young couple expecting their first child. Their net worth about $40,000.
(b) A couple with children in high school. Buying a home, planning for children's college. Their net worth about $120,000.
(c) A couple whose children are grown and out of their house. Both are nearing retirement, will both have good joint-survivor pensions and some investments, the home will be paid for by the time of retirement. Their net worth about $350,000.
(d) Wealthy couple, children grown and out of the house. Both retired, good pensions, ABC estate plan. Their net worth about $10,000,000. Enough wealth to cover estate taxes but would like to cover a portion of it with insurance. They still qualify for insurance and obviously can afford it.

12. (a) Describe the characteristics of the irrevocable life insurance trust.
(b) What are its advantages?

13. What special problem might arise for a community property couple who set up a life insurance trust that provides income for life to the survivor? How is the problem avoided?

14. Five years ago, Mary assigned ownership of an insurance policy on the life of her husband, Bud, to the trustee of Bud's living trust. The trustee is beneficiary, and terms of the trust provide that at Bud's death Mary is entitled to a life estate in the trust income. If Mary survives Bud, could there be an estate tax problem?

15. Why is an ILIT more likely to hold a whole life policy rather than a term policy? Since the insured is likely to be the creator of the ILIT, how is it possible that the trust (and hence the life insurance) is not included in the insured's estate?

16. Dianne Reis is a Texas board Certified Estate Planning and Probate Law attorney. To answer the questions that follow, visit her website: <http://willsandprobate.com/FAQ/life-ins-trust.htm> (a) What happens if the

ILIT allows the insured to borrow against the policy? (b) How does one avoid §2035(a) life insurance three-year inclusion rule? (c) How does one avoid using up AEA? (d) Who does attorney Reis suggest might serve as a trustee? Why might the trustee initially charge a reduced fee?

17. Pamela has a rare blood disease that is likely to take her life within the next couple of years. She has no great desire to continue to pay the annual $15,000 premiums on the $500,000 life insurance policy that she received when she sold her interest in a closely held business to her co-owners. The cash surrender value of the policy is about $100,000. An ABD provision would allow her to take $75,000 from the company and stop paying premiums. A viatical company has offered to buy the policy for $290,000. She would like to do a world cruise while she still is well enough to enjoy it. Consider each of the following means of using the policy to obtaining money for this and other expenses. Explain how she would obtain the cash and the relative merits of each option. (a) Cash out the policy. (b) Accept the ABD. (c) Enter into a viatical agreement.

18. Read the article by JJ MacNab titled Viatical Settlements: Myths & Misconceptions found at <http://deathandtaxes.com/viatical.htm>. Note that the article was written in 1999 so the examples assume higher estate tax rates and lower AEA than are true today but most of what is described concerning these arrangements is still true. Taking information and opinion from the article, answer these questions: (a) Who are the three parties likely to be involved in a viatical contract and which party is most likely to benefit? (b) What is the source and the meaning of the term "viatical"? (c) Is the insured restricted as to the use of the funds if he or she exercises an ADB option? Why, at least from the standpoint of the terminally ill person's beneficiaries, is an ADB option better than a viatical settlement? (d) What is the viator's maximum life expectancy if he or she is to have the settlement money be tax-free? How is the life expectancy verified? What is the other important qualifying requirement? (e) What is the tax treatment of the insurance proceeds received by the investors?

ANSWERS TO THE QUESTIONS AND PROBLEMS *(odd numbered only)*

1. (a) The traits that distinguish cash value insurance from term insurance are: (1) The pattern of the *premiums* over time (cash value: constant premiums; term: increasing premiums). (2) Whether the proceeds are *certain* to be paid (cash value: certain; term: uncertain).

   (b) The traits that distinguish universal life (UL) insurance from other types of cash value insurance are: (1) degree of flexibility - UL policies permit the policyholder to vary the face value and premium payments; and (2) investment yield - UL policies offer a variable yield, based on shorter-term investment rates.

3. Gift taxation of life insurance can arise either when a policy is assigned, or at the insured's death, whenever the insured, owner, and beneficiary are all different parties.

5. Foxtail's gain is the difference between the proceeds collected and what it paid: $100,000 - ($20,000 + $5,000) = $75,000. This is ordinary income. This is an example of the transfer for value rule representing one of the rare situations where proceeds of insurance are subject to income taxes.

7. To establish an asset base to provide income to her children in the event of her premature death, April should establish an irrevocable life insurance trust, a device that can function reasonably free from the control of her ex-husband. The trustee would be the policy beneficiary, directed to provide for the children's needs. The trustee ought to be instructed to pay funds, whenever possible, directly to the provider.

9. The major question in deciding whom to insure is whose death will result in financial loss that should be replaced.

   (a) *Spouses in their 30's; husband working; wife at home with two young children:* Both spouses may need term insurance: for the husband to replace his lost income; for the wife to finance day care services, etc., while the widower is working. Probably term insurance makes the most sense in all of these cases. It is cheaper and the need that is being addressed is temporary and will disappear by the time the individuals reach retirement age.

(b) *Spouses in their 30s; both working; no children:* Often, neither spouse needs coverage, because the income (modest) loss from the death of either is assumable. However, this depends on their relative current standard of living and desired standard of living when the first one dies. Spouses who live modestly and save a lot may not need life insurance if the survivor can live on one salary and the expected investment income. On the other hand, spouses who save little and live expensively (costly home, cars, lifestyle, etc.) and want the surviving spouse to continue enjoying this lifestyle will probably need a considerable amount of insurance on the lives of both spouses.

(c) *Spouses in their 50's; both working; children are self-supporting adults living elsewhere:* Essentially same answer as part b, except less insurance usually necessary because the surviving spouse's expected life span is lower and expected investment income is often greater.

(d) *Single adult; no children:* No insurance usually necessary.

(e) *Single parent of one six-year old child:* Considerable insurance would ordinarily be needed for the parent to provide funds needed to raise the child.

(f) *Retired couple; self-supporting adult children living elsewhere:* Answer depends on surviving spouse's other expected sources of income. To the extent that retirement benefits will continue and investment income will be high, less insurance is needed.

11. (a) Term insurance, both as insured, ownership less important since estate tax is not an issue hence either or both for each policy. They need to replace wage earner and/or homemaker in the event of either death; term buys the most insurance to cover immediate needs.

(b) Term insurance, both as insured, ownership less important since estate tax is not an issue hence either or both for each policy. Their financial needs are likely to be greatest over the next several years until children are through school and working.

(c) They might not have a need for insurance since they seem to have sufficient resources without it. Perhaps decreasing term to cover the remaining balance on their home mortgage.

(d) Whole life policy held in an ILIT, either both as insured or it could be a last to die policy. The premiums paid reduce their taxable estate and the insurance itself is not taxed in either estate.

13. The surviving spouse may be treated as if he or she owned half of everything that went into the trust. To avoid this have the independent trustee buy the life insurance and have it deemed separate property of the insured.

15. Generally an ILIT is created only if the person (couple) is quite wealthy and has a desire to keep significant insurance proceeds from being subjected to estate tax. If the purpose is to pay a portion of the estate taxes, then it is important that the insurance actually be there when the insured dies. Only whole life policies assure that to be the case. Term insurance is generally used for income replacement and is a good buy for a family that is not really wealthy. It is generally understood that once family obligations decrease (e.g., kids are raised and educated) and wealth increases, term policies will be allowed to lapse as the premiums become quite expensive.

17. (a) She would get the $100,000 but the insurance would be at an end. This is not as good an idea as the viatical option if she really doesn't care whether proceeds are eventually paid to her family members.
(b) This option gives her the least cash but would allow payment, when she dies, of the balance of the policy to her family.
(c) This gives her the greatest cash to do with as she pleases but of course the proceeds go to the investors and not to her family members.

ENDNOTES

1. In this chapter, the word *insurance* will be used as shorthand to mean life insurance.

2. *Theodore H. Cohen*, 39 TC 1055 (1963), acq. 1964-1 CB 4.

3. IRC § 101.

4. *Swanson*, 33 TCM 296, (1974), aff'd. 518 F2d 59 (8th Cir., 1975); Rev. Rul. 85-13 1985-1 CB 184.

5. IRC § 101(*a*)(2).

6. IRC § 677(a)(3).

7. *Baptiste*, TCM 1992-198; IRC § 6324(a)(2).

8. IRS § 2642(c)(2).

CHAPTER 14

Planning for Closely Held Business Interests

OVERVIEW

For most people, identity and self-worth are closely tied to family, friends, and career. Meeting someone for the first time, we are curious about what they do for a living as much or more than who the person is on a personal level, meaning, whether they have children, a significant other, what hobbies they enjoy, and whether religion plays a significant role in the person's life. Given the positive reinforcement from family, friends, and society, is it any wonder that the successful businessperson has a great deal more than money invested in his or her business? Or that parting with, or even thinking about parting with, his or her business is difficult? Adding to the emotional elements are other complicating factors such as how to fairly divide what may be the largest asset one owns, especially if some family members show an interest in the business and others do not. There are also tax and valuation issues. These may overlap to some extent given that from a division standpoint, family members inheriting a business and planning to continue its operation would prefer it be valued low for estate tax purposes and because it will be part of their share of the estate, other family members may wish to have it valued high even if it means more taxes, since valuing it high means that they will receive a greater share of the non-business estate assets.

TRANSFER ISSUES

Transfer issues center around the questions of when and to whom. Should the transfer start (and maybe finish) while the owner is alive to oversee the transition or should it be postponed until after the owner's death? Will the transfer be by gifts to family or will it be by sale? If sold, will it be to co-owners or to outsiders? Even when these questions are answered, there are matters to resolve. For example, if transferred to family, how can assets be fairly divided if the business is worth more than any child's share of the parents' estate, especially if some of the children work in the business while others do not?

Timing: Lifetime or After?

The owner's basis in a successful business is likely to be quite low compared to its worth. If sold while the owner can guide the selling, the price might be higher for two reasons: first, by staying around for a while, the owner-seller might be able to transfer some of the business's goodwill to the new owners; second, prospective buyers are less likely to perceive an air of desperation if the owner who developed the business (or ran it for years) is the seller, rather than if the sale is being made by the deceased owner's estate or heirs. On the other hand, selling after the death of the owner is likely to produce lower capital gains, given the step-up in basis that occurs when property is part of an estate. Given the recent increases in the estate applicable exclusion amount (AEA), many estates that include a significant business asset will not have to pay estate taxes. If there is a surviving spouse, the estate tax may be postponed until the surviving spouse dies; perhaps by then the AEA will be even larger.

If estate tax is a worry, lifetime gifts that divide the business interest may greatly reduce the overall transfer taxes by lowering the value for tax purposes without seriously disrupting the estate planning goal of eventual transfer of the business to the next generation. For estates that cannot completely avoid the estate tax, if there are significant business interests, a number of estate tax relief provisions may be available.

During Life to Family, Co-owners, or Outsiders?

Where other family members are not interested in, or in some cases not capable of, running the business, the owner may decide to sell it. This is obviously a very different situation than if the transfer will eventually be to family members. Where the sale is to non-family, generally one is seeking the highest price, and hence the highest valuation possible. The most likely buyers are co-owners, assuming they wish to continue in the business. If a buy-sell agreement is in place, then following it is likely to be straightforward as it is likely to have rules on how to value the business and the manner in which the leaving co-owner will be compensated, e.g., some cash up-front and a note payable over time, or perhaps some form of profit participation for a period of time together with a note. One of the blessings of having a buy-sell agreement is that such are almost always drafted when the co-owners' interests parallel, meaning that at the time of drafting none of them knows who will be the sellers and who the buyers, hence they want fairness to both sides—a fair price and terms that don't make the leaving co-owner wait too long to be paid while at the same time are not so burdensome that the continuing owners suffer undue financial stress, perhaps forcing them to sell the business. Buy-sell agreements are discussed in detail below.

Where a sole proprietor or co-owners join to sell to outsiders, the eventual buy-sell contract will be negotiated from different points of view, with the seller wanting the highest price and the buyer wanting the lowest price. There are likely to be negotiations concerning how the price is to be paid, what is included in the sale, and whether the seller will be paid something for agreeing not to compete with the buyers and/or for consulting with them for a transition period. Generally, the price paid for the business is capital gain for the seller and might not be deductible for the buyer although the buyer may be able to allocate some of the purchase price to depreciable assets and to inventory. As part of the negotiation, the seller might agree to a lower price and payments for not competing and for consulting. These payments, generally set to last for a specific period of time, are ordinary income for the seller and deductible by the buyer. The seller should take into account that these payments will end if he or she dies, whereas purchase price installment payments are collected by his or her estate until fully paid.

Where the transfer is made without consideration (in the contract sense) to family members, it is a very different paradigm. The goals and interests of donor and donee are likely to parallel, with neither seeking the highest possible valuation. Indeed, if transfer taxes are a concern, then the lowest valuation will be sought. Later, under the heading "Valuation Issues," we will discuss how decreasing the value for gift tax purposes might be accomplished.

At Death to Family, Co-owners, or Outsiders?

Obviously, with the death of a business owner the question of whether to transfer an interest in the business also dies. The question that is left is to whom and how. If there is a buy-sell agreement, those two questions may have already been answered. They are also answered if there is an estate plan that leaves the business interest to family members that will continue the operation of the business. Where there is no buy-sell agreement and no family members interested in continuing the business, assuming the business can survive without the decedent, the estate or heirs will sell it. At least the business's basis is stepped-up to its fair market value as of the owner's date of death, hence the sale of the business is not likely to generate any capital gains tax.

VALUATION ISSUES

Valuation issues for selling a business are very different from those that arise in transferring the business to family members through gift or bequest. When selling, the owner generally is after highest price that can be obtained, whereas when the transfer is to family, there are two–perhaps conflicting–valuation issues that arise. If the owner's estate exceeds the estate AEA, then reducing the value of the business for tax purposes without reducing its utility to the family is one goal but family members that do not work in the business and expect to receive non-business assets may object to having a low value placed on the business assets.

Transfer to Family: Discounts to Reduce Transfer Tax Value

Where estate taxes are a concern, reducing the value of the transferred property for tax purposes without decreasing its utility to the recipient is a goal. Much of the discounting that is done is based on the fact that for transfer taxes the value of what is transferred is its fair market vale (FMV), i.e., value based upon the "willing seller-willing buyer" fiction.

Lack of control discounts. Hence the value of a partial interest in a business, or in a parcel of land, that is given to a child is based on the price that partial interest would bring if sold on the open market. Court cases support the argument that one does not look beyond (or behind) the immediate transaction to find that the pieces will eventually be put back together by the family. It stands to reason, even if objective evidence is difficult to come by, that selling a 1/10th interest in a business does not bring a price equal to 1/10th of what the business as a whole would fetch. One who has a business interest of less than 50% does not control the business, hence in valuing a transfer of a fractional interest of less than 50%, what is referred to as a "lack of control" discount (sometimes referred to as a minority interest discount) is widely accepted. While it is important that one documents how the particular discount was determined, (generally by attaching to the gift or estate tax return the report of an experienced appraiser who specializes in the valuation of fractional interests) the mechanics of such appraisals is beyond the scope of this text. Appraisals for lack of control generally establish a discount between 20 and 40 percent. Factors influencing the size of the discount include the overall quality of management, composition of other share holdings, size of the business, history of profitability, existence of business opportunities not currently being exploited by management, and degree of the company's financial leverage.[1]

The corollary to the lack of control discount is the control premium, meaning that if one owns more than 50% of a business, but less than 100%, that interest, being a controlling interest, is worth more than its proportionate share; hence a 60% share of a business that has an underlying value of $1,000,000 might be worth 75% of that underlying value, i.e., $750,000 rather than its proportionate share of $600,000. Control premiums tend to be associated with estates and not with gifts. It seldom comes up with gifts because the donor can avoid making a gift of a controlling interest. Each gift is considered separately meaning that only what is transferred is valued. Therefore, a parent giving a series of fractional interests in a business to a child might, over the course of several years, transfer 100% of that business but each transfer qualifies for a lack of control discount, including the transfer that gives the donee-child a total interest in excess of 50%.

EXAMPLE 14 - 1. Ester's 1,200 shares in KNOCK Corporation were the only shares of the corporation. The underlying value of the corporation was $1,200,000 and she could have sold her shares for that amount. In year one, she gave 400 shares to her son, Ryan. Reporting this gift, she claimed a lack of control discount of 20%, hence the gift's value was shown as $320,000 (i.e., 80% * $400,000). In year two, she again gave him 400 shares, and again took the discount even though Ryan owned 2/3 of the shares. In year three, she gave him the last of her shares, again taking the discount even though the gift made Ryan the sole owner of the corporation. With each gift, the focus is on what is being given rather than on what the donee has after the gift is complete.

EXAMPLE 14 - 2. In the prior example, if Ester died after making the first gift but before making the second, her remaining 800 shares, representing 2/3 of the shares, would result in a valuation control premium, hence, assuming that the underlying value is still $1,200,000, they might be valued for estate tax purposes at 75% or 80% of that value, i.e., at $900,000 or $960,000 rather than $800,000.

In community property states, control premiums cannot apply to stock held as community property since neither spouse has majority control. Indeed, the decedent's half interest should be discounted for lack of control, but one finds that, where there is no estate tax, the estate's personal representative is unlikely to claim a discount since doing so lowers the basis of the property in the hands of the survivor without saving any estate tax.

Lack of marketability discounts. Related to the lack of control discount is the lack of marketability discount. Indeed, the two often go hand in hand but the concept is slightly different. For certain business interests, such as shares in a closely held corporation or limited partnership interests, there is no established market, making them more difficult to sell than shares that can be sold in an established market such as the New York Stock Exchange or the Pacific Stock Exchange. Securities listed on one of these exchanges are easy to buy and easy to sell; there is information contained in publicly available reports that these listed companies must file with the Securities and Exchange Commission. With closely held companies, such information is not so easily obtained, and selling may be more restricted, perhaps limited to knowledgeable investors. In any event, the seller must comply with the state and federal regulations in selling stock or limited partnership interests. To factor in this decrease in value associated with selling business interests for which there is no ready market, a lack of marketability discount is allowed. Again, one hires appraisers well versed in this sort of appraisal, but generally one sees discounts for lack of marketability of between 20 and 30 percent.

> EXAMPLE 14 - 3. In the prior example, in addition to the lack of control discount, Ester would claim a lack of marketability discount. Assuming her appraiser established a discount for this of 35%, the result would be a final gift value for the first year of $208,000, i.e., $400,000 * 80% * .65%. Note, this gift also qualifies for the annual exclusion, dropping the taxable gift below $200,000.

Discounts and imperfect unification. Earlier we discussed the fact that the federal "unified" transfer tax system is not perfectly unified. Imperfections include the allowance of an annual exclusion for lifetime gifts, failure to include post-gift appreciation in the estate tax base, and the ability to avoid grossing-up gift taxes on gifts made more than three years before death. To these we add the ability to obtain valuation discounts for certain lifetime gifts that would not be available to transfers at death.

> EXAMPLE 14 - 4. Fiore owns 100% of the stock in a closely held corporation worth $900,000. In 2007, he gave each of his three children one-third of the stock. Taking a 25% lack of control discount and a 30% lack of marketability discount on each transfer, Fiore will report on Form 709 three taxable gifts of $145,500, i.e., $300,000 * 75% * 70% - $12,000. Thus, the total subject to transfer taxes was $436,500 rather than $900,000. Had Fiore kept the stock and bequeathed it to the three children, these discounts would not have been available and the entire $900,000 (plus any appreciation) would have been part of the transfer tax base.

If an interest is whole at the moment of death but broken into fractional shares as part of the distribution, there is no minority interest discount. The asset is valued at its fair market value as of the moment of the owner's death. Thus, valuation discounts create a fourth instance of imperfect unification.

Fractional Interest Discount for Real Property

Undivided interests in real property can receive a fractional interest discount, analogous to the minority interest and lack of marketability discounts for stock, because such interests are neither easily partitioned nor readily marketable.

EXAMPLE 14 - 5. Jones died owning a 58% interest in common in commercial real property that was appraised for $2,000,000. His estate was allowed a 25% fractional interest discount that resulted in his estate listing a value of $870,000 on the estate tax return [i.e., 58% * 75% * $2,000,000].[2]

The fractional interest discount for real property is strongly opposed by the IRS. It has taken the position that the only discount allowed should be the cost of a partition action.[3] It should be noted that the issue of control premiums does not arise with real property because all owners must agree on significant property decisions.

Other Valuation Discounts

Worth mentioning briefly are two other valuation discounts:

- Securities, even publicly traded ones, that are subject to special securities law restrictions can be discounted. Restrictions include lack of registration and the need to sell the stock by private placement.
- Large quantities of a stock listed on an exchange can receive a *blockage discount* if their sale all at one time could have a depressing effect on the market price. However, if the block represents a controlling interest in the corporation, possibly triggering an even higher price, a *premium* may be attached to its value; this is called a control premium. Blockage discounts may be available for other property, such as a large number of paintings left in the estate of a prominent artist.[4]

Valuation discounts can generate significant transfer tax savings. For estates, there can be a tradeoff because the lower value for estate tax gives less step-up in basis, but there is often a net benefit. This tradeoff does not apply to gifts since the basis is a carryover of the donor's basis.

FAMILY LIMITED PARTNERSHIPS

Family limited partnerships (FLPs) have been used by families in agricultural areas for decades to involve children in running a ranch or farm. Recently they have become a popular planning tool for other family-run businesses and offer many attractive estate planning advantages. However, due to the costs of establishing them and the appraisal costs associated with making multiple transfers of the limited partnership interests, they usually are not recommended unless the parents owning the business have a net worth in excess of two or three million dollars. For those that qualify, an FLP has numerous advantages: (1) the parents can give away wealth and still retain control; (2) transfers can be made at substantial discounts compared to the value of underlying assets, thus saving unified credit and gift taxes; (3) restrictions can be placed on transfers by children; and (4) there is some protection from creditors.

Family partnerships are sanctioned by the IRC with requirements set forth in § 704(e). Among other things, the income and tax benefits must be distributed or allocated according to each owner's percentage in the partnership. The general partners may be paid for their personal services to the partnership. Also, capital must be "a material income-producing factor," meaning that a family partnership cannot be used to redistribute income generated from the personal services of general partners.

Establishing a family limited partnership. To establish a family limited partnership, one must follow the requirements of the state's limited partnership act. This will probably require publication of the names of the general partner and the limited partners. The Uniform Limited Partnership Act requires that there be at least one general partner and one limited partner. With an FLP, it is common for one or both parents to serve as the general partners. They may start by owning all but a very small portion of the limited partnership units. Over time, the parents transfer by gift a significant portion of the limited partnership units to the children. Given the wealth of the parents, it is unlikely that this transfer can be accomplished by annual exclusion gifts alone. Thus, often parents both use up their unified credits, and perhaps pay some gift tax.

Under unusual circumstances, such as the death or bankruptcy of the general partner, most limited partnership agreements give the limited partners the right to elect a new general partner. As with most real estate limited partnerships, a limited partner cannot take assets from the partnership or otherwise force liquidation before the partnership term is up. The term is commonly 50 years. However, these agreements usually provide that after both general partners are deceased, the limited partners can vote to liquidate the partnership. The terms of the agreement would determine the necessary vote percentage.

The major costs are attorneys' fees to establish the partnership, generally in the $5,000 to $20,000 range depending on the nature of the business assets, and appraisal fees probably in the $5,000 to $30,000 range to establish the underlying value and the appropriate discounts. In addition, when partnership shares are transferred as gifts, an appraisal will again have to be performed. The high cost of appraisals is one reason that the parents should consider large initial gifts right after the partnership is established. The appraisal then serves a dual function. However, subsequent appraisal fees by the same appraisal firm should be considerably lower than the first ones, since the company will be familiar with the business. There will also be annual accounting fees for preparation of the partnership returns and the K-1s that must be distributed to all partners. There may also be annual state fees for the right to do business as a limited partnership.

Applying the discounts. The two types of valuation discounts discussed earlier in the chapter play a significant role in making the use of an FLP attractive. Limited partnership units are transferred at a huge discount because the units have limited marketability and control.

> EXAMPLE 14 - 6. In the year 2002, the Wilson family created a family limited partnership with Jack and Lilly Wilson as general partners. The net value of their combined estates was $18,000,000, which includes their ranch valued at $6,000,000. The limited partnership interests represented 95% of the total value of the ranch. The other 5% was allocated to the general partnership interest. The limited partnership portion was divided into 95 limited partnership units. Immediately after formation of the limited partnership, 20 units were transferred to each of the three children.
>
> The lack of marketability discount was determined to be 30% and the minority interest discount was 25%. The following was reported by each parent as the taxable gift to each child: ($6,000,000 * 70% * 75% * 20% * 50%) - $10,000 = $305,000 [FMV ranch * (1 - 30%) * (1 - 25%) * 20% interest * 50% because split between two parents, - annual exclusion = taxable gift.] Each parent reports three such gifts (for a total taxable gift of $915,000) but pays no gift tax because the taxable gifts are less than the AEA for 2002. The Wilsons moved 60% [$3,600,000 at FMV] of the ranch to their children.

If Jack dies in 2006, Trust B receives assets worth $2 million and the rest of the estate goes into Trusts A and C. Jack's executor QTIPs Trust C expecting Lilly to outlive the estate tax. Unfortunately she died in 2008. (Assume no change in value of any assets.) The ranch was discounted for estate tax purposes because Trusts A and C held only a 40% interest in the ranch, therefore: 40% * $6,000,000 * 70% * 75% = $1,260,000. Lilly's estate then was $13,175,000 [assets other than the ranch, $12,000,000, less $85,000 in Trust B (remember, Jack used up most of his AEA on gifts), plus the discounted value of the minority interest in the ranch, $1,260,000]

Compare the two scenarios with and without the gifts assuming values remain the same between the deaths and all estate tax is postponed to the second death. In both cases, only S2's estate owes taxes. Note that in the gifts alternative one must show adjusted gifts of $915,000. In a real situation, any post-gift appreciation escapes estate tax.

No gifts, tax on $16,000,000 [exclude Tr. B @ $2,000,000] $6,300,000
Gifts, tax on $13,175,000 [exclude Tr B @ $1,085,000] $4,990,500
Taxes saved $1,309,500

Challenges to taking the discounts. The IRS has made numerous attempts to disallow discounts for intra family transfers, losing most of the cases.[5] It has finally conceded the discounts, provided the taxpayer can back them up by credible professional appraisals using relevant market data for the discounts. The appraisals to establish the discount are in addition to the appraisal of the underlying assets owned by the partnership.

In recent years the IRS has had some success in getting all of the FLP's assets included in the transferor's estate on the argument that the parent retained enjoyment of the property during his or her lifetime, hence IRC § 2036 applies.[6] It also argues, sometimes successfully, that transfers of investment assets (stocks and bonds), as opposed to business assets, to a FLP constitutes an indirect gift to the limit partners (e.g., the children) for which no discount is allowed.[7]

Ability to control gifted assets. In addition to the discounts, the most attractive feature of the FLP is the ability of the donor to retain control over the assets. While key rights of a limited partner must be recognized, the general partner maintains all the managerial control over the partnership assets, determining when and whether to make income distributions to all the partners or to reinvest the income into additional assets. To keep control in the family, the partnership agreement should give the family a first right of refusal for any attempted sale by the limited partners.

For most wealthy individuals, the biggest roadblocks to making substantial gifts are the donor's reluctance to lose control of his or her business or other important valuable assets and concern about how well the donee-children will use the gifts. The control offered to the parent-general partner makes this an acceptable vehicle to give assets now, especially when one can use the tax benefits of valuation discounts and lowered values on appreciating assets.

Getting the children involved. Once the children have a vested interest in the business, they may take a greater interest in how it works. Annual reports must be given to all partners and formal partnership meetings with all the family partners present are a good time to discuss the family investments and why they performed well or poorly. To avoid having the children liable as general partners, they cannot be involved in the actual management of the business and they must not appear to outsiders to be general partners.

Income shifting. One benefit of a family limited partnership is that it is possible to shift income into the lower tax brackets of the children in proportion to the percentage interest the child actually owns in the partnership. When a parent is in the 38.6% federal income tax bracket and the child is in the 15% tax bracket, this can make a significant difference.

Asset protection. One important benefit of the FLP is its asset protection capabilities. Most states have some form of fraudulent transfers act that allows creditors to attach property transferred by debtors for inadequate consideration when the transfer takes place in the face of mounting financial pressure. However, if sufficient time has passed, the parent is generally the only one liable to his or her personal creditors and, as general partner, the only one liable to the creditors of the partnership. Limited partnership units given several years before the parents have financial difficulty should not be subject to levy by the parents' creditors.

In the past, creditors of limited partners collected their debts by using a court-issued *charging order* that allowed them to collect the money distributed to a partner. The partnership income tax liability of the partner whose interest was seized was also passed on to the creditor. One strategy available to a partnership that wants to make a creditor negotiate to reduce a debt is for the general partner to not make distributions even though there are profits. That would leave a creditor with a charging order with a tax liability but no distribution.

Some state court decisions have held that if a charging order does not result in timely payment of the debt, the creditor can foreclose on the debtor's partnership interest, forcing the liquidation of enough of the underlying assets to pay the creditor, provided the foreclosure does not unreasonably interfere with the partnership business. If other courts adopt this approach, then a charging order could delay the creditors but would eventually allow them to be fully paid by means of foreclosure.

Another consideration is that the assets can be held as the separate property of each child. While the income distributed is usually commingled with the child's other assets, the partnership interest is usually clearly identified as the child's separate property. In community property states, only the community property is divided in a divorce proceeding. While everything is presumed to be community property unless it can be traced to a gift, an inheritance, or to property owned prior to the marriage, it should be easy to establish that the units were acquired as gifts and therefore stay in the family. Of course, a child who is not worried about divorce can change them into joint tenancy or community property by written agreement with a spouse.

Loss of the step-up in basis on gifted assets. One disadvantage of giving assets is that the donees (the children) lose the ability to get a step-up in basis at the death of the parent on the partnership shares that were pre-death gifts. When the assets have a very low tax basis, this reduces the tax benefits of the family limited partnership. Of course, if the children do not intend to sell the business, then the low basis is a price worth paying to avoid the transfer tax costs.

LIMITED LIABILITY COMPANIES

The limited liability company (LLC) has similar uses in estate planning to the family limited partnership without some of its problems. It does not have common law roots as the partnership does, but every state (and the District of Columbia) has adopted an LLC statute since Wyoming led the way in 1977. Why the sudden popularity? An LLC offers business owners the limited liability of a corporation with the tax passthrough advantages of a partnership. Each owner-investor is called a *member* and his or her ownership share is called a *membership interest*.

Creating a Limited Liability Company. Owners must comply with the state statute, and they must consider the IRS rules concerning taxation of business entities. On January 1, 1997, Treasury regulations became effective that made the old rules of trying to avoid looking like a corporation obsolete. Most business entities can select for themselves whether to be classified for tax purposes as a corporation, a partnership, or disregarded as a separate entity by checking the appropriate boxes on federal Form 8832. The new regulations[8] (called the *check-the-box regulations*) make it much easier for owners to choose the tax status of their businesses. A business entity with two or more owners can elect to be taxed as either a corporation or a partnership. A business owned by just one person (or a married couple filing jointly) can elect to be taxed as a corporation or be disregarded as a separate tax entity (i.e., be taxed as a sole proprietorship) regardless of the actual business organization. Hence, in a state that allows a single owner LLC, the owner could choose to be taxed as a corporation or as a sole proprietor. An LLC owned by two or more people can choose between being taxed as a partnership or as a corporation. The default classification (one need not file the form) is partnership treatment for eligible domestic entities with two or more owners and sole proprietorship (disregarded as a separate entity) for businesses with just one owner (or a married couple). [9]

Compared to corporations. Both the LLC and the corporate form give the owners the protection of limited liability. An owner is liable only for torts in which he or she is actually involved. If one drives the company car on business and causes an accident in which others are injured, only the business and the owner-driver are liable. The other co-owners are not liable. Furthermore, none of the co-owners are liable for contracts entered into in the company's name. Of course, for either of these business forms the owners may be asked to personally guarantee certain contracts, such as leases and loans, which will create personal liability. However, absent some personal guarantee by the owners, contractual liability attaches solely to the business entity and not to the owners.

LLCs have a single level of taxation at the membership level. Of course, S corporations also have this characteristic, but LLCs do not have the restrictions on stock ownership that S corporations have. Trusts, foreign individuals, and other corporations can be members. Although LLCs are most likely to be closely held, there is no restriction on the number of owners, whereas federal law limits to 75 the number of S corporation shareholders. S corporations are limited to one class of stock, whereas LLCs can have membership interests with different rights to income allocation, capital preferences, and voting.[10]

Compared to partnerships. Both LLCs and partnerships share the advantage of single-level taxation, but partnerships have the disadvantage of all partners being fully liable for all contracts taken in the partnership name and any torts that arise out of the partnership business whether committed by a partner or by a partnership employee. Both allow withdrawal of assets, subject to the partnership or LLC agreement, without such withdrawals being deemed income. Of course, withdrawals do affect the owners' capital accounts. Some states require LLCs to pay some minimal annual fee (generally less than $1,000) whereas general partnerships are usually exempt from such fees.

Compared to limited partnerships. The advantages and disadvantages are similar to those stated for the general partnership, except limited partners enjoy limited liability. Unlike LLCs, the limited partnership must have at least one person, the general partner, exposed to unlimited personal liability. Furthermore, limited partners must not be involved in the day-to-day management of the partnership, or they will lose their limited liability insofar as third parties rely on their appearance as general partners in extending credit to the partnership.

Tax considerations in liquidation of a business entity. Prior to the 1986 Tax Reform Act, a corporation distributing assets as part of a liquidation of the corporation was able to avoid tax at both the corporate and shareholder level.[11] The 1986 Tax Reform Act changed the rule so a corporation distributing appreciated property, whether or not the distribution is pursuant to a liquidation, must recognize the capital gain.[12] Thus, many existing corporations holding significant amounts of appreciated assets, whether the corporation is a C type (taxed as a separate entity) or S type (taxed as if a partnership), may find it too costly from a tax standpoint to convert to LLC status. Partnerships and LLCs do not recognize gain on their dissolution, nor will an owner be taxed on the liquidation unless he or she receives cash in excess of his or her basis.

BUSINESS BUYOUT AGREEMENTS

Placing the burden of selling the business on the survivors after the owner's death creates problems that would be avoided by a business buyout agreement. Executed by the owner and prospective purchasers (usually co-owners), the buyout agreement obligates the other parties to purchase the owner's interest on the occurrence of specific events, such as at the onset of disability or on death.

Tax Considerations

The most critical taxation issues in buyout agreements arise in the estate tax area.

Gift tax. Generally, the execution of a buyout agreement does not result in a taxable gift unless it gives a purchaser an unqualified present purchase right at a contract price below fair market value.

Income tax. Income tax effects of buyout agreements will depend on the type of the agreement.

Estate tax. The deceased owner's gross estate will include some value attributable to the decedent's ownership interest held at the moment of death. Ordinarily, the estate executor will prefer to avoid a dispute with the IRS over this value. One method has been to establish a selling price in the buyout agreement that will, by law, fix the value for estate tax purposes. Only half-jokingly, one commentator has said that in the absence of a price "set" by a buyout agreement, the "value" of the business can be said to be the amount agreed on by "a willing IRS agent and a willing executor, neither of whom has ever owned a business."

Structuring the Agreement

The three most common types of buyout agreements are distinguished by the identity of the contracting parties. First, the *cross-purchase* agreement provides that the other owners purchase the interest of a particular owner. Many owners use a reciprocal cross-purchase agreement, in which each owner agrees to purchase a pro rata share of the interest of any owner that dies. Second, the *entity*, or *redemption* agreement has the business itself purchase the interest of one or more owners. Third, the *mixed* agreement gives the business an option to purchase an owner's interest and gives the other owners the option or obligation to purchase the balance. A hybrid, the mixed agreement has characteristics of both cross-purchase and entity-redemption agreements and is the most flexible

Cross-purchase. The selling owner, usually the estate of a decedent-business owner, sells a capital asset subject to capital gain treatment. But the step-up in basis at the decedent's death means the only gain recognized is on appreciation after the date of death that is reflected in the sale price. The buyer's new basis will be the purchase price of the business interest acquired.

Entity-redemption. The acquiring business's new basis will be its purchase price, which is not tax deductible. If the business has been paying premiums on life insurance to fund the arrangement, it will not be allowed a tax deduction for those premiums. They must be paid with after-tax dollars.[13] Further, any cash value buildup on a policy and any receipt of proceeds, while not included as ordinary income, may be subject to the alternative minimum tax.[14]

The selling party, again usually the decedent-owner's estate, will be taxed on the sale proceeds as a dividend, to the extent of the corporation's earnings and profits. Dividend treatment can be avoided if the sale can qualify for favorable redemption treatment under IRC § 302 or § 303. Both sections permit the redeeming party to treat the sale as a disposition of a capital asset rather than the receipt of a dividend. The step-up in basis means that there is generally little or no taxable gain. Without this favorable treatment, the entire receipt would be taxable as ordinary income.

Mixed. Tax under a mixed agreement follows the above patterns.

EXAMPLE 14 - 7. Stan and Oliver, equal owners of a corporation, are trying to decide whether to arrange a cross-purchase or an entity-redemption buyout plan. Each has an adjusted basis of $20,000 in his respective shares. They project that the business is worth $2,000,000. Thus, under either arrangement, if a death occurred in the near future, the purchase price would be about $1,000,000, and the total value of the surviving owner's stock would be $2,000,000, i.e., the total value of the business. However, the survivor's basis will be different, depending on which arrangement is selected. If a cross-purchase plan is chosen, the surviving shareholder's total basis will increase to $1,020,000, of which $20,000 is the basis of the survivor's own stock, and $1,000,000 is the price of the decedent's stock. If an entity-redemption arrangement is chosen, the total basis of the surviving shareholder's stock will remain $20,000, because he will not have purchased any additional shares.

Common valuation methods. Prior to October 9, 1990, the effective date of IRC § 2703, fixing the value of the business for estate tax purposes was simpler because case law was quite generous in allowing fixed values that were below fair market value.

Three valuation methods are commonly included in buyout contracts. First, a specific dollar amount is specified, with a provision made for periodic review so the owners can revise the amount as conditions change. Without provision for a review, if the value of the business increased, the purchasing owners would receive a windfall at the expense of the selling owner. Unfortunately, inertia can reduce the likelihood of periodic reviews.

Second, the selling price can be determined by appraisal, with the agreement specifying that a qualified appraiser will determine the value of the business at the time of sale. The appraisal method has the advantage of ensuring that a current value is used.

Third, business buyout agreements can use a valuation formula determined by an expert appraiser. Its terms ordinarily call for valuation to be a specified percentage of book value or a multiple of current earnings. A formula is more flexible and often more accurate than setting a specific amount since the selling price will vary with economic conditions. However, because a formula is more arbitrary than an appraisal, it may later turn out not to reflect current economic conditions.

Impact of IRC § 2703. To set the estate tax value of a business equal to its buyout agreement price, agreements executed after October 8, 1990, must meet § 2703(b) requirements.

1. The agreement must be a bona fide business arrangement.
2. The agreement cannot be a device to transfer property to members of the decedent's family for less than full and adequate consideration in money or money's worth.
3. The terms of the agreement must be comparable to similar arrangements entered into by persons in arm's length transactions.

The thrust of these requirements is to ensure a value reasonably close to the value of the business interest at the moment of the transfer. Thus, an agreement under which the surviving owner, a son, is obligated to purchase the parent's $1 million business interest (current value) for a fixed $300,000 (historical contract value) would be currently labeled a "disguised bequest," and not meet the first two requirements.[15] On the other hand, prices set between unrelated owners are not usually subject to intense scrutiny by the IRS if the transaction otherwise appears to be made at arm's length. IRS regulations provide that a buyout agreement will meet all three requirements if more than 50% of the value of the property subject to the agreement is owned by persons who are not "natural objects of the transferor's bounty."[16]

> EXAMPLE 14 - 8. Dad's will incorporated an AB trust plan. He executed a business buyout agreement with his son, who was obligated to buy Dad's 1,000 shares of closely held stock for $1 million. When Dad died in 2002, in addition to the stock, he owned other property worth $1.5 million. Son paid Dad's estate $1 million for the stock and Dad's executor distributed $1 million to the bypass trust and $1.5 million to the marital trust. After an IRS audit, Dad's executor agreed that the stock's fair market value was $2 million. Thus, Dad's gross estate totaled $3.5 million not $2.5 million as had been shown on the estate tax return. Only the $1.5 million that went into the marital trust qualified for the martial deduction, thus the taxable estate was actually $2 million, resulting in estate taxes of $435,000. The additional $1 million is considered as having been left to the son and, in the absence of a clause allocating taxes to the credit shelter trust, since the taxable estate is divided equally between him and the bypass trust, each would pay half of the tax. The tax could have been avoided had the buyout agreement provided for a realistic selling price. Consider the two alternatives.

	Alternative Values Given the Stock			
	Sales Agreement $1 million		Realistically Valued $2 million	
Gross Estate	$3,500,000	1	$3,500,000	
Less Marital Deduction	$1,500,000	2	$2,500,000	3
Taxable Estate	$2,000,000		$1,000,000	
Tentative Tax	$780,800		$345,800	
Less Unified Credit	($345,800)		($345,800)	
Estate Tax	$435,000		$0	

> notes:
>
> 1 $3,500,000 = stock @ $2 million & other property @ $1,500,000
>
> 2   marital deduction = $2,500,000 - AEA into Trust B
>
> 3   marital deduction = $3,500,000 - AEA into Trust B

The comparability condition of §2703's third requirement creates considerable uncertainty and the additional expense of having to obtain appraisals because typically buyout agreements are not public documents. However, for businesses in some industries, agreements may be able to specify a formula, such as a multiple of sales or earnings, if that formula is known to be the predominant valuation method for the industry.

Even though valuation discounts may be available, the estate could wind up paying more estate tax than it should if valuation is not set for estate tax purposes. Planners must consider the § 2703 valuation rules carefully. It may not work to include a "savings" clause that increases the selling price, in the event of an audit, to the final determination of estate tax value. The IRS has challenged such clauses as contrary to public policy because it sees them as attempts to pass property at less than its true value.[17]

Funding the Agreement

A business buyout agreement can require survivors to pay a cash lump sum or periodic installments at the triggering event. The choice sometimes depends on the nature of the triggering event.

Lump-sum payment. Buyout agreements that require a cash lump sum are likely to be funded with life insurance and/or lump-sum disability insurance.

Life insurance. The choice of life insurance to fund a business buyout agreement will be influenced by the type of buyout chosen. Under an *entity* agreement, the firm purchases and acts as beneficiary of a policy on the life of each business owner. Each policy is in the amount that is necessary to buy out that owner's interest. In a reciprocal *cross-purchase agreement*, each contracting party purchases and acts as beneficiary of a policy on the life of each of the other contracting owners, in an amount that is their pro-rata share of the buyout price.

> EXAMPLE 14 - 9. Sol and Harry are equal shareholders of a corporation that has a net worth of $300,000. The men have executed an entity buyout arrangement. The corporation will own and be the beneficiary of two $150,000 face value policies, one on Sol's life and one on Harry's life. The men plan to review and update this amount periodically as the value of the business changes.

> EXAMPLE 14 - 10. Facts are the same as the prior example, except that a reciprocal cross-purchase plan is adopted. Sol will own and be beneficiary of a $150,000 policy on Harry's life, and Harry will own and be a beneficiary of a $150,000 policy on Sol's life.

A reciprocal cross-purchase arrangement funded with life insurance becomes unwieldy when the agreement includes numerous owners, because each contracting party will have to purchase a policy on the life of each other contracting owner. For example, although only two policies would have to be purchased for a firm with two contracting owners, six policies would have to be purchased for three owners, and 12 policies for four owners. In general, the number of policies purchased under a cross-purchase plan would be $n(n - 1)$, where n equals the number of contracting owners. Under an entity plan, the business itself would simply purchase one policy on the life of each contracting owner. Thus, only n policies would have to be purchased.

The number of policies needed under a cross-purchase arrangement can be reduced somewhat by using one of two specialized life insurance contracts. First, two contracting parties may be able to purchase a *first to die* joint lives policy that pays the proceeds to the survivor on the first death of the two insured parties. The premium cost should be less than the total cost for two separate policies because only one payout will be made. Second, some companies offer a policy covering more than two insured owners for different amounts based on their respective ownership interests.

An entity agreement funded with life insurance might trigger a corporate alternative minimum tax because the "book income" of the corporation will include the insurance proceeds whereas its taxable income will not. For any buyout agreement, insurance premiums are not deductible from income, even if paid by the firm.[18] Thus, all premiums are paid with after-tax dollars.

With a cross-purchase agreement between owners who are not close in age (or who have unequal interests), a larger premium will likely be paid by the younger owner (or the owner with the smaller interest). The greater burden falls on this owner, who is probably less affluent, to insure an older person or to buy out a larger share.

Using the firm's assets. A second method of funding a lump-sum payment under an entity arrangement is with the firm's own cash or noncash assets. This can make life insurance unnecessary, but too often the business will not own sufficient distributable assets, particularly the amount of cash that may be needed to pay estate debts.

Lump-sum disability insurance. To accommodate buyout agreements, more insurance companies are offering disability policies paying a lump sum at the onset of disability, rather than an income stream.

Installment payments. Many events can trigger a buyout and most cannot be covered by insurance, e.g., a co-owner's retirement, divorce, insolvency, criminal activity, or loss of a professional license. None of these other events is likely to generate cash flow for the owners who remain with the company, and a full-cash buyout under such circumstances may be difficult. The parties can agree to an installment sale, making life insurance unnecessary and providing income to the seller or their family. On the other hand, installment payments carry the risk that the purchasers will be unable to make the payments, returning a failing business to the family. The estate may need immediate liquidity at death. An installment note can create a potentially stressful creditor-debtor relationship between the decedent's surviving family and the successor. It could also give the successor but not the family leverage to renegotiate terms.

In conclusion, the advantages of the business buyout agreement include business continuity, liquidity, a guaranteed market, and possibly greater certainty over the selling price. The preceding overview material merely highlights the general principles of this complex subject. A business buyout agreement should not be drafted or executed without expert legal advice.

ESTATE TAX RELIEF SECTIONS

When the owner of a closely held business dies, severe liquidity problems can arise. The largest portion of the estate may be the interest in the business that usually is very illiquid. The need to pay the estate tax nine months after date-of-death may compel surviving family members to sell the business. Some advanced planning by the business owner and some special Code sections may help the heirs get through the transition crisis.

Estate Tax Installment Payments

Congress added § 6166 to the Code, applicable to estates of decedents dying after 1976, to lessen the liquidity crisis that often accompanies the death of a business owner. If the estate is eligible and the executor makes the election, the estate tax for a closely held business interest can be paid over 14 years. The portion deferrable is the ratio of the net value of the business to the value of the adjusted gross estate. The first four annual installments are interest-only payments starting on the one-year anniversary of the original due date. Starting in the fifth year, the estate pays the estate tax in 10 installments, each one equal to one-tenth of the deferred tax, plus the interest accrued since the last annual payment. Although the estate must pay interest on the deferred tax, it is at a lower rate than the regular rate for underpaid (i.e., late or deferred) tax payments.

Three conditions must be met for qualification under § 6166. First, the value of the decedent's interest in the business must be at least 35% of the value of the *adjusted gross estate* (AGE). The AGE is the gross estate reduced by debts, expenses, losses, and certain taxes (i.e., accrued income taxes and property taxes, but not the death taxes).[19] Second, the decedent's interest must have been in a *closely held business*, which is defined as: (1) a sole proprietorship; or (2) a partnership in which at least 20% of the capital interest is included in the decedent's gross estate or that has 15 or fewer partners; or (3) a corporation in which at least 20% of the voting stock is included in the decedent's gross estate or that has 15 or fewer shareholders. Third, the business must have been actually carrying on a trade or business at the time of the decedent's death.

> EXAMPLE 14 - 11. Jack died in the year 2006, owning stock in a closely held corporation. His shares had a value of $2,000,000. Jack's gross estate was worth $6 million. There were debts and expenses that totaled $500,000. The federal estate tax was $1,610,000. Since the closely held business interest was slightly more than 36% of AGE, the estate qualifies for § 6166 extended payments. The amount of the tax that may be deferred is $585,455 [i.e., 2/5.5 * $1,610,000].

In the past, the executor had the option of deducting the interest paid on the § 6166 extended tax payments either on the estate tax return (Form 706) or on the estate income tax return (Form 1041).[20] This deduction has been eliminated for estates of decedents dying after 1997, but continues to be available for estates that are already on an extended payment plan.[21]

For § 6166 interest, the executor claims the deduction using Form 843 (Refund Claim) since the deduction can only be taken after the interest is paid.[22] Estates often wait until after the seventh or eighth principal payment (out of the 10 scheduled for the § 6166 extension) to claim the deduction because it reduces the estate tax to the extent that the last couple of payments are eliminated. A complex interrelated calculation is required because the interest paid reduces the estate tax, which in turn reduces the interest owed, which in turn increases the estate tax, etc.[23]

Deducting interest on the estate tax return continues to be available for interest on estate taxes paid late, regardless of whether the executor obtained an extension to pay based on reasonable cause (i.e., § 6161) or negligently paid them late without obtaining an extension. The interest that must be paid on late or deferred estate taxes should be deducted on the estate tax return because it saves more tax than claiming it for income tax purposes, since the estate tax rate is higher than the income tax rate.

Late payment interest on a portion of the deferred estate tax is charged at a mere 2% rate. The Taxpayer Relief Act of '97 reduced the rate for eligible estates of persons who die after December 31, 1997. The *2% portion*, as it is now called (previously 4%), is the amount of deferred tax that equals the tentative tax generated on the quantity $1,000,000 plus the AEA, less the unified credit.[24] Thus, in 1998 the 2% portion would be the tentative tax on $1,625,000 less the unified credit, i.e., $612,050 - $202,050 = $410,000. The $1,000,000 amount is indexed for inflation starting in 1999, using 1997 as the base year. By 2003 it reached $1,120,000 and is likely to continue to increase by 20 to 30 thousand dollars a year in the near future. The balance of any deferred tax also incurs interest higher than the special 2% rate but still reduced. The reduced deferred rate on the balance is equal to 45% of the regular "underpayment" rate imposed by § 6601(a).[25] Estates that are still paying on pre-1998 § 6166 payment plans can elect to take advantage of the new lower interest rates, but only if the estate's representative waives the right to claim a deduction for any remaining interest payments. This waiver is likely to be advantageous for estates with deaths after 1994. For estates of decedents with earlier deaths, more dollars will probably be saved by claiming the interest deduction than will be saved by using the lower interest rates.

EXAMPLE 14 - 12. Hitch died in 2005, leaving to his children an estate that included a closely held business. The estate qualified under § 6166 to extend $1,800,000 of its federal estate tax. Because of indexing, the $1,000,000 base for the 2% portion had increased to $1,170,000. The tentative tax on $2,670,000 (i.e., AEA for 2005 + $1,120,000) is $1,095,700. Subtracting the unified credit for 2005 (i.e., minus $555,800) gives us $539,900 as the 2% portion. If, during the first year's deferral period, the regular underpayment rate is 6%, the balance of the deferred taxes would be charged interest at a 2.7% rate (i.e., 45% * 6%). Hence, the first interest payment (due one year after the regular due date of the estate tax return) is $44,821 [2% * $539,900 + 2.7% * $1,260,100]. Assuming the regular late payment interest rate remained at 6%, the payment due on the fifth-year anniversary would be $224,821 (10% of the deferred taxes plus a year of interest). Even though the estate tax might be repealed for years after 2009, any payments that fall due after that year must still be paid and the recapture will occur if the heirs abandon the special use or sell the property within the 10-year recapture period.

Estate tax deferral under § 6166 reduces the estate's immediate cash needs. Since this is a relief provision designed to reduce the likelihood of a forced sale, the sale, redemption, or other disposition of all, or a significant portion of the business, or the unauthorized failure to make timely interest or principal payments, causes the deferred taxes to be immediately due.

Special Use Valuation

Another relief provision available to the business owner's estate, called *special use valuation*, is provided by § 2032A. This Code section permits qualifying estates to value at least a portion of the real property in the estate at its "qualified use" value, i.e., its value as a farm or other trade or business rather than at its highest and best use.

Suppose a person has owned her farm for many years and her children want to continue to work the farm for the foreseeable future. The farm was originally located outside the city limits, but urban growth is beginning to approach the area and, hence, the farm's FMV is considerably greater than the capitalized value of the farm income. Valuation at its highest and best use might force the survivors to sell the land to pay the estate tax. On the other hand, valuation at its use as a farm might enable the survivors to continue to carry on the business.

Requirements. The five major requirements under § 2032A are listed below.

1. The property must have been held for "qualified use" and actively managed by the decedent or the decedent's family for five out of the eight years prior to the decedent's death.
2. The net value of the real and personal property devoted to the qualifying use must equal at least 50% of the adjusted value of the gross estate.[26] The adjusted value of the gross estate is the gross estate reduced by mortgages and liens (not unsecured debts or expenses).
3. The net value of the real property portion must constitute at least 25% of the adjusted value of the gross estate.[27]

4. The qualifying property must pass to qualifying heirs. The heirs must sign a recapture agreement that acknowledges that a lien will be placed on the property and that the taxes saved will be recaptured by the government if the heirs do not continue the qualified use for at least 10 years after the decedent's death. A qualified heir is a member of the decedent's family who acquired the property from the decedent.[28] A qualified use is one in conjunction with farming or other trade or business. Generally, the qualified heir must actively participate. The mere leasing of the farmland to others will not qualify.[29]

5. The executor must make the election on the estate tax return and attach the recapture agreement. The return must show how the special use value was determined. The rules and a § 2032A checklist immediately follow Schedule A in the estate tax return.

If the election is made, the maximum amount by which the value of the special use real estate can be reduced is $750,000.[30] The $750,000 amount is indexed for inflation for years after 1998, with 1997 being the base year. By the year 2003, the amount reached $840,000. Assuming 50% as the maximum marginal estate tax rate, the maximum that can be saved by this election is $420,000 on a $840,000 special use reduction in the value of the real estate. While this is not an insignificant amount, if there is a big difference between values, the heirs may decide the tax savings are not enough to compensate for the burden of continuing to run the business for 10 more years.

Since the election applies only to real property and has some onerous requirements, it is not used often. Business owners dying after 1997 and before 2004 may be able to use § 2057, the family-owned business interest deduction, which requires that the business interest, not necessarily including real estate, meets a 50% of AGE threshold. If § 2032A or § 2057 is available, the estate will also qualify for § 6166 deferral since its threshold is only 35% of AGE. The family-owned business interests deduction is repealed for decedents dying after 2003.

Recapture. If the qualified heir discontinues the special use or sells his or her interest (other than to another qualified heir) within 10 years, the taxes saved are recaptured. For example, if the qualified heir allows others to lease the property for cash, it will result in a cessation of the qualified use and the recapture of the taxes saved.[31] However, there is an important exception that allows a surviving spouse or lineal descendant of the decedent to rent on a "net cash basis" the property to another member of the family of the spouse or descendant without it causing recapture.[32] Net cash basis evidently means that rent is per acre rather than a share-crop arrangement, though it is hard to imagine why the government would care. Once an event occurs that triggers the recapture, the heirs (remember they had to sign a recapture agreement when the § 2032A election was made) have just six months to file Form 706-A, *United States Additional Estate Tax Return*, and pay the additional tax. If the special use is discontinued, then the amount recaptured is the amount of tax saved. If the property is sold, the recaptured amount is the lesser of the taxes saved or the difference in the proceeds from the sale and the special use valuation. The application of these recapture rules to partial sales is beyond the scope of this text. Two examples will help clarify recapture in general.

> EXAMPLE 14 - 13. When Gerard died in 2005, his estate included a persimmon farm that qualified for special use valuation. The real estate had a fair market value of $4,000,000 and a special use valuation of $2,400,000. The $870,000 reduction in the value of the real estate reduced the federal estate taxes by $408,900. Three years after her father's death, Julie (the sole heir) decided to turn the farm into a dude ranch. The cessation of use caused the $408,900 to be recaptured. It had to be paid six months after the change was made.

> EXAMPLE 14 - 14. Suppose, instead of changing the use, Julie sold the farm. The amount of recapture would depend on the price. Since the special use value shown on the return was $3,130,000, a price up to $3,538,900 [the scheduled value plus the taxes saved] would recapture the difference between $3,130,000 and the sales price. A sale above $3,538,900 would recapture all of the taxes saved. Hence, a sale for $3,500,000 would result in a recapture of $370,000, whereas a sale for $4,200,000 would result in the recapture of the entire $408,900.

When recapture occurs, the heir does not have to pay interest on the recaptured taxes. However, the heir can elect to pay the interest (going back to the original due date, i.e., nine months after the date of death) and in exchange take a step-up in the basis to what it would have been had special use not been elected.[33] One must compare the capital gains taxes saved to the cost of paying the interest. In general, the closer the sale is to the original due date of the return, the less the interest and the more likely the benefit of the increase in basis will exceed the interest expense. If one makes this election there is no deduction for the interest on the recaptured taxes, unlike the general rule that allows an estate tax deduction for late payment interest.

If the qualified heir dies before the 10-year recapture period has ended, the heir's estate could sell the property immediately without causing a recapture. The sale to another qualified family member avoids recapture, but the buyer must also agree to the recapture provisions for the remainder of the 10-year period. The recapture rules for changes in ownership or changes in use are complex and beyond the scope of this text.

Redemption of Stock to Pay Estate Taxes

The Internal Revenue Code provides another method to lessen the impact of taxes on the estates of decedents whose businesses are incorporated. The general rule is that when a closely held corporation buys back the shares of its stockholders, the proceeds must be treated as dividend income unless the transaction falls within one of the special redemption Code sections, including § 303. That section allows a closely held corporation to redeem some of a decedent's shares with the transaction treated as a sale of the stock rather than the receipt of a dividend. Since the owner's death steps-up the adjusted basis of the stock, very little, if any, gain is likely.

> EXAMPLE 14 - 15. Polly's estate included 1,000 shares of stock in a closely held corporation. Each share was valued at $150 for estate tax purposes. Immediately before her death, each share had an adjusted basis of just $10. Eight months after her death, to help the estate pay some of its expenses, the board of directors of the corporation agreed to redeem 300 shares from the estate at a price of $160 per share. Business was good, and the $160 was a realistic share price at the time of the purchase. If the entire redemption qualifies under § 303, the estate will have a taxable long-term gain of $3,000 (reflecting a $10 gain on each share purchased). If the redemption does not qualify under Section 303, the estate will be deemed to have received a dividend of $48,000 (300 shares at $160 per share), all of which will be treated as ordinary income.

There are three major requirements to qualify under § 303. First, as with the § 6166 deferral, the value of the decedent's interest in the stock must be at least 35% of the adjusted gross estate. Second, the amount paid by the corporation in redemption of the shares may not exceed the sum of federal and state death taxes, generation-skipping transfer taxes, and funeral and administration expenses.

Notice that the limit does not include the decedent's debts, although they are used in calculating the adjusted gross estate. Third, the shareholder (usually the estate) must be obligated to pay the taxes and/or the expenses.[34]

If more is paid, the excess will be treated as a dividend payment by the corporation. If the excess distributions exceed the amount of the corporation's earnings and profits, the excess is considered a nontaxable return of capital. However, if the firm distributes appreciated property instead of cash, the distribution will probably be considered a sale by the corporation, with the corporation forced to recognize a taxable gain.

Lifetime planning may assure that §§ 6166 and 303 are available to an estate that might not otherwise meet the 35% test. The owner can increase his or her interest in the firm, or reduce the size of his or her nonbusiness estate by making gifts, thereby reducing the adjusted gross estate and increasing the portion represented by the business. These strategies require advance planning. Section § 2035(c) requires that the date-of-death value of any gifts made within three years of death be included in the gross estate to determine whether the percentage requirements of §§ 6166 and 303 are met but not for calculating the actual tax. Bringing gifts back into the gross estate enlarges the denominator, making qualification less likely.

> EXAMPLE 14 - 16. Gabe's estate included his closely held corporation. His gross estate was valued at $5,000,000. Debts and expenses were $1,000,000 and the value of his shares was $1,500,000. The estate meets the 35% requirements of both §§ 303 and 6166 since the shares represent 37.5% of the AGE.

> EXAMPLE 14 - 17. Same as the prior example, except Gabe gave his daughter real estate worth $250,000 two years before he died. At his death, the property was worth $300,000. Inclusion of this property in the gross estate for purposes of determining the percentage brings the AGE to $4,300,000 and drops the percentage to 34.8%. For calculating the estate tax, the gift is simply a $240,000 adjusted taxable gift. The date-of-death value was used only to determine whether the estate qualified for the benefits of §§ 303 and 6166.

CONCLUSION

This chapter has considered the additional planning necessary when working with a business owner. Some of it is tax driven and some is family dynamics driven. It is unfortunate that tax considerations sometimes compel families to complicate their lives by creating complex business arrangements, e.g., limited partnerships, overlaid by multiple trust planning, e.g., ABC Trust plans. Some of the relief code sections, while well intended, offer too little to be of much help, e.g., special use valuation might save $450,000 in estate tax but that may not be enough to save the farm when the estate tax might measure in the millions. If the estate tax remains with us, perhaps Congress can find better solutions to preserving family held businesses, e.g., full value deduction with a 10-year recapture period coupled with a carryover basis for the business would greatly ease the burden for those families that truly intend to continue the business. Indeed, even a carryover basis would be a fair exchange for being able to avoid the estate tax since capital gains tax is significantly less than the estate tax. The next chapter gets personal; we consider how medical and property management decisions are handled when one is no longer able to speak for oneself.

QUESTIONS AND PROBLEMS

1. Minnie and Mark, parents of two adult children, Betty and Bryan, own a closely held business. It is clearly their most valuable asset making up about 75% of their net worth. Betty pretty much runs the business and would like to continue to do so after her parents are gone, whereas Bryan has no interest in it. Minnie and Mark wish to leave equal value to their children and have Betty receive the business. Suggest several ways they might accomplish these goals.

2. What unique estate planning problems are common to owners of closely held businesses?

3. (a) One of your friends is considering selling her business to a third party. Describe the benefits of selling now, rather than waiting and letting her heirs sell it. (b) Is planning for a sale after death always unwise? Explain.

4. Visit the website of Robert J. Mintz, a California attorney who focuses on asset protection, estate and tax planning to answer the questions from the "Asset Protection Law Library" about family limited partnerships (FLP) and limited liability companies (LLC). <http://www.rjmintz.com/appch5.html>

(a) In the estate tax benefit example, how much would the Smith's $5 million estate be reduced to by discounting? What amount would be transferred in the first year of setting up the FLP? Approximately how much tax is saved by doing this? What additional benefit is achieved by making the large transfers immediately rather than just relying on the annual exclusion amount? (b) For this question and the next click on "New Developments" on the upper bar to locate the summary on the <u>Hacki</u> and <u>Strangi</u> case discussion. In the <u>Hacki v. Commissioner</u> tax court case, what benefit was lost in transferring the limited partnership interests and why was it lost? How can this negative result be avoided? (c) In the tax court case of <u>Albert Strangi</u>, what benefit was lost in transferring the limited partnership interests and why was it lost? How can this negative result be avoided? (d) On the left side, under Asset Protection Law Library, click on "Asset Protection Planning to answer this question: What is meant by a "dangerous asset"? How are the risks associated with such assets contained?

5. The Fontilea family owned and worked a ranch in Idaho. It was valued at $5,000,000 when the parents created a FLP. The parents served as general partners and their three children (all adults) each received limited partnership interests. The general partnership share of the assets was valued at 10% of the total and 90 limited partnership units were each valued at 1%. Immediately after the creation of the FLP the parents transferred 15 units to each child. Gift tax returns were filed, with appropriate appraisals attached, reporting the transfer as follows: the underlying value at 45% of the $5,000,000 = $2,250,000; a lack of marketability discount of 35%; a lack of control discount of 25%; and an annual exclusion for each gift of $10,000. (a) What was the total taxable gift (for all three gifts) shown on the return? Note, the parents could continue to make annual gifts to bring down their holdings. (b) Besides the cost of having a FLP established, what is the main negative aspect of this kind of planning?

6. To answer the questions that follow visit the website of Financial Valuation Group (FVG), professional valuations experts on a wide range of transactions and interests who have made available tax cases where valuation is an issue. Click on *Estate of Bigelow* TCM 2005-65, March 30, 2005. <http://www. fvginternational.com/newsletters/2005_eflash.html> If an important goal of establishing a family limited partnership is to reduce estate taxes, this case is

a lesson in what not to do. Summary: Virginia Bigelow died August 8, 1997. She was survived by two daughters and a son. The son, referred to in the case as Mr. Bigelow, was her co-trustee and the holder of a durable power of attorney for financial matters. Virginia had placed her former residence in a limited partnership but retained the obligation to pay the mortgage. The home was exchanged for another residence, the Padaro Lane rental. Again, Virginia retained the obligation to pay the mortgage and an equity line of credit secured by the property. When she died she still owned 44% of the limited partnership. (a) How old was Virginia when she established the limited partnership? Who was the general partner? What code section was argued by the IRS to cause inclusion of the limited partnership property in her gross estate? [see p. 2]; (b) In 1990 (or 91) decedent (Virginia) gave each of her children a 1/175th interest in her home. Why that particular fractional interest? How might she have given a larger fraction, say 1/150th, and not used up AEA? [see p. 3]; (c) From 1994 - 97, what did Mr. Bigelow do with the power of attorney? [see pp. 10-11]; (d) On the estate tax return, what was the value of adjusted taxable gifts and of the gross estate? How does the combined total compare to the AEA for 1997? [see p. 16]; (e) How did the executor reduce the value of the property from $1,475,000 to an estate inclusion value of just $135,079.88 for the limited partnership interest (and another $19,912.50 for the general partnership interest)? How much would the inclusion at full value increase the estate tax? [for the first question see pp. 18-19 and for the second use ETAX, zeroing the value of the gifts of limited partnership interest but take into account the gift to Mr. Bigelow of loan forgiveness in the amount of $150,000]; (f) Summarize the courts opinion and the reasons for it. [see pp. 19-29].

7. To answer the questions that follow use the FVG case library (see prior problem) and click on the "2004 cases" to find and open Estate of Thompson, T. C. Memo 2004-174, July 26, 2004.
(a) For each of the following, show how they started with the value for the company, multiplied the value by the interest, then applied a minority interest discount (MI) and/or a lack of marketability discount (LOM) to arrive at a value. (i) The taxpayer's expert [see p. 30]; (ii) IRS's expert [answer pp. 38-39]; and (iii) the court [see pp. 49-50]. (b) What was the dollar amount of the penalty sought by the IRS and how was it calculated? (c) What would the penalty have been, based on the court's determination of additional liability,

and why did the court find the penalty to be inapplicable? Note, you can estimate the tax deficiency by multiplying 53% times the difference between the estate-reported value of the TPC shares and the value as determined by the court.

8. Javier started his real estate business years ago. He now owns the building on Main Street that houses the business and has 20 agents working for him. He has had several offers to buy the business for as much as $7 million without the building and $10 million with the building. In both cases, non-compete clauses and a transition period of consulting were discussed. His non-business assets are worth about $5 million. At the age of 75 he is in fair health but would like to wind down his involvement in the business. Two of his children work for him and his third child teaches. As you answer the questions that follow, discuss the factors that would push in one direction or the other. (a) What are the advantages of selling the business now? (b) What are the advantages of holding the business until he dies?

9. (a) How have check-the-box regulations made it easier for closely held businesses to select the appropriate organization with less worry about tax implications? (b) For a business with just a few owners, why is the LLC likely to be favored over the corporate form? Can all of the advantages of the LLC be obtained by making a Subchapter S election? (c) What is likely to keep the owners of an S corporation from liquidating it and reforming as an LLC?

10. Explain what tax advantages the ideal recapitalization was designed to provide. Why is it more difficult with the "anti-freeze" code sections to dramatically increase the value of the preferred shares by using high dividend rates and things like voting rights and liquidation bonuses?

11. Mandy has established a very successful adventure travel agency, estimated to be worth $2,000,000. Mandy has used a corporate recapitalization to turn the future value of her business over to her children, both of whom are involved in running the business. She has retained voting preferred shares and the children were given non-voting common stock. If the corporation is liquidated within five years of the recapitalization, Mandy will receive 110% of the preferred's stated par value before the common will receive anything.

(a) For transfer tax purposes, what is the maximum amount that Mandy can value stock she retains? (b) What happens if the corporation fails to pay dividends on the preferred stock? (c) For transfer tax purposes, does the liquidation bonus in the event of liquidation within five years increase the value of the preferred shares?

12. What is the tax advantage of including a method for determining the selling price in a properly drafted business buyout agreement?

13. At his death in 2005, Silva owned a successful farm near an expanding metropolitan area. As a farm, the land was worth $650,000, but a real estate developer is now willing to pay Silva's estate $2,200,000 for it. The rest of his estate has a value of $1,700,000. What is Silva's total gross estate if: (a) the executor does not elect § 2032A, and (b) an election is made?

14. At his death in 2005, Pedro owned a little farm on the outskirts of town, where he grew a variety of fruits and vegetables. His kids would like to continue the family farming tradition. A realistic appraisal of his farm real estate as plain old farm property is $900,000, yet a major developer would like to purchase the land for a very important project and has offered Pedro's estate $2,300,000 for the land. The farm equipment and livestock is valued at $220,000. The rest of Pedro's estate is valued at $2,380,000. Finally, the mortgage on the farmland is $110,000, unsecured debts are $35,000, and estate expenses are $40,000. Show the § 2032A percentage thresholds, and determine the taxable estate with and without the election. Use the indexed value for the deduction.

15. When he died in 2006, Nicolas Emery's estate included a small private lake that he and his family ran as a private resort where families enjoyed boating and fishing. Capitalization of the earnings of the present enterprise gives a value of $1,150,000 for the land. There was a $430,000 mortgage on the land. The boats, several utility vehicles, fishing equipment, portable concession stands, picnic tables, etc., are valued at $1,300,000. His home and other investments (not related to the business) were worth $2,800,000. Nicolas owed miscellaneous debts of $150,000 and estate expenses were $25,000. Developers would like to buy the property from the estate, put in a hotel and golf course at one end, and subdivide the rest as exclusive residential sites.

The beneficiaries of his estate are § 2032A qualified heirs and wish to continue the present business use. (a) What is the minimum fair market value that would have to be assigned to the real estate for Nicolas's estate to qualify for special use? (b) Suppose the FMV is determined to be $2,000,000; what would be the special use value, i.e., what value would be shown on the estate tax return? Use the inflation adjusted § 2032A amount. (c) Use the ETAX program to determine the estate tax savings.

16. At Mabel's death in 2005 her farmland, Creek Side Acres, was appraised at $3 million. The milk cows, tractors, milk-machines and other farm equipment were valued at $1.3 million and the non-farm assets at $4 million. Debts and expenses were negligible. Mabel actively worked the farm right up to her death at the age of 83. Her son and daughter wish to continue the farming operations. (a) Does the farm qualify for a 2032A election? Explain. (b) Does it qualify for a 6166 election? Explain. If so, how much of the tax would qualify for the 2% interest rate on deferral? (c) What is the tax savings if the farm's special use value is $2 million? What is it if the value is $2.2 million?

17. At farmer Brown's death in 2006 his farmland, Brown Hills Orchards, was appraised at $2.5 million. The value of the harvesting and apple processing equipment was $2.3 million. His non-farm assets were valued at $4.5 million. Debts and expenses were negligible. Mr. Brown had actively worked the farm until he had a stroke about three years before he died. Shortly before he became ill, he gave investments worth $500,000 to his two children Due to his health problems his two children began running the operation. The children wish to continue the farming operations. (a) Explain how the date of the gift to his children determines whether the estate qualifies for the 2032A election. (b) Does it qualify for a 6166 election? Explain. If so, how much of the tax would qualify for the 2% interest rate on deferral? (Assume the indexed amount for 2006 is $1,200,000) (c) If the farm qualifies for special use, what is the tax savings if the special use value is $1.1 million? What is it if the value is $1.5 million? (Assume the indexed amount for 2006 is $890,000)

18. Farmer Rice died in January of 2002. His estate saved $336,200 by making a § 2032A election on the 706 timely filed in October of 2002. The farmland

had a FMV of $3,000,000 but only $2,000,000 as a farm, hence it was scheduled on the 706 at $2,180,000. The heirs sold the farm for $3,500,000 in June of 2008. Assuming interest on the underpayment of tax has averaged 6% from October of 2002 to October of 2008 and that the gain will be taxed at 20%, compare whether the heirs should pay interest and step-up the basis or pay no interest and keep the basis as shown on the return.

19. When Sheila died in 2009 she was a majority shareholder in the software company QuikBite. Her estate can be summarized as follows:

Item	FMV DOD	Secured Debt
personal residence	$2,000,000	$500,000
apartment building	$5,000,000	$2,700,000
QuikBite shares	$4,000,000	
vested pension/401k	$3,000,000	.
miscellaneous personal	$400,000	
Debts and expenses		
credit card, bills, etc.		$20,000
estate transfer expenses		$75,000
funeral expense		$10,000
Totals	$14,400,000	$3,305,000
Debts and expenses	($3,305,000)	
Net	$11,095,000	

There were no state death taxes. (a) Explain how §303 applies to this estate. (b) What is the maximum dollar amount the corporation can pay for shares without the purchase being treated as dividend income by the estate? (c) How much would be treated as dividends if the corporation buys out the estate's entire interest at $4 million?

20. Repeat the prior problem parts "b" and "c" assuming one change: the state enacted an estate tax equal to 50% of what the federal state death tax credit would have been had it not been repealed. Note, you can calculate the state

death tax by using ETAX just enter an earlier year before the credit began phasing out and, for this problem, divide the number so determined by two. However, to answer these questions, you will then need to recalculate the federal estate tax taking this state death tax into account.

21. (a) What are the main tax breaks available to decedents' estates that include a closely held business? (b) What is the common thread that determines whether an estate can avail itself of one or more of these benefits? (c) Are any of these available only to estates holding shares of stock?

22. When Chet died in 2007, his estate consisted of the following: a controlling interest in Helter Shelter, Inc., a corporation that makes prefabricated homes (his shares are worth more than a million dollars and the estate is in the process of having them appraised), a home worth $900,000, and other assets worth $1,750,000. The estate has debts of $300,000, funeral expenses of $15,000, and estate administration expenses of $50,000. What is the minimum appraised value of the corporate shares that will allow the estate to use §303 and §6166? Assuming that the value comes out to be just above the minimum rounded to the next higher $100,000 (e.g. if the minimum amount is $820,000, the next higher rounded figure would be $900,000), calculate the estate taxes in order to determine (1) the maximum share value (i.e., the dollar amount) that qualifies for §303 capital buy back, and (2) the maximum federal taxes that would qualify for §6166 long-term deferral.

ANSWERS TO THE QUESTIONS AND PROBLEMS *(odd numbered only)*

1. The problem is that an equal distribution of the estate would mean a portion of the business to Bryan, an asset he does not want. A survivorship (second death) life insurance policy sufficient to equalize the benefit to each child could be arranged such that Betty would receive the business and Bryan receive more of the insurance proceeds. Thus, life insurance can simplify distribution of "lumpy" estate assets to survivors with widely different lifestyles and preferences. It might be wise, even though there is no estate tax problem, to have all assets held in trust and the insurance paid to the trust as doing so would facilitate making the equal division.

3. (a) Benefits of sale to a third party while person is still alive:
    1. Eliminate potential friction between survivors and other owners and managers.
    2. Survivors receive more liquid assets.
    3. A higher selling price.
    (b) Planning for a post-death sale may not be unwise if a buyout agreement is executed since it enhances the potential proceeds from the business transferable to the owner's survivors.

5. (a) $2,250,000*65%*75% = $1,096,875; less $30,000 (three annual exclusions) = $1,066,875. (b) Since much of the transfer is by gift, the children will have a carryover basis. However, given the new lower capital gains rate this may be less of a concern, indeed, of no concern if the family intends to keep the ranch forever.

7. (a) The various valuations:

    i. estate's expert:

$25,784,000		
$5,303,769	Value after discount	
$3,182,261	0.6	minority discount
$1,750,244	0.55	lack of marketability

    Court's comment: As noted, the estate's experts based their minority and lack of marketability discounts on general studies and not on the facts of this case.

The experts for the estate selected discount rates that were extreme and highly favorable for the estate, without any credible substantive discussion of how the facts of this case support such particular discounts.

ii IRS's expert:

$225,000,000		
$46,282,500		IRS - no minority discount
$32,397,750	0.7	lack of marketability

Court's comment: Turning to respondent's expert's valuation, respondent's expert appeared to be concerned with numbers only and did not appear to make an effort to base his valuation of TPC on a real company. His sterile approach is reflected both in his comparable public company analysis and in his discounted cashflow analysis. The court also disagreed with the IRS expert's failure to allow a minority interest discount.

iii court's decision:

$110,508,000		
$22,731,496		
$19,321,771	0.85	minority discount
$13,525,240	0.7	lack of marketability

(b) A substantial understatement penalty is 20% of the tax deficiency if the understatement is more than 50% but less than 75%, and is 40% if the understatement is greater than 75%, i.e., if the value on the return is 25% or less than the actual value. The estate's value was only 5.4% of the IRS determined value. This is how the IRS figured the penalty:

$32,393,000	IRS expert
-$1,750,000	estate expert
$30,643,000	difference
$16,326,408	tax deficiency
$6,530,563	penalty@ 40%

(c) The estate's value was only 12.9% of the value determined by the court. The penalty would have been over $2.5 million if the court had not found that there was a good faith belief by the estate representative in the figures supplied (hard to believe).

$13,525,240	court
($1,750,244)	estate
$11,774,996	difference
$6,276,073	@53.3%
$2,510,429	penalty @ 40%

9. (a) The regulations allow the owners to choose to be taxed as a partnership or corporation, if two or more owners, or as a corporation or sole proprietorship if just one owner (or a married couple) regardless of the actual structure. Since closely held businesses usually prefer to have a pass-through entity in order to avoid having tax at the entity level and again at the owner level, the check-the-box regulations have made it very easy for new businesses to avoid the corporate tax. (b) Even though the check-the-box regulations allow a corporation to be taxed as a partnership, the recognition of capital gains tax on the distribution of appreciated assets from a corporation (§ 311) will cause many to favor the LLC. A Subchapter S corporation is taxed as a partnership for the most part. However it also has the § 311 problem and, compared to the LLC, it is much more restricted as to capital structure (only one class of stock) and as to who may own shares (75 limit, generally only individuals can own it, no non-resident aliens allowed). (c) The Code § 311 requirement that gain be recognized on distribution of appreciated assets.

11. Mandy: (a) The minimum value of the junior interest must be at least 10% of the value of the business interest, hence the maximum value for the cumulative preferred stock is $1,800,000 ($2,000,000 * 90%). (b) The dividends may be skipped (the board of directors decides this) for five years even though the corporation has income or retained earnings out of which it can legally pay them. If it goes beyond that time, it will be considered a gift from Mandy to her children. The gift is the amount that she should have been paid. (c) Since the liquidation within five years is an event that might not happen, it is give a zero value, hence it does not increase the value of the retained interest. (Remember, the goal in this type of planning is to give the retained interest the highest value allowed since doing so reduces the value of the transferred shares.)

13. (a) If the property does not qualify for special use valuation, the land will be valued at $2,200,000, its highest and best use value, making the gross estate equal to $2,900,000.

(b) If the property does qualify for special use valuation, the land will be valued at $1,330,000 (which is the $2,200,000 highest and best use value, reduced by $870,000, the maximum amount allowed for 2005), making the gross estate equal $3,030,000.

15. (a) Answer: $1,930,000. The minimum value could be determined by trial and error or by using algebra. Let the value of the business land be X. We know that to qualify, the net value of the real estate must equal 25% of the adjusted value of the gross estate and the real estate plus the other business property must equal 50% of the adjusted value of the gross estate. Only the mortgage is taken into account in making these determinations. Algebra: we must solve for X in the following two equations: (X - $430,000) = (X - $430,000 + $1,300,000 + $2,800,000)/4; and (X - $430,000 + 1,300,000) = (X - $430,000 + $1,300,000 + $2,800,000)/2. The first gives a value of $1,797,000 and the second one $1,970,000. Only the higher value will satisfy both percentages, i.e., using the first would result in 25% and 48.8% (and would not qualify), whereas the second would be 26.8% and 50% (and would qualify). (b) Since the FMV is $2,000,000 and special use value is $1,150,000, the difference being less that the indexed § 2032A value, maximum reduction can only bring the real estate down to the special use value. (c) Without the election, the taxable estate would be $5,495,000 [$2,000,000 + $1,300,000 + $2,800,000 - $430,000 - $150,000 - $25,000] and the tax would be $1,607,700. With the election the taxable estate is $4,645,000, the tax is $1,216,700 and the difference is $391,000.

17. (a) The AGE is $9.3 million. Without the gifts included in the AGE, the land at 26.9% of AGE meets the 25% requirement and the farm as a whole at 51.6% meets the 50% requirement. However, if one adds back the $500,000 in gifts, the land at 25.5% still meets the requirement but the total value of the business falls just short at 49%. If the gifts were within 3 years, they must be added back to the AGE to determine whether the estate qualifies and it would not. If they occurred more than three years before farmer Brown died, then it would qualify.

(b) Whether gifts are added back or not, the estate's business interest is still well over the 35% threshold for 6166 so it qualifies. The 2% portion is the tax on an estate equal to the AEA plus the indexed $1 million. If the indexed amount is $1,200,00 in 2006, then the 2% portion is the tax on an estate of $3,600,000 and would be $736,000.

(c) At $1.1 million, the difference between the special use and the FMV is $1.4 million and the reduction is the full $1.2 million; at a marginal rate of 46% the taxes would be decreased by $552,000. On the other hand, a special use valuation of $1.5 million is only $1 million less, hence the reduction in value would be limited to that amount and savings would be $460,000.

19. (a) The threshold is met because the closely held shares equal 35% or more of the gross estate reduced by secured debts (but not unsecured debt), funeral, and expenses, i.e., $4,000,000/($14,400,000 - ($3,200,000 + $75,000 + $10,000)) = 36% . (b) The buy back as a capital transaction equals all estate expenses, funeral expenses, and death taxes. The taxable estate is $11,095,000 determined as follows: $14,400,000 - ($3,200,000 + $20,000 + $75,000 + $10,000). The estate tax is $3,417,750. Therefore, the buy back that receives capital treatment: $75,000 + $10,000 + $3,417,750 = $3,502,750. (c) If the estate buys all the shares for $4 million, the excess of $497,250 is dividend income to the estate.

21. Tax-break Code sections: (a) Transfer at death allows the use of several techniques that may reduce the estate tax (§2032A, § 2057), make it easier for the estate to obtain money to pay the taxes (§303), or allow the taxes to be paid over an extended period of time(§6166). Also, the ownership interest may receive a step-up in basis for income taxes. (b) The value of the business interest must be a significant part of the estate, generally meeting minimum threshold, e.g., 35% for 303 and 6166; 50% for 2032A and 2057. (c) Only 303, given that it deals with the buyback of stock, is specifically aimed at corporate interests.

ENDNOTES

1. *John and Viola Moore v. Commissioner*, 62 TCM 1128 (1991) (35% discount on gift of partnership interest); *Estate of Winkler v. Commissioner*, 62 TCM 1514 (1991) (20% discount on nonvoting stock); *Estate of Catherine Campbell v. Commissioner*, 62 TCM 1514 (1991) (56% discount); *Estate of Lenheim v. Commissioner*, 60 TCM 356 (1990); *Nancy Moonyham v. Commissioner*, TC Memo 1991-178.

2. *Smythe v. U.S.* 86-1 U.S. Tax Cases (CCH).

3. See TAM 9336002.

4. *G.O'Keeffe Estate* TC ¶12,886(M) (50% blockage discount allowed).

5. *Estate of Bright v. U.S.*, 658 F.2d 999 (5th Cir. 1981).

6. *Estate of Morton B. Harper v. Comm.*, T.C. Memo. 2002-121; Estate of *Theodore R. Thompson, et al. V. Comm.*, T.C. Memo. 2002-246.

7. TAM 200212006; *J.C. Shepherd v. Comm.*, 283 F.3d 1258 (11th Cir. 2002).

8. Reg. § 301.7701-1 through § 301.7701-4. See *US v. Kintner*, 216 F. 2d 418 (9th Cir. 1954). *Kintner* lead to the old regulations based on corporate characteristics.

9. Reg. § 301.77013(b)(1).

10. IRC § 1361(b)(1) sets forth the restrictions for S corporations.

11. *General Utilities & Operating Co.*, 296 U.S. 200, 56 S.Ct. 185 (1935).

12. IRC § 311.

13. IRC § 264(a)(1).

14. IRC § 56(g)(4)(B).

15. Reg. § 25.2703-1(d), Example 1.

16. Reg. § 25.2703-1(b)(3).

17. In *Commissioner vs. Procter* 142 F.2d 824 (4th Cir. 1944).

18. IRC § 264(a)(1).

19. IRC §§ 6166(b)(6); 2053(d).

20. IRC § 163(h)(2)(E).

21. IRC § 2503(d) added by the Taxpayer Relief Act of 1997.

22. Rev. Rul. 80-250, 1980-2 CB 278.

23. Cecil Cammack, Jr., at Cammack Computations Co., 1-800-594-5826, will do these computations at a very reasonable price.

24. IRC § 6601(j)(2).

25. IRC § 6601(j)(1)(B)

26. IRC § 2032A(b)(1)(A).

27. IRC § 2032A(b)(1)(B).

28. IRC § 2032A(e)(1).

29. IRC § 2032A(b)(2).

30. IRC § 2032A(a)(2).

31. *J. Fisher*, TC CCH 12,923 (1993).

32. IRC § 2032A(c)(7)(E).

33. IRC § 1016(c).

34. IRC § 303(b)(3).

CHAPTER 15

Surrogate Decision Makers

OVERVIEW

What could be more important than answering the questions, "If something happens to me, who will care for my children, manage my property, and make sure I receive appropriate care?" The common thread that runs though this chapter is that only by planning can we guide the process of selecting the person or persons who will perform these important services. Given the advances in medicine, one who is virtually braindead can live for years, presumably with no awareness of his or her surroundings. Given the choice, once any realistic chance of recovery has passed, most people would prefer to die naturally. It is important that each adult choose the degree of intervention with which he or she is comfortable. Because one cannot anticipate every eventuality, it is best to choose someone to speak on one's behalf in the event one cannot speak for oneself.

Choosing the appropriate surrogate decision-maker depends on the tasks he or she is expected to perform. The person will need guidance if we expect our wishes to be carried out. Wills and trusts are the major documents used in estate planning, but there are others such as directives to physicians and durable powers that in many respects are just as important.

PLANNING FOR THE CARE OF DEPENDENT CHILDREN

The chance of disability or premature death should compel everyone to do some planning. A serious injury or illness may require someone to care for the person and his or her property. The death of a parent might require the selection of one or more persons to care for children. Planning should document one's wishes as to the selection of the caregivers and in the care given.

Planning for the care of an orphaned child and for one's own incapacity have three common factors. First, if ones preferences are not documented a court generally selects the caregiver. Probate codes have lists as to who, all else being equal, should be given priority to serve in each of the various fiduciary capacities, e.g., guardian, conservator, or executor. The lists typically put in the highest category close family members, then more remote family members, next friends, and finally a public administrator or guardian. Without a written expression by the parent or the person incapacitated, the court will select from among those in the group at the highest priority level who have indicated a willingness to serve. Conflict may result if someone from a lower priority level really wants to serve but a person at a higher level agrees to take on the task out of a sense of duty, or when persons of the same level strongly disagree as to who should serve.

Second, the law differentiates two types of care: of the person and of the property. Fiduciaries serving in the former capacity provide for the everyday physical and psychological needs of the person and the latter safeguards, invests, and generally takes care of financial matters.

Third, because care of the person and care of the property entail such dissimilar responsibilities, different parties may be nominated and appointed to perform them. It is not unusual for one person to serve in both capacities.

Care of Minor Children

The material below explores the arrangements that are undertaken to provide care for minor children in the event both parents are incapacitated or die prematurely.

Guardian of the person. In the traditional household, the parents of a child are the natural and legal guardians of their children. Thus, on the death of one parent, generally the surviving parent continues as sole guardian. Only in the most unusual situations will the courts deny this right. On the other hand, when a minor child survives the death of both parents, the state must select a successor guardian. The selection process typically culminates in an order by a judge of the probate court after a noticed hearing. The court will appoint the person nominated in the parent's will, unless the nominee is unwilling, unable, or unsuitable to perform. If the will contains no nomination, or if there is no will, the court seeks information about willing relatives and friends, generally giving preference to the persons in the highest category level as a tie-breaker. If the child is sufficiently mature to have and express an opinion the court will consider it. Since the court's main criterion is the best interests of the child, it seeks to appoint a person who is capable of providing for the psychological well-being of the child, offering love and attention as well as such basics as food, clothing, shelter, medical care, and schooling.

Parents should nominate guardians in their wills. Although it may be the most difficult to make, choosing a guardian for one's children may be the most important estate planning decision that one makes. It might keep family peace by avoiding court contests over who will serve as guardian.

Who should be nominate to care for one's children? An ideal parental guardian possesses the following qualities:

1. The integrity, maturity, physical stamina, and experience expected of a parent.
2. A strong concern for the child's welfare.
3. The ability to provide a stable personal environment conducive to raising a child in a manner consistent with the parent's particular moral, religious, social, and financial situation.

A nomination greatly reduces the risk of an undesired appointment. Nominating successor guardians is wise since the first choice may be unwilling or unable to serve, or, once appointed, unable to continue to serve. The nomination is not carved in stone; the parents should periodically review the nomination in light of the child's changing needs and the nominee's changing personal and financial situation.

Managing the estate. While most states allow a minor to receive outright a modest amount of property, larger amounts are required to be turned over to a fiduciary legally responsible for their care and custody. What acceptable fiduciary arrangements are available? While the law recognizes parental guardianships as the only legal arrangement for a child's personal care, it recognizes several arrangements for managing the child's property, including a guardian of the estate, a trust, or a custodianship under the Uniform Transfer to Minors Act.

Financial guardianship. A financial guardian, also called the estate guardian or guardian of the estate, is typically appointed by the court in a manner similar to the procedures used for appointment of a parental guardian. Usually required to file a formal accounting with the court every one or two years, the financial guardian must obtain written permission from the court to undertake transactions that are out of the ordinary, such as the sale of real property. Reflecting the general trend in probate reform, some states have enacted streamlined guardianship proceedings to minimize court involvement.

In general, the criteria for selecting a financial guardian are quite different from those used in selecting a parental guardian. The primary consideration in selecting the parental guardian is parenting ability, whereas the primary focus in selecting the financial guardian is skill in financial matters.

Trustee. Instead of a financial guardian, a trustee can be chosen to manage the property left for the benefit of a minor child. Whether a living trust or a testamentary trust, the trust may be part of the parents' overall estate plan, with the children named as remaindermen. A trust is a private arrangement, not usually subject to court supervision, while a guardianship requires the filing of a bond, periodic accountings, and court approval for asset transfers; a trust can avoid these costly and time-consuming activities. Some states might still require ongoing probate court supervision of testamentary trusts, but the trend has been to eliminate this requirement unless the terms of the trust call for such supervision.

A trust offers great flexibility as the parent-settlors tailor it to their personal wishes. For example, while guardianship property usually must be surrendered outright to the minor when he or she reaches the age of majority, trust property can be retained in trust until the age specified in the trust. Indeed, for a disabled child, the trust might last his or her lifetime. Further, while a separate guardianship must be established for each minor, a single trust can have multiple beneficiaries and the trustee can be given discretion to distribute different amounts of trust assets to different beneficiaries at different times. For example, the trustee can be given the power to distribute principal to an income beneficiary, to accumulate income and add it to principal, or to "sprinkle" income among the beneficiaries, i.e., giving more income to some beneficiaries than to others perhaps because individual needs or outside resources differ.

A financial guardianship usually arises by default when parents die without having an estate plan in place. Guardianships are rarely preferred over trusts because they tend to be more expensive and, for the fiduciary, more cumbersome.

UTMA Custodian. Parents can leave property to a custodian for the benefit of a minor child under the Uniform Transfers to Minors Act in the manner described in Chapter 11. Like trusts, custodianships offer greater privacy than financial guardianships since they are not subject to court supervision. However, like guardianships, custodianships are quite inflexible because they are usually controlled by statute. For example, in most states property held by the custodian must be turned over to the minor when he or she reaches the maximum age set by statute, e.g., 21 or 25 years old.

SELECTION OF EXECUTOR AND THE EXECUTOR'S POWERS

An executor is responsible for representing and managing a decedent's probate estate. Tasks of this multifaceted job include marshaling and valuing the decedent's assets, filing tax returns, paying taxes and debts, distributing assets, and accounting for the entire process. It also involves dealing with grieving family members, distributing personal effects, and resolving family conflicts, all of which can be emotionally taxing. Finally, the executor must keep assets invested, sell them to pay taxes, and possibly manage or liquidate the decedent's business.

Selection. Who should be nominated for the job of executor? An ideal nominee possesses the following qualities:

1. Longevity, that is the likelihood of being able to serve after the death of the testator, perhaps many years after the will is executed.
2. Skill in managing legal and financial affairs.
3. Familiarity with the testator's estate and the testator's wishes.
4. Strong integrity coupled with loyalty to the testator.
5. Impartiality and absence of conflicts of interest.

An ideal financial guardian will also possess these qualities. Let us use these criteria to evaluate the candidates who are most likely available to serve.

Family member or a friend. Nominating a family member or a friend to be executor might reduce administration costs paid to people who are not beneficiaries. Family members and friends usually possess a strong degree of familiarity and loyalty. However, they often have only modest legal and financial skills, which may compel them to pay for professional advice. While they can normally delegate some of their work to the estate attorney, they cannot delegate their legal responsibility, since the executor cannot avoid personal liability for certain types of mistakes that might occur in administration. Nonetheless, in small estates most mistakes are not costly, and, in general, nominating as executor the spouse, an adult child, or a good friend makes sense.

Corporate executor. The testator may prefer to select a corporate executor such as a bank trust department. Reasons include inability to find and select a responsible family member or friend, conflict among family members, or a complex estate. Banks usually do a good job of managing estate assets. However, because they are usually unfamiliar with the decedent's family, they might not offer as much of a personal touch in the administration process. For example, they may have difficulty deciding who should be given minor personal effects that the decedent did not specifically devise. A cooperative family, or use of limited powers of appointment to delegate certain decision-making responsibility to a family member, increases the likelihood that the nominated corporate executor will accept the position. Finally, many banks will not agree to be executor if the estate is too small, if they dislike certain provisions of the will, or if they are not also nominated trustee under the estate plan's trust arrangements.

Attorney. Should an attorney, such as the testator's attorney, be considered for nomination as executor? Probate attorneys usually do a good job in managing assets during the probate period, because they commonly possess a substantial degree of expertise acquired over the years by doing the work delegated by their many executor-clients. Nomination of the testator's attorney, however, may increase the risk of a will contest. Dissatisfied with the will provisions, a dissatisfied beneficiary might allege that the nomination is further evidence that the testator was subject to "undue influence" and intimidation, and might petition that the will not be admitted to probate. However, keep in mind that successful will contests are rare. California specifically forbids the attorney who drafts the will from naming him or herself (or any associates, staff, or persons related to the attorney, associates or staff) as fiduciary of a will or trust. There are several exceptions to this rule. The nomination is acceptable if: (1) the attorney is related to the person for whom the estate plan is drafted; (2) the person has another attorney, one independent of the first, review with him or her the appropriateness of the nomination and determines that the person really wants the attorney to serve as fiduciary; (3) after the person dies, a court determines that it is in the best interest of the estate to have the nominated attorney serve.[1] Nominating the testator's attorney might increase efficiency in estate management, but it might not reduce administration costs since the attorney-executors may hire another attorney to represent the estate.

Other considerations. Especially where a friend or family member is nominated, the testator should also nominate an alternate executor to serve in case the primary nominee is unwilling or unable to serve. A corporate executor is a good alternate because one can be fairly confident that it will be available to serve. Regardless of the choice of executor, the testator should always consult with the nominees to get their consent, and should periodically review the choice in light of changing circumstances.

Executor's powers. What powers should be explicitly granted to an executor? Most simple wills either do not delineate the powers of the executor or list just a few powers. The will in Exhibit 3-1 explicitly grants to the executor the powers to distribute principal and income; to sell, lease, mortgage, pledge, assign, invest, and reinvest estate property; and to operate a business.

When a will "is silent" regarding a specific proposed action of the executor, we look for authority first to the provisions of the state's estates and trusts or probate code, which usually delineate many executor's powers. In the absence of explicit permission in the will, executors may seek a court order authorizing certain action, e.g., spending money to paint or repair a house before putting it on the market. Specifying powers explicitly in the will can offer the executor greater flexibility by minimizing unnecessary delays in probate but one cannot expect them to cover every eventuality.

SELECTION OF TRUSTEES AND TRUSTEE'S POWERS

It should become clear that the factors in selection of rustee are quite similar to those mentioned earlier, in the section dealing with the selection of an executor.

Selection. We saw that a good executor (and financial guardian) is characterized by longevity, skill in managing, familiarity, integrity, loyalty, and impartiality. In general, these traits also apply to selecting a trustee, except that in the case of a trustee, greater weight is accorded to skill in ongoing financial management since the trustee's job is often long-term. As in the case of the executor, potential nominees include family members, friends, the family attorney, and a corporate fiduciary.

Selecting a family member or friend to be trustee can minimize costs, maximize administrative speed, and may ensure a personal relationship with the survivors. Selecting a family member to be trustee can also result in mismanagement, since few family members have much experience in maintaining, investing, and accounting for an investment portfolio, all critical responsibilities of the trustee. Thus, family members may feel compelled to hire professionals for advice. In addition, family conflicts can arise. For example, nominating the person's children from a former marriage to be trustees of a QTIP trust can create a difficult situation for the surviving spouse.

Selecting a trust beneficiary to be trustee can also cause problems of proper distribution. For example, in one case, the trustee, who was also a remainder beneficiary, was ordered by the court to make additional distributions to the decedent-trustor's disabled son, under a trust that allowed such distributions.[2] In this situation, a conflict of interest resulted in a breach of fiduciary obligation that nearly frustrated the deceased trustor's dispositive intent to provide care for his disabled son.

Selecting an attorney to be trustee can create the same minor risk of a will contest as in nominating an attorney to be executor. In addition, since management of the trust may be a long-term assignment, the client should determine whether the attorney has the time and expertise required to perform effectively. Finally, anticipating trusteeship, the attorney may be tempted to include unconventional self-serving clauses in the trust instrument, similar to the problems described earlier in the selection of the attorney as executor.[3]

Selecting a corporate trustee, such as a bank trust department or a trust company, increases the likelihood that an impartial satisfactory job will be performed. Most corporate trustees try to match the investment strategy for the trust assets to the needs of the beneficiaries, balancing both the income beneficiary's needs with the interests of the remaindermen. The trust instrument can give some guidance as to the settlor's view of appropriate asset allocation.

Most trust departments try to build long-term personal relationships with the beneficiaries. Again, using family members as holders of limited powers might make the corporate trustee's job easier while allowing more creative responses to family needs and desires.

A common choice is the cotrusteeship of family member and corporate trustee. It can combine the advantages of each: personal knowledge of the family situation and competent asset management. Also, naming the surviving spouse to be a cotrustee can be psychologically uplifting to that spouse.

Ordinarily, cotrusteeships do not save management fees, since the corporate trustee will probably charge its customary fee. There may be some situations where corporate trustees will turn down cotrustee arrangements, particularly when they anticipate that the other trustee may be difficult to accommodate. When cotrustees disagree, they may have to seek a resolution in court, unless the trust instrument authorizes a less formal method, such as giving the corporate trustee the final say.

As in nominating an executor, the settlor should always nominate a successor trustee and should consult with the proposed trustees to ensure that the job will be accepted. Many bank trust departments set minimum asset amounts, which creates the possibility that they may refuse to manage small trusts. Minimum amounts vary and a corporate trustee may have discretion to lower the amount from its standard minimum depending on the relationship that has been established between it and the family. It might also be influenced by the ease or difficulty it is likely to encounter in managing the estate's assets.

Trustee's powers. The settlor has at least three commonly used options in deciding what trustee powers to confer in a trust document. The settlor can specify no powers, relying entirely on implied powers, and on that state's statutory and case-law framework, which explicitly confers some powers to trustees. Many states have adopted the Uniform Trustees Powers Act, which codifies numerous trustee powers. Another approach is to rely on the state's laws in general and explicitly grant in the trust instrument other desirable powers not found in the statute. Such an approach may facilitate asset administration. An example of this is found in Exhibit 3-2, the living trust, and in Exhibit 3-3, the trust-will. Finally, some trusts set forth a long list of the powers given to the trustee. Making a long detailed list creates the presumption that anything not included is unauthorized even though it might be something that state law would ordinarily approve and that trustees commonly do, e.g., the long list does not include the authority to borrow; if the list appears to be exhaustive, the trustee probably cannot borrow even if doing so would be prudent. To avoid this presumption, the trust might state that the list is not intended to be exclusive and that the trustee has all other powers allowed by state law and/or commonly held by trustees.

Trust distributions. Trust documents should specify how and when the trust will end. Most commonly, this is when the beneficiaries have reached the age specified in the document, but it could be conditioned on something else, such as when all of the children have graduated from college or when the youngest turns 30, whichever event happens first. Determining in advance the appropriate time to terminate a trust can be difficult for a parent with minor children because the parent may not be able to accurately predict their rates of maturation or eventual degree of sophistication. It might make sense to delay distribution of corpus to a later age, such as age 30 or 40, or to stagger the distribution in stages, e.g., distribute one-third of the trust at age 21, half the balance at age 25, and the remainder at age 30. Other parents, seeking an alternative to mandatory distribution, simply give the trustee or a family member the power to decide the timing of the termination of the trust once the beneficiary reaches some specified age. Thus, the trustee would continue to manage the property indefinitely if the beneficiary became unable to manage the property.

Some people prefer to leave much of their wealth to charity. They may fear the potentially devastating impact the anticipation of inherited wealth can have on children. Some children of wealthy families are prone to a malady, which one commentator has called "affluenza," whose symptoms include a lack of connection between work and reward, inadequate self discipline, a distorted view of money, lack of motivation, feelings of guilt, and low self-esteem. For this, and a variety of other reasons, some people choose to limit the wealth they leave to their children.[4]

Single versus multiple trusts. For parents with more than one child, a separate trust can be established for each child, or a single trust can include all children. How much each child will receive may depend on how many trusts are created. Creating immediately, upon the death of a parent, a separate trust for each child adds flexibility but increases administration costs and may be, in some circumstances, considered unfair to the younger children. If the parents had lived, the expenses in raising all their children probably would have come from the whole of family assets and not from separate shares reserved for each child. Thus, expenses to raise even the youngest child would come from what could be called the family "pot" of wealth. On the other hand, if separate trusts are immediately created, each child's living expenses will be charged to his or her separate share, rather than from the collective wealth. Consequently, the younger children might receive a relatively smaller distribution upon reaching adulthood. A single trust, at least for a period of time, might be more appropriate.

Family trust. The "family trust" is the name commonly given to a single trust created to benefit all of the children of a deceased couple. This used to be called the family pot trust because all expenses are paid from the same "pot" so to speak. Under its usual terms, the trust remains undivided until the youngest child reaches age 21, the age at which parental obligations are commonly perceived to terminate. At that time, the assets are divided into equal separate shares, one for each child. The assets are distributed outright, or they are held for distribution at some older age. The age that triggers division is decided by the parents when the trust is drafted. It can be set at older or younger than 21, and it does not have to be when the youngest reaches that age but could be when the oldest reaches it. As was mentioned earlier, it can even be left to the discretion of a surrogate decision-maker, whether the trustee or a family member, so long as the guidelines for distribution and termination are set forth in the trust document.

The choice of the age at which the assets in a family trust are divided into separate shares or separate trusts involves a trade-off between inequality and delay. The younger that age, the more unequal will be the total cumulative amounts distributed to the children, but the sooner will the older children be certain of the size of their shares. Conversely, the older the age at which the assets are divided into separate shares, the less the inequality, but the later the share amounts will be determined.

EXAMPLE 15 - 1. Mrs. Hunsaker, a widow, is pondering the type of distribution clause for her trust. She has two children, Colleen, age 20, and Nancy, age 15. Colleen is a senior in college and is engaged to be married, and Nancy, still in high school, is headed for college. One alternative would be to split the trust into two equal shares immediately on her death, with outright distribution to each child at age 21. Another alternative would be to delay dividing the assets into equal shares until Nancy reaches age 21, at which time both children would receive equal shares outright. If Mrs. Hunsaker dies just after the trust is executed, with the first alternative, Colleen will receive her distribution in less than one year and none of it will have been used to finance Nancy's living expenses. With the second alternative, Colleen will have to wait until age 26 to receive her distribution, and the entire corpus will have been available to meet Nancy's living expenses, including most of her college education.

Some attorneys recommend dividing the corpus of a family trust into separate shares sooner rather than later, i.e., when the oldest child reaches age 18 rather than when the youngest reaches age 21, reasoning that parents would probably prefer that each child bear subsequent (perhaps very unequal) costs (e.g., college, graduate school) only out of his or her own share. This, of course, reflects a very different philosophy of family financial planning. The planner should determine the preferences of each client rather than using boiler plate language.

Restrictions on assignment. As mentioned in Chapter 3, the settlor may wish to include a spendthrift clause, insulating the trust from the claims of the beneficiaries' creditors and restricting beneficiaries from transferring their interests in trust income or principal prior to trust termination. Spendthrift clauses are legally recognized in the majority of American jurisdictions. They can help a financially prudent beneficiary (e.g., a professional) by protecting trust assets from most creditors. However, such clauses are not foolproof. Although they may deny a creditor the right to demand that the trustee directly hand a distribution over to it, they do not prevent the creditor from exercising the usual legal remedies (i.e., action in court) against a beneficiary after the beneficiary receives a distribution. In addition, the law generally recognizes as enforceable a beneficiary's promise to a creditor to deliver trust property once it is received. Thus, while a spendthrift clause can discourage excessive spending, it cannot completely prevent the beneficiary from "spending" trust property prior to receiving it, as long as there are creditors willing to wait. Spendthrift clauses work best in discretionary trusts, ones in which the beneficiary has no legally enforceable right to income or principal.

PLANNING FOR PARTICULAR NEEDS

There are a number of planning techniques designed to provide care for disabled individuals. Generally the goal is to stretch the financial resources available so as to maximize the quality of the care given to the disabled person.

Special needs trust. Special needs trust, also known as supplemental needs trusts, are created to give extra help to a disabled beneficiary without diminishing what the beneficiary receives from other sources. For instance an adult child with resources of less than $2,000 might qualify for $800 per month in state and federal disability payments. The person would be ineligible for benefits if he or she has assets greater than $2,000. Generally, each dollar of income decreases dollar for dollar one's monthly benefits. A carefully crafted special needs trust (SNT) can provide life enrichment funds while allowing the public assistance to take care of very basic needs. To avoid having the trust income decrease the benefits, a SNT will generally directs the trustee to pay helpers directly or to reimburse other family members for money spent to enrich the life of the disabled person. For instance, the money might be used to hire a reader for a beneficiary who has lost the ability to read, or to be a companion to one living in a care facility, perhaps taking the person on outings to the beach, museums, or movies.

The key to drafting a SNT is that the beneficiary has no right to force the payments from the trust. Indeed, when these trusts were first proposed, years ago, it was thought to be necessary to have an implosion clause that would cause the trust to terminate in favor of other relatives in the event a governmental agency sought to attach the trust assets to gain reimbursement for governmental expenditures on behalf of the beneficiary. It is now well established by both state and federal regulations that these trusts, if properly drafted, do not constitute assets of the disabled beneficiary, and that neither the trust income nor expenditures made on behalf of the beneficiary are counted in determining the beneficiary's eligibility so long as the expenditures are not mandatory and are not for necessities. However, since even gifts count to reduce some kinds of government benefits, most of the spending must be indirect, such as that paid to helpers. Even the purchase of food, clothing, or shelter is considered as payment "in kind" and will reduce benefits. It is unlikely that benefits will be cut for incidental expenditures that fall into the aforementioned categories, e.g., the paid companion purchases a hot dog and souvenir baseball cap for the beneficiary while the two of them enjoy watching a game at the ballpark.

The trust can be established by the parents while they are alive or, as is often done, be created after the death of both parents, as part of an overall estate plan. Sometimes these are funded with life insurance, especially if the parents' estate is fairly modest. If the child's basic needs are being taken care of by other means, it might be appropriate to limit the amount going into a SNT to what can realistically be used to enrich the child plus some extra to allow for the unexpected.

EXAMPLE 15 - 2. Ann had three children, Jerry, Diane, and Kristin. After a serious head injury from a motorcycle accident, Kristin began receiving $350 per month in state disability benefits, lived in a state supported group-living home, and, most importantly, qualified for Medicaid. State law decreased her aid money by one dollar for every two dollars that she received above $50 during the month whether such money was through earnings, gifts, or investments. Ann often took Kristin for rides in the country, to the beach, or they would go out for lunch and then take in a movie. As part of her estate plan, Ann created a special needs trust, naming Jerry and Diane as co-trustees. The trustees were authorized (but not required) to use the income for any kind of enrichment that they thought appropriate. If the income proved to be insufficient, they were also authorized to use corpus for these activities. When Ann died, the SNT was funded with the proceeds from a $300,000 life insurance policy. The balance of her estate, valued at a little over a million dollars, was divided equally between Jerry and Diane. The SNT provided that upon Kristin's death, any remaining trust property would be distributed to Jerry and Diane, or their issue. Although, this creates the appearance of a conflict of interest, i.e., the less the trustees spend for Kristin's benefit, the more they can expect to eventually receive, Ann had faith that the two would do the right thing insofar as their sister was concerned. With the SNT, the trustees arranged for college students to make regular visits to engage Kristin in interesting activities much to her delight.

Self-settled special needs arrangements. In addition to SNTs created by other family members, usually parents, there are similar trusts created with the beneficiary's own funds; these are referred to as "self-settled" trusts. Perhaps the beneficiary-settlor received a personal injury monetary settlement arising out of an accident or from medical malpractice. Both Medicaid and SSI permit the creation of a self-settled SNT if the trust meets certain requirements. Generally an SNT will be established specifically for the individual disabled person, or the funds will become part of a pooled trust fund, the latter managed by a state agency or by a not-for-profit foundation. The beneficiary of a pooled fund can be any age, whereas the non-pooled self-settled SNT beneficiary must be under age 65 when the trust is established.[5] If the SNT is established just for the settlor-beneficiary, then when the beneficiary dies, the state will have a claim against the remaining trust assets for the Medicaid payments made on his or her behalf.[6] If there are assets remaining after government claims, the trustee can distribute them as directed by the trust document, e.g., to family members. With a pooled fund, there are many beneficiaries, each beneficiary with a subaccount based upon his or her contribution. When a pooled fund beneficiary dies, the state does not make a claim for Medicare or SSI payments that were made on behalf of the decedent, rather the contribution stays with the state agency or foundation and is used to help other disabled individuals.

Persons who impoverish themselves by giving away assets in order to qualify for government assistance programs are generally "punished" by being ineligible for that assistance for a period of time. Transfers that occur within five years of making application for assistance, referred to as the "look back" period, trigger this penalty, however state and federal rules generally exempt correctly drafted self-settled SNTs from the look back penalties. However, given the complexity of this area of the law, it is very important to engage experienced legal counsel when incorporating an SNT into an estate plan.

Incentive trusts. One concern about leaving significant wealth to young adults is that it will kill incentive to lead a productive life. This concern is multiplied if a child has had difficulties with holding a job, especially if this has been coupled with addition to drugs or alcohol. One way to create an incentive to stay sober, at least clean enough to hold a job, is to create what is called an incentive trust. Rather than leaving a portion of the parent's estate outright to the child with difficulties, his or her share is held in what is called an *incentive trust*. The trustee (or a family member with a power of appointment) is given discretion to withhold income and corpus, making distributions to the child based upon criteria placed in the trust document by the settlor-parent. In addition to paying for expenses related to higher education, a bonus distribution might be made for graduating. Other incentive distributions might be periodic matching of the beneficiary's earned income. In general, these trusts set forth criteria for distributions that can be easily verified, such as class enrollment and progression, graduation, wages, etc., rather than requiring the trustee to verify that the beneficiary is staying sober. However, without requiring the trustee to be a detective, there might be penalties for wrongdoing that comes to light, such as heavy drinking, drug use, or criminal behavior. The trustee might be given authority to terminate the trust in favor of the beneficiary if he or she matures to be a responsible person or in favor of the settlor's other issue if he or she seems lost forever, e.g., in prison with no possibility of parole.

Spend-down planning. The medical profession has been tremendously successful in prolonging the life of the seriously ill, often at great economic cost. Such patients often need *custodial care* for help with feeding, bathing, dressing, and transportation. Later, they may need *skilled nursing care* provided in a licensed facility, and costing $3,000 per month or more. Their condition may finally require a lengthy period of hospitalization, costing far more. Private and public insurance can help pay these costs, but often not entirely. Long-term care insurance is available, but policies usually are expensive and contain significant restrictions and exclusions, so few people are willing to buy it. Federal Medicare insurance for persons with Medicare Part A coverage receive up to 100 days of skilled nursing care. The conditions for obtaining this coverage are quite stringent such that most illnesses will be determined not to require skill nursing. These limitations in private and public insurance raise the possibility that a person will totally deplete the wealth acquired over a lifetime, thereby preventing any significant amount going to the children.

To prevent this, some people are turning to attorneys who specialize in elder law. Many recommend "spending down" assets through the use of gifts and trusts. This action seeks to accomplish two goals. First, it strives to insulate the person's assets from the claims of health care providers and government agencies. Second, it attempts to impoverish the person sufficiently to qualify for certain types of federal and state assistance, including Supplemental Security Income, In-Home Supportive Services, In-Home Medical Care Services, and perhaps most importantly, Medicaid. While Medicare is considered an "entitlement" for those who have paid into the system, Medicaid is not. It is considered a form of welfare, hence one can have too much wealth or too much income to qualify for Medicaid. Each state, in exchange for matching federal Medicaid grants, imposes federally influenced limits on both 1) assets a recipient can own, and 2) the his or her income beyond that needed for the actual cost of medical and custodial care. These levels do vary by state so only general statements can be made. Generally, the person's home is not factored into the asset value limitation so long as the person intends to return to it (regardless of how improbable that might be). To reduce asset value, especially if the person has meager income, he or she can purchase a single premium annuity. Although distributions from the annuity do count for purposes of the income test, the overall value of the annuity does not count under the assets test.

As part of a spending-down strategy, an individual may wish to make outright gifts of property to children. However, outright gifts have the major drawback that the donor loses total control over the property. Also, the gifts must be made well in advance of the person entering a nursing home since a "Transfer Penalty" applies to gifts made within 36 months prior to the Medicaid application (or 60 months if the transfer was made to certain kinds of trusts).[7] The penalty is a period of ineligibility to receive benefits. The period is determined by dividing the value of the gifts during the 36 months leading up to the application by the average private-pay nursing home rate in the applicants state.

> EXAMPLE 15 - 3. The year prior to going into a nursing home, Mildred gave her son John cash, stocks, and bonds worth $40,000. The average private-pay nursing home rate was $4,000 at the time. Because of the transfer penalty, Mildred will have to pay her own way for ten months.

In addition, after the beneficiary's death, the state must attempt to recoup from the recipient's estate the benefits it paid for the recipient's care. It can recoup from the probate estate as well as other assets that once belonged to the recipient, including those conveyed to a survivor, heir, or transferred through joint tenancy, tenancy in common, survivorship, life estate, or living trusts. Property in the estate of the surviving spouse is exempt.

Helping a client who owns a sizable estate to impoverish him or her self so as to qualify for public assistance funds is a controversial subject and raises ethical issues. Many planners will not recommend it, because they see it as taking unfair advantage of an imperfect system designed for truly needy people. It also encourages children to treat Medicaid as if it were "their personal inheritance insurance." Many wealthy people are not interested in spending down their estates. Most will want a higher quality of care and may not like being regarded as a "welfare case." Others find no moral dilemma, and consider it no different from tax planning, such as recommending a credit shelter bypass trust to minimize estate tax. Perhaps all planners would agree that clients should be encouraged to consider, at a minimum, other basic protective planning steps, such as purchasing an effective long-term care insurance policy or saving for their future care.

PLANNING FOR NONTRADITIONAL RELATIONSHIPS

From time to time, planners will be asked for advice by unmarried clients involved in nontraditional, long-term relationships with members of the same or opposite sex. These relationships present some unique planning challenges. Being unmarried, the partners are not be entitled to the advantages offered by law to married couples. If the partners do not have children in common, they probably have totally different sets of surviving kin. Thus, while they may have a strong desire to leave most or all property for the benefit of the partner, they will not want the partner to be able to control disposition of their property at or after the partner's death.

Greater Attention to Legal Documents

Unmarried partners are not included as heirs in intestate succession statutes, making written estate planning documents even more important. Intestacy will have the undesired effect of disinheriting the surviving partner, who is hardly ever a blood relative.

In the event of a medical emergency, unless domestic partners have written agency documents, medical practitioners might not follow the requests of one partner trying to intervene on behalf of his or her significant other.

Estate Tax Concerns

In theory, the largest combined estate size that unmarried partners can transfer to survivors, estate tax-free, with a credit shelter bypass is two times the applicable exclusion amount (AEA), e.g., $4 million in 2006, 2007, or 2008, just as for married couples. However, in fact, the true maximum is usually less, to the extent that one of the partners owns less than the AEA. While the AEA will be sheltered at the first death by the unified credit, any excess amount cannot be sheltered by the marital deduction. Thus, estate planning cannot "zero out" the estate tax for any first partner to die (P1) owning greater than the AEA. Since P1 will incur an estate tax whether the excess is left to the surviving partner (P2) or to a bypass trust, P1 may prefer to leave the entire estate to the bypass trust, in order to minimize P2's estate tax, and to ensure that the property will ultimately pass to P1's surviving kin.

As a partial solution, the partners may agree to arrange separate wills leaving everything to one another, and agreeing that at P2's death, property originating from P1 will pass to P1's surviving kin. However, short of executing a joint and mutual will, P1 has no way to prevent P2 from revising the instrument later on. Thus, the surest plan requires use of bypass trusts to minimize P2's estate tax and ensure that each will have selected his or her own remaindermen as the ultimate beneficiaries of their respective estates.

Life insurance. Since a taxable estate exceeding the AEA will owe an estate tax, liquidity planning will often require life insurance on P1 as well as P2. The proceeds can still be kept out of both partners' gross estates with irrevocable life insurance trusts.

Lifetime giving . The inability to use a marital deduction to avoid estate tax might prompt unmarried partners to engage in greater gift planning. Although unmarried partners will not be able to utilize the gift tax marital deduction, they can still take advantage of one annual exclusion per donee per year. Thus, they can still undertake an ongoing program of lifetime giving to reduce their estate tax base. Careful planning should avoid outright gifts to the partner, however, to enable the donor, as a potential P1, to retain final dispositive control. Instead, the planner should encourage gifting in trust, with provisions granting a life estate in the income to the partner and the remainder to the trustor's surviving relatives. As future interests, however, the remainder interest portion of such gifts in trust will not qualify for the annual exclusion and will either use up the settlor's unified credit or result in an actual gift tax.

PREPARING FOR INCAPACITY

As life expectancy increases so too the probability that one will endure a serious disability. The percentage of persons 65 and older is projected to grow from 12.4% in 2000, to 13.0% in 2010, and 16.3% in 2030.[8] A person's disability creates the need for surrogate decision-makers. It makes more sense to choose the person who will care for you and set forth guidelines rather than having the person chosen for you and forced to guess at the care you might desire.

Property Management

Techniques available to direct the management of the incapacitated person's property include guardianships or conservatorships, revocable living trusts, and durable powers of attorney.

Guardianship or conservatorship. Similar to the guardianship of the estate of a minor, all states provide a court-supervised arrangement to manage the property of an incapacitated individual. Called a *guardianship* or a *conservatorship*, depending on the state, establishment of either normally requires a court hearing, and the appointment of a guardian who is ordinarily subject to continuing court supervision. The guardian or conservator is required to give periodic accountings to the court and is typically required to obtain court permission before engaging in most property transactions. Most guardians and conservators have little or no discretionary authority. However, some states are reducing court involvement in guardianships and conservatorships in much the same way they are reducing court involvement for probate proceedings.[9]

For reasons similar to those for avoiding probate, many people will plan to avoid the necessity of having a property guardian or conservator. Some individuals, however, may prefer the protection offered from their closer court supervision. People owning larger estates, or those who cannot recommend a friend or relative to manage property, might prefer a court-administered alternative. Most people will prefer one or both of the arrangements described next.

Revocable living trust. In planning for incapacity, a person could create a revocable living trust, funding it with family assets, and serving as its initial trustee. The trust instrument could provide for a successor trustee when the person became unable to manage the trust's financial affairs. The successor trustee could be the spouse, an adult child, another relative, a trusted friend, or a corporate trustee. In comparison with a guardianship or conservatorship, a living trust offers the advantages of privacy, flexibility, and freedom from court appearances and accountings. On the other hand, since the trust is a private, unsupervised arrangement, there exists greater potential for undiscovered fraud and mismanagement by the successor trustee.

One additional disadvantage of the trust arrangement with regards to handling incapacity is the possible requirement of a formal legal determination of the settlor-trustee's incapacity before a successor trustee can take over the job. Embarrassing litigation can develop between the settlor and a family member who is attempting to establish that the settlor-trustee is incompetent. However, this conflict can also arise if a guardianship or conservatorship is being established. The trust can contain a clause providing for a private determination of incapacity, in a manner similar to that provided by the springing durable power of attorney for property, discussed next.

Durable power of attorney. Creation of a trust can be relatively expensive. Persons owning smaller estates may prefer to execute a simpler document, known as a *durable power of attorney for property*, also called a *financial durable power* of attorney. Popularized by the Uniform Probate Code, the durable power of attorney for property has been recognized by the statutes of every state. Generally, all of these documents that set forth guidelines for care and management in the event one becomes incapacitated are referred to as *advance directives*. The durable power of attorney for property is different from the durable power of attorney for health care, described in the next section. Since state laws vary, the reader is strongly urged to examine the law of his or her particular state.

A power of attorney is a written document executed by one person, called the *principal*, authorizing another person, called the *agent* or the *attorney-in-fact*, to perform designated acts on behalf of the principal. A durable power of attorney for property (DPOA) creates an agency relationship that allows the agent to perform acts to protect the principal's property interests, even if the principal becomes incapacitated.

Powers of attorney can be either durable or nondurable. A nondurable power of attorney is not a practical alternative for caring for the property of elderly individuals because the power becomes legally invalid at the onset of the principal's incapacity, just when the agency is needed most.

The *durable* power of attorney was developed by the states to overcome this deficiency. Thus, a DPOA is durable because its authority continues even during the principal's incapacity. Exhibit 15-1 illustrates the common provisions of a DPOA. The italicized statement near the end of the document makes it "durable."

EXHIBIT 15-1 Durable Power of Attorney (for property)[10]

DURABLE POWER OF ATTORNEY

JOHN JONES, PRINCIPAL

TO WHOM IT MAY CONCERN:

I, John Jones, a resident of Anytown, Anystate, in the county of Anycounty, do hereby constitute and appoint Aaron Agent, a resident of Anytown, Anystate, to be my agent with full power to act on my behalf and with full power to substitute at any time or times for the purposes described below one or more agents and to revoke the appointment of my agents so substituted and to do the following:

1. To manage my affairs; handle my investments; arrange for the investment, reinvestment, and disposition of funds; exercise all rights with respect to my

---

EXHIBIT 15-1 Durable Power of Attorney *continued*

---

investments; accept remittances of income and disburse the same, including authority to open bank accounts in my name and to endorse checks for deposit therein or in any bank where I may at any time have money on deposit and sign checks covering withdrawals therefrom.

2. To endorse and deliver certificates for transfer of bonds or other securities to be sold for my account and receive the proceeds from such sale.

3. To sign, execute, acknowledge, and deliver on my behalf any deed of transfer or conveyance covering personal property or real estate wherever situated (including transfers or conveyances to any trust established by me), any discharge or release of mortgage held by me on real estate or any other instrument in writing.

4. To negotiate and execute leases of any property, real or personal, which I may own, for terms that may extend beyond the duration of this power and to provide for the proper care and maintenance of such property and pay expenses incurred in connection therewith.

5. To subdivide, partition, improve, alter, repair, adjust boundaries of, manage, maintain, and otherwise deal with any real estate held as trust property, including power to demolish any building in whole or in part and to erect buildings.

6. To enter into a lease or arrangement for exploration and removal of minerals or other natural resources or to enter into a pooling or unitization agreement.

7. To hold securities in bearer form or in the name of a nominee or nominees and to hold real estate in the name of a nominee or nominees.

8. To continue or participate in the operation of any business or other enterprise.

9. To borrow money from time to time in my name and to give notes or other obligations therefore, and to deposit as collateral, pledge as security for the payment thereof, or mortgage any or all my securities or other property of whatever nature.

10. To have access to any and all safe deposit boxes of which I am now or may become possessed, and to remove therefrom any securities, papers, or other articles.

11. To make all tax returns and pay all taxes required by law, including federal and state returns, and to file all claims for abatement, refund, or other papers relating thereto.

12. To demand, collect, sue for, receive, and receipt for any money, debts, or property of any kind, now or hereafter payable, due or deliverable to me; to pay or contest claims against me; to settle claims by compromise, arbitration, or otherwise; and to release claims.

EXHIBIT 15-1 Durable Power of Attorney *continued*

---

13. To employ as investment counsel, custodians, brokers, accountants, appraisers, attorneys-at-law, or other agents such persons, firms, or organizations, including my said attorney and any firm of which my said attorney may be a member or employee, as deemed necessary or desirable, and to pay such persons, firms, or organizations such compensation as is deemed reasonable and to determine whether to act on the advice of any such agent without liability for acting or failing to act thereon.

14. To expend and distribute income or principal of my estate for the support, education, care, or benefit of my dependents and me.

15. To make gifts to any one or more of my spouse and my descendants (if any) of whatever degree (including my said attorney who is a spouse or descendant of mine) in amounts not exceeding $10,000 annually with respect to any one of them and gifts to charity in amounts not exceeding 20% of my federal adjusted gross income in any one year.

16. To renounce and disclaim any interest otherwise passing to me by testate or intestate succession or by inter vivos transfer.

17. To exercise my rights to elect options and change beneficiaries under insurance and annuity policies and to surrender the policies for their cash value.

In general I give to my said attorney full power to act in the management and disposition of all my estate, affairs and property of every kind and wherever situated in such manner and with such authority as I myself might exercise if personally present.

This power of attorney shall be binding on me and my heirs, executors, and administrators and shall remain in force up to the time of the receipt of my attorney of a written revocation signed by me.

This power of attorney shall not be affected by my subsequent disability or incapacity.

IN WITNESS THEREOF, I have set forth signature on November 19, 2005.

_____ *John Jones* _____

EXHIBIT 15-1 Durable Power of Attorney *continued*

STATE OF ANYSTATE

COUNTY OF ANYCOUNTY

On November 19, 2005, the above named John Jones appeared and acknowledged the foregoing instrument to be his/ free act and deed.

Mary D. Notary
_____
Notary Public

My commission expires: January 1, 2007

Some commentators recommend having the designated agent (and alternate agents) sign the document below a statement that expresses the agent's willingness to serve. Of course, there is little that can be done if the agent "resigns" when the principal becomes incapacitated, hence the need to have alternates designated.

Springing DPOAs. There are two common types of DPOAs. The first type becomes effective as soon as it is executed. The second type, called a "springing" DPOA, becomes effective at the principal's incapacity. Some attorneys recommend that a physician or a "trusted committee" of three of the client's trusted friends and relatives should be empowered to determine when the power of attorney becomes effective. It might contain a clause similar to the one that follows:

EFFECTIVE DATE OF POWER OF ATTORNEY. This Power of Attorney shall become effective on the date that any two (2) of the following named persons has delivered to my agent(s) a dated statement, signed under penalty of perjury, that, in their opinion, (i) I am incapacitated, and (ii) that it is their opinion that my interests would be best served by having my agent(s) act for me as my attorney-in-fact under this durable power of attorney. The persons are: [followed by the identification of the persons selected].

To be valid, of course, any DPOA must be executed prior to the principal's incapacity. To ensure competent execution, many advisers recommend the preparation of a DPOA for an older client at the time the will is prepared.

Advantages of the DPOA. The DPOA has several advantages over the other devices designed to manage an incapacitated person's property. Compared to a guardianship or conservatorship, the DPOA is less expensive to create and to administer. The non-springing type can avoid the necessity of a court-held incompetency proceeding, an event that can be painful and embarrassing to all parties, especially the proposed conservatee. Compared with the living trust, the DPOA is also less expensive to create and administer. Some individuals who refuse to set up a trust may be willing to execute a DPOA, because of its relative simplicity. Yet a trust can continue long after the settlor's death, whereas a DPOA, being based on agency law, must terminate when the principal dies. It may be durable but it is not that durable.

The trust and the DPOA need not be considered alternatives. Greater flexibility may result if a DPOA authorizes the agent to add newly acquired property (by gift, inheritance, etc.) to the principal's partially living trust, or to fund an existing unfunded revocable living trust (a "standby trust") with the principal's assets, at the onset of incapacity. Thereafter, the agent may perform other duties that were not given to the trustee, including making gifts or disclaimers, and signing the principal's personal tax returns.

Regarding the power of the agent to make gifts, one court has ruled that failure to explicitly include that power in the document will totally frustrate gift planning. In that case, the agent did make gifts before the principal's death. Relying on Virginia's narrow construction of powers-of-attorney law, the appellate court treated the gift as revocable at the time of the principal's death, resulting in inclusion of gifted assets in the gross estate under §§ 2036(a) and 2038.[11] However, in a more recent Virginia case, the Tax Court allowed gifts by an agent because Virginia law authorizes agents to make gifts "in accordance with the principal's personal history of making or joining in lifetime gifts."[12]

Drawbacks of the DPOA. The DPOA has a potential drawback for the agent. If the agent dies first, the IRS might claim that the principal's property part of the agent's gross estate on the theory that the agent held a general power of appointment over the property. The fact that the agent has a fiduciary duty to use the power only for the best interest of the principal should be enough to prevent this argument from being successful.

A non-tax drawback to the DPOA concerns its acceptance. Certain financial institutions may be unwilling to honor the DPOA if they cannot satisfy themselves that it is currently valid. The power, they reason, may already have been revoked by the principal or the principal may be dead. Due to their uncertainty about the validity of custom-drafted DPOAs, they may insist on the use of their own form. The industry's increasing use of the DPOA should substantially lessen these concerns. The attorney can minimize acceptance problems with careful and specific custom drafting of enumerated powers, and by having the principal periodically re-execute the DPOA to prevent it from appearing outdated. Nevertheless, some institutions refuse to accept a DPOA, and some banks and the IRS will, but might require the use of their own forms.

Other helpful techniques to maximize acceptability include a provision in the document that empowers the agent to bring legal action against a recalcitrant third party and indemnifies the third party when it acts in reliance on the document and the agent's instructions. However, pursuing legal action can be expensive and time consuming. Finally, the person, while still competent, can show the document to banks, insurance companies, health care providers, etc., to find out whether it will be accepted, and to stop dealing with those institutions that refuse. New York has a statute making it unlawful to refuse to recognize the New York statutory form DPOA and indemnifying banks that honor them. California's statute permits one to bring suit to compel the honoring of a statutory durable power and specifies that a refusal is unreasonable if the sole reason for the refusal is that it is not on the third party's (e.g., a bank's) own form.[13]

The second non-tax drawback of the DPOA is that it can be misused. Lawyers will attest to situations where agents have used a disabled client's property in a manner clearly contrary to the principal's best interest. Although such behavior is actionable, it is rarely challenged. Because the DPOA delegates very fundamental property rights, a person considering signing one should first think long and hard about the possible consequences.

Personal Care During Incapacity

Who should the person nominate to provide personal care in the event of his or her incapacity? How should one express the kind and degree of care? Documentation is needed to assure that one's wishes are carried out when he or she is no longer able to attend to these matters.

Society generally expect a spouse to step into that role if he or she is able to do so. Next come other family members, especially adult children. However, the children may lead busy lives and may not be capable or willing to do all the work required. This problem is even more likely to arise for a person in an advanced stage of incapacity, such as extreme mental confusion coupled with incontinence. Prior to this degree of impairment, the individual may simply need home delivery of meals, housekeeping services, or adult day care, all of which are commercially available. While these services are not inexpensive, some programs are government subsidized. Services can be arranged for a fee by a "private geriatric care manager," who is often a social worker or nurse. Helpful sources of information include: County and local departments for the aging, for referrals on services for elders; the National Association of Area Agencies on Aging, which has an "elder care locator" (http://www.n4a.org/); the National Association of Professional Geriatric Care Managers (http://www.caremanager.org/); the National Academy of Elder Law Attorneys (http://www.naela.com/); and the Children of Aging Parents (http://www.caps4caregivers.org/), which is designed to provide "caregivers of the elderly or chronically ill with reliable information, referrals and support, and to heighten public awareness that the health of the family caregivers is essential to ensure quality care of the nation's growing elderly population."

Nursing home. As a person gets older, it may be wise to visit residential health care facilities for the elderly. Such facilities vary widely in cost, extent of services offered, and the degree of incapacity permitted. At one end of the spectrum is the traditional nursing home, which offers complete care, but is quite expensive. Some critics feel entering a nursing home is tantamount to "a life sentence to mental and physical imprisonment," where patients lose nearly all of their independence in a dehumanizing environment.

Assisted living. Other less structured facilities offer a new and increasingly popular style of housing called assisted living for elderly people without serious medical problems. Private apartments are provided, as well as meals, laundry, housekeeping, social activities, transportation, and regular visits by nurses. Such facilities usually cost considerably less than nursing homes and offer the greatest degree of independence possible.[14]

Life care facility. Finally, one other type of organization called a life-care facility offers, at a hefty price, the right to lifetime occupancy of an apartment in a residential health-care facility, which also provides, on the premises, all meals and around-the-clock nursing, medical, and hospital services.

Some figures from the U.S. Census Bureau shows how the percentage of elderly living in nursing homes increases dramatically after the age of 84. In 2000, approximately 1.6 million people over the age of 65 lived in nursing homes. The percentage residing in nursing homes by age group were as follows: 1.1% of the 65 to 74 year olds; 6.1% of the 75 to 84 year olds; and 24.5% of those 85 years of age and older.[15]

Guardian or conservator. Similar to the procedure for selecting the guardian of a minor child, the procedure for selecting the person who will care for an incapacitated adult is usually undertaken in the county probate court after a noticed hearing. Some states call this fiduciary a *guardian*, while others use the term *conservator*. In any case, the court selects the fiduciary after a formal hearing. In some states, such as California, a conservator is a person appointed by the court to manage the personal care and the property of an adult (called the *conservatee*) who is unable to provide for his or her own personal needs and/or is unable to manage his or her financial resources, whereas a *guardian* is appointed to perform such services for a minor. In other states, such as New York, the term guardian is used whether the incapacitated person is an infant or an adult.[16] The UPC and California Probate Code are similar, however it does not appear that the UPC uses the term conservatee, rather the person who has a conservator or guardian appointed is referred to as the protected person.[17]

Delegation of health care decisions. Until recently, people have not had the ability to delegate the power to make medical decisions. Today, almost all states recognize an individual's ability either to delegate important medical decisions or at least to state in writing what those decisions should be.

An *advance directive* is a general term that refers to written instructions about a person's desire concerning medical care in the event the person becomes unable to speak for his or herself. The state laws may differ somewhat but all generally authorize the use of advance directives. The two major types of advance directives are the living will and the medical power of attorney.

A *living will* is a type of advance directive in which a person puts in writing his or her wishes about medical treatment should he or she be unable to communicate. These generally address end of life issues. State law may define when the living will goes into effect, or the triggering event may be set forth in the document, e.g., a diagnosis by two physicians that a condition is terminal and likely to result in death with ten days. Depending upon the jurisdiction, the document may be called a directive to physician, a declaration under the [state's] natural death act, a medical directive, or a durable power for health care. One can download state-specific advance directives in PDF format from Partnership for Caring's website <http://www.partnershipforcaring.org/>.

Terri Schiavo case. The need to state medical choices clearly and in writing is dramatically illustrated by Terri Schiavo's tragic story that starts with her collapse on February 25, 1990 and ends, more or less, with her death on March 31, 2005. Apparently, problems associated with an eating disorder caused her heart to stop, depriving her brain of oxygen. In the fifteen years that followed, a court battle raged between Terri's husband, Michael, and her parents Bob and Mary Schindler. Michael, contending that Terri had told him that she would not want to live if she had to be kept alive artificially, sought to have her feeding tube removed; her parents, contending that there was hope for meaningful recovery, sought to have Michael removed as her personal guardian so that the feeding tube could be kept in place. The courts, based on the evidence and the law, consistently sided with Michael, as did most medical experts and the vast majority of the public but that did not stop the matter from being taken up by Washington lawmakers, the President of the United States, the Governor of Florida, and the Florida legislature.

It was reminiscent of the 1990 U.S. Supreme Court decision, *Cruzan v. Missouri*.[18] A victim of an automobile accident that occurred on January 11, 1983, Nancy Cruzan remained for seven years in a persistent vegetative state, with functioning respiratory and circulatory systems but little else. She could not swallow food, she was unable to recognize her relatives, and there was no reasonable hope of any improvement in her condition. Unlike the Terri Schiavo situation, Nancy's family was united and sought to let her die naturally by withdrawing her feeding tube. However, the State of Missouri would not allow it, despite the fact that a year before the accident, Nancy had told a friend that "if sick or injured she would not wish to continue her life unless she could live at least halfway normally." On appeal, the U.S. Supreme Court affirmed, approving the Missouri requirement that the family would have to show "clear and convincing evidence" of Nancy's wishes to remove life sustaining equipment, something the jury determined that the Cruzans did not establish.

After the Supreme Court decision, the Cruzans requested another hearing in the local court, claiming they had new evidence showing that Nancy would not wish to live under the conditions that were keeping her alive. Before the hearing, the state attorney general withdrew as a party to the case. This meant that there was no longer anyone to oppose removing Nancy's feeding tube; and the court granted the family's request. On December 26, 1990, Nancy died at age 33, twelve days after the tube was removed. Terri Schiavo's journey had barely begun. In many ways it was even more heart breaking than the Cruzan case because it was fought by a family divided.

The "clear and convincing evidence" standard of proof will often be difficult to meet without documentation. Obviously, a durable power of attorney for health care and/or a living will would supply this evidence.

Durable power of attorney for health care. Like the durable power of attorney for property (DPOA), the durable power of attorney for health care (DPOAHC) appoints a person to serve as agent to make decisions on behalf of the principal. However, the documents are different in three important respects. First, the DPOAHC concerns medical, not property decisions. Examples of medical decisions listed in this type of "advance directive" include the power to secure the placement in or removal from a medical facility, to withhold future medical treatment, to use or not use medication, to perform or not perform surgery, and the power to use or not use artificial life-sustaining methods, such as respiration, nourishment, and hydration. As one might expect, this last power is quite controversial, and some legal commentators have defended it ardently. Reflecting an increasingly popular dissatisfaction with the zealous use of artificial life-sustaining methods, some have argued that rapid advances in medical technology, combined with the implicit premise of medicine to "do everything" for patients, violate patients' rights. These advances in medicine may actually condemn the very sick to an existence void of relationship in antiseptic hospital-like settings, an existence that many feel is worse than death.

Designating a surrogate with the power to terminate life support can be helpful in situations where the physician in charge refuses to act. One study has shown that physicians are reluctant to terminate life support in cases where the patient would take a relatively long time to die, where the life support became necessary because of medical errors, and in cases where the patient has already been on life support for a relatively long period of time.[19]

The DPOAHC differs from the DPOA in that the DPOAHC is always a springing power, while the DPOA can be non-springing. Thus, the DPOAHC becomes effective only on the principal's incapacity, that is, on his or her inability to make health care decisions. The DPOAHC does not apply just to situations where the principal is terminally ill, but to all situations where the principal is unable to give "informed consent" with respect to a particular medical decision.

While it is possible to include the legal content of a DPOAHC within a DPOA document they are usually drafted as separate documents. They involve very different situations, different evolving law, and possibly different agent. In addition, many attorneys prefer to use a preprinted state medical association form for health care because of its widespread acceptance by the medical profession. In contrast, a custom-drafted form can generate decision-making delays when a hospital requires its own lawyers to carefully evaluate it.

The DPOAHC is statutorily recognized in almost every state. State law varies in terms of both the scope of the authority of the attorney in fact to act on behalf of the principal and the protection afforded to health care providers who act on those instructions. Some states such as California have statutes permitting health care providers to assume that a DPOAHC is valid in the absence of knowledge to the contrary. Offering some support, the American Medical Association has ruled that it is appropriate for doctors to withdraw life-supporting, artificial feeding systems from hopelessly comatose patients.

One drawback of the DPOAHC concerns the fact that it is so powerful. It can place reluctant family members in the difficult position of having to make critical life or death decisions, ones they may regrettably relive in their minds over and over, long after the crisis has ended. Nevertheless, the durable power of attorney for health care has become one of the most popular estate planning devices.

Living will. The DPOAHC has become widely accepted in the United States. Before then, most states only recognized some variation of the living will, which typically addresses just one of the two features of the DPOAHC. Typically the living will detail those health care interventions that the person does or does not wish to be subjected to in situations when he or she is no longer capable of making those decisions, but did not designate an agent to make medical decisions for the person signing the document.

When compared to the DPOAHC, living wills have at least five limitations. First, a traditional living will does not appoint a surrogate decision-maker, which restricts its flexibility considerably, especially in view of the rapid advances in medical technology. Second, living wills are typically very brief, covering only a few possible outcomes, mostly in the area of life-sustaining treatment. No living will, no matter how detailed, can spell out all of the possible treatment decisions that may be needed. Third, most living will statutes apply only to terminal patients, not those who are just incurably ill, such as a person in a persistent vegetative state. Many states require that death be "imminent." Fourth, the language of living wills is usually quite vague, failing to define important terms, leaving the physician and the family to disagree over proper care. Finally, a number of states' living will statutes provide that a physician is obligated to comply with the directives in a living will concerning withdrawal or withholding of life-sustaining procedures. In the event the physician chooses not to comply, he or she must transfer the patient to another physician.

With regard to the second and fourth limitations, more and more attorneys are drafting quite specific living wills (and DPOAHCs, for that matter). For example, the client may be asked to enter preferences in writing in a matrix-table depicting alternative medical scenarios and procedures. The rows of the matrix might list ten to fifteen medical procedures, such as invasive diagnostic tests; CPR; pain medication; artificial nutrition and hydration; mechanical breathing, and the like. The columns of the matrix might list alternative physical scenarios, such as coma or persistent vegetative state with no chance of regaining awareness, irreversible brain damage or disease, irreversible brain damage or disease combined with terminal illness, coma with small chance of recovery and greater chance of surviving with severe brain damage, etc. Then, for each cell in the matrix-table, the client would insert one of several letters signifying a desired action, such as U = uncertain; N = do not want procedure; T = yes, try procedure but have it stopped if no clear improvement is shown; and Y = yes, try procedure for as long as possible. The danger in documenting this detail is that the person may thoughtlessly and hastily fill in the blanks on a written instrument that may wind up being the only hard evidence available, thereby ruling out the possibility of an alternative choice which may reflect the careful contemplation of the person's sincere loved ones.

Miscellaneous factors. In some states, planners recommend that clients execute both a living will and a DPOAHC, particularly in states where DPOAHCs are not written to include the main characteristic of the living will. Finally, in their attempt at coordination, more and more states are adopting integrated statutes that deal with both types of advance directive.

Several states, including Virginia, recognize a variation on the living will called the *directive to physicians*, giving instructions with regard to the use of life-sustaining treatment. The directive to physicians has been largely rendered obsolete in most other states by the common acceptance of the DPOAHC.

Whatever documents are used, they should be updated periodically, for three reasons. First, state law may require it. Second, the person's wishes may have changed. And third, the planner should make sure the documents remain consistent with the rapidly changing law in this area.

END OF LIFE DECISIONS

Natural death directive. Many states have what are called Natural Death Acts that affirm a person's right to die without life prolonging measures being taken if the person requests such in writing.[20] Generally, this matter can be addressed in a person's advance directive for health care regardless of whether the state of domicile has enacted one of these statutes. Only Oregon has gone so far as to authorize physician assisted suicide; the "Oregon Death with Dignity Act" was approved by the voters in 1994 and has survived numerous court challenges. However in November of 2001, U. S. Attorney General John Ashcroft, claiming the Federal Controlled Substances Act preempted the Oregon law, initiated a policy aimed at prosecuting physicians who prescribe life ending drugs under the Oregon law. Physicians in Oregon obtained an injunction preventing the enforcement of the Justice Department's policy, and the Ninth Circuit Court of Appeals upheld the injunction. However, the Justice Department appealed, and the U. S. Supreme Court granted certiorari, setting the matter to be heard during the Court's autumn of 2005 session, with a decision likely during the summer of 2006.[21]

Do-not-resuscitate orders. A person with a terminal illness, especially if elderly and in pain, might request what is called a "do-not-resuscitate order." This order is a written directive from the person's physician to all medical professionals, telling them not to perform cardiopulmonary resuscitation (CPR) in the event of heart failure, i.e., do not perform procedures to restart the person's heart if it stops beating. Without the order, medical personnel are likely to implement CPR by mouth to mouth breathing and rhythmic chest compression, by electric shock to the chest, or injection of drugs that stimulate the heart muscle. If the person is in a hospital or nursing home, the order will be noted on the person's chart and the staff should all be aware of it. If the person is not in a facility, he or she might want to wear a special do-not-resuscitate bracelet intended to let medical professionals know that an order has been signed. Most states, perhaps all, have laws making it clear that honoring the order does not constitute the offense of aiding suicide. A designated health care agent, acting on behalf of the disabled principal, has the authority to request a do-not-resuscitate order unless the durable power specifically withholds this authority.

Hospice. Hospice is the term given to specialized care given to dying patients and their loved ones. With hospice care, the focus is not on curing the patient but rather on allowing the person to die pain-free and with dignity. Trained hospice caregivers, some paid and some as volunteers, work with other medical personnel to ease the stress on the dying patient and his or her family. Most, if not all, of the services provided by hospice are covered if the patient qualifies for Medicare. In addition, most private health plans cover the care, and almost all states have programs that cover the care for some patients that lack Medicare coverage. Generally, reimbursement sources, whether government or private, require a prognosis of six months or less if the illness runs its normal course. Obviously, if the patient lives longer than six months the care continues if it is needed.

The National Hospice and Palliative Care Organization (NHPCO) is the oldest and largest nonprofit membership organization representing hospice care programs in the United States. The American Hospice Foundation (AHF), another nonprofit, supports programs that serve the needs of terminally ill and grieving individuals. It sponsors workshops, the creation of educational materials, and research related to end-of-life care. While NHPCO and AHF are nonprofit charitable organizations, many of the local programs that provide the hospice care operate for profit, thus donations to NHPCO and AHF are tax deductible whereas a donation to the local program might not be. Nevertheless, it takes special nurturing people to perform the front-line work of these caregivers and most people who have used their services are profoundly grateful.

Rest In Peace. Making plans for disposing of one's body after death is difficult for most people. Funeral homes label it as nicely as can be with "pre-need" packages. The idea is a good one as it lessens the likelihood of grieving family members being talked into spending more than is reasonable. Rather than spending money on burial or cremation, one should consider donation. There are many programs that will accept the body for medical training and research. Often, it is organ and tissue not suitable for transplant that is taken for medical research in areas such as Alzheimer's, cancer, Parkinson's disease.

Most programs pay the cost of transporting the body from anywhere in the United States to the medical facility; after the intended use is completed the body is cremated and, depending on arrangements made with the deceased or with the family, the ashes are returned to the family or other disposition made.

All states have enacted the Uniform Anatomical Gift Act (UAGA). One should also consider donating organs for transplant. There is a waiting list for hearts, livers, and kidneys. Corneas are used to improve sight for persons with damaged eyes and skin is used for burn victims. Almost all states have an organ donation registry; over half of these are through the state's department of motor vehicles. Many of these state programs are run by United Network for Organ Sharing (UNOS), a nonprofit organization. According to the UNOS website, at the end of 2004, there were approximately 90,000 waiting for transplants yet the number of transplants performed that year was about 27,000. On average, 17 people die each day while waiting for a transplant.[22] UNOS's simple motto is "Donate Life." There are not many gifts greater.

CONCLUSION

This chapter has described miscellaneous lifetime estate planning techniques, most of them directed at how to prepare for possible incapacity, addressing such issues as the importance of selecting, in advance of need, the persons to make medical decisions and manage property. With proper planning, not only will the appropriate persons be designated, but the documents will also give guidance to those surrogate decisions makers making their job easier.

The next chapter considers the tasks that must be addressed almost immediately after a person dies. The family and estate representative must make numerous arrangements such as letting the decedent's friends know of his or her passing, following the decedent's wishes regarding burial or cremation, and perhaps planning a memorial service. In addition, tax matters must be attended to, such as the decedent's last income tax returns, and if there is a trust or estate, fiduciary tax returns. For large estates, there is the estate tax return with various elections that must be considered.

QUESTIONS AND PROBLEMS

1. (a) Describe the attributes of an effective parental guardian, executor, and trustee. (b) Why are they different?

2. Describe the legal alternatives available to provide for an orphaned child's financial care. Be sure to mention the advantages and disadvantages of each.

3. In planning for one's own possible incapacity, what are the main estate planning alternatives for taking care of financial matters? Describe the advantages and disadvantages of each.

4. Your 86-year-old mentally competent client wishes to plan for her incapacity but refuses to immediately transfer her assets to anyone. Is planning impossible, or does this refusal merely create a particular problem?

5. Describe the family trust and the trade-off involved in determining the age of distribution to young adult beneficiaries.

6. At Partnership for Caring's website you will find a wealth of information about end-of-life issues. To answer the questions that follow, use the site at <http://www.partnershipforcaring.org>. (a) The Minnesota Health-care Directive has three parts, name them and state their respective purposes. Can a relative of the principal serve as a witness? Can the agent serve as a witness? (b) What are Vermont's two advanced care directives called? Are they alternative documents or is it recommend that both be used? Do both create an agency? Do either nominate a conservator?

7. At Partnership for Caring's website you will find state specific living wills and durable powers of attorney for health care. Visit the site to download the "advance directive package" appropriate for your state of domicile. You will first need to download Adobe Acrobat Reader if it is not already on your computer. See <http://www.adobe.com/products/acrobat/readstep2.html> to obtain a free copy of the program.

8. To answer the questions that follow, visit the United Network for Organ Sharing 's website at <http://www.unos.org/>. Click on the Newsroom, then fact sheet, and finally Donor Designation to find a table on state registration programs. (a) In your state, where does one register? (b) What is meant by "first person consent legislation?" (c) How many states have not passed first person consent legislation? How many of those appear to be moving towards passage? Which state has neither passed such legislation nor has a registry?

9. To answer the questions that follow, visit the website of National Hospice and Palliative Care Organization (NHPCO) at <http://www.nhpco.org/>. (a) From the history of hospice section: what is the origin of the term "hospice"? In modern times, when was it first applied to a facility that provided care for dying patients? (b) At the NHPCO home page, click on "Inside the NHPCO" to find the "awards and contests" section, and finally, the 2004 winning essay by Becky Lindenmyer, "Why do I do this? Reflections of a Hospice Social Worker." What gift did Max give his wife?

10. To answer the questions that follow, visit the American Hospice Foundation website at <http://www.americanhospice.org/index.htm>. (a) In the Free Articles section, open "Debunking the Myths of Hospice." What is "myth # 9" and what is the related reality? (b) Using the site's IICN MegaSearch feature put in the term "palliative care" to find the article "What is Palliative Care?" How does the World Health Organization (WHO) answer the question? When a hospital children's cancer program called its palliative care program the "advanced cancer support program" who objected and why?

ANSWERS TO THE QUESTIONS AND PROBLEMS *(odd numbered only)*

1. (a) Attributes of a good parental guardian, executor, and trustee. Parental Guardian: (1) Integrity, maturity, physical stamina and experience needed to be a permanent parent; (2) strong concern for the minor's welfare, and (3) a stable personal situation. Executor: (1) Longevity; (2) skill in managing legal and financial affairs; (3) familiarity with the testator's estate and wishes; (4) integrity and loyalty. Trustee: Same as those for executor, except greater weight on skill in financial management. (b) The attributes are different because of the differing responsibilities. Parental skills are most important for a personal guardian. On the other hand, property management skills are most important for an executor and trustee, with even greater significance for the trustee, because of the possible time span of the job.

3. Alternative in property planning for incapacity:
   (a) Conservatorship: Advantage: Substantial court supervision.
   Conservatorship: Disadvantages: (1) Relatively expensive; (2) inflexible; and (3) public. (b) Trust: Advantages: (1) Private; (2) flexible; and (3) potentially less expensive. Trust: Disadvantage: Not court supervised. (c) Durable Power of Attorney for property: Advantages: (1) Private; (2) flexible; and (3) potentially less expensive. Durable Power Disadvantage: Not court supervised. NOTE: The trust and the durable power of attorney for property need not be considered alternatives; they can be used by the same person.

5. The family trust is a single trust originally for the benefit of two or more beneficiaries, at least one of whom is a minor. Corpus is typically not divided into separate shares for the beneficiaries until the youngest reaches a certain age, such as 21. Selecting that age involves a tradeoff between inequality and delay. The older the predetermined age, the more equitable is the distribution, but the longer the older beneficiaries may have to wait for that distribution.

7. The Partnership for Caring website is an excellent resource. I recommend assigning this task as it is worth reviewing the advance directives with students.

9. The American Hospice Foundation site is well worth the visit.

ENDNOTES

1. California Probate Code § 15642(b)(6)(B)

2. *Pollock v. Phillips* 41 S.E. 2d 242 (W. Va., 1991).

3. In *Marsman v. Nasca* 573 N.E. 2d 1025 (Mass. App. 1991), the court exonerated an attorney-trustee's "abuse of discretion," where a trust clause exculpated the trustee from liability except for "willful neglect or fraud." For a contrary holding see, *First Alabama Bank of Huntsville v. Spraquins* 515 S. 2d 962 (Ala. 1987).

4. "How much sharper than a serpent's tooth it is to have a thankless child." *King Lear*, Act 1, Scene V.

5. 42 U.S.C. § 1396p(c)(2)(B)(iv).

6. 42 U.S.C. § 1396p(d)(4)(A).

7. 42 USC § 1396. The Omnibus Budget Reconciliation Act of 1993, besides increasing the period from thirty months, made several other restrictive changes, reflecting Congressional interest in discouraging spend down planning.

8. See Table 2b at: <http://www.census.gov/ipc/www/usinterimproj/>.

9. For example, see California Probate Code § 2590-95.

10. Modified version of the sample form contained in Charles M. Hamann. "Durable Powers of Attorney," *Trusts and Estates*, February 1983, pp. 30-31.

11. *Estate of Casey v. Commissioner*, 948 F2d. 895 (1991). Also see LR 9231003.

12. *J. Ridenour Estate*, 46 TCM 1850 (1992).

13. California Civil Code § 2480.5.

14. Wall Street Journal articles on December 3 and 4, 1992. Both on page A1.

15. See U.S. Census Bureau Census 2000 Brief, "The 65 Years and Over Population:2000" at <http://www.census.gov/prod/2001pubs/c2kbr01-10.pdf>.

16. NY Consolidated Laws, Chapter 27, Mental Hygiene, Art. 81.

17. UPC §§ 5-103(3), 5-103(6), and 5-103(7)

18. 110 S.Ct. 2841 (1990)

19. *Lancet*, Sept. 11, 1993, p. 645.

20. See for instance Washington Codes, Chapter 70.122 RCW Natural Death Act and Idaho Statutes, Title 39, Chapter 45, The Medical Consent and Natural Death Act

21. *Gonzales v. Oregon*, No. 04-623; originally *Ashcroft v. Oregon*, the case takes on the name of Ashcroft's successor, Attorney General Alberto R. Gonzales.

22. <http://www.unos.org/helpSaveALife/promoteOrganDonation/>.

CHAPTER 16

Postmortem Planning

OVERVIEW

The estate planning process does not end at the client's death. Assets must be marshaled, conserved, insured, and held or distributed by the decedent's representatives. Tasks are performed by family, executors, trustees, accountants, attorneys, and others. After a short discourse on attending to various non-tax related matters, the chapter focuses on postmortem tax compliance and planning devices that reduce income taxes, including estate expense elections, choice of tax year, and distribution-planning strategies. Finally, the chapter presents planning devices that reduce estate taxes, including the alternate valuation date, the use of disclaimers, and the QTIP election.

TRANSITIONS

A death in the family is sure to result in transitions. Depending on the circumstances, the survivors may feel a mixture of grief, sadness, loss, and, if there has been a long period of suffering, some relief. Professional advisors must be ready to ease the burdens associated with such trying times without being too cold and detached. While the focus for estate planning advisors is likely to be on property matters, one must also be aware of what the surviving family is going through and their needs. The greater the extent of pre-death planning, the less will be the need to collect financial information needed to carry out tasks such as changing accounts and determining date of death values. The family will appreciate the professional advisors who are able to take on tasks without burdening the family with multiple requests for information during a time when they might rather not deal with these matters.

Survivors' Needs

Recognize that the survivors, whether a surviving spouse, parents, or children, generally need a time to grieve. Hopefully, decisions concerning burial or cremation, and whether to have a service, were made by the decedent. Nevertheless, dealing with estate matters is likely to take a backseat to these very personal matters whether elaborate or simple. If hospice care was initiate before the person died, the hospice service person is likely to continue working with the family for as long as they seek the help. At the appropriate time, the advisors must help the estate representative take control of estate matters.

Securing Property

One of the first things that must be done is to secure the decedent's property. How and by whom depends on how title was held. If the person was collecting social security, the local office must be notified. Since social security is paid "forward" the last payment has to be returned. Likewise, if the decedent was receiving a pension, the payer must be notified. Depending on the circumstances, the personal representative might want to cancel magazine and newspaper subscriptions, cable television and cell phone service, and the like.

Initiate the transfer process. Without repeating entire chapters, obviously the trustee or successor trustee takes charge of trust property, the nominated executor might need to obtain temporary letters of administration if such are necessary to sell an asset readily declining in value, e.g., decedent's medical practice, and surviving join tenants usually need not hurry as they already are on title. In some cases, summary procedures can be used, e.g., small estate claiming by persons entitled, and in others a probate may need to be initiated.

Marshal assets. The estate representative must quickly become familiar with the estate assets to assure that property insurance is in place, that the property is as physically secure as is possible, and that holders of intangible property are aware of the transition. This might be important if there was an agent under a durable financial power different from the nominated personal representative. The agency ends with the death of the principle, but the agent continues to have apparent power to deal with the property until third parties who have dealt with the agent, such as the decedent's stock broker, are informed that the agency has come to an end.

Determining the date of death value of investment assets, and certain personal assets such as the home, is important as this will determine the income tax basis for the assets. Generally, it is easier to collect this information if it is done within several months of the owner's death.

Collect insurance. This is generally done by the beneficiary of the insurance policy. The needed contact information is probably in a file with the insurance policy. Occasionally a policy is misplaced and unknown to the beneficiary and the estate representative, in which case either a premium notice or an annual statement from the company alerts the representative of the existence of the policy. Once the beneficiary is identified, he or she follows the insurance company's procedures for obtaining the proceeds. Usually, one submits a certified death certificate and proof that the person submitting the claim is indeed the beneficiary.

Awareness. Professional advisors should be aware that most surviving spouses and adult children want the people they work with to acknowledge their loss. Rather than starting the first post-death meeting with a checklist of what must be done and how to do it, it is important to take the time to express condolences. If the advisor had a long relationship with the deceased, remembrances might be in order. The best advice is to take the first meeting slowly, letting the family members signal when they are ready to proceed.

Obviously, there are limits to how long one can take. Wait too long and the nominated executor may find someone else seeking appointment. A trustee who fails to keep beneficiaries informed or who delays distributions beyond what is reasonable may end up in court as beneficiaries seek his or her removal. Of course, hardly anyone is more impatient than the IRS. Failure to pay taxes, file returns, and/or obtain extensions, may result in the personal representative being personally liable for taxes, interest, and penalties.

TAX RETURNS AFTER DEATH

We already know that the death of an individual may trigger estate and inheritance taxes. But can the transfer of a decedent's property be done free of income tax? Will the death of an income-earning individual terminate the obligation to pay taxes on all income received thereafter? Of course, the answer to both questions is no, because income ordinarily subject to taxation will be received by survivors, estates, and trusts. If income ordinarily subject to taxation is being received, you can be sure that the Internal Revenue Code imposes a tax on that income in the year it is received.

Usually, income tax returns, and perhaps estate or inheritance tax returns, must be filed after the person has died. This section will introduce principles of postmortem federal tax compliance, that is, the completion of federal tax returns and the payment of federal taxes on income and on property of a decedent.

Transfer Taxes

With regard to transfer taxes, the decedent's representatives may be required to file a state inheritance or estate tax return, and a federal estate tax return. The federal return is due nine months after the date of death. As discussed previously, a federal estate tax return must be filed if the total gross estate plus adjusted taxable gifts equals or exceeds the estate applicable exclusion amount (AEA) for the year of death (e.g., equal to, or over, $2 million for the years 2006 to 2008). For example, a decedent who dies in 2007, leaving a gross estate of $1,300,000 and adjusted taxable gifts of $800,000 must file a return because the sum exceeds the AEA by $100,000. Filing is required even if no estate tax will be due, as in the case where the entire estate is left to a surviving spouse or debts drop the taxable estate below the AEA. Given the increase in the AEA over the past several years, a very small portion of estates (about 1%) will have to file estate tax returns.

Income Taxes

For many estates, the personal representatives will be required to file at least two sets of state and federal income tax returns. First, the decedent's final income tax return will be reported on Federal Form 1040 and on the comparable state income tax form (unless the state of domicile was one of the few that has no state income tax). Only seven states have no state income tax: Alaska, Florida, Nevada, South Dakota, Texas, Washington, and Wyoming. New Hampshire and Tennessee tax dividend and interest income but not other types of income, such as wages and rents. The decedent's last income tax returns will cover all income for the last tax year up to, and including, the date of death.

If the decedent leaves a probate estate or a living trust, an estate fiduciary income tax return, Form 1041 and its state counterpart, will be filed for each tax year of the estate's existence. The fiduciary return for the first year will report all income starting with the day after the decedent's date of death to the end of the first tax year. When the estate is terminated, usually by final distribution, the last estate income tax return will be filed for a "short" year, from the beginning of the tax year to the date of distribution. After the estate terminates, the beneficiaries will report the income from distributed estate property on their own tax returns.

The following example summarizes these federal income tax rules and assumes that all taxpayers report taxes on a calendar year basis; that is, their tax year begins January 1 and ends December 31. Actually, an estate need not use a calendar year. Planning the use of a fiscal rather than a calendar year will be discussed later in the chapter.

EXAMPLE 16 - 1. Farley, a widower, died on May 12, 2005. In his will, Farley left 100 shares of XYZ stock outright to his son Jordan, and the residue of his estate in trust for the benefit of his granddaughter Sheila. The date of final estate distribution to Jordan and to the trust was February 25, 2007. The following post-death tax returns were filed. All income earned by the decedent from January 1 through May 12, 2005 was reported by the executor on the decedent's final income tax return, Form 1040. All income earned by the estate between May 13 and December 31, 2005 was reported by the executor on the first estate income tax return, Form 1041. The executor filed a second Form 1041 return for all estate income for the entire year 2006, and a third for income earned during the period from January 1 to February 25, 2007. Jordan reported on his Form 1040 all income received on the stock after February 25, 2007. Trust distributable income, or DNI, earned after that date will either be reported by the trust on Form 1041 or by Sheila on her Form 1040, to the extent the income is actually distributed to her.

All capital gains income on trust property will be reported by the trust except in the trust's last year, when these gains will be "carried out" and reported by the beneficiaries.

A joint return may be filed for a decedent and the surviving spouse for the year of death, covering income of the decedent to the date of death and income of the spouse for the entire year.[1] Alternatively, returns may be filed for each spouse separately. In most situations, filing jointly will save total taxes in the same way it does when both spouses are alive. The greater the difference between the two spousal incomes, the greater the tax usually saved by filing jointly. The surviving spouse will also be permitted to enjoy the lower rates applicable to joint returns for two years after the decedent's death, provided that he or she (a) has not remarried and (b) maintains a home for one or more dependent children.[2]

Reducing income taxes. Some postmortem planning strategies are primarily undertaken to reduce income taxes. They include various expense elections, selection of the estate tax year, and distribution planning. Before examining these techniques, let us survey three tax principles on which most of them will be based.

First, income tax is reduced when taxable income can be spread among taxpaying entities. Proper pre-death planning can result in the creation of additional taxpaying entities after the client's death. These tax entities can include the estate, several trusts (with at least one trust for each beneficiary), and the beneficiaries themselves. After death, proper timing of distributions among these entities can often save significant tax dollars, as we shall see.

A second tax principle on which postmortem income tax planning is based is the notion of the conduit. The conduit principle prevents double taxation of estate or trust income. It is derived from the concept of distributable net income, or DNI, which is roughly equal to the estate or trust's fiduciary accounting income. DNI constitutes the maximum amount of income taxable to the beneficiaries, as well as the maximum amount deductible by the estate or trust. The amount taxable to an estate or trust roughly equals its total income, including capital gains and losses, reduced by the distribution deduction, which roughly equals the lesser of the amount distributed or its DNI. Thus, a trust or estate that distributes all of its income will be taxed only on its capital gains. Consequently, under the conduit principle, DNI earned by an estate or trust which is distributed to the beneficiaries in the year earned will be taxed to the beneficiaries and not to the estate or trust, which simply acts as a conduit for delivering income from the source to the beneficiaries. Conversely, any DNI retained by the estate or trust will not be offset by a distribution deduction, which will make that DNI taxable to the trust or estate rather than to the beneficiaries.

A third tax principle on which postmortem income tax planning is based is that in the year in which an estate or trust makes its final distribution, all income, including capital gains, will be carried out to and taxed to the beneficiaries. Thus in its termination year, a trust or estate will have no taxable income.

Expense Elections Available to the Executor

During administration, the executor is able to make several informal elections with regard to estate expenses. We will refer to the executor's ability to make elections because the executor is the person having that legal authority. Of course, most executors rely on their attorney or accountant to apprize them of the tax alternatives. These elections include the medical expense election, the administration expense and losses election, and the election to waive the executor's commission. They are covered next.

Medical expense. Any of the decedent's medical expenses, unreimbursed by insurance or Medicare, that are unpaid at death may be deducted either on the decedent's final income tax return (provided they are paid within one year of the death) or on the federal estate tax return, but not on both.[3] The choice of where to deduct unpaid medical expenses will depend on which alternative will yield the greater tax savings. The amount of tax saved is a function of the marginal tax rates. It is highly unlikely that an estate would benefit by claiming an income tax deduction rather than an estate tax deduction if the estate is also subject to estate tax. This is because the effective estate tax rate is at least 45% (even more if there is a state death tax that is based on the federal taxable estate) and the top federal income tax rate is only 35%. Note that funeral expenses (e.g., burial, memorial services, flowers, etc.) are deductions, if at all, only on an estate tax return (Form 706), never on an income tax return.

Smaller estates may be unable to benefit from a deduction on either return. If deducted on the income tax return, only the excess of the medical expense amount over 7.5% of adjusted gross income is deductible. Any nondeductible amount may not be deducted on the estate tax return. With regard to the estate tax return, most estates pay no estate tax, either because no estate tax return need be filed or because other deductions, particularly the marital deduction, may reduce the taxable estate to zero.

Expenses and losses. Expenses in administering the decedent's estate, including executor's commission, attorney's fees, and casualty losses, are deductible either on the federal estate tax return or on the estate income tax return, or partly on each.[4] However, double deductions are not allowed.

Again, the choice of where to deduct these items will depend on which return will produce the greater tax savings. Casualty losses are deductible against income only to the extent that they exceed 10% of adjusted gross income whereas there is no such percentage reduction when casualty losses are claimed on an estate tax return. Larger estates that owe estate taxes generally will claim all available deductions on the estate tax return because the marginal rate for estate taxes will almost always be higher than the marginal rate for income taxes. However, it is usually imprudent to claim a deduction on an estate tax return that will avoid estate tax by using the unified credit or the marital deduction.

The executor's commission, as a deductible administration expense, is taxable as income to the executor. However, the executor may elect to waive (i.e., refuse) the commission. Waiver of the commission may be worthwhile if the executor is a residuary beneficiary of the estate, and if his or her personal marginal income tax rate exceeds the marginal tax rate for both the estate tax and the estate income tax. If the executor is not a residuary beneficiary of the estate, a waiver of the commission will mean a complete forfeit of that amount. Thus, the non-residuary executor will usually prefer to receive the commission, regardless of the tax cost.

> EXAMPLE 16 - 2. An estate has been left entirely to the decedent's daughter, who is the executor. The executor's commission will be $10,000. The estate's marginal estate tax rate is 45% and its marginal income tax rate is 28%. The daughter's marginal income tax rate is 31%. Claiming the commission and deducting it on the estate tax return will lower the estate tax by $4,500 and raise daughter's income tax by $3,100, for a net tax saving of $1,400.

> EXAMPLE 16 - 3. Facts similar to the last example, except that the decedent left his entire estate to his spouse, who is executor. Due to the unlimited marital deduction, the effective marginal estate tax rate is 0%. Regarding income tax rates, assuming that the spouse's effective marginal rate is 31%, and the estate's marginal rate is 28%, waiving the commission will in essence raise the estate income tax by $2,800 and lower the spouse's income tax by $3,100, for a net tax saving of $300.

EXAMPLE 16 - 4. Facts similar to the prior example, except that the entire estate has been left outright to the decedent's children by a former marriage. Waiving the executor's commission would mean forfeiting the $10,000. As executor, the spouse elects to take the commission. Instead of receiving nothing, the spouse will receive $6,900, after tax, from the estate. Because the commission is also an estate tax deduction the children's loss is $5,500 rather than $10,000.

Selection of Estate Taxable Year

The executor of a probate estate has considerable flexibility in choosing the estate's income tax year. Although all income tax years except the first and the last must be 12 months long, the executor can choose the estate's tax year to end on the last day of any month. If it ends on December 31, the estate is said to be on a *calendar year* with the first tax year from the date of death to December 31. All other tax years will then run from January 1 to December 31, except for the year of final distribution of the estate assets, which will run for a "short year" from January 1 to date of distribution. Alternatively, if the estate's elected tax year ends on the last day of any month other than December, it is said to be on a *fiscal year*.

Whether an estate is on a calendar year or fiscal year, two basic income tax benefits are available to it. First, the estate is a separate taxpaying entity, capable of splitting income with the other tax entities involved in the estate distribution process. However, by increasing tax rates and by radically compressing bracket amounts for estates, tax reform since 1986 has reduced the tax saving benefit of splitting income.

Second, tax saving can be realized in the first and last tax years of an estate's life, since both years are usually shorter than 12 months. The first tax year is shorter because date of death does not usually coincide with the last day of the tax year. The last tax year is shorter than 12 months because the date of final distribution seldom coincides with the last day of the tax year. A short tax year produces income tax savings because proportionately less income is ordinarily taxed in those years.

In contrast to the tax benefits available to all estates, some benefits are available only to estates having a carefully selected fiscal year. Regardless of when income is actually distributed to a beneficiary, it will be treated for tax purposes as though it was distributed on the last day of the estate's tax year.

EXAMPLE 16 - 5. Lucille died March 12, 2006. Her executor is planning the distribution of income to Nathan, the estate's sole beneficiary. The executor elects a fiscal year ending January 31. If the estate distributes income earned during June of 2006 to Nathan during the month of November, 2006, it will be treated as though he received it on January 31, 2007, and he will not have to report the income until April 15, 2008, almost two years after the income was initially received by the estate.

If the executor of an estate expects an unusually large income receipt shortly after the period of administration begins, he or she may wish to elect a year end which would give it a rather short first year, so that other taxable income received later will be taxed during the following year rather than lumped with the large receipt and taxed at a higher rate.

EXAMPLE 16 - 6. Decedent Malley was an accountant who died on May 19 owning, among other things, account receivables amounting to $50,000. The estate elects a fiscal year ending June 30 to include some of this income in the first tax year, with the rest of it taxed in the second year.

Distribution Planning

Although federal tax reform since 1986 reduced income tax rates substantially for all tax entities, an estate or trust may be able to save some income tax for its beneficiaries by properly planning the amount and timing of beneficiary distributions. Much of distribution planning hinges on the existence of differentials in marginal tax rates, and thus one of the planner's tasks is to compare the tax rates of the various entities and allocate taxable income to those in lower brackets. In this section, we will consider situations where the beneficiaries are, alternatively, in a higher bracket and in a lower bracket in comparison with the distributing estate or trust. This section will also examine the income tax advantage of prolonging the estate's life.

Goal to tax in the lowest bracket. When the estate or trust is in a lower income tax bracket than its beneficiaries, consideration should be given to distribution arrangements that will generate a greater taxable income to itself and a correspondingly lesser taxable income to its beneficiaries. The main limitation is the very compressed estate and trust tax brackets that result in the estate or trust being in the top income tax bracket with income of less than $10,000.

The most common device used accumulates income by reducing and delaying distributions of DNI. However, with the very compressed marginal rates for estates and trusts, the amount of tax savings is minimal.

> EXAMPLE 16 - 7. Jonathan died earlier this year, leaving his entire estate to his wife, Kathleen. This year, Kathleen, who has earned considerable income herself, is also recipient of a large lump-sum pension distribution from Jonathan's employer. Consequently, her income is taxed at the very highest marginal rates. Of the income received by the estate, the executor might wish to hold back nine thousand dollars to at least use up the estate's lower marginal rates.

Another way to benefit from the estate or trust having a lower tax rate than the beneficiaries is through the realization of a gain. If an estate asset has appreciated after death and is expected to be sold soon after its receipt by the designated beneficiary, the executor of a lower-bracket estate should give consideration to selling the asset prior to distribution so that the estate can recognize the gain. The after-tax proceeds can be distributed to the beneficiary tax-free, assuming all DNI has already been distributed. However, to be taxed to the estate, the sale will have to be made before its last taxable year so that the gain is not automatically "carried out" to the beneficiary.

Despite having a lower marginal tax rate, the executor of an estate may wish to distribute rather than sell the asset if the beneficiary has a realized loss that is presently unusable for lack of any offsetting gains. The beneficiary, who could sell the asset, then would not have to carry over an unused loss to future years.

In cases where an estate or trust is subject to a higher marginal income tax rate than one or more of its beneficiaries, the executor or trustee may prefer to distribute income to them in the year the income is received, so that it is taxed at the beneficiaries lower rate. In addition, when the estate or trust's tax year overlaps those of the beneficiaries, the executor or trustee can time the distribution so that it is made in the year in which the beneficiaries' tax rate is lower.

> EXAMPLE 16 - 8. In the month of November, Arleen, the sole beneficiary of her dad's estate, resigned from her job as a law firm associate. She is contemplating either opening her own office or going to business school for a year. To help her out, the executor elects a fiscal year end of February 28 and distributes $50,000 (out of income) to her in early December. Since the estate's fiscal year ends February 28, the distribution is treated as having been made on that date, hence Arleen will

report the income in a year in which she expects to be in a low tax bracket, even though she received it in a year in which she was in a high tax bracket.

Unduly prolonging the probate estate. By now, the reader is aware of several potential income tax advantages to having a probate estate remain open. This will encourage some executors to delay closing their estates. Since termination of an estate by final distribution cuts off the tax benefits available to this separate taxpayer, tax planning would suggest undertaking this ploy by delaying the estate's date of final distribution. However, the IRS has authority to treat an estate as terminated for tax purposes if it concludes that the estate's life had been "unduly" prolonged.[5]

How long can an estate usually be kept open without generating IRS disapproval? Some authorities believe that a reasonable life is about three to four years for an ordinary estate, and as long as 15 years for an estate which elects to defer payment of taxes under § 6166. However, the income tax benefit from prolonging an estate's life has been significantly curtailed in recent years due to tax reform's compression of income tax rates.

PLANNING DEVICES TO REDUCE DEATH TAXES

We turn now to an examination of several postmortem tax planning strategies that have their greatest impact on death taxes. They include the alternate valuation date election, disclaimers, the QTIP election, and several other miscellaneous techniques discussed briefly in earlier chapters.

Alternate Valuation Date Election

The size of the estate tax for an estate is a direct function of the value of the interests includible in the gross estate. An intelligent executor or estate adviser will try to keep valuation as low as possible. Often, conflicts with the IRS arise regarding the correct valuation of particular estate assets and deductions. While such conflicts make the entire subject of estate valuation seem quite subjective, there is one specific rule in this field that offers some objective certainty. The Code allows the executor the option to value estate assets and deductions at one of two different points in time.

Under § 2032, the value of the assets included in the gross estate (and corresponding liabilities) may be determined as of the date of death, or they may be determined as of the alternate valuation date (AVD), which is six months after the date of death. This section was enacted after the Great Depression to limit the adverse tax and liquidity effects that radical changes in market values could have on an estate. For example, consider a decedent who died just before the 1929 crash owning a considerable amount of stock, which had to be included in the gross estate at high, pre-crash date-of-death values. By the time the taxes were due, the value of the estate might be less than the taxes owed.

Under AVD rules, the executor may not pick and choose which assets to value at which of the two dates. If the election is made, all assets (and deductions) must be valued at the AVD. However, any assets sold or distributed after death and before the AVD must be valued as of that sale or distribution date.

Prior to 1984, the AVD election was permitted in situations where it increased the gross estate, thereby resulting in a greater step-up in basis for assets owned at death. For income tax purposes, this strategy was attractive for estates completely sheltered by the unified credit and/or marital deduction. Section 2032(c) now permits the AVD election only if it reduces both the value of the gross estate and the estate tax (and GST tax, if any).

Of course making the AVD election has income tax ramifications; with a smaller step-up (or greater step-down), a lower estate tax value will save estate tax but it might also result in additional income taxes when assets are sold. Since the minimum effective marginal estate tax rate (i.e., just above the AEA) is 46% in 2006 and 45% for later years while the maximum capital gains tax rate is likely to be around 15% (more if state tax is included), the AVD election should lower net taxes by as much as 30 cents for every dollar of reduced valuation. In addition, if the inherited asset is not sold, the AVD advantage increases to at least 45 cents per dollar. Finally, even if the heir chooses to sell the asset, a time value of money savings results to the extent that the income tax is likely to be paid later than the estate tax.

Effective Disclaimers

A disclaimer is an unqualified refusal to accept a gift. We have already studied disclaimers in two earlier chapters. First, in Chapter 7, covering the federal gift tax, we examined the transfer tax aspects of disclaimers, including the requirements for a valid disclaimer. Second, in Chapter 10, surveying marital deduction and bypass planning, we saw how a disclaimer provision could be included in a bypass arrangement to add postmortem flexibility to the client's estate plan. That discussion also mentioned several disadvantages of the use of disclaimers. The purpose of the present discussion is to provide additional detail on disclaimer planning, in the context of general postmortem planning.

Because of the requirement that the disclaiming donor cannot have accepted any interest in the benefits, the client's survivors must be told as soon as possible not to accept the decedent's property or income if a disclaimer is anticipated. The following material describes three general situations where disclaimers can be effectively utilized. They include spousal disclaimers to reduce the marital deduction, disclaimers by a nonspouse to increase the size of the marital deduction, and disclaimers to correct defective or inefficient dispositive documents.

To fully use decedent's applicable exclusion amount. We have seen how a spousal disclaimer of a marital deduction bequest can add postmortem flexibility by enabling the surviving spouse to choose the amount of the marital bequest to disclaim to the bypass share, thereby self-determining the amount of estate tax to defer to the second death. What is described as an AdB Trust plan has all of S1's estate pass to the survivor's Trust A, qualifying for the marital deduction unless S2 files a disclaimer, thereby pushing assets into Trust B, the bypass trust.

The marital deduction disclaimer can be used for any size estate but is probably most needed for modest estates that may or may not exceed the AEA for estates. For example, a plan for an estate that is currently too small to justify the use of a bypass could include a disclaimer provision, available in the event that the estate grew large enough to warrant a bypass distribution. It also makes sense for couples who wish to leave everything to the survivor but for the estate tax. If the estate tax is eliminated, then there will be no need for the survivor to make a disclaimer.

On the other hand, the disclaimer can also work well in larger estates in which S1 has under-utilized the GST exemption. The surviving spouse, at S1's death, may be able to disclaim assets being received outright into a GST exemption credit shelter bypass trust or QTIP trust.

Factors that may help the surviving spouse decide whether and how much to disclaim include S2's needs and his or her income tax bracket. First, the greater S2's perceived need for S1's assets to live comfortably, the less S2 will probably be willing to disclaim. This, in turn, will depend on the size of S2's estate. Of course, by disclaiming, S2 would not ordinarily be relinquishing all interests in the property, since the typical recipient bypass or QTIP trust provides for some invasion powers and for most or all income to be paid to S2. However, many S2s are still likely to react emotionally that, by disclaiming, they are in reality making a complete relinquishment.

Second, S2's willingness to disclaim might also depend on his or her marginal income tax rate. If S2's rate is high, a disclaimer can redirect taxable income to other family members who might be in lower tax brackets.

By others to increase surviving spouse's marital share. A disclaimer can be used to raise a marital deduction that is subsequently found to be inadequate. For example, a client may have died with an estate plan that neither included a bypass nor took full use of the unlimited marital deduction. This can occur when a person dies intestate or dies owning a considerable amount of property in joint tenancy with someone other than a spouse. The nonspouse beneficiary may be encouraged to disclaim the interest so that it may qualify for the marital deduction by passing to the surviving spouse. However, problems in implementation may arise. First, only a donee of property held in joint tenancy may disclaim.[6] Thus, such a disclaimer will work only if the decedent was the original donor of the property. Second, courts may be unwilling to allow the guardian of a minor child (or unborn child) to disclaim rights to property, reasoning that full relinquishment of property is not in the child's best interest. However, since a disclaimer cannot be made by a person until he or she reaches age 21, a disclaimer that is delayed until the disclaimant reaches majority might be effective.

Third, until recently, the IRS had been taking the position that the disclaimer had to be made within nine months of the date the joint tenancy was created, rather than the date of death. After losing in the courts, the IRS acquiesced with regard to joint tenancies where state law gives the joint tenant the right to sever the joint tenancy or cause the property to be partitioned.[7] In other words, disclaimers of joint interests may not be valid in some states. For example, a qualified disclaimer is not permitted for tenancy by the entirety property because it cannot be partitioned by one spouse without the permission of the other.[8]

Disclaimers to tweak the estate plan. Occasionally, wills and trusts are drafted erroneously. One always hopes that these mistakes will be discovered during the client's lifetime. If not, they can still often be corrected by disclaimer. For example, a disclaimer may also be used to refuse an undesirable bequest of a general power of appointment.

> EXAMPLE 16 - 9. Barbara died seven months ago leaving a will that provides for a bypass trust for the benefit of her husband, Jake. The will gives Jake the right to invade the trust for reasons of "health or happiness." Since courts have consistently held that the term happiness does not constitute an ascertainable standard, Jake will be deemed to be the holder of a general power of appointment over the entire trust corpus, which will be includible in Jake's gross estate when he dies. Jake can prevent this result by properly disclaiming his power over the corpus.

A disclaimer can also be used to overcome an inefficient disposition, thereby increasing the size of a charitable contribution.

> EXAMPLE 16 - 10. Sally, a widow, was 90 years old when she died six months ago, leaving her multi-million dollar estate entirely to her only child, Abbott, who at 73 is in failing health. Sally's will reads, "All my estate is left to my son, Abbott, but if he does not survive me by 30 days, then to the Girl Scouts of America." Abbott, who has no issue and would not mind the Girl Scouts receiving his mother's estate, files a disclaimer. Consequently, the property passes to the Girl Scouts without being subject to taxation in Sally's (or Abbott's) estate.

A disclaimer may be made with respect to an undivided portion of an interest, which the IRS defines as a fraction or percentage of each and every substantial interest owned by the disclaimant extending over the entire term of the disclaimant's interest.[9]

> EXAMPLE 16 - 11. Lynn survived her husband, who bequeathed her 100 shares of stock outright and a life estate in trust property producing $10,000 in annual income. Lynn may disclaim fewer than 100 shares of the stock, and she may disclaim a life estate in less than $10,000 annually of the trust property. But she may not disclaim only a remainder interest in the stock, or only a term for years portion of her life estate, such as for the first five years of the income.

These examples are merely illustrative of the many situations where post-mortem disclaimers can be used to alter estate dispositions to obtain more desirable results.[10] Disclaimers are generally considered to be an extremely powerful estate planning tool. It should be noted that since the stakes can be quite high in this technical area of the law, the person contemplating using one is encouraged to seek competent counsel prior to attempting to make a qualified disclaimer.

QTIP Election Planning

As covered in detail previously, property normally can qualify for the marital deduction only if it "passes" to the spouse. In other words, the spouse cannot ordinarily receive an interest that might terminate; the interest cannot be terminable. Over the years, however, the code has carved out several exceptions to this rule. Up to 1982, the most commonly used marital trust designed to take advantage of an exception was the power of appointment trust, i.e., the one giving the spouse a life estate in the income and a general power of appointment over the corpus.[11] Since then, the QTIP trust, based on the QTIP election exception, has become far more popular. It is found in § 2056(b)(7) and provides that property subject to a terminable interest can qualify for the marital deduction if it meets the following two requirements for "qualified terminable interest property:"

1. The surviving spouse must be entitled to receive all income from the property for life, payable at least annually.
2. No person may have the power to appoint the property to anyone other than the surviving spouse.

Why might a person wish to bequeath only a terminable interest to his or her spouse? Why might a person prefer not to give marital deduction property to the spouse outright, or in trust with the spouse receiving a general power of appointment over the property? Why restrict a spouse's ability to control disposition of the property? There are several possible reasons, including the desire to protect the estate from the consequences of S2's immaturity or senility and the goal of protecting assets from the surviving spouse's creditors. But perhaps the most common reason is a desire by S1 to absolutely guarantee the ultimate disposition to an intended remainder beneficiary. The typical S1 choosing a QTIP arrangement has children of a former marriage and wishes to provide for the surviving spouse's income needs during lifetime, yet still absolutely ensure that his or her own children will eventually receive the property after the surviving spouse's death. Only a QTIP-type arrangement will do all this and still qualify the property for the marital deduction.

Some planners also recommend the QTIP plan for clients still married to their first spouse to eliminate the risk that their surviving spouse might remarry and leave substantial property to the new spouse rather than the children. Others disagree, pointing out that most S2s either do not remarry or act prudently when they do.

Uniqueness of the QTIP election. In contrast with the decision as to who will ultimately receive the property outright, the final decision whether to claim a marital deduction for QTIP property is not be up to S1, and in contrast with the spousal disclaimer, it is not up to S2; instead, S1's *executor* makes the choice on S1's estate tax return. Obviously, this is an election that is made after the first spouse is dead.

Deferral versus equalization revisited. If the election is made, the QTIP property can qualify for the S1 marital deduction, and S1's taxable estate and estate tax will be reduced. However, at S2's death, the S2 date-of-death value of the qualifying property must be taxed as though it were includible in S2's gross estate.[12] The estate of S2 will receive reimbursement from the QTIP trust for the tax incurred by it.[13]

Thus, in considering the QTIP election, the S1 executor must choose one of the following two tax consequences: (1) making the election will defer the estate tax by reducing the S1 taxable estate and increasing the S2 taxable estate; or, alternatively, (2) not making the election will accelerate the estate tax by producing a larger S1 taxable estate, but can result in a smaller S2 taxable estate, via bypass. The choice whether to make the election essentially boils down to a tax issue: whether to defer or to equalize spousal estate tax. As we approach 2010, most estates will choose to defer with the hope that no estate tax will ever have to be paid. Keep in mind that the S1 executor's QTIP election has nothing to do with determining who will receive the property; the trust terms decide that and, except for the possibility of disclaimer by a beneficiary, it is no longer subject to change by anyone.

QTIP election versus disclaimer. The use of disclaimers and of the QTIP election enable a surrogate decision maker to decide on behalf of the deceased client whether to defer the estate tax. One advantage of the QTIP alternative over the disclaimer is the ability to delay the decision an additional six months. While a disclaimer must usually be made within nine months after date of death, a QTIP election is made on the federal estate tax return which, when including a 6-month extension to file, allows up to 15 months after the date of death before a decision must be made.

Perhaps the most fundamental difference between the disclaimer and the QTIP arrangement concerns the amount of control S2 is given over the assets involved. Often, it is the single deciding factor in making the choice. Thus, if the client wishes the spouse to have complete control, an outright transfer anticipating the possibility of a disclaimer will be preferred. If, on the other hand, minimal S2 control is desired, a transfer to a QTIP trust will be the better choice.

Additional Postmortem Tax-Saving Devices

Three other postmortem tax elections often available to the estates of business owners include the IRC § 6166 election to pay the estate tax in installments, the § 303 redemption of stock, and the § 2032A special-use valuation election. These elections were covered in some detail in Chapter 14 and are mentioned here just as a reminder that the elections are not made until after the business owner dies.

CONCLUSION

This chapter has focused on postmortem planning designed to collect and protect the decedent's property, as well as to reduce income and estate taxes. These steps represent the final phase of planning undertaken on behalf of an individual.

The next and final chapter discusses advanced material that is less likely to be needed for most estate planning tasks, even where one is working with relatively wealthy families. Given the nature of the material, mastery of it is not expected of professionals just starting out in some aspect of estate planning. Depending upon the course objective the chapter might be skipped, skimmed, assigned in part, or expected to be mastered.

QUESTIONS AND PROBLEMS

1. List the federal tax returns that may have to be filed during a period of administration of a decedent's property.

2. Maxie, a widower, died recently, leaving his $3 million gross estate to his brother Morey. Maxie spent the last six months in a hospital, paying $50,000 of the $80,000 hospital bill before he died. Marginal tax rates for the taxpaying entities are as follows: Maxie's final Form 1040, 31%; the Form 1041, 28%; the Form 706, 45%. Determine how much tax Maxie's estate will save if the allowable expense is deducted, alternatively, on: (a) Form 706; (b) Form 1040; and (c) Form 1041.

3. Moose died recently, leaving his entire $3 million gross estate to his wife, Trixie, who is named executor. Assume that the only estate expense is the executor's commission of $100,000. Marginal tax rates for the taxpaying entities are: Trixie's Form 1040, 31%; the final Form 1040, 15%; the Form 1041, 28%; the Form 706, 41%.

   (a) Should Trixie accept or waive the commission? Why?
   (b) Where, if at all, should the estate deduct the commission? Why?
   (c) Would your answers to parts "a" and "b" change if Moose's net estate was $200,000?
   (d) Would your answers to parts "a" and "b" probably change if Trixie, the executor, was Moose's cousin to whom Moose left nothing by will or otherwise? Assume a $3 million taxable estate that goes to Moose's adult children.

4. Describe the income tax advantages available to all estates and those advantages available only to estates having a carefully chosen fiscal year.

5. How can the executor of an estate or the trustee of a trust reduce income taxes by planning the distributions to beneficiaries if the beneficiaries marginal tax rates are: (a) Higher than that of the estate or trust? (b) Lower than that of the estate or trust?

6. What is the benefit of prolonging an estate's life, and what is the tax consequence if it is "unduly" prolonged?

7. What two conditions must be met before an estate can make the alternate valuation date election? What is the tax advantage? When are assets valued?

8. Give two specific examples where a disclaimer can reduce the estate tax.

9. Describe the unique contribution of a QTIP arrangement to estate planning.

10. Is it clearly erroneous for an executor to fail to take the marital deduction on QTIP property when doing so would eliminate taxes on S1's estate?

11. (a) Can a QTIP arrangement and a disclaimer provision be alternative methods of achieving a common objective? Why or why not? (b) Which places greater property rights in the hands of S2? Explain.

12. Brunk owned three assets at his death. Their description and appraised values at date of death, six months after death and nine months after death, respectively, are as follows: Home and furnishings, $400,000, $450,000, $475,000; securities, $1,000,000, $800,000, $900,000; and an interest in a closely held business, $900,000, $850,000, $750,000. Brunk bequeathed all assets to his son, who, as executor, sold the home for $430,000 four months after Brunk died and sold the business for $775,000 eight months after Brunk died. If Brunk's executor makes a § 2032 election, calculate Brunk's gross estate.

13. With regard to the QTIP election: (a) Who makes it? (b) If the election is made, will it influence either the ultimate disposition of the property, or taxation of the qualifying property, or both? (c) If the election is not made, how will the tax result change?

ANSWERS TO THE QUESTIONS AND PROBLEMS *(odd numbered only)*

1. Federal tax returns:

   (a) Estate tax: Form 706, due nine months after date of death.
   (b) Income tax:

      1. Form 1040: Decedent's final income tax return, for all income for the last year up to the date of death.
      2. Form 1041: Estate income tax return (if there is a probate estate), for each tax year of the estate's existence.
      3. Form 1041: Trust income tax return for each tax year of any trust created by the decedent.

3. (a) If Trixie accepts the $100,000 commission, that amount will be taxable income to her, resulting in an income tax outlay of 31 % * ($100,000) = $31,000. If the expense is deducted on the 706, estate tax will not be reduced, because the entire estate is already sheltered by the marital deduction and the exemption equivalent of the unified credit.

   If, alternatively, the expense is deducted on the estate's 1041, there will be an estate income tax saving of ($100,000) * 28% = $28,000. Thus, Trixie should waive the commission because it will result in a net increase in her after-tax proceeds of $31,000 - $28,000 = $3,000.
   (b) The estate should not pay or deduct the commission, for the reasons mentioned above.
   (c) The results would change. Trixie would be indifferent between waiving and accepting the commission. At equal marginal tax rates, the tax saved on the form 1041 would just equal the higher tax on Trixie's 1040. However, cutting the hypothetical gross estate to $200,000 would not in itself alter the results. For any size estate, a 100% marital deduction would prevent additional tax savings with other deductions. Thus, the effective marginal estate tax rate would still be 0%.
   (d) The answers would very likely change. Trixie would probably rather accept the commission. Her after-tax proceeds would be $69,000, which is far better than receiving nothing.

5. Tax planning for distributions to beneficiaries:
   (a) When the estate or trust is in a lower bracket than the beneficiaries, it should consider accumulating income, realizing gains, and, if it is an estate, prolonging its life.
   (b) When the estate is in a higher bracket, it should use the conduit principle to distribute income in the year received.

7. The alternate valuation date election can reduce the value of assets in the gross estate, and therefore the estate tax, if their total value six months after date of death is lower (higher) than the date-of-death value.

9. The unique contribution of a QTIP arrangement to estate planning is to enable property that will not pass to S2 to qualify for the marital deduction.

11. (a) Yes, a QTIP arrangement and a disclaimer provision can be alternative methods of achieving the same objective, which is estate tax minimization. Both typically enable S2 to decide whether to qualify certain property for the marital deduction and, consequently, to determine the size of the bypass share.
    (b) The disclaimer provision will place greater property rights in the hands of S2 because, if S2 does not disclaim, he or she will receive it. On the other hand, the QTIP election only influences estate taxation, not property disposition; disposition of the property is in complete control of S1.

13. (a) The executor of the estate of S1 makes the election, since S1 is the decedent whose document qualifies for the QTIP election.
    (b) If the QTIP election is made, it will influence taxation of the qualifying property, but not its disposition. Except for adjustments for payment of estate tax, all named beneficiaries will still receive their designated shares. Taxwise, the property will be deductible from S1's gross estate and included in S2's gross estate at his or her later death.
    (c) If the QTIP election is not made, the qualifying property will be included in S1's taxable estate and not included (via bypass) in S2's estate. Thus, a greater bypass may increase S1 estate tax (but only if, under simple assumptions, the bypass becomes greater than the AEA.

ENDNOTES

1. IRC § 6013(a)(2).

2. IRC §§ 1(a)(2); 2(a)(1).

3. IRC §§ 213; 2053

4. Reg. § 1.642 (g)-2.

5. Reg. § 1.641(b)-3(a).

6. Reg § 25.2518-2(c)(4)(I).

7. LR 9106016; TAM 9208003.

8. LR 9208003.

9. Reg. § 25.2518-3(b).

10. For an example of an unsuccessful disclaimer to correct a defect in a trust intended to achieve QTIP treatment, see *Estate of Bennett*, 100 TC No. 5 (1993).

11. IRC § 2056(b)(5).

12. IRC § 2044.

13. IRC § 2207(a).

CHAPTER 17

Advanced Topics in Estate Planning

OVERVIEW

This chapter takes on the task of covering disparate estate planning topics that, for the most part, are beyond what one would be expected to master in a first course in estate planning. Whether these topics are assigned and, if so, whether to be mastered or merely skimmed, is left to the individual instructor or program.

ESTATE PLANS SELDOM SEEN

Next, we cover several estate plans that you are not likely to see in your practice, but they are of interest because they will come up from time to time at continuing education seminars or in discussions with colleagues. The Estate Trust was never popular because of its limitations; the Traditional AB Trust was very popular until 1982, when the 100% marital deduction and the QTIP election made it obsolete. The QTIP election and the lowering of the top marginal rates made the inflexible Estate Equalization Trust less desirable than ABC Trusts, since the latter can accomplish the same tax savings but gives S1 greater control over who will be the remaindermen and gives S1's executor more options.

Estate Trust

An unusual type of marital trust called the Estate Trust is almost never used. Its unique feature is that during S2's lifetime the terms of the trust allow the trustee discretion as to how much income to distribute to S2, but at S2's death all accumulated income and corpus must be distributed to S2's probate estate. Consequently, trust income can be accumulated and taxed at trust rates, but given the compressed nature of those rates, there is little reason to use this trust in an attempt to save income taxes. The reason this plan qualifies for the marital deduction is that it is not considered a terminable interest since the interest of S2 does not shift to someone else (see the definition of a terminable interest found at IRC § 2056(b)(1)). Given the greater flexibility of the QTIP trust, which allows the marital deduction while letting S1 control the remainder interest, it is difficult to imagine a reason to use one of these trusts.

Traditional AB Trust

The Traditional AB Trust (TAB) is the name now given to those estate plans drafted between 1948 and 1981 that were designed to use the maximum marital deduction then available. For large estates, the maximum marital deduction was 50% of the adjusted gross estate (AGE). That amount was "given" to S2 by way of a marital deduction trust (Trust A), and that portion of S1's estate that could not escape taxation at S1's death was left to a bypass trust (Trust B), thus avoiding S2's estate. The tax savings for these plans came not at the first death but at the second death. The idea was to transfer into Trust A, in addition to S2's property, so much of S1's estate as exactly equaled the maximum marital deduction available to S1's estate, and to pass the rest of S1's estate (the taxed portion) into Trust B. Smaller estates (those under $500,000) could use the alternate minimum marital deduction of $250,000 for decedents dying between 1977 and 1981, inclusive, but for larger estates, even during that time frame, the 50% AGE was the controlling factor. Because the pre-1982 marital deduction was limited to 50% of AGE, the property going into Trust B would have been taxed even if it passed directly to S2, therefore, placing it in Trust B did not increase the estate tax at S1's death, but doing so did allow it to avoid S2's estate when S2 died.

As with the more modern plans, Trust A generally held all S2's property; in addition it received from S1's estate the maximum marital deduction amount. In common law states this would be equal to 50% of S1's net estate. In community property states, because the marital deduction was not allowed for the community property, the marital deduction was 50% of S1's separate property.

The names given the two trusts are similar to the names now used for the modern AB Trust plan. Trust A might have been called the Survivor's Trust, the Marital Deduction Trust, or General Power of Appointment Trust. S2 had to receive all income for life and hold a general power of appointment over it.[1] The names and characteristics of Trust B were similar to those for the Trust B of the modern AB Trust except instead of being equal to the AEA, the trust was funded with all that property which would not qualify for the marital deduction, hence, 50% of S1's separate property and S1's half of the community property. The trust was likely to be called Trust B or the Bypass Trust. Like the credit shelter trust of the modern AB plan, it could be a sprinkling trust benefiting the children as well as S2, but it was much more common that all income was given to S2. A sprinkling trust with S2 as both the trustee and as one of the potential beneficiaries has all the trust income taxed to S2 anyway. This defeats one of the primary reasons for having a sprinkling provision in a trust, namely the ability to lower overall income taxes within a group of beneficiaries by distributing more income to the lower tax bracket members. It was very common to give S2 invasion rights limited to an ascertainable standard. Also common were B trusts in which S2 had limited powers to appoint among the children, and, less commonly, S2 was given a 5 & 5 power.

EXAMPLE 17 - 1. Compare two pre-1982 estate plans. The first one is a simple will plan in which S1 leaves everything to S2 and, on S2's death, everything goes to their children. The second one is a TAB in which, after S1's death, S1's taxable estate goes into a bypass trust (Trust B) and the maximum marital deduction amount, plus all S2's property goes into Trust A, a general power of appointment trust. On S2's death, Trusts A and B terminate and go to their children. When S1 died in 1965, S1 owned separate property worth $1,800,000 and S2 owned separate property worth $200,000; in addition they had community property worth $300,000. S2 died in 1976 and between deaths the assets doubled in value. (Pre-1977 tax rates are used.)

With plan one, all S1's estate (less the estate tax) was transferred to S2. With plan two, Trust A was funded with property worth $1,250,000 (the one-half of S1's separate property that qualifies for the marital deduction, plus S2's separate property and S2's half of the community property) and Trust B with property worth

$1,050,000 out of S1's estate (half S1's separate property, plus S1's half of the community property). All estates claimed the $60,000 estate tax exemption that was available at the time.

	S1 100%> S2		TAB Trust	
	S1	S2	S1	S2
	d1965	d1976	d1965	d1976
GE	$1,950,000	$3,956,000	$1,950,000	$2,500,000
MD	(900,000)	0	(900,000)	0
EstEx	(60,000)	(60,000)	(60,000)	(60,000)
TxE	$990,000	$3,896,000	$990,000	$2,440,000
tax	$322,000	$1,776,800	$322,000	$968,800

The entire estate tax savings of $808,040 [$1,776,800 - $968,800] occurred at the second death; the bypass trust kept Trust B property from being taxed again in S2's estate. The value of Trust B [$1,050,000 - $322,000 = $728,000] doubled; therefore, $1,456,000 avoided the second tax. The tax saved is equal to 55.5% of the latter figure, corresponding roughly to the pre-1977 average marginal rate between $2,500,000 and $4,000,000.

Note that with a TAB the marital deduction for Trust A is in terms of a dollar amount (not as a QTIP fraction) because part of S1's separate property is transferred from S1's estate into Trust A, the trust over which S2 has a general power of appointment; therefore, the marital deduction is automatic, unlike the QTIP trust for which an election must be made in order to claim a marital deduction. Furthermore, at S2's death, all Trust A is included in S2's estate, not just a fraction of it. Some plans written prior to 1981 still exist, and as demonstrated in the above example, Trust B may exceed the AEA at S1's death. Even though it makes little sense today to have S1's separate property split equally between Trusts A and B, neither the executor, the surviving spouse, nor the trustee can rewrite the decedent's estate plan. However, the tax laws allow the executor of S1's estate to obtain a marital deduction on Trust B by making the QTIP election, provided S2 has the requisite income interest in the trust. Fortunately, most of the old TAB plans give S2 a life estate in Trust B. As discussed before, the QTIPed portion is expressed as that fraction of Trust B necessary to bring S1's taxable estate down to the desired taxable estate (e.g., down to the AEA). It is that same fraction that determines the amount of Trust

B that is later included in S2's estate; therefore, the election must be expressed as a fraction rather than as a dollar amount.

Estate Equalization AB Trust

The funding of the two trusts created at S1's death required the executor of S1's estate to have S2's property valued too. Trust B was funded such that it exactly equaled half of the combined values. These plans enjoyed some popularity for very large estates when the maximum marginal rate was 77% for estates over $10 million. With the QTIP trust and the possibility of using a partial QTIP election there is much greater flexibility in allocation between the two estates, and if S2 is healthy at the time S1's estate tax return is prepared it is likely that Trust C will be fully QTIPed; therefore there is no need to have S2's property valued, whereas with the old Estate Equalization AB Trusts, all assets had to be valued to determine the funding amount for Trust B. With an ABC plan, an AsuperB plan, or an ABdC plan, S2's property needs to be appraised at S1's death only if the executor of S1's estate desires to use the QTIP election to equalize (or optimize) the two taxable estates.

THE GENERATION-SKIPPING TRANSFER TAX

Up to now, we have focused our tax planning discussion on how gifts and trusts are used to reduce transfer taxes for the nuclear family, i.e., S1, S2, and their children. Similar planning works for transfers to more remote family members. For example, a childless couple could develop a bypass plan for nephews and nieces. A bypass trust plan works well for any survivors who belong to the same, or to the next generation, but complexity arises when a bypass trust (or an outright transfer) skips the estates of the transferor's children and goes to grandchildren, great-grandchildren, or even more remote descendants. The Generation-Skipping Transfer Tax (GST tax) is designed to capture additional taxes such that the total transfer tax approximates that which would have been collected had the property been taxed at each generation. It is imposed on direct skips, taxable terminations, and taxable distributions to, or for the benefit of, a skip person. A skip person is a beneficiary who is at least two generations younger than the transferor. For this discussion, think in terms of grandparent, parent, and grandchild, with the grandchild being the skip person vis-a-vis the grandparent. Keep in mind that this GST tax is not appreciably "unified" with gift and estate taxes; it is a separate tax having its own unique rules. To report the transfer and calculate the tax Form 706 is used for transfers at death and Form 709 is used for gifts. These forms are on the Teaching Aids CD ROM in "pfd" format.

Purpose of the GST Tax

The purpose of the GST tax is to assure that large estates are subjected to a transfer tax as they pass from one generational level to the next. Prior to the mid-1980's, a common method for the very wealthy to pass their estates through many generations with a minimum of transfer tax was to create trusts that would benefit first the children for their lives, then the grandchildren for their lives, and then the great-grandchildren for as long as the rule against perpetuities would allow. Transfer tax (either the estate tax or the gift tax) would be levied only when the trust was initially funded. Because the income beneficiaries had no powers to appoint corpus, nor any other interest in the trust that would cause it to be included in their estates, no new taxes were levied as the interests shifted from one generation to the next. These were the ultimate bypass trusts designed to last a hundred years or more.

The first generation-skipping transfer tax was enacted in 1976. Although planners found it very complicated, they quickly learned that the tax was easy to circumvent. As a result, in 1986, Congress acknowledged its error by repealing it retroactively, and at the same time, enacting a more comprehensive version as described below.

EGTRRA not only eliminates the GST tax in 2010 but dramatically changes it pending repeal. The GST exemption, $1 million when the present GST system was enacted in 1986, will increase to the AEA for transfers after 2003. The exemption keeps most GST transfers from being taxed. The delay in tying the exemption to the AEA avoids a temporary decrease in the exemption. Indexing, which started in 1999, increased the exemption to $1,060,000 in 2001, whereas the AEA for 2002 and 2003 is $1 million. The GST tax rate is equal to the estate tax top marginal rate, which EGTRRA has decreased over the years from a top rate of 55% in 2001 to 50% in 2002, then another point each year until it reaches 45% in 2007. Like the rest of the EGTRRA changes, the sunset provision applies to the repeal of the GST tax, almost guaranteeing that Congress will change the GST tax law between now and 2011.

The GST Tax Scheme

The solution devised by Congress is to tax transfers that skip a generation even if they are subject to the regular gift or estate tax. *Generation-skipping Transfer Tax* (GST tax) is the tax levied on what is called a *generation-skipping transfer*, which is a transfer to a *skip person*, defined as a person two or more generations below the transferor. A transfer to a trust whose beneficiaries are all skip persons is also considered a generation-skipping transfer.[2] The basic rule for determining the tax is as follows:

$$\text{GST tax} = \text{the taxable amount} * \text{the applicable rate}[3]$$

Think of the taxable amount as the value of the gift or estate that is given to a skip person or to skip persons. Complications set in because the taxable amount depends on whether the transfer is a direct skip, a taxable termination, or a taxable distribution. The *applicable rate* is the maximum federal estate tax rate multiplied by the inclusion ratio. The *inclusion ratio* is determined by the amount of the donor's GST exemption allocated by the donor to a particular transfer. We will start by covering the calculation of the tax for each of the three types of skips. To keep this as simple as possible, the initial examples will assume that the donor does not allocate any of his or her GST exemption to the transfer. Later we will consider the allocation of the exemption and look at examples where it is a factor.

Credit for state taxes. For transfers prior to 2005, there was a federal credit for state GST taxes triggered by a generation-skipping transfer (other than a direct skip) that occurred as a result of the death of an individual. The credit allowed against the federal GST tax was equal to the lesser of the state GST tax or 5% of the federal GST tax.[4] Most states have simply adopted a state GST "pickup" tax equal to 5% of the federal GST tax for such indirect skips. Congress eliminated this credit for transfers from decedent's estates where the death occurs after December 31, 2004.[5]

Transfers excluded from the GST tax. The annual exclusion applies to GST tax present interest inter vivos gifts. Those inter vivos gifts that would not be treated as taxable gifts because of IRC § 2503(e) (payments directly to educational institutions or to medical providers) are also excluded from the definition of a GST tax.[6]

Grandfathered trusts. Some generation-skipping trusts that were around when the GST tax laws went into effect are exempt from the GST tax. To be grandfathered, a trust had to be irrevocable as of September 25, 1985, or the skip must be caused by a will, a testamentary trust, or a trust in existence on October 21, 1986, that became irrevocable as a result of the testator or trustor's death before January 1, 1987. A grandfathered trust will lose its exempt status if after the dates just mentioned, the trust is modified. An addition to the corpus after September 25, 1985 will cause a proportionate part of the corpus, including future appreciation and income to be subject to the GST tax.[7]

Taxable Transfers

The taxable amount depends on whether the transfer is a direct skip, a taxable termination, or a taxable distribution. Keep in mind that the goal is to approximate the transfer tax that would be levied if the property passed through each generational level. Generally, unless the governing instrument (e.g., a will or a trust) by specific reference to the GST tax provides otherwise, the GST tax must be charged to the property transferred.

Direct skips. A direct skip is a transfer to a skip person where that transfer is subject to estate or gift tax.[8] These are likely to be outright gifts or bequests from grandparents to grandchildren. For all direct skips, other than a direct skip from a trust, the liability for paying the GST tax is placed on the transferor.[9] The taxable amount, in the case of a direct skip, is the value of the property received by the transferee.[10] This means that in the case of a bequest, the taxable amount is the bequest net of its share of debts, expenses, etc., and death taxes (both federal and state). Where the direct skip property is included in the transferor's estate that makes alternate valuation or special use valuation election, the value of the property for purpose of the GST tax is the same as used for estate tax.[11] For gifts of a present interest, the annual exclusion also reduces the taxable amount for GST tax purposes.

> EXAMPLE 17 - 2. In 2006, Barry made a gift of Bucky Company common stock, worth $750,000, to his granddaughter Julie. He had applied his GST exemption to taxable gifts to other grandchildren, and the annual exclusion was applied to a gift made earlier in the year to Julie. Because of those earlier gifts, the gift of Bucky Company stock required Barry to pay gift taxes of $322,750 and GST tax of $345,000 [$750,000 * 0.46]. Had Barry waited until 2007 to make the gift, he could apply the $500,000 increase in the GST exemption to the transfer such that only $250,000 would be subject to the tax and the rate would be 45% instead of 46%.

Things get a little more complicated with decedent's direct skips. The GST tax is paid by the decedent's estate and the GST tax should not itself be subjected to the GST tax, i.e., multiplying the net estate by the top rate (e.g., 46% in 2006) will produce a tax that is too high. The result for an estate should be the same as if the transfer was a direct skip gift. Let's look at the last example; after the regular gift tax had been paid, Barry (the donor) parted with assets worth $1,095,000 to make a gift to Julie of $750,000. The $1,095,000 is the gift of $750,000 plus the GST tax of $345,000. Leaving a skip person $750,000 by way of a bequest (instead of a gift) requires a net estate (after estate taxes, but before the GST tax) of $1,095,000. The GST tax of $345,000 divided by $1,095,000 equals 0.315068497, which is the GST tax rate for direct skips from a decedent, i.e., a tax rate of 31.5% when the top transfer marginal rate is 46%.

> EXAMPLE 17 - 3. Tisha died in 2006. She had made gifts the year before that used up her GST exemption. Out of her estate, she left property worth $1,095,000 to her favorite grandson, Frank. This bequest was made free of estate tax (i.e., it is charged to the residue of the estate) but charged with any GST tax. The estate must pay $345,000 in GST tax [0.315068497 * $1,095,000] and Frank will actually receive just $750,000.

The steps that a decedent's estate must take to calculate the GST tax for a direct skip are found in Schedule R, Part 2, of the U.S. Estate Tax Return, Form 706. Notice that, after subtracting debts, regular death taxes, and the exemption, the net amount left is divided by the number we call the "706 divisor" (see the table to the right) to determine the GST tax (see line 6 of Schedule R). How does 3.173917 relate to the 0.315068497 rate given above as the marginal tax rate? The answer: dividing "1" by 0.315068497 equals 3.173917, therefore the result will be the same whether one divides the net transfer (net after regular tax) by 3.173917 or whether one multiplies it by 0.315068497.

Taxable terminations. A taxable termination means that a shift in interest from one generation to the next has occurred as a result of: (1) the death of a person, (2) the release of an interest, (3) the passage of time, or (4) for some other reason. As is the case of a direct skip from a trust, it is the trustee who must pay the GST tax in the case of a taxable termination. The taxable amount is the value of the property with respect to which the taxable termination has occurred, reduced by any expenses or indebtedness that would be deductible

year	max. rate	GST rate	706 divisor
01	55%	0.354838687	2.818182
02	50%	0.333333333	3.000000
03	49%	0.328859096	3.040816
04	48%	0.324324359	3.083333
05	47%	0.319727848	3.127660
06	46%	0.315068497	3.173913
07	45%	0.310344849	3.222222
08	45%	0.310344849	3.222222
09	45%	0.310344849	3.222222

under IRC § 2053 (debts and expenses). The § 2032 alternate valuation election is available (assuming it will reduce the GST tax) if the taxable termination is the result of the death of an interested party.[12] Such would be the case if the settlor established a trust, giving his children income for life, then income for the life of grandchildren, and finally distribution to the great-grandchildren. Once the last of the settlor's children died and the income interest in the trust shifted to grandchildren, there would be a taxable termination. If the value of the trust had decreased in the six months following the death of the last of the settlor's children to die, the trustee could elect the alternate valuation date in order to reduce the GST tax.

Just because a GST tax trust terminates does not mean that a taxable termination has occurred. Whether it is also a taxable termination depends on whether the termination results in a shift from one generation to another. Furthermore, as shown in the examples that follow, a taxable termination may occur without the trust itself terminating. Once the interests of all members of a generational level terminate and a tax is levied, the younger generations are considered to have moved up a generation such that individuals at the new top generation level are no longer skip persons. This "move-up" avoids having the GST tax apply again when transfers are made to members of said generation, since it was already imposed when the property interest shifted to that generation.[13]

> EXAMPLE 17 - 4. When grandpa Xuyen died in 2000 his estate plan created a trust that income for life to his son Ha, remainder to Ha's issue by right of representation, except that if any of Ha's children were under age 35, the assets were to remain in trust until the youngest reached age 35. Because the executor allocated the $1,030,000 GST exemption[14] to direct skips, none of the exemption was allocated to the trust. When Ha died in 2004, the trust was worth $2,000,000 and Ha's youngest child, Yi Yun, was 32 years old. Because the death of Ha causes the interest to shift to a younger generation, a taxable termination occurs even though the trust itself does not terminate. The tax payable by the trustee is at the highest marginal rate for taxable transfers, i.e., 48%, hence the tax of $960,000 leaves just $1,040,000 in the trust.

> EXAMPLE 17 - 5. Continuing the prior example: In 2007, shortly after Yi Yun's 35th birthday, the trust corpus, valued at $1,190,000, was distributed to him and his brother Sui-on. Since this is not a shift in generations (Yi Yun and Sui-on are in the oldest generation and not considered skip persons), there is no new GST tax (nor any other transfer tax) resulting from the trust's actual termination. Had Yi Yun died after his father, but before his 35th birthday, with the result that his interest went to his children, there would be a GST tax on his share. On the other hand, if he died before his 35th birthday, but left no issue with the result that Sui-on received his share, there would be no additional GST tax because the two brothers are in the same generation.

Taxable distributions. The Code gives a functional definition for a *taxable distribution*: "the term 'taxable distribution' means any distribution from a trust to a skip person (other than a taxable termination or a direct skip)."[15] This covers situations where a trust has beneficiaries in two or more generations, and the trustee can, and does, distribute to one of the beneficiaries in one of the lower generations. The transferee (i.e., distributee-beneficiary) is liable for the GST tax. The taxable amount is the value of the property received by the transferee, reduced by any expenses or indebtedness that would be deductible under IRC § 2053.

EXAMPLE 17 - 6. Using the facts from the prior two examples, if while Ha (the son of the trustor) is still alive, the trustee, using powers given to her by the terms of the trust, makes a $100,000 distribution in the year 2003 to grandson Yi Yun, it would be a taxable distribution. The GST tax in the amount of $49,000 (i.e., 49% * $100,000) is charged to Yi Yun with the result that he only gets $51,000.

Because the GST tax liability is placed on the transferee, if the trustee pays the GST tax, it is treated as a taxable distribution. The amount that must be "distributed" to achieve a desired net distribution can be solved algebraically. Let the gross distribution be Dg and the net distribution be Dn, then solve for Dg as follows:

Dg - GST tax = Dn
GST tax = Dg * GST tax rate
Dg = Dn/(1-GST tax rate)

EXAMPLE 17 - 7. Suppose that in the prior example, the trustee was required by the terms of the trust to distribute $100,000 to Yi Yun and pay the tax on it. This will require the trustee parting with $196,078.40 whether the trustee pays the GST tax of $96,078.40 [0.49 * $196,078.40] and distributes $100,000 to Yi Yun or the trustee distributes $196,078.40 and lets Yi Yun pay the tax on it.

EXAMPLE 17 - 8. Suppose the trustee distributed trust corpus worth $500,000 to Siu-on (Yi Yun's brother) after Ha's death (i.e., after the taxable termination had occurred), but before the trust had terminated. This distribution is not a taxable distribution for GST tax purposes, because by that time the two brothers were in the oldest generation of living beneficiaries having an interest in the trust, hence they were no longer skip persons.

Applicable Rate

The applicable rate is made up of two components: the maximum federal estate tax rate and the inclusion ratio. Remember, the GST tax is equal to the taxable amount (a reference to the transferred property) times the applicable rate (a tax rate modified to take into account the allocation of the GST exemption). The term maximum federal estate tax rate is the maximum imposed by IRC § 2001, e.g., 55% in 2001 decreasing to 45% in 2007.[16]

Inclusion ratio and the GST exemption. Think of the inclusion ration as that portion of the transfer that is not saved from the dreaded GST tax by the GST exemption. The GST exemption is $1,000,000 indexed for inflation for transfers occurring after 1998 and before 2004. Increases are rounded down to the next lowest multiple of $10,000. The base year for measuring the change is 1997.[17] The GST exemption increased to $1,060,000 in 2001, $1,100,000 in 2002, and $1,120,000 in 2003. EGTRRA tied the exemption to the estate AEA, hence it became $1,500,000 in 2004, and has tracked the estate AEA since. The inclusion ratio, i.e., the portion that will be subjected to the GST tax, is defined as the value one minus the "applicable fraction,"[18] or

$$1 - \frac{GSTT\ exemption\ allocated}{Net\ FMV\ of\ property\ tranferred}$$

The "net FMV of the property transferred" means net of debt, expenses, liens, death taxes (federal and state) charged to the property, as well as any charitable deduction. Generally, the allocation of the exemption is an elective one made by the donor in the case of gifts and by the executor in the case of estates. It is not unusual to make allocations within a multiple trust estate plan such that all the GST tax trusts have inclusion ratios of either zero or one.

EXAMPLE 17 - 9. When Ruben died in 2007, $3,000,000 of his estate (net of regular death taxes) was left to his grandchildren. The executor allocated the entire $2,000,000 GST exemption to this bequest, resulting in an applicable fraction of one-third ($2,000,000/$3,000,000) and an inclusion ratio of one-third (1 - 2/3). The GST tax would be $3,000,000 * 0.45 * .3333333, which is $450,000.

EXAMPLE 17 - 10. When Josephine died in 2007, she left her $3,000,000 estate (net of regular death taxes) in trust for her son Albert, with remainder to his issue. Since this was her entire net estate, the exemption was allocated to this trust. While Albert was still alive, the trustee made a distribution out of corpus in the amount of $360,000 to Albert's daughter, Martha. This, of course, was a taxable distribution. Given the inclusion ratio, the applicable rate would be 0.45 * .3333333. Therefore, the tax on the distribution would be: $360,000 * 0.45 * .3333333 = $54,000.

EXAMPLE 17 - 11. Continuing the prior example, when Albert died in 2009, the trust was worth $4,500,000. His death caused a taxable termination. The applicable rate is 0.45 * .3333333. The GST tax is: $4,500,000 * 0.45 * .3333333 = $675,000.

Generations and the GST Tax

There are a number of special rules related to GST tax, some of which we will cover here; others are beyond the scope of this text even for an advanced topics chapter.

Generation assignment. Where transferees are related to the transferor the assignments are fairly straightforward. The Code requires that one start with the transferor's grandparents and count down generations to the transferee and compare the number to the number of generations between the grandparent and the transferor. If the difference is greater than one, the transferee is a skip person.

> EXAMPLE 17 - 12. Jack wishes to leave half of his multi-million dollar estate to his brother's daughter Alice (Jack's niece) and the other half to Alice's two children, Martin and Paula. Are any or all of them skip persons? Jack's grandfather is two generations above him. From the grandfather to Alice is three generations. Three minus two equals one, so Alice is not a skip person. It is four generations from the grandfather to Martin and Paula. Four minus two equals two, therefore, both Martin and Paula are skip persons.

Predeceased parent exception. A special rule (called the *predeceased parent exception)* allows a skip person to "move up" a generation if his or her parent is a lineal descendant of the transferor (or the transferor's spouse) and the parent dies before the transfer occurs that is subject to a gift tax or an estate tax.[19] If there are two taxable events, then the person must have predeceased the earliest taxable event. It does not apply to skip persons not related to the transferor, nor to collateral heirs (e.g., nieces and nephews), with one exception, and that is if the transferor has no lineal descendants, a transfer to a collateral relative (e.g., a nephew or niece) whose parent is deceased qualifies for the predeceased parent exception.[20] The move-up exception also applies if the parent (of the person who would otherwise be a skip person) dies within 90 days of the transferor, provided the parent is treated as having predeceased the transferor, either because of a survivorship clause in the transferor's estate planning documents (i.e., the grandparent's will or trust) or because applicable state law has a statutory survivorship period.[21] This is another good reason to include a general survivorship clause of at least 90 day in estate planning documents.

> EXAMPLE 17 - 13. Sarah's will left her multimillion dollar estate to her issue. All three children survived her, but one child, named Richard, died 75 days after her.

Richard left two children who were entitled to inherit his entire estate. Sarah's will had a 60-day survivorship clause. Since Richard lived beyond the 60 days, he was entitled to a one-third share of Sarah's estate. Richard's executor disclaimed Richard's share so that it could pass directly to his children. This share is subject to the GST tax because insofar as Sarah's will (and her state of domicile) is concerned he did not predecease her. Had her will included a 90-day survivorship clause (or an even longer one), Richard would have been considered to have predeceased Sarah and there would be no GST tax.

A disclaimer will not work insofar as the predeceased parent exception is concerned, i.e., it will not move the disclaimant's children up a generation.[22] Thus, in the above example, even though the disclaimer worked for other purposes (e.g., avoiding Richard's gross estate for regular estate tax and avoiding his probate estate), for GST tax purposes the disclaimer will not cause Richard to be treated as though he had predeceased Sarah. In the typical estate plan for wealthy couples that use multiple trusts, it is very likely that the contingent remaindermen are skip persons. This may cause a GST tax problem.

EXAMPLE 17 - 14. S1 and S2 had an ABC trust estate plan. The remaindermen of all trusts were the couple's issue by right of representation. There were four children who had children of their own. When S1 died in 2004, his $1,500,000 GST exemption was allocated to Trust B, giving it a zero inclusion ratio. The executor of S1's estate QTIPed Trust C to postpone the tax on it until after S2's death. When S2 died in 2007, Trust C was worth $10 million. One son died eleven months after S1's death. He was survived by two children. When S2 died, the three living children each received a one-fourth share and the two grandchildren a one-eighth share. The GST tax does not apply to the grandchildren's share of Trust C because it is S2's death that triggers the estate tax insofar as Trust C is concerned, hence the predeceased parent exception moves them up a generation. Trust B is not subjected the GST tax because of the allocation of S1's exemption to it

EXAMPLE 17 - 15. Same facts as in the prior example except S1's executor did not make a QTIP election, hence Trust C was taxed after S1's death. Since the son died more than 90 days after S1 and Trust C was "subject to a tax," the predeceased parent exception does not apply and the GST tax is imposed on the portion of Trust C going to the grandchildren. The shift in interest to the two grandchildren is a taxable termination. Trust B again avoids the tax because of the allocation of the exemption to it.

Marital relationships. A transfer to one who is related to the transferor's spouse is in the generation level determined as if the transfer was from the spouse rather than from the transferor. The counting up (and down) from the spouse to her (or his) grandparent is just for the purpose of determining whether a donee is a skip person. For all other purposes the transfer is treated as coming from the transferor, unless the couple elect to "split the gift"[23] in which case both spouses are treated as being donors.

A spouse or ex-spouse of a transferor is treated as in the same generation as the transferor, regardless of age difference. This "same-generation-treatment" will continue even if a marriage ends due to the transferor's death or ends by divorce, which some people say is a little like death. Likewise, anyone married to a lineal descendant of the transferor's grandparents (or a lineal descendant of the transferor's spouse's grandparents) is in the same generation as that person's spouse (i.e., the lineal descendant) even if the marriage ends.

> EXAMPLE 17 - 16. Jennifer wishes to leave a portion of her estate to the widow of her uncle's grandson. Would this be a generation-skipping transfer? The widow of the grandson is in the same generation as was the grandson. The parent of the grandson is at the same generation level (count up and count back down) as Jennifer. Therefore, the grandson was (and his widow is) just one generation below Jennifer and no generation-skipping transfer will occur.

Transferees who are not lineal descendants. If the lineal descendant rules and the spouse rules do not apply, then assignment to generations is based on the difference in age between the transferor and the transferee. A person older than, or not less than 12.5 years younger than, the transferor is considered to be in the same generation as the transferor. A person 12.5 to 37.5 years younger is in the next generation below, and similar rules apply to assign individuals to still younger generations based on 25-year increments. Obviously, a person 40 years younger is a skip person and a person 30 years younger is not.

GST Exemption Allocation

As indicated earlier in this discussion, the allocation of the exemption is not automatic unless a direct skip is involved. Generally, at the death of a transferor, one should allocate in a manner that is most likely to reduce the GST tax, taking into account the present value of money. Because most taxpayers would prefer to postpone taxes of whatever variety, the Code has as a default position the automatic allocation of the exemption to lifetime direct skips unless the donor elects not to have the automatic allocation apply.[24] Where a transfer is not a direct skip (e.g., a transfer into trust with the surviving spouse as the immediate income beneficiary and grandchildren as remaindermen) the donor (or executor) must elect to allocate all or a portion of the exemption to the transfer (e.g., to the trust).

Discretionary allocations. Given a choice, the person making the decision would like to accomplish two or three things, some of which may be in opposition or which may require the use of a functioning crystal ball. Consider the following examples:

EXAMPLE 17 - 17.   Eunice never trusted her two boys to wisely handle investments. The oldest, Jimmy, she had given up on, but for the youngest boy, Billie, she wanted to provide a good living, while making sure he could not squander the estate that she had put together. She loved her grandchildren, who have turned out to be fine adults. When she died in 2006, she left her estate in equal shares, one share immediately to Jimmy's children and the other in trust for Billie for his lifetime, the remainder, free of trust, to Billie's issue. The plan specifically gave her executor authority to allocate the exemption as the executor deemed appropriate. Her net estate, after payment of all federal estate and state death taxes, had a value of $3,000,000. Her executor could allocate $1,500,000 of the $2,000,000 exemption to the direct skip or to the trust and $500,000 to the other, or half to each, or in any other combination that adds up to full allocation. If it is fully allocated to the trust, the trust will have a zero inclusion ratio such that, even if it is worth more than the GST exemption amount when it terminates, no GST tax will be due. However, doing so will cause an immediate GST tax for the portion of the S1,000,000 direct skip not covered by the exemption. Allocating $1,500,000 to the direct skip will postpone all GST tax until the trust ends, but the trust will have an inclusion ratio of two-thirds, i.e., $500,000 allocated to a $1,500,000 trust leaves two-thirds unprotected.

EXAMPLE 17 - 18. Accept this oversimplification that somewhat ignores the payment of estate taxes out of Trusts B and C. Mark and Wilma Smith had an ABC Trust estate plan. Their three children, Arthur, Betty, and Cathy, were remaindermen of all three trusts. The trust document called for the values of the three trusts to be aggregated at the second death, with the share going any skip person to be satisfied first out of trust property not subject to the GST tax. Mark died in 2004. Their estate was worth $8,000,000. Trust A received $4,000,000, Trust B $1,500,000, and Trust C $2,5000,000. The GST exemption was allocated to Trust B. In 2005, daughter Cathy died, leaving a son named Sam. Wilma died in 2006. At that time the trusts had the following values: A $4,500,000; B $1,800,000; and C $2,700,000. Since the total value is $9,000,000 each remainderman will receive $3,000,000. If at Mark's death, Trust C was QTIPed, then none of the distributions would be subject to GST tax regardless since Trusts A and C are taxed and Sam has moved up a generation vis-a-vis those two trusts, and the allocation of the GST exemption to Trust B avoids the tax on any distribution from it. On the other hand, if Trust C was not QTIPed, then it was taxed when Mark dies, and, since Cathy died more than 90 days after Mark, the predeceased parent rule was not applicable, hence Sam is a skip person insofar as Trust C is concerned. By the provisions of the trust document, Sam's share will be satisfied out of Trusts A and B since distributions to from these two trusts will not be subject to the GST tax. He is not a skip person vis-a-vis Trust A because Cathy died before Wilma making the predeceased parent rule applicable and Trust B is sheltered by the GST exemption.

Delayed allocations. In the case of inter vivos gifts, if the property would be included in the donor's estate due to a retained interest (§§ 2036-2038), the allocation cannot be made until the close of the *estate tax inclusion period* (ETIP). The ETIP is the point at which the retained interest either ends (released or ends by the terms of the transfer) or the donor dies.

EXAMPLE 17 - 19. In 1994, sixty-year old Stacie funded a 10-year qualified personal residence trust (QPRT) with her $950,000 home. The trust included a contingent reversion in the event Stacie died before the trust ended. The 7520 rate was 8% so she reported a gift of $406,615. The remainderman is her son, Charlie, or his issue. Charlie died in 2000. In 2004, at the end of the 10-year term the house is worth $1,750,000. Because Charlie died more than 90 days after the taxable gift was made, his three children do not move up under the predeceased parent exception. However, the ETIP ends with the termination of the trust, and she can allocate her $1,500,000 exemption to the transfer. Even though the gift escaped tax because it was under the gift AEA, the delay in being able to allocate the exemption exposes $250,000 of this transfer to the GST tax, resulting in a tax of $120,000, i.e., $250,000 * 48%.

EXAMPLE 17 - 20. Suppose, in the prior example that Stacie died in 2001 and the home was worth $1,525,000. The trust would revert to Stacie's estate. The taxable gift would drop to zero since the house is in her estate; the children would move up a generation since Charlie, having died in 2000, predeceased Stacie. The house would be subject to estate tax but not to the GST tax even though it passes to grandchildren.

Efficient utilization of the exemption. Generally, one would like the exemption to reduce GST tax sooner, rather than later, to cover completely a GST tax trust that is likely to grow, and to limit its allocation to trusts that will actually go to skip persons.

EGTRRA modified the exemption allocation rules. Under the old rules, there was no automatic allocation to trusts that have both skip and nonskip beneficiaries. It may be a waste of exemption to allocate it to a trust with both skip and nonskip beneficiaries if there is a possibility that the GST tax will not apply. Furthermore, under the old rules, once a taxable termination took place it was too late to allocate exemption to the trust.

> EXAMPLE 17 - 21. Matthew creates a trust that gives income to his sister, Kara, for her life with her issue named as remaindermen. Kara has three living children when the trust is established. If her children are still living when she dies, no skip will occur since her children are just one generation below Matthew. If any of Kara's children die before she does, and leaves issue, then at her death a taxable termination will result. In the first instance (all children survive), allocation exemption to the trust would have wasted it, whereas in the second (at least one child died leaving issue) failing to allocate it results in a GST tax that could have been avoided.

EGTRRA allows a retroactive allocation in situations like the one just described. The inclusion ratio is calculated using the values of the previous transfers at the time they were made rather than the values at the time of the taxable termination. The retroactive allocation must be made on a gift tax return that is timely for a gift made in the year of the beneficiary's death (Kara in the above example). Failure to file on time and a late allocation can be made but it will be based on the value of the trust at the beneficiary's death (or alternate valuation date). The IRS is given authority to prescribe regulations for granting relief from failures to make the retroactive allocation in a timely manner.[25] After 2009, if repeal of the estate tax and GST tax is made permanent, all of this will be mute as there will be no GST tax, not even on distributions from, or terminations of, exiting trusts.

The Need for GST Tax Planning

It should be evident by now that planning for the lifetime GST exemption requires careful thought and attentive drafting of complex will or trust clauses, and can add considerably to the expense of estate planning. It also forces the planner to openly discuss with the client an unpleasant fact: the eventual death of the client's children. Which wealthier families are most likely to need careful GST tax planning? Any of the following:

- ▸ "dynastic"-oriented families wishing to perpetuate their wealth
- ▸ families with wealthy children

- ▸ families who believe that their children cannot handle large amounts of money maturely
- ▸ families who wish to give to their grandchildren things that their children cannot or will not give

Which wealthier families most probably do not need GST tax planning? First, families with estates not expected to exceed the GST exemption when combined with taxable gifts need not worry about a GST tax. They may, however, wish to do some trust planning to skip a generation by transferring some property for the benefit of their grandchildren, confident that GST tax will not apply so long as the amount is under the GST exemption.

Second, those who do not wish to directly include grandchildren in their plan. For example, families preferring a 100% marital deduction plan, as in a simple will, probably want their property to pass entirely to the surviving spouse and then to the children, all nonskip persons. Even families anticipating a bypass may have no wish to provide for grandchildren so long as their children are living. Of course, with either plan the property may wind up passing under the instrument to grandchildren (i.e., "descendants" or "issue") if a child predeceases a grandchild. However, the property is likely to be sheltered from the GST tax under the predeceased parent exception, with the help of some careful drafting, to ensure that a direct skip will in fact occur or that the interest is covered by the GST exemption, e.g., allocated to Trust B in the ABC Trust plan.

Third, in some situations, GST tax trust planning will suggest that a person leave the estate outright to the children, perhaps with expectation that the children will preserve the property for ultimate disposition to the grandchildren. Having a large estate divided among the transferor's children may actually result in a greater amount finally landing in the hands of the grandchildren. This might occur because the use of each child's unified credit can reduce the overall estate tax (and there would be no GST tax).

BASIS AFTER ESTATE TAX REPEAL

To set new basis rules for property acquired from a decedent, EGTRRA added § 1022, Treatment of Property Acquired From a Decedent Dying After December 31, 2009. It starts with a general rule that, beginning in 2010 (after the estate, gift, and generation-skipping transfer taxes have been repealed), the present-law rule providing for a fair market value basis for property acquired from a decedent is repealed and replaced with a carryover basis as if the property had been transferred by gift. But the section goes on to make a couple of exceptions such that the general rule will become the exception, applying only to estates of the very wealthy. Probably 98 to 99 percent of all estates will receive the same "step-up" at death as they would have received under pre-EGTRRA law.

Limiting basis increase. The new law applicable to estates of decedents dying after 2009 allows an executor to increase, within limits, the basis in assets owned by the decedent and acquired by the beneficiaries at death.[26] Each decedent's estate is permitted to increase the basis of assets transferred by up to a total of $1.3 million. The $1.3 million limit is increased by the amount of unused capital losses, net operating losses, and certain "built-in" losses of the decedent. In addition, the basis of property transferred to a surviving spouse can be increased by an additional $3 million. Thus, the basis of property transferred to surviving spouses can be increased by a total of $4.3 million.

> EXAMPLE 17 - 21. When Marjorie died in 2010 the executor of her estate had the task of allocating the allowable basis increase. Marjorie had lived in her home for years and it qualified for § 121 gain non-recognition. There was a vacation home that the family planned to keep and a vacant lot that they planned to develop into a small commercial center that would probably be kept as a rental. The apartment building was in a desirable area; some family members wanted to sell it and others want to keep it, so no decision has been made on that property. With these matters in mind, the executor created the following table for the allocation of the increase in basis:

Item	old basis	FMV	added	new
home	$175,000	$400,000	$0	$175,000
apartment building	$400,000	$1,000,000	$600,000	$1,000,000
IRA	$0	$250,000	$0	$0
ABC stock	$150,000	$500,000	$350,000	$500,000
MOP stock	$200,000	$100,000	$0	$100,000
XYZ stock	$90,000	$340,000	$250,000	$340,000
vacation cabin	$25,000	$300,000	$0	$25,000
vacant lot	$50,000	$180,000	$100,000	$150,000
misc. household	$120,000	$70,000	$0	$70,000
			$1,300,000	

Since the estate can take advantage of § 121 to avoid recognition of $250,000 in gain, there is no point to allocating additional basis to it. The apartment building is a depreciable asset; therefore the maximum allocation possible should be made. The IRA is income in respect of a decedent and, just as under the old rules, no step-up in basis is allowed. ABC and XYZ stock are stepped-up to the maximum possible as they might be sold. The value of MOP at Marjorie's death is less than her basis hence it is stepped-down to its date-of-death value. If the family had been planning to sell the vacation cabin sooner than they planned to sell the appreciated stock, then it would be wise to allocate some increase to it rather than to the stock, but this allocation makes sense given their plans to keep it in the family. In general, the miscellaneous household property has gone down in value and the allocation cannot bring basis higher than its date-of-death value. Even the individual personal items that have gone up in value (e.g., collectibles) are likely to remain in the family, hence no increase is allocated to them. The vacant lot receives $100,000 to use up the balance of the $1.3 million allowed increase. Given that neither the lot nor the appreciated stock can be depreciated, and that the $1.3 million increase allowed falls short of bringing the basis of all assets up to their full fair market value, the choice of how to allocate falls on the executor. It makes sense to allocate the remaining basis increase in the order in which one expects asset to be sold.

Nonresidents who are not U.S. citizens will be allowed to increase the basis of property by up to $60,000. The $60,000, $1.3 million, and $3 million amounts are adjusted annually for inflation occurring after 2010. Executors of large estates will be required to file returns reporting how the allocation has been made.[27]

Property eligible for basis increase. In general, the basis of property may be increased above the decedent's adjusted basis in that property only if the property is owned, or is treated as owned, by the decedent at the time of the decedent's death. In the case of property held as joint tenants or tenants by the entireties with the surviving spouse, one-half of the property is treated as having been owned by the decedent and is thus eligible for the basis increase. In the case of property held jointly with a person other than the surviving spouse, the portion of the property attributable to the decedent's consideration furnished is treated as having been owned by the decedent and will be eligible for a basis increase. The decedent also is treated as the owner of property (which will be eligible for a basis increase) if the property was transferred by the decedent during his lifetime to a revocable trust that pays all of its income during the decedent's life to the decedent or at the direction of the decedent. The decedent also is treated as having owned the surviving spouse's one-half share of community property (which will be eligible for a basis increase) if at least one-half of the property was owned by, and acquired from, the decedent.[28] The decedent shall not, however, be treated as owning any property solely by reason of holding a power of appointment with respect to such property.

Property not eligible for a basis increase includes: (1) property that was acquired by the decedent by gift (other than from his or her spouse) during the three-year period ending on the date of the decedent's death; (2) property that constitutes a right to receive income in respect of a decedent; (3) stock or securities of a foreign personal holding company; (4) stock of a domestic international sales corporation (or former domestic international sales corporation); (5) stock of a foreign investment company; and (6) stock of a passive foreign investment company (except for which a decedent shareholder had made a qualified electing fund election).

Basis increase will be allocable on an asset-by-asset basis (e.g., basis increase can be allocated to a share of stock or a block of stock). However, in no case can the basis of an asset be adjusted above its fair market value. If the amount of basis increase is less than the fair market value of assets whose bases are eligible to be increased under these rules, the executor will determine which assets and to what extent each asset receives a basis increase.

Carryover basis for the wealthy. For estates in excess of $1.3 million (above $4.3 million for property to a surviving spouse), a modified carryover basis regime generally takes effect. After the executor of the estate has applied the increase allowed, e.g., the $1.3 or $4.3 million, the rest of the property transferred at the decedent's death will receive a basis equal to the lesser of the adjusted basis of the decedent or the fair market value of the property on the date of the decedent's death.

The modified carryover basis rules apply to property acquired by bequest, devise, or inheritance, or by the decedent's estate from the decedent, property passing from the decedent to the extent such property passed without consideration, and certain other property to which the present law rules apply.[29] Property acquired from a decedent is treated as if the property had been acquired by gift. Thus, the character of gain on the sale of property received from a decedent's estate is carried over to the heir. For example, real estate that has been depreciated and would be subject to recapture if sold by the decedent will be subject to recapture if sold by the heir.

The modified carryover basis rules apply to property acquired from the decedent. Property acquired from the decedent is (1) property acquired by bequest, devise, or inheritance, (2) property acquired by the decedent's estate from the decedent, (3) property transferred by the decedent during his or her lifetime in trust to pay the income for life to or on the order or direction of the decedent, with the right reserved to the decedent at all times before his death to revoke the trust,[30] (4) property transferred by the decedent during his lifetime in trust to pay the income for life to or on the order or direction of the decedent with the right reserved to the decedent at all times before his death to make any change to the enjoyment thereof through the exercise of a power to alter, amend, or terminate the trust,[31] (5) property passing from the decedent by reason of the decedent's death to the extent such property passed without consideration (e.g., property held as joint tenants with right of survivorship or as tenants by the entireties), and (6) the surviving spouse's one-half share of certain community property held by the decedent and the surviving spouse as community property.

Reporting requirements after repeal. To document the basis of transferred property, there will be reporting requirements for both gifts and estates.

Lifetime gifts. A donor is required to report to the Internal Revenue Service the basis and character of any non-cash property transferred by gift with a value in excess of $25,000 (except for gifts to charitable organizations). The donor is be required to report to the IRS:

1. the name and taxpayer identification number of the donee, an accurate description of the property,
2. the adjusted basis of the property in the hands of the donor at the time of gift,
3. the donor's holding period for such property,
4. sufficient information to determine whether any gain on the sale of the property would be treated as ordinary income, and
5. any other information as the Treasury Secretary may prescribe.

Similar information (including the name, address, and phone number of the person making the return) is required to be provided to recipients of such property.

For transfers at death of non-cash assets in excess of $1.3 million and for appreciated property the value of which exceeds $25,000 received by a decedent within three years of death, the executor of the estate would report to the IRS:

1. the name and taxpayer identification number of the recipient of the property,
2. an accurate description of the property,
3. the adjusted basis of the property in the hands of the decedent and its fair market value at the time of death,
4. the decedent's holding period for the property,
5. sufficient information to determine whether any gain on the sale of the property would be treated as ordinary income,
6. the amount of basis increase allocated to the property, and
7. any other information as the Treasury Secretary may prescribe.

The above rules also apply to the trustee of a revocable trust once the settlor dies.

Penalties for failure to report. Any donor required to report the basis and character of any non-cash property with a value in excess of $25,000 who fails to do so is liable for a penalty of $500 for each failure to report such information to the IRS and $50 for each failure to report such information to a beneficiary.

Any person required to report to the IRS transfers at death of non-cash assets in excess of $1.3 million in value who fails to do so is liable for a penalty of $10,000 for the failure to report such information. Any person required to report to the IRS the receipt by a decedent of appreciated property valued in excess of $25,000 within three years of death who fails to do so is liable for a penalty of $500 for the failure to report such information to the IRS. There also is a penalty of $50 for each failure to report such information to a beneficiary.

No penalty is imposed with respect to any failure that is due to reasonable cause. If any failure to report to the IRS or a beneficiary under the bill is due to intentional disregard of the rules, then the penalty is five percent of the fair market value of the property for which reporting was required, determined at the date of the decedent's death (for property passing at death) or determined at the time of gift (for a lifetime gift).

FREEZING THE VALUE OF A BUSINESS INTEREST

The United States has many owners of very successful closely held businesses. Some have amassed a degree of wealth that they themselves consider to be more than adequate to provide for their income and capital needs for the rest of their lives. Nevertheless, few of them look forward to relinquishing control of their business interests, even though they realize that someday their wealth must be transferred. When the time comes, most want the transfer tax to be as low as possible. Indeed, many consider living beyond 2009 to be an integral part of their estate plan.

Prior to 1987, entrepreneurs had several relatively safe but complicated methods of freezing the transfer tax value of their businesses without giving up control. The two most common methods were the corporate recapitalization and the partnership capital freeze. Through a reorganization of the firm's capital structure, the owner could retain voting control of the firm, continue to receive about the same amount of income from the firm, and freeze the value of his or her own interest for transfer tax purposes, while assuring that any future appreciation in the value of the business would benefit other (usually younger) family members.

By adding Chapter 14 (IRC §§ 2701-2704) to the Internal Revenue Code in 1990,[32] the government has substantially restricted the ability to freeze the value of a business interest and retain control of it. The material that follows first discusses the use of business estate freezing during its heyday and then reviews the present law.

Corporate Recapitalization Freeze

Prior to Congress's "anti-freeze" legislation, a corporate recapitalization (a "recap") might be structured as follows: Prior to the recap, the owner had a controlling interest in a company through the ownership of most or all of the common stock. The owner exchanged the common stock for a combination of common stock and voting preferred shares. The preferred stock was given high dividend rates so it was worth almost as much as the underlying value of the firm. The owner would then transfer the common stock to younger-generation family members. The common shares were deemed to have very little value, given the high value placed on the preferred shares. The retained voting preferred shares meant the transferor would be able to outvote the new common stock shareholders. Any future growth of the business inured to the common stock, because the preferred shares had a fixed upper limit to their income and a fixed value in liquidation. In the following three examples, assume the date is 1987, i.e., before Congress passed its first anti-freeze legislation.

EXAMPLE 17 - 22. Alfred owns all 1,000 shares of the common stock of a highly successful computer software corporation called AlfSoft, Inc. Each share is valued at $2,000. The company will have $260,000 in net income this year, however, within the next six months, the company expects to be releasing a revolutionary new software package that might triple the company's sales and double its net worth. Alfred is divorced and has two children, Kyle and Maude. Kyle, age 37, has worked for the firm for 10 years and shows great promise to take over when Alfred departs. Maude, age 34, a tenured biology professor, has never been interested in working for the company. At his death, Alfred wishes to leave his entire estate in approximately equal shares to the children.

A recapitalization of the firm is undertaken. In exchange for Alfred's 1,000 shares of common stock, the corporation issues three classes of new stock:

1. 20,000 shares of nonvoting noncumulative preferred stock, with a par value of $100, are retained by Alfred. These are valued at close to $2 million.
2. 480 shares of nonvoting common stock, 230 shares to Kyle, 230 shares to Maude, and 20 shares to Alfred. These shares have almost no value.
3. 20 shares of voting common stock, to Alfred.

Both types of common stock will share, pro rata, in any income available after payment of preferred dividends and in any increase in the firm's value. Alfred's estate plan is changed to leave his preferred shares equally to his two children, the 20 shares nonvoting common to Maude, and the 20 shares voting common to Kyle.

Assume that when Alfred dies (about 10 years after the recap), the business is worth $6 million. Assuming the preferred stock's value remains at $2 million, the total value of the common shares will be $4 million, or $8,000 per share. Included in his gross estate is the value of the preferred stock ($2 million), plus the value of the 40 shares of common stock ($320,000). Thus, nearly all of Alfred's interest in the firm remained frozen at its value as of date of recapitalization, and nearly the entire post-recapitalization appreciation inured tax-free to the interests held by Kyle and Maude.

EXAMPLE 17 - 23. In the prior example, instead of passing the voting common shares at his death, Alfred could make periodic gifts of them to Kyle in amounts not exceeding the annual gift tax exclusion. In this way, Alfred would have both given additional incentive to Kyle to remain with the firm and, at the same time, reduced even further the value of the business interest taxable in his estate at his death.

The ideal recap was designed to have the following tax-related benefits:

1. No taxation to the corporation arising from the recap.
2. No taxable income to the owner on receipt of the new shares.
3. Little or no taxable gift by the owner.
4. At death, the amount included in the owner's taxable estate attributable to the firm would approximately equal the value of the owner's interest in the business at the date of the recap.

Even prior to the passage of anti-freeze legislation in 1987, the IRS took the position that the value of the common shares transferred could not possibly equal zero because the value of the preferred shares could not be made to equal the total value of the firm. Consequently, it argued, some positive value remained in the common stock, value that was therefore transferred as a taxable gift to the other family members.

Old law: IRC § 2036(c). Enacted in 1987, and repealed retroactively by the 1990 Act, § 2036(c) virtually eliminated the use of the estate freezing recapitalizations after December of 1987. We can skip the details, but when owners retained income-producing assets that had limited growth potential (i.e., preferred stock) and gave away assets with great growth potential (i.e., common stock), the transaction was treated as though there was a retained interest in the gift. Hence when the owner-transferor died, the gross estate included the date-of-death value of the entire business, even the part that had been given away.

Current law: IRC § 2701. Section 2701 takes a different approach to limiting the use of business estate freezes. IRC § 2701 imposes a gift tax at the time of the transfer, presumptively increases the value of the gift, and diminishes the value of retained interests. Remember, the lower the value of the retained interest, the higher the value of the taxable gift, and vice versa.

Unless the retained interest has a right to a "qualified payment" it is valued at zero and the gift is equal to the entire value of the business. Such "qualified payments" are periodic, cumulative dividends. Their value is subtracted from the total value of the business in determining the value of the gift of common stock.

If the business fails to make the qualified payments, the law includes the value of the missed payments plus interest in the estate of the owner of the retained interest (e.g., the preferred shares held by the parent), or sooner if the retained interest is transferred during the owner's lifetime. The § 2701 valuation rules apply to any post-October 8, 1990, transfer of junior equity interests in a corporation or partnership to a member of the transferor's family, if the transferor or family member retains an interest in the corporation or partnership immediately after the transfer. This area of the law has many technical terms with very specific meanings, however it is easiest to understand if you by thinking of the following typical scenario: the parents keep the preferred shares and the children take the common shares, the parent is the "applicable family member," each child is a "member of the transferor's family," the preferred shares are the "retained interest," and the common shares are the "junior equity interest."

Transfer. A transfer of a business interest can be direct or indirect. Examples of an indirect transfer include a contribution to capital, a redemption and a recapitalization or other change in capital structure.[33]

Junior equity interest. A junior equity interest includes common stock, or, in the case of a partnership, any interest in which the rights to income and capital are junior to the rights of other equity interests.

Member of the transferor's family. Members of the transferor's family include the transferor's spouse, descendants of the transferor and the transferor's spouse, and any spouse of such descendants.[34] These are people likely to receive the common stock from the transferor. Note that nieces and nephews are not included.

Applicable family member. An applicable family member of the transferor includes the transferor's spouse, ancestors of the transferor or the transferor's spouse, and any spouse of such ancestor.[35] These are the people likely to be trying to shift wealth to the younger generation family members.

Applicable retained interest. An applicable retained interest is any interest (except publicly traded stock) having either (a) a distribution right, but only if the transferor and applicable family members hold control (50% or more) of the business immediately before the transfer, or (b) a liquidation, put, call or conversion right, irrespective of the degree of control held by the parties.[36]

> EXAMPLE 17 - 24. If undertaken today, the AlfSoft, Inc., corporate recapitalization described earlier would fall within the rules of § 2701. Alfred transferred a junior equity interest (common stock) in a corporation to members of his family (his son and daughter), and retained an applicable retained interest (preferred stock) with respect to a business over which Alfred had control immediately before the transfer.

Section 2701 does not apply when the transferred interest is of the same class as the retained interest, or if market quotations are "readily available" for the retained interest, or if the retained interest is proportionally the same as the transferred interest.[37]

> EXAMPLE 17 - 25. Up to now, Rocky has been the sole owner of RR Corporation, which has issued only one class of stock. Today, Rocky gives 10% of his common stock to his daughter, retaining the remaining 90%. Section 2701 does not apply, and the usual rules pertaining to gifts would be used to value the transferred shares.

Effect of valuation treatment under IRC § 2701. When § 2701 applies, three specific valuation rules must be observed:

1. The junior equity must be assigned a value of at least 10 percent of the value of the business.[38] This is the "minimum value rule."
2. The transferred interest must be valued by the "subtraction method."
3. The retained rights other than "qualified payments" must be assigned a value of zero.[39] This is the so-called "zero valuation rule." However, the transferor can elect to have certain nonqualified payment rights treated as "qualified."

Under the second rule, a simplified application of the subtraction method starts with the value of the entity and subtracts the value of all family-held senior equity interests (with nonqualifying retained interests valued at zero), to arrive at the gift amount that must be allocated to the transferred interests.[40]

EXAMPLE 17 - 26. Based on the AlfSoft, Inc., recapitalization in the preceding examples, the value of Alfred's gift equals $2 million, which is the value of the entity reduced by zero, the value of Alfred's retained interest because it is nonqualifying. Since Alfred's son receives all transferred interests, the entire $2 million is allocated to those interests. Thus, Alfred has made a $2 million gross gift to his son.

Under the third rule, retained rights to *qualified payments* have value and do not fall within the zero valuation rule. A qualified payment is defined as "any dividend payable on a periodic basis under any cumulative preferred stock (or a comparable payment under any partnership interest) to the extent that such dividend (or comparable payment) is determined at a fixed rate." The Section goes on to state that, "a payment shall be treated as fixed as to rate if such payment is determined at a rate which bears a fixed relationship to a specified market interest rate."[41] In addition, on the gift tax return, the donor can elect to treat a nonqualified payment right as though it was a qualified one, with the result that the retained interest would have a value greater than zero.

EXAMPLE 17 - 27. Had Alfred, in the above examples, retained a right to cumulative preferred stock with a set dividend rate (e.g., 8% of par), the payment right would be treated as a qualified payment so the value of the retained preferred stock could be subtracted from the value of the business in determining the value of Alfred's gift. Even for noncumulative preferred stock, Alfred could elect to have it treated as if it had a qualified payment right. Either way, if the value of the qualifying preferred stock was $1,500,000, Alfred would have made a gross gift of $500,000. Even if the preferred stock was worth $1,950,000, Alfred's gift could not be given a value below $200,000, under the rule that the "junior equity" interests must be assigned a minimum value of 10% of the value of the entire business.

If the qualified payments are not made when due, their value (increased as though the payment had been made on time and reinvested) will, at some point, be treated as though it is a taxable gift by the transferor or as though the value is part of the transferor's gross estate. The holder of the retained interest (the preferred) can elect to have the missed dividend payments treated as gifts to the junior equity holders rather than having them treated as received and "reinvested."[42] Making the election avoids having the phantom reinvestment value taxed in the preferred shareholder's estate.

If not for this rule, the payments, and thus the value of the retained interest, would be illusory and the real value of the gift would be higher than its taxable value because of the unmade payments.

The increase in value for payments not timely made is the amount that would have been earned had the payments been timely made, and then invested at the interest rate originally used to determine the value of the retained interest. The forgoing treatment of missed payments is also true where the transferor elected to treat nonqualifying payments as qualifying, and the business then fails to make the payments. Recognizing that there are good business reasons for not declaring dividends, Congress (through the code) allows a grace period of four years. If a payment is made within four years of its due date, it will be treated as having been timely made.

If the transferor dies still owning an applicable retained interest (e.g., the preferred shares) for which there are cumulated unpaid dividends, his or her gross estate will be increased by the amount that should have been paid, with the amount further increased as though it had been reinvested since its payment due date at the yield rate originally used to value the retained interest. If the transferor gives away the retained interest (e.g., the preferred stock) while there are cumulated unpaid dividends, then the unpaid amount (increased as though invested) is treated as a gift. In addition, if payments are received more than four years after they are due, the taxpayer (holder of the shares) can elect to treat the hypothetical increase in value (the increase that would have been there had the payment been timely received and invested) as a gift made during the year.

EXAMPLE 17 - 28. Richard holds all the outstanding stock of RichGold Company, Inc. He exchanges his shares in a recapitalization for 19,000 shares of cumulative voting preferred stock, each with a $100 par paying 8%, and 1,000 shares of no-par voting common stock. He then transfers the common stock to his daughter Maureen. Section 2701 applies to the transfer and the gift is calculated using the subtraction method. The preferred shares should pay dividends of $152,000 each year. After not paying any dividends for three years, the corporation's board of directors declared a dividend payment on the preferred shares and Richard received a payment of $152,000. The payment, because it came within the four-year grace period, is treated as if it was timely made.

EXAMPLE 17 - 29. Continuing with the prior example, assume that the second $152,000 payment is made exactly five years late and that Richard decides to treat as a gift the hypothetical increase in value that investing the dividends would have produced. The amount of the gift is the additional amount that Richard would now have if the $152,000 had been invested at 8% compounded annually for the five years, i.e., $152,000 * (1.08)^5 - $152,000 = $71,338.

EXAMPLE 17 - 30. Suppose Richard dies in 2005 and the dividends for the prior three years are the only ones past due. Since his death is a taxable event, each payment that is past due must be included in Richard's gross estate (i.e., 3 * $152,000), plus the income that would have been generated on each payment invested on the due date. Thus, there would be three years of hypothetical income for the earliest missed payment, two years on the next, and one year for the last. Had the three payments been received on time and reinvested so as to earn 8%, Richard's estate would have had an additional $532,929 (i.e., $152,000 * (1.08)^3 + $152,000 * (1.08)^2 + $152,000 * (1.08)). This amount must be added to his gross estate.

Note that a corporation is not legally required to pay dividends even if it has the money to do so. Any unpaid dividends are "past due" only in an Internal Revenue Code sense. The general rule is that only the board of directors can declare a dividend.

EXAMPLE 17 - 31. Same facts as in the prior example, except instead of dying, Richard gave all of the preferred shares to Maureen when dividends for the prior three years were past due. The result would be nearly the same, with the value of the missed dividends (i.e., 3 * $152,000), and their related hypothetical investment return (i.e., $76,929) added to Richard's taxable gifts for the year.

To avoid double taxation of the retained interest, the Code allows a deduction from the donor's taxable gifts (if the taxable event is a gift) or the donor's adjusted taxable gifts (if the taxable event is the donor's death). The deduction is the lesser of–

(1) the amount by which the value of the initial gift was increased due to the application of the § 2701 subtraction method; or

(2) the amount "duplicated" in the tax base at a subsequent transfer, whether the transfer is a gift of the preferred stock or occurs because the preferred stock is included at the transferor's death in his or her taxable estate.[43]

EXAMPLE 17 - 32. Martha owned 10,000 shares of $100 par value noncumulative preferred stock (bearing an annual dividend of $10 per share) of Ahtram Company, Inc., and 500 shares of its common stock. The underlying value of the company was $1,500,000 and the preferred and common stock had values of $1,000,000 and

$500,000, respectively. On March 10, 2003, she transfers all of the common shares to her son Ethan. Since § 2701 applies to the transaction and Martha does not elect to treat the retained shares as having "qualified rights," the subtraction method results in a transfer valued at $1,500,000. Notice that the increase is $1,000,000 since the common stock is valued at $500,000.

EXAMPLE 17 - 33. On May 2, 2006, Martha died still owning the preferred stock. An appraisal determined that the value is $950,000. Given that this is less than the $1,000,000 increase in value of the initial transfer, her adjusted taxable gifts are reduced by $950,000 to reflect this duplicated amount. If, on the other hand, the stock is valued in her estate at $1,050,000, then the earlier increase in the taxable gifts is the lesser amount, and the decrease to her adjusted taxable gifts is $1,000,000.

Certain rights and restrictions disregarded: IRC § 2703. Section 2703 requires that the value of any property subject to rights and restrictions shall be valued for transfer tax purposes without regard to the reduced valuation effect of those rights or restrictions.

EXAMPLE 17 - 34. Shortly before his death this year, Hansen, sole shareholder of the common stock of his $1 million closely held corporation, executed a contract with his daughter, who is obligated to purchase all of Hansen's stock at Hansen's death for $400,000. Under § 2703, Hansen's gross estate will include the stock at a value of $1 million; the reduction in actual value attributable to the obligation to sell the stock must be disregarded.

More specifically, the rights and restrictions that must be disregarded under § 2703 include:

1. Any option, agreement, or other right to acquire or use the property at a price less than the property's fair market value (determined without regard to such option, agreement, or right).
2. Any restriction on the right to sell or use the property.[44]

Section 2703 does not apply to any agreement, option, right, or restriction, which meets all of the following requirements:

1. It is a bona fide business arrangement.
2. It is not a device to transfer the property to members of the decedent's family for less than full and adequate consideration in money or money's worth.

3. Its terms are comparable to similar arrangements entered into by persons in an arm's length transaction.[45]

> EXAMPLE 17 - 35. Shortly before his death this year, Trafalgar, sole owner of the common stock of his $1 million closely held corporation, executed a contract with a non-relative business associate, who is obligated to purchase all of Trafalgar's stock at Trafalgar's death for $960,000. The valuation rules under § 2703 are not applicable and the value of $960,000 should be accepted for estate tax purposes.

Treatment of certain lapsing rights and restrictions: IRC § 2704. Section 2704 is of relatively limited application. It addresses the transfer taxation of the lapse of a voting or liquidation right in a corporation or partnership.

In general, if there has been a lapse and the person holding the right before the lapse and the members of that person's family hold control of the entity both before and after the lapse, then the lapse is treated as gift or a transfer at death and subject to tax. The value of the transfer subject to taxation is the reduction in value due to the lapse. The reader is referred to Reg. § 25.2704-1(f) for examples.

The present status of business freezes. Estate freezing recaps of the type created prior to § 2036(c) still work for some families since § 2701 does not apply to transfers benefiting nieces and nephews, or anyone not related to the transferor. The definition of "applicable family members" includes only the transferor's spouse, descendants, descendants of the spouse, and their respective spouses.[46] In lieu of a recap the owner might consider a simple outright gift of the business. Gifting is simple, and control can be retained by transferring nonvoting stock.

Additional Freeze Techniques

Finally, some other types of business freeze techniques are not affected by the antifreeze rules because no form of lifetime gifting is involved.

Testamentary freeze. A bequest of common stock to younger generation beneficiaries and preferred stock to the spouse.

Postmortem recapitalization freeze. A recapitalization after the owner's death, in which the marital trust receives the preferred stock and the bypass trust receives the common stock. Remember, the bypass trust is not taxed again when

S2 dies, so any appreciation that pushes up the value of the common shares escapes estate taxation.

Generation-skipping freeze. The children receive preferred stock, by gift or bequest, and the grandchildren receive the common stock. The GST exemption is applied to the transfer to the grandchildren.

Notwithstanding these possible opportunities, the current limitations and restrictions are numerous, and commentators have been guarded about the extent to which corporate recapitalizations will be used in the future. If the repeal of the estate tax is made permanent, most of this type of planning will become obsolete.

Partnership Capital Freeze. It may be possible to reorganize an unincorporated firm to achieve the same results as the estate-freezing recap. Under the partnership capital freeze, two classes of partnership interests are created, one for the older, wealthier, family members and one for the younger family members. The interests of the older family members are restricted in ways that limit the upside value, thus assuring that future appreciation in the business will accrue to the shares of the younger generation. As with the corporate recap, the partnership capital freeze is a complex, rapidly changing area of tax law, subject to the provisions of § 2701 and also to frequent IRS attack. Planning should be approached carefully, with the help of competent counsel.

MISCELLANEOUS ESTATE PLANNING ITEMS

A place for estate planning items that either do not fit well elsewhere, have limited application, or interesting (and come up in discussion) but are out of date.

Qualified conservation easement: § 2031(c). The Taxpayer Relief Act of 1997 added a provision that allows some tax relief for estates that include land that is appropriate for a conservation easement. The complicated rules will just be summarized here. Basically, the executor can donate (this had better be done with the blessing of all beneficiaries whose interest would be affected) a conservation easement to certain organizations and exclude a portion of the value of the land, up to certain dollar limits, from the gross estate. The election is made by the executor on the estate tax return. This election is available even if the decedent's estate plan made no provision for a conservation easement.

A *conservation easement* is one that protects the natural habitat of fish, wildlife, or plants, a historical site (land and/or structures), or open space for public benefit, i.e., a scenic or recreational benefit. The easement must be donated to a charitable organization or government agency. As originally enacted the land had to meet certain location requirements, e.g., within a national park or wilderness area. The 2001 tax legislation changed the rules, and for the estates of decedents dying after December 31, 2000, a conservation easement can be claimed for land located anywhere in the United States or its possessions. The decedent or a member of the decedent's family must have owned the property for three years prior to the decedent's death.

If the executor makes the election, donates the easement, and fulfills all of the other requirements of the section, then the estate can deduct the lesser of: (A) the applicable percentage of the value of the land subject to the easement, reduced by any charitable deduction that results from said donation, or (B) the easement exclusion limitation. The *applicable percentage* is 40% times the value of the land reduced by two percentage points for each percentage point (or fraction thereof) by which the value of the qualified conservation easement is less than 30% of the value of the land (determined without regard to the value of the easement). The easement exclusion limitation starts at $100,000 for estates of decedents dying in 1998 and increases $100,000 each year until it reaches $500,000 for the year 2002 and beyond.

> EXAMPLE 17 - 36. When she died in 1999, Alice Le Mond's estate included acreage near a national park. Without a conservation easement, it was worth $450,000 for estate tax purposes. An easement for riding and hiking was negotiated with the Park Service. Appraisers determined that the value of the easement to the park was $160,000. Since this is greater than 30% of the value of the land, there is no percentage reduction. The estate can deduct the lesser of 40% [$180,000] times the value of the land or the exclusion limit for 1999 [$200,000]. If the easement was valued at $117,000 (i.e., 26% of the value of the land) the deduction would be 32% [i.e., 40% - 2 * (30% - 26%)] times the value of the land, resulting in an exclusion of $144,000 [i.e., 32% * $450,000]. Had she died in 1998, the limit would have been $100,000.

There is a recapture provision that takes effect if the easement agreement has not been implemented within the earlier of two years after the decedent's death or the sale of the land by the estate or the heirs.

Asset protection foreign trusts. Individuals owning substantial liquid assets and wishing to more completely protect them from their own creditors may consider creating a foreign "protection of assets" trust. Certain jurisdictions including the Bahamas, Bermuda, and the Cayman Islands offer great protection from pre- and post-judgment remedies of creditors. Drawbacks include setup costs in excess of $25,000, considerable reporting requirements, and ethical issues. An in-depth discussion of asset protection is beyond the scope of this text.

Flower bonds. A topic clearly past its "sell-by" date, this is not so much an advanced topic as a bit of estate planning trivia. It could come under the heading: "Sometimes Congress Does the Darnedest Things." In the 1950s and early 1960s, the federal government issued Treasury bonds that could be used at their par value, plus accrued interest, to pay the federal estate tax, provided the bonds were part of the decedent's estate, i.e., owned at the time of death. Since the bond yields, while reasonable when issued, were quite low (3% to 5%) compared to other investments in the 1970s and 1980s, they began selling at deep discounts. This created some estate planning opportunities for persons with terminal illnesses to purchase bonds at as little as 85% of par shortly before death. The decedent's executor could use them to pay the estate tax, achieving an increase in value in a short time span. Because the worth of the bonds jumped from their discounted value to their par value when the owner died, the bonds were called flower bonds. Of course, to the extent the bonds could be used to pay estate taxes, their value in the estate was the par value. Thus, some of that 15% increase in value was lost to increased estate taxes. The last of the flower bonds matured November 15, 1998, which means the estate planning opportunities are gone.

CONCLUSION

For those working in any of the estate planning fields, the study of estate planning is never really over. Mastery of this textbook is just the beginning. New ideas lead to new planning strategies. As laws change, estate planning professionals need to adapt to the changes in a continuing effort to aid clients in achieving their goals. Continuing education seminars, estate planning journals, and consultations with colleagues will create the knowledge base needed to be a successful estate planner. Hopefully you will find that helping individuals and families achieve predictability, security, and satisfaction with results as they move through life's many transitions is very rewarding both financially and psychologically.

QUESTIONS AND PROBLEMS

1. What peculiar aspect of the estate trust allows it to qualify for the marital deduction?

2. Why was the bypass trust (Trust B) of the Traditional AB Trust plan defined in such a way as to receive just 50% of S1's adjusted gross estate?

3. What 1981 change in the law caused the Estate Equalization AB Trust to go out of fashion? Explain.

4. A bypass trust provides for income to the trustor's wife for her life, then remainder outright to his daughter, if she survives her mother; otherwise, to the daughter's issue.
   (a) What is the potential GST tax problem?
   (b) Is the size of the trust a factor?
   (c) Can you suggest a solution to the problem?

5. Which clients do not need to worry too much about GST tax planning and which ones do need to worry about it? Why is it becoming less of a worry?

6. Darryl, having not previously used his GST exemption, allocates it to his 2007 gift of stock worth $2,024,000 to his son's two children (Darryl's grandchildren). (a) What is the gift tax? The GST tax? (b) What does the allocation of the GST exemption to this gift tell you about Darryl's son? Explain.

7. What is the advantage in allocating the GST exemption such that a trust either has a zero inclusion ratio (i.e., completely covered by the exemption) or an inclusion ratio of one?

8. Richard died in 2010, leaving his entire estate to his two children. His executor must allocate basis increase among the assets of his estate. The overall appreciated value of his estate is such that not all assets that qualify for a step-up will receive a full step-up. What determines whether a full step-up should be allocated insofar as the following items (just a small portion of

his estate) are concerned? Explain. (a) ZMP stock purchased for $75,000 now worth $250,000. (b) A small rental house that was once Richard's home. He bought it for $45,000 and its date-of-death value was $200,000. (c) A painting purchased for $2,000 but now worth about $500,000.

9. Penny died in 2010, leaving her entire estate to Jake, her long time live-in lover. Jake claims that the two of them were married by a sea captain on one of the cruises they took, but he can't find the papers to prove it. He has photos from what he claims to be the wedding, but it is hard to tell whether they show the two being married or whether it was just costume night on the cruise. The state would recognize the marriage if Jake can prove it took place. Penny's estate is worth millions and is highly appreciated. (a) Given that the estate tax is repealed and no one is contesting the validity of Penny's will, why does it matter whether they are married? (b) Assuming the maximum allowable basis increase is allocated to each of the following, what would be Jake's basis in each? WEB stock purchased for $40,000, date-of-death value (DODV) $95,000; a sailboat purchased for $100,000, DODV $60,000; and owned an IRA with a basis of $16,000, DODV $70,000.

10. Perla's corporation, presently worth $6,000,000, is increasing in value. Recapitalizing the corporation she causes it to issue to her preferred shares with a stated capital of $5,600,000, paying a 6% cumulative annual dividend, and with a liquidation preference of $5,900,000; her children receive all of the common stock. The preferred share holders (i.e., just Perla) have the right to force liquidation if the preferred dividends are not paid for two or more consecutive years. (a) Assuming the preferred shares avoid the zero valuation rule, what is the minimum value assigned to the common shares? (b) Is the liquidation preference given any value, i.e., does it increase the value of the retained interest? Explain. (c) Given the dividend rate, what dividends should be paid each year to avoid having the lack of payment accumulated for inclusion in Perla's estate? If Perla elects to treat non-payment as a gift, to whom is it a gift?

11. Joshua did a recapitalization of his closely held corporation in 2002. At the time the corporation's value was $3,000,000. He retained preferred 5% non-cumulative shares with a stated value of $2,500,000. The common shares

were issued to his two children. Although he reported the gift of the common shares at a value of $500,000 (less two annual exclusions), the IRS at audit put the gross value of the gift at $3,000,000 and assessed a gift tax of $920,000. When Joshua died in 2007, the preferred shares were still in his estate and valued for estate tax purposes at $2,500,000. His taxable estate including the preferred shares at full value was $7,000,000. (a) Why was the total value of the corporation treated as a gift in 2002 and not just the $500,000 Joshua assigned to common shares? (b) Given the preferred shares are included in Joshua's estate, is there any relief from double taxation? Explain.

12. When Amel died intestate in 2006, her estate included acreage in Montana. Emilo and Elena are the only heirs. Emilo, while serving as administrator, has been approached by an environmentalist group that would like to see the estate set aside about 400 acres as part of a conservation easement. The acres include a stream at the base of a mountain where the state is considering releasing endangered condors. The group wants to put Emilo together with representatives of the State Park and Game Department as there is apparently an interest on their part to accept the easement. (a) Emilo asks how it is possible to gain an estate tax benefit, given that granting an easement was not part of his mother's estate plan. Explain. (b) Briefly, what must be established to obtain an estate tax benefit? Does it matter that the property is not located next to a state or national park? (c) In general, what might be accomplished by granting the easement? (d) Suppose they reduce the estate taxes by $200,000, will any of the taxes saved be recaptured if they sell the Montana property (including the 400 acres subject to the easement) 20 months after their mother's death? Explain.

13. Why were certain government bonds called "flower bonds?" From an estate planning standpoint, why are they no longer useful?

ANSWERS TO THE QUESTIONS AND PROBLEMS (odd numbered only)

1. Estate trusts qualifying for the marital deduction:
   Because it must be distributed to S2 or S2's estate at some point, it is not considered a terminal interest, hence it qualifies for the marital deduction. It is a peculiar aspect because it is hard to conceive of a reason to use this in an estate plan.

3. Why equalization AB trust plans disappeared:
   The old equalization plans were popular when the marginal rates were extremely high and large estates were forced to pay a tax even if most of the estate was left to S2. With the advent of the 100% marital deduction and the possibility of the QTIP election, mandating a tax at the first death, as is required with an Estate Equalization AB Trust, does not seem wise, especially when a QTIP election can equalize the estates if S1 is the wealthier spouse and equalization seems appropriate. The fact that the QTIP decision is not made until after S1 dies makes the ABC Trust plan much more attractive than the old equalization plan that was fixed once S1 died.

5. Worrying about the GST tax:
   Clients whose estates are not expected to exceed the estate AEA, and those who do not wish to directly include grandchildren in their plan, do not need to worry too much about the GST tax. For example, clients preferring a 100% marital deduction plan, as in a simple will, probably want their property to pass entirely to the surviving spouse and then to the children. Even clients anticipating a bypass may have no wish to provide for grandchildren. Of course, with most plans, property may wind up passing under the instrument to grandchildren (i.e., "issue") if a child predeceases a grandchild. However, the property involved can usually be sheltered from the GST tax under the predeceased parent direct skip rule or, with the help of careful drafting distributions to skip persons can be made from trust not subject to the GST tax.
   Clients who should do some GST tax planning include: "dynastic" oriented clients wishing to perpetuate themselves through multi-generation trusts, clients with very wealthy children, clients who believe that their children cannot handle large amounts of money maturely, and clients who

wish to give to their grandchildren significant amounts of wealth. The GST tax has become less of a worry since the GST exemption has increased dramatically in step with the estate AEA.

7. Allocating the GST exemption:

By having at least one trust with a zero inclusion ratio, one can direct that any distributions to skip persons first come from that source and to non-skip persons from the trusts with an inclusion ratio of one. If the inclusion ratio is some fraction, then all distributions to skip persons will have at least some GST tax to pay.

9. Penny's estate and basis rules:

(a) Where the transfer is to a surviving spouse, the executor gets to allocate up to $4.3 million as additional basis instead of just $1.3 million. (b) WEB stock, full step-up to $95,000 (c) basis cannot be more than the DODV, i.e., just $60,000 for the sailboat (a case where one would prefer a carry-over basis); (d) an IRA is an example of income in respect of a decedent (IRD) and as such it receives no step-up in basis, hence, it stays at $16,000.

11. Joshua's attempted corporate freeze:

(a) Because the preferred shares are non-cumulative the interest represented by the dividend rate is non-qualified, hence the zero valuation rule applies (not a good thing) and the entire value of the corporation is treated as having been given (attaches to the common shares). (b) There will be a credit based upon the preferred shares being taxed as a gift and again as part of the estate. To the extent the transfer generates both an estate and a gift tax, a deduction is allowed equal to the lesser of the extra inclusion as a gift, due to the zero valuation method or the property's value in the estate. By removing the shares' value from the estate, the taxable amount is $4,500,000 instead of $7,000,000. The tax of $1,590,000 is $1,125,000 less than if the preferred shares are included. If duplicating this example using ETAX, use $2,980,000 as the gift in 2002 since the annual exclusion should be allowed for the portion of the gift represented by the common stock (i.e., there is a present interest there), and the gift tax payable would be $876,000 not the $920,000 actually paid.

13. Flower bonds:

They are called such because they "blossomed" when the owner died. Meaning that their face value could be used to pay the federal estate tax rather than their discounted market value. Since the last of these matured in the late 1990s, they are no longer around.

ENDNOTES

1. IRC § 2056(b)(5).

2. IRC § 2613(a).

3. IRC § 2602.

4. IRC § 2604.

5. EGTRRA, P.L. 107-16, § 503(c)(10) adding new subsection (c) to IRC § 2604.

6. IRC § 2611(b)(1).

7. Reg. § 26.2601-1(b)(1)(ii).

8. IRC § 2612(c)(1).

9. IRC § 2603(a)(3).

10. IRC § 2623.

11. IRC § 2624(b).

12. IRC § 2624(c).

13. IRC § 2612(a)(1).

14. See Appendix A, Table 7, Estate Planning Indexed Values.

15. IRC § 2612(b).

16. IRC § 2641(b).

17. IRC § 2631(c)(1).

18. IRC § 2642(a).

19. IRC § 2651(e)(1).

20. IRC § 2551(e).

21. Reg. § 26.2612-1(a)(2)(i).

22. Proposed Reg. § 26.2651-1(a)(2)(iv).

23. IRC § 2513.

24. IRC § 2632(b)(1) - (b)(3).

25. IRC § 2642(g) added by EGTRRA.

26. IRC § 1022(b).

27. IRC § 6018.

28. Thus, similar to the present law rule in IRC § 1014(b)(6), both the decedent's and the surviving spouse's share of community property would change.

29. IRC § 1014(b)(2) and (3).

30. This is the same property the basis of which is stepped up to date-of-death fair market value under present law IRC § 1014(b)(2).

31. This is the same property the basis of which is stepped up to date-of-death fair market value under present law IRC § 1014(b)(3).

32. Revenue Act of 1987.

33. IRC § 2701(e)(5).

34. IRC § 2701(e)(1).

35. IRC § 2701(e)(2).

36. IRC § 2701(b).

37. IRC § 2701(a)(2).

38. IRC § 2701(a)(4).

39. IRC § 2701(a)(3)(A).

40. Reg. § 25.2701-3(b).

41. IRC § 2701(a)(3)(A).

42. IRC § 2701(d)(3)(A)(iii).

43. IRC § 2701(e)(6); Reg. § 25.2701-5.

44. IRC § 2703(a).

45. IRC § 2703(b).

46. IRC § 2701(e)(1).

Tax and Valuation Tables

TABLE 1 Federal Unified Transfer-Tax Rates - Since 1/1/77

If the Amount is:		Tentative Tax:		
Over	But Not Over	Base Amount +	Percent	On Excess Over
For years (1976-2009) the marginal rates are the same for taxable transfers up to $2,000,000.				
$0	$10,000	$0	18%	$0
$10,000	$20,000	$1,800	20%	$10,000
$20,000	$40,000	$3,800	22%	$20,000
$40,000	$60,000	$8,200	24%	$40,000
$60,000	$80,000	$13,000	26%	$60,000
$80,000	$100,000	$18,200	28%	$80,000
$100,000	$150,000	$23,800	30%	$100,000
$150,000	$250,000	$38,800	32%	$150,000
$250,000	$500,000	$70,800	34%	$250,000
$500,000	$750,000	$155,800	37%	$500,000
$750,000	$1,000,000	$248,300	39%	$750,000
$1,000,000	$1,250,000	$345,800	41%	$1,000,000
$1,250,000	$1,500,000	$448,300	43%	$1,250,000
$1,500,000	$2,000,000	$555,800	45%	$1,500,000
Top Rates: 1977 through 1981				
$2,000,000	$2,500,000	$780,800	49%	$2,000,000
$2,500,000	$3,000,000	$1,025,800	53%	$2,500,000
$3,000,000	$3,500,000	$1,290,800	57%	$3,000,000
$3,500,000	$4,000,000	$1,575,800	61%	$3,500,000
$4,000,000	$4,500,000	$1,880,800	65%	$4,000,000
$4,500,000	$5,000,000	$2,205,800	69%	$4,500,000
$5,000,000		$2,550,800	70%	$5,000,000
Top Rates: 1982				
$2,000,000	$2,500,000	$780,800	49%	$2,000,000
$2,500,000	$3,000,000	$1,025,800	53%	$2,500,000
$3,000,000	$3,500,000	$1,290,800	57%	$3,000,000
$3,500,000	$4,000,000	$1,575,800	61%	$3,500,000
$4,000,000		$1,880,800	65%	$4,000,000
Top Rates: 1983				
$2,000,000	$2,500,000	$780,800	49%	$2,000,000
$2,500,000	$3,000,000	$1,025,800	53%	$2,500,000
$3,000,000	$3,500,000	$1,290,800	57%	$3,000,000
$3,500,000		$1,575,800	60%	$3,500,000
Top Rates: 1984 - 1986				
$2,000,000	$2,500,000	$780,800	49%	$2,000,000
$2,500,000	$3,000,000	$1,025,800	53%	$2,500,000
$3,000,000		$1,290,800	55%	$3,000,000

(Rate Table Continued)

Top Rates: 1987 - 1997

$2,000,000	$2,500,000	$780,800		49%	$2,000,000
$2,500,000	$3,000,000	$1,025,800		53%	$2,500,000
$3,000,000	$10,000,000	$1,290,800		55%	$3,000,000
$10,000,000	$21,040,000	$5,140,800	**	60%	$10,000,000
$21,040,000		$11,764,800		55%	$21,040,000

Top Rates: 1998 - 2001

$2,000,000	$2,500,000	$780,800		49%	$2,000,000
$2,500,000	$3,000,000	$1,025,800		53%	$2,500,000
$3,000,000	$10,000,000	$1,290,800		55%	$3,000,000
$10,000,000	$17,184,000	$5,140,800	**	60%	$10,000,000
$17,184,000		$9,451,200		55%	

Top Rates: 2002

$2,000,000	$2,500,000	$780,800	49%	$2,000,000
$2,500,000		$1,025,800	50%	$2,500,000

Top Rate: 2003

$2,000,000	$780,800	49%	$2,000,000

Top Rate: 2004

$2,000,000	$780,800	48%	$2,000,000

Top Rate: 2005

$2,000,000	$780,800	47%	$2,000,000

Top Rate: 2006

$2,000,000	$780,800	46%	$2,000,000

Top Rate: 2007-2009

$2,000,000	$780,800	45%	$2,000,000

2010 and beyond

Repealed for Estates. The maximum rate for gifts is 35% starting at $500,000.

** From 1988-1997, transfers between $10,000,000 and $21,040,000 were subject to a 5% surcharge imposed until the benefit of the unified credit and of lower marginal rates was taken back. Transfers taking place 1998-2001 have the 5% surcharge applied to transfers between $10,000,000 and $17,184,000 taking back the benefit of the lower rates, but not the benefit of the unified credit. The surcharge is eliminated for transfers after 2001.

TABLE 2 Unified Credits (UCr), Applicable Exclusion Amounts (AEA), and the End of the Bubble by Year Since 1977

Year	UCr Estates	AEA Estates	End of Bubble	UCr Gifts	AEA Gifts
1977	$30,000	$120,667		$30,000	$120,667
1978	$34,000	$134,000		$34,000	$134,000
1979	$38,000	$147,333		$38,000	$147,333
1980	$42,500	$161,563		$42,500	$161,563
1981	$47,000	$175,625		$47,000	$175,625
1982	$62,800	$225,000	*The 5%*	$62,800	$225,000
1983	$79,300	$275,000	*surcharge*	$79,300	$275,000
1984	$96,300	$325,000	*started in*	$96,300	$325,000
1985	$121,800	$400,000	*1988*	$121,800	$400,000
1986	$155,800	$500,000		$155,800	$500,000
1987	$192,800	$600,000		$192,800	$600,000
1988	$192,800	$600,000	$21,040,000	$192,800	$600,000
1989	$192,800	$600,000	$21,040,000	$192,800	$600,000
1990	$192,800	$600,000	$21,040,000	$192,800	$600,000
1991	$192,800	$600,000	$21,040,000	$192,800	$600,000
1992	$192,800	$600,000	$21,040,000	$192,800	$600,000
1993	$192,800	$600,000	$21,040,000	$192,800	$600,000
1994	$192,800	$600,000	$21,040,000	$192,800	$600,000
1995	$192,800	$600,000	$21,040,000	$192,800	$600,000
1996	$192,800	$600,000	$21,040,000	$192,800	$600,000
1997	$192,800	$600,000	$21,040,000	$192,800	$600,000
1998	$202,050	$625,000	$17,184,000	$202,050	$625,000
1999	$211,300	$650,000	$17,184,000	$211,300	$650,000
2000	$220,550	$675,000	$17,184,000	$220,550	$675,000
2001	$220,550	$675,000	$17,184,000	$220,550	$675,000
2002	$345,800	$1,000,000		$345,800	$1,000,000
2003	$345,800	$1,000,000	*and it*	$345,800	$1,000,000
2004	$555,800	$1,500,000	*ended in*	$345,800	$1,000,000
2005	$555,800	$1,500,000	*2002*	$345,800	$1,000,000
2006	$780,800	$2,000,000		$345,800	$1,000,000
2007	$780,800	$2,000,000		$345,800	$1,000,000
2008	$780,800	$2,000,000		$345,800	$1,000,000
2009	$1,455,800	$3,500,000		$345,800	$1,000,000
after 2009	Estate tax repealed. Gift tax at the top individual income tax rate.			$330,800	$1,000,000

TABLE 3A Credit For State Death Taxes 1977 - 2001

Taxable Estate(TA)		Base	Rate	R Applied to
At Least	But Not Over	Amount	(R)	TA Over
$100,000	$150,000	$0	0.8%	$100,000
$150,000	$200,000	$400	1.6%	$150,000
$200,000	$300,000	$1,200	2.4%	$200,000
$300,000	$500,000	$3,600	3.2%	$300,000
$500,000	$700,000	$10,000	4.0%	$500,000
$700,000	$900,000	$18,000	4.8%	$700,000
$900,000	$1,100,000	$27,600	5.6%	$900,000
$1,100,000	$1,600,000	$38,800	6.4%	$1,100,000
$1,600,000	$2,100,000	$70,800	7.2%	$1,600,000
$2,100,000	$2,600,000	$106,800	8.0%	$2,100,000
$2,600,000	$3,100,000	$146,800	8.8%	$2,600,000
$3,100,000	$3,600,000	$190,800	9.6%	$3,100,000
$3,600,000	$4,100,000	$238,800	10.4%	$3,600,000
$4,100,000	$5,100,000	$290,800	11.2%	$4,100,000
$5,100,000	$6,100,000	$402,800	12.0%	$5,100,000
$6,100,000	$7,100,000	$522,800	12.8%	$6,100,000
$7,100,000	$8,100,000	$650,800	13.6%	$7,100,000
$8,100,000	$9,100,000	$786,800	14.4%	$8,100,000
$9,100,000	$10,100,000	$930,800	15.2%	$9,100,000
$10,100,000		$1,082,800	16.0%	$10,100,000

Note: the brackets found in §2011 have been adjusted by adding $60,000 at each
level, hence you use the taxable estate without adjustment, i.e., do not subtract $60,000.

TABLE 3B Credit For State Death Taxes 2002 - 2004

Taxable Estate(TA)		Year 2002		Year 2003		Year 2004	
At Least	But Not Over	Base Amount	Rate (R)	Base Amount	Rate (R)	Base Amount	Rate (R)
$100,000	$150,000	$0	0.6%	$0	0.4%	$0	0.2%
$150,000	$200,000	$300	1.2%	$200	0.8%	$100	0.4%
$200,000	$300,000	$900	1.8%	$600	1.2%	$300	0.6%
$300,000	$500,000	$2,700	2.4%	$1,800	1.6%	$900	0.8%
$500,000	$700,000	$7,500	3.0%	$5,000	2.0%	$2,500	1.0%
$700,000	$900,000	$13,500	3.6%	$9,000	2.4%	$4,500	1.2%
$900,000	$1,100,000	$20,700	4.2%	$13,800	2.8%	$6,900	1.4%
$1,100,000	$1,600,000	$29,100	4.8%	$19,400	3.2%	$9,700	1.6%
$1,600,000	$2,100,000	$53,100	5.4%	$35,400	3.6%	$17,700	1.8%
$2,100,000	$2,600,000	$80,100	6.0%	$53,400	4.0%	$26,700	2.0%
$2,600,000	$3,100,000	$110,100	6.6%	$73,400	4.4%	$36,700	2.2%
$3,100,000	$3,600,000	$143,100	7.2%	$95,400	4.8%	$47,700	2.4%
$3,600,000	$4,100,000	$179,100	7.8%	$119,400	5.2%	$59,700	2.6%
$4,100,000	$5,100,000	$218,100	8.4%	$145,400	5.6%	$72,700	2.8%
$5,100,000	$6,100,000	$302,100	9.0%	$201,400	6.0%	$100,700	3.0%
$6,100,000	$7,100,000	$392,100	9.6%	$261,400	6.4%	$130,700	3.2%
$7,100,000	$8,100,000	$488,100	10.2%	$325,400	6.8%	$162,700	3.4%
$8,100,000	$9,100,000	$590,100	10.8%	$393,400	7.2%	$196,700	3.6%
$9,100,000	$10,100,000	$698,100	11.4%	$465,400	7.6%	$232,700	3.8%
$10,100,000		$812,100	12.0%	$541,400	8.0%	$270,700	4.0%

Note: the brackets found in §2011 have been adjusted by adding $60,000 at each level, hence you use the taxable estate without adjustment, i.e., do not subtract $60,000.

TABLE 4 Federal Gift Tax Rates prior to January 1, 1977

Taxable Gift*		Gift Tax		
At Least	But Not Over	Base Amount	Plus Percent	On Excess Over
$0	$5,000	$0	2.25%	$0
$5,000	$10,000	$113	5.25%	$5,000
$10,000	$20,000	$375	8.25%	$10,000
$20,000	$30,000	$1,200	10.50%	$20,000
$30,000	$40,000	$2,250	13.50%	$30,000
$40,000	$50,000	$3,600	16.50%	$40,000
$50,000	$60,000	$5,250	18.75%	$50,000
$60,000	$100,000	$7,125	21.00%	$60,000
$100,000	$250,000	$15,525	22.50%	$100,000
$250,000	$500,000	$49,275	24.00%	$250,000
$500,000	$750,000	$109,275	26.25%	$500,000
$750,000	$1,000,000	$174,900	27.75%	$750,000
$1,000,000	$1,250,000	$244,275	29.25%	$1,000,000
$1,250,000	$1,500,000	$317,400	31.50%	$1,250,000
$1,500,000	$2,000,000	$396,150	33.75%	$1,500,000
$2,000,000	$2,500,000	$564,900	36.75%	$2,000,000
$2,500,000	$3,000,000	$748,650	39.75%	$2,500,000
$3,000,000	$3,500,000	$947,400	42.00%	$3,000,000
$3,500,000	$4,000,000	$1,157,400	44.50%	$3,500,000
$4,000,000	$5,000,000	$1,378,650	47.25%	$4,000,000
$5,000,000	$6,000,000	$1,851,150	50.25%	$5,000,000
$6,000,000	$7,000,000	$2,353,650	52.50%	$6,000,000
$7,000,000	$8,000,000	$2,878,650	54.75%	$7,000,000
$8,000,000	$10,000,000	$3,426,150	57.00%	$8,000,000
$10,000,000		$4,566,150	57.75%	$10,000,000

* Taxable amount after the annual exclusion and the gift exemption.

WARNING:

THESE ARE **PRE-1977 GIFT** TAX RATES

TABLE 5 Federal Estate Rates prior to January 1, 1977

Taxable Estate*		Estate Tax		
At Least	But Not Over	Base Amount	Plus Percent	On Excess Over
$0	$5,000	$0	3.0%	$0
$5,000	$10,000	$150	7.0%	$5,000
$10,000	$20,000	$500	11.0%	$10,000
$20,000	$30,000	$1,600	14.0%	$20,000
$30,000	$40,000	$3,000	18.0%	$30,000
$40,000	$50,000	$4,800	22.0%	$40,000
$50,000	$60,000	$7,000	25.0%	$50,000
$60,000	$100,000	$9,500	28.0%	$60,000
$100,000	$250,000	$20,700	30.0%	$100,000
$250,000	$500,000	$65,700	32.0%	$250,000
$500,000	$750,000	$145,700	35.0%	$500,000
$750,000	$1,000,000	$233,200	37.0%	$750,000
$1,000,000	$1,250,000	$325,700	39.0%	$1,000,000
$1,250,000	$1,500,000	$423,200	42.0%	$1,250,000
$1,500,000	$2,000,000	$528,200	45.0%	$1,500,000
$2,000,000	$2,500,000	$753,200	49.0%	$2,000,000
$2,500,000	$3,000,000	$998,200	53.0%	$2,500,000
$3,000,000	$3,500,000	$1,263,200	56.0%	$3,000,000
$3,500,000	$4,000,000	$1,543,200	59.0%	$3,500,000
$4,000,000	$5,000,000	$1,838,200	63.0%	$4,000,000
$5,000,000	$6,000,000	$2,468,200	67.0%	$5,000,000
$6,000,000	$7,000,000	$3,138,200	70.0%	$6,000,000
$7,000,000	$8,000,000	$3,838,200	73.0%	$7,000,000
$8,000,000	$10,000,000	$4,568,200	76.0%	$8,000,000
$10,000,000		$6,088,200	77.0%	$10,000,000

* Taxable amount after the estate exemption.

WARNING:

THESE ARE **PRE-1977 ESTATE** TAX RATES

TABLE 6   Federal Income Tax Rates: Estates and Trusts - 2005

Taxable Income

Over	But not over	Base amount	+ percent	On excess over
$0	$2,000	$0.00	15%	$0
$2,000	$4,700	$300.00	25%	$2,000
$4,700	$7,150	$975.00	28%	$4,700
$7,150	$8,900	$1,661.00	33%	$7,150
$9,750	....	$2,519.00	35%	$9,750

Table 7   Estate Planning Indexed Values

Year	Annual Exclusion Regular	Annual Exclusion Non-US Spouse	GST Tax Exemption	6601j 2% portion on 6166 payments	2032A Special Use	"Kiddie Tax" Threshold
1987						**$1,000**
1997	**$10,000**	**$100,000**	**$1,000,000**	**$1,000,000**	**$750,000**	$1,300
1998	$10,000	$100,000	$1,000,000	$1,000,000	$750,000	$1,400
1999	$10,000	$101,000	$1,010,000	$1,010,000	$760,000	$1,400
2000	$10,000	$103,000	$1,030,000	$1,030,000	$770,000	$1,400
2001	$10,000	$106,000	$1,060,000	$1,060,000	$800,000	$1,500
2002	$11,000	$110,000	$1,100,000	$1,100,000	$820,000	$1,500
2003	$11,000	$112,000	$1,120,000	$1,120,000	$840,000	$1,500
2004	$11,000	$114,000	$1,500,000	$1,140,000	$850,000	$1,600
2005	$11,000	$117,000	$1,500,000	$1,170,000	$870,000	$1,600

Numbers in bold indicate the base amount and the base year for indexing. Shown are only those years in which a change occurred for at least one of the items. For years after 2003, the GST tax exemption will equal the estate applicable exclusion amount for the year. The 2% portion is the indexed $1 million plus the applicable exclusion amount, e.g., in 2005 it is $1,170,000 plus $1,500,000.

ACTUARIAL VALUE TABLES

Note: Tables that follow are taken from Department of the Treasury's *Internal Revenue Service Publication 1457* (7-1999), *Actuarial Values Book Aleph*. We will use the designation for each table as is used by the Treasury, i.e., Tables K, S, B, and 90CM. The Mortality Table (90 CM) is drawn from the 1990 census. We can expect Table S and Table 90 CM to be updated once the 2000 census information is digested by the U.S. Department of Health and Human Services, Public Health Service, National Center for Health Statistics, however, the 1990 updates were not published until April of 1999.

Table K

Adjustment Factors for Annuities Payable at the End of Each Interval

Interest Rate	Annually	Semi-Annually	Quarterly	Monthly	Weekly
3%	1.0000	1.0074	1.0112	1.0137	1.0146
4%	1.0000	1.0099	1.0149	1.0182	1.0195
6%	1.0000	1.0148	1.0222	1.0272	1.0291
8%	1.0000	1.0196	1.0295	1.0362	1.0387
10%	1.0000	1.0244	1.0368	1.0450	1.0482
12%	1.0000	1.0292	1.0439	1.0539	1.0577

The factors in Table K are used to adjust the values for annuities when the payments are made other than annually.

TABLE B -Term Certain

PV of Annuity (A), Income Interest (Inc. Int.), & Remainder Interests

	(3%) Three Percent				(4%) Four Percent		
Year	A	Inc.Int.	REM	Year	A	Inc.Int.	REM
1	.97090	.029126	.970874	1	0.9615	.038462	.961538
2	1.9135	.057404	.942596	2	1.8861	.075444	.924556
3	2.8286	.084858	.915142	3	2.7751	.111004	.888996
4	3.7171	.111513	.888487	4	3.6299	.145196	.854804
5	4.5797	.137391	.862609	5	4.4518	.178073	.821927
6	5.4172	.162516	.837484	6	5.2421	.209685	.790315
7	6.2303	.186908	.813092	7	6.0021	.240082	.759918
8	7.0197	.210591	.789409	8	6.7327	.269310	.730690
9	7.7861	.233583	.766417	9	7.4353	.297413	.702587
10	8.5302	.255906	.744094	10	8.1109	.324436	.675564
15	11.9379	.358138	.641862	15	11.1184	.444735	.555265
20	14.8775	.446324	.553676	20	13.5903	.543613	.456387
25	17.4131	.522394	.477606	25	15.6221	.624883	.375117
30	19.6004	.588013	.411987	30	17.2920	.691681	.308319
35	21.4872	.644617	.355383	35	18.6646	.746585	.253415
40	23.1148	.693443	.306557	40	19.7928	.791711	.208289
45	24.5187	.735561	.264439	45	20.7200	.828802	.171198
50	25.7298	.771893	.228107	50	21.4822	.859287	.140713
55	26.7744	.803233	.196767	55	22.1086	.884344	.115656
60	27.6756	.830267	.169733	60	22.6235	.904940	.095060

TABLE B -Term Certain

PV of Annuity (A), Income Interest (Inc. Int.), & Remainder Interests

	(6%) Six Percent				(8%) Eight Percent		
Year	A	Inc.Int.	REM	Year	A	Inc.Int.	REM
1	.09434	.056604	.943396	1	0.9259	.074074	.925926
2	1.8334	.110004	.889996	2	1.7833	.142661	.857339
3	2.6730	.160381	.839619	3	2.5771	.206168	.793832
4	3.4651	.207906	.792094	4	3.3121	.264970	.735030
5	4.2124	.252742	.747258	5	3.9927	.319417	.680583
6	4.9173	.295039	.704961	6	4.6229	.369830	.630170
7	5.5824	.334943	.665057	7	5.2064	.416510	.583490
8	6.2098	.372588	.627412	8	5.7466	.459731	.540269
9	6.8017	.408102	.591898	9	6.2469	.499751	.500249
10	7.3601	.441605	.558395	10	6.7101	.536807	.463193
15	9.7122	.582735	.417265	15	8.5595	.684758	.315242
20	11.4699	.688195	.311805	20	9.8181	.785452	.214548
25	12.7834	.767001	.232999	25	10.6748	.853982	.146018
30	13.7648	.825890	.174110	30	11.2578	.900623	.099377
35	14.4982	.869895	.130105	35	11.6546	.932365	.067635
40	15.0463	.902778	.097222	40	11.9246	.953969	.046031
45	15.4558	.927350	.072650	45	12.1084	.968672	.031328
50	15.7619	.945712	.054288	50	12.2335	.978679	.021321
55	15.9905	.959433	.040567	55	12.3186	.985489	.014511
60	16.1614	.969686	.030314	60	12.3766	.990124	.009876

TABLE B -Term Certain

PV of Annuity (A), Income Interest (Inc. Int.), & Remainder Interests

	(10%) Ten Percent				(12%) Twelve Percent		
Year	A	Inc.Int.	REM	Year	A	Inc.Int.	REM
1	0.9091	.090909	.909091	1	0.8929	.107143	.892857
2	1.7355	.173554	.826446	2	1.6901	.202806	.797194
3	2.4869	.248685	.751315	3	2.4018	.288220	.711780
4	3.1699	.316987	.683013	4	3.0373	.364482	.635518
5	3.7908	.379079	.620921	5	3.6048	.432573	.567427
6	4.3553	.435526	.564474	6	4.1114	.493369	.506631
7	4.8684	.486842	.513158	7	4.5638	.547651	.452349
8	5.3349	.533493	.466507	8	4.9676	.596117	.403883
9	5.7590	.575902	.424098	9	5.3282	.639390	.360610
10	6.1446	.614457	.385543	10	5.6502	.678027	.321973
15	7.6061	.760608	.239392	15	6.8109	.817304	.182696
20	8.5136	.851356	.148644	20	7.4694	.896333	.103667
25	9.0770	.907704	.092296	25	7.8431	.941177	.058823
30	9.4269	.942691	.057309	30	8.0552	.966622	.033378
35	9.6442	.964416	.035584	35	8.1755	.981060	.018940
40	9.7791	.977905	.022095	40	8.2438	.989253	.010747
45	9.8628	.986281	.013719	45	8.2825	.993902	.006098
50	9.9148	.991481	.008519	50	8.3045	.996540	.003460
55	9.9471	.994711	.005289	55	8.3170	.998037	.001963
60	9.9672	.996716	.003284	60	8.3240	.998886	.001114

TABLE S - Single Life

PV of Annuity (A), Life Estate (LE), & Remainder Interests (REM)

Age	(3%) Three Percent A	LE	REM	Age	(4%) Four Percent A	LE	REM
0	28.7622	.86287	.13713	0	22.9703	.91881	.08119
5	28.5292	.85588	.14412	5	22.9427	.91771	.08229
10	27.8101	.83430	.16570	10	22.5352	.90141	.09859
15	26.9749	.80925	.19075	15	22.0381	.88152	.11848
20	26.0939	.78282	.21718	20	21.5071	.86028	.13972
25	25.1194	.75358	.24642	25	20.9018	.83607	.16393
30	23.9844	.71953	.28047	30	20.1625	.80650	.19350
35	22.6701	.68010	.31990	35	19.2658	.77063	.22937
40	21.1893	.63568	.36432	40	18.2139	.72856	.27144
45	19.5621	.58686	.41314	45	17.0155	.68062	.31938
50	17.8164	.53449	.46551	50	15.6868	.62747	.37253
55	15.9842	.47952	.52048	55	14.2490	.56996	.43004
60	14.0854	.42256	.57744	60	12.7141	.50856	.49144
65	12.1758	.36527	.63473	65	11.1278	.44511	.55489
70	10.2706	.30812	.69188	70	9.5020	.38008	.61992
75	8.4310	.25293	.74707	75	7.8926	.31570	.68430
80	6.6699	.20010	.79990	80	6.3132	.25253	.74747
85	5.1450	.15435	.84565	85	4.9172	.19669	.80331
90	3.9270	.11781	.88219	90	3.7835	.15134	.84866
95	3.0148	.09044	.90956	95	2.9223	.11689	.88311
100	2.4636	.07391	.92609	100	2.3989	.09596	.90404
105	1.9446	.05834	.94166	105	1.9058	.07623	.92377
109	0.4854	.01456	.98544	109	0.4808	.01923	.98077

TABLE S - Single Life

PV of Annuity (A), Life Estate (LE), & Remainder Interests (REM)

	(6%) Six Percent				(8%) Eight Percent		
Age	A	LE	REM	Age	A	LE	REM
0	16.1278	.96767	.03233	0	12.2534	.98027	.01973
5	16.1718	.97072	.02928	5	12.3295	.98636	.01364
10	16.0350	.96210	.03790	10	12.2666	.98133	.01867
15	15.8450	.95070	.04930	15	12.1759	.97407	.02593
20	15.6441	.93865	.06135	20	12.0859	.96687	.03313
25	15.3981	.92389	.07661	25	11.9728	.95782	.04218
30	15.0780	.90468	.09532	30	11.8146	.94517	.05483
35	14.6737	.88042	.11958	35	11.6027	.92821	.07179
40	14.1646	.84987	.15013	40	11.3191	.90553	.09447
45	13.5237	.81142	.18858	45	10.9390	.87504	.12496
50	12.7497	.76498	.23502	50	10.4515	.83612	.16388
55	11.8459	.71075	.28925	55	9.8543	.78834	.21166
60	10.8279	.64967	.35033	60	9.1507	.73206	.26794
65	9.7151	.58291	.41709	65	8.3490	.66792	.33208
70	8.4988	.50993	.49007	70	7.4325	.59460	.40540
75	7.2349	.43409	.56591	75	6.4407	.51526	.48474
80	5.9340	.35604	.64396	80	5.3768	.43015	.56985
85	4.6961	.28177	.71823	85	4.3268	.34614	.65386
90	3.5847	.21508	.78492	90	3.3518	.26814	.73186
95	2.7346	.16408	.83592	95	2.5872	.20698	.79302
100	2.1130	.12678	.87322	100	2.0188	.16151	.83849
105	1.5468	.09281	.90719	105	1.4939	.11951	.88049
109	0.4717	.02830	.97170	109	0.4630	.03704	.96296

TABLE S - Single Life

PV of Annuity (A), Life Estate (LE), & Remainder Interests (REM)

	(10%) Ten Percent				(12%) Twelve Percent		
Age	A	LE	REM	Age	A	LE	REM
0	9.8484	.98484	.01516	0	8.2240	.98688	.01312
5	9.9225	.99225	.00775	5	8.2908	.99490	.00510
10	9.8897	.98898	.01103	10	8.2712	.99254	.00746
15	9.8383	.98383	.01617	15	8.2377	.98852	.01148
20	9.7921	.97921	.02079	20	8.2108	.98529	.01471
25	9.7344	.97344	.02656	25	8.1783	.98139	.01861
30	9.6485	.96485	.03515	30	8.1274	.97529	.02471
35	9.5282	.95282	.04718	35	8.0539	.96646	.03354
40	9.3589	.93589	.06411	40	7.9464	.95357	.04643
45	9.1183	.91183	.08817	45	7.7860	.93431	.06569
50	8.7963	.87963	.12037	50	7.5628	.90753	.09247
55	8.3843	.83843	.16157	55	7.2672	.87206	.12794
60	7.8804	.78804	.21196	60	6.8944	.82732	.17268
65	7.2860	.72860	.27140	65	6.4421	.77305	.22695
70	6.5796	.65796	.34204	70	5.8863	.70636	.29364
75	5.7877	.57877	.42123	75	5.2438	.62926	.37074
80	4.9061	.49061	.50939	80	4.5044	.54053	.45947
85	4.0066	.40066	.59934	85	3.7271	.44725	.55275
90	3.1453	.31453	.68547	90	2.9613	.35535	.64465
95	2.4540	.24540	.75460	95	2.3332	.27999	.72001
100	1.9322	.19322	.80678	100	1.8524	.22229	.77771
105	1.4443	.14443	.85557	105	1.3976	.16771	.83229
109	0.4545	.04545	.95455	109	0.4464	.05357	.94643

TABLE 90 CM - Mortality Table

Age x	L(x)	Age x	L(x)	Age x	L(x)	Age x	L(x)
0	100,000						
1	99,064	31	96,934	61	84,490	91	14,466
2	98,992	32	96,791	62	83,368	92	12,066
3	98,944	33	96,642	63	82,169	93	9,884
4	98,907	34	96,485	64	80,887	94	7,951
5	98,877	35	96,322	65	79,519	95	6,282
6	98,850	36	96,150	66	78,066	96	4,868
7	98,826	37	95,969	67	76,531	97	3,694
8	98,803	38	95,780	68	74,907	98	2,745
9	98,783	39	95,581	69	73,186	99	1,999
10	98,766	40	95,373	70	71,357	100	1,424
11	98,750	41	95,156	71	69,411	101	991
12	98,734	42	94,928	72	67,344	102	672
13	98,713	43	94,687	73	65,154	103	443
14	98,681	44	94,431	74	62,852	104	284
15	98,635	45	94,154	75	60,449	105	175
16	98,573	46	93,855	76	57,955	106	105
17	98,497	47	93,528	77	55,373	107	60
18	98,409	48	93,173	78	52,704	108	33
19	98,314	49	92,787	79	49,943	109	17
20	98,215	50	92,370	80	47,084	110	0
21	98,113	51	91,918	81	44,129		
22	98,006	52	91,424	82	41,091		
23	97,896	53	90,885	83	37,994		
24	97,784	54	90,297	84	34,876		
25	97,671	55	89,658	85	31,770		
26	97,556	56	88,965	86	28,687		
27	97,441	57	88,214	87	25,638		
28	97,322	58	87,397	88	22,658		
29	97,199	59	86,506	89	19,783		
30	97,070	60	85,537	90	17,046		

TABLE §7520 Monthly Rates - Factors for Valuing Split Interests (i.e., Annuities, Life Estates, and Remainders)

	91	92	93	94	95	96	97	98	99	00	01	02	03	04	05	06	07
Jan	9.8	8.2	7.6	6.4	9.6	6.8	7.4	7.2	5.6	7.4	6.8	5.4	4.2	4.2	4.6		
Feb	9.6	7.6	7.6	6.4	9.6	6.8	7.6	6.8	5.6	8.0	6.2	5.6	4.0	4.2	4.6		
Mar	9.4	8.0	7.0	6.4	9.4	6.6	7.8	6.8	5.8	8.2	6.2	5.4	3.8	4.0	4.6		
Apr	9.6	8.4	6.6	7.0	8.8	7.0	7.8	6.8	6.4	8.0	6.0	5.6	3.6	3.8	5.0		
May	9.6	8.6	6.6	7.8	8.6	7.6	8.2	6.8	6.2	7.8	5.8	6.0	3.8	3.8	5.2		
Jun	9.6	8.4	6.4	8.4	8.2	8.0	8.2	7.0	6.4	8.0	6.0	5.8	3.6	4.6	4.8		
Jul	9.6	8.2	6.6	8.2	7.6	8.2	8.0	6.8	7.0	8.0	6.2	5.6	3.0	5.0	4.6		
Aug	9.8	7.8	6.4	8.4	7.2	8.2	7.6	6.8	7.2	7.6	6.0	5.2	3.2	4.8	4.8		
Sep	9.6	7.2	6.4	8.4	7.6	8.0	7.6	6.6	7.2	7.6	5.8	4.6	4.2	4.6			
Oct	9.0	7.0	6.0	8.6	7.6	8.0	7.6	6.2	7.2	7.4	5.6	4.2	4.4	4.4			
Nov	8.6	6.8	6.0	9.0	7.4	8.0	7.4	5.4	7.4	7.2	5.0	3.6	4.0	4.2			
Dec	8.4	7.4	6.2	9.4	7.2	7.6	7.2	5.4	7.4	7.0	4.8	4.0	4.2	4.2			

§7520 rates are available at: http://www.irs.gov/businesses/small/article/0,,id=112482,00.html

Teaching Aids
CD ROM Contents

The Table that follows lists the files found on the Estate Planning and Taxation Teaching Aids CD ROM. The ETAX 2006 program is an EXCEL (Microsoft) spreadsheet file that will make estate and gift tax calculations through the year 2009. The next several files are Federal tax forms in "pdf" format, hence require Adobe Acrobat Reader to open. The Adobe program is available free at <http://www.adobe.com/products/acrobat/readermain.html>.

The code files are all in MS Word format so they can be searched using key words. The Internal Revenue Code file contains selected code sections deemed most relevant to estate planning. The Uniform Codes are reprinted with the permission of the National Conference of Commissioners on Uniform State Laws, 211 East Ontario Street, Suite 1300, Chicago, Illinois 60611.

TEACHING AIDS CD ROM
TABLE OF FILES ON ESTATE PLANNING AND TAXATION

Name of File	Type
Teaching Aid CD ROM list	Microsoft Word
Good Estate Planning weblinks	Microsoft Word
ETAX 2006	Microsoft Excel
1041 Form U.S. Income Tax Return for Estates and Trusts	Adobe Acrobat
1041 Instructions	Adobe Acrobat
1041sd Form Capital Gains and Losses	Adobe Acrobat
1041sj Form Accumulation Distribution for Certain Complex Trusts	Adobe Acrobat
1041sk1 Form Beneficiary's Share of Income, Deductions, Credits,	Adobe Acrobat
1041t Form Allocation of Estimated Tax Payments to Beneficiaries	Adobe Acrobat
2848 Form Power of Attorney and Declaration of Representative	Adobe Acrobat
4768 Form Application for Extension of Time To File a Return	Adobe Acrobat
556 Examination of Returns, Appeal Rights, and Claims for Refund	Adobe Acrobat
559 Survivors, Executors, and Administrators (Treas-Pub)	Adobe Acrobat
594 The IRS Collection Process (Treas-Pub)	Adobe Acrobat
706 Form United States Estate (and Generation-Skipping Transfer)	Adobe Acrobat
706 Instructions	Adobe Acrobat
706-A Form United States Additional Estate Tax Return	Adobe Acrobat
706A Instructions	Adobe Acrobat
706GS(D) Instructions	Adobe Acrobat
706GS(D-1) Form Notification of Distribution From a Generation-	Adobe Acrobat
706GS(T) Form Generation-Skipping Transfer Tax Return For	Adobe Acrobat
706GS(T) Instructions	Adobe Acrobat
706NA Form Nonresident Not a Citizen	Adobe Acrobat
706NA Instructions	Adobe Acrobat
706QDT Form QDOT	Adobe Acrobat
706QDT Instructions	Adobe Acrobat
709 Form United States Gift (and Generation-Skipping Transfer) Tax	Adobe Acrobat
709 Instructions	Adobe Acrobat
712 Form Life Insurance Statement	Adobe Acrobat
746 Notice Penalties and Interest	Adobe Acrobat
843 Form Claim for Refund and Request for Abatement	Adobe Acrobat
843 Instructions	Adobe Acrobat
8736 Application for Automatic Extension of time to File U.S.	Adobe Acrobat

Teaching Aids CD ROM files (*continued*)

8800 Form Application for an Additional Extension for Certain	Adobe Acrobat
8892 Form Payment of Gift/GST Tax and/or Application for	Adobe Acrobat
947 Practice Before the IRS and Power of Attorney (Treas-Pub)	Adobe Acrobat
950 Introduction to Estate and Gift Taxes (Treas-Pub)	Adobe Acrobat
IRC ESTATE PLANNING SELECTION	Microsoft Word
NCCUSL Uniform Laws Copyright 2005	Microsoft Word
REVISION OF UPC SEC 3-916 (apportionment of estate taxes)	Microsoft Word
TOD SECURITY REGISTRATION ACT	Microsoft Word
UNIFORM ANATOMICAL GIFT ACT	Microsoft Word
UNIFORM CUSTODIAL TRUST ACT	Microsoft Word
UNIFORM DETERMINATION OF DEATH ACT	Microsoft Word
UNIFORM ESTATE TAX APPORTIONMENT ACT	Microsoft Word
UNIFORM FRAUDULENT TRANSFER ACT	Microsoft Word
UNIFORM HEALTH-CARE DECISIONS ACT	Microsoft Word
UNIFORM PARENTAGE ACT	Microsoft Word
UNIFORM PREMARITAL AGREEMENT ACT	Microsoft Word
UNIFORM PRINCIPAL AND INCOME ACT	Microsoft Word
UNIFORM PROBATE CODE	Microsoft Word
UNIFORM PROBATE CODE without comments	Microsoft Word
UNIFORM STATUTORY DURABLE POWERS FORM	Microsoft Word
UNIFORM TRANSFERS TO MINORS ACT	Microsoft Word
UNIFORM TRUST CODE 2005	Microsoft Word
Wyoming Distribution by Affidavit	Microsoft Word

GLOSSARY

Abatement The legal process of reducing or eliminating the bequests of a decedent-testator who died owning insufficient assets to pay all bequests, debts and administration expenses.

Ademption The failure to fulfill a specific bequest in a will because the property bequeathed was sold, given away or lost before the testator's death.

Adjusted basis The dollar amount subtracted from the amount realized to calculate gain or loss on the sale or exchange of property. It is generally thought of as the price paid for property, but an owner's basis is generally determined by how the person acquired the property, e.g., by purchase, by gift, or by inheritance. It is also increased by capital improvements and decreased by depreciation.

Adjusted taxable gifts In federal estate tax, the sum of post-1976 taxable gifts, other than those included in the gross estate. It is added to the taxable estate on the federal estate tax return to arrive at the estate tax base.

Administrator A personal representative of a decedent's estate who was not nominated in the decedent's will.

Administrator with will annexed A personal representative of an estate where the decedent's will is admitted to probate but the personal representative was not nominated in the will as the executor.

Advance directive A document (e.g., a living will or durable power of attorney) in which a person expresses his or her wishes regarding medical treatment in the event of incapacitation.

Advancement Property given to a donee with the expressed intention by the donor that it will reduce or eliminate a bequest to the donee.

Adverse party In the Internal Revenue Code, a person having a substantial interest in property that is subject to a power of appointment, where that person's interest would be diminished if the holder of the power exercised it.

Affidavit A sworn statement in writing made esp. under oath or on affirmation before an authorized magistrate or officer

After-born child A child who was born after the execution of his or her parent's will.

Alternate valuation date Under Federal estate tax law assets are usually valued as of the date of death, but the personal representative may elect to value them as of six months after the date of death if doing so will reduce the value of the gross estate and the estate tax.

Ancillary administration Ancillary means having a subordinate, subsidiary, or secondary nature. In this context it refers to a probate in a state other than the decedent's state of domicile.

Annual exclusion Under the federal gift tax, a deduction up to $10,000 (indexed after 1997) from gross gifts by a donor to any donee in a given calender year.

Annual exclusion gift A gift of property worth no more than the gift tax annual exclusion.

Annuitant A person entitled to receive benefits or payments from an annuity.

Annuity An amount payable at regular intervals (as yearly or quarterly) for a certain or uncertain period. A contract (as with an insurance company) under which one or more persons receive annuities in return for prior fixed payments made by themselves or another (as an employer).

Antilapse statute A state statutory provision that specifies, in the absence of a provision in the will, to whom a lapsed testamentary bequest will pass.

Applicable exclusion amount (AEA) Also known as the credit shelter amount, is the amount that can be transferred over a person's lifetime and/or at death free of gift tax and estate tax, e.g., $2 million in 2006 for estates and $1 million for gifts made after 2001.

Appointee (of a power of appointment) The party or parties whom the holder of a power of appointment actually appoints property.

Apportionment statute *See Equitable apportionment statute.*

Ascertainable standard Wording in a will or trust intentionally limiting the freedom of a holder of a power of appointment over property to assure that the property subject to the power will not be included in the holder's gross estate. The most common words of limitation (derived from Section 2041) are that the holder can withdraw property from a trust for his or her benefit if such is needed for "health, education, support, or maintenance."

Assignment Any transfer of a claim, right, or interest in property.

Assignment of income doctrine Under income tax law, a doctrine holding that earnings from services performed will always be taxed to the person performing those services.

Attestation clause A clause at the end of a will in which the witnesses state that the will was signed and witnessed with all the formalities required by law and which often sets forth those requirements.

Attested will A will signed by the testator in front of witnesses who sign below the attestation clause.

Attorney-in-fact An agent who may or may not be a lawyer who is given written authority to act on another's behalf, esp. by a power of attorney. The agent acts on behalf of a principal.

Augmented estate A deceased person's probate estate increased in accordance with statutory provisions. Although it varies by state, this may require the addition of any property transferred as a gift by the deceased within two years of death, any joint tenancies, and any transfers in which the deceased retained either the right to revoke or the income for life. In some states, the surviving spouse's elective share is determined by the augmented estate.

Average tax rate The tax rate determined by dividing the tax by value of what is being taxed. Compare this to the marginal tax rate which is the rate of tax on each dollar within a tax bracket.

Bargain sale Part-gift, part-sale of an asset for some amount that the parties know is less than what would be regarded as full and adequate consideration. The difference between the consideration received by the seller-donor and the value of the asset transferred constitutes a gift, for tax purposes.

Basis *See adjusted basis.*

Beneficial interest An interest in property that carries an economic benefit. Examples of beneficial interests in property include the temporary or permanent right to possess, consume, and pledge the property.

Beneficiary A person who is receiving or will receive a gift of a beneficial interest in property. *See Donee.*

Bequest A gift, by will, of personal property. Also called a legacy.

Blockage discount A valuation discount given to a large quantity of a stock listed on an exchange, or certain other property, if its sale all at one time could have a temporarily depressing effect on the market price.

Bond In probate, an agreement under which an insurance company guarantees that the personal representative will faithfully perform required probate duties.

Business buyout agreement An agreement between one or more owners of a closely held business and one or more other persons that obligates one or more of the parties to purchase the interest of one of the others upon the occurrence of specific future events, such as the latter's death and, often, the onset of his or her permanent disability.

Buyout agreement *See Business buyout agreement.*

Buy-sell agreement *See Business buyout agreement.*

Bypass An arrangement under which property owned by a decedent and intended for the lifetime benefit of the surviving spouse does not actually pass to the surviving spouse, thereby avoiding inclusion in the latter's gross estate.

Bypass trust A trust designed to contain property that bypasses the surviving beneficiary's estate. *See Bypass.*

By right of representation The distribution of a decedent's estate whereby the children of the decedent share equally, with the share of a deceased child who left issue going to his or her children in equal shares, again with the share of a deceased child who left issue passing in like manner to his or her issue.

Carryover basis Generally applied to gifts. The person receiving property has a basis in the property equal to the basis of the asset when it was in the hands of the donor or transferor.

Cash value life insurance policy A policy that accumulates economic value because the insurer charges a constant premium that is considerably higher than mortality costs requires during the earlier years. Part of this overpayment accumulates as a cash surrender value which, prior to the death of the insured, can be enjoyed by the owner, basically in one of two ways. First, at any time the owner can surrender the policy and receive this value in cash. Second, the owner can make a policy loan and borrow up to the amount of this value.

Charitable lead trust (CLT) A trust under which the settlor donates an asset's income interest to a charity for a period of time, at the end of which the remainder interest passes to a private party, typically children or grandchildren for a specified term of years. The settlor (or the settlor's estate) will receive an income tax deduction for the value of the income interest.

Charitable remainder annuity trust (CRAT) A trust into which the settlor transfers assets in exchange for a fixed annuity income of at least 5 percent of the original value of the assets transferred into trust, payable at least annually, usually for life. The value of the remainder is deductible on the income tax return.

Charitable remainder unitrust (CRUT) A trust that is much like the charitable remainder annuity trust, except that the annual income depends on a fixed percentage of the current fair market value of the assets in the trust, determined annually.

Check-the-box regulations Treasury Regulations that allow businesses significant freedom in determining whether to be taxed as a partnership or a corporation.

Chose in action A claim or debt recoverable in a lawsuit.

Clifford trust A grantor trust lasting at least ten years with income payable to a beneficiary and principal reverting to the settlor upon termination. Prior to the Tax Reform Act of 1986, a Clifford trust could be used as a tax shelter that diverted income from the settlor, who was in a higher tax bracket, to a beneficiary, often a child, who was in a lower tax bracket.

Closely held business A firm privately owned by no more than a few individuals or families.

Codicil A written document that amends or revokes a will.

Collateral A relative who shares a common ancestor with a person but who is neither a descendant nor an ascendant of that person, e.g., a cousin. Contrast with issue.

Common disaster clause A clause in a will or trust that specifies which spouse is to be presumed to have died first in the event both are killed in an accident. It may specify that the wealthier spouse is to be presumed to have died first or that each spouse's property is to be distributed as though the other spouse died first.

Common law A body of law that is based on custom and general principles and embodied in case law. It serves as precedent or is applied to situations not covered by statute. In the case of property law it refers to laws developed in England up to the time of the Revolutionary War and is followed by most states in the North, the East Coast, and the South. In contrast, community property law is followed by most of the states on the Pacific Coast and South-West.

Community property In the eight states recognizing it, all property that has been acquired by the efforts of either spouse during their marriage while living in a community property state, except property acquired by only one of the spouses by gift, devise, bequest or inheritance, or, in most of the community property states, by the income therefrom. The eight states are: Arizona, California, Idaho, Louisiana, Nevada, New Mexico, Texas, and Washington. In addition, Wisconsin adopted a form of community property known as "marital partnership property."

Completed gift A gift in which the donor has so parted with dominion and control over an interest in property that the donor has no power to change its disposition, whether for his or her own benefit or for the benefit of another.

Complex trust A nongrantor trust which, in a given year, either (a) accumulates some fiduciary accounting income (FAI) (i.e., does not pay out all of that year's FAI to the beneficiaries) or (b) distributes principal.

Conduit principle In the income taxation of estates and trusts, the rule that fiduciary accounting income distributed to beneficiaries will be taxed to them, rather than to the estate or trust.

Consanguinity Degree of blood relationship between one person and another.

Conservatee A person who is cared for or whose property is managed by a conservator.

Conservator A court-appointed fiduciary responsible for the protection of the person and/or the person's property after the court has determined that the person is mentally incapable of handling such matters on his or her own.

Consideration furnished test Under the federal estate tax, the proposition that includes in a decedent's gross estate the entire value of property held by the decedent in joint tenancy, reduced only by an amount attributable to that portion of the consideration in money or money's worth which can clearly be shown to have been furnished by the survivors.

Constructive fraud Conduct that is considered fraud under the law despite the absence of an intent to deceive, because it has the same consequences as an actual fraud would have and is against public interests. Examples include a violation of a public or private trust or confidence, the breach of a fiduciary duty, or the use of undue influence.

Contingent interest A future interest that is not vested; that is, an interest whose possession and enjoyment are dependent on the happening of some future event, not on just the passage of time.

Corpus The property in a trust. Also called principal or the *res* (Latin for a thing or object).

Creator The person, also called grantor, settlor, or trustor, who creates a trust and transfers property into it (technically transfers it to the trustee).

Creditor claim form A written statement that sets forth a claim against the probate estate of a deceased debtor.

Creditor claim period Time set by state law in which a creditor must present his or her creditor claim form or lose the right to collect on a debt owed by a decedent. In probate it is usually quite short, e.g., four months.

Credit shelter bypass Property equal in value to the applicable exclusion amount that is taxed when the owner of the property dies, but the unified credit matches the tentative tax, so no tax is actually paid. The property may be held in trust, benefitting certain individuals for a period of time, before eventually being transferred, without being taxed again, to someone else.

Crummey provision A general power clause found in some trusts that give one or more beneficiaries the right to withdraw, for a limited period of time each year, the lesser of the amount of the annual exclusion or the value of the gift property transferred into the trust. Allows the donor to claim an annual exclusion. Often found in trusts for minors and in irrevocable life insurance trusts.

Cumulative gift doctrine The requirement that all lifetime gifts be accumulated; that is, that prior taxable gifts be added to current taxable transfers to determine the estate or gift tax base.

Curtesy A husband's right under common law to a life estate upon the death of his wife in the real property that she owned, provided that they bore a child capable of inheriting the property.

Custodial gift A gift to a custodian for the benefit of a child, under the Uniform Gifts to Minors Act or the Uniform Transfers to Minors Act.

Custodianship An arrangement whereby one person, the custodian, cares for the person or property of another, e.g., a person named to manage a child's property under the Uniform Transfers to Minors Act.

Cy pres **rule** a rule in the law of trusts and estates that provides for the interpretation of instruments as nearly as possible in conformity with the intention of the testator when literal construction is illegal, impracticable, or impossible.

Death certificate A written document issued by the state that verifies the death of a person. In most states these are issued by the health department for the county in which the person died.

Death tax A tax levied on certain property owned or transferred by the decedent at death. Either an estate tax or an inheritance tax.

Decedent In estate planning nomenclature, the person who has died.

Degrees of consanguinity A measure of how closely related two people are.

Depreciation Any decrease in the value of property (as machinery) for the purpose of taxation that is carried on company books as a yearly charge amortizing the original cost over the useful life of the property.

Demand note A note with no fixed period that is due upon the creditor's demand for payment.

Descendant *See issue.*

Devise A gift, by will, of real property.

Devisee A beneficiary, under a will, of a devise, i.e., a gift of real property.

Direct skip A generation-skipping transfer of an interest in property to a skip person, i.e., a person two or more generations below the person making the transfer or to a trust in which all interest is held by such persons and that is subject to generation-skipping transfer taxes.

Disclaimant One who disclaims an interest in property.

Disclaimer An unqualified refusal to accept a gift, bequest, or the right to exercise a power of appointment. In estate planning, a tax-effective disclaimer must meet the requirements of both local law and IRC Section 2518. Tax-effective means that the disclaimant will not be treated as having made a gift.

Dispositive provisions Parts of a will or trust that set forth how property is to be distributed.

Distributable net income (DNI) An amount more or less equal to fiduciary accounting income (FAI) that acts as the measuring rod for estate and trust income taxation.

Distribution deduction In the income taxation of estates and trusts, an amount equal to the lesser of distributable net income or the amount actually distributed to beneficiaries.

Distribution planning Planning the amount and timing of beneficiary distributions from an estate or irrevocable trust, usually with the objective of reducing income tax.

DNI *See Distributable net income.*

Donative intent The person transferring property to another has the intention of making a gift.

Donee A person who receives a gift of a beneficial interest in property. *See Beneficiary.*

Donor A person who make a gift.

Dower A surviving wife's interest in a portion of the real property owned by her deceased husband. Usually, the interest was a life estate.

Durable power of attorney A written agency agreement that continues to have validity even during the principal's incapacity. At common law an agent's authority ceased as soon as the principal was mentally incapacitated.

Durable power of attorney for health care (DPOAHC) A written power of attorney granting to an agent (sometimes called the attorney-in-fact) the authority to make medical decisions on behalf of the principal during such times as the principal is unable to make such decisions.

Durable power of attorney for property A durable power of attorney granting to the attorney-in-fact the power to make decisions concerning the property of the principal.

Dynasty Trust A trust, expected to last for generations, established in a state that has abolished the Rule Against Perpetuities or in a state that has greatly extended the allowable duration.

Economic Growth and Tax Relief Reconciliation Act (EGTRRA) Legislation passed in 2001 that lowers estate and gift tax rates, increases the applicable exclusion amount, and eliminates the estate tax as of 2010. A sunset provision repeals EGTRRA as of 2011.

Elective share The share (e.g., one-third) of an estate set by statute that a widow or widower or sometimes a child is entitled to claim in lieu of any provisions made in a will or in the event of being disinherited unjustifiably. It is also called a forced share.

Endowment insurance Life insurance in which the benefit is paid to the policyowner if he or she is still living at the end of the policy's term (as 20 years).

Equalization A term used in this text to mean a plan of property disposition by the spouses so that the taxable estates (or estate tax bases) of the two are more or less equal as of the first death.

Equitable apportionment statute A state statute that spreads the death tax burden in direct proportion to each beneficiaries share of the taxable estate.

Equitable interest An interest (as a beneficial interest) that is held by virtue of equitable title or that may be claimed on the ground of equitable relief.

Escheat The transfer of an intestate decedent's property to the state, because either the decedent left no next of kin, or all surviving relatives are considered under state law to be too remote for purposes of inheritance.

Estate A quantity of wealth or property. *See also Net estate, Gross estate, and Probate estate.*

Estate planning The arranging for the disposition and management of one's estate at death through the use of wills, trusts, insurance policies, and other devices

Estate pour autre vie A life estate measured by the life of a third person rather than that of the person enjoying the property. Also known as a life estate based upon the life of another.

Estate tax A federal or state tax on the decedent's right to transfer property.

Estate planning The study of the principles of planning for the use, conservation, and efficient transfer of an individual's wealth.

Estate tax base On the federal estate tax return, it is the sum of the taxable estate plus adjusted taxable gifts. It is the amount used to calculate the tentative estate tax.

Estate trust One type of marital trust, rarely if ever used, under which the corpus (and any accumulated income) is made payable to the estate of the surviving spouse at his or her death. Its unique feature is that it qualifies for the marital deduction even though the surviving spouse may not receive all of the income during his or her lifetime. However, income cannot be payable to anyone else.

Excise tax A tax levied on the manufacture, sale, consumption, or transfer of a commodity.

Execute To complete a document (i.e., to do what is necessary to render it valid).

Executor A personal representative of a decedent's estate who was nominated in the will.

Executrix A woman who is an executor. Modern usage uses executor without regard to gender.

Exercise a power of appointment To invoke the power by appointing a permissible appointee.

FAI *See Fiduciary accounting income.*

Family limited partnership A limited partnership meeting the requirements of §704(e) for the benefit of family members, generally with parents as the general partners and children as the limited partners. Used to take advantage of lack of control discounts and lack of marketability discounts as the parents transfer limited partnership units to the children.

Family-owned business interest deduction The estate tax deduction that combines with the applicable exclusion amount to shelter property worth up to $1,300,000 from federal estate taxes. IRC §2057 makes the deduction available for estates that meet certain requirements, such as that the value of the family owned business interest equals or exceeds 50% of the decedent's adjusted gross estate. EGTRRA repeals the deduction as of 2004.

Family pot trust *See Pot trust.*

Fee simple An ownership interest in property (called a fee) that is alienable (i.e., transferrable by deed, will, or intestacy) and of potentially indefinite duration. Sometimes referred to as *fee simple absolute*.

Fee simple absolute A fee that is freely inheritable and alienable without any limitations or restrictions on transfers and is of indefinite duration.

Fiduciary A person in a position of trust and confidence; one who has a legal duty to act for the benefit of another. Examples include executor, trustee, agent, custodian, and attorney.

Fiduciary accounting income (FAI) In the income taxation of estates and trusts, most sources of federal gross income, including cash dividends, interest, and rent (reduced by certain expenses) but not including stock dividends and capital gains.

Fiscal year An income tax year that ends on the last day of any month except December.

Flower bonds Certain long-term U.S. Treasury bonds (no longer in circulation) which, if owned by the decedent at death, were redeemable at par value to pay the federal estate tax.

Fractional interest discount A valuation discount for a partial interest in real property (e.g., a 25% interest as a tenant in common) because it is neither easily partitioned nor readily marketable.

Fraud Any act, expression, omission, or concealment calculated to deceive another to his or her disadvantage. A misrepresentation or concealment with reference to some fact material to a transaction that is made with knowledge of its falsity or in reckless disregard of its truth or falsity and with the intent to deceive another and is reasonably relied on by the other who is injured thereby.

Fraud in the execution Fraud in which the deception causes the other party to misunderstand the nature of the transaction in which he or she is engaging, especially with regard to the contents of an instrument (as a will or promissory note). It is also called fraud in the factum.

Fraud in the inducement Fraud in which the deception leads the other party to engage in a transaction the nature of which he or she understands. Compare this to fraud in the execution.

Freezing the estate tax value Using estate planning transfer techniques to effectively ensure that the future value of certain appreciating property includible in the estate tax base will not be significantly higher than its current value.

Future interest A beneficial interest in property in which the right to possess or enjoy the property is delayed, either by a specific period of time or until the happening of a future event, e.g., a remainder or reversionary interest.

General bequest A gift payable out of the general assets of the estate, but not one that specifies one or more particular items.

General power of appointment The holder of a power has the right to use the property that is subject to the power for his or her own benefit or for the benefit of his or her estate. The property subject to the power at the holder's death will be included in the holder's gross estate even if the power is unexercised.

General power of attorney A document executed by one person called the principal, authorizing another person called the attorney-in-fact, to perform designated acts on behalf of the principal.

Generation-skipping transfer tax (GST tax) A federal or state tax on certain property transfers to a skip person, that is, someone who is two generations or more younger than the donor.

Generation-skipping trust A trust in which the principal will eventually go to a skip person usually following payment of income for life to a non-skip person.

Gift A completed lifetime or deathtime transfer of property by an individual in exchange for any amount that is less than full consideration.

Gift tax A tax on a completed lifetime transfer of property for less than full consideration.

Grantor A person who creates a trust and whose property is transferred into it. Also called creator, settlor, or trustor.

Grantor retained annuity trust (GRAT) A grantor retained trust that pays the grantor a fixed income for a specified period and meets all other requirements of IRC §2702.

Grantor retained income trust (GRIT) An irrevocable trust into which the settlor transfers appreciating property in exchange for the right to receive income for a period of years. Under most GRITs, distribution of corpus at the end of the period depends upon whether or not the settlor survived the period, and if not, the corpus likely reverts to the settlor's estate; if the settlor does survive the period, the corpus likely passes to younger-generation beneficiaries.

Grantor retained unitrust (GRUT) A grantor retained trust that pays the grantor a fixed percentage of the trust's principal, revalued each year, for a specified period and meets all other requirements of IRC §2702.

Grantor trust A trust in which the settlor has retained sufficient interest to make the income received by the trust taxable to the grantor, not to the trust or its other beneficiaries.

Grantor trust rules The federal income tax rules concerning grantor trusts located in Internal Revenue Code §§671-78.

Gross estate An estate tax term meaning all property in which the decedent had an interest at the time of his or her death, any property transferred by the decedent under which the decedent retained an interest or control, and any life insurance transferred, or any retained interests released, within three years of death.

Grossing up Inclusion in the gross estate of gift taxes paid on any gifts made within three years of death. Review IRC §2035(b).

GST tax *See Generation-skipping transfer tax.*

Guardian A court-appointed fiduciary responsible for the person or property of a minor or, in some cases, an incompetent adult, or both. In some states, a guardian is called a committee, in others, a guardian for an incompetent adult is called a conservator.

Heir One who inherits or is entitled to succeed to the possession of property after the death of its owner: as one who by operation of law inherits the property from a person who dies without leaving a valid will. Also called an heir at law, heir general, or legal heir. The term is used even if the person is disinherited by a valid will.

Holder (of a power of appointment) A person who has received a power of appointment, i.e., the one who has the right to appoint designated property to a permissible appointee. Also called the donee of the power.

Holding period In income tax law, the length of time that property is held. It determines whether a gain is short term or long term. The current threshold is one year for long term capital gains, however, property received from a decedent is automatically long term.

Holographic will A will, recognized as valid in most states even though it is not witnessed. The state law is likely to require that at least the dispositive portions of the will be the testator's handwriting.

Incapacity The quality or state of being incapable. Lack of legal qualifications due to age or mental condition.

Incidents of ownership Powers and interests over an insurance policy on decedent's life that would subject the proceeds to inclusion in the decedent's gross estate under Section 2042.

Income beneficiary The beneficiary of a trust who has a life estate or estate for years in the trust income.

Income shifting In estate planning, saving income tax by enabling income otherwise taxable to a high income tax individual to be taxed to a lower tax bracket family member.

Income tax A tax levied on income earned by a taxpayer during a given year.

Incompetence The state or fact of being incompetent.

Incomplete transfer A gift made without total relinquishment of dominion and control. i.e., it is rescindable or amendable.

Informed consent Consent to medical treatment or to participation in a medical experiment after achieving an understanding of what is involved and of the risks.

Inherit To receive property by intestate succession or by a bequest.

Inheritance The acquisition of real or personal property under the laws of intestacy or sometimes by a will. The succession either by will or by operation of law to all the estate, rights, and liabilities of the decedent. Something that is or may be inherited .

Inheritance tax A state tax on the right of a beneficiary to receive property from a decedent.

Installment sale The sale of an asset in exchange for an installment note, in which the buyer agrees to make periodic payments of principal and interest, based on a fair market rate of interest.

Insurable interest An interest or stake in property or in a person that arises from the potential for financial loss upon the destruction of the property or the death of the person. In many states one cannot obtain an insurance policy without showing that one has an insurable interest. The purpose of requiring an insurable interest is to prevent the use of insurance as a form of gambling or as a method of profiting from destruction.

Insurance The action, process, or means of insuring or the state of being insured usu. against loss or damage by a contingent event (as death, fire, accident, or sickness).

Intangible personal property Property (as a stock certificate or professional license) that derives value not from its intrinsic physical nature but from what it represents.

Intentionally defective grantor trust A funded irrevocable trust that is complete for estate tax purposes and incomplete for income tax. The purpose of this arrangement is to give have the grantor pay the income tax rather than having it paid by the trustee or by the beneficiary.

Inter vivos transfer A transfer made while the transferor is alive.

Inter vivos trust *See living trust.*

Interest by the entirety *See tenancy by the entirety.*

Interest for years A property interest for a fixed period of time.

Interest-free loan A loan, having no interest charge, usually to a family member in a lower income tax bracket. TRA 1986 limited its use by requiring lenders to impute interest income for many of these low-interest, no-interest family loan arrangements.

Interest in common *See tenancy in common.*

Intestate Having died leaving probate property not disposed of by a valid will.

Instrument Any legal document.

Inventory and appraisement A probate document that delineates all probate assets at their fair market value as of the date of death.

Irrevocable Subject to no right to rescind or amend (the terms of a transfer of one or more interests in property).

Irrevocable trust A trust that cannot be revoked by the settlor after its creation except upon the consent of all the beneficiaries.

Issue A person's direct offspring, including children, grandchildren, great-grandchildren, and the like. Also called descendants or lineal descendants.

Itemized deductions In federal income tax law, deductions from adjusted gross income that are specifically listed, and taken in lieu of the standard deduction.

Joint and mutual will A single will jointly executed by two or more persons and containing reciprocal provisions for the disposition of property owned jointly, severally, or in common upon the death of one of them. It may also be called a *joint and reciprocal will.*

Joint tenancy A form of equal, undivided ownership in property that, upon death of one owner, automatically passes to the surviving owner(s). All interests must be equal, therefore, there cannot be a joint tenancy held 25% by one person and 75% by another. The co-owners are called joint tenants.

Joint will A single will jointly executed by two or more persons and containing their respective wills. In most states the execution of a joint will or mutual wills does not create a presumption of a contract not to revoke the will or wills. See mutual wills.

Kiddie tax The term given to the federal income tax law that requires the unearned income of a child under the age of 13 be taxed at the parent's top marginal rate.

Lack of marketability discount A valuation discount given stock in a closely held business arising from the lack of an established market making the stock more difficult to sell.

Lapse The result when a beneficiary named in a will fails to survive the testator. Also, a power of appointment is said to lapse if the holder does not exercise it within the permitted period.

Leasehold An interest in property entitling the lessee to possess and use the property for a specified time, usually in exchange for a series of payments.

Legacy A gift, by will, of personal property. Also called a bequest.

Legal interest An interest that is recognized in law (as by legal title). Compare equitable interest or beneficial interest neither of which require the person benefitted to have title.

Legatee A beneficiary, under a will, of a gift of personal property.

Letters testamentary A formal court document used as evidence of the probate court's authorization of the estate's personal representative to act on behalf of a decedent's estate.

Leveraging The process by which a given amount of exclusion, exemption, or credit can shelter more than that amount from future transfer taxation.

Lineal Consisting of or being in a direct male or female line of ancestry, e.g., a lineal descendant.

Life estate An estate in property held only during or measured in duration by the lifetime of a specified individual, usually the individual enjoying the property. The life of the person who determines the duration is referred to as the measuring life.

Life insurance Insurance providing for the payment of money to a designated beneficiary upon the death of the insured.

Life insurance policy A contract in which the insurance company agrees to pay a cash lump-sum amount (the face value or policy proceeds) to the person named in the policy to receive it (the beneficiary) upon the death of the subject of the insurance (the insured).

Limited liability companies A business organization in which the owners, called members, do not have personal liability for the contracts or the torts of the business, yet the organization is taxed like a partnership. Those owning an interest in the company are called members.

Limited power of appointment The holder of a power cannot use it to transfer the property that is subject to the power for his or her own benefit or for the benefit of his or her estate. It is not considered a gift if the holder exercises the power and the property subject to the power is not included in the holder's gross estate when the holder dies.

Living trust A trust funded during the lifetime of the trustor. Also called an inter vivos trust.

Living will A document in which the signer indicates preferences or directions for the administration of life-sustaining medical treatment (including the withdrawal or withholding thereof) in the event of terminal illness or permanent unconsciousness. It may be in the form of a directive to physicians.

Marital deduction In federal gift and estate taxation, the deduction for certain transfers to a spouse.

Marital trust A trust structured to receive property that will qualify for the marital deduction, e.g., a "power of appointment trust" or a QTIP trust. Also called a *marital deduction trust.*

Members in a limited liability company Investors/owners in a limited liability company.

Minority discount A valuation discount allowed for an interest in a business because the interest is not a controlling interest.

Mutual will One of two separate wills that share reciprocal provisions for the disposition of property in the event of death by one of the parties. They may be executed in connection with an agreement based on sufficient consideration such that neither will can be revoked without mutual consent of the parities. These may also be called reciprocal or mirror wills.

Net estate The net worth of a person; i.e., total assets minus total liabilities.

No contest clause A clause inserted in a will that causes a legacy to be forfeited if the legatee challenges the will by bringing a will contest.

Non-recourse note A note whose satisfaction upon default may be obtained only out of the collateral securing it.

Nuncupative will A will allowed in some states that is dictated orally before witnesses and set down in writing within a statutorily specified time period (e. g., 30 days before the testator's death) and that is allowed only for one in imminent peril of death from a terminal illness or from military or maritime service.

Obligor One who is bound by an obligation to another.

Omitted child *See Omitted heir.*

Omitted heir A descendant of a testator who would be an heir under the laws of intestacy but who is not named under the will. Many states have statutes requiring a share of the estate to go to a pretermitted heir on the assumption that the omission was unintentional.

Omitted spouse *See Omitted heir.*

Opportunity shifting The transfer of a rapidly appreciating wealth- or of an income-producing opportunity to another family member.

Outright transfer A transfer in which the transferee receives both legal interests and all beneficial interests, subject to no restrictions or conditions.

Partnership capital freeze Like a recapitalization, the reorganization of a partnership for the purpose of freezing the estate value of a partner's partnership interest. Severely restricted by the Revenue Reconciliation Act of 1990.

Permissible appointee (of a power of appointment) A party whom the holder may appoint by exercising the power.

Per capita Equally to each individual. Per capita distribution of an estate, although it follows the line of descent, provides each descendant (providing there is no ascendent relative in between the person and the decedent) with an equal share of the estate's assets regardless of the degree of his or her kinship. Children, grandchildren, great-grandchildren, etc., all receive equal shares.

Perfect unification When applied to the estate and gift tax laws, a set of conditions in which an individual would be indifferent, from a total transfer tax planning point of view, between making lifetime and deathtime gifts. It helps identify the factors that make the current system imperfect, which serves as the basis for some transfer tax planning.

Per stirpes *See right of representation.*

Perpetuities saving clause A clause in a will or trust that prevents interests from being ruled invalid under the rule against perpetuities.

Personal exemption In federal income tax law, amounts deductible on behalf of the taxpayer, the spouse, and each dependent, in calculating taxable income.

Personal property Property other than real estate. It is property that is movable (not including crops or other resources still attached to land). Also called personalty.

Personal representative The person appointed by the probate court to represent and manage the estate. If nominated in the will, called an executor.

Pickup tax A state death tax set as exactly equal to the federal credit for state death taxes.

Pooled income fund An investment fund created and maintained by the target charity, which "pools" property from many similar contributors. This arrangement ordinarily provides that the charity will pay to the grantor an income for life and, if desired, for the life of the grantor's spouse, based on the rate of return actually earned by the fund as a whole. At their death, the property passes to the charity.

Postmortem Referring to events that happen after a person's death.

Possessory interest An interest (as a right) involving or arising out of the possession of property. A possessory interest is based on control rather than use. Thus a lessee who occupies and controls the use of property has a possessory interest, while a party who has an easement does not.

Pot trust A trust established at the death of parents for the benefit of their minor children. Typically, the trust corpus remains undivided until the youngest child reaches an age specified in the trust, e.g., age 18 or 21. At that time, the assets are divided into equal separate shares, one for each child. The assets are distributed outright, or they are held for distribution at some older age. Also called a Family Pot Trust.

Pour-over trust A trust that receives the assets that make up its principal by operation of a testamentary disposition to it upon the settlor's death.

Pour-over will A will that distributes at the testator's death probate assets to a trust previously created.

Power of appointment A power to name someone to receive a beneficial interest in property.

Power of appointment trust A marital trust that provides a surviving spouse with a life estate in the property and with a power of appointment allowing appointment of the property to the surviving spouse or to his or her estate, e.g., Trust A of the ABC or AB estate plans. To obtain a marital deduction the trust must comply with IRC § 2056(b)(5).

Power of attorney A document executed by one person, called the principal, authorizing another person, called the attorney-in-fact, to perform designated acts on behalf of the principal.

Precatory language Language in a will that does not direct or command, but merely expresses a wish, hope or desire, e.g., $50,000 to Martin with the expectation that he will use the money to go to college. Precatory language is not enforceable.

Present interest An immediate right to possess or enjoy property.

Pretermitted heir *See omitted heir.*

Principal The property in a trust. Also called corpus.

Private annuity A transfer of property under which the seller receives an unsecured promise of a life annuity.

Probate The legal process of administering the estate of a decedent. It focuses on the probate estate, that is, property which will be disposed of by, and only by, either the decedent's will or by the state laws of intestate succession. More narrowly and less commonly, probate is used to mean certifying or proving the validity of the will after the death of the testator.

Probate estate All of the decedent's property passing to others by means of the probate process. This includes all property owned by the decedent except joint tenancy interests. The probate estate does not include property transferred by the decedent before death to a trustee, life insurance proceeds on the decedent's life when paid directly to a beneficiary, nor the decedent's interest in pension and profit sharing plans. The latter are said to "pass outside of probate."

Promissory note A note containing an unconditional promise to pay on demand or at a fixed or determined future time a particular sum of money to or to the order of a specified person or to the bearer.

Qualified terminable interest property (QTIP) Property passing to a surviving spouse that qualifies for the marital deduction if the executor so elects providing that the spouse is entitled to receive income in payments made at least annually for life, and that no one has a power to appoint any part of the property to any person other than the surviving spouse.

QTIP election An election by the executor of the estate of the first spouse to die to treat certain property as QTIP property, thereby qualifying it for the marital deduction.

QTIP trust A marital trust for which a federal estate tax election can be made so as to qualify the trust property for the marital deduction. It must provide that the surviving spouse is entitled to all of the income from the trust property, payable at least annually. In addition, the trust cannot give anyone a power to appoint any of the property to anyone other than to the surviving spouse so long as he or she is alive. Its uniqueness lies in the fact that it qualifies for the marital deduction even though its property neither passes to nor is controlled by the surviving spouse.

Qualified charitable remainder trust A trust that is either a charitable remainder annuity trust or a charitable remainder unitrust.

Real property Property consisting of land, buildings, crops, any other resources still attached to or within the land, improvements or fixtures permanently attached to the land or a structure on it.

Recapitalization A reorganization of a closely held corporation for the purpose of freezing the value of a primary owner's interest in the company. Severely restricted by enactment of Revenue Reconciliation Act of 1990.

Reciprocal wills Wills for two people (usually a married couple) that are virtually identical; each leaves all (or substantially all) property to the other if the latter survives, otherwise to third persons. Sometimes called *mirror wills* or *mutual wills*. Reciprocal wills are usually simple wills; more complex wills are more likely to have unique features.

Remainder In the context of trusts, the future interest to the remaining trust assets at the termination of all other interests. More technically, the right to use, possess and enjoy property after a prior owner's interest ends, in a situation where both interests were created at the same time and in the same document.

Remainderman The beneficiary of a trust who will receive the trust corpus (i.e., that which remainders) at the termination of all other interests.

Res From the Latin for "the thing." In the context of estate planning it generally refers to the property held in trust. Also called *corpus*.

Residuary bequest A gift by will of that part of the testator's estate that remains after taking care of all specific and pecuniary bequests.

Residuary estate All of what is left of an estate once the deceased person's debts and administration costs have been paid and all specific and general bequests and devises have been distributed. It is also called the residual estate.

Resulting trust An implied trust based upon the presumed intentions of the parties as inferred from all the circumstances that the party holding legal title to trust property holds it for the benefit of the other party.

Reversion A future interest in property that is retained by the transferor; it will become a present interest (revert back to the transferor) when all other interests created at the time of the transfer have ended. Usually used in connection with trusts established for a limited duration.

Revocable Subject to the right to rescind or amend (the terms of a transfer of one or more interests in property).

Revocable trust A trust over which the settlor has retained the power of revocation.

Right of survivorship The right of the surviving owners of property held jointly to take the entire property and exclude the deceased owner's heirs and estate beneficiaries, e.g., the right of the survivor of joint tenants to sole ownership of the entire property, or of the surviving spouse to own the property the couple held as tenants by the entirety.

Rule against perpetuities A common law principle invalidating a dispositive clause in a will or a trust if the contingent interest transferred might vest in a transferee too long after the settlor's death.

S1 Shorthand nomenclature for the first spouse to die.

S2 Shorthand nomenclature for the second spouse to die.

Sale A transfer of property under which each transferor exchanges consideration that the parties regard as equivalent in value.

Self-canceling installment note (SCIN) An installment note which provides that no further payments will be made after the seller's death.

Self-proved will A will containing a formal affidavit by witnesses stating that all formalities have been complied with. It eliminates the need for the witnesses to verify the correctness of the execution of the document after the testator dies.

Separate property In community property states, all property that is not community property. That is, all property acquired by a person prior to marriage, and all property acquired during a marriage by gift, devise, bequest or inheritance, or, in most community property states, income earned on property so acquired. Community property may be converted to separate property by the written agreement of the couple.

Settlor The person who creates the trust and whose property is transferred to it. Also called creator, grantor, or trustor.

Shifting income *See Income shifting.*

Short-term trust An irrevocable trust that reverts to the grantor sometime after 10 years or after the life of the income beneficiary. The income was taxed to the beneficiary, not to the settlor. TRA 86, in subjecting this trust to the grantor trust rules, virtually eliminated its further use.

Simple trust A trust under which all current income must be distributed and no principal may be distributed.

Simple will A will prepared for a family having a small estate, one for whom death tax planning is not a significant concern, with the typical pattern being "everything to my spouse, if she survives, and if she does not, then to my children per stirpes."

Skip person In federal generation-skipping transfer tax law, a beneficiary who is at least two generations younger than the transferor.

Soak-up tax *See sponge tax.*

Special use valuation A provision in federal estate tax law (Section 2032A) that permits qualifying estates to value farmland or business use real estate at its "qualified-use value" rather than at its "highest and best use" value. The maximum decrease is $750,000 (indexed after 1997).

Specific bequest A gift of a particular item of property which is capable of being identified and distinguished from all other property. Contrasted with general bequest and residuary bequest.

Spendthrift clause A clause in a trust that restricts the beneficiary from transferring any of his or her future interest in the corpus or income. For example, a typical spendthrift clause would not permit the beneficiary to pledge the interest as collateral against a loan.

Spendthrift trust A trust that is created for the benefit of a spendthrift who is paid income therefrom but it cannot be reached by creditors to satisfy the spendthrift's debts.

Splitting a gift Treating a gift of the property owned by one spouse, on the federal gift tax return, as if it were made one-half by each spouse.

Sponge tax Where a state's inheritance tax produces total death taxes for a decedent's estate that are less than that estate's allowable federal credit for state death taxes, the state collects the difference between the total and the allowable credit. Because the federal credit is a dollar for dollar credit, this sponge tax does not increase the overall taxes for a decedent's estate.

Spousal remainder trust An irrevocable trust providing for income for a period to a lower-income tax bracket family member, then remainder to the trustor's spouse. Use of this trust was virtually eliminated by TRA 86, which subjected it to the grantor trust rules.

Springing durable power of attorney A durable power of attorney that becomes effective at the onset of the principal's mental incapacity.

Standard deduction In federal income tax law, a fixed amount that may be deducted from adjusted gross income. It may be used instead of specifically subtracting actual "itemized" deductions.

Standby trust An unfunded living trust whose principal financial management and control provisions do not come into effect until the grantor dies or is determined to be incapacitated. At that point, the trust is usually funded by the probate process or, if the grantor is still alive but incapacitated, by the grantor's attorney-in-fact.

Step-up in basis Shorthand for the change in basis that occurs when the owner of property dies. Technically, it will only be a "step-up" in basis if, at the owner's death, the property has a fair market value that is higher than the basis was immediately before his or her death.

Subrogation An equitable doctrine holding that when a third party pays a creditor or obligee the third party succeeds to the creditor's rights against the debtor or obligor. A doctrine holding that when an insurance company pays an insured's claim of loss due to another's tort, the insurer succeeds to the insured's rights (as the right to sue for damages) against the tortfeasor (the person who did the harm).

Surrogate decision makers Individuals capable of making decisions regarding a person's property and family at times when the person is unable, either due to incapacity or death. Examples include attorney-in-fact, trustee, and executor.

Survival clause A disposition provision in a will or trust naming an alternate taker of certain property if the donee fails to survive the donor for some period of time.

Takers in default Persons who receive property subject to a power of appointment if the holder permits the power to lapse unexercised.

Tangible personal property Personal property which has value because of its physical characteristics.

Taxable estate In federal estate tax law, the gross estate reduced by all allowable deductions.

Taxable distribution In federal generation-skipping transfer tax law, any distribution of property out of a trust to a skip person (other than a taxable termination or a direct skip).

Taxable gift In federal gift tax law, for a given year, total gross gifts reduced by all allowable deductions, exemptions, and exclusions.

Taxable termination In federal generation-skipping transfer tax law, the termination of all the interests of one generation in the income or principal of a trust, with the result that the interest shift to another lower generation of skip persons.

Tax clause A provision in a will specifying which property bears the burden of paying taxes.

Tenancy by the entirety An tenancy in property similar to a joint tenancy; however, it can be created only between husband and wife. Unlike joint tenancy, neither spouse may transfer or encumber the property without the consent of the other.

Tenancy in common An interest in property held by two or more persons, each having an undivided right to possess property. Unlike a joint interest, however, an interest in common may be owned in unequal percentages, and when one owner dies the remaining owners do not automatically succeed in ownership. Instead, the decedent's interest passes through his or her estate, by will, by some other document, or by the laws of intestate distribution. The co-owners are called "tenants in common."

Terminable interest An interest which might terminate or fail on the lapse of time, on the occurrence of an event or contingency, or on the failure of an event or contingency to occur. Property otherwise qualifying for the marital deduction will not qualify if the interest passing to the spouse is terminable, unless there is an exception such exists for QTIP property.

Terminal value Used to indicate the value of a cash value life insurance policy that is currently in force. Formally called the policy's interpolated terminal reserve value, its amount is nearly equal to its cash surrender value.

Term life insurance A type of life insurance policy that has no value prior to the death of the insured because the premium charged, which increases over time with increasing risk of death, just covers the risk of death for that period. Term insurance simply buys pure protection: if the insured dies during the policy term, the company will pay the face value; otherwise, it will pay nothing.

Testamentary capacity The mental ability required of a testator to validly execute a will.

Testamentary transfer A transfer at death by will.

Testamentary trust A trust established by a will. The funding mechanism is the probate process.

Testate Dying with a valid will.

Testator The person who executes a will.

Throwback rules In the income taxation of trusts, rules that, prior to being repealed by TRA '97, subjected income accumulated by a trust in one year and distributed to a beneficiary in another year to possible additional taxation to the beneficiary.

Totten trust A pay on death bank account. The owner of the account specifies that, if the owner dies while the account is still open, it should be transferred (without probate) to a named beneficiary. Also known as a *bank account trust, savings bank trust,* or a *tentative trust.*

TOD account A bank account or brokerage account that is set up to follow the requirements of the Uniform Transfer on Death Act, such that upon the owners death the account is transferred to a named beneficiary without probate. *See Totten trust.*

TRA '86 Tax Reform Act of 1986.

TRA '97 Taxpayer Relief Act of 1997.

Transfer Any type of passing of property in which the transferor gives up some kind of interest to the transferee. Sometimes called an assignment.

Transfer Penalty, Medicaid Gifts made during the 36 months prior to applying for Medicaid may result in a period of ineligibility to receive benefits.

Trust A legal arrangement between trustor and trustee that divides legal and beneficial interests in property among two or more people. In estate planning the trust agreement is likely to be many pages long, and to spell out in detail the trustees obligations concerning the management and distribution of the trust income and corpus.

Trust beneficiary A person who is named to enjoy a beneficial interest in the trust.

Trust-will *See Testamentary trust.*

Trustor The person who creates a trust and whose property is transferred to the trustee. Also called creator, grantor, or settlor.

Underwriter A person (or a company) who underwrites an insurance policy. A person who assesses risks to be covered by an insurance policy.

Undue influence Influence by a confidante which has the effect of impeding the testator's free will. A will can be denied probate (or at least certain clauses will be disregarded) if it can be established that the testator, at execution, was subject to undue influence. To be undue, the influence must be wrongful in some way.

Unification of gift and estate taxes Partially successful efforts by Congress in 1976 to tax lifetime and deathtime transfers equally, so that an individual would be indifferent, from a total transfer tax planning point of view, between making lifetime and deathtime gifts.

Unified credit The credit allowed against the tentative tax that results in sheltering modest taxable gifts and modest taxable estates from the transfer tax.

Uniform Gifts to Minors Act Like the Uniform Transfers to Minors Act, a statute in many states permitting custodial gifts for the benefit of a minor.

Uniform Probate Code (UPC) A complete set of probate laws originally promulgated by legal scholars and practitioners and currently adopted in whole or in part by about two fifths of the states.

Uniform Simultaneous Death Act (USDA) A statute providing that when transfer of title to property depends on the order of deaths, and that when no sufficient evidence exists that two people died other than simultaneously, the property of each is disposed of as if each had survived the other.

Uniform Transfer on Death Act A uniform law adopted by many states that allows accounts at financial institutions (e.g., banks, savings and loans, thrifts, credit unions) and at brokerages to have a designation that allows the account to be transferred to a named beneficiary, without passing through probate, if the account is still open when the owner dies.

Uniform Transfers to Minors Act Like the older Uniform Gifts to Minors Act, this provides a means of transferring property to young people through the use of a custodian.

Universal life insurance Life insurance characterized by flexible premiums, benefits, and payment schedules, by the indexing of cash value to money market interest rates, and by the periodic reporting of current value and company costs charged to the account.

Variable life insurance Life insurance in which all or part of the cash value of the policy is located in a tax-deferred investment portfolio with risk assumed by the insured for investment losses.

Variable universal life insurance Universal life insurance that includes the investment component of variable life insurance.

Vested interest A nonforfeitable future interest whose possession and enjoyment are delayed only by time and not dependent on the happening of any future event.

Wait-and-see statute A provision in some state statutes that can overcome the effect of the rule against perpetuities by finding an interest void only if its turns out, in fact, not to vest within the required period, e.g., within 60 years.

Whole life insurance Life insurance that provides coverage over the life of the insured and that can be sold for surrender value or used as the basis of low-interest loans. It is also called ordinary life insurance, cash value life insurance, and straight life insurance.

Will A written document disposing of a person's probate property at death.

Will substitute A device (as a trust) used instead of a will to transfer property upon death.

Witnessed will A written will, recognized in all states, that must be signed by two or more witnesses who acknowledge, among other things, that the testator asked them to witness the will, that they in fact did witness the testator's signing, and that the testator is mentally competent to execute a will (in accordance with state law).

Index